Marketing communications

Contexts, contents and strategies

Second edition

CHRIS FILL

An imprint of Pearson Education

Harlow, England · London · New York · Reading, Massachusetts · San Francisco · Toronto · Don Mills, Ontario · Sydney
Tokyo · Singapore · Hong Kong · Seoul · Taipei · Cape Town · Madrid · Mexico City · Amsterdam · Munich · Paris · Milan

First published 1995
Second edition published 1999
Pearson Education Limited
Edinburgh Gate
Harlow
Essex CM20 2JE
England

and Associated Companies throughout the world

Visit us on the World Wide Web at:
http://www.pearsoneduc.com

Typeset in 9½/12 by Goodfellow & Egan Limited

Printed and bound by Grafos S.A.,
Arte sobre papel, Barcelona - Spain

Library of Congress Cataloguing-in-Publication Data

Fill, Chris.
Marketing communications: contexts, contents and strategies / Chris Fill.
p. cm.
Includes bibliographical references and indexes.
1. Communication in marketing. 2. Marketing channels. Sales promotion.
I.Title.
HF5415. 123 F55 1998 98-29818
658.8'02-dc21 CIP

British Library Cataloguing in Publication Data

A catalogue record for this book is available from the British Library

ISBN 0-13-010229-6

10 9 8 7 6 5 4 3
04 03 02 01 00

This book, like me, is dedicated to Karen
and our lads John and Michael.

Marketing communications

Contents

Preface

This book has been written as a second edition to *Marketing Communications: Frameworks, Theories and Applications*. It builds upon the first edition and introduces new issues and aspects associated with this fast developing subject.

There are any number of practical books describing marketing communications from a 'how to do it' perspective. In addition there are some edited 'readers' which can serve to provide useful considered discussion about aspects across the subject. This book has been written deliberately from an academic perspective and seeks to provide a suitably consistent appraisal of the ever-expanding scope of marketing communications. This book seeks to stimulate thought and consideration about a wide range of interrelated issues, and to help achieve this aim a number of theories and models are advanced. Some of these theories reflect marketing practice, while others are offered as suggestions for moving the subject forward. Many of the theories are abstractions of actual practice, some are based on empirical research and others are pure conceptualisation. All seek to enrich the subject, but not all need carry the same weight of contribution. Readers should form their own opinions based upon their reading, experience and judgement.

There are a number of themes running through the text, but perhaps the main one concerns integrated communications. I am of the view that organisations will in the future perceive communications as a core activity, central to strategic management and thought. Corporate and marketing communications will inevitably merge and integrate, the need to build and sustain relationships with a variety of stakeholders inside and outside the organisation will become paramount and communications will be a vital source in making it all work.

In this light, this text assumes relationship marketing to be essential and sees communication in the context of relational exchanges (see Chapters 1 and 2). Corporate and marketing communications are considered as important components of the total process. Finally, a new chapter on integrated marketing communications is deliberately positioned at the end of the text as symbolic of the range of activities and the need to bring all communications together.

Many fresh topics are included in this edition: internal marketing communications, cross-border communications, integrated marketing communications, direct marketing and interactive communications, sponsorship and how advertising works are just some of the ten new chapters in the book. However, while the material has been revised and extended the basic structure has also been reviewed. There are now three major parts: contexts, contents and strategies.

Part 1 considers the *contexts* within which communications are developed: the situations facing communication planners in which communication strategies are developed.

Part 2 examines the individual promotional methods or *contents* available to communicate with target audiences.

Part 3 explores some of the *strategies* available to organisations in the light of their contextual positions. This part also examines integrated marketing communications and concludes with a presentation of a marketing communications plan and an overview of how components of marketing communications interlink.

Part 1: Contexts

This part considers the individual elements that underpin or contribute to marketing communications. The situations in which communications occur influence current communications and the way they are received, interpreted and used by people. Only through understanding the context in which communications are developed, conveyed and understood by receivers can effective communications evolve.

Developing a contextual perspective based upon a thorough understanding of the market and the target audience is imperative if appropriate objectives, strategies, promotional methods and resources are to be determined, allocated and implemented.

A number of contexts are explored. First, the *ethical* context is considered. By examining some of the responsibilities that participants in the marketing communication process hold, it assists understanding of what could, should and often is conveyed through marketing communication messages.

Second is the *buyer's* context. By understanding how buyers process information and the way they make purchasing decisions in particular situations for particular product categories and brands, is it possible to design communication strategies and messages that are relevant to members of the target audience and their needs.

The third context to be considered is that of the interrelationships between the different organisations and *stakeholders* who impact on an organisation's marketing communications. First, the networks of stakeholders are considered primarily from a 'marketing channel' perspective, with a particular emphasis upon the relationships that are of increasing importance. Second, attention is given to the communications industry and specifically the strategic and operational issues of advertising agencies and their interaction with client organisations.

The *external environment* is the focus of the next context to be considered. Here the environment and market research activities are reviewed.

The final context to be considered is the *internal* situation: those factors that influence and are influenced by communication activities within organisations. Ideally these should blend with an organisation's external communications. Three main areas of analysis are considered. The first concerns the marketing strategy of the organisation and the relationship with marketing communications, the second considers internal marketing issues and the third deals with the management of the resources, mainly financial, available to support marketing communications.

Through a consideration of these individual elements and by developing a view of the overall context facing marketing communication planners it is possible to begin building coherent and consistent marketing communications plans.

Part 2: Contents

This part looks at the promotional methods that are available to organisations to communicate with its external and internal audiences.

First, attention is given to how advertising might work. Following a consideration of some traditional and some more contemporary explanations, a cognitive association model is offered as a means of consolidating recent research and conceptual thinking. Messages, media, media planning and methods of evaluation then follow.

Sales promotion, public relations, sponsorship, personal selling, and direct and interactive marketing are the other primary methods explored in this part. The approach remains the same with each chapter; consideration of the theoretical aspects is interspersed with examples and illustrations.

Part 3: Strategies

The final part of the book presents some strategies for marketing communications and ends with an operational approach to devising, formulating and implementing a strategic marketing communications plan.

In particular, generic communication strategies, pull, push and profile are considered in turn, followed by issues concerning cross-border communications.

Integrated marketing communications concepts are presented and explored from a strategic perspective, and the book closes with ideas about how to write marketing communication plans. It is hoped that this chapter will help draw together much of the overall thinking and material introduced in the book. It should be of use to practitioners as well as students studying for the Chartered Institute of Marketing diploma.

Despite the misuse and often laboured understanding of the term, this book presents marketing communications from a strategic perspective. The interlinking of corporate, marketing and promotional strategy, the blend of internal and external communications, the relational aspects of network communications, and the various objectives and strategies that flow from understanding the context within which marketing communications emanates, functions and forms a part of the fabric within which audiences frame and interpret marketing messages are presented to readers for consideration.

The book contains many examples to help explain and illustrate points. In addition, it includes a number of case illustrations, usually in the form of mini-case histories, which are presented to illustrate practical applications of theoretical concepts.

I have written some of these case illustrations, but the majority have been written by my students. These are some of the people who have enjoyed the subject and been stimulated to take their involvement with the subject further. One MBA student changed his total career path and embarked upon the exciting world of Corporate Identity. These people are either ex-BA Business Studies, CIM, MBA or MA Marketing students whom I have had the pleasure to teach. Their material is presented in the style and tone in which they wrote it; very little has been changed. I hope this small innovation adds character and interest to the book and the chapters to which they contribute.

Acknowledgements

It is common practice to thank all those people who contributed to the publication of a book. I see no reason to change this custom.

There is no doubt in my mind that this book would not have been possible without the goodwill and kind assistance of a wide range of people. There are those who have written and contributed sections of the book, those who have provided information, pictures and advice and those who have read, reviewed and provided moral support and encouragement.

Using this format my thanks are first directed to Richard Christy for contributing an important new chapter on Ethics in Marketing Communications and for up-dating his chapter on Marketing Research. For this edition I decided to include examples written by some of my former students. I hoped this would provide richness and variety to the book. Therefore my thanks to Jo Crotty, Jane Lockwood, Mark Barrett, Martin Sparkes, Nigel Markwick, Paul Priddy and Janet Chard for helping to bring the book to life. In addition, my thanks are forwarded to Pat Dade, not a student of mine but someone who is a loyal supporter and contributor to the book.

I have had the pleasure of meeting and speaking to a variety of organisations in the quest for information, examples and pictures. I have tried to list them all but should I have omitted anyone or any organisation then please accept my apologies. Everyone who has answered telephone calls, put things in the post or liaised with others in the cause of the book, thank you, your efforts are very much appreciated.

In addition there are those who have supported the project, such as Julia Helmsley at Prentice Hall, Gordon Oliver at the University of Portsmouth and all those who gave hours reviewing manuscripts and making constructive comments. Finally, materials and advice have been provided by many including the following:

Will Arnold-Baker – Rainey Kelly Campbell Rolf
George Ashby – Vauxhall Motors
Daniela Beltz – Hugo Boss AG
Mark Bleathman – Wella GB Ltd
Jamie Bowden – British Airways
Tony Billsborough – Cadbury's
Breda Bubear – Virgin Atlantic
Rita Campbell – Kimberly-Clark
Martin Chand – London Taxis
Mark Chapman – IBM UK
Janet Chard – University of Portsmouth

Richard Christy – University of Portsmouth
Pat Dade – Synergy Brand Values
Sir Peter Davis – The Prudential Corporation
Richard Davis – Bose
Catherine Ede – BBC
Joanna Essex – Virgin Atlantic
Sarah Farmer – Association of Publishing Agents
Herr Flosdorf – Hugo Boss AG
Liz Fox – Orange
Sarah Fitch – Gieves and Hawkes
Louise Friend – JWT
John Gusthart – Scottish Courage
Anna Hales – TBWA Simons Palmer
Nicky Horton – Renault UK
Lucy Jones – Hill & Knowlton
Tony Key – BBC
Tom Lucas – AMVBBDO
Nigel Markwick – Wolf Olins
Stuart McGuire – Catalina Systems
Sarah Marshall – Inland Revenue
Sophie Maunder – Ogilvy and Mather
Miles Millington – Skoda
Ian Muir – Coca Cola Great Britain
Tim Ossler – RAC
Roger Paice – Dennis Fire Engines
Neil Perrot – Cable and Wireless Communications
Steve Pike – Photographer
Anne Seabrook – Royal and SunAlliance
Linda Semarck – Britvic Soft Drinks
Mark Schultz – WCRS
Susan Turner – Britvic Soft Drinks
Sara Tye – Yellow Pages
Penny Vince – Allied Domecq
Andrea Ward – The Prudential Corporation
Louise Watts – Adshel
David Weddel – JWT
Robin Wight – WCRS
Mark Williamson – Rapier Communications
Mike Wiltshire – HMS Victory

And thanks to:

Direct Line
Millward Brown
Kellogg Company Great Britain Ltd

for their support and contribution

However, above all others, my love and thanks to my wife Karen, who allowed me the time and space to produce this second edition.

Grateful acknowledgement is made for permission to reproduce material in this book. Every effort has been made to trace the correct copyright holders but if any have been inadvertently overlooked the publisher will be pleased to make the necessary arrangement at the first opportunity.

chapter 1

Marketing communications: an introductory perspective

Marketing communications is a management process through which an organisation enters into a dialogue with its various audiences. To accomplish this, the organisation develops, presents and evaluates a series of messages to identified stakeholder groups. The objective of the process is to (re)position the organisation and/or its offerings in the mind of each member of the target audience. This seeks to encourage buyers and other stakeholders to perceive and experience the organisation and its offerings as solutions to some of their current and future dilemmas.

AIMS AND OBJECTIVES

The aims of this introductory chapter are to explore some of the concepts associated with marketing communications and to develop an appreciation of the key characteristics of the main tools of the communications mix.

The objectives of this chapter are:

1. To examine the concept of exchange in the marketing context.
2. To assess the role of promotion in the context of the marketing mix.
3. To consider the range and potential impact of marketing communications.
4. To identify the key characteristics of each major tool in the communications mix.
5. To examine the effectiveness of each communication tool.
6. To establish a need for marketing communications.

Introduction

Wella, the hair care company, operates across a number of countries and uses a variety of marketing communications tools to communicate with its various audiences. These audiences consist not only of people who use hair care products, but also of people and organisations who might be able to influence Wella, who might help and support them by providing, for example, financial, manufacturing, distribution and legal advice.

Wella is part of a network of companies, suppliers, retailers, hair salons and other retailers, who join together freely so that each can achieve its own goals. Effective communication is critically important to Wella, which is why it uses a variety of promotional tools. Advertising, sales promotion, public relations, direct marketing, personal selling and added-value media such as sponsorship are used in different combinations to 'talk' to Wella's customers, potential customers, suppliers, financiers, distributors, hairdressers and employees, among others.

Marketing communications provides the means by which brands and organisations are presented to their audiences with the goal of stimulating a dialogue leading to a succession of purchases, in this case of Wella hair care products. This interaction represents an exchange between Wella and each consumer, and, according to the quality and satisfaction of the exchange process, will or will not be repeated. It follows therefore, that presentation is a very important and integral part of the exchange process, and it is the skill and judgement of management that determines, in most cases, success or failure.

The concept of marketing as an exchange

The concept of exchange, according to most marketing academics and practitioners, is central to our understanding of marketing. For an exchange to take place there must be two or more parties, each of whom can offer something of value to the other and who are prepared to enter freely into the exchange process, a transaction. It is possible to identify four forms of exchange: market and relational exchanges, redistributive exchanges and reciprocal exchanges (Andersson, 1992).

Market exchanges (Bagozzi, 1978; Houston and Gassenheimer, 1987) are transactions that occur independently of any previous or subsequent exchanges. They have a short-term orientation, and are primarily motivated by self-interest. In contrast to this, *relational exchanges* (Dwyer *et al.*, 1987) have a longer-term orientation and develop between parties who wish to build long-term supportive relationships. This is the basis of relationship marketing and is the platform on which the material in this book is presented.

Pandya and Dholkia (1992) have observed that *redistributive exchanges* can exist among parties who work as a collective unit. Members of a unit or group of organisations enter into exchanges because they wish to share resources with the other members of the group. Pandya and Dholkia offer the example of the tax system of a country as an example of this type of exchange. Here a central unit collects resources and redistributes them to 'authorized beneficiaries according to the prevailing laws'.

Reciprocal exchanges (Mauss, 1974) are essentially gift transactions. Gift-giving usually occurs between members of a unit who share a close relationship and it is the frequency of the act of giving a gift that symbolises the strength of the relationship. The act of giving suggests a need to return a gift; a sense of mutuality rather than the self-interest which characterises market exchanges.

There are, therefore, a range of exchange transactions, but in industrial societies market exchanges tend to dominate. All four can be observed at the interpersonal level, at the organisation to individual level or between organisations. As we shall see later, these member units can form together as a network. This may take the form of a dyad, triad or larger group, in order that exchanges may take place.

The role of communication in exchange transactions

Bowersox and Morash (1989) demonstrated how marketing flows, including the information flow, can be represented as a network which has as its sole purpose the satisfaction of customer needs and wants. Communication plays an important role in these exchange networks. At a basic level, communication can *inform* and make potential customers aware of an organisation's offering. Communication may attempt to *persuade* current and potential customers of the desirability of entering into an exchange relationship.

Communications can also *remind* people of a need they might have or remind them of the benefits of past transactions and so convince them that they should enter into a similar exchange. This *reassurance* or comfort element of marketing communications is of vital importance to organisations, as it helps to retain current customers. This approach to business is much more cost-effective than constantly striving to lure new customers. Finally, marketing communications can act as a *differentiator*, particularly in markets where there is little to separate competing products and brands. Mineral water products, such as Perrier and Highland Spring, are largely similar: it is the communications surrounding the products that have created various brand images, enabling consumers to make purchasing decisions. In these cases it is the images created by marketing communications that disassociates one brand from another and positions them so that consumers' purchasing confidence and positive attitudes are developed. Therefore, communication can inform, persuade, remind and build images to delineate a product or service.

Marketing communications can be used to:
D*ifferentiate* products and services
R*emind* and *reassure* customers and potential customers
I*nform* and
P*ersuade* targets to think or act in a particular way
DRIP

At a higher level, the communication process not only supports the transaction, by either informing, persuading, reminding or differentiating, but also offers a means of exchange itself; for example, communication for entertainment, for potential solutions and concepts for education and self-esteem. Communications involve intangible benefits, such as the psychological satisfactions associated with, for example, the entertainment value of television advertisements. Communications can also be seen as a means of perpetuating and transferring values and culture to different parts of society or networks. The form and characteristics of the communication process adopted by some organisations (both the deliberate and unintentional use of signs and symbols used to convey meaning) help to provide stability and continuity.

Other examples of intangible satisfactions can be seen in the social and psychological transactions involved increasingly with the work of the National Health Service (NHS), charities, educational institutions and other not-for-profit organisations, such as housing associations. Not only do these organisations increasingly recognise the need to communicate with various audiences, but they also perceive value in being seen to be 'of value' to their customers. There is also evidence that some brands are trying to meet the emerging needs of some consumers who want to know the track record of manufacturers with respect to their environmental policies and actions. For example, Ty-phoo tea had the quality of its product assessed by an independent body and also commissioned an assessment of the working conditions and pay given to its pickers. The outcome of this five-year process has resulted in Premier Brands claiming on their packaging: 'care for tea and our tea pickers' (Slingsby, 1993).

The notion of value can be addressed in a different way. All organisations have the opportunity to develop their communications to a point where the value of their messages represents a competitive advantage. This value can be seen in the consistency, timing, volume or expression of the message.

Communication can be used for additional reasons. The tasks of informing, persuading, reminding and differentiating are, primarily, activities targeted at consumers or end users. Organisations do not exist in isolation from each other: each one is part of a wider system of corporate entities, where each enters into a series of exchanges to secure raw material inputs or resources and to discharge them as value-added outputs to other organisations in the network.

The exchanges that organisations enter into require the formation of relationships, however tenuous or strong. Andersson looks at the strength of the relationship between organisations in a network, and refers to them as 'loose or tight couplings'. These couplings, or partnerships, are influenced by the communications that are transmitted and received. The role that organisations assume in a network and the manner in which they undertake and complete their tasks are, in part, shaped by the variety and complexity of the communications in transmission throughout the network. Issues of channel or even network control, leadership, subservience and conflict are implanted in the form and nature of the communications exchanged in any network.

Marketing communications can be used to persuade target audiences in a variety of ways. For example, speaking on BBC Radio 4, Bob Waller claimed that publicity had been used effectively by the Peak District National Park. However, instead of using publicity to attract tourists, they had deliberated used their publicity opportunities to divert visitors away from particular areas in the Park, in order to repair, preserve and protect them for visitors in the future.

Waller (1996)

Within market exchanges, communications are characterised by formality and planning. Relational exchanges are supported by more frequent communication activity. As Mohr and Nevin (1990) state, there is a bidirectional flow to communications and an informality to the nature and timing of the information flows. This notion of relational exchange has been popularised by the term 'relationship marketing' and is a central theme in this text.

Marketing communications and the process of exchange

The exchange process is developed and managed by researching consumer/stakeholder needs; identifying, selecting and targeting particular groups of consumers/stakeholders who share similar discriminatory characteristics, including needs and wants; and developing an offering that satisfies the identified needs at an acceptable price, which is available through particular sets of distribution channels. The next task is to make the target audience aware of the existence of the offering. Where competition or other impediments to positive consumer action exist, such as lack of motivation or conviction, a promotional programme is developed and used to communicate with the targeted group.

Collectively, these activities constitute the marketing mix (the 4Ps as McCarthy (1960) originally referred to them), and the basic task of marketing is to combine these 4Ps into a marketing programme to facilitate the exchange process (see Figure 1.1). The use of these 4Ps has been criticised as limiting the scope of the marketing manager. The assumption by McCarthy was that the tools of the marketing mix allow adaptation to the uncontrollable external environment. It is now seen that the external environment can be influenced and managed strategically. To do this, Kotler (1984) suggests the addition of two further Ps to McCarthy's four. These are political power

Figure 1.1 The marketing communications mix.

and public opinion formation. He advocates the deliberate use of certain communication tools to create and frame the environments in which the organisation wishes to operate. This corporate perspective is one that is adopted in this book.

Promotion, therefore, is one of the elements of the marketing mix and is responsible for the communication of the marketing offer to the target market. While recognising that there is implicit and important communication through the other elements of the marketing mix (through a high price, for example, symbolising quality), it is the task of a planned and integrated set of communication activities to communicate effectively with each of the organisation's stakeholder groups. Marketing communications is sometimes perceived as dealing with communications that are external to the organisation. It should be recognised that good communications with internal stakeholders, such as employees, are also vital if, in the long term, successful favourable images, perceptions and attitudes are to be established. This book considers the increasing importance of suitable internal communications (Chapter 11) and their vital role in helping to form a strong and consistent corporate identity (Chapter 27).

The promotional mix is traditionally perceived to consist of four elements: advertising, sales promotion, public relations and personal selling. New forms of promotion have been developed in response to changing market and environmental conditions. For example, public relations is now seen by some to have a marketing and a corporate dimension (Chapter 20). Direct marketing is now recognised as an important way of developing personal relationships with buyers, both consumer and organisational (Chapter 23), while new and innovative forms of communication through sponsorship (Chapter 21), floor advertising, video screens on supermarket trolleys and check-out coupon dispensers (Chapter 15) mean that effective communication requires the selection and integration of a variety of communication tools. The marketing communication mix depicted in Figure 1.1 attempts to reflect these developments and represents a new promotional configuration for organisations.

There is no universal definition of marketing communications and there are many interpretations of the subject. Delozier's (1976) definition is that it is:

> *The process of presenting an integrated set of stimuli to a market with the intent of evoking a desired set of responses within that market set and setting up channels to receive, interpret and act upon messages from the market for the purposes of modifying present company messages and identifying new communication opportunities.*

This is a useful perspective as it introduces the concept of feedback – two-way communication – and also the concept that the stimuli, or message set, should be integrated, if the required reaction of the target audience is to be successfully generated. What it fails to draw out is the opportunity that marketing communication provides to add value through enhanced product and organisational symbolism. It also fails to recognise that it is the context within which marketing communications flow that impacts upon the meaning and interpretation given to such messages. Its ability to frame and associate offerings with different environments is powerful.

Key characteristics of the tools of the promotional mix

Traditionally, the tools of marketing communications are regarded as advertising, sales promotion, public relations and personal selling. Collectively these are referred to as the promotional mix. However, there have been some major changes in the environment and in the way organisations communicate with their target audiences. New approaches to the promotional mix see fresh combinations of communication tools being used. For example, there has been a dramatic rise in the use of direct-response media as direct marketing becomes adopted as part of the marketing plan for many products. An increasing number of organisations are using public relations to communicate messages about the organisation (corporate public relations) and also messages about their brands (marketing public relations).

What has happened therefore is that the promotional mix has developed such that the original emphasis on heavyweight mass communication (above-the-line) campaigns has given way to more direct and highly targeted promotional activities using direct marketing and the other tools of the mix. Using the jargon, through-the-line and below-the-line campaigns are used much more these days. Figure 1.1 brings these elements together.

Advertising is a non-personal form of mass communication and offers a high degree of control for those responsible for the design and delivery of the advertising message. However, the ability of advertising to persuade the target audience to think or behave in a particular way is suspect. Furthermore, the effect on sales is extremely hard to measure. Advertising also suffers from low credibility in that audiences are less likely to believe messages delivered through advertising than they are messages received through some other tools.

The flexibility of this tool is good because it can be used to communicate with a national audience or a particular specialised segment. Although the costs can be extremely large, a vast number of people can be reached with the message, so the cost per contact can be the lowest of the tools in the mix. Advertising and related media are considered at some depth in Chapters 13–17.

Sales promotion comprises various marketing techniques, which are often used tactically to provide added value to an offering, with the aim of accelerating sales and gathering marketing information. Like advertising, sales promotion is a non-personal form of communication, but has a greater capability to be targeted at smaller audiences. It is controllable and, although it has to be paid for, the associated costs can be much lower than those of advertising. As a generalisation, credibility is not very high, as the sponsor is, or should be, easily identifiable. However, the ability to add value and to bring forward future sales is as strong as it is important in an economy which focuses upon short-term financial performance. Sales promotion techniques and approaches are the subject of Chapters 18 and 19.

Personal selling is traditionally perceived as an interpersonal communication tool which involves face-to-face activities undertaken by individuals, often representing an organisation, in order to inform, persuade or remind an individual or group to take appropriate action, as required by the sponsor's representative. A salesperson engages in communication on a one-to-one basis where instantaneous feedback is possible. The costs associated with interpersonal communication are normally very large.

This tool, the focus of Chapter 22, differs from the previous two in that, while still lacking in relative credibility and control, the degree of control is potentially lower. This is because the salesperson is free at the point of contact to deliver a message other than that intended (Lloyd, 1997). Indeed, many different messages can be delivered by a single salesperson. Some of these messages may enhance the prospect of the salesperson's objectives being reached (making the sale), or they may retard the process and so incur more time and hence costs. Whichever way it is viewed, control is lower than with advertising.

A growing area of interest concerns the use of *direct marketing*, in particular direct mail, telemarketing and the fast developing area of interactive communications, such as the Internet. By removing the face-to-face aspect of personal selling and replacing it with a telephone conversation, many facets of the traditional sales persons' tasks can be removed, freeing them to concentrate on their key skill areas. Aspects of direct marketing are developed below and in Chapter 23.

Public relations is 'the art and social science of analysing trends, predicting their consequences, counselling organisations' leadership, and implementing planned programmes of action which will serve both the organisation's and the public interest' (the Mexican Statement, 1978). This definition suggests that public relations should be a part of the wider perspective of corporate strategy, and this is discussed at length in Chapter 20. The increasing use of public relations, and in particular publicity, is a reflection of the high credibility attached to this form of communications. Publicity involves the dissemination of messages through third-party media, such as magazines, newspapers or news programmes. There is no charge for the media space or time but there are costs incurred in the production of the material. (There is no such thing as a free lunch or a free promotion.) There is a wide range of other tools used by public relations, such as event management, sponsorship and lobbying. It is difficult to control a message once placed in the channels, but the endorsement offered by a third party can be very influential and have a far greater impact on the target audience than any of the other tools in the promotional mix.

This non-personal form of communication offers organisations a different way to communicate, not only with consumers but also with many other stakeholders.

The four elements of the promotional mix discussed so far have a number of strengths and weaknesses. As a response to some of the weaknesses which revolve around costs and effectiveness, direct marketing is emerging as a new and effective way of building relationships with customers over the long term.

Direct marketing seeks to target individual customers with the intention of delivering personalised messages and building a relationship with them based upon their responses to the direct communications. In contrast to conventional approaches, direct marketing attempts to build a one-to-one relationship, a partnership with each customer, by communicating with the customers on a direct and personal basis. If an organisation chooses to use direct marketing then it has to incorporate the approach within a marketing plan. This is because distribution is different and changes in the competitive environment may mean that prices need to change. For example, charges for packing and delivery need to be incorporated. The product may also need to be altered or adapted to the market. For example, some electrical products are marketed through different countries on home shopping channels. The electrical requirements of each country or region need to be incorporated within the product specification of each country's offering. In addition to these changes, the promotion component is also different, simply because communication is required directly with each targeted individual. To do this, direct-response media must be used.

In many cases direct-response media are a derivative of advertising, such as direct mail, magazine inserts, and television and print advertisements which use telephone numbers to encourage a direct response. However, direct response can also be incorporated within personal selling through telemarketing and sales promotions with competitions to build market knowledge and develop the database which is the key to the direct marketing approach.

Table 1.1 A summary of the key characteristics of the tools of marketing communications

	Advertising	Sales promotion	Public relations	Personal selling	Direct marketing
Communications					
Ability to deliver a personal message	Low	Low	Low	High	High
Ability to reach a large audience	High	Medium	Medium	Low	Medium
Level of interaction	Low	Low	Low	High	High
Credibility given by target audience	Low	Medium	High	Medium	Medium
Costs					
Absolute costs	High	Medium	Low	High	Medium
Cost per contact	Low	Medium	Low	High	High
Wastage	High	Medium	High	Low	Low
Size of investment	High	Medium	Low	High	Medium
Control					
Ability to target particular audiences	Medium	High	Low	Medium	High
Management's ability to adjust the deployment of the tool as circumstances change	Medium	High	Low	Medium	High

This text regards direct marketing as the management process associated with the marketing objective of building mutually satisfying customer relationships through a personal and intermediary-free dialogue. Direct-response media are the primary communication tools when direct marketing is an integral part of the marketing plan.

Further discussion of direct marketing and direct-response communications can be found in Chapters 15 and 23. Reference is made to direct marketing throughout the book. The communication mix is changing: no longer can the traditional grouping of promotional tools be assumed to be the most effective forms of communication.

This brief outline of the elements of the promotions mix signals some key characteristics. These are the extent to which each element is controllable, whether it is paid for by the sponsor, and whether communication is by mass medium or undertaken personally. One additional characteristic concerns the receiver's perception of the credibility of the source of the message. If the credibility factor is high then there is a greater likelihood that messages from that source will be accepted by the receivers.

Table 1.1 represents the key characteristics and shows the relative effectiveness of the tools of promotion across a number of different characteristics. The three primary groupings are the ability of each to communicate, the costs involved and the control that each tool can maintain.

Effectiveness of the promotional tools

Each element of the promotions mix has different capacities to communicate and to achieve different objectives. The effectiveness of each tool can be tracked against the purchase decision process. Here consumers can be assumed to move from a state of unawareness through product comprehension to purchase. Advertising is better for creating awareness, and personal selling is more effective at promoting action and purchase behaviour.

Readers are encouraged to see the elements of the mix as a set of complementary ingredients, each drawing full potential from the other. The tools are, to a limited extent, partially interchangeable and in different circumstances different tools are used to meet different objectives. For example, network marketing organisations such as Amway Inc. use personal selling to complete the majority of activities in the purchase decision sequence. The high cost of this approach is counterbalanced by the effectiveness of the communications. However, this aspect of interchangeability only serves to complicate matters. If management's task was simply to identify problems and then select the correct precision tool to solve the problem, then the issue of the selection of the 'best' promotions mix would evaporate (Figure 1.2).

These five elements of the promotional mix are supplemented by one of the most effective forms of marketing communication, *word-of-mouth* recommendation. As we shall see later, word-of-mouth recommendation is one of the most powerful marketing communication tools and, if an organisation can develop a programme to harness and accelerate the use of personal recommendation effectively, the more likely it will be that the marketing programme will be successful.

Selection criteria

The key criteria governing an organisation's selection and use of each tool are as follows:

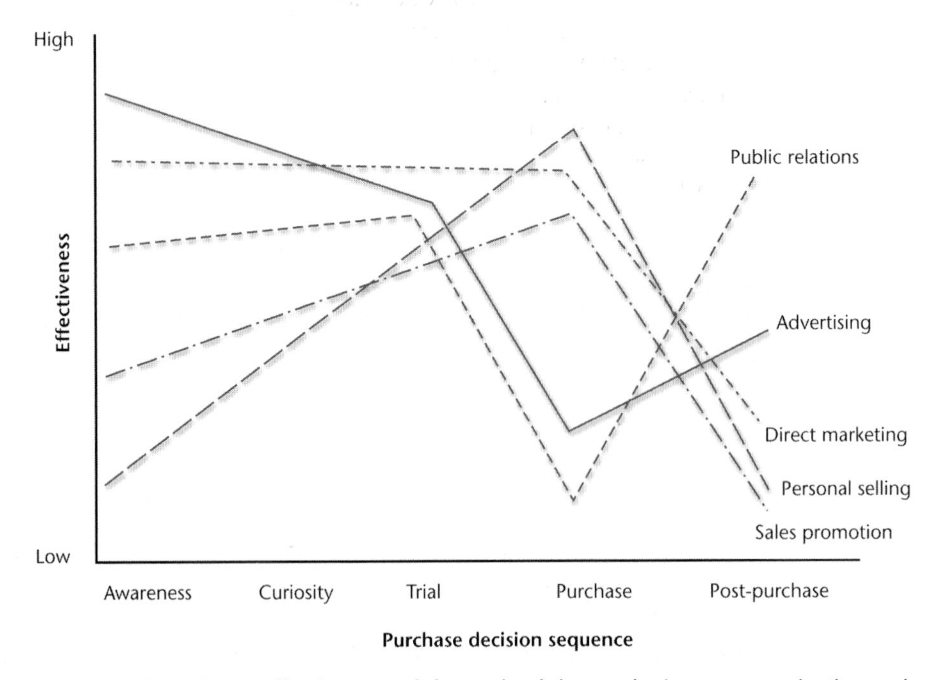

Figure 1.2 The relative effectiveness of the tools of the marketing communications mix.

1. The degree of control required over the delivery of the message.
2. The financial resources available to pay a third party to transmit messages.
3. The level of credibility that each tool bestows on the organisation.
4. The size and geographic dispersion of the target audiences.

Control

Control over the message is necessary to ensure that the intended message is transmitted and received by the target audience. Furthermore, this message must be capable of being understood in order that the receiver can act appropriately. Message control is complicated by interference or negative 'noise' which can corrupt and distort messages. For example an airline's advertising may be discredited by a major news story about safety checks or even an accident.

Advertising and sales promotion allow for a high level of control over the message, from design to transmission. Interestingly, they afford only partial control or influence over the feedback associated with the original message.

Financial resources

Control is also a function of financial power. In other words, if an organisation is prepared to pay a third party to transmit the message, then long-term control will rest with the sponsor for as long as the financial leverage continues. However, short-term message corruption can exist if management control over the process is less than vigilant. For example, if the design of the message differs from that originally agreed, then partial control has already been lost. This can happen when the working relationship between an advertising agency and the client is less than efficient and the process for signing off work in progress fails to prevent the design and release of inappropriate creative work.

Advertising and sales promotion are tools which allow for a high level of control by the sponsor, whereas public relations, and publicity in particular, are weak in this aspect because the voluntary services of a third party are normally required for the message to be transmitted.

There is a great variety of media available to advertisers. Each media type (for example television, radio, newspapers, magazines, posters) carries a particular cost, and the financial resources of the organisation may not be available to use particular types of media, even if such use would be appropriate on other grounds.

Credibility

Public relations scores heavily on credibility factors. This is because receivers perceive the third party as unbiased and to be endorsing the offering. They view the third party's comments as objective and trustworthy in the context of the media in which the comments appear.

At a broad level, advertising, sales promotion and, to a slightly lesser extent, personal selling are tools that can lack credibility, as perceived by the target audience. Because of this, organisations often use celebrities and 'experts' to endorse their offerings. The credibility of the spokesperson is intended to distract the receiver from the sponsor's prime objective: to sell the offering. Credibility, as we shall later, is an important aspect of the communication process and of marketing communications.

Size and geographic dispersion

The final characteristic concerns the size and geographic dispersion of the target audience. A consumer audience, often national, can only be reached effectively if tools of mass communication are used, such as advertising and sales promotion. Similarly, various specialist businesses require personal attention to explain, design, demonstrate, install and service complex equipment. In these circumstances personal selling, one-to-one contact, is of greater significance. The tools of marketing communications can enable an organisation to speak to vast national and international audiences through advertising and satellite technology, or to single persons or small groups through personal selling and the assistance of word-of-mouth recommendation.

Management of the promotional tools

Traditionally, each of the promotional tools has been regarded as the domain of particular groups within organisations:

1. Personal selling is the domain of the sales director, and traditionally uses an internally based and controlled sales force.
2. Public relations (PR) is the domain of the chairperson, and is often administered by a specialist PR agency.
3. Advertising and sales promotion are the domain of the marketing manager or brand manager. Responsibility for the design and transmission of messages for mass communications is often devolved to an external advertising agency.

Many organisations have evolved without marketing being recognised as a key function, let alone as a core philosophy. There are a number of reasons why this might be so. First, the organisation may have developed with a public relations orientation in an environment without competition, where the main purpose of the organisation was to disperse resources according to the needs of their clients. The most obvious examples are to be drawn from the public sector: local authorities and the NHS in particular. A second reason would be because a selling perspective ('our job is to sell it') dominated. There would invariably be no marketing director on the board, just a sales director representing the needs of the market.

It is not surprising that these various organisational approaches have led to the transmission of a large number of different messages. Each function operates with good intent, but stakeholders receive a range of diverse and often conflicting messages.

The role of marketing communications

Marketing communications are about the promotion of both the organisation and its offerings. Marketing communications recognise the increasing role the organisation plays in the marketing process and the impact that organisational factors can have on the minds of consumers. As the structure, composition and sheer number of offerings in some markets proliferate, so differences between products diminish, to the extent that differentiation between products has become much more difficult. This results in a decrease in the number of available and viable positioning opportunities. One way to resolve this problem is to use the parent organisation as an umbrella, to provide greater support and leadership in the promotion of any offerings.

A view which is becoming increasingly popular is that corporate strategy should be supported by the organisation's key stakeholders if the strategy is to be successful. Strategy must be communicated in such a way that the messages are consistent through time and targeted accurately at appropriate stakeholder audiences. Each organisation must constantly guard against the transmission of confusing messages, whether this be through the way in which the telephone is answered, through the impact of sales literature or the way salespersons approach prospective clients. These and other stakeholder issues are discussed at length in Chapter 6.

Many organisations recognise the usefulness and importance of good PR. PR's key characteristics of high credibility and relatively low cost are seen to be critical in the battle not only to secure a position in the consumer's mind but also to restrain promotional costs. As a result, the growth of corporate advertising, the combination of the best of advertising and public relations, has been significant. The repositioning activities by British Airways in 1997 were based on the astute use of corporate advertising and an apparently integrated corporate communications campaign.

Finally, marketing communications recognise the development of channel or trade marketing. Many organisations have moved away from the traditional control of a brand manager to a system which focuses upon the needs of distributors and intermediaries in the channel. The organisations in the channel work together to satisfy their individual and collective objectives. The degree of conflict and cooperation in the channel network depends upon a number of factors, but some of the most important factors are the form and quality of the communications between member organisations. This means that marketing communications must address the specific communication needs of members of the distribution network and those other stakeholders who impact on or who influence the performance of the network. Indeed, marketing communications recognise the need to contribute to the communications in the channel network, to support and sustain the web of relationships.

For example, many organisations in the computer industry have shifted their attention to the needs of distributors, software houses and systems integrators, with the express intent of creating 'business partners' who in turn add value in the form of software, support and general services (Crane, 1994). IBM, Digital and others have changed their approach, attitude and investment priorities to channel partnerships because the environment in which they previously operated has changed in a radical way. Now there is a clear emphasis on working with their partners and their competitors (e.g. Microsoft moving to support Apple in July 1997), and this entails agreement, collaboration and joint promotional activity in order that all participants achieve their objectives.

A definition of marketing communications

Marketing communications is a management process through which an organisation enters into a dialogue with its various audiences. To accomplish this the organisation develops, presents and evaluates a series of messages to identified stakeholder groups. The objective of the process is to (re)position the organisation and/or its offerings in the mind of each member of the target audience. This seeks to encourage buyers and other stakeholders to perceive and experience the organisation and its offerings as solutions to some of their current and future dilemmas.

This definition has three main themes. The first concerns the word *dialogue*. The use of marketing communications enables organisations to communicate with their audiences in such a way that multi-way communications are stimulated (Chapter 2). Promotional messages should encourage members of target audiences to respond to the focus organisation (or product/brand). This response can be immediate through, for example, purchase behaviour or use of customer care lines, or it can be deferred as information is assimilated and considered for future use. Even if the information is discarded at a later date, the communication will have prompted attention and consideration of the message. Dialogue can also be stimulated in such a way that members of the various audiences communicate with one another, primarily by way of word-of-mouth communications.

The second theme is *positioning*, and implies that the communications of the organisation affect all offerings in the opportunity set. Positioning can only work if there are two or more offerings for the receiver to position. Communications from one organisation/offering will hold attention to the extent that competitor organisations are temporarily put aside in the mind of receiver. The length of time that this temporary position lasts is, to some degree, determined by the quality of the 'blocking' communication. Furthermore, if rivals attempt to adjust or reinforce their positions then a number of competitive offerings are also going to be automatically repositioned. Positioning, therefore, is a matter of context. This is the context in which receivers perceive and understand product-based messages relative to other products which they regard as appropriate. Management attention to positioning and marketing communications is therefore of considerable importance.

The third theme from the definition is *cognitive response*, that is receivers are viewed as active problem solvers and they use marketing communications to help them in their purchasing and organisation-related activities. For example, brands are developed partly to help consumers and partly to assist the marketing effort of the host organisation. A brand can quickly inform consumers that, among other things, 'this brand means *x* quality', and through experience of similar brand purchases consumers are assured that their risk is minimised. If the problem facing a consumer is 'which new soup to select for dinner', by choosing one from a familiar family brand the consumer is able to solve it with minimal risk and great speed.

It follows that a brand that provides solutions on a continuous basis for a consumer may become integral to a long-term relationship. A partnership might develop whereby the brand, among other things, reassures the consumer and the consumer supports the brand by paying the price premium that the brand demands. The huge investments made by organisations in the promotion of brands, especially in the fast-moving consumer goods (FMCG) industry, is a testimony to the potential strength of these brand partnerships and to the power of marketing communications.

Mention has been made of the 'cognitive response' that buyers use. There are others, such as the behavioural approach, and these are not totally rejected. Indeed, aspects from a number of different approaches will be utilised to aid understanding of consumer behaviour, as no single theory is applicable to all circumstances.

Context and marketing communications

Organisations can be seen as open social systems (Katz and Kahn, 1978) in which all of the components of the unit or system, are interactive and interdependent (Goldhaber, 1986). Modify one part of a system and adjustments are made by all the other components to accommodate the change. This effect can be seen at the micro and macro levels. At the macro level the interdependence of organisations has been noted by a number of researchers. Stern and El-Ansary (1992) depict distribution channels as 'a network of systems', and so recognise organisations as interdependent units. At the micro level, the individual parts of an organisation accommodate each other as the organisation adjusts to its changing environment. By assembling the decisions associated with the development and delivery of a marketing communications strategy (Figure 1.3), it becomes possible to see the complexity and sensitivity of each of the decision components.

The marketing communications undertaken by organisations within these systems can be regarded as a series of communication episodes. These episodes constitute a dialogue and can be seen to have a certain continuity. The amount of time between episodes may vary from the very small, such as those associated with many major

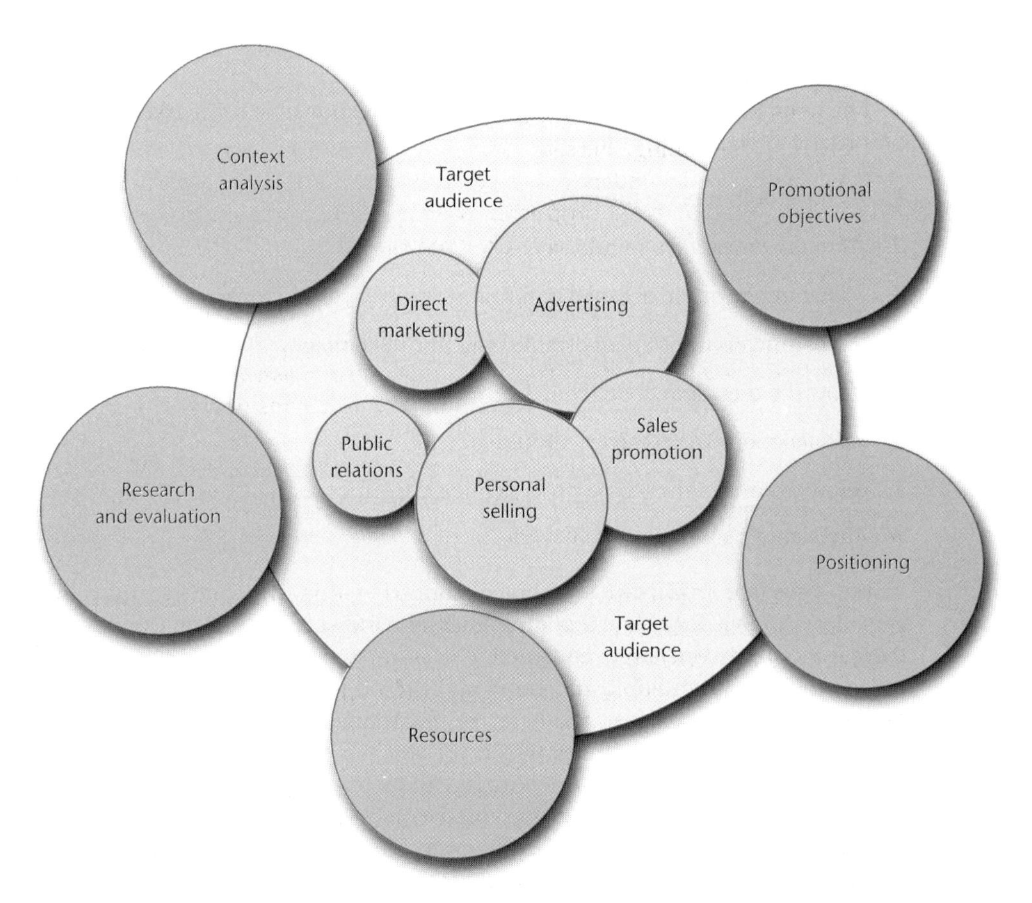

Figure 1.3 The system of marketing communications.

FMCG brand campaigns, which run and run, or very large, such as those associated with some business-to-business campaigns or one-off events associated with a single task, such as government drink-driving campaigns held annually each Christmas period.

These episodes occur within situations where specific factors can be identified and where the circumstances are characteristically individual. Indeed, it is unlikely that any two episodes will occur with exactly the same circumstances. The use of marketing communications as a means of influencing others is therefore determined by the specific circumstances or the context in which the episode is to occur. Marketing communications become part of the context and influences and are influenced by the particular circumstances.

It is important therefore, when considering the elements and factors that contribute to marketing communications, to account for the context in which the communications will contribute. For example, falling sales often provoke a response by management to increase or change the advertising. The perception of the brand by the target audience might be inaccurate or not what was intended, or a new product might be launched into a competitive market where particular positions have been adopted by competitors. These contexts contain a set of specific circumstances in which a marketing communication episode might (will) occur. It should be borne in mind that the list of possible contexts is endless and that the task facing marketing communications managers is to identify the key aspects of any situation and deliver promotional messages that complement the context. This enables audiences to interpret messages correctly and maintain a dialogue.

The main tasks facing the management team responsible for marketing communications are to decide the following:

1. Who should receive the messages.
2. What the messages should say.
3. What image of the organisation/brand receivers are to form and retain.
4. How much is to be spent establishing this new image.
5. How the messages are to be delivered.
6. What actions the receivers should take.
7. How to control the whole process once implemented.
8. Determining what was achieved.

These tasks are undertaken within a context within which there may be many episodes or only a few. Note that more than one message is often transmitted and that there is more than one target audience. This is important, as recognition of the need to communicate with multiple audiences and their different information requirements, often simultaneously, lies at the heart of marketing communications. The aim is to generate and transmit messages which present the organisation and its offerings to their various target audiences, encouraging them to enter into a dialogue and relationship. These messages must be presented consistently and they must address the points stated above. It is the skill and responsibility of the marketing communications manager to blend the communication tools and create a mix that satisfies these elements.

CASE ILLUSTRATION

Wella UK

Wella is a German company whose main business activity is hair care and which has a strong heritage in the sector. The company has grown geographically through organic development and acquisition, and now has a number of wholly owned subsidiaries throughout Europe. It is also represented in South America and parts of Asia-Pacific.

Wella's overall goal is to be number one in the hairdressing market.

The market

The hair care market is growing at about 9.3% p.a. and was worth approximately £841million in 1997. The market consists of a number of sectors, but the largest sector is the shampoo and conditioner market, which is worth approximately £457 million.

Traditionally, the shampoo and conditioner (S&C) market sector consisted of a range of products that were functionally led and which offered convenience as the primary benefit. The market underwent a major revolution in 1993 when *Pantene*, a Procter & Gamble brand, launched a product positioned on technological benefits. They had developed a vitamin-based ingredient that had already been present in most shampoos. The vitamin focus was developed into an attribute that enabled the user to have healthy and shining hair. In other words, Pantene shampoo was presented as a beauty brand, one whose technological strength was the Pro-V factor.

This brand was extremely successful and was quickly followed by *Organics* from Elida Fabergé, a Unilever company. The technological factor in their formulation was Glucasil.

Wella launched their brand, *Experience*, with Liquid Hair and L'Oréal launched *Elvive* with Ceramide R, Cera Protein and Neutra Vitamin as their technological formulations for three different types of hair.

The market had moved forward, with these premium brands adding value and helping to grow the category. These main players had repositioned themselves in similar ways, to some extent imitating the lead taken by Procter & Gamble.

Growth projections over the next twelve months indicated that the total hair care market would grow by 10%, the shampoo market by 5% and the conditioner market by 9%. The faster growth in conditioners was driven by an increasing number of female consumers switching from 2-in-1s to stand-alone higher value specialist conditioners, and also through increased frequency of use.

The target market

The market for Wella Experience is largely female in the 20–40 age group. Wella Experience is perceived as a strong brand, particularly for solving hair problems, such as damaged, dry and fine hair. This segment has shown a strong specific usage propensity to switch from convenience brands to beauty brands. However, repertoire buying in the sector is rampant, with high levels of promiscuity as buyers switch from brand to brand, sometimes attracted by promotional offers and sometimes driven by curiosity.

Early adopters have been critical to Wella's performance and the young female BC1C2 group has been identified as a socioeconomic group in which there are a high proportion of opinion leaders. These are people who value the key strengths of the brand and who, by word of mouth, speed the communication process.

The trade sector is important to Wella to achieve its penetration goals. One of the goals of the retail outlets is to generate increased profits per square metre. In a market such as shampoo that is static in terms of volume growth, increased profitability can only be derived from increased price premiums and switching to higher value brands. Shelf space is increasingly important and a critical aspect of Wella's strategy.

Marketing communications at Wella: background

Of the main players in the market it is interesting to note that Wella is the only one to have a pure pedigree in hair care. Both Procter & Gamble and Unilever deliver a vast range of branded FMCG products and L'Oréal has a cosmetic and fragrance background. Only Wella has the heritage in hair care, operating through salons and the consumer market. With changes in the market very often first detectable in the salons, Wella is well placed to discern market developments early and to utilise the information and deliver new products to meet changing customer needs ahead of the competition.

One of the overriding influences on marketing communications has been the influence of the market leader. Pantene Pro-V has dominated the above-the-line communications to the extent that the beauty and shine proposition has become generic. This means that all brands in the sector are perceived to possess these attributes and that competitor brands must find additional brand equity if they are to compete successfully.

It is interesting to consider the communication strategies of the other players. Pantene rely on a strong above-the-line advertising spend to communicate the key brand messages of beauty and shine. Some in-store work supports the brand advertising. Organics attempted to emulate Pantene, but has failed to achieve the growth and market share expected, largely because it did not offer the additional brand value.

The launch of Elvive in March 1997 was led through a sales promotion in-store offer which was used to create volume and a wide number of trialists. This was then supported with an above-the-line campaign featuring Jennifer Aniston, from the television comedy *Friends*, as a potent brand endorser encouraging people to 'wash the strength back in'. This key message presents strong brand value and a reason to buy which is totally different from all other propositions. Aniston has since been replaced by David Ginola and Claudia Schiffer.

Wella Experience was launched in 1996 with an advertising campaign, excellent distribution and strong in-store point of purchase activity. Awareness ratings were high, but the branding struggled to sustain sufficient levels of loyalty and repertoire buying within the largely promiscuous group of consumers.

In January 1997 a bonus pack was introduced to gain a greater number of users. But the lack of branding and a point of identification was still lacking. Looked at in terms of triggers and associations, Elvive had a stronger trigger and Pantene had the volume through share of voice (SOV).

Wella had used broadcast sponsorship very successfully with the popular *Baywatch* programme, and it was decided to consider this strategy again. In 1996 the American comedy *Friends* was selected as a programme (or brand) whose values mirrored those of the target market and were close to those deemed important for Wella Experience. *Friends* is accessible to the target market, is humorous, is of high quality, stands out and is fashionable.

Research indicated that the brand was used to solve hair care problems rather than be purchased for everyday use. Experience has a strong consumer profile and is well placed within areas where the market is growing. The primary marketing objective at this stage was to develop market penetration and secure higher levels of brand loyalty.

The amount of financial resources that Wella could draw upon is small relative to those of Pantene Pro-V, which is supported by Procter & Gamble, and Organics, supported by Lever Brothers. This support is reflected in the advertising spend used to promote their respective brands: see Table 1.2.

Table 1.2 Market share and media spend by the principal brands in the UK shampoo and conditioner market

Brand	Market share (%)		Advertising spend	Share of voice
	Shampoo	Conditioner	1997 (£m)	1997
Pantene Pro-V	16.7	14.9	20.4	30
Organics with Glucasil	8.6	6.1	15.8	23
Elvive with Ceramide R	7.0	10.6	7.1	10
Head & Shoulders	8.8	N/A	6.3	9
Wash & Go	4.7	N/A	5.0	7
Wella Experience	3.2	4.0	4.3	6
Others	51.0	35.6	3.1	15

Source: Register-Meal.

Marketing communications: the next phase

Awareness levels for Wella Experience are good and much of this can attributed to in-store as well as television activity. Partly as a result of this, one of Wella's communication strengths lies with its in-store promotional activities (in-store mechanics). However, it was necessary to build the values associated with the brand, and television advertising would be a strong mechanism to deliver brand values and inform about sales promotion tie-ups. There would be additional benefits through support for the trade, as well as providing consumer interest and motivation.

The marketing communication objectives were to generate high levels of awareness and interesting campaigns that add consumer value. The real goal was to build the personality of the brand and develop its equity.

The brand was positioned on both a rational and an emotional basis. The rational platform was the delivery of beautiful hair with more body and more shine, while the emotional benefits focused on giving women the confidence to look beautiful through an understanding of their lifestyle.

The promotional methods used to deliver the strategy focused on the two main target audiences: the consumer and the trade. For the consumer market, television sponsorship from January to June in 1998 provided an anchor around which television advertising, sales promotion and direct marketing activities were levered. Videos of past television series under sponsorship were used to drive further associations with the brand and to generate widespread national promotional activity. Public relations was used to develop knowledge and understanding of the role of Liquid Hair. Advertorials, national newspaper tie-ups and press releases were the primary mechanisms.

For the trade, consumer-orientated promotions such as buy-one-get-one-free (BOGOF) and special packs of shampoo with free conditioner were used to generate trials and retrieve lapsed users. In addition, in-store point of purchase mechanics which linked with the public relations activities were also used to develop brand personality. The key aspect of these in-store promotions was that they were supported by television and radio. Wella developed coordinated marketing communications that used a strong theme, specific objectives and clear strategy.

This brief history of the S&C market and Wella's participation seeks to demonstrate a number of important points. The market is dynamic: it is constantly changing, and as such the objectives and strategies pursued by the players are adapted to the context in which each organisation finds itself.

The promotional tools are the same, but the way they are used by each brand is different. This reflects their history, skills, resources, objectives, strategies and the needs of the part of the target market. It is also a reflection of the way each brand is perceived and the way each brand (manager) perceives its part of the market. Marketing communications cannot and should not be seen or used as a prescriptive tool. Marketing communications is as much a part of the market as the products and people that populate it. Marketing communications is a part of the S&C market context – it is not a detached element that can be used to finely manipulate market shares. If only it was that simple!

This book endeavours to uncover different aspects of marketing communications, some of which have been represented in the Wella example.

The author would like to express his thanks to Wella UK for its willingness to provide materials and to assist with the accuracy of the information in this case illustration. In particular, thanks are due to Mark Bleathman, Senior Product Manager, Wella UK, for his insight, advice and technical support.

Consequently, contexts are not independent or isolated sets of easily identifiable circumstances, but are interrelated and overlapping circumstances in which it is rare for any one organisation to have total knowledge of any single context. Management make judgements based upon their experience, marketing research and limited knowledge of any one identifiable part context, and it might be said that each time a marketing communications programme is rolled out management takes an educated leap into the unknown.

Summary

The concept of exchange transactions is seen by many commentators as underpinning the marketing concept. Of the different types of exchange, market and relational are the two that can be observed most often in industrial societies.

Marketing communications have a number of roles to play in the context of both these types of exchange, but as will be seen later in this text, there is a strong movement away from the reliance on market exchanges to the longer-term perspective that relational exchanges enjoy and to the development of partnerships. This approach is referred to as 'relationship marketing', and it is here that changes in the use and deployment of marketing communications can be best observed.

There are four traditional elements to the promotional mix: advertising, sales promotion, public relations and personal selling. Each has strengths and weaknesses, and these tools are now beginning to be used in different ways to develop relationships with customers, whether they be consumers or organisational buyers. An example of these changes is direct marketing, which has grown rapidly over the past decade, and the direct-response media used are, essentially, a reconfiguration of the traditional promotional tools.

Marketing communications have an important role to play in communicating and promoting the products and services not only to customers but also to organisations who represent the channel partners and other stakeholders. The development of partnerships between brands and consumers and between organisations within distribution channels or networks is an important perspective of marketing communications. Communications in this context will be an important part of this text.

Finally, marketing communications can be seen as a series of episodes that occur within a particular set of circumstances or contexts. Marketing managers need to be able to identify principal characteristics of the context they are faced with and contribute to the context with a suitable promotional programme.

Review questions

1. Briefly compare and contrast the different types of exchange transaction.
2. How does communication assist the exchange process?
3. Name the five main elements of the marketing communications mix.
4. Write a brief description of each element of the marketing communications mix.
5. How do each of the elements compare across the following criteria: control, communication effectiveness and cost?
6. How does direct marketing differ from the other elements of the mix?
7. Identify five different advertisements that you think are using direct-response media. How effective do you think they might be?
8. Explain contexts and episodes. Describe the main tasks facing the management team responsible for marketing communications.
9. What is systems theory and how might it apply to marketing communications?
10. Explain how marketing communications supports the marketing and business strategies of the organisation.

References

Andersson, P. (1992) Analysing distribution channel dynamics. *European Journal of Marketing*, **26**(2), 47–68.

Bagozzi, R. (1978) Marketing as exchange: a theory of transactions in the market place. *American Behavioural Science*, **21**(4), 257–61.

Bowersox, D. and Morash, E. (1989) The integration of marketing flows in channels of distribution. *European Journal of Marketing*, **23**, 2.

Crane, A. (1994) Tuning the Channel. *Financial Times*, 14 March, p.11.

Delozier, M. (1976) *The Marketing Communication Process*. London: McGraw Hill.

Dwyer, R., Schurr, P. and Oh, S. (1987) Developing buyer–seller relationships. *Journal of Marketing*, **51**(April), 11–27.

Goldhaber, G.M. (1986) *Organisational Communication*. Dubuque: W.C. Brown.

Houston, F. and Gassenheimer, J. (1987) Marketing and exchange. *Journal of Marketing*, **51** (October), 3–18.

Katz, D. and Kahn, R.L. (1978) *The Social Psychology of Organisations*, 2nd edn. New York: John Wiley & Sons.

Kotler, P. (1984) Kotler: rethink the marketing concept. *Marketing News*, 14 September.

Lloyd, J. (1997) Cut your rep free. *Pharmaceutical Marketing* (September), 30–2.

McCarthy, E.J. (1960) *Basic Marketing: A Managerial Approach*. Homewood IL: Richard D. Irwin.

Mauss, M. (1974) *The Gift: Forms and Functions of Exchange in Archaic Societies*. London: Routledge & Kegan Paul.

Mexican Statement (1978) *The Place of Public Relations in Management Education*. Public Relations Education Trust, June.

Mohr, J. and Nevin, J. (1990) Communication strategies in marketing channels. *Journal of Marketing* (October), 36–51.

Pandya, A. and Dholkia, N. (1992) An institutional theory of exchange in marketing. *European Journal of Marketing*, **26**(12), 19–41.

Slingsby, H. (1993) Firms gain heart from new values. *Marketing Week*, 12 March, p. 17.

Stern, L. and El-Ansary, A. (1992) *Marketing Channels*, 4th edn. Englewood Cliffs NJ: Prentice Hall.

Waller, R. (1996) BBC Radio 4 *Today* programme, 29 July.

chapter 2

Communication theory

Only by sharing meaning with members of the target audience can it be hoped to create a dialogue through which marketing goals can be accomplished. To share meaning successfully may require the support of significant others: those who may be expert, knowledgeable or have access to appropriate media channels.

AIMS AND OBJECTIVES

The aims of this chapter are to introduce communication theory and to set it in the context of marketing communications.

The objectives of this chapter are:

1. To understand the basic model of the communication process.
2. To appreciate how the components of the model contribute to successful communications.
3. To provide an analysis of the linkages between components.
4. To examine the impact of personal influences on the communication process.
5. To introduce more recent explanations of communication theory, including networks.
6. To explain how communication theory underpins our understanding of marketing communications.

An introduction to the communication process

It was established in the previous chapter that marketing communications is partly an attempt by an organisation/brand to create and sustain a dialogue with its various constituencies. Communication itself is the process by which individuals share meaning. Therefore, for a dialogue to occur each participant needs to understand the meaning of the other's communication.

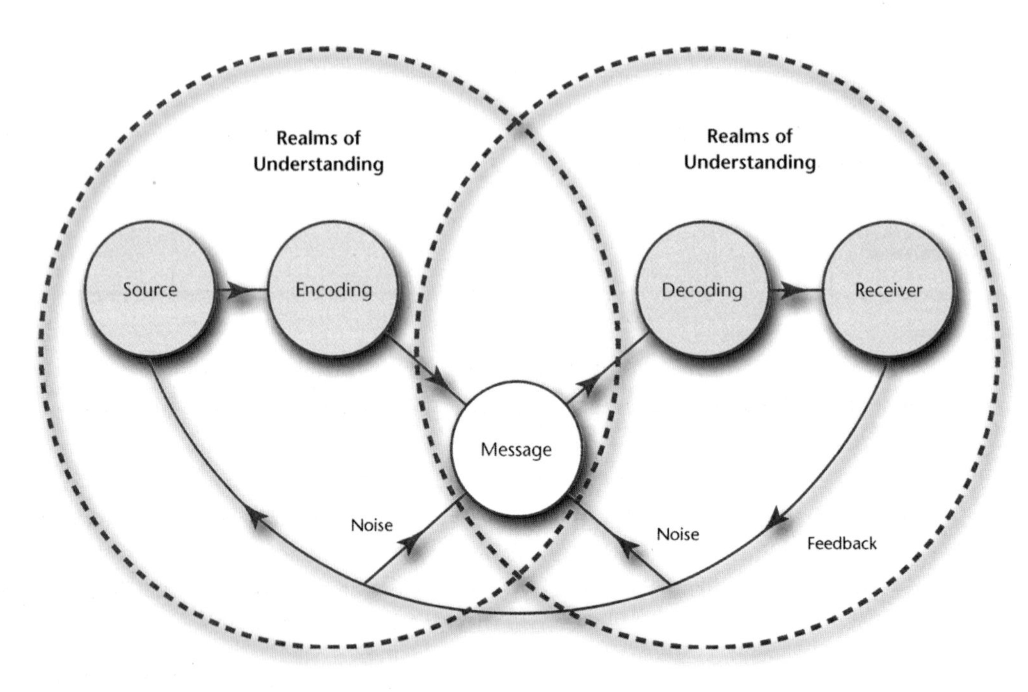

Figure 2.1 A linear model of communication (based on Schramm (1955) and Shannon and Weaver (1962)).

For this overall process to work, information needs to be transmitted (Dibb *et al.*, 1991) by all participants. It is important, therefore, that those involved with marketing communications understand the complexity of the transmission process. Through knowledge and understanding of the communications process, they are more likely to achieve their objective of sharing meaning with each member of their target audiences and so have an opportunity to enter into a dialogue.

In the previous chapter the point was established that there are a variety of reasons why organisations need to communicate with various groups. Of these, one of the more prominent is the need to influence or persuade.

As an initial observation, persuasive communications can be seen in three different contexts. First, persuasion can be viewed in the form of the negotiations that occur between individuals. Here persuasion is based upon a variety of overt and subtle rewards and punishments.

Second, persuasion can be seen in the form of propaganda. Organisations seek to influence their target audiences through the use of symbols, training and cultural indoctrination. The third and final context is that of a speaker addressing a large group. Influence in this context is achieved through the structure of the material presented, the manner in which the presentation is delivered and the form of evidence used to influence the group.

These three perspectives focus upon persuasion, but there is a strong need for organisations also to inform and remind. Furthermore, these approaches are too specific for general marketing purposes and fail to provide assistance to those who wish to plan and manage particular communications.

Linear model of communication

Wilbur Schramm (1955) developed what is now accepted as the basic model of mass communications (Figure 2.1). The components of the linear model of communication are:

1. Source: the individual or organisation sending the message.
2. Encoding: transferring the intended message into a symbolic style that can be transmitted.
3. Signal: the transmission of the message using particular media.
4. Decoding: understanding the symbolic style of the message in order to understand the message.
5. Receiver: the individual or organisation receiving the message.
6. Feedback: the receiver's communication back to the source on receipt of the message.
7. Noise: distortion of the communication process, making it difficult for the receiver to interpret the message as intended by the source.

This is a linear model which emphasises the 'transmission of information, ideas, attitudes, or emotion from one person or group to another (or others), primarily through symbols' (Theodorson and Theodorson, 1969). The model and its components are straightforward, but it is the quality of the linkages between the various elements in the process that determine whether the communication will be successful.

Source/encoding

The source, an individual or organisation, identifies a need to transmit a message and then selects a combination of appropriate words, pictures, symbols and music to represent the message to be transmitted. This is called encoding. The purpose is to create a message that is capable of being understood by the receiver.

There are a number of reasons why the source/encoding link might break down. For example, the source may fail to diagnose a particular situation accurately. By not fully understanding a stakeholder's problem or level of knowledge, inappropriate information may be included in the message, which, when transmitted, may lead to misunderstanding and misinterpretation by the receiver. By failing to appreciate the level of education of the target receiver, a message might be encoded in words and symbols that are beyond the comprehension of the receiver.

Some organisations spend a great deal of time and expense on marketing research, trying to develop their understanding of their target audience. This is a point that we shall return to later. The source of a message is an important factor in the communication process. A receiver who perceives a source lacking conviction, authority, trust or expertise is likely to discount any message received from that source, until such time that credibility is established.

Most organisations spend a great deal of time and expense recruiting sales representatives. The risk involved in selecting the wrong people can be extremely large. Many high-tech organisations require their new sales staff to spend over a year receiving both product and sales training before allowing them to meet customers.

From a customer's perspective, salespersons who display strong product knowledge skills and who are also able to empathise with the individual members of the decision-making unit (DMU) are more likely to be perceived as credible. Therefore, the organisation that prepares its sales staff and presents them as knowledgeable and trustworthy, is more likely to be successful in the communication process than those that do not take the same level of care.

The source is a part of the communication process, not just the generator of detached messages. Patzer (1983) determined that the physical attractiveness of the communicator, particularly if it is the source, contributes significantly to the effectiveness of persuasive communications.

This observation can be related to the use, by organisations, of spokespersons and celebrities to endorse products. Spokespersons can be better facilitators of the communication process if they are able to convey conviction, if they are easily associated with the object of the message, if they have credible expertise and if they are attractive to the receiver, in the wider sense of the word.

This legitimate authority is developed in many television advertisements by the use of the 'white coat', or product-specific clothing, as a symbol of expertise. By dressing the spokesperson in a white coat, he or she is perceived immediately as a credible source of information ('they know what they are talking about'), and so is much more likely to be believed.

Signal

Once encoded, the message must be put into a form that is capable of transmission. It may be oral or written, verbal or non-verbal, in a symbolic form or in a sign. Whatever the format chosen, the source must be sure that what is being put into the message is what is wanted to be decoded by the receiver. The importance of this aspect of the communication process will be developed later when different message strategies are examined in Chapter 14.

The channel is the means by which the message is transmitted from the source to the receiver. These channels may be personal or non-personal. The former involves face-to-face contact and word-of-mouth communications, which can be extremely influential. Non-personal channels are characterised by mass media advertising, which can reach large audiences.

Information received directly from personal influence channels is generally more persuasive than information received through mass media. This may be a statement of the obvious, but the reasons for this need to be understood. First, the individual approach permits greater flexibility in the delivery of the message. The timing and power with which a message is delivered can be adjusted to suit the immediate 'selling' environment. Second, a message can be adapted to meet the needs of the customer as the sales call progresses. This flexibility is not possible with mass media messages, as these have to be designed and produced well in advance of transmission and often without direct customer input.

Decoding/receiver

Decoding is the process of transforming and interpreting a message into thought. This process is influenced by the receiver's realm of understanding, which encompasses the experiences, perceptions, attitudes and values of both the source and the receiver. The more the receiver understands about the source and the greater his or her experience in decoding the source's messages, the more able the receiver will be to decode the message successfully.

Feedback/response

The set of reactions a receiver has after seeing, hearing or reading the message is known as the response. These reactions may vary from the extreme of dialling an enquiry telephone number, returning a coupon or even buying the product, to storing information in long-term memory for future use. Feedback is that part of the response that is sent back to the sender, and is essential for successful communication. The need to understand not just whether the message has been received but also which message has been received is vital. For example, the receiver may have decoded the message incorrectly and a completely different set of responses elicited. If a suitable feedback system is not in place then the source will be unaware that the communication has been unsuccessful and is liable to continue wasting resources. This represents inefficient and ineffective marketing communications.

The evaluation of feedback is, of course, vital if sound communications are to be developed. Only through evaluation can the success of any communication be judged. Feedback through personal selling can be instantaneous, through overt means such as questioning, raising objections or signing an order form. Other means, such as the use of gestures and body language, are less overt, and the decoding of the feedback needs to be accurate if an appropriate response is to be given. For the advertiser, the process is much more vague and prone to misinterpretation and error.

Feedback through mass media channels is generally much more difficult to obtain, mainly because of the inherent time delay involved in the feedback process. There are some exceptions, namely the overnight ratings provided by the Broadcasters' Audience Research Board (BARB) to the television contractors, but as a rule feedback is normally delayed and not as fast. Some commentators argue that the only meaningful indicator of communication success is sales. However, there are many other influences that affect the level of sales, such as price, the effect of previous communications, the recommendations of opinion leaders or friends, poor competitor actions or any number of government or regulatory developments. Except in circumstances such as direct marketing, where immediate and direct feedback can be determined, organisations should use other methods to gauge the success of their communications activities, for example the level and quality of customer inquiries, the number and frequency of store visits, the degree of attitude change and the ability to recognise or recall an advertisement. All of these represent feedback, but, as a rough distinction, the evaluation of feedback for mass communications is much more difficult to judge than the evaluation of interpersonal communications.

Noise

A complicating factor which may influence the quality of the reception and the feedback is noise. Noise, according to Mallen (1977), is 'the omission and distortion of information', and there will always be some noise present in all communications. Management's role is to ensure that levels of noise are kept to a minimum, wherever it is able to exert influence.

Noise occurs when a receiver is prevented from receiving the message. This may be because of either cognitive or physical factors. For example, a cognitive factor may be that the encoding of the message was inappropriate, so making it difficult for the receiver to decode the message. In this circumstance it is said that the realms of understanding of the source and the receiver were not matched. Another reason why noise may enter the system is that the receiver may have been physically prevented from decoding the message accurately because the receiver was distracted. Examples of distraction are that the telephone rang, or someone in the room asked a question or coughed. A further reason could be that competing messages screened out the targeted message.

Some sales promotion practitioners are using the word 'noise' to refer to the ambience and publicity surrounding a particular sales promotion event. In other words, the word is being used as a positive, advantageous element in the communication process. This approach is not adopted in this text.

Realms of understanding

The concept of the 'realm of understanding' was introduced earlier. It is an important element in the communication process because it recognises that successful communications are more likely to be achieved if the source and the receiver understand each other. This understanding concerns attitudes, perceptions, behaviour and experience: the values of both parties to the communication process. Therefore, effective communication is more likely when there is some common ground, a realm of understanding between the source and receiver.

Some organisations, especially those in the private sector, spend a huge amount of money researching their target markets and testing their advertisements to ensure that their messages can be decoded and understood by the target audience. The more organisations understand their receivers, the more confident they become in constructing and transmitting messages to them. Repetition and learning, as we shall see later, are important elements in marketing communications. Learning is a function of knowledge and, the more we know, the more likely we are to understand.

Kelman's model of source characteristics

Kelman (1961) developed a simple scheme for examining the characteristics of a source. Figure 2.2 indicates that these are source credibility, source attractiveness and the degree of compliance required by the source. Each characteristic involves a different process by which the source influences attitudinal or behavioural change in the receiver.

Source credibility refers to the extent that receivers perceive the source, or a participant in the communication process, as able and willing to give an objective opinion and as having sufficient relevant expertise. As explained earlier, a high level of perceived expertise in a source is often more persuasive than if the expertise is perceived as low. Trustworthiness is important, as the impact of the source will be reduced if receivers perceive the source to be biased.

A high level of source credibility is not always an asset, nor is a low-credibility source always a liability. Eagly and Chaiken (1975) found high- and low-credibility sources to be of equal effectiveness when the source is arguing for a position opposing

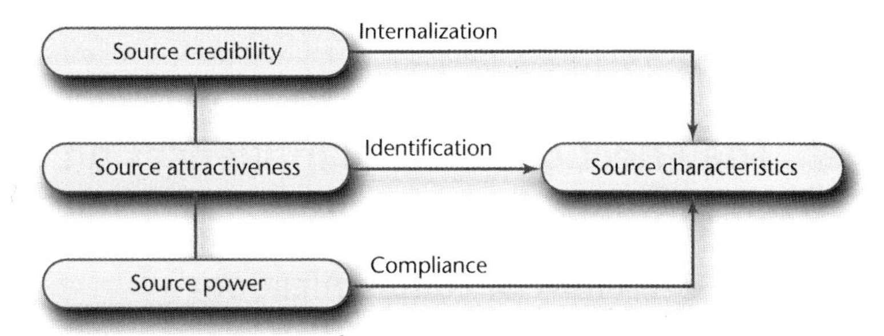

Figure 2.2 Kelman's model of source characteristics (Kelman (1961); used with kind permission).

their own best interest. The use of a high-credibility source is of less importance when the receivers have a neutral position. Recent advertisements in the United Kingdom (e.g. Lombard North, Parcelforce) suggest that source credibility and attractiveness need not necessarily be high in order to be effective.

While a great deal of empirical work indicates that the credibility of a message source correlates strongly with a message's ability to induce attitude change there are a number of factors that can moderate this change (Newell and Shemwell, 1995). Factors such as involvement, product type, message type, experience and expectations are some of the more notable influences.

Source attractiveness develops when a source is perceived as attractive, and persuasion, according to Kelman, occurs through a process known as identification. This is apparent when the receiver is motivated to seek some type of relationship with the source and so adopts a similar position. The receiver may only maintain the attitude or behaviour as long as it is supported by the source or as long as the source remains attractive.

Organisations often select sales staff whose characteristics have a strong correlation with their customers or who have similar backgrounds to those of the target audience. This is thought to be an appropriate way to help build a bond or area of common interest between the two parties. This bond of similarity can also be established through what is referred to as 'slice of life' advertising. This is a technique where the target audience is exposed to a series of messages which represent an everyday occurrence or problem. The receiver is encouraged to believe 'I can see myself in that situation'. Credibility is established by inviting receivers to identify themselves with the situation and by showing how the promoted product can resolve their problem. Oxo have promoted their gravy and stock cubes using this approach. Advertisements that depict a family in which everyday events are portrayed are used to associate the Oxo product so that the target audience can identify easily and naturally with the overall scene.

Source power is said to be present when the source of a message is able to reward or punish. When the receiver perceives source power, the influence process occurs through compliance. In an attempt to be rewarded and to avoid punishment, the receiver complies with the request of the source.

Such power is difficult to apply in advertising, but is more easily identifiable in personal selling, where sales staff, through use of a lavish expense account, for example, may exert power over a buyer. Alternatively, if the seller's organisation is perceived as dominating a market, buyers may comply with the requests of the source to ensure continuity of supply.

The effect of personal influences on the communications process

One-step flow of communication

Having looked at the traditional model of communication, attention must now be given to the effect that personal influences may have on the process. The traditional view of communication holds that the process consists essentially of one step. Information is directed and shot at prospective audiences, rather like a bullet is propelled from a gun. The decision of each member of the audience to act on the message or not is the result of a passive role or participation in the process (Figure 2.3).

Organisations can communicate with different target audiences simply by varying the message and the type and frequency of channels used. The one-step model has been criticised for its oversimplification, and it certainly ignores the effect of personal influences on the communication process.

Two-step flow of communication

This model depicts information flowing via media channels to particular types of people (opinion leaders and opinion formers; see later) to whom other members of the audience refer for information and guidance. Through interpersonal networks, opinion leaders not only reach members of the target audience who may not have been exposed to the message, but may reinforce the impact of the message for those members that did receive the message (Figure 2.4). For example, editors of travel sections in the Sunday press and television presenters of travel programmes fulfil the role of opinion former and can influence the decision of prospective travellers. It can be seen that targets 5 and 6 were not exposed to the original message, so the opinion leader (OL; T_4) acts as an original information source for them and as a reinforcer for targets 1, 2 and 3.

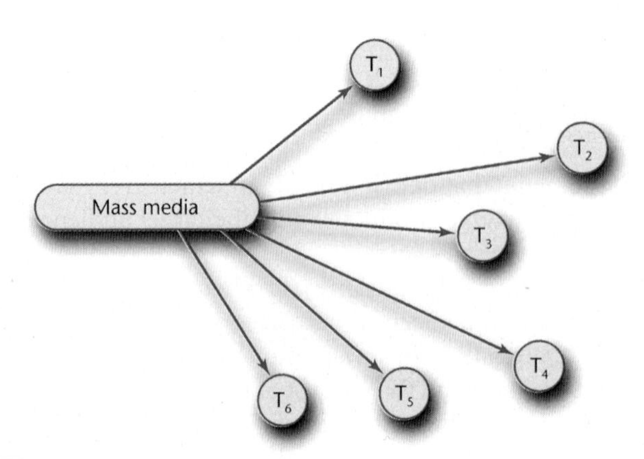

Figure 2.3 One-step model of communication. T = member of the target audience.

The implication of the two-step model is that the mass media do not have a direct and all-powerful effect over their audiences. If the primary function of the mass media is to provide information, then personal influences are necessary to be persuasive and to exert direct influence on members of the target audience.

CASE ILLUSTRATION

Dennis fire engines

Kelman's model can be used to interpret the source characteristics associated with the promotion of Dennis fire engines. The number of fire engines sold in the United Kingdom was 233 (1997). Each fire unit costs each of the 63 fire brigades approximately £140,000. Of the chassis that are built, Dennis are market leaders with a 40% share and Volvo second with 32%. The other players are Mercedes and Scania.

Dennis fire engines can be observed in current affairs and news programmes, such as the *News at Ten* on ITV and the BBC's *9 O'clock News*, plus various films, television series and documentaries (see Plate 2.1). The use of Dennis engines in films began in the mid-1980s when two old S and D engines from the London Fire Brigade were converted. Since then, other engines have been refurbished and used in similar ways. The reasoning behind this type of exposure is that the name Dennis, prominently displayed across the front of each tender, serves to reinforce the brand name. In addition, this visibility also helps to provide buyer confidence by reducing risk through familiarity and association.

The high source credibility bestowed on Dennis through on-screen exposure is an important part of its overall approach to marketing communications. First, any news event, such as a major fire, road traffic accident or terrorist incident, may present opportunities for television coverage, where Dennis engines can be observed in action. Source expertise is bestowed because of the bravery and skill of those involved in attending to the incident. Trustworthiness is represented through the continued presence and reliability of the equipment: Dennis equipment.

Source attractiveness is more difficult to attribute, but should Dennis be featured in a documentary or film any ensuing success may prompt potential buyers to desire a relationship with Dennis, simply because of a wish to be associated with success.

The primary promotional tool in the market is personal selling, and each manufacturer tries to develop strong relationships with the buyers of each brigade. It is here that source power can also be identified, because, through the process of personal selling, reference to the fact that Dennis fire engines can be observed in various credible media may be of benefit in much the same way that some used to say 'no one ever got fired for buying IBM'. Such pressure to comply and reinforce the market leader's position can be strong.

To support personal selling, Dennis places advertisements on a regular basis in the two main trade magazines, *Fire Magazine* and *Fire International*. These serve to maintain awareness, provide more detailed information and help defend its leadership position.

Dennis uses many of the tools in the promotional mix and a variety of media in delivering its messages. To be successful in this, and other markets, it is important that it and its messages are perceived to be credible. Kelman's model, while not perfect, can be used to interpret and understand the source characteristics of Dennis's marketing communications.

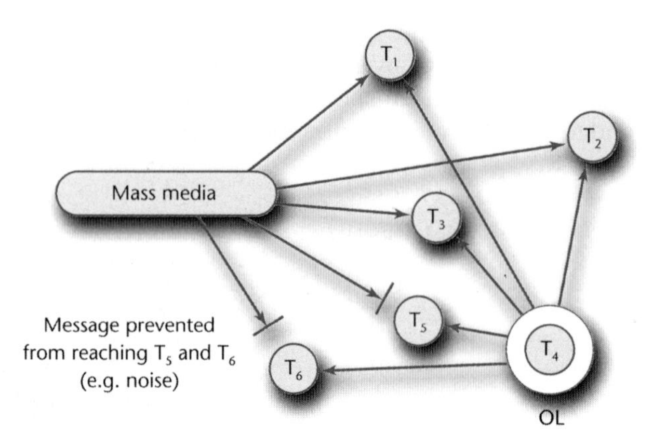

Figure 2.4 Two-step model of communication. OL = opinion leader.

Multi-step flow of communications

This model proposes that the process involves interaction among all parties to the communication process; see Figure 2.5. This interpretation closely resembles the network of participants that are often involved in the communication process.

Word-of-mouth communications

The multi-step model suggests that opinion leaders/formers and members of the target audience all influence each other. The communication process is two-way, and interaction by word-of-mouth communications assists and enriches the communication process.

We can see, therefore, the importance of personal influences upon the communication process. Customers use word-of-mouth recommendations to provide information and to support and reinforce their purchasing decisions. At the heart of this approach is the source credibility that is assigned to people whose opinions are sought after and used in the purchase decision process.

People like to talk about their product experiences, for a variety of reasons that are explored in the next section. However, by talking with a neighbour or colleague about the good experiences associated with a new car, for example, the first-hand 'this has actually happened to someone I know' effect will be instrumental in the same views being passed on to other colleagues, irrespective of their validity or overall representation of similar cars.

But why do people want to discuss products or advertising messages? Dichter (1966) determined that such motivation fell into four categories:

1. *Product involvement*
   People, he found, have a high propensity to discuss matters that are either distinctly pleasurable or unpleasurable. Such discussion serves to provide an opportunity for the experience to be relived, whether it be the 'looking for' or the 'use' experience, or both.

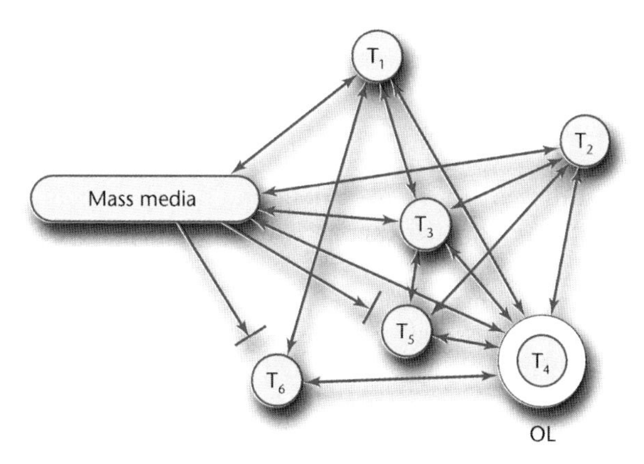

Figure 2.5 Multi-step model of communication.

2. *Self-involvement*
   Discussion offers a means for ownership to be established and signals aspects of prestige and levels of status to the receiver. More importantly perhaps, dissonance can be reduced as the purchaser seeks reassurance about the decision.
3. *Other involvement*
   Products can assist motivations to help others and to express feelings of love, friendship and caring. These feelings can be released through a sense of sharing the variety of benefits that products can bestow.
4. *Message involvement*
   The final motivation to discuss products is derived, according to Dichter, from the messages that surround the product itself, in particular the advertising messages and, in the business-to-business market, seminars, exhibitions and the trade Press, which provide the means to provoke conversation and so stimulate word-of-mouth recommendation.

It is interesting to note that Dichter's various forms of involvement, in particular the 'self' and 'other' categories, bear a strong similarity to the market exchanges and reciprocal exchanges explored in Chapter 1.

These motivations to discuss products and their associative experiences vary between individuals and with the intensity of the motivation at any one particular moment. For organisations it is important to target messages at those individuals who are predisposed to such discussion, as this may well propel word-of-mouth recommendations and the success of the communications campaign. The target, therefore, is not necessarily the target market, but those in the target market who are most likely to volunteer their positive opinions about the offering or those who, potentially, have some influence over members. There are three types of such volunteers: opinion leaders, formers and followers.

Opinion leaders

Katz and Lazerfeld (1955) first identified individuals who were predisposed to receiving information and then reprocessing it to influence others. Their studies of

American voting and purchase behaviour led to their conclusion that those individuals who could exert such influence were more persuasive than information received directly from the mass media. These opinion leaders, according to Rogers (1962), tend 'to be of the same social class as non-leaders, but may enjoy a higher social status within the group'. Williams (1990) uses the work of Reynolds and Darden (1971) to suggest that they are more gregarious and more self-confident than non-leaders and, importantly, have a greater exposure to relevant mass media.

Opinion leadership can be simulated in advertising by the use of product testimonials. Using ordinary people to express positive comments about a product to each other is a very well-used advertising technique. For example, Stork used to show ordinary people being asked if they could taste the difference between Stork margarine and butter.

The importance of opinion leaders, in the design and implementation of communication plans should not be underestimated. Midgley and Dowling (1993) refer to *innovator communicators*: those who are receptive to new ideas and who make innovation-based purchase decisions without reference to or from other people. However, while the importance of these individuals is not doubted, a major difficulty exists in trying to identify just who these opinion leaders and innovator communicators are. While they sometimes display some distinctive characteristics, such as reading specialist media vehicles, often being first to return coupons, enjoying attending exhibitions or just involving themselves with new, innovative techniques or products, they are by their very nature invisible outside their work, family and social groups.

Opinion formers

Opinion formers are individuals who are able to exert personal influence because of their authority, education or status associated with the object of the communication process. Like opinion leaders, they are looked to by others to provide information and advice, but this is because of the formal expertise that opinion formers are adjudged to have. For example, community pharmacists are often consulted about symptoms and medicines, and film critics carry such conviction in their reviews that they can make or break a new production.

Opinion formers

The BBC radio programme *The Archers*, an everyday story of country folk, has been used to deliver messages about farming issues. The actors in the programme are opinion formers and they direct messages to farmers about farming techniques and methods. The educational use was very important after the Second World War.

Popular television programmes, such as *Eastenders*, *Brookside* and *Coronation Street*, all of which attract huge audiences, have been used as vehicles to bring to attention and open up debates about many controversial social issues, such as contraception, abortion, drug use and abuse, and serious illness and mental health concerns.

CASE ILLUSTRATION

Opinion formers – Durogesic

To relieve pain caused through cancer a new drug, Durogesic, was launched in 1995. This drug offered patients an improved quality of life by reducing the impact of side-effects such as constipation and nausea. However, this drug failed to gain the expected market penetration, partly because of the strong loyalty and attitudes held by doctors towards the traditional pain relief, morphine.

A marketing communications campaign was developed to change these attitudes. It was decided that three abstracts should be published: one focused on GPs' underestimation of cancer patient pain, the second highlighted cancer in teenagers and the third looked at the benefits of Durogesic in the adult population.

To ensure the speedy dissemination of these abstracts, it was necessary to develop educational materials providing accurate information for the media and to convince opinion leaders. Three main types were identified: first, qualified nurses working with the Pain Society, the National Cancer Alliance and the Pain Network; second, eminent doctors working in the therapeutic area; and third, cancer patients who had been using the drug.

Many cancer charities would be approached when the campaign broke, so they were advised in advance, but otherwise there was a strict embargo on TV, radio and press coverage to ensure that the story broke with maximum impact. Advertising for the drug was increased to capitalise on the increased attention the drug was to receive.

In order for the campaign to break with impact it was necessary to gain the support of opinion formers, many of whom were in the media. One of the more notable and influential is the ITN's *News at Ten* programme, and they decided to interview various opinion leaders nominated in the press kits. From this high-profile media exposure considerable media coverage developed: TV (BBC1: *Good Morning with Anne and Nick* and *South Today*), radio (Radio 5 Live: *The Breakfast Programme*) and press (*Daily Mail*, *The Independent*, *The Times*).

Source: Sparkes (1997)

The influence of opinion formers can be great. For example, the editor of a journal or newspaper may be a recognised source of expertise, and any offering referred to by the editor in the media vehicle is endowed with great credibility. In this sense the editor acts as a gatekeeper, and it is the task of the marketing communicator to ensure that all relevant opinion formers are identified and sent appropriate messages.

Many organisations constantly lobby key members of parliament in an effort to persuade them to pursue 'favourable' policies. Opinion formers are relatively easy to identify, as they need to be seen shaping the opinion of others, usually opinion followers.

Opinion followers

The vast majority of consumers can be said to be opinion followers. The messages they receive via the mass media are tempered by the opinions of the two groups of personal influencers just discussed. Some people actively seek information from those they believe are well informed, while others prefer to use the mass media for information and guidance (Robinson, 1976). However, this should not distract from the point that, although followers, they still process information independently and use a variety of inputs when sifting information and responding to marketing stimuli.

Ethical drug manufacturers normally launch new drugs by enlisting the support of particular doctors who have specialised in the therapy area and who are recognised by other doctors as experts. These opinion leaders are invited to lead symposia and associated events to build credibility and activity around the new product. At the same time, public relations agencies prepare press releases with the aim that the information will be used by the mass media (opinion formers) for editorial purposes and create exposure for the product across the target audience, which, depending upon the product and/or the media vehicle may be GPs, hospital doctors, patients or the general public. All these people, whether they be opinion leaders or formers, are active influencers or talkers (Kingdom, 1970).

Process of adoption

An interesting extension to the concept of opinion followers and the discussion on word-of-mouth communications is the process by which individuals become committed to the use of a new product. Rogers (1983) has identified this as the process of adoption and the stages of his innovation decision process are represented in Figure 2.6. These stages in the adoption process are sequential and are charac-

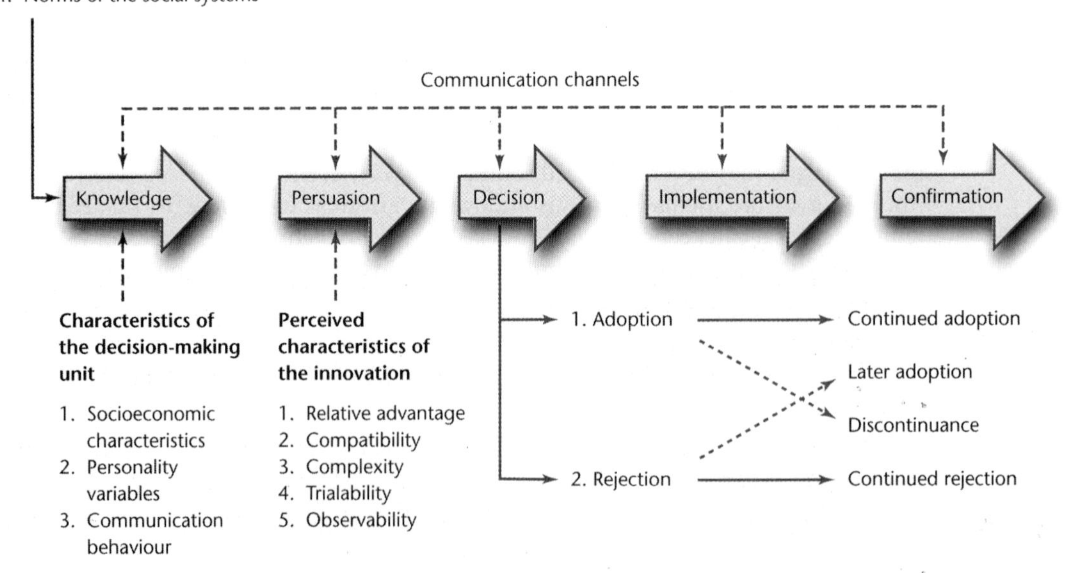

Figure 2.6 Stages in the innovation decision process of adoption (reprinted from Rogers (1983) with the permission of the Free Press. Copyright 1962, 1971, 1983 by the Free Press).

terised by the different factors that are involved at each stage (e.g. the media used by each individual).

1. *Knowledge*
   The innovation becomes known to consumers, but they have little information and no well-founded attitudes. Information must be provided through mass media to institutions and people that active seekers of information are likely to contact. Information for passive seekers should be supplied through the media and channels that this group habitually uses to look for other kinds of information (Windahl *et al.* 1992).

   Jack cleans his teeth regularly, but he is beginning to notice a sensitivity to both hot and cold drinks. He becomes aware of an advertisement for Special Paste on television.

2. *Persuasion*
   The consumer becomes aware that the innovation may be of use in solving known and potential problems. Information from those who have experience of the product becomes very important.

   Jack notices that the makers of Special Paste claim that their brand reduces the amount of sensitive reaction to hot and cold drinks. Special Paste has also been recommended to him by someone he overheard in the pub last week. Modelling behaviour predominates.

3. *Decision*
   An attitude may develop and may be either favourable or unfavourable, but as a result a decision is reached whether to trial the offering or not. Communications need to assist this part of the process by continual prompting.

   Jack is prepared to believe (or not to believe) the messages and the claims made on behalf of Special Paste. He thinks that Special Paste is potentially a very good brand (or not). He intends trying Special Paste because he was given a free sample (or because it was on a special price deal).

4. *Implementation*
   For the adoption to proceed in the absence of a sales promotion, buyers must know where to get it and how to use it. The product is then tested in a limited way. Communications must provide this information in order that the trial experience be developed.

   Jack buys 'Special Paste' and tests it.

5. *Confirmation*
   The innovation is accepted or rejected on the basis of the experience during trial. Planned communications play an important role in maintaining the new behaviour by dispelling negative thoughts and positively reaffirming the original 'correct' decision. McGuire, as reported in Windahl *et al.* (1992), refers to this as postbehavioural consolidation.

   It works, Jack's teeth are not as sensitive to hot and cold drinks as they were before he started using 'Special Paste'. He reads an article that reports that large numbers of people are using these types of products satisfactorily. Jack resolves to buy 'Special Paste' next time.

This process can be terminated at any stage and, of course, a number of competing brands may vie for consumers' attention simultaneously, so adding to the complexity and levels of noise in the process. Generally, mass communications are seen to be more effective in the earlier phases of the adoption process for products that buyers are actively interested in, and more interpersonal forms are more appropriate at the later stages, especially trial and adoption. This model assumes that the stages occur in a predictable sequence, but this clearly does not happen in all purchase activity, as some information that is to be used later in the trial stage may be omitted, which often happens when loyalty to a brand is high or where the buyer has experience in the market-place.

Process of diffusion

The process of adoption in aggregate form, over time, is diffusion. According to Rogers, diffusion is the process by which an innovation is communicated through certain channels over a period of time among the members of a social system. This is a group process and Rogers again identified five categories of adopters. Figure 2.7 shows how diffusion may be fast or slow and that there is no set speed at which the process occurs. The five categories are as follows:

1. *Innovators*: these groups like new ideas and have a large disposable income. This means they are more likely to take risks associated with new products.
2. *Early adopters*: research has established that this group contains a large proportion of opinion leaders and they are therefore important in speeding the diffusion process. Early adopters tend to be younger than any other group and above average in education. Other than innovators, this group takes more publications and consults more salespeople than all others. This group is important to the marketing communications process because they can determine the speed at which diffusion occurs.

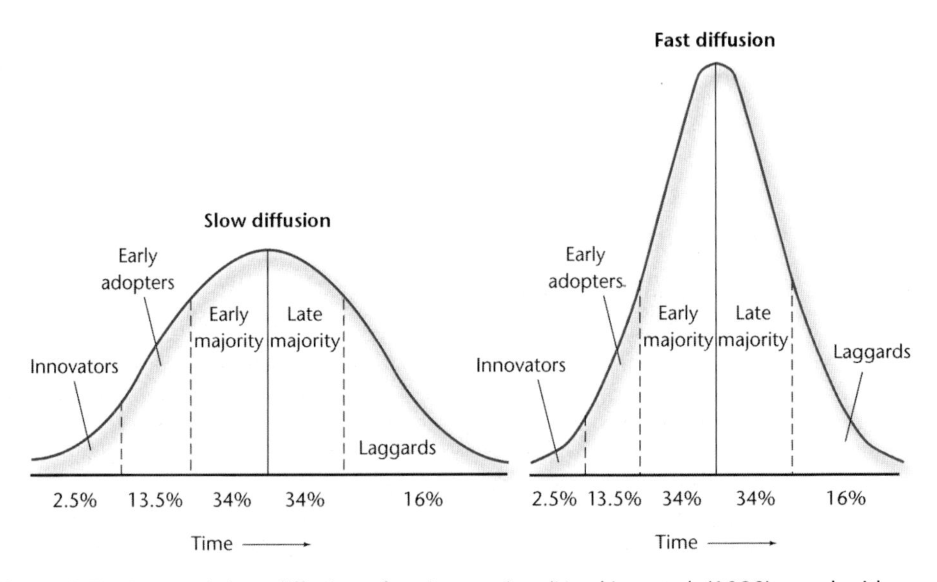

Figure 2.7 Fast and slow diffusion of an innovation (Hawkins *et al.* (1989); used with kind permission).

3. *Early majority*: usually, opinion followers are a little above average in age, education, social status and income. They rely on informal sources of information and take fewer publications than the previous two groups.
4. *Late majority*: this group of people is sceptical of new ideas and only adopts new products because of social or economic factors. They take few publications and are below average in education, social status and income.
5. *Laggards*: a group of people who are suspicious of all new ideas and set in their opinions. Lowest of all the groups in terms of income, social status and education, this group takes a long time to adopt an innovation.

This framework suggests that, at the innovation stage, messages should be targeted at relatively young people in the target group, with a high level of income, education and social status. This will speed word-of-mouth recommendation and the diffusion process. Mahajan *et al.* (1990) observe that the personal influence of word-of-mouth communications does not work in isolation from the other communication tools. Early adopters are more likely to adopt an innovation in response to 'external influences' and only through time will the effect of 'internal influences' become significant. In other words, mass media communications need time to work before word-of-mouth communications can begin to build effectiveness.

A major difficulty associated with the use of this framework, however, is the inability to define which stage of the diffusion process is operating at any time. Furthermore, Gatignon and Robertson (1985) suggest that there are three elements to the diffusion process which need to be taken into account, particularly for the FMCG sector:

1. The rate of diffusion or speed at which sales occur.
2. The pattern of diffusion or shape of the curve.
3. The potential penetration level or size of the market.

Care should be taken to ensure that all three of these elements are considered when attempting to understand the diffusion process. It can be concluded that if a promotional campaign is targeted at innovators and the early majority and is geared to stimulating word-of-mouth communications, then the diffusion process is more likely to be successful than if these elements are ignored.

Interactional approaches to communications

The models and frameworks of the communication process discussed to date can be interpreted as an abstraction. The one-step model is linear and unidirectional, and suggests that the receiver plays a passive role in the process. The two-step and multi-step models attempt to account for the interactive nature of communication and they proffer a mutually participative role for all parties to the communication process. These models emphasise individual behaviour and exclude the social behaviour implicit in the process. Goffman (1969) advocates an 'interactional' approach which focuses on the roles adopted by the players in the communication process. Through mutual understanding of each other's behaviour, the rules of the communication process are established. McEwan (1992) suggests that this permits formal and informal communication procedures to be established, and that mutual understanding (Rogers and Kincaid, 1981) and increased levels of trust can be developed by the participants.

This is an interesting perspective, as strands of the importance of source credibility can be identified in this approach. Evidence of Goffman's approach can be seen in personal selling. Sellers and buyers, meeting for the first time, often enter negotiations at a formal level, each adopting a justifiable, self-protective position. As negotiations proceed, so the two parties adjust their roles, and as the likelihood of a mutual exchange increases, so the formal roles give way to a more informal ones.

Relational or contextual approaches to communications

The previous model accounts for social behaviour, but does not account for the context within which the behaviour occurs. Communication events always occur within a context (Littlejohn, 1992) or particular set of circumstances, which not only influence the form of the communication but also the nature and the way the communication is received, interpreted and acted upon. There are a huge number of variables that can influence the context, including the disposition of the people involved, the physical environment, the nature of the issue, the history and associated culture, the goals of the participants and the anticipated repucussions of the dialogue itself.

Littlejohn identifies four main contextual levels. These are interpersonal, group, organisational and mass communication. These levels form part of a hierarchy whereby higher levels incorporate the lower levels but 'add something new of their own'.

The relational approach means that communication events are linked together in an organised manner, one where the events are 'punctuated' by interventions from one or more of the participants. These interventions occur whenever the participants attempt cooperation or if conflict arises.

Soldow and Thomas (1984), referring to a sales negotiation, state that a relationship develops through the form of negotiations rather than the content. An agreement is necessary about who is to control the relationship or whether there will be equality. Rothschild (1987) reports that 'sparring will continue' until agreement is reached or the negotiations are terminated. In other words, without mutual agreement over the roles of the participants, the true purpose of the interaction, to achieve an exchange, cannot be resolved.

An interesting aspect of relational communication theory is social penetration (Taylor and Altman, 1987). Through the disclosure of increasing amounts of information about themselves, partners in a relationship (personal or organisational) develop levels of intimacy which serve to build interpersonal (interorganisational?) relationships. The relationship moves forward as partners reveal successive layers of information about each other and, as a greater amount or breadth of information is shared, confidence grows. These levels can be seen to consist of orientation, exploratory affective exchange, affective exchange and stable exchange; see Table 2.1. These layers are not uncovered in a logical, orderly sequence. It is likely that partners will return to previous levels, test the outcomes and rewards and reconsider their positions as the relationships unfolds through time. This suggests that social penetration theory may lie at the foundation of the development of trust, commitment and relational exchanges between organisations.

Table 2.1 Layers of social penetration

Orientation: the disclosure of public information only.
Exploratory affective exchange: expansion and development of public information.
Affective exchange: disclosure, based upon anticipated relationship rewards, of deeper feelings, values and beliefs.
Stable exchange: high level of intimacy where partners are able to predict each other's reactions with a good level of accuracy.

Source: Adapted from Taylor and Altman (1987).

Relationships need not be just dyadic, as the interactional approach suggests, but could be triadic or even encompass a much wider network or array of participants. Through this perspective a 'communication network' can be observed, through which information can flow. Participants engage in communication based upon their perception of the environment in which the communication occurs and the way in which each participant relates to each other.

Rogers (1986) identifies a communication network as 'consisting of interconnected individuals who are linked by patterned communication flows'. This is important, as it views communication transcending organisational boundaries. In other words, it is not only individuals within an organisation that develop patterned communication flows but also individuals across different organisations. These individuals participate with one another (possibly through exchanges) and use communication networks to achieve their agenda items.

The extent to which individuals are linked to the network is referred to as connectedness. The more a network is connected, the greater the likelihood that a message will be disseminated, as there are few isolated individuals. Similarly, the level of integration in a network refers to the degree to which members of the network are linked to one another. The greater the integration the more potential channels there are for a message to be routed through.

Systems theory, as discussed in the previous chapter, recognises that organisations are made of interacting units. The relational approach to communications is similar to systems theory. The various 'criss-crossing' flows of information between reciprocating units allow individuals and groups to modify the actions of others in the 'net', and this permits the establishment of a pattern of communication (Tichy, 1979).

Network approaches to communications

The regular use of these patterned flows leads to the development of communication networks, which have been categorised as prescribed and emergent (Weick, 1987). Prescribed networks are formalised patterns of communication, very often established by senior management within an organisation or by organisational representatives when interorganisational communications are considered. It follows that emergent networks are informal and emerge as a response to the social and task-orientated needs of the participants.

Undoubtedly some of these more recent approaches have made significant contributions to our understanding of communication. They need to be developed further, and for a fuller account of these approaches to communication readers are referred to McEwan (1992). These later approaches, like their predecessors, have been developed as a result of our understanding of individual behaviour, often within an organisational context.

Summary

An appreciation of the way in which communication works is important to understanding and developing planned communications. The classic approach to communication views the process as linear, similar to the actions of a hypodermic syringe injecting its audience with information. Here the sender, message, channel, receiver approach is prevalent. Subsequent models have attempted to reflect the two-way perspective and to account for the interpersonal components of communications, which in themselves stress mutuality and shared perceptions (Windahl *et al.*, 1992).

The linear approach is not rejected, as there are circumstances where a one-way transmission of information is required, such as a flood warning by the National Rivers Authority or the announcement that a product specification has been altered to meet new legislative requirements. However, in the context of developing relational exchanges (Chapter 1) the network approach to communications is both justified and compatible. Individuals are seen to engage in patterned flows of communication which partly reflect the diversity of their interests.

This text recognises the importance of the linear and interactional approaches to communication, but uses the concept of communication networks, a contextual perspective, to explore marketing communications.

Review questions

1. Name the elements of the linear model of communication and briefly describe the role of each element.
2. What is source credibility and what are the two main components?
3. How does Kelman assist our understanding of the source of a message?
4. Select four television and four print advertisements and identify how the advertisers attempt to establish credibility. Do they succeed?
5. Discuss the differences between one-step, two-step and multi-step communications.
6. How do opinion leaders differ from opinion formers and opinion followers?
7. Why is word-of-mouth communication so important to marketing communications?
8. Draw a graph to show the difference between fast and slow diffusion.
9. What is the relational approach to communications? How might social penetration theory assist our understanding of this interpretation of how communication works?
10. Identify two forms of communication networks.

References

Dibb, S., Simkin, L., Pride, W. and Ferrel, O. (1991) *Marketing: Concepts and Strategies*. New York: Houghton Mifflin.

Dichter, E. (1966) How word-of-mouth advertising works. *Harvard Business Review*, **44** (November/December), 147–66.

Eagly, A. and Chaiken, S. (1975) An attribution analysis of the effect of characteristics on opinion change. *Journal of Personality and Social Psychology*, **32**, 136–44.

Gatignon, H. and Robertson, T. (1985) A propositional inventory for new diffusion research. *Journal of Consumer Research*, **11**, 849–67.

Goffman, E. (1969) *Strategic Interaction*. University of Pennsylvannia, New York: Doubleday.

Hawkins, D.I., Best, R.J. and Coney, K.A. (1989) *Consumer Behaviour: Implications for Marketing Strategy*. Homewood IL: Richard D. Irwin.

Katz, E. and Lazarfeld, P.F. (1955) *Personal Influence*. Glencoe IL: Free Press.

Kelman, H. (1961) Processes of opinion change. *Public Opinion Quarterly*, **25** (Spring), 57–78.

Kingdom, J.W. (1970) Opinion leaders in the electorate. *Public Opinion Quarterly*, **34**, 256–61.

Littlejohn, S.W. (1992) *Theories of Human Communication*, 4th edn. California: Wadsworth.

McEwan, T. (1992) Communication in organisations, in *Hospitality Management* (ed. L. Mullins). London: Pitman.

Mahajan, V., Muller, E. and Bass, F.M. (1990) New product diffusion models in marketing. *Journal of Marketing*, **54** (January), 1–26.

Mallen, B. (1977) *Principles of Marketing Channel Management*. Massachusetts: Lexington Books.

Midgley, D. and Dowling, G. (1993) Longitudinal study of product form innovation: the interaction between predispositions and social messages. *Journal of Consumer Research*, **19** (March), 611–25.

Newell, S.J. and Shemwell, D.J. (1995) The CEO endorser and message source credibility: an empirical investigation of antecedents and consequences. *Journal of Marketing Communications*, **1**, 13–23.

Patzer, G.L. (1983) Source credibility as a function of communicator physical attractiveness. *Journal of Business Research*, **11**, 229–41.

Reynolds, F.D. and Darden, W.R. (1971) Mutually adaptive effects of interpersonal communication. *Journal of Marketing Research*, **8** (November), 449–54.

Robinson, J.P. (1976) Interpersonal influence in election campaigns: two step flow hypothesis. *Public Opinion Quarterly*, **40**, 304–19.

Rogers, E.M. (1962) *Diffusion of Innovations*, 1st edn. New York: Free Press.

Rogers, E.M. (1983) *Diffusion of Innovations,* 3rd edn. New York: Free Press.

Rogers, E.M. (1986) *Communication Technology: The New Media in Society*. New York: Free Press.

Rogers, E.M. and Kincaid, D.L. (1981) *Communication Networks: Toward a Paradigm for Research*. New York: Free Press.

Rothschild, M. (1987) *Marketing Communications*. Lexington MA: D.C. Heath.

Schramm, W. (1955) How communication works, in *The Process and Effects of Mass Communications* (ed. W. Schramm). Urbana IL: University of Illinois Press, pp. 3–26.

Shannon, C. and Weaver, W. (1962) *The Mathematical Theory of Communication*. Urbana IL: University of Illinois Press.

Soldow, G. and Thomas, G. (1984) Relational communication: form versus content in the sale interaction. *Journal of Marketing*, **48** (Winter), 84–93.

Sparkes, M. (1997) Unpublished dissertation, BA (Hons) Business Studies. University of Portsmouth.

Taylor, D. and Altman, I. (1987) Communication in interpersonal relationships: social penetration theory, in *Interpersonal Processes: New Directions in Communication Research* (eds. M.E. Roloff and G.R. Miller). Newbury Park CA: Sage, pp. 257–77.

Theodorson, S.A. and Theodorson, G.R. (1969) *A Modern Dictionary of Sociology*. New York: Cromwell.

Tichy, N. (1979) Social network analysis for organisations. *Academy of Management Review*, **4**, 507–19.

Weick, K. (1987) Prescribed and emergent networks, in *Handbook of Organisational Communication* (ed. F. Jablin). London: Sage.

Williams, K. (1990) *Behavioural Aspects of Marketing*. Oxford: Heinemann.

Windahl, S., Signitzer, B. and Olson, J.T. (1992) *Using Communication Theory*. London: Sage.

part *i*

Contexts

Ethics in marketing communications

Richard Christy

Ethical considerations – questions of right and wrong – are an inseparable part of real-life marketing communications. Any part of an organisation's marketing communications can send messages about its ethical stance, either intentionally or otherwise. Organisations need to cultivate an active awareness of the ethical consequences of their marketing communications.

AIMS AND OBJECTIVES

The aim of this chapter is to introduce the ideas of business ethics and to review how they are relevant to marketing communications.

The objectives of this chapter are:

1. To review briefly the main ideas in ethics and the way they are applied to business in general.
2. To discuss the differing viewpoints of the ethics of marketing communications as a whole.
3. To understand how ethical considerations affect specific issues in marketing communications, such as truth-telling, respect for personal privacy, the treatment of vulnerable groups and questions of taste and decency.
4. To introduce frameworks and models that can help managers to think through these issues in planning their marketing communications.

Introduction

In this book, the word 'good' is probably used dozens of times, often in the sense of 'likely to contribute to effective marketing communications', or similar. 'Good', however, can also have a moral, or ethical (the two words are used interchangeably here), connotation, which may be quite distinct: something that is functionally effective may or may not be ethically acceptable. This chapter looks at how ethical questions of good and bad or right and wrong might be applied to marketing communications.

Familiar concerns

How do these questions make themselves felt in real life? Everyone will have their own list, but common concerns include:

- misleading or false advertising
- shocking, tasteless or indecent material in marketing communications
- high-pressure sales techniques, particularly when applied to vulnerable groups
- telesales calls that seem to intrude on personal privacy
- PR communications that seem to distract and obfuscate, rather than inform
- the payment of bribes to win business

Why is it worth paying attention to these matters? For many, the main reason for wanting to understand how ethics may bear upon marketing communications will be a natural desire to know how good things can be promoted and bad things avoided. For others, interest in these questions will result from a realisation that if a company conducts its marketing communications (or any other aspect of its business) in a way that others find unethical, then it may have negative consequences that can outweigh any functional benefits. Finally, many may believe that there is no necessary contradiction between being effective in business and behaving ethically, and perhaps even that true long-term effectiveness in business is more likely to be achieved by companies who set and stick to high ethical standards.

Importance of judgement and experience

There has been a growing emphasis on business ethics in recent years, partly as a consequence of an increased public interest in how businesses behave (i.e. not just in the products and services they produce) and a more sceptical and less respectful attitude to the place of business and business people in society. Business ethics as a subject addresses itself to the complete range of activities of an organisation, part of which is to do with the ethical implications of the way an organisation approaches its marketing communications. As we shall see, many of the issues that arise are not simple 'black and white' questions, but more complex situations in which judgement and experience have to be applied to arrive at an ethically acceptable solution.

For example, most would presumably object to a sales presentation whose content was designed to mislead consumers about a product or make deliberately false claims about its benefits, but few would go as far as to require every marketing communication to provide full 'warts and all' detail about the advantages and possible disadvantages of buying and using the product. Finding the balance between these two extremes is not wholly an ethical question – practical and legal issues, for example, are also likely to intrude – but one in which an understanding of ethics as applied to the conduct of business can be very valuable.

This chapter provides a brief introduction to some of the main ideas in ethics and to the way in which ethical thinking can be applied to business. For all that common sense plays a major role in the resolution of many real-life ethical questions, these issues can be highly complex, with solutions sometimes depending strongly on the approach adopted to analysis. Understanding moral concepts may help a decision-maker to analyse the ethical ramifications of a situation in order to make a better ethical choice. Sometimes, in real-life business situations, resolving to do the right thing can be easier than determining what the right thing actually *is*.

Ideas in business ethics

Ethics is the study of morality: those practices and activities that are importantly right and wrong (De George, 1995); business ethics considers the application of ethical principles to the conduct of business. This distinction may seem obvious, but it makes an important point: just as medical ethics considers the application of ethics to medicine, business ethics is about the way general ethical principles should be applied to business. In particular, business is not 'exempt' from the moral considerations that apply to human affairs in general, nor should a separate set of moral standards be developed for the set of human activities that fall under the heading of business (or 'marketing communications' in particular).

Questions of right and wrong have occupied thinkers and writers over many millennia, and it is impossible to provide anything but a superficial overview in the space available here. Those who wish to follow up in more detail some of the theoretical ideas mentioned here should consult a specialist business ethics text: De George's (1995) book, for example, is one of many in the field that provide a clear and accessible account of the application of ethical principles to business.

Duties and consequences

Two major schools of thought can be distinguished in ethics, which broadly lie on either side of the means/ends debate:

- The first is concerned with *duties*, and argues that some actions are always bad and others always good.
- The second approach focuses on *consequences*, holding that whether an act is good or bad depends on what happens as a result of taking that action, no matter what the action is. Utilitarianism is a well-known form of this approach, seeking to identify actions that (very broadly) can be expected to result in the greatest good of the greatest number.

Problems of the main approaches

To make this distinction is to oversimplify a very complex and long-running debate and also to overlook the many sophisticated variants and hybrid theories that have been developed. In the course of this debate, the problems inherent in either approach have been well rehearsed – an approach to ethics based on duty alone is likely to be inflexible and difficult to put into practice in a complex real world. By contrast, the alternative approach of considering only outcomes seems unsatisfactory to many. Crude utilitarianism, for example, is (by definition) 'unprincipled' and insufficiently concerned with the idea of justice. In practical terms, it can also be very difficult to arrive at a satisfactory assessment of 'the greatest good', however that is defined.

Neither approach on its own seems to offer a practical and foolproof guide to ethical business decision-making. As has been suggested above, a simple and apparently unarguable duty-based rule like 'Always tell the truth in marketing communications' may cause problems as soon as we start to plan an advertising campaign. Is it our duty to provide a detailed and reasoned discussion of all of the reasons for and against buying the product, whatever the medium we are using? Must we refrain from using ironic statements that are plainly designed to entertain, rather than inform? For example, Heineken's famous '... refreshes the parts that other beers cannot reach' campaign would have to be excluded by this rule. The simple rule is unworkable: it must either be made platitudinously general (e.g. 'Do no intentional harm') or it must be expanded to a long list of qualifications, definitions and exceptions.

Basing the ethical evaluation of our actions only on the expected consequences brings a separate set of problems. If, for example, a company designs an advertising campaign that most people will find mildly amusing but which a small religious minority will (quite foreseeably) find highly offensive, then the publication of research data showing a weighted average calculation of approval for the adverts will be unlikely to reassure most people's intuitive concerns about the campaign. In practical terms, it can also be extraordinarily difficult to forecast all of the consequences of a proposed action, however concerned one may be to achieve a balanced assessment.

Other approaches to business ethics

These practical difficulties in applying simple rules or methods to complex real-life situations have caused many writers in business ethics to leave the theoretical ends/means argument to one side and to propose alternative bases for judging the ethical implications of proposed business actions. Jackson (1996), for example, explains how a focus on moral virtues in business life can provide a much more practical basis for assessing good conduct in business. The concept of virtues seeks to express those qualities and dispositions in a person that will help to ensure a good life, often seeking a 'mean' between two undesirable poles. Courage, for example, can be defined as a virtue that lies between the extremes of cowardice on the one hand and foolhardiness on the other. One of the strengths of this approach is the way in which it helps to temper the absolutism to which a duty-based approach to ethics is prone as well as the unprincipled expedience of crude utilitarianism. Finding the 'mean', however, is far from straightforward.

A different alternative is proposed by Sternberg (1994), in which the assessment of business ethics is based upon a definition of the *purpose* of the company (for this reason, her approach to business ethics is described as teleological):

> *To be an ethical business, an organisation must be a business and must conduct its activities ethically. An organisation is a business if its objective is maximising long-term owner value; a business acts ethically, if its actions are compatible with that aim and with distributive justice and ordinary decency* (p. 93)

In this definition, 'distributive justice' refers to the principle by which rewards are allocated in proportion to the contribution made to organisational ends, while the constraint of 'ordinary decency' obliges a firm to refrain from coercion, lying, cheating and so on, whether or not they appear at the time to further the business purpose. These two restrictions acknowledge the vital importance of confidence and trust in the business world.

In adopting this approach, a manager would be mainly concerned with the consequences of a proposed action, but would concentrate on those consequences that are directly or indirectly relevant to the firm's long-term interests, rather than seeking to judge what is in the general interest. On first reading, this may seem to some be nothing more than a formal statement of the 'Greed is good' values which are sometimes associated with the aggressive 'Anglo-Saxon' model of capitalism of the 1980s. The teleological approach, however, is importantly different from the excesses of that era:

- The concept of 'long-term owner value' is not the same thing as that of short-term rewards: the pursuit of long-term value may require very different actions from a policy designed to maximise, say, the next dividend payment.
- The requirement to behave with 'common decency' firmly excludes actions on the part of the firm such as lying, cheating, stealing and coercion, no matter how expedient or financially attractive they may seem in the short term: these things are always unethical.
- An intelligently self-interested firm will generally not wish to pursue activities that give it a bad reputation among customers, suppliers, potential recruits and so on, because to do so would be to fail to maximise long-term owner value. This is not to say that individual employees may have no other reasons for this restraint, but rather to suggest that the teleological principle will often provide sufficient reason to behave ethically in business.

Stakeholder theories

Although it is framed in terms that may seem to be disconcertingly stark – even provocative – this teleological principle may help to provide a bridge between the ideas of 'stakeholder' theory and the narrower concerns of the 'agency' theorists. One example of agency theory is provided by Milton Friedman's (1970) suggestion that the social responsibility of business is to use its resources to engage in activities designed to increase its profits, within the 'rules' of free competition and without deception or fraud. This type of approach views directors and managers as agents of the owners, with a prime duty to maximise their wealth. By contrast, some forms of stakeholder theory define a far wider set of external interests, to which the firm is in some way 'accountable' (see Chapter 6 for a fuller discussion of the implications of stakeholder theory).

Whatever view is taken of a firm's relationship to and duties towards its various stakeholders, the mere acknowledgement of complexity and plurality does not of itself help managers to know what to *do* about this plurality in practice. Managers seeking to 'balance' stakeholder interests will quickly encounter the very practical problem of how that 'balance' should be defined. Consider, for example, opportunities for a firm to contribute to or become involved with charitable causes. The available range of local, national and global causes will in total outweigh any conceivable budget. What is needed is both an ethical basis for deciding whether to lend support at all and, if so, which causes to support. Asking the question 'Which actions best support the long-term goals of this firm?' in an intelligent and enlightened way may well help to illuminate the complex ethical issues facing firms today. The word 'enlightened' is used here to describe an outlook that deliberately considers the long term as well as the short term, that thinks more broadly than the immediate transactions carried out by the firm, and is active and searching, rather than passive.

The teleological principle requires that stakeholder interests be acknowledged and taken into account, because not to do so would be a violation of the principle. Importantly, it also provides guidance on *how* those interests are to be taken into account (i.e. by assessing their impact on the long-term interests of the owners of the firm). As Sternberg (1994, p. 50) points out, however, 'taking something into account' is not the same being accountable to it.

The scope of ethical issues in marketing communications

Before looking at the application of these ideas to marketing communications, one or two things need to be clarified. The first of these is the importance of distinguishing between:

- those critiques of marketing communications that are based upon a belief that the activity as a whole is undesirable
- criticisms of some aspects of marketing communications in practice that are based on an acceptance that the activity is in principle justifiable

The next section provides a brief review of some of the first type of critique, not least because these arguments are very frequently encountered in public debate; in effect, they are part of the world in which marketing takes place. The rest of the chapter, however, concerns itself with the second category of criticisms – ethical issues that are raised by the practice of marketing communications, with a clear implication that advertising, selling, PR and so on are things that can be done ethically or unethically, depending upon the choices that are made.

It is also important to clarify that the review concentrates on marketing communications in particular, rather than marketing in general, meaning that many issues relating to marketing as a whole have been excluded. It is certainly unethical to advertise a product that is known to be so badly designed or manufactured as to be dangerous, for example, but the ethical issue in this case has more to do with the practice of product management than advertising. Those interested in ethical issues affecting marketing in general should consult a specialised text such as Chonko (1995), or the review of the literature presented in Tsalikis and Fritzsche (1989).

The final clarification is to point out that the main ethical questions in marketing communications are considered one by one in this chapter, rather than looking at the individual elements of the promotional mix in turn. Questions of truth-telling, decency, privacy and so on have some bearing on every part of the promotional mix, although the context of each medium may affect the way in which ethical considerations have to be applied.

Marketing communications: a diabolical liberty?

In the 1968 comedy film *Bedazzled*, Peter Cook plays a jaded, weary devil, who complains that since introducing the Seven Deadly Sins, he has done very little except invent advertising. The line is no more than a joke, of course, but does rely upon one familiar view of advertising: that it is inherently bad, manipulative, corrupting or whatever. Nor is this disapproval confined to advertising: the image of the smooth, fast-talking 'snake oil' salesman is an enduring one, with many modern counterparts. Similarly, the public relations industry has suffered from some extremely *poor* PR in recent years: the term 'PR' sometimes seems to be used in a way that is almost synonymous with half-truths, insincerity and manipulation.

If these views – in effect, that marketing communications is inherently undesirable and unworthy – are taken seriously, then the ethical response must presumably be to indulge in these activities as little as possible, if at all. Happily, however, this is not the only view that can be taken: an alternative view regards marketing communication as playing a key role in the market economy, assisting the process through which consumer needs are identified and satisfied. From this perspective, the ethics of advertising, PR and so on depend upon how they are carried out: in themselves, these activities are ethically neutral. Most of this chapter takes the latter perspective, but it is certainly worth briefly highlighting the more fundamental critiques of advertising.

Advertising as mass manipulation?

Vance Packard's famous book about mass communications *The Hidden Persuaders* (Packard, 1960) had a major impact. His concern was what he saw as the manipulative widespread use of psychological techniques in advertising, PR, politics and so on:

> *... many of us are being influenced and manipulated – far more than we realise – in the patterns of our everyday lives. Large-scale efforts are being made, often with impressive success, to channel our unthinking habits, our purchasing decisions, and our thought processes by the use of insights gained from psychiatry and the social sciences. Typically these efforts take place beneath our level of awareness, so that the appeals which move us are often, in a sense, 'hidden'.* (p. 11)

Today's hard-pressed advertisers, trying to engage the attention of a sophisticated, knowing and demanding public, might be forgiven for wryly wishing that anything like that level of influence could be achieved. However, Packard's book provided a powerful expression of a point of view that is often found in press and academic commentaries on advertising, sometimes linked to more fundamental political critiques of the capitalistic society in which advertising takes place.

Pollay's (1986) review of social science commentaries on advertising drew together a wide range of material into a general framework. This synthesis suggested that advertising was seen – by social scientists – as a powerful and intrusive means of communication and persuasion, whose (unintended) effects could be to reinforce materialism, cynicism, irrationality, selfishness and a number of other undesirable outcomes.

Holbrook's (1987) reply to this paper challenged some of its implicit assumptions (e.g. that advertising is monolithic, somehow acting in concert; that it appeals to a mass audience; that it manipulates social values; that it relies mainly upon emotional impact) and suggested that the 'conventional wisdom or prevailing opinion' represented in the Pollay model was unfairly destructive of a much more diverse reality.

Space does not permit anything like an adequate discussion of these serious and important arguments. The important point to be taken forward is that this discussion of ethics in marketing communications takes for granted a number of much broader issues to do with the ethical acceptability of marketing as an activity and of the capitalist system which engendered it. As Robin and Reidenbach (1993) point out:

> *The degree to which the basic marketing functions are seen to be ethical or unethical must ... be measured within our understanding of their history, the times in which they are applied, the context in which they are applied, the expectations of society, the requirements of capitalism and our best understanding of human behaviour*
>
> (p. 104)

Similarly, Thompson (1995) recommends a 'contextualist' model of marketing ethics, in which ethical dilemmas are to be recognised and addressed through the interplay of social values, cultural meanings, stakeholder interests and values and the organisational contexts within which individual marketing agents operate. At a practical level, Vallance (1995) observes that it is usually more valuable in business to ask a specific question like 'Is it ethical for us to run this advert now?' than to wonder more generally 'Is advertising ethical?'.

Truth-telling

The general ethical requirement to tell the truth is one that bears upon every type of marketing communication. Reflecting the widespread public distaste for lying and deceit, there are plenty of legal and other regulatory deterrents to this type of unethical conduct in advertising, selling, public relations and so on. Clearly, no responsible business will wish to be found on the wrong side of these requirements, but there remains plenty of scope for judgement in respect of which aspects of the truth are to be presented in marketing communications and how they are to be put across.

As discussed at the beginning of this chapter, we expect a salesperson not to lie to us, but few would require from a salesperson a full and balanced account of the advantages and disadvantages of our entering into the proposed transaction. There are perhaps two reasons why: mainly, it is unreasonable to expect the salesperson or advertiser to have enough information about us to be able to carry this out; also, however, there is a general acceptance that the principle of *caveat emptor* ('let the buyer beware') should play some sort of moderating role.

As Sternberg (1994) observes, the aim of a salesperson is to sell the company's products, not to provide consumer guidance. Both buyer and seller have their own interests and it is normally up to either party to look after these interests during the purchase process. Thus there is no ethical requirement that customers should ensure that the transaction is profitable for the seller, nor – in every case – that the seller must go to great lengths to ensure that the buyer is making a wise and prudent purchase (although many sellers will choose to provide some advice of this nature, in order to appeal more effectively to customers). Much depends on the context of the sales dialogue: the nature of the product or service, the awareness and expectations of the customer and so on.

Misrepresentation and 'puffery'

Some way short of the extreme of deceit or lying, but nonetheless the wrong side (for most people) of the ethical divide, is the problem of deliberate or reckless misrepresentation in selling. Chonko (1995) defines misrepresentation as occurring when sales people make incorrect statements or false promises about a product or service. The dividing line is not always absolutely clear: a salesperson can be generally expected to show enthusiasm for the product, which may result in some degree of exaggeration. Up to a point, of course, a sales negotiation can be seen as a performance in which both buyer and seller may make some claims that do not represent their actual or final position. Most, however, would accept this as perfectly normal, perhaps even seeing it as an effective way of identifying and delineating the area within which both buyer and seller are prepared to participate.

Misrepresentation in advertising is likely to be condemned by codes of practice, if not by actual statute. Much advertising, however, contains some degree of what might be called 'embellishment' or 'puffery' – the enthusiastic use of language and images to convey the most optimistic view of the product or service being portrayed. Those who find embellishment to be a natural, obvious and harmless aspect of advertising language will have some difficulty in providing a firm dividing line between harmless embellishment and deception. Chonko (1995) points out that the American Federal Trade Commission regards puffery as acceptable because such statements are not likely to be relied upon by consumers in making their choice. However, this approach seems itself to place great reliance upon being able to identify those parts of a marketing communication that *are* likely to be relied upon. Similar issues are raised by the visual images created for advertising, which naturally seek to show the product as appealingly as possible. Images of sports cars parked outside large country houses are unlikely to delude any potential buyers as to the lifestyle benefits of the model. Nor can there be any serious concern about using mashed potato to represent easily melted ice cream in an advertising photo session. However, for some products aimed at some audiences – and children's toys are often mentioned in this context – exaggerated images may have a greater potential to delude.

The importance of context: selling complex products

The importance of context in judging ethical behaviour can be seen in the debate in the UK over the problems arising from the selling of private pensions during the 1980s. In many cases, customers were persuaded by salespeople to switch out of existing pension schemes into new schemes whose subsequent performance left them worse off. In these cases, the complex nature of the services, together with the unfamiliarity of many of the customers with the various types of product and how to choose between them, led them to place an unusually great reliance on the advice provided by the salesperson. Put another way, the extent to which the buyer was foreseeably *able* to 'beware' in these cases was very limited, which in turn should have placed a greater than normal ethical duty on the salesperson to ensure that the customers were properly informed of the consequences and implications of the switch. The fact that these ethical standards were clearly not met in a large number of cases has caused a great deal of loss, anxiety and inconvenience for the customers who lost out, but also a great deal of difficulty, expense and embarrassment for the pensions industry as a whole. At the time of writing, the UK Government has adopted a policy of publicly 'naming and shaming' formerly well-respected financial services companies who are failing to meet regulatory targets for compensating these customers.

Writing about ethical issues in insurance selling in general, Diacon and Ennew (1996) point out that marketing transactions in financial services have greater than normal potential for ethical complications. The unavoidable complexity of many financial services products is heightened by the fact that the evaluation may depend upon individual calculations carried out for the customer by the salesperson; also, risk for the customer may be significant, in that the actual benefits received will often depend upon the performance of the economy over a long period. The authors highlight a number of other ethical issues relevant to insurance selling, including:

- the issue of 'fitness for purpose' in both the design of the products and the way in which they are matched to customer needs
- the transparency of the price for these products, such that any commissions payable to the intermediary organisation or individual salesperson are clearly visible
- the need for truth in promotion, not only in terms of strict factual correctness, but also in terms of what the consumer might be expected to understand from a phrase
- the effect of the sales targeting and reward systems of the selling organisation on the behaviour of salespeople, particularly in view of the important advisory component of this type of selling

In their survey of the industry, the authors found some awareness of these ethical issues and also evidence of initial moves to address the main cause of problems: the potentially dangerous combination of commission-based selling and imperfect information on the part of customers.

In the teleological approach to business ethics described above, businesses are encouraged to act in ways that can be expected to maximise the long-term wealth of owners. The serious problems arising from personal pension selling during the 1980s provide an example of how important it is for businesses to maintain an active awareness of the likely effects of their actions. A decade later, it is all too clear that a failure to address problems that should have been quite foreseeable has caused misery and distress for many customers and – tellingly – major disadvantage for the industry as a whole. It is difficult to escape the conclusion that a more enlightened assessment of the long-term interests of the business on the part of financial service providers would have helped to avert many of the problems, to the great benefit of all involved. This is easy to conclude with hindsight: the effective ethical businesses are those that manage to cultivate this type of foresight.

The relational context and expectations

The importance of the buyer/seller context in which the statement is made is also reflected in Gundach and Murphy's (1993) paper on the ethics of relational marketing exchanges. In these relational exchanges, the value of the arrangement for both sides depends critically upon the mutual maintenance of trust, equity, responsibility and commitment (i.e. as opposed to the more contractual regulation of shorter term transactional relationships). Clearly, the expectations as regards the content and openness of marketing communications in the former would be different from the latter. A customer might, for example, feel upset if a car salesperson with whom he had dealt for many years failed to tell him that the model he was buying was about to be superseded, because that would seem to be inconsistent with the trust built up over the years. The same customer might not be at all upset to find the same thing happen with a personal computer bought from a discount store in London, not only because computers are known to date more quickly than models of cars, but also because there was no long-term relationship to be brought into question.

Truth-telling and PR

The practice of public relations (PR) is also likely to raise many truth-telling issues. The purpose of PR is to create and manage relationships between the firm and its various publics and there must always be a temptation in so doing to place undue emphasis on the positive aspects of the firm's actions. The question of what is 'due' emphasis is no easier in this area of marketing communications than in selling or advertising: a firm must strike an ethical balance, based upon its understanding of its impact on others and its own long-term interests and reputation. Firms that make a habit of using PR techniques to mislead stakeholder groups are in effect consuming in the short term the trust upon which their long-term profitable existence may depend.

Botan (1997) distinguishes between the 'monologic' and 'dialogic' approaches to PR, suggesting that dialogue is a more ethical basis for planning PR campaigns, particularly in an information society. More pragmatically, Barton (1994) warns that, following the major business scandals of the 1980s, courts may increasingly hold PR firms liable for making false or misleading statements on behalf of their clients, placing a prudential burden of proof and research on the PR firms themselves. Onerous though such burdens may turn out to be, they appear to be little different from that which an enlightened view of long-term self-interest on the part of PR firms might indicate – PR firms above all must rely upon a basic level of public trust in their activities if they are to do any good for their clients at all.

Vulnerable groups

The question of truth-telling leads directly to the special requirements for the treatment of vulnerable groups in marketing communication campaigns. Many countries, for example, have much stricter controls on the content and timing of advertising to children, based upon an enhanced concern for the potential of advertisements and other promotional material to delude and disturb these audiences.

These special regulations, however, should not distract attention from the general ethical requirement to design marketing communications that show an enlightened understanding of and concern for the needs of the recipient of the communication. The often-discussed tragic problems resulting from the sale of baby milk products in some developing countries had much to do with marketing and other communications from the seller that simply did not take adequate account of the reality of life in developing countries. As De George (1995) observes:

In an attempt to increase sales, Nestlé, as well as other producers of infant formula (milk), extended the sale of their product to many countries in Africa. They followed some of the same marketing techniques that they had followed with success and without customer complaint elsewhere.

One standard technique was advertising on billboards and magazines. A second was the distribution of free samples in hospitals to new mothers as well as to doctors. In themselves, these practices were neither illegal nor unethical. Yet their use led to charges of following unethical practices and to a seven-year worldwide boycott of all Nestlé products.

In retrospect, it is easy to point out that the company should have paid greater attention to the likelihood in this environment of the product being made up with water from a contaminated source or of the product being over-diluted by users who were unfamiliar with it. Again, firms that cultivate an enlightened awareness of their impact on their surroundings will have a greater chance of perceiving and anticipating these issues before they become problems.

Vulnerable groups: children or parents?

According to press reports, UK children represent a major marketing opportunity, with disposable income valued at £1.6bn per year, with influence over a further £8bn or so of expenditure. Elsewhere in Europe, the focus is on the ethics of advertising to children, but in the UK, advertisers are homing in on the opportunity.

Children are significant consumers of TV (very high proportions have their own set) and seem to have much better advertising recall than adults. Parents on the receiving end of the demands of these assertive and sophisticated media consumers could be forgiven for feeling that they are being held to ransom.

Adapted from Lisa Buckingham, *The Guardian*, 20 April 1996

Privacy and respect for persons

One aspect of the duty-based view of ethics referred to at the beginning of this chapter is the importance of treating others as ends in themselves, rather than merely as means: in other words, not merely using others, but treating them with the respect they deserve as fellow human beings. This ethical requirement finds a number of potential applications in the world of marketing communications, for example:

- avoiding the annoyance and harassment that can result from the inappropriate application of high-pressure sales techniques
- respecting the wish that some may have at some times to be private; not to be approached with sales calls and – for some – not to be sent unsolicited direct mail communications
- refraining from causing unwarranted distress or shock by ensuring that the content of any marketing communication remains within generally-accepted boundaries of taste and decency

The first of these issues is perhaps easiest to deal with here: harassment is something that can be subjectively defined (i.e. by the recipient of the unwelcome attention) and no ethical business will wish to cross that line. The reason for this is both to do with the standards of common decency that an ethical firm will wish to maintain, but also the view that harassing customers is unlikely to be consistent with the long-term interests of the business. The fact that sales harassment does take place – at the time of writing, for example, there is discussion of the need for further curbs on the activities of time-share touts – does not undermine the principle, but rather suggests that some businesses have a flawed view of their long-term interest, or, in the most opportunistic cases, that they are making no plans to have a long-term future. As in some of the other cases discussed above, the need for regulation is primarily to support and reinforce the action that an ethical company would be likely to choose anyway.

Responding to individual preferences for privacy

The issue of privacy is a little more complex, especially if it is treated as a question of 'rights'. It is not very easy to define a separate and defensible right to privacy in respect of direct marketing approaches. Privacy is essentially a subjective concept, to do with not being perceived or disturbed at a particular time or while engaged in a particular activity. To express this as a right seems to involve a corresponding obligation on others to sense in some way that a person is in a private state and then not to perceive or disturb that person, which sounds impractical in many circumstances. In the context of a capitalist society, it is also difficult to think about general prohibitions on the making of commercial approaches.

This is not at all to argue that concerns about privacy in respect of direct marketing have no basis, but rather to suggest that they can be more productively addressed by regarding them as a reasonable request (rather than the assertion of a right) and then considering how an ethical firm ought to respond. Privacy-related concerns in this area seem to fall into two main categories: unwelcome sales approaches (e.g. teleselling calls in the evening) and a more general concern about the implications of large amounts of personal data being collected, stored and processed for sale to those involved in direct marketing.

In the first case, the ethical response is the same as for sales harassment: ethical firms will refrain as far as possible from making unwelcome approaches, for reasons of enlightened self-interest. They will, for example, support and encourage the development of general schemes through which individuals can signify their general wish not to be contacted. They will also seek out and use mailing lists that are a very close match with their target segments, which will both make the mailing more effective and also reduce the chance of the mailing piece being seen as 'junk'. They will also provide a clear means for those who do not wish to be contacted to indicate their wish.

An ethical company can also respond to the second and more general concern about privacy, both by offering clear opportunities to individuals to have their details excluded from files and also by ensuring as far as possible that information about individuals used in direct marketing has been ethically collected, processed and stored (e.g. such that it is still up to date, thus minimising the risk of, say, causing distress by inadvertently mailing to deceased people). Sometimes, even these efforts may not be enough to avoid causing offence inadvertently, and an ethical firm will ensure that it has in place clear and effective systems to receive and respond to the complaint.

Taste and decency

The question of taste and decency in the content of marketing communications is also one which may have an ethical aspect. This is not only to do with the use of 'pin-up' images in corporate calendars and trade advertising; separate, but related concerns may apply to the use by a charity of particularly distressing images in order to raise funds or even the apparently innocent use of stereotypical images in advertising.

Images of women and men in advertising

The first point to be made is that public standards of what is acceptable in this area do clearly change over time. The portrayal of women in early TV advertisements, for example, now often seems so obviously inappropriate as to be hilarious: no advertiser adopting a similar tone today could expect to communicate effectively (except perhaps as a spoof). The extent to which contemporary images of women and men in advertising may also be creating stereotypes is beyond the scope of this chapter, but it should be clear that an advertisement that annoys or alienates its target audience is unlikely to be effective. Effective (and ethical) advertisers will wish to treat their prospective audiences with respect, if only because in a competitive market they cannot afford to behave otherwise. David Ogilvy's (1963, p. 96) often-quoted remark that:

> *the consumer isn't a moron; she is your wife*

provided a much-needed reminder to fellow advertisers of the need to avoid insulting the intelligence of their audiences. The fact that this (no doubt entirely well-intentioned) advice would probably be expressed differently today also underlines the point that standards and expectations do change over time. Ethical advertisers will seek to understand their target audiences well enough to be able to communicate effectively, without giving inadvertent offence.

The interplay of public taste and choices made by advertisers

The annual reports of the Advertising Standards Authority (ASA) provide a crude barometer of public attitudes towards advertising images.

In its commentary on complaints received in 1996, the ASA pointed out that complaints had fallen by 12% from the record 1995 level of 12,804. Complaints about the portrayal of women, however, doubled during that period, causing the ASA to recommend that 'Advertisers need to be more sensitive to public opinion when portraying women, especially when such images appear on posters'.

In the following year, the general level of complaints continued to fall and the complaints about the portrayal of men had almost halved. In the same year, significant numbers of complaints were received about the portrayal of men in advertising, together with complaints about violent and sexist advertisements for computer games.

These changes reflect a number of influences: the choices made by advertisers about which images to use (based upon their perceptions of what will be effective), the effect of codes of practice on those choices and the short- and long-term shifts in public opinion about what is acceptable.

ASA Web site (http://www.asa.org.uk/), accessed 31 March 1998;
Alison Boshoff, *Daily Telegraph*, 31 March 1988

Images designed to shock

The question of the use of shocking images in marketing communications is one in which an organisation would do well to consider its own long-term interest as broadly as possible. In the short term, a shocking image may be effective, but used to excess the tactic will be counter-productive for a growing number of recipients of the message. The controversy resulting from the famous Benetton poster campaign certainly succeeded in gaining publicity for the knitwear company: the long-term benefit for the company in a case like this may be less easy to discern.

The same is likely to hold true for a charity: those appealing for funds to help alleviate distressing problems around the world may be tempted to make use of shocking real-life images of the situations that they encounter. Being aware of the ever-present risk of 'compassion fatigue' on the part of donors, as well as the possibility of causing unwarranted distress to some recipients of the message, most charity fund-raising communications remain within limits of taste and decency for what are likely to be purely prudential reasons.

Hospitality, incentives, inducements and bribery and extortion

The ethical questions surrounding the payment of bribes in business feature prominently in most textbooks on business ethics. These difficult issues need to be mentioned here both because they are important and because they may well involve sales staff. Bribes are unofficial – and usually illegal – payments to individuals 'to procure services or gain influence' (*Collins Concise English Dictionary*). These payments may be to secure orders, for example, or to expedite deliveries.

Distinguishing between bribery and extortion

It is useful to draw a distinction between extortion and bribery: the former is demanded by the would-be receiver, while the latter is offered by the individual or organisation wishing to buy the influence. In a situation in which informal payments of this nature are thought to be commonplace, a company's decision to go along with extortion is ethically different from a decision to offer a bribe. But in either case, the familiar distinction between short-term and long-term benefits is important.

CASE ILLUSTRATION

Finding the balance

A recent example of shocking images illustrates the tension between the desire to make a point powerfully and the need to avoid undue offence. The UK-based Vegetarian Society ran a brief press advertising campaign in 1997 which drew attention to recently published research findings of possible links between diets that are high in red meat and an increased risk of some types of cancer: readers were recommended to reduce or eliminate meat consumption and to eat more vegetables and fruit.

Expressed in this way, the proposition seems to be a reasonable and unsurprising communication from an organisation with the aims of the Vegetarian Society. The campaign, however, attracted an adverse adjudication from the Advertising Standards Authority in December 1997, for reasons that were mainly to do with *how* the point was made, rather than the underlying proposition. The advertisements were deliberately hard-hitting in style, showing photographs of cancer operation scars and including headlines such as 'It's much easier to cut out meat'. Objectors – who included bodies such as the Meat and Livestock Commission and the National Farmers Union – claimed that the advertisements had in a number of ways exaggerated the research findings and government recommendations alluded to in the text and that the advertisements were shocking to those directly or indirectly affected by cancer and unduly distressing.

Most of these complaints – including that of undue distress – were upheld by the ASA. The adjudication was followed by a defiant response from the Vegetarian Society, maintaining that the evidence upon which the advertisements were based was robust and pointing out that the Society had received around 2500 telephone calls responding positively to the advertisement. The purpose of this example is not to comment on the decisions made, but rather to illustrate the complex issues that have to be weighed in these situations in marketing communications. The Vegetarian Society and other cause-promoting organisations are not businesses in the normal sense, but they do need to make similarly broad and balanced judgements in deciding how to communicate their ideas.

ASA Web site (http://www.asa.org.uk/), accessed 19 January 1998;
Vegetarian Society press release of 9 December 1997

Difficult choices

The ethical company will need to take account of the effects on its image and wider relationships of taking part in bribery or extortion: these illegal practices have harmful effects on local economies and are likely to be regarded negatively by most stakeholders. The normal conduct of business relies heavily upon trust and the rule of law, both of which are undeniably jeopardised by corruption.

Even where these practices are in fact commonplace, the position of a company that makes informal payments while at the same time actively pressuring the government to take action against corruption is likely to be seen as different from one that pays bribes on the basis of short-term expediency. Sometimes, companies may consider some sort of arm's-length arrangement, in which local agents are required to 'look after' any needs of this sort, with payments eventually appearing under headings such as 'consultancy fees'. Although expectations and practices may well vary from one industry to another, an ethical analysis of these arm's-length arrangements cannot fail to take account of the fact that corrupt payments are being made, however well they are hidden in the short term.

For Sternberg (1994), offering a bribe is an attempt to cheat and a violation of ordinary decency, while taking a bribe is a violation of distributive justice: decisions are made because of the bribe, rather than the relevant merits of the business offering. These are difficult questions in practice, which may involve hard choices, including the choice of whether to take part in markets in which corruption is endemic.

Corporate hospitality: what are the limits?

Far less serious than actual bribery, but arguably on the same continuum, is the question of the scale of entertainment and hospitality that should be provided by the selling organisation to the buying organisation. It is entirely natural for a company to seek to build up closer relationships with its major customers, and corporate hospitality would normally be seen as an entirely legitimate part of this process. Even in this area, however, sales staff may be conscious of 'grey areas', in which the lavishness of the hospitality or gift-giving may seem to be out of proportion to the purpose of building a business relationship. Many companies recognise this potential hazard by providing guidelines to staff on what is to be regarded as acceptable in accepting and offering corporate hospitality. Those guidelines will naturally take account of normal practice within the industry and may well differ from one industry to another and – within any given industry – from one period to another.

No such thing as a free lunch

According to the Law Commission, the current legislation on corruption is 'outmoded, uncertain and inconsistent'. New proposals would broaden the definition of corruption to include hospitality that could be shown to have led to the award of a contract, together with 'excessive hospitality', such as expensive holidays. By contrast, entertaining whose purpose is to pass on information about the company, talk business or to cement business relationships is legitimate.

Reaction to the proposals by those involved in the provision of corporate entertainment highlighted the practical difficulties of making these distinctions in some cases. In many cases, respondents gave the proposals a cautious welcome, because they provided a basis for affirming the legitimate role of corporate hospitality: that of building business relationships.

Adapted from Business Monitor, *Daily Telegraph*, 9 March 1998

Again, however, the appropriate judgement about corporate entertainment is likely to be the one that maximises the company's long-term interests, within the limits of common decency and distributive justice: hospitality expenditure, like any other business expense, needs to be assessed in terms of its intended purpose and in the context of the long-term aims of the business. At one extreme, to ban all corporate entertainment would damage a firm's commercial relationships and hence its interests in most situations; at the other end of the scale, however, a different type of damage to the firm's long-term interests would be caused by practising over-lavish hospitality.

Ethical influence of supervisory and reward systems in sales management

The previous section mentioned the beneficial role that company codes can play in promoting and facilitating ethical decision-making on the part of sales and other staff. It is also worth highlighting that the management framework itself can also exert a powerful positive or negative influence on the ethical decision-making environment. Sales recruitment, training and briefing systems, for example, can be designed to encourage ethical behaviours on the part of sales staff, but equally may (e.g. through neglect) provide an uncertain context for individual employees, in which inexperienced or opportunistic staff may start to take decisions that are against the long-term interest of the company.

Fostering ethical behaviour by the sales force

The same is true, of course, of the approach taken to sales motivation and reward: a sales targeting and reward system that has been designed without due consideration of the long-term reputation of the company may have the effect of encouraging and rewarding some highly damaging behaviours on the part of staff, especially in the run-up to year-end with everyone under pressure to meet targets. Ethical companies design sales motivation and reward systems that encourage sales behaviour that maximises the long-term company interest. In an empirical study in this area, Hunt and Vasquez-Parraga (1993) found that sales managers did consider both the behaviours of sales staff and the consequences of those behaviours: unethical behaviour was likely to be more severely disciplined, for example, if the consequences were negative for the organisation. The authors suggest that:

> *A culture emphasizing ethical values may be best developed and maintained by having sales people and their supervisors internalising a set of* [duty-based] *norms proscribing a set of behaviours that are inappropriate, 'just not done', and prescribing a set of behaviours that are appropriate, 'this is the way we do things'. In both cases, sales people and their supervisors should know that when ethical issues are involved, rewards (or punishments) flow from following (or violating) the* [duty-based] *norms, not from organisationally desirable or undesirable outcomes.* (p. 87)

This suggestion, with its emphasis on duties for salespeople, rather than consequences, may at first sight seem to be at odds with the Sternberg's (1994) general recommendation that a business should take that course of action that is consistent with maximising long-term owner value within the constraints of common decency and distributive justice. There is, however, no necessary contradiction: the recommended sales management framework may well be the best way for the firm to maximise long-term owner value, reflecting, for example, the difficulty that individual salespeople may have in judging the long-term interests of the firm reliably.

Ethical decision-making models in marketing

A number of contributions to the literature have proposed models to facilitate ethical decision-making in business in general and in marketing in particular. In looking at these models, we necessarily stray beyond the specific topic of this chapter: the models offer approaches to decision-making that are certainly applicable to marketing communications, but can also be applied more widely in business affairs.

At a general business level, for example, Sternberg (1994) proposes a four-stage process for identifying and resolving ethical issues in business:

- clarify the question (e.g. look carefully for unintentional vagueness or false assumptions)
- determine the relevance for *this* business (i.e. is this actually a problematic issue relevant to this particular business?)
- identify the circumstantial constraints (which may include legal and regulatory issues, but also contractual, cultural, economic, physical and technical considerations)
- assess the available options (i.e. against the tests of maximising long-term owner value and respecting distributive justice and common decency)

Chonko (1995) characterises the ethical decision-making process in marketing as comprising:

- the ethical situation itself (e.g. the opportunity, or scope for action, the ethical decision history and the moral intensity of the situation)
- characteristics of the decision-maker (for example, knowledge, experience, achievement motivation, need for affiliation)
- significant influences (e.g. the organisation, the law, economics, technology)
- the decision itself
- the outcomes of the decision (e.g. in terms of performance, rewards, satisfaction, feedback)

From a different point of view, Smith (1995) suggests that marketing ethics can be seen as depending upon the prevailing outlook, ranging along a continuum from *caveat emptor* ('let the buyer beware') at one end, moving through intermediate points of industry standards, ethics codes and consumer sovereignty to the position of *caveat venditor* ('let the seller beware'). In his view, ethics in marketing has for some time been moving away from the simple *caveat emptor* position towards the position of consumer sovereignty. He proposes a consumer sovereignty test for companies to apply:

- *Consumer capability:* is the target market vulnerable in ways that limit consumer decision-making?
- *Information:* are consumer expectations at purchase likely to be realised? Do consumers have sufficient information to judge?
- *Choice:* can consumers go elsewhere? Would they incur substantial costs or inconvenience in transferring their loyalty?

The answers to these test questions in any situation will help the firm to realise what actions it needs to take in order to behave ethically.

Laczniak and Murphy (1991, p. 264) also list some rules of thumb for marketers facing what appears to be an ethical dilemma:

- The *Golden Rule* – act in a way that you would expect others to act towards you.

- The *Professional Ethic* – take only actions which would be viewed as proper by an objective panel of your professional colleagues.
- Kant's *Categorical Imperative* – act in a way such that the action taken under the circumstances could be a universal law of behaviour for everyone facing those same circumstances.
- The *TV Test* – a manager should always ask, would I feel comfortable explaining this action on TV to the general public?
- The outcomes of the decision (e.g. in terms of performance, rewards, satisfaction, feedback).

Laczniak and Murphy also propose a set of questions for marketers to help to analyse an issue in ethical terms. The questions cover issues of law, moral obligations, consequences and intent. As they point out, exploring the sometimes conflicting answers to these questions is likely to enhance the moral reasoning capabilities of managers, which – in parallel with company and other codes of ethics – is likely to result in better ethical decisions.

In these decision models, the literature provides a checklist of questions or characteristics which aim to help a firm think its way through ethical issues. As should be clear, the answers to the questions are very much up to the judgement made by the managers involved in the process.

Why strive to be ethical in marketing?

In closing this chapter, it is perhaps worth highlighting some of the research that has been conducted into the ethical behaviour of real-life marketing people. As Goolsby and Hunt (1992) point out, marketing as a function is often linked in the public mind with ethical abuse, mainly because of the way marketing operates at the boundary between the firm and its customers. In their study, however, the authors found that marketing people (and especially marketing women) compared favourably with those from other functions in terms of cognitive moral development (broadly, an individual's capacity for independent moral reasoning).

Singhapakdi *et al.* (1995) concluded from a survey of US marketing professionals that marketers seem to believe that ethics and social responsibility are important components of organisational effectiveness. The survey also partly indicated that ethical corporate values seem to sensitise marketers to the need to include ethics and social responsibility in marketing decisions.

These findings would seem to indicate that there may be a positive reception within the marketing profession for Thompson's (1995, p. 188) suggestion:

> *For marketers, adopting a more caring orientation offers an opportunity to become ethical innovators within their organisation. In most firms, those in marketing positions are closest to consumers, in terms of direct interaction and knowledge of their lifestyles. One role for marketers would be to regard themselves as more explicit advocates of consumer interests – both immediate and long term*

This general proposal about the role of marketing in general has special relevance for the activities of marketing communications.

Summary

This chapter has provided a brief introduction to the main ideas in business ethics and looked at some of the implications of these ideas for the practice of marketing communications. Just as there are no special ethical rules for business in general, ethics in marketing communications is a matter of applying normal ethical principles to the practice of marketing communications. Some of the difficulties in business of deciding between general ethical systems based upon duties and those based upon consequences may be avoided by taking a teleological or purpose-based approach, seeking to identify actions which will have the effect of maximising the long-term interest of the firm and its owners, remaining always within the important constraints of common decency and distributive justice. Done properly, this approach obliges managers to take an intelligent and enlightened view of the likely consequences of their actions on others.

It is sometimes argued that practices such as advertising are inherently undesirable: powerful means of manipulation, with destructive consequences. This chapter, however, has taken the view that ethics in marketing communications need to be considered in the context of a market economy, meaning that advertising, selling and so on are activities that are in themselves ethically neutral, but can be carried out in ethical or unethical ways. Applying the teleological approach helps to resolve many problems in marketing communications, including those to do with truth-telling, behaviour towards vulnerable groups, privacy and respect for persons, taste and decency, inducements and approaches to sales supervision and reward.

Marketing communications managers, with their special responsibility for the dialogue between the firm and the outside world, have every reason to take business ethics seriously (and generally seem, in fact, to do so) and may well have the opportunity to play an influential role in this respect within the firm as a whole.

Review questions

1. What are the practical problems of adopting a simple duties-based or consequences-based approach to ethics in marketing communications?
2. What are the limitations, if any, of the principle *caveat emptor* (let the buyer beware) as a guide to ethics in personal selling?
3. What guiding principles can help a company to decide about the proposed use of a shocking image in its advertising?
4. What ethical lessons for marketing communications managers in financial services companies should be learned from the private pensions scandal in the UK in the 1980s?
5. What is the difference between lying, misrepresentation and puffery in advertising? What tests should an advertiser apply to avoid misrepresentation?
6. You are the public relations manager for a medium-sized engineering company, which is the largest employer in the area. Over the last four weeks, your firm has received three requests for charitable donations or support: one from a local youth club, which serves the children of many of the employees of your firm; the second from a national charity whose aim is to promote employment opportunities for people with disabilities; and the third from an international charity concerned with

famine relief. Your firm's trading environment is tight at present and funds for any such donations are very limited. What guiding principles would you recommend to your board in considering these (and similar) requests and why?

7. Your company manufactures soft drink products and has successfully entered a number of new markets in the former Soviet republics, using mass advertising on posters, press and TV. A recent TV documentary in the UK has attacked your firm and its competitors for taking advantage of (what it described as) consumers who are unused to the blandishments of Western-style advertising and who may now be spending too much of their limited incomes on your products, to the detriment of their diet as a whole. A UK-based lobbying organisation is now threatening to call for a boycott of your products in the UK. What are the ethical issues that are apparent in this example and how should your firm evaluate them?
8. What is the distinction between monologic and dialogic approaches to public relations?
9. You are the sales director of an international company that has recently acquired another firm in the same sector. The acquired firm has an established presence in a number of markets where you were not formerly represented. In reviewing these operations, you discover that two of the local offices routinely make 'informal payments' to government officials in order to maintain the vital cooperation of the relevant departments. You know of no other such instances in your organisation and have prohibited any such practice in past cases. The local sales managers have said to you that these payments are essential to the continuing presence of your company in these markets; in both cases the operations are also very profitable and good growth prospects appear to exist. What are the ethical issues in this case? What choices should your company consider and how should it evaluate these options?
10. Explain Sternberg's four-stage process for identifying and resolving ethical issues in business.

References

Barton, L. (1994) A quagmire of ethics, profit and the public trust: the crisis in public relations services. *Journal of Professional Services Marketing*, **11**(1), 87–99.

Botan, C. (1997) Ethics in strategic communication campaigns: the case for a new approach to public relations. *Journal of Business Communication*, **34**(2), 188–202.

Chonko, L.B. (1995) *Ethical Decisions in Marketing*. Thousand Oaks CA: Sage.

De George, R.T. (1995) *Business Ethics*, 4th edn. Englewood Cliffs NJ: Prentice Hall.

Diacon, S.R. and Ennew, C.T. (1996) Ethical issues in insurance marketing in the UK. *European Journal of Marketing*, **30**(5), 67–80.

Friedman, M. (1970) The social responsibility of business is to increase its profits. *New York Times Magazine*, 13 September, pp. 32 *et seq*.

Goolsby, J.R. and Hunt, S.D. (1992) Cognitive moral development and marketing. *Journal of Marketing*, **56** (January), 55–68.

Gundach, G.T. and Murphy, P.E. (1993) Ethical and legal foundations of relational marketing exchanges. *Journal of Marketing*, **57** (October), 35–46.

Holbrook, M.B. (1987) Mirror, mirror, on the wall, what's unfair in the reflections on advertising? *Journal of Marketing*, **51** (July), 95–103.

Hunt, S.D. and Vasquez-Parraga, A.Z. (1993) Organisational consequences, marketing ethics and salesforce supervision. *Journal of Marketing Research* (February), 78–90.

Jackson, J.C. (1996) *An Introduction to Business Ethics*. Oxford: Blackwell.

Laczniak, G.R. and Murphy, P.E. (1991) Fostering ethical marketing decisions. *Journal of Business Ethics*, **10**, 259–71.

Ogilvy, D. (1963) *Confessions of an Advertising Man*. London: Longman.

Packard, V. (1960) *The Hidden Persuaders*. Harmondsworth: Penguin.

Pollay, R.W. (1986) The distorted mirror: reflections on the unintended consequences of advertising. *Journal of Marketing*, **50** (April), 18–36.

Robin, D.P. and Reidenbach, R.E. (1993) Searching for a place to stand: toward a workable ethical philosophy for marketing. *Journal of Public Policy and Marketing*, **12**(1), 97–105.

Singhapakdi, A., Kraff, K.L., Vitell, S.J. and Rallapalli, K.C. (1995) The perceived importance of ethics and social responsibility on organisational effectiveness: a survey of marketing. *Journal of the Academy of Marketing Science*, **23**(1), 49–56.

Smith, N.C. (1995) Marketing strategies for the ethics era. *Sloan Management Review*, Summer, pp. 85–97.

Sternberg, E. (1994) *Just Business*. London: Warner.

Thompson, C.J. (1995) A contextualist proposal for the conceptualization and study of marketing ethics. *Journal of Public Policy and Marketing*, **14**(2), 177–91.

Tzalikis, J. and Fritzsche D.J. (1989) Business ethics: a literature review with a focus on marketing ethics. *Journal of Business Ethics*, **8**, 695–743.

Vallance, E.M. (1995) *Business Ethics at Work*. Cambridge: Cambridge University Press.

Buyer information processing

Understanding how buyers use and process information is vital if effective communications are to be developed. The way in which buyers view their world and through that picture learn, develop attitudes and respond to marketing communication stimuli is a foundation for a range of promotion-related activities.

AIMS AND OBJECTIVES

The aim of this chapter is to provide an introduction to the main elements of buyer information processing, in order that readers develop an appreciation of the complexities associated with understanding and using information provided through marketing communications.

The objectives of this chapter are:

1. To introduce cognitive theory as an important element in the development of planned communications.
2. To examine personality as a main factor in the determination of successful communications.
3. To explore perception in the context of marketing communications.
4. To understand the main differences between conditioning and cognitive learning processes.
5. To appraise the role of attitudes and the different ways in which attitudes are thought to be developed.
6. To appreciate the importance of understanding an individual's intention to act in a particular way and its part in the decision process.
7. To provide a brief overview of the other environmental influences that affect the manner in which individuals process information.

Introduction

This chapter will explore the elements that influence the information processing behaviour of two different types of buyer: consumers and organisational buyers. It will then establish how the identification of different behaviour patterns can influence marketing communications.

Marketing is about many things, but one of its central themes is the management of behaviour, in particular behaviour prior to, during and after an exchange. Therefore it makes sense to underpin marketing activities with an understanding of buyer behaviour, in order that marketing strategies and plans be more effective. It is not the intention to provide a deep or comprehensive analysis of buyer behaviour, since there are many specialist texts that readers can refer to. However, a basic understanding of the context in which buyers process information, the way they behave, their decision-making processes and the ways in which such knowledge can be utilised in promotional plans is important.

There are a number of theoretical approaches that have been developed to assist our understanding of human behaviour, but the majority have their roots in one of three psychological orientations. These three (Freud's psychoanalytical theory, reinforcement theory and cognitive theory) can be seen to have influenced thinking about buyer behaviour over the last fifty years. This book will explore cognitive theory in the context of marketing communications.

Cognitive theory

Mainstream psychology has moved from a behaviourist to a cognitive orientation. Similarly, the emphasis in understanding and interpreting consumer behaviour has progressed from a reinforcement to a cognitive approach.

Cognitive theory is based upon an information processing, problem-solving and reasoning approach to human behaviour. Individuals use information that has been generated by external sources (e.g. advertisements) and internal sources (e.g. memory). This information is given thought, processed, transferred into meanings or patterns and then combined to form judgements about behaviour (based on Rumelhart in Belk (1975).

The cognitive orientation considers the consumer to be an adaptive problem solver, one who uses various processes in reasoning, forming concepts and acquiring knowledge. There are several determinants that are important to our understanding of the cognitive orientation because they contribute to the way in which individuals process information. These are personality, perception, learning, attitudes, certain environmental influences and issues pertinent to an individual's purchase situation (Figure 4.1). Each of these will now be considered.

Personality

Personality is, essentially, concerned with the inner properties of each individual, those characteristics that differentiate each of us. Consideration is given to two main approaches: the Freudian and Trait theories of personality.

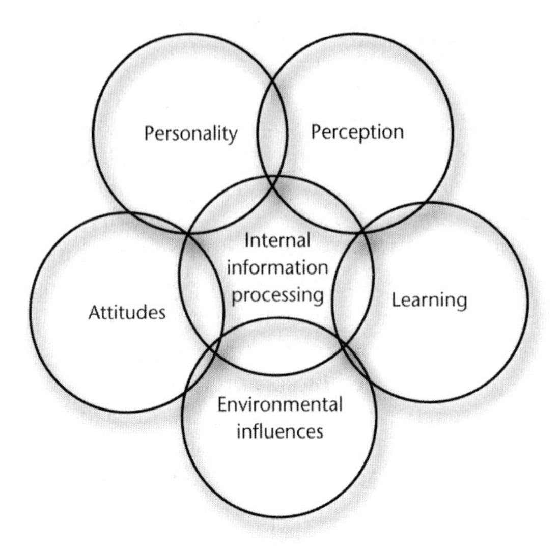

Figure 4.1 Elements of information processing.

Freudian theory

Freud believed that the needs which motivate human behaviour are driven by two primary instincts: life and death. The life instincts are considered to be predominantly sexual in nature, whereas the death instincts are believed to be manifested through self-destructive and/or aggressive behaviour.

The personality of the individual is assumed to have developed in an attempt to gratify these needs, and consists of the id, superego and ego; this approach is termed psychoanalytic theory. The id is the repository for all basic drives and motivations. Its function is to seek pleasure through the discharge of tension. The superego acts to restrain the id, to inhibit the impulses of the pleasure-seeking component, partly by acting within the rules of society. These two are obviously in conflict, which the ego attempts to mediate by channelling the drives of the id into behaviour acceptable to the superego.

The application of psychoanalytic theory to buyer behaviour suggests that many of the motives for purchase are driven by deeply rooted sexual drives and/or death instincts. These can only be determined by probing the subconscious, as in work undertaken by motivation researchers, the first of whom were Dichter and Vicary. Motivation research attempts to discover the underlying motivations for consumer behaviour. A variety of techniques have been developed, including in-depth interviews, projective techniques, association tests and focus groups.

Psychoanalytic theory has been criticised as too vague, unresponsive to the environment and too reliant on the early development of the individual. Furthermore, because the samples used are very often small and because of the emphasis on the unconscious, verification and substantiation of the results of experiments are often difficult – and some say impossible.

However, the psychoanalytic approach has been used as the basis for many advertising messages, aimed at deeply rooted feelings, hopes, aspirations and fears. For example, many life assurance companies use fear in their advertising messages to motivate people to invest in life and pension policies. Advertisements for cars often

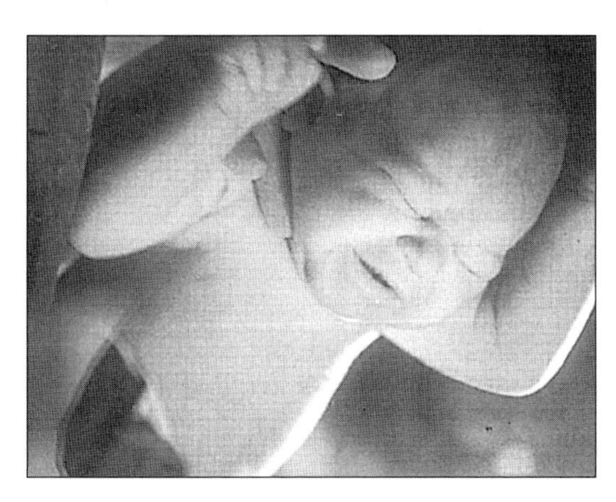

Exhibit 4.1 Audi advertisement using symbols of life (picture supplied and used with the kind permission of Audi UK).

depict symbols: those of life and death in the Audi advertisement in Exhibit 4.1, and that of safety in the Volvo advertisement in Exhibit 4.2. We also know that buyers can be motivated by symbolic as well as functional motives in their purchases. Thus the use of sexual appeals and symbols in advertisements is often undertaken with this information in mind. In addition, many commentators agree that motivation research is the forerunner of the psychographics research often used for market segmentation (see Chapter 10).

Exhibit 4.2 Volvo advertisement using safety as the main motivation (picture supplied and used with the kind permission of Volvo UK).

Trait theory

In contrast with the largely qualitative approach of the Freudian school is the empirical perspective. Under this approach, personality is measured and quantified. What is being measured are the traits or 'distinguishing, relatively enduring ways in which one individual differs from another' (Guildford, 1959). Personality tests invariably seek to measure individual differences in respect of specific traits. The end result is a label that is applied to the particular traits observed in the individuals being tested. These labels, for example, consider aspects such as the degree of assertiveness, responsiveness to change or the level of sociability an individual might exhibit.

Of specific interest to marketing communicators is the relationship between broad personality traits and general styles of behaviour. Consumer psychologists, working on behalf of advertising agencies in particular, have spent a great deal of time trying to identify specific traits and then develop consumer profiles which enable a distinct market segment to be determined. The 4Cs was one such programme, developed by Young and Rubicam in the late 1980s. Four distinct types of consumer were identified: aspirers, succeeders, mainstreamers and reformers, each of whom had particular psychographic characteristics.

Mainstreamers are motivated by a basic need for security and belonging. To satisfy that drive, they tend to buy established products and manufacturers' brands, as they perceive purchase risk to be lower. Aspirers seek status and self-esteem and this is directed through identification with materialism. Aspirers are able to express themselves through the possession of goods, which act as symbols of achievement, such as the latest hi-fi or designer clothes. Succeeders are people who are successful but who need to control the events in their lives. Typically they read the *Financial Times* or the *Daily Telegraph* and consume products that have proven quality. Reformers are the antithesis of the aspirers, in that they seek self-fulfilment rather than status. Own brands and natural products are sought by them, as it is the quality of life that is their underlying motivation (QED, 1989).

Brand personality: Beamish

Beamish is a traditional Irish ale, and a campaign was launched in October 1997 which presented two sides of life, the red and the black. These are intended to reflect two aspects of the Irish personality.

The black is represented by a swarthy tousle-haired man who symbolises contemplation and romance. Love for this character is a burning heart and marriage is not a word but more of a sentence, and failure is more interesting than success.

The red is represented by a bright, eccentric red haired Irishman who is humorous, extrovert and depicts the livelier Irish character.

The Beamish ale is available as both a red and a black drink and in being so allows drinkers to satisfy complementary attitudes, tastes and occasions. See Plates 4.1 and 4.2.

Adapted from Hall (1997)

By combining the qualitative approach of the motivational researchers with the quantitative approach of the trait theorists, psychographic variables can be determined. Over the last twenty years this has developed into a popular segmentation technique, called psychographics. This particular technique is discussed in Chapter 10, from both a consumer and organisational buyer perspective.

Perception

Perception is concerned with how individuals see and make sense of their environment. It is about the selection, organisation and interpretation of stimuli by individuals so that they can understand the world.

Individuals are exposed, each day, to a tremendous number of stimuli. Leslie de Chernatony (1993) suggests that research has shown that on a typical day each consumer is exposed to over 550 advertisements, notwithstanding the thousands of other non-commercial stimuli that we encounter. To cope with this bombardment, our sensory organs select those stimuli to which attention is given. These selected stimuli are organised in order to make them comprehensible and are then given meaning, in other words, there is an interpretation of the stimuli which is influenced by attitudes, values, motives and past experiences as well as the character of the stimuli themselves. Stimuli, therefore, are selected, organised and interpreted.

Perceptual selection

The vast number of messages mentioned earlier need to be filtered, as we cannot process them all. The stimuli that are selected result from the interaction of the nature of the stimulus with the expectations and the motives of the individual. Attention is an important factor in determining the outcome of this interaction: 'Attention occurs when the stimulus activates one or more sensory receptor nerves and the resulting sensations go to the brain for processing' (Hawkins *et al.*, 1989).

The nature of the stimuli, or external factors such as the intensity and size, position, contrast, novelty, repetition and movement, are factors that have been developed and refined by marketing communicators to attract attention. Animation is used to attract attention when the product class is perceived as bland and uninteresting, such as margarine or tea-bags. Unexpected camera angles and the use of music can be strong methods of gaining the attention of the target audience, as used successfully by the Peugeot 405 and 406 commercials. Sexual attraction can be a powerful means of attracting the attention of audiences and when associated with a brand's values can be a very effective method of getting attention (for example, the Diet Coke advertisement (Plate 4.3)).

The expectations, needs and motives of the individual, or internal factors, are equally important. Individuals see what they expect to see, and their expectations are normally based on past experience and preconditioning. From a communications perspective the presentation of stimuli that conflict with the individual's expectations will invariably receive more attention. The attention-getting power of erotic and sexually driven advertising messages (jeans manufacturers often promote their brands, such as Levi 501s and Diesel, using this stimulus) is well known, but, as we shall see later, readers only remember the attention-getting device (e.g. the male or female), not the offering with which an association was intended. Looked at in terms of Schramm's model of communication (Chapter 2), the process of encoding was inaccurate, hence the inappropriate decoding.

Of particular interest is the tendency of individuals to select certain information from the environment. This process is referred to as selective attention. Through attention, individuals avoid contact with information which is felt to be disagreeable in that it opposes strongly held beliefs and attitudes.

Individuals see what they want or need to see. If they are considering the purchase of a new car there will be heightened awareness of car advertisements and a correspondingly lower level of awareness of unrelated stimuli. Selective attention allows individuals to expose themselves to messages that are comforting and rewarding. For example, reassurance is often required for people who have bought new cars or expensive technical equipment and who have spent a great deal of time debating and considering the purchase and its associated risk. Communications congratulating the new owner on his or her wise decision often accompany post-purchase literature such as warranties and service contracts. If potentially harmful messages do get through this filter system, perceptual defence mechanisms help to screen them out after exposure.

Perceptual organisation

For perception to be effective and meaningful, the vast array of selected stimuli needs to be organised. The four main ways in which sensory stimuli can be organised are figure–ground, grouping, closure and contour.

Figure–ground

Each individual's perception of an environment tends to consist of articles on a general background, against which certain objects are illuminated and stand proud. Williams (1981) gives the examples of trees standing out against the sky and words

Exhibit 4.3 A picture using the foreground to highlight the object (car) against a general background (picture kindly supplied by Renault UK Ltd, and Publicis. Photograph Steve Hoskins).

on a page. This has obvious implications for advertisers and the design and form of communications, especially advertisements, to draw attention to important parts of the message, most noticeably the price, logo or the company/brand name (see Exhibit 4.3: Renault Mégane Liberté).

Grouping

Objects which are close to one another tend to be grouped together and a pattern develops. Grouping can be used to encourage associations between a product and specific attributes. For example, food products which are positioned for a health market are often displayed with pictures that represent fitness and exercise, the association being that consumption of the food will lead to a lifestyle that incorporates fitness and exercise, as these are important to the target market.

Volvo: change of perception

Volvo cars have been regarded as safe, reliable and environmentally friendly. However, a recent print advertisement proclaiming that 'The Porsche will be along in a couple of seconds', and showed a Volvo 850 estate car outpacing a Ferrari. The message is part of an attempt to change public opinion and perception of Volvo cars and appeal to new markets in addition to the core family segments. The shift is from 'boxy and boring' to 'safe but sexy' (Carnegy, 1995). The aim is to attract younger, 'pre-family' and older, 'post-family' buyers, without losing the core reputation of Volvo and family customers.

The strategy to overhaul the way Volvo is perceived includes reviewing the design of the cars. It is regarded as important to preserve the Scandinavian element in the design, and may be compared with Ikea, the furniture retailer, which utilises the Scandinavian character as a worldwide selling point. In contrast, Electrolux, the household appliance maker, makes no special merit of its Swedish roots.

Adapted from Carnegy (1995)

Closure

When information is incomplete individuals make sense of the data by filling in the gaps. This is often used to involve consumers in the message and so enhance selective attention. Advertisements for American Express charge cards or GM credit cards ('if invited to apply'), for example, suggest that ownership denotes membership, which represents exclusiveness and privilege.

Television advertisements that are run for 60 seconds when first launched are often cut to 30 or even 15 seconds later in the burst. The purpose is two-fold: to cut costs and to remind the target audience. This process of reminding is undertaken with the assistance of the audience, who recognise the commercial and mentally close the message even though the advertiser only presents the first part.

Contour

Contours give objects shape and are normally formed when there is a marked change in colour or brightness. This is an important element in package design and, as the battle for shelf space in retail outlets becomes more intense, so package design has become an increasingly important aspect of attracting attention.

The battles between Sainsbury's and Coca-Cola in the mid 1990s regarding the introduction of an alleged 'copy-cat' (Glancey, 1994) own-label product serves to illustrate this point. This and other own-label products are often packaged in a very similar way to the branded item. This serves to diffuse the impact of the branded item on the shelves and enhances the position and credibility of the own-label item.

United Biscuits took Asda (a multiple retailer) to court when the retailer launched an own-brand chocolate biscuit (Puffin) with very similar packaging to the bar owned by United Biscuits (Penguin). The court ruled that the colour, typography and use of the Puffin character were deceptively similar to those of Penguin and Asda were required to change the packaging.

Adapted from Murphy (1997)

These methods are used by individuals in an attempt to organise stimuli and simplify their meanings. They combine in an attempt to determine a pattern to the stimuli, so that they are perceived as part of a whole or larger unit. This is referred to as Gestalt psychology.

Perceptual interpretation

Interpretation is the process by which individuals give meaning to the stimuli once they have been organised. As Cohen and Basu (1987) state, by using existing categories, meanings can be given to stimuli. These categories are determined from the individual's past experiences and they shape what the individual expects to see. These expectations, when combined with the strength and clarity of the stimulus and the motives at the time perception occurs, mould the pattern of the perceived stimuli.

The degree to which each individual's ascribed meaning, resulting from the interpretation process, is realistic, is dependent upon the levels of distortion that may be present. Distortion may occur because of stereotyping: the predetermined set of images which we use to guide our expectations of events, people and situations. Another distortion factor is the halo effect which occurs when a stimulus with many attributes or dimensions is evaluated on just a single attribute or dimension. Brand extensions and family branding strategies are based on the understanding that if previous experiences with a different offering are satisfactory, then risk is reduced and an individual is more likely to buy a new offering from the same 'family'.

Marketing and perception

Individuals, therefore, select and interpret particular stimuli in the context of the expectations arising from the way they classify the overall situation. The way in which individuals perceive, organise and interpret stimuli is a reflection of their past experiences and the classifications used to understand the different situations each individual frames every day. Individuals seek to frame or provide a context within which their role becomes clearer. Shoppers expect to find products in particular situations, such as rows, shelves or display bins of similar goods. The context is a relevant purchase situation and does not contradict a shopper's expectations. Consequently, the likelihood that a sale will result is improved.

Marketing communications should attempt to present products (objects) in a frame or 'mental presence' (Moran, 1990) that is recognised by a buyer, such as a consumption or purchase situation. A product has a much greater chance of entering an evoked set if the situation in which it is presented is one that is expected and relevant.

Javalgi *et al.* (1992) point out that perception is important to product evaluation and product selection. Consumers try to evaluate a product's attributes by the physical cues of taste, smell, size and shape. Sometimes no difference can be distinguished, so the consumer has to make a judgement on factors other than the physical characteristics of the product. This is the basis of branding activity, where a personality is developed for the product which enables it to be perceived differently from its competitors. The individual may also set up a separate category or evoked set in order to make sense of new stimuli or satisfactory experiences.

Goodrich (1978) discusses the importance of perception, which can be seen in terms of the choices tourists make when deciding which destination to visit. The decision is influenced by levels of general familiarity, levels of specific knowledge and perception. It follows that the more favourable the perception of a particular destination, the more likely it is to be selected from its competitors.

Finally, individuals carry a set of enduring perceptions or images. These relate to themselves, to products and to organisations. The concept of positioning the product in the mind of the consumer is considered to be fundamental to marketing strategy, according to Schiffman and Kanuk (1991) and is a topic that will be examined in greater depth in Chapter 24. The image an individual has of an organisation is becoming recognised as increasingly important, judging by the proportion of communication budgets being given over to public relations activities and corporate advertising in particular.

Organisations develop multiple images to meet the positioning requirements of their end-user markets and stakeholders. They need to monitor and adjust their identities constantly in respect of the perceptions and expectations held by the other organisations in their various networks. For example, Stern and El-Ansary (1991) state that the level of channel coordination and control is a function of the different perceptions of channel members. These concern the perception of the channel depth, processes of control and the roles each member is expected to fulfil. Furthermore, the perception of an organisation's product quality and its associated image (reputation) is becoming increasingly important. Both end-user buyers and channel members are attempting to ensure that the intrinsic and extrinsic cues associated with their products are appropriate signals of product quality (Moran, 1990).

Learning

There are two mainstream approaches to learning: behavioural and cognitive.

Behavioural learning

The behaviourist approach to learning views the process as a function of an individual's acquisition of responses. There are three factors important to learning: association, reinforcement and motivation. However, it is the basic concept of the stimulus–response orientation which will be looked at in more detail.

It is accepted that for learning to occur all that is needed is a 'time–space proximity' between a stimulus and a response. Learning takes place through the establishment of a connection between a stimulus and a response. Marketing communications is thought to work by the simple process of people observing messages and being stimulated/motivated to respond by requesting more information or purchasing the advertised product in search of a reward. Behaviour is learned through the conditioning experience of a stimulus and response. There are two forms of conditioning: classical and operant.

Classical conditioning

Classical conditioning assumes that learning is an associative process that occurs with an existing relationship between a stimulus and a response. By far the best-known example of this type of learning is the experiment undertaken by the Russian psychologist, Pavlov. He noticed that dogs began to salivate at the sight of food. He stated that this was not taught, but was a reflex reaction. This relationship exists prior to any experimentation or learning. The food represents an unconditioned stimulus and the response (salivation) from the dogs is an unconditioned response.

Pavlov then paired the ringing of a bell with the presentation of food. Shortly the dogs began to salivate at the ringing of the bell. The bell became the conditioned stimulus and the salivation became the conditioned response (which was the same as the unconditioned response).

From an understanding of this work it can be determined that two factors are important for learning to occur:

1. To build the association between the unconditioned and conditioned stimulus there must be a relatively short period of time.
2. The conditioning process requires that there be a relatively high frequency/repetition of the association. The more often the unconditioned and conditioned stimuli occur together, the stronger will be the association.

Classical conditioning can be observed operating in each individual's everyday life. An individual who purchases a new product because of a sales promotion may continue to buy the product even when the promotion has terminated. An association has been established between the sales promotion activity (unconditioned stimulus) and the product (conditioned stimulus). If product quality and satisfaction levels allow, long-run behaviour may develop despite the absence of the promotion. In other words, promotion need not act as a key purchase factor in the long run.

Advertisers attempt to associate their products/services with certain perceptions, images and emotions that are known to evoke positive reactions from consumers. Image advertising seeks to develop the associations that individuals have when they think of a brand or an organisation, and hence its reputation. Messages of this type show the object with an unconditioned stimulus that is known to evoke pleasant and favourable feelings. The product becomes a conditioned stimulus eliciting the same favourable response. The advertisements for Bounty Bars use images of desert islands to evoke feelings of enjoyment and pleasure.

Operant conditioning

In this form of conditioning, sometimes known as instrumental conditioning, learning occurs as a result of an individual operating or acting on some part of the environment. The response of the individual is instrumental in getting a positive reinforcement (reward) or negative reinforcement (punishment). Behaviour that is rewarded or reinforced will be continued, whereas behaviour that is not rewarded will cease.

B.F. Skinner was a pioneer researcher in the field of operant conditioning. His work, with rats who learned to press levers in order to receive food and who later only pressed the lever when a light was on (discriminative stimulus), highlights the essential feature of this form of conditioning: that reinforcement follows a specific response.

Many organisations use reinforcement in their communications by stressing the benefits or rewards that a consumer can anticipate receiving as a result of using a product or brand. For example, Sainsbury's offer 'Reward Points' and Asda offer a reward of money savings which 'makes the difference'. Reinforcement theories emphasise the role of external factors and exclude the individual's ability to process information internally. Learning takes place either through direct reinforcement of a particular response or through an associative conditioning process.

However, operant conditioning is a mechanistic process which is not realistic, as it serves only to simplify an extremely complex process.

Cognitive learning

This approach to our understanding of learning assumes that individuals attempt to control their immediate environments. They are seen as active participants in that they try to resolve problems by processing information that is pertinent to each situation. Central to this process is memory. Just as money can be invested in short-, medium- and long-term investment accounts, so information is memorised for different periods of time. These memories are sensory, short-term and long-term; see Figure 4.2.

Sensory storage refers to the period in which information is sensed for a split second, and if an impression has been made the information will be transferred to short-term memory where it is rehearsed before transfer to long-term memory. *Short-term* memory lasts no longer than approximately eight seconds and a maximum of four or five items can be stored in short-term memory at any one time. Readers will probably have experienced being introduced to someone at a social event only to forget the name of the guest when they next meet them at the same event. This occurs because the name was not entered into *long-term* memory. Information can be stored for extended periods in long-term memory. This information is not lying dormant, however, it is constantly being reorganised and recategorised as new information is received.

There are four basic functions by which memory operates. These are, first, *rehearsal*, where information is repeated or related to an established category. This is necessary so that the second function, *encoding*, can take place. This involves the selection of an image to represent the perceived object. Once in long-term memory it is *categorised and stored*, the third function. *Retrieval* is the final function, a process by which information is recovered from storage.

Cognitive learning is about processing information in order that problems can be resolved. These information-handling processes can range from the simple to the complex. There are three main processes: iconic, modelling and reasoning.

Iconic rote learning involves understanding the association between two or more concepts when there is an absence of a stimulus. Learning occurs at a weak level through repetition of simple messages. Beliefs are formed about the attributes of an offering without any real understanding of the source of the information. Advertisers of certain products (low value, frequently purchased) will try to remind their target audiences repeatedly of the brand name in an attempt to help consumers learn. Through such repetition, an association with the main benefits of the product may be built, if only via the constant reminders by the spokesperson.

Learning through the *modelling* approach involves the observation and imitation of others and the associated outcomes of their behaviour. In essence, a great deal of children's early learning is developed in this way. Likewise, marketing communicators use the promise of rewards to persuade audiences to act in a particular way. By using positive images of probable rewards, buyers are encouraged to believe that they can receive the same outcome if they use the particular product. For example, clothing advertisements often depict the model receiving admiring glances from passers-by. The same admiration is the reward 'promised' to those who wear the same clothing. A similar approach is used by Kellogg's to promote their Special K breakfast cereal. The commercial depicts a (slim) mother and child playing on a beach. The message is that it is important to look after yourself and to raise your family through healthy eating, an outdoor life and exercise.

Reasoning, according to Hawkins *et al.* (1989), is the most complex form of cognitive learning. Through this process, individuals need to restructure and reorganise information held in long-term memory and combine it with fresh inputs in order to generate new outputs. Because of legislation, cigarette advertisers have had to find new ways of reaching their audiences. Benson & Hedges have used innovative

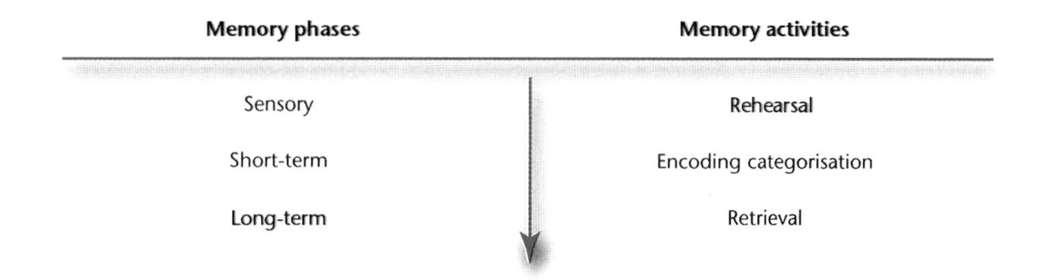

Figure 4.2 Aspects of internal information processing.

complex messages to reach smokers of their Silk Cut brand. The complex messages associated with this brand require much thought and reasoning to deduce the relationship between the image (scissors and silk ribbon) and the brand. The same type of complexity and reasoning can be applied to some of the late 1980s and early 1990s Guinness commercials.

Kellogg's All-Bran, a shredded fibre breakfast cereal, began to lose market share in the late 1980s after achieving brand leadership. Research revealed that buyers understood the importance of fibre in their diet, but had assumed that fresh fruit, vegetables and wholemeal bread were suitable and easier alternative sources of fibre. In 1990, Kellogg's used a campaign which compared the fibre content with a variety of commonly assumed rich sources of fibre, such as nine slices of brown bread (see Exhibit 4.4), twenty-one new potatoes and eight bananas. The success of this campaign was largely due to both current and lapsed buyers having to re-think their view of All-Bran. They were challenged to reason why they were not using All-Bran when it is the richest source of an ingredient that they value. Buyers were encouraged to make a judgement about their current diet and an alternative that was being presented as patently superior.

Of all the approaches to understanding how we learn, cognitive learning is the most flexible interpretation. The rational, more restricted approach of behavioural learning, where the focus is external to the individual, is without doubt a major contribution to knowledge. However, it fails to accommodate the complex internal thought processes that individuals utilise when presented with various stimuli.

Attitudes

The perceptual and learning processes may lead to the formation of attitudes. These are predispositions, shaped through experience, to respond in an anticipated way to an object or situation. Attitudes are learned through past experiences and serve as a link between thoughts and behaviour. These experiences may relate to the product itself, to the messages transmitted by the different members of the channel network (normally mass media communications) and the information supplied by opinion leaders, formers and followers.

Attitudes tend to be consistent within each individual: they are clustered and very often interrelated. This categorisation leads to the formation of stereotypes, which is

Exhibit 4.4
All Bran advertisement – an example of the use of reasoning in an advertisement appeal (picture supplied and used with the kind permission of Kellogg Company of Great Britain Ltd. All rights reserved).

extremely useful for the design of messages as stereotyping allows for the transmission of a lot of information in a short time period (thirty seconds) without impeding learning or the focal part of the message.

Attitude components

Attitudes are hypothetical constructs, and classical psychological theory considers attitudes to consist of three components:

1. *Cognitive component (learn)*
   This component refers to the level of knowledge and beliefs held by individuals about a product and/or the beliefs about specific attributes of the offering. This represents the learning aspect of attitude formation.
2. *Affective component (feel)*
   By referring to the feelings held about a product – good, bad, pleasant or unpleasant – an evaluation is made of the object. This is the component that is concerned with feelings, sentiments, moods and emotions about an object.
3. *Conative component (do)*
   This is the action component of the attitude construct and refers to the individual's disposition or intention to behave in a certain way. Some researchers go so far as to suggest that this component refers to observable behaviour.

This three-component approach (Figure 4.3) to attitudes is based upon attitudes towards an object, person or organisation. The sequence of attitude formation is learn, feel and do. This approach to attitude formation is limited in that the com-

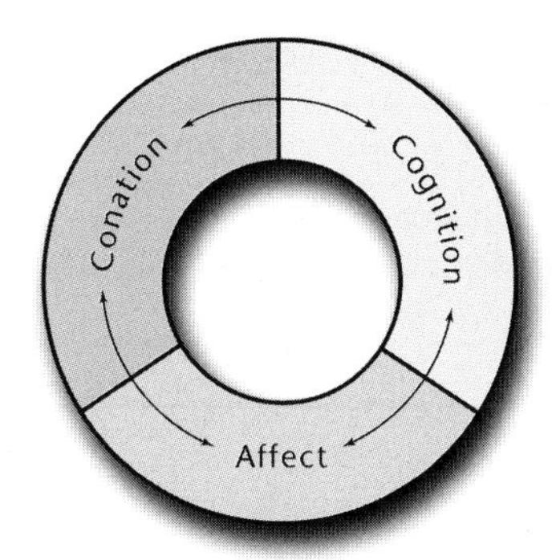

Figure 4.3 The three-component attitude model.

ponents are seen to be of equal strength. A single-component model has been developed where the attitude only consists of the individual's overall feeling towards an object. In other words, the affective component is the only significant component.

Multi-attribute attitude models

One of the difficulties with the three- and single-component attitude models is that they fail to explain why an individual has a particular attitude. A different approach views objects possessing many different attributes, all of which are perceived and believed by individuals with differing strengths and intensity.

Attribute analysis is an important factor in the design and consistency of marketing communication messages. For example, the UK toilet tissue market has been dominated by two main players, Andrex and Kleenex Velvet.

For many years Andrex has used a puppy to symbolise the softness, strength and length of their product. Table 4.1 indicates how the softness and strength attributes valued by consumers in 1992 have changed so that by 1996 the key attributes had become slightly less significant than they were. However, strong attitudes held by Andrex's loyal customers have enabled market share to rise steadily and market leadership has been maintained. This has been achieved in the light of the increased number of high quality products (often own label) that are now available, all of which communicate softness and strength as the key attributes; see Plate 4.4.

Of the many advances in this area, those made by Ajzen and Fishbein (1980) have made a significant contribution. They reasoned that the best way of predicting behaviour was to measure an individual's intention to purchase (the conative component). Underlying intentions are the individual's attitude towards the act of behaviour and the subjective norm. In other words, the context within which a proposed purchase is to occur is seen as important to the attitude that is developed towards the object.

The subjective norm is the relevant feelings others are believed to hold about the proposed purchase, or intention to purchase. Underpinning the subjective norm are the beliefs held about the people who are perceived to 'judge' the actions an individual might take. Would they approve or disapprove, or look favourably or unfavourably upon the intended action?

Underpinning the attitude towards the intention to act in a particular way are the strengths of the beliefs that a particular action will lead to an outcome. Ajzen and Fishbein argue that it is the individual's attitude to the act of purchasing, not the

Table 4.1 Attributes valued by consumers when purchasing toilet tissue

Attributes	1992	1995	Change 1992–95 (%)
Softness	66	57	-9
Colour to match decor	47	48	1
Price	45	45	0
Brand loyalty	39	36	−3
Special offers	24	32	8
Strength	42	29	−13
Length of roll	25	24	−1
Own label	6	14	8

Source: Adapted from a Mintel Report (1996).

object of the purchase, that is important. For example, a manager may have a positive attitude towards a particular type of expensive office furniture, but a negative attitude towards the act of securing agreement for him to purchase it.

The theory of reasoned action (Ajzen and Fishbein, 1980; Figure 4.4) shows that intentions are composed of interrelated components: subjective norms, which in turn are composed of beliefs and motivations about relevant others, towards a particular intention, and attitudes, which in turn are made up of beliefs about the probable outcomes that a behaviour will lead to.

This approach recognises the interrelationship of the three components of attitudes and that it is not attitude but the intention to act or behave that precedes observable behaviour that should be the focus of attention. It should be understood that attitudes do not precede behaviour and cannot be used to predict behaviour, despite the attempts of a number of researchers. Attitudes are important, but they are not the sole determinant of behaviour, and intentions may be a better indicator of behaviour.

Attitudes impact on consumer decision-making, and the objective of marketing communications is often to create a positive attitude toward a product and/or to reinforce or change existing attitudes. An individual may perceive and develop a belief that British Airways has a friendly and informal in-flight service and that the service provided by Lufthansa is cold and formal. However, both airlines are perceived to hold a number of different attributes, and each individual needs to evaluate these attributes in order that an attitude can be developed. It is necessary, therefore, to measure the strength of the beliefs held about the key attributes of different products. There are two main processes whereby beliefs can be processed and measured: compensatory and non-compensatory models.

Compensatory models

Through this approach, attributes that are perceived to be weak can be offset by attributes that are perceived to be strong. As a result, positive attitudes are determined in the sense that the evaluation of all the attributes is satisfactory. For example, Table 4.2 sets out a possible evaluation of three package holidays. Despite the weakness on hotel cleanliness, the strength of the other attributes in Package 2 scores this the highest, so the strongest attitude is formed towards this product. Some individuals

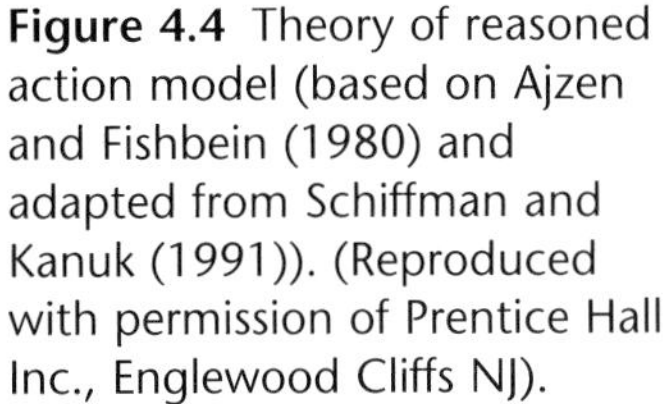

Figure 4.4 Theory of reasoned action model (based on Ajzen and Fishbein (1980) and adapted from Schiffman and Kanuk (1991)). (Reproduced with permission of Prentice Hall Inc., Englewood Cliffs NJ).

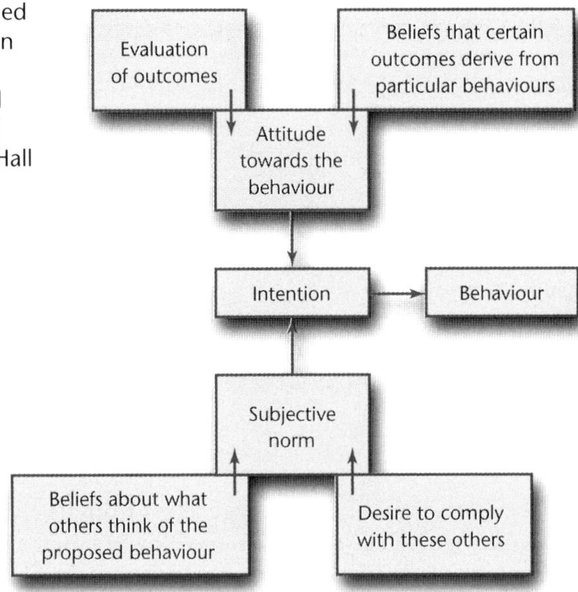

make decisions about products on the basis that their attributes must not contain any weaknesses. Therefore Package 2 would not be considered, as it fails to reach a minimum level of expected satisfaction on cleanliness; thus, despite its strengths, it is relegated from the decision alternatives.

An understanding of attitude components and the way in which particular attributes can be measured not only enables organisations to determine the attitudes held towards them and their competitors, but also empowers them to change the attitudes held by different stakeholders, if it is thought necessary.

There are a number of ways in which attitudinal change can be implemented. The first approach would be to change the beliefs held about the object and the performance qualities of the object. Beliefs can be adjusted through appropriate marketing communications. For example, by changing the perceptions held about the attributes, it is possible to change the attitudes about the object.

It should be possible to change the way the importance ratings are determined. By stressing the importance of travel times, Package 2 might raise the importance of this attribute in the minds of potential holiday-makers and so gain an advantage over its rivals, using the non-compensatory decision rule.

A further opportunity might exist for Package 3 where it currently fails to win under either of the decision models. The solution may be to introduce a fourth attribute, one in which the suppliers of Package 3 know they have an advantage over the competition. This may be that they have a no-surcharge guarantee and Packages 1 and 2 do not. By making prominent the new no-surcharge guarantee in the promotional messages transmitted by Package 3, the introduction of a new significant attribute may lead to greater success.

Further options for Package 3 include changing the perception of Packages 1 and 2 or changing the association of their packages with the others. This could be achieved

Table 4.2 Compensatory and non-compensatory models

Attribute	Weighting	Package 1		Package 2		Package 3	
		Rating	Score	Rating	Score	Rating	Score
Price	5	5	25	6	30	5	25
Hotel cleanliness	3	3	9	2	6	4	12
Travel times	2	7	14	9	18	4	8
Attitude rating			48		54		45
Possible decisions							
Compensatory model		Not considered		*Winner*		Not considered	
Non-compensatory model		*Winner*		Not considered		Considered	

by using messages that set the package apart from its rivals, suggesting for example, that not all package holidays are the same. This is a theme used by Thomson Holidays, where their copy reads, 'We go there, we don't stay there'.

By understanding the attitudes held by an object, person or organisation, it becomes possible to change perception, beliefs and hence attitudes to the advantage of the sponsoring organisation.

Environmental influences

Neither organizations nor consumers exist in a vacuum. They exist in an 'open' system and therefore act upon and are affected by various environmental factors (Figure 4.5). There are a number of externally generated influences that impact upon buyer information processing and decision-making. The main factors are described below.

Culture

Culture has been referred to as the unique characteristics that identify the acceptable patterns of behaviour and social relations within a particular society. Culture embodies the norms, beliefs, artefacts and customs that are learned from society and that constitute its values. It is these values that influence consumer behaviour and are of increasing importance to the international advertiser. Indeed, a more detailed consideration of the role of culture on marketing communications can be found in Chapter 28.

Culture is learned and acquired, it is not instinctive. Culture defines acceptable behaviour within a society and so sets the rules for all members who belong to the culture. For marketing communications, culture should be seen as a communication system in its own right. Through verbal and non-verbal actions a society is able to maintain stability, to bind all members with a sense of identity and to provide them with a means of continuity.

Sub-cultures

There are a number of sub-cultures within any given culture. These include age, geography, race, religion and ethnic groupings.

CASE ILLUSTRATION

Attitude Change – Skoda

Skoda, the East European car manufacturer, has long suffered an inferior reputation in Western Europe for the poor quality and reliability of their cars. However, Volkswagen bought shares in Skoda in 1991 and set about changing the attitudes of people in the important markets. To do this they first set about changing the quality of the cars by introducing new design and manufacturing techniques. Their first new product was the Felicia, launched in 1994 and this was followed by the Octavia which was launched at the Paris International Motorshow in October 1996. Its UK launch was in January 1998.

The launches of the Felicia and Octavia are interesting because Skoda had 100% unprompted name awareness. The first task was therefore not to build awareness of the name Skoda, unlike the recent launch of the Korean car manufacturer Daewoo, who spent £150m on advertising in the first 12 months. Skoda spent a mere £7 million informing the market about changes in the ownership of Skoda. In May 1995 the Felicia was launched with the line, 'We have changed the car, can you change your mind?' Here was a direct challenge to car buyers to revisit their attitude towards the Skoda name.

In October 1995 they launched a campaign based upon the line, 'Who's behind the changes at Skoda?'. To support the question a Volkswagen badge was depicted in the background as a shadow of the Skoda badge. This was an important and risky move as for many VW stands for reliability, the result of a long positioning approach.

In February 1996, advertising was used that showed the Felicia being used by representatives of the Territorial Army, and no immediate reference to Skoda was provided. In January 1997 the line changed to 'Judge for yourself', inviting buyers and the media to test drive and encouraging action (a behavioural and cognitive move) towards changing their attitudes.

Typical comments from the motoring press (opinion formers) were:

> 'The Octavia is a sound car with plenty to recommend it and little against it... [which] represents a big step forward for the company' Chadderton (1996) and 'The new Octavia will be able to look any of its rivals in the eye while it undersells them' Marshall (1996) 'on the road it feels, responds, as you would expect a car from the VW stable, with a taut, composed road manner' Hunston (1996).

Whilst attitudes towards Skoda have not been completely changed there is evidence that Volkswagen have embarked upon a strategy to alter attitudes and one that leans towards product enhancement and association with established and acceptable standards; this is very likely to be achieved in the longer term.

(Adapted from materials supplied by Skoda UK and an unpublished dissertation from the University of Portsmouth)

Social class

Virtually all societies are stratified by class, based upon power, wealth and prestige. Society values individuals and groups on criteria such as education, occupation and level of income. This information is distilled into a social class system, such as upper,

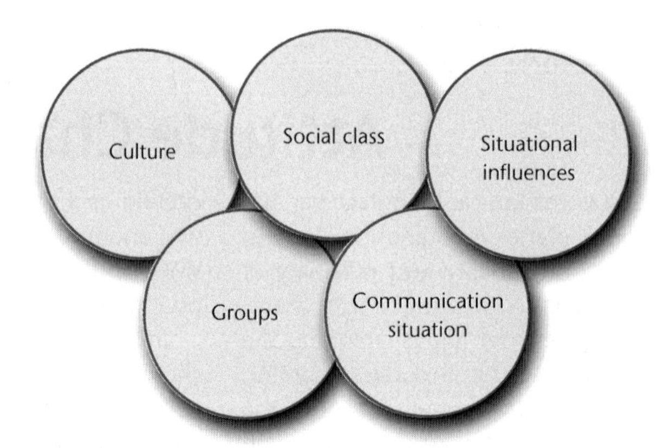

Figure 4.5 Environmental influences on buyer information processing.

middle and lower class, which for a long time has been a main characteristic of UK society.

Marketeers have developed a socioeconomic categorization which is used as a primary means of segmenting markets. Communications planners have always used symbols to reflect the values, lifestyles, norms and family roles associated with each perceived stratum. Among the many benefits this brings is the ability to transfer a lot of information relatively quickly and so communicate effectively. The process also allows for the continuity of the core values of society.

However, as discussed in Chapter 10, this traditional approach to segmentation is becoming increasingly difficult to utilise as consumers' purchasing habits become more complex and their lifestyles become less rigid and more open. McMurdo (1993) discusses some of the research by the advertising agency J. Walter Thompson. It is now necessary for advertisers to recognise the speed at which consumers can move between purchasing styles, even in the space of a single shopping trip. This is because the requirements of each purchase can be so different that tailor-made segmentation by product is necessary. For example, Dulux recognises that its market for paints consists of 'sloshers' and 'craftsmen'. Paint can be bought for the attic, where it will be 'sloshed', or for the lounge, where it will be applied like a 'craftsman', by the same individual.

Groups

Groups are one of the primary factors influencing learning and socialization. An individual may simultaneously be a member of several groups, each having a different degree of effect. These groups can be categorized as follows:

1. Ascribed groups: one automatically belongs, e.g. family.
2. Primary/secondary groups: where interaction is on a one-to-one basis, e.g. family and friends.
3. Formal/informal groups: where the presence or absence of structure and hierarchy define the group activity.

4. Aspirational/membership groups: groups to which the individual wishes to belong or does belong.

All these act as reference groups for the individual and influence the individual's behaviour.

Situational influences

The design, encoding and media channels used to transmit communication messages must take into account that buyers are influenced by factors that are unique to each buying situation and are not related specifically to the product or the individual. The situational context impacts on the information-processing capabilities of the buyer. For example, the amount of light in the store or the level of store traffic can influence the amount of time given to decision-making. While this factor will normally have been accounted for in the formulation of the marketing strategy, it must be revisited if the communications are to be effective.

When considering the impact that situational influences might have on information processing, the type of situation needs to be considered. A situational determinant is a factor that is unique to each buying act. These situational influences are connected neither to the purchase object nor to the buyer, and are independent of them. Hansen (1972) identified three types of situation: usage, purchase and communications.

Usage situation

When and where is the offering to be consumed and is consumption to be largely a private act, orientated to the individual (such as chocolate bars) or part of a social activity (such as beer)? For example, some manufacturers of breakfast cereals have been repositioning (Chapter 24) their brands in an attempt to encourage use at other times of the day. Communications need to reflect this strategy and encapsulate the situation in which the desired eating behaviour occurs.

Purchase situation

The act of purchase and the associated environment can influence the behaviour of the target individual. Is shopping a monthly, biannual, weekly or last-minute activity? Hawkins *et al.* (1989) state that mothers shopping with children are more likely to be influenced by product preferences of their children than when shopping without them. This may be due not only to the amount of time available to complete the physical act of shopping but also to the time to process the information. Engel *et al.* (1990) cite information load, format and form as important criteria. Too much information (information overload) can reduce the accuracy of an individual's decision-making, whereas the order in which information is presented both on packages and in terms of store layout can seriously retard the amount of time taken to process information, and this can also influence the motivation of the shopper.

The manner in which information is presented will affect the decision style. For example, the ease of comparing brands, perhaps on an individual attribute basis (e.g. diabetics determining the amount of carbohydrate in competing brands), will influence both perception and purchase behaviour.

What is the environment of the shop like? Are there opportunities to influence the target with in-store promotions and advertising messages? Different individuals prefer different supermarkets and price is not the sole criterion. Store loyalty is a function of a number of issues, among them convenience, layout, product range, car parking facilities and whether packers are available. Associated with this is the concept of corporate image. Each of the supermarket chains has a particular range of images held by its consumers. Consumer perception of store efficiency and value for money and the totality of corporate communications need to reflect, deflect or reinforce particular images. This element is pursued in greater depth in Chapter 27.

Communications situation

The settings in which marketing communications are received will affect the degree to which the message is understood and acted upon. For example, salespersons cold-calling on organisations (arriving at an organisation and requesting a sales interview without a prior appointment) are not usually received in a positive way. Furthermore, having gained an appointment through a prior arrangement does not mean that the information provided during the visit will be received as intended. The buyer may have been advised of some bad news prior to the meeting and his or her thoughts are not focused on the object of the sales meeting or presentation. Television commercials may be zipped or zapped, clutter may prevent key points of the message getting home or general noise in the form of conversation may also affect the effectiveness of the message. One of the central issues concerning the situation in which communications are received is the need to gain the attention of the receiver.

Having determined that there are particular types of situations where the consumption process occurs, Belk (1975; used with kind permission), proposes that there are five main situation variables that should be considered. These are the physical aspects, the social surroundings, the time, the task and the antecedent states.

Physical aspects refer to the store design and layout, the location, the lighting, music, smells and sounds associated with the situation. The *social surroundings* refer to all those involved in the purchase, usage or communications. For example, a child was described in one type of situation as accompanying a mother on the shopping activity, and children have a degree of influence on such an event.

Time was considered in the context of the time available to complete the activity, but it could also be considered in the context of time of day, year or season, or time elapsed since the last purchase. The *task* itself is pertinent. Is the purchase for a third party as a present, or is it for personal consumption? Finally, *antecedent states* are the influences each individual experiences, but state is transitional. For example, states of high elation, despondency, bitterness or pleasure are experienced by all individuals, but they are not enduring characteristics.

The particular impact of various environmental influences can affect the behaviour of buyers during purchase activity, during usage and when information is being processed. Understanding the impact of the physical, time and social influences, together with the nature of the task and antecedent states, provides the marketing communications planner with fresh inputs to the exercise of positioning the product appropriately.

Summary

This chapter has reviewed some of the recent and current thinking about how individuals process information. Cognitive theory provides a valuable insight into the manner in which buyers use externally and internally generated stimuli to solve problems. Personality, perception, learning, attitudes and aspects pertinent to the wider environment and each purchase situation have been considered as major elements of the problem-solving approach adopted by both consumers and organisational buyers.

Marketing communication planners need to be aware of these elements and to understand how they operate in the target audience. Messages can be created to match the cognitive needs of the intended audience and change, for example, perception or attitudes, in such a way that communication with the target audience is likely to be more successful.

Review questions

1. Write a short description of cognitive theory. How does it differ from behaviourism?
2. What are the main elements of information processing?
3. How does trait theory differ from Freudian theories of personality?
4. Describe a purchase repertoire (or evoked set) and suggest how marketing communications might assist perceptual selection.
5. To what extent are perception and positioning interlinked?
6. Choose three printed advertisements where the user is promised a reward.
7. Attitudes are believed to comprise three elements. Name them.
8. Write a brief explanation of the theory of reasoned action.
9. How might the environment influence marketing communications?
10. Identify the different types of situational influences on the purchase process.

References

Ajzen, I. and Fishbein, M. (1980) *Understanding Attitudes and Predicting Social Behaviour*. Englewood Cliffs NJ: Prentice Hall.

Belk, R. (1975) Situational variables in consumer behaviour. *Journal of Consumer Research*, **2** (December), 57–64.

Carnegy, H. (1995) Volvo shifts on to the fast track: the Swedish car group is trying to widen its appeal with a more adventurous image. *Financial Times*, 21 July, p. 15.

Chadderton, P. (1996) Worth Czeching out. *Auto Express*, 20 September.

Cohen, J. and Basu, K. (1987) Alternative models of categorisation. *Journal of Consumer Research* (March), 455–72.

de Chernatony L. (1993) The seven building blocks of brands. *Management Today* (March), 66–7.

Engel, F., Blackwell, R. and Minniard, P. (1990) *Consumer Behaviour*, 6th edn. New York: The Dryden Press.

Glancey, J. (1994) The real thing put to the test. *Independent on Sunday*, 24 April, News Analysis, p. 5.

Goodrich, J.N. (1978) The relationship between preferences for and perceptions of vacation destinations: application of a choice model. *Journal of Travel Research*, **17**(2).

Guildford, J. (1959) *Personality*. New York: McGraw-Hill.

Hall, E. (1997) Beamish work takes comparative approach. *Campaign*, 3 October, p. 4.

Hansen, F. (1972) *Consumer Choice Behaviour: A Cognitive Theory*. New York: Free Press.

Hawkins, D., Best, R. and Coney, K. (1989) *Consumer Behaviour*. Homewood IL: Richard D. Irwin.

Hunston, H. (1996) Skoda takes the Asians head on. *Daily Telegraph*, 14 September.
Javalgi, R., Thomas, E. and Rao, S. (1992) US travellers' perception of selected European destinations. *European Journal of Marketing*, **26**(7), 45–64.
McMurdo, M.W. (1993) Chasing butterflies. *Marketing Week*, 21 May, pp. 28–31.
Marshall, P. (1996) Rivals under the same roof. *Financial Times*, September, pp. 21–2.
Moran, W. (1990) Brand preference and the perceptual frame. *Journal of Advertising Research* (October/November), 9–16.
Murphy, C. (1997) Penguin forces Asda redesign. *Marketing*, 20 March, p. 1.
QED (1989) It's not easy being a dolphin. BBC TV.
Schiffman, L. and Kanuk, L. (1991) *Consumer Behavior*. Englewood Cliffs NJ: Prentice Hall.
Stern, L. and El-Ansary, A. (1991) *Marketing Channels*, 4th edn. Englewood Cliffs NJ: Prentice Hall.
Williams, K.C. (1981) *Behavioural Aspects of Marketing*. London: Heinemann.

chapter 5

Buyer decision-making processes

Knowledge of the ways in which buyers make decisions and the contextual elements that frame their view of the world are important if the correct type of information is to be conveyed to them at the right time and in the right manner.

AIMS AND OBJECTIVES

The aim of this chapter is to consider some of the different processes consumers and organisational buyers use to make purchase decisions.

The objectives of this chapter are:

1. To present a general process for purchase decision-making.
2. To examine the sequence and methods used by consumers to make decisions.
3. To explore the components of perceived risk.
4. To introduce and explain involvement theory and relate it to planned communication activities.
5. To consider the different types of individual who contribute to purchase decisions made by organisations.
6. To understand the stages which organisations use to make purchase decisions.
7. To appreciate the differences in approaches and content of marketing communications between consumer and organisational buying.

Introduction

An understanding of the contextual elements that impact upon individual purchase decision-making and the overall process through which individuals behave and ultimately make decisions is an important first stage in the development of any marketing communications plan. Knowledge of a buyer's decision-making processes is vital if the correct type of information is to be transmitted at the right time and in the right or appropriate manner. There are two broad types of buyer: consumers and organisational buyers. First, consideration will be given to a general decision-making process and then an insight into the characteristics of the decision-making processes for consumers and organisational buyers will be presented.

A general buying decision-making process

Figure 5.1 shows that there are five stages to the general process whereby buyers make purchase decisions and implement them. Marketing communications can impact upon any or all of these stages with varying levels of potential effectiveness.

Problem recognition

Problem recognition occurs when there is a perceived difference between an individual's ideal state and reality. Advertisers often induce 'problem recognition' by suggesting that the current state is not desirable, or by demonstrating how consumers can tell if they have a similar problem (e.g. 'Is your hair dull and lifeless?'). The difficulty in getting buyers to recognise that they have a problem invites the question: do

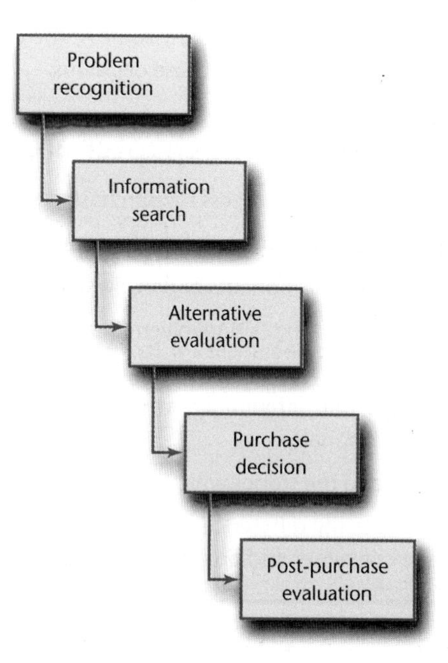

Figure 5.1 Five general stages of a buyer's purchase decision process.

they actually have a problem? If there is no identified need, then it is not marketing but selling that is being practised.

Information search

Having identified a problem a prospective buyer will search for information in an attempt to resolve it. There are two main areas of search activity:

1. The internal search involves a memory scan to recall experiences and knowledge, utilising the perceptual processes to see if there is an 'off-the-shelf' solution.
2. If there is no 'off-the-shelf' solution the prospective buyer will resort to an external search. This will involve family and friends, reference sources and commercial guides and advertising.

Alternative evaluation

Potential solutions need to be evaluated in order that the optimum choice be made. Products considered feasible constitute the *preference set*, and it is from these seven or eight products that a smaller group of products is normally assembled. This is referred to as the *evoked set* (or repertoire) and it is from this that consumers make a choice. Attributes used to determine the sets are referred to as evaluative criteria. Very often these attributes are both objective and subjective in nature.

Purchase decision

Having evaluated various solutions, the buyer may develop a predisposition to make a purchase. This will involve matching motives and evaluative criteria with product attributes. This necessitates the use of the processes of learning and attitude formation, discussed in the previous chapter.

Post-purchase evaluation

Direct experience of the product is an important part of the decision process. Feedback from use helps learning and attitude development and is the main contributor to long-run behaviour. Communication activity must continue to provide satisfaction and prevent the onset of cognitive dissonance. This is a state where, after the purchase decision has been made, a buyer might feel tension about a past decision either because the product fails to reach expectations or because the consumer becomes aware of a superior alternative.

Marketing communications, at this stage, should be aimed at reinforcing past decisions by stressing the positive features of the product or by providing more information to assist its use and application. For example, much of the advertising undertaken by car manufacturers seeks to prevent the onset of tension and purchase dissatisfaction.

Types of consumer decision-making

Buyers do not follow the general decision sequence at all times. The procedure may vary depending upon the time available, levels of perceived risk and the degree of involvement a buyer has with the type of product. Perceived risk and involvement are issues that will be covered later. At this point three types of problem solving behaviour (extended problem solving, limited problem solving and routinised response) will be considered.

Extended problem solving (EPS)

Consumers considering the purchase of a car or house undertake a great deal of external search activity and spend a lot of time reaching a solution that satisfies, as closely as possible, the evaluative criteria previously set. This activity is usually associated with products that are unfamiliar, where direct experience and hence knowledge is weak, and where there is considerable financial risk.

Marketing communications should aim to provide a lot of information to assist the decision process. Sales brochures, access to salespersons and advertisements are just some of the ways in which information can be provided.

Limited problem solving (LPS)

Having experience of a product means that greater use can be made of internal memory-based search routines, and the external search can be limited to obtaining up-to-date information or to ensuring that the finer points of the decision have been investigated.

Marketing communications should attempt to provide information about any product modification or new attributes and convey messages which highlight those key attributes known to be important to buyers. By differentiating the product, marketing communications provide the buyer with a reason to select that particular product.

Routinised response behaviour (RRB)

For a great number of products the decision process will consist only of an internal search. This is primarily because the buyer has made a number of purchases and has accumulated a great deal of experience. Therefore, only an internal search is necessary, so little time or effort will be spent on external search activities. Low-value items which are frequently purchased fall into this category, for example, toothpaste, soap, tinned foods and confectionery.

Some outlets are perceived as suitable for what are regarded as distress purchases. Alldays and Happy Shopper outlets position themselves as convenience stores for distress purchases (for example, a pint of milk at ten o'clock at night). Many garages have positioned themselves as convenience stores suitable for meeting the needs of RRB purchases. In doing so they are moving themselves away from the perception of being only a distress purchase outlet.

Communicators should focus their activities upon keeping their product within the evoked set or getting it into the set. Learning can be enhanced through repetition of messages, but repetition can also be used to maintain attention and awareness.

Perceived risk

An important factor associated with the purchase decision process is the level of risk perceived by the buyer. This risk concerns the uncertainty of the proposed purchase and the outcomes that will result from a decision to purchase a product.

Risk is perceived because the buyer has little or no experience of the performance of the product or the decision process associated with the purchase. Buyers may lack the ability to make what they see as the right decision and they may be forced to trade the decision to purchase one product in lieu of another because resources, such as time and money, are restricted. Settle and Alreck (1989) suggest that there are five main forms of risk that can be identified; the purchase of a hi-fi unit demonstrates each element (see Plate 5.1).

1. Performance risk: will the unit reproduce my music clearly?
2. Financial risk: can I afford that much or should I buy a less expensive version?
3. Physical risk: will the unit damage my other systems or endanger me in any way?
4. Social risk: will my friends and colleagues be impressed?
5. Ego risk: will I feel as good as I want to feel when listening to or talking about my unit?

A sixth element, time, is also considered to be a risk factor (Stone and Gronhaug, 1993). Using the hi-fi example, will purchase of the unit lead to an inefficient use of my time? Or can I afford the time to search for a good hi-fi so that I will not waste my money?

What constitutes risk is a function of the contextual characteristics of each situation, the individuals involved and the product under consideration:

1. Each situation varies according to perceptions of the shopping experience, the time the purchase is to be made in the context of the other activities that need to be completed (last chance to buy a birthday present, only fifteen minutes left before meeting my partner), and the image different stores have and the risk that is associated with the products offered by the store.
2. Each individual has a propensity to higher or lower levels of risk. These levels may vary according to their experience of purchasing particular products, demographic factors such as age, level of education and religion, and various personality factors.
3. The product may, if only for price, convey a level of risk to the purchaser. For example, the purchase of a car is not only a large financial commitment for most people, but is also a highly emotive decision that has significant ego and social risks attached to it.

Perceived risk need not be constant throughout the decision process. Mitchell and Boustani (1994) suggest that the level of perceived risk may vary as depicted in Figure 5.2, although more work is required to determine the validity of their initial findings.

The main question is, how can buyers be helped to alleviate high levels of risk during the pre- and post-purchase stages in the decision process? The main method used by buyers is the acquisition of information. Information through the mass media, through word-of-mouth communications and through personal selling (usually sales representatives) are used to set out the likely outcomes and so reduce the levels of risk. Brand loyalty can also be instrumental in reducing risk when launching new products. The use of guarantees, third-party endorsements, money-back offers (Rover offer the opportunity to return a car within 30 days or exchange it for a different model) and trial samples (as used by many hair care products) are well-used devices to reduce risk.

CASE ILLUSTRATION

Airline travel – Virgin Atlantic

The airline business is notoriously competitive with over 50 airlines advertising above-the-line; between 1992 and 1996 airline advertising spend increased by 27%.

When Virgin Atlantic first launched, its business class product was regarded as innovative and ahead of the competition. During 1996/97, however, British Airways changed market expectations with the launch of its 'cradle seat', and an increasing number of airlines were copying the Virgin Atlantic product and service propositions. One of the key difficulties for Virgin was that the more conservative business travellers did not feel at ease with their image of the airline. A campaign was devised to change this situation by highlighting competitive product advantages and innovations. It was also necessary to keep reminding current business passengers of the benefits of flying Upper Class. The first endorser was the actor Terence Stamp, and this was followed by Helen Mirren. The television campaign was supported with national press advertising.

The campaign led to a 12% increase in passengers in the month following the spring burst in 1997 and 20% following the autumn burst. Research shows that business flyers have a 50% recall of Upper Class, while BA recall stands at 60%, but this is also a reflection of the increased weight of spend that British Airways is able to afford. For example, BA spent five times as much as Virgin Atlantic on advertising in 1995 and three times as much in 1996.

See Plate 5.1.

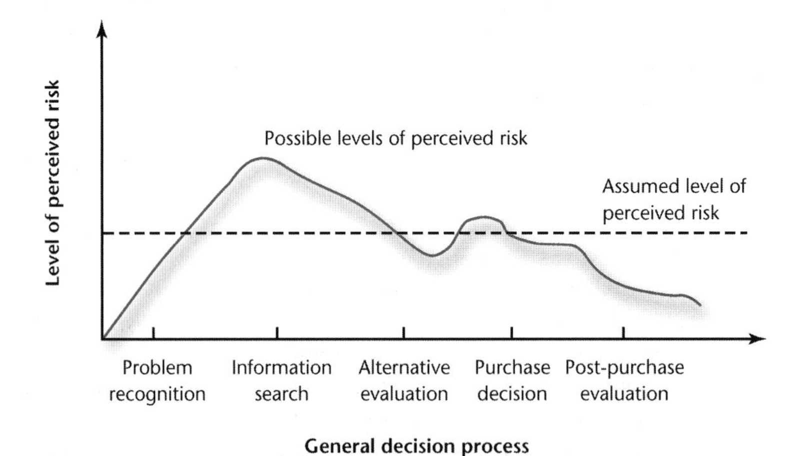

Figure 5.2 Varying levels of perceived risk through the purchase decision process (adapted from Mitchell and Boustani (1994); used with kind permission).

Involvement theory

A central framework, vital to understanding consumer decision-making behaviour and associated communications, is involvement theory. Purchase decisions made by consumers vary considerably, and one of the factors thought to be key to brand choice decisions is the level of involvement (in terms of importance and relevance) a consumer has with either the product or the purchase process.

The term 'involvement' has become an important concept in the consumer behaviour literature. The concept has its roots in social psychology, but its current form and interpretation by researchers is both interesting and revealing. There is no consensus on a definition of involvement. Kapferer and Laurent (1985) argue that involvement has five different facets. These are interest, risk importance, risk probability, sign value and hedonic value. Their approach tends to be all-consuming, whereas Ratchford (1987), quoting Zaichkowsky (1985) and others, does not perceive involvement as such a broad matter. The majority of researchers do not recognise the importance of hedonic and sign value elements in this context. To some, involvement is about the ego, perceived risk and purchase importance – a cognitive perspective. To those who favour a behavioural perspective, the search for and evaluation of product-orientated information is pertinent (Schiffman and Kanuk, 1991).

Laaksonen (1994) draws three perspectives of involvement from the literature. These are the cognitive, predisposition to act and response-based interpretations.

He proposes that the *cognitive view* of involvement regards the perceived personal relevance of an object to an individual as of paramount importance. This approach refers to the strength or extent of the cognitive/attitude structure towards an object. The strength of the psychological linkage between an individual and a stimulus object determines the intensity of involvement. How important is it to purchase Levi 501 jeans? This intensity of attitude is seen to have originated from social judgement theory, where involvement is seen as a variable affected by how others might interpret a purchase; that is, their predisposition to respond to Levi 501s.

The second perspective regards involvement as an individual state or *predisposition to act*. Here, involvement focuses on the mental state of an individual, evoked by a stimulus. It is the degree of perceived importance, the interest or level of emotional attachment, arousal, drive or motivation that defines the intensity of involvement, either present in an individual or present in any given situation. Using the jeans analogy, how motivated is the individual to purchase 501s? Therefore, involvement refers to the motivational state of an individual in a specific situation. The goals and their importance (hierarchy) defined by individuals determine the direction (towards an object/advertisement or perhaps the act of purchasing) and the level (high, medium, low) of involvement. Again, involvement is regarded as a mediating variable in information processing and a predisposition to act.

The third perspective is the *response view*. Here involvement is regarded as a reaction to an external stimulus or stimuli such as marketing communications. These responses are typically characterised by the form of cognitive and behavioural processing (learn–feel–do) directed to accomplishing a task. So the response view of involvement is based on the reaction of an individual to a stimulus, which will affect the learn–feel–do sequence and the depth to which processing occurs. Therefore, the impact of promotional messages for Levi 501s is likely to be most important in determining the direction and purchase intentions of potential jeans purchasers. Here, involvement is considered as a cognitive response to the marketing communication messages (Batra and Ray, 1983). These views do not see involvement as a mediating variable, simply because involvement is regarded as 'an actualised response in itself' (Laaksonen).

Of these three, no one view can be determined as a correct interpretation. In a way all are wrong and all are right simultaneously. There is agreement among many researchers that involvement should be seen in the context of three main states. These are high, low and zero involvement. The last of these is self-explanatory and requires no additional comment. The other two states are portrayed as two discrete ends of a continuum.

Consumers are thought to move along this continuum, from high to low, as purchase experience increases, perceived risk is reduced and levels of overall knowledge improves.

The approach taken here is that involvement is about the degree of personal relevance and risk perceived by members of the target market in a particular purchase situation (Rossiter *et al.*, 1991). This implies that the level of involvement may vary through time as each member of the target market becomes more (or less) familiar with the purchase and associated communications. At the point of decision-making, involvement is either high or low, not some point on a sliding scale or a point on a continuum between two extremes. Involvement is a cognitively bound concept, the strength and depth of which varies among and between individuals.

High involvement occurs when a consumer perceives an anticipated purchase which is not only of high personal relevance but also represents a high level of perceived risk. Cars, washing machines, houses and insurance polices are seen as 'big ticket' items, infrequent purchases that promote a great deal of involvement. The risk described is financial, but as we saw earlier, risk can take other forms. Therefore, the choice of perfume, suit, dress or jewellery may also represent high involvement, with social risk dominating the purchase decision. The consumer, therefore, devotes a great deal of time to researching the intended purchase and collecting as much information as possible in order to reduce, as far as possible, levels of perceived risk.

A *low-involvement* state of mind regarding a purchase suggests little threat or risk to the consumer. Low-priced items such as washing powder, baked beans and breakfast cereals are bought frequently, and past experience of the product class and the brand cues the consumer into a purchase that requires little information or support. Items such as alcoholic and soft drinks, cigarettes and chocolate are also normally seen as low-involvement, but they induce a strong sense of ego risk associated with the self-gratification that is attached to the consumption of these products.

There is a range of products and services that can evoke high levels of involvement based upon the emotional impact that consumption provides the buyer. This is referred to as hedonic consumption, and Hirschmann and Holbrook (1982) describe this approach as 'those facets of consumer behaviour that relate to the multi sensory, fantasy and emotive aspects of one's experience with products'. With its roots partly in the motivation research and partly in the cognitive processing schools, this interpretation of consumer behaviour seeks to explain how and why buyers experience emotional responses to the act of purchase and consumption of particular products. *Historical imagery* occurs when, for example, the colour of a dress, the scent of a perfume or aftershave, or the aroma of a restaurant or food, can trigger an individual's memory to replay an event. In contrast, *fantasy imagery* occurs when a buyer constructs an event, drawing together various colours, sounds and shapes to compose a mental experience of an event that has not occurred previously. Consumers imagine a reality in which they derive sensory pleasure. The cigarette brand 'Strand' probably failed because the advertisement depicted a lone individual ('you're never alone with a Strand'): individuals projected themselves into the scene and found it unsatisfactory. The imagined scene (cold, damp and isolated) was unattractive and did not satisfy a sensory need. Some smokers imagine themselves as 'Marlboro Men': not just masculine, but as idealised cowboys (Hirschmann and Holbrook, 1982).

Whereas the traditional view of consumption observes products to be objective in nature and stresses the tangible attributes, hedonic consumption regards certain types of products (classes) as subjective symbols. The image of the product, or what it represents, is more important than what the product is. Therefore, the intangible elements of certain products are recognised as strong motivators for consumption. Products such as the cinema, opera, a football match, rock concerts and fashion shows are often cited, as they draw on aesthetic qualities.

There are a number of problems with the hedonic approach, namely measurement factors of reliability and validity, but, nevertheless, appreciating the hedonic needs of the target audience can be an important contribution to the creation of promotional messages.

Consumer decision-making processes

From this understanding of general decision-making processes, perceived risk and involvement theory, it is possible to identify two main approaches to consumer decision-making.

High-involvement decision-making

If an individual is highly involved with the initial purchase of a product, EPS is the appropriate decision sequence, as information is processed in a rational, logical order. Individuals who are highly involved in a purchase are thought to move through the process shown in Figure 5.3. When high-involvement decision-making is present, individuals perceive a high level of risk and are concerned about the intended purchase. The essential element in this sequence is that a great deal of information is sought initially and an attitude is developed before a commitment or intention to trial is determined.

Information search is an important part of the high-involvement decision-making process. Because individuals are highly motivated, information is actively sought, processed and evaluated. Many media sources are explored, including the mass media, word-of-mouth communications and point-of-sale communications. As individuals require a lot of information, print media are more appropriate as a large volume of detailed information can be transmitted and this allows the receiver to

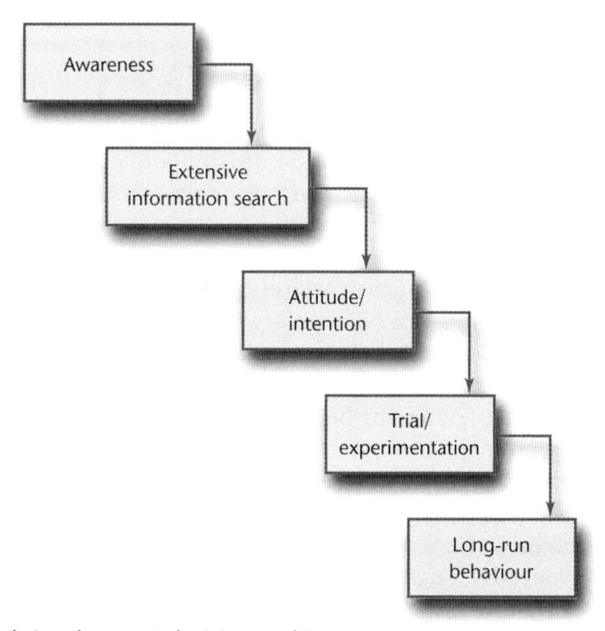

Figure 5.3 High-involvement decision-making process.

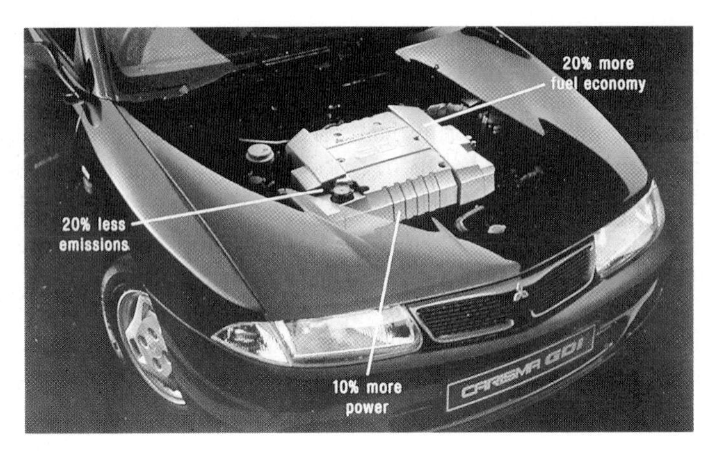

Exhibit 5.1
A print advertisement for a product that often evokes high involvement. Permission to reproduce this advertisement kindly given by Mitsubishi.

digest the information at a speed which they can control. Exhibit 5.1 depicts an advertisement for a car. Note the amount of information presented and the balance between the copy and the visual elements of the message.

Evaluation of the information and of the alternatives that have been derived from the information search needs to be undertaken. By comparing and implicitly scoring the different attributes of each alternative, a belief about the overall competitiveness of each alternative can be established. In Chapter 4 a compensatory model was examined. In this approach, individuals do not reject products because an attribute scores low; rather, a weakness is offset or compensated for by the strength and high scores accredited to other attributes. An individual's attitude to a purchase is the sum of the scores given to the range of evaluative criteria used in the decision-making process. As we saw in Chapter 4, Fishbein states that an attitude towards the act of purchasing and the subjective norm (the perceived attitude of others to the act being considered) combine to form an *intention* to act in a particular way. This part of the process is facilitated by the use of credible sources of information. Therefore, personal selling is important to bring individuals closer to the product, in order that it may be demonstrated and allow intense learning to occur.

Trial behaviour will follow if the perceived quality of the product is satisfactory and sufficient triggers, from internal searches, stimulate experimentation. Likewise, long-run behaviour, the goal of all marketing activities, will be determined if the guarantees and product quality combine to meet the expectations of the individual, generated by the information search.

Low-involvement decision-making

If an individual has little involvement with an initial purchase of a product, LPS is the appropriate decision process. Information is processed in a passive, involuntary way because of the low personal relevance and perceived risk associated with the purchase. Individuals who have a low involvement with a purchase decision choose not to search for information and are thought to move through the process shown in Figure 5.4.

Communications can assist the development of awareness in the low-involvement decision-making process. However, as individuals assume a passive problem-solving role, messages need to be shorter than in the high-involvement process and should contain less information. Broadcast media are preferred as they complement the passive learning posture adopted by the individual. Repetition is important because the receiver has little or no motivation to retain information, and his or her perceptual selection processes filter out unimportant information. Learning develops through exposure to repeated messages, but attitudes do not develop at this part of the process (Harris, 1987).

Where low involvement is present, each individual relies upon internal, rather than external, search mechanisms, often prompted by point-of-purchase displays. Using non-compensatory decision rules (Chapter 4), where product weaknesses are not offset by strengths, individuals make decisions, often at the point-of-purchase, to try established or new brands.

Price can be a very important factor by which individuals can discriminate between low-involvement purchase decisions. In high-involvement decisions there is a wide

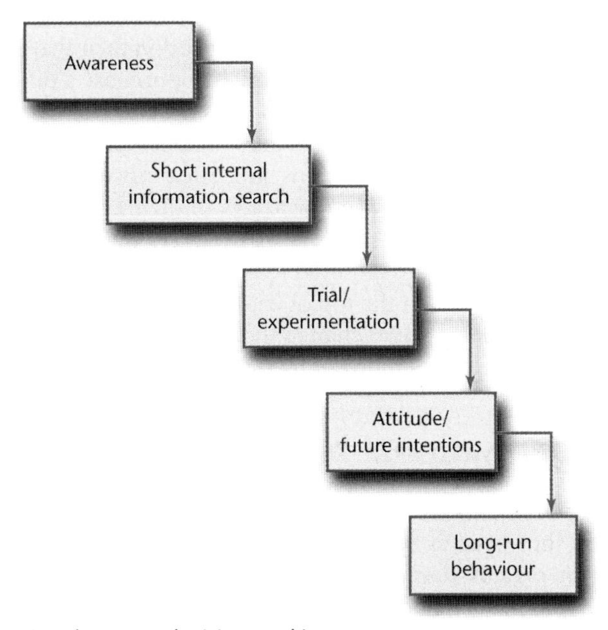

Figure 5.4 Low-involvement decision-making process.

variety of attributes which individuals can use to discriminate between purchase decisions. In low involvement purchases, price, packaging and point-of-purchase displays, and promotions work together to cue and stimulate an individual into trying a product.

As a direct result of trying a product (or experimenting) and hence product experience, an attitude develops. By judging the quality of the experience an attitude is formed which acts as the basis for future decisions. Long-run behaviour is a function of promotional messages, product quality and the degree of loyalty that can be sustained towards the brand.

Subsequent purchase activity

The initial purchase decision process frames all subsequent decisions in the product category. If a high-involvement decision process ends satisfactorily, then levels of brand loyalty are normally high, which means that subsequent decisions can be processed much more quickly. Routinised response behaviour occurs safely, as any risk associated with a purchase can be dispelled through the security associated with a brand. Brand loyalty is the normal outcome of a successful high-involvement decision-making process.

If the high-involvement process ends in partial satisfaction, then depending upon the nature and extent of the outstanding risk, the next decision may also be EPS. For example, if the purchase of a first savings or investment product results in total dissatisfaction, any second purchase of a similar or financially related product will require a review of the critical attributes to provide up-to-date product and provider information, but not necessarily to inform about what a savings/investment policy is.

If the initial decision was motivated by a low level of involvement and the outcome was satisfactory, then subsequent decisions will be based upon a state of brand ambivalence. This means that individuals relegate these decisions to a habitual process but will consider a number of different brands, and will switch to one of them if they perceive that the circumstances in which the decision is being made are changing. For example, a typical habitual decision concerns the purchase of tinned tomatoes. Most consumers will decide upon their usual brand until they notice a price promotion, special offer or incentive to purchase a different brand. A switch may also be actuated by different merchandising and positioning within the store, different personal requirements (e.g. dietary changes) and levels of brand awareness.

Repeat purchase decisions are often unstable on the grounds that buyers are content to switch between products in their evoked set unless there is a high level of brand loyalty. Manufacturers of products that are associated with low-involvement decision-making are required to engage in promotional activities that keep the awareness of the brand at the top of each individual's mind-set. Otherwise there is a danger that a competitor may change the circumstances in which an individual makes a decision and trigger a motivation to try its offering.

Organisational buying decision processes

Organisations have so far been viewed in the context of sellers, but in order to function they need to buy materials, parts, general supplies and services from a range of other organisations. Some texts refer to this as industrial marketing or, in the more current terminology, business-to-business marketing, reflecting the growth and importance of the public sector and the increasing use of the services sector within mature economies. However, the term 'organisational marketing' is used here to reflect the wide range of organisations involved with such activities.

Organisational buying processes need to be understood, just as consumer buying processes do, in order that appropriate and effective communication plans can be developed to complement and support the marketing mix.

Organisational buying, according to Webster and Wind (1972), is 'the decision making process by which formal organisations establish the need for purchased products and services and identify, evaluate and choose among alternative brands and suppliers'. Of particular significance is the relationship that develops between organisations who enter market exchange transactions. As mentioned previously, the various networks that organisations belong to will influence the purchase decisions that other organisations in the network make. However, before exploring these issues it is necessary to review the context in which organisational decisions are made.

One way of examining the context is to compare organisational decisions with those made in consumer markets. There are far fewer buyers in the organisational context than in the consumer market, although there can be a number of people associated with a buying decision in an organisation. Orders are invariably larger and the frequency with which they are placed is much lower. It is quite common for agreements to be made between organisations for the supply of materials over a number of years. Similarly, depending upon the complexity of the product (photocopying paper or a one-off satellite), the negotiation process may also take a long time.

Many of the characteristics associated with consumer decision-making processes can be observed in the organisational context. However, organisational buyers make decisions which ultimately contribute to the achievement of corporate objectives. To make the necessary decisions, a high volume of pertinent information is often required. This information needs to be relatively detailed and is normally presented in a rational and logical style. The needs of the buyers are many and complex, and some may be personal. Goals, such as promotion and career advancement within the organisation, coupled with ego and employee satisfaction combine to make organisational buying an important task, one that requires professional training and the development of expertise if the role is to be performed optimally.

Buyclasses

Organisational buyers make decisions that vary with each buying situation and buyclass. Buyclasses, according to Robinson *et al.* (1967), comprise three types: new task, modified rebuy and straight rebuy (Table 5.1).

1. *New buy*
   As the name implies, the organisation is faced with a first-time buying situation. Risk is inevitably large at this point, and partly as a consequence there are a large number of decision participants. Each participant requires a lot of information and a relatively long period of time is required for the information to be assimilated and a decision to be made.
2. *Modified rebuy*
   Having purchased a product, the organisation may request through their buyer that certain modifications be made to future purchases, for example, adjustments to the specification of the product, further negotiation on price levels or perhaps the arrangement for alternative delivery patterns. Fewer people are involved in the decision process than in the new task situation.

Table 5.1 Main characteristics of the buyclasses

Buyclass	Degree of familiarity with the problem	Information requirements	Alternative solutions
New buy	The problem is fresh to the decision-makers	A great deal of information is required	Alternative solutions are unknown, all are considered new
Modified rebuy	The requirement is not new but is different from previous situations	More information is required but past experience is of use	Buying decision needs new solutions
Rebuy	The problem is identical to previous experiences	Little or no information is required	Alternative solutions not sought or required

3. *Straight rebuy*
In this situation, the purchasing department reorders on a routine basis, very often working from an approved list of suppliers. No other people are involved with the exercise until different suppliers attempt to change the environment in which the decision is made. For example, they may interrupt the procedure with a potentially better offer.

These phases bear a strong resemblance to the extended, limited and routinised response identified by Howard with respect to the consumer market.

Buying centres

Reference has been made on a number of occasions to organisational buyers, as if these people are the only representatives of an organisation to be involved with the purchase decision process. This is not the case, as very often a large number of people are involved in the purchase decision. This group is referred to as either the decision-making unit (DMU) or the buying centre.

Buying centres vary in size and composition in accordance with the nature of each individual task. Webster and Wind (1972) identified a number of people who make up the buying centre.

Users are people who not only initiate the purchase process but will use the product, once it has been acquired, and evaluate its performance. *Influencers* very often help set the technical specifications for the proposed purchase and assist the evaluation of alternative offerings by potential suppliers. *Deciders* are those who make purchasing decisions. In repeat buying activities the buyer may well also be the decider. However, it is normal practice to require that expenditure decisions involving sums over a certain financial limit be authorised by other, often senior, managers. *Buyers* (purchasing managers) select suppliers and manage the process whereby the required products are procured. As identified previously, buyers may not decide which product is to be purchased but they influence the framework within which the decision is made. *Gatekeepers* have the potential to control the type and flow of information to the organisation and the members of the buying centre. These gatekeepers may be technical personnel, secretaries or telephone switchboard operators.

The size and form of the buying centre is not static. It can vary according to the complexity of the product being considered and the degree of risk each decision is perceived to carry for the organisation. Different roles are required and adopted as the nature of the buying task changes with each new purchase situation (Bonoma, 1982). It is vital for seller organisations to identify members of the buying centre and to target and refine their messages to meet the needs of each member of the centre.

The task of the marketing communications manager and the respective sales team is to decide which key participants have to be reached, with which type of message, with what frequency and to what depth should contact be made. Just like individual consumers, each member of the buying centre is an active problem solver and processes information so that personal and organisational goals are achieved.

Influences on the buying centre

Three major influences on organisational buyer behaviour can be identified as stakeholders, the organisational environment and those aspects which the individual brings to the situation (Table 5.2).

Stakeholders develop relationships between the focus organisation and other stakeholders in the network. The nature of the exchange relationship and the style of communications will influence buying decisions. If the relationship between organisations is trusting, mutually supportive and based upon a longer-term perspective (a relational structure) then the behaviour of the buying centre may be seen to be co-operative and constructive. If the relationship is formal, regular, unsupportive and based upon short-term convenience (a market structure-based relationship) then the purchase behaviour may be observed as courteous yet distant.

Without doubt the major determinant of the organisational environment is the cost associated with switching from one supplier to another (Bowersox and Cooper, 1992). When an organisation chooses to enter into a buying relationship with another organisation an investment is made in time, people, assets and systems. Should the relationship with the new supplier fail to work satisfactorily then a cost is incurred in switching to another supplier. It is these switching costs that heavily influence buying decisions. The higher the potential switching costs, the greater the loss in flexibility and the greater the need to make the relationship appropriate at the outset.

Behaviour within the buying centre is also largely determined by the interpersonal relationships of the members of the centre. Participation in the buying centre has

Table 5.2 Major influences on organisational buying behaviour

Stakeholder influences	Organisational influences	Individual influences
Economic conditions	Corporate strategy	Personality
Legislation	Organisational culture and values	Age
Competitor strategies	Resources and costs	Status
Industry regulations	Purchasing policies and procedures	Reward structure and systems
Technological developments	Interpersonal relationships	
Social and cultural values		
Interorganisation relationships		

Source: Based on Webster and Wind (1972).

been shown to be highly influenced by individuals' perceptions of the personal consequences of their contribution to each of the stages in the process. The more that individuals think they will be blamed for a bad decision or praised for a good decision, the greater their participation, influence and visible DMU-related activity (McQuiston and Dickson, 1991). The nature and dispersal of power within the unit can influence the decisions that are made. Power is increasingly viewed from the perspective of an individual's ability to control the flow of information and the deployment of resources (Spekman and Gronhaug, 1986). This approach reflects a network approach to, in this case, intraorganisational communications.

Buyphases

The organisational buying decision process consists of several stages or buyphases (Robinson *et al.*, 1967). The following sequence of six phases or events is particular to the new task buyclass. Many of these buyphases are ignored or compressed when either of the other two buyclasses are encountered.

Need/problem recognition

Products or services are purchased because of two main events (Cravens and Woodruff, 1986). Difficulties may be encountered first as a result of a need to solve problems, such as a stock-out or new government regulations, and secondly, as a response to opportunities to improve performance or enter new markets. Essentially, the need/recognition phase is the identification of a gap. This is the gap between the benefits an organisation has now and the benefits it would like to have. For example, when a photocopier breaks down or fails to meet the needs of the organisation, the communication benefits it offers are missed by the users. This gap can be bridged by using a different machine on a temporary basis or by buying a new machine that provides the range of benefits required.

Product specification

As a result of identifying a problem and the size of the gap, influencers and users can determine the desired characteristics of the product needed to resolve the problem. This may take the form of a general description or may require a much more detailed analysis and the creation of a specification for a particular product. What sort of photocopier is required? What is it expected to achieve? How many documents should it copy per minute? Is a collator or tray required? This is an important part of the process, because if it is executed properly it will narrow the supplier search and save on the costs associated with evaluation prior to a final decision.

Supplier and product search

At this stage the buyer actively seeks organisations who can supply the necessary product. There are two main issues at this point. Will the product reach the required performance standards and will it match the specification? Secondly, will the potential supplier meet the other organisational requirements? In most circumstances organisations review the market and their internal sources of information and arrive at a decision that is based on rational criteria.

Organisations, as we have seen before, work wherever possible to reduce uncertainty and risk. By working with others who are known, of whom the organisation has direct experience and who can be trusted, risk and uncertainty can be reduced substantially. This highlights another reason why many organisations seek relational exchanges and operate within established networks and seek to support each other.

The quest for suppliers and products may be a short task for the buyer; however, if the established network cannot provide a solution, the buying organisation has to seek new suppliers, and hence new networks, to be able to identify and short-list appropriate supplier organisations.

Evaluation of proposals

Depending upon the complexity and value of the potential order(s), the proposal is a vital part of the communication plan and should be prepared professionally. The proposals of the short-listed organisations are reviewed in the context of two main criteria: the product specification and the evaluation of the supplying organisation. If the organisation is already a part of the network, little search and review time need be allocated. If the proposed supplier is new to the organisation, a review may be necessary to establish whether it will be appropriate (in terms of price, delivery and service) and whether there is the potential for a long-term relationship or whether this is a single purchase that is unlikely to be repeated.

Once again, therefore, is the relationship going to be a market exchange or a relational exchange? The actions of both organisations, and of some of the other organisations in the network to the new entrant, are going to be critical in determining the form and nature of future relationships.

Supplier selection

The buying centre will undertake a supplier analysis and use a variety of criteria depending upon the particular type of item sought. This selection process takes place in the light of the comments made in the previous section. A further useful perspective is to view supplier organisations as a continuum, from reliance on a single source to the use of a wide variety of suppliers of the same product.

Jackson (1985) proposed that organisations might buy a product from a range of different suppliers, in other words a range of multiple sources are maintained (a practice of many government departments). She labelled this approach 'always a share', as several suppliers are given the opportunity to share the business available to the buying centre. The major disadvantage is that this approach fails to drive cost as low as possible, as the discounts derived from volume sales are not achieved. The advantage to the buying centre is that a relatively small investment is required and little risk is entailed in following such a strategy.

At the other end of the continuum are organisations who only use a single source supplier. All purchases are made from the single source until circumstances change to such a degree that the buyer's needs are no longer being satisfied. Jackson referred to these organisations as 'lost for good', because once a relationship with a new organisation has been developed they are lost for good to the original supplier. An increasing number of organisations are choosing to enter alliances with a limited number or even single source suppliers. The objective is to build a long-term relationship, work together to build quality and help each other achieve their goals. Outsourcing manufacturing activities for non-core activities has increased, and this has moved the focus of communications from an internal to an external perspective.

Evaluation

The order is written against the selected supplier and immediately the supplier is monitored and performance is evaluated against such diverse criteria as responsiveness to enquiries and modifications to the specification and timing of delivery. When the product is delivered it may reach the stated specification but fail to satisfy the original need. This is a case where the specification needs to be rewritten before any future orders are placed.

Organisational buying has shifted from a one-to-one dyadic encounter, salesperson to buyer, to a position where a buying team meets a selling team. The skills associated with this process are different and are becoming much more sophisticated, and the demands on both buyers and sellers are more pronounced. The processes of buying and selling are complex and interactive.

Developments in the environment can impact on a consumer or organisation buyer and change both the way decisions are made and their nature. For example, the decision to purchase new plant and machinery requires consideration of the future cash flows generated by the capital item. Many people will be involved in the decision, and the time necessary for consultation may mean that other parts of the decision-making process are completed simultaneously.

There are a number of other issues concerned with the manner in which the members of a buying centre interact and make choices. An interesting new approach to strategic management considers the subjective, cognitive thoughts of the strategist to be more important than has been considered previously. Porter (1980), Ansoff and McDonnell (1990) and others, in what is referred to as the design school of thought, assume that strategic decisions result from rational, logical analysis and interpretation of the environment.

An alternative view is that as environments are too complex and dynamic for objective analysis to be any practical use (Simon, 1976), then strategy or choices are fashioned from individuals' interpretations of their environment. Projections of historical data in uncertain highly unpredictable environments mean that strategists, or members of the buying centre in this case, will rely more on knowledge and experience as the main platform for decision-making and selection among options (Rutter, 1994).

Communication differences

There are a number of differences between organisation and consumer-orientated marketing communications. Some writers (Brougaletta, 1985; Gilliand and Johnston, 1997) have documented a variety of differences between consumer and business-to-business markets. The following is intended to set out some of the more salient differences. See also Table 5.3.

1. *Message reception*
   The contextual conditions in which messages are received and ascribed meanings is very different. In the organisational setting the context is much more formal, and as the funding for the purchase is to derived from company sources (as opposed to personal sources for consumer market purchases) there may be a lower orientation to the price as a significant variable in the purchase decision. The purchase is intended to be used by others for company usage, whereas products bought in a consumer context are normally intended for personal consumption.
2. *Number of decision makers*
   In consumer markets a single person very often makes the decision. In organisational markets decisions are made by many people within the buying centre.

Table 5.3 Differences between consumer and business-to-business marketing communications

	Consumer orientated markets	Business-to-business markets
Message reception	Informal	Formal
Number of decision makers	Single or few	Many
Balance of the promotional mix	Advertising and sales promotions dominate	Personal selling dominates
Specificity and integration	Broad use of promotional mix with a move towards integrated mixes	Specific use of below-the-line tools but with a high level of integration
Message content	Greater use of emotions and imagery	Greater use of rational, logic and information-based messages although there is evidence of a move towards the use of imagery
Length of decision time	Normally short	Longer and more involved
Negative communications	Limited to people close to the purchaser/user	Potentially an array of people in the organisation and beyond
Target marketing and research	Great use of sophisticated targeting and communication approaches	Limited but increasing use of targeting and segmentation approaches
Budget allocation	Majority of budget allocated to brand management	Majority of budget allocated to sales management
Evaluation and measurement	Great variety of techniques and approaches used	Limited number of techniques and approaches

This means that the interactions of the individuals needs to be considered. In addition, a variety of different individuals need to be reached and influenced and this may involve the use of different media and message strategies.

3. *The balance of the communications mix*
The role of advertising and sales promotions in business-to-business communications is primarily to support the personal selling effort. This contrasts with the mix which predominates in consumer markets. Personal selling has a relatively minor role and is only significant at the point of purchase in some product categories where involvement is high (cars, white goods and financial services), reflecting high levels of perceived risk. However, the increasing use of direct marketing in consumer markets suggests that personal communications are becoming more prevalent and in some increasingly similar to the overall direction of business-to-business communications.

4. *The constituents of the marketing communications mix*
Business-to-business markets have traditionally been quite specific in terms of the promotional tools and media used to target audiences. While the use of advertising literature is very important, there has been a tendency to use a greater proportion of below-the-line activities. This compares with consumer markets, where a greater proportion of funds have been allocated to above-the-line activities. It interesting that the communications in the consumer market are moving towards a more integrated format, more similar in form to the business-to-business model than was previously considered appropriate.

5. *Message content*
   Generally, there is high involvement in many business-to-business purchase decisions, so communications tend to be much more rational and information-based than in consumer markets. However, there are signs that businesses are making increased use of imagery and emotions in the messages (see Chapter 25).

6. *Length of purchase decision time*
   The length of time taken to reach a decision is much greater in the organisation market. This means that the intensity of any media plan can be dissipated more easily in the organisational market.

7. *Negative communications*
   The number of people affected by a dissatisfied consumer, and hence negative marketing communication messages, is limited. The implications of a poor purchase decision in an organisational environment may be far-reaching, including those associated with the use of the product, the career of participants close to the locus of the decision and, depending upon the size and spread, perhaps the whole organisation.

8. *Target marketing and research*
   The use of target marketing processes in the consumer market has been more advanced and sophisticated than the organisational market. This impacts on the quality of the marketing communications used to reach the target audience. However, there is much evidence that the business-to-business markets are using advanced techniques such as the use of psychographics, the Wilson learning 'social style' model and the 'cube' model (Eisenhart, 1988), which use lifestyle and values as a means of segmentation and the formulation of effective messages.

9. *Budget allocation*
   The sales department receives the bulk of the marketing budget in the organisation market and little is spent on research in comparison with the consumer market.

10. *Measurement and evaluation*
    The consumer market employs a variety of techniques to evaluate the effectiveness of communications. In the organisation market, sales volume, value, number of enquiries and market share are the predominant measures of effectiveness.

There can be no doubt that there are a number of major differences between consumer and organisational communications. These reflect the nature of the environments, the tasks involved and the overall need of the recipients for particular types of information. Information need, therefore, can be seen as a primary reason for the differences in the way promotional mixes are configured. Advertising in organisational markets has to provide a greater level of information and is geared to generating leads which can be followed up with personal selling, which is traditionally the primary tool in the promotional mix.

Summary

The processes which buyers use to make purchase decisions differ according to a variety of factors. These vary with the nature of the purchase situation; that is, whether the purchase is orientated to consumer or organisational buying and the depth of experience held by the buyer. Other factors concerned are the levels of perceived risk, involvement, knowledge and the number of others who are contributing to the final outcome.

Some of the decision processes that have been presented in this chapter appear to be linear and based upon logic and reason. This is not the case, as decisions are often the result of experience, knowledge and an interpretive view of the environment. Therefore, the decision processes used by buyers are not always sequential, nor do they reflect a rational approach to resolving problems and needs.

Marketing communications need to be based on an understanding of the decision processes used by buyers in the targeted market. This means that the content and style of messages and the form of delivery by the tools of the promotional mix (Chapters 12–23), can be dovetailed closely to the needs of the receivers. This also demonstrates how the realm of understanding is an important issue in effective communications.

Review questions

1. Describe the general decision-making process.
2. What are EPS, LPS and RRB?
3. Select a product and a service which you have used recently and relate the six elements of perceived risk to both of them. How do the elements of risk differ?
4. Explain the three broad interpretations of involvement. How does involvement differ from perceived risk?
5. Describe the high- and low-involvement decision-making processes.
6. Highlight the differences between consumer and organisational buying.
7. What are buyclasses and buying centres?
8. How might a salesperson successfully utilise knowledge about the buying centre?
9. Explain the components of the various buyphases.
10. What are the main communication differences between consumer-orientated and business-to-business orientated marketing communications?

References

Ansoff, H.I. and McDonnell, E.J. (1990) *Implanting Strategic Management*. 2nd edn, Hemel Hempstead: Prentice Hall.

Batra, R. and Ray, M.L. (1983) Operationalizing involvement as depth and quality of response, in *Advances in Consumer Research* (eds. R.P. Bagozzi and A.M. Tybout), **10**, pp. 309–13. Ann Arbor MI: Association for Consumer Research.

Bonoma, T.V. (1982) Major sales: who really does the buying?. *Harvard Business Review* (May/June), 113.

Bowersox, D. and Cooper, M. (1992) *Strategic Marketing Channel Management*. New York: McGraw-Hill.

Brougaletta, Y. (1985) What business-to-business advertisers can learn from consumer advertisers. *Journal of Advertising Research*, **25**(3), 8–9.

Cravens, D. and Woodruff, R. (1986) *Marketing*. Reading MA: Addison-Wesley.

Eisenhart, T. (1988) How to really excite your prospects. *Business Marketing* (July), 44–55.

Gilliand, D.I. and Johnston, W.J. (1997) Toward a model of business-to-business marketing communications effects. *Industrial Marketing Management*, **26**, 15–29.

Harris, G. (1987) The implications of low involvement theory for advertising effectiveness. *International Journal of Advertising*, **6**, 207–21.

Hirschmann, E.C. and Holbrook, M.B. (1982) Hedonic consumption: emerging concepts, methods and propositions. *Journal of Marketing*, **46** (Summer), 92–101.

Jackson, B. (1985) Build customer relationships that last. *Harvard Business Review*, **63**(6), 120–8.

Kapferer, J.N. and Laurent, G. (1985) Consumer involvement profiles: a new practical approach to consumer involvement. *Journal of Advertising Research*, **25** (6), 48–56.

Laaksonen, P. (1994): *Consumer Involvement: Concepts and Research*. London: Routledge.

McQuiston, D.H. and Dickson, P.R. (1991) The effect of perceived personal consequences on participation and influence in organisational buying. *Journal of Business*, **23**, 159–77.

Mitchell, V.W. and Boustani, P. (1994) A preliminary investigation into pre and post-purchase risk perception and reduction. *European Journal of Marketing*, **28**(1), 56–71.

Porter, M.E. (1980) *Competitive Strategy: Techniques for Analysing Industries and Competitors*. New York: Free Press.

Ratchford, B.T. (1987) New insights about the FCB grid. *Journal of Advertising Research* (August/September), 24–38.

Robinson, P.J., Faris, C.W. and Wind, Y. (1967) *Industrial Buying and Creative Marketing*. Boston MA: Allyn & Bacon.

Rothschild, M. (1987) *Marketing Communications*. Lexington MA: D.C. Heath.

Rutter, K.A. (1994) Strategy formulation in turbulent times: the need for counselling methods. Unpublished Working Paper, University of Portsmouth.

Schiffman, L. and Kanuk, L. (1991) *Consumer Behavior*. Englewood Cliffs NJ: Prentice Hall.

Settle, R.B. and Alreck, P. (1989) Reducing buyers' sense of risk. *Marketing Communications* (January), 34–40.

Simon, H.A. (1976) *Administrative Behaviour: A Study of Decision Making Processes in Administrative Organisations*. New York: Free Press.

Spekman, R.E. and Gronhaug, K. (1986) Conceptual and methodological issues in buying centre research. *European Journal of Marketing*, **20**(7), 50–63.

Stone, R.N. and Gronhaug, K. (1993) Perceived risk: further considerations for the marketing discipline. *European Journal of Marketing*, **27**(3), 39–50.

Webster, F.E. and Wind, Y. (1972) *Organizational Buying Behaviour*. Englewood Cliffs NJ: Prentice Hall.

Zaichkowsky, J. (1985) Measuring the involvement constraint. *Journal of Consumer Research*, **12**, 341–52.

Networks and stakeholders

It is necessary to consider the whole system of relationships between organisations because the relationship of any two is contingent upon the direct and indirect relationships of all the actors (Andersson, 1992). A network of relationships therefore provides the context within which exchange and associated marketing communication behaviour occurs.

AIMS AND OBJECTIVES

The aims of this chapter are to introduce the concept of networks and stakeholders with a view to understanding marketing channel networks and associated inter-organisational relationships.

The objectives of this chapter are:

1. To introduce fundamental issues concerning network analysis.
2. To develop a methodology for stakeholder analysis and network mapping.
3. To show how organisations combine to form partnerships with particular stakeholders, coordinating their efforts to provide buyer satisfaction.
4. To establish marketing communications as a vital management process between stakeholders in a network of organisations.
5. To introduce two main common distribution networks, the conventional and vertical marketing systems.
6. To examine some of the behavioural issues involved with the management of channel networks, including conflict and leadership.

7. To explain how planned communications, in both network and intra-organisational contexts, can be improved by focused responsibilities and integration of communications activities.

Introduction

Distribution is a vital part of the marketing mix and accounts for a large percentage of the cost of a product. Its importance, however, is often overlooked by managers and students of marketing, and marketing communications in particular.

The distribution of products concerns two main elements. The first is the management of the tangible or physical aspects of moving a product from the producer to the end user. This must be undertaken in such a way that the customer can freely access an offering and that the final act of the buying process is as easy as possible. The second element is the management of the intangible aspects or issues of ownership, control and flows of communication between parties responsible for making the offering accessible to the customer. The focus of this chapter will be on the second of these elements, commonly referred to as channel management.

Products flow through a variety of organisations, who coordinate their activities to make the offering readily available to the end user. Coordination is necessary to convert raw materials into a set of benefits that can be transferred and be of value to the end user. These benefits are normally bundled together and represented in the form of a product or service. The various organisations who elect to coordinate their activities each perform different roles in a chain of activity. Some perform the role of manufacturer, some act as agents, and others may be distributors, dealers, value-added resellers, wholesalers or retailers. Whatever their role, it is normally specific and geared to refining and moving the offering closer to the end user.

Each organisation is a customer to the previous organisation in an industry's value chain. Some organisations work closely together, coordinating and integrating their activities, while others combine on a temporary basis. In both cases, however, these organisations can be observed to be operating as members of a partnership (of differing strength and dimensions) with the express intention of achieving their objectives with their partner's assistance and cooperation. So, in addition to the end user, a further set of customers (partners) can be determined: all those who make up the channel of distribution.

It was seen in Chapter 2 that effective communications are developed by building a positive realm of understanding with all those who impact upon the organisation and with whom communication is necessary and important: the target audiences. It is important, therefore, to identify who these other organisations (the target audiences) are, what their needs are and how important they are to the focus organisation and its products. Further questions include what the aims and objectives of these other organisations are and what the nature of the relationships between them is. Having undertaken this analysis it is then possible to develop complementary messages, to coordinate their transmission and to monitor and assess their effectiveness.

To help accomplish this, organisations must not only understand which other organisations interact with them but also determine the nature and the form of the relationships between organisations both inside and outside of the distribution channel. For example, organisations operating within the 'fast-moving consumer goods' (FMCG) or 'over-the-counter' (OTC) markets will invariably be able to identify two particular clusters: first, all those that contribute to the value-adding activities and directly affect the performance of the focus organisation, such as dealers, distributors, wholesalers and retailers, and second, all those that affect the performance in an indirect way, such as banks, market research agencies, recruitment organisations and local authorities.

Networks

Marketing channels consist of those organisations that coordinate their activities in such a way that their individual goals are achieved. Much of the literature depicts these channels as a vertical alignment of organisations which is linear and essentially bipolar. That is, the inter-organisational relationships are regarded as one-to-one or dyadic in nature, as if to exclude the impact and influence that other organisations bring to the relationship.

One of the difficulties of this approach is that organisations are regarded out of the true context in which they operate. It is necessary to consider the whole system of relationships because the relationship of any two actors (organisations) is contingent upon the direct and indirect relationships of all the actors (Andersson, 1992). A network of relationships therefore provides the context within which exchange behaviour occurs.

Stern and El-Ansary (1992) refer to a systems view that accepts that the actions of an organisation impact, to a greater or lesser degree, upon many other organisations, not just the one to whom action is directed. Indeed, it is the interdependency and web of relationships that organisations develop with one another that characterises the nature and intensity of network behaviour.

Networks hold together partly through 'an elaborate pattern of interdependence and reciprocity' (Achrol, 1997). Indeed, the development of relationship marketing appears to coincide with the emergence of network approaches to interorganisational analysis. This approach is referred to as industrial network analysis, and has evolved from its original focus on dyadic relationships (Araujo and Easton, 1996). Now the position of an organisation in a network is regarded as important. Positions are determined by the functions performed, their importance, the strength of relationships with other organisations and the identity of the organisations with which there are direct and indirect relationships (Mattsson, 1989). The position an organisation has and the degree to which an organisation is connected or coupled to other organisations partly determines the extent to which organisations are able to mobilise resources and achieve corporate goals. As Achrol states, the strength and duration of a relationship is partly dependent upon 'the network of relationships that collectively define and administer the norms by which dyadic relationships are conducted'. He goes on to quote Macneil (1978) who suggested that the more relational an exchange becomes the more it takes on the properties of 'a minisociety with a vast array of norms beyond those centred on the exchange and its immediate processes'.

Network approaches provide a more dynamic interpretation of the relationships that organisations have with one another. Networks provide a context for understanding the actions that actors take and in particular provide a means for understanding or interpreting the communications used to maintain or enhance relationships. This text uses a network approach to understand the context within which organisations interact.

Stake	Formal or voting	Economic	Political
Equity	Shareholders Directors Minority interests	Employers/owners	Dissident shareholders
Economic	Preferred debt holders	Suppliers Debt holders Customers Employees Competitors	European Union Local governments Foreign governments Consumer lobbies Unions
Influencers	Outside directors Licensing bodies	Regulatory agencies	Trade associations Environmental groups

Power

Figure 6.1 Participant stakeholders: the grid location denotes the primary but not necessarily sole orientation of the stakeholder (Freeman (1984); used with kind permission).

The stakeholder concept

All organisations develop a series of relationships with a wide variety of other organisations, groups and indeed consumers who buy their products. These relationships and individual partnerships vary considerably in their intensity, duration and function. Nevertheless these partnerships are entered into on the grounds that each organisation anticipates benefit from mutual cooperation.

The concept of different groups influencing an organisation and in turn being influenced is an important element in the development of integrated marketing communications. The concept enables an organisation to identify all those other organisations and individuals who can be or are influenced by the strategies and policies of the focus organisation. Understanding who the stakeholders are also helps to determine where power is held, and this will in turn influence strategy at a number of levels within the focus organisation. According to Freeman (1984), stakeholders are 'any group or individual who can affect or is affected by the achievement of an organisation's purpose'. These stakeholders may be internal to the organisation, such as employees or managerial coalitions, or external to the organisation in the form of suppliers, buyers, local authorities, shareholders, competitors, agencies or the government.

The essential purpose of stakeholder analysis is to determine which organisations influence the focus organisation and what their aims, objectives and motivations are. This enables the development of a more effective strategy, one that considers the power and interests of those who have a stake in the focus organisation. Freeman suggested that the stake held by any organisation could be based upon one of three forms. The first is a stake based upon the equity held in the organisation; the second is a stake based upon an economic perspective, reflecting a market exchange-based relationship; and the third is a stake based upon the influence of organisations who affect the focus organisation but 'not in market-place terms'.

The horizontal dimension reflects the type of power that stakeholders can have over the focus organisation. Again, Freeman highlights three elements. The first is the formal power to control the actions of the organisation. The second is economic power to influence the organisation through the markets in which they operate, and the final element is political power generated by the stakeholders' ability to influence an organisation through legislation and regulation. He constructed a matrix, Figure 6.1, which represents the dominant influence of each stakeholder. This acknowledges that stakeholders could be placed in a number of different cells, but as Stahl and Grigsby (1992) point out, by showing their dominant role the focus organisation is in a better position to gauge the influence of each stakeholder group.

Stakeholder models

There are two main models which reflect how organisations can cope with the diversity of interests of a variety of stakeholders. The first of these is the autocratic model shown in Figure 6.2, which clearly suggests that the power and the right to lead a channel are placed in a single organisation.

The second model, Figure 6.3, is the integrator model. This interpretation suggests that the power and right to govern the organisation or channel are vested among many stakeholders and sub-groups. The organisation, as a networker or channel leader (see later), attempts to balance the conflicting aims and objectives and hence 'weave' a path through the conflicting influences on the organisation. The Integrator model clearly shows the two-way relationship between the organisation and each of the stakeholders. It also illuminates the direct and indirect interaction among the different stakeholders and the power positions relative to the focus organisation.

Stakeholder analysis

The first step in stakeholder analysis is to list all stakeholders and then position them on a map. Those organisations with a primary relationship are then linked together so that 'patterns of interdependence emerge' (Rowe *et al.*, 1994). Figure 6.4 is a

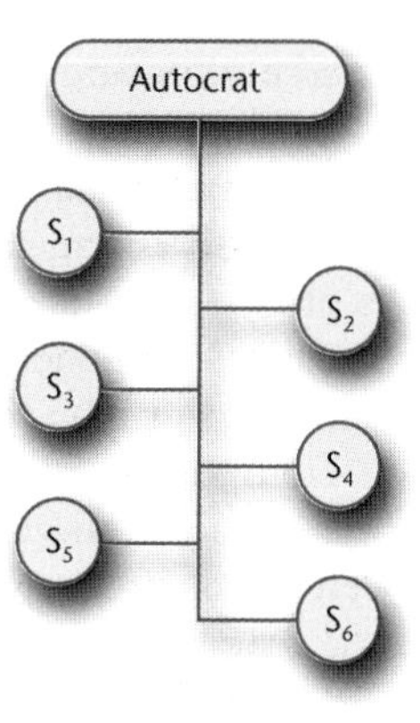

Figure 6.2 The autocrat model of stakeholder management (adapted from Rowe *et al.* (1994)).

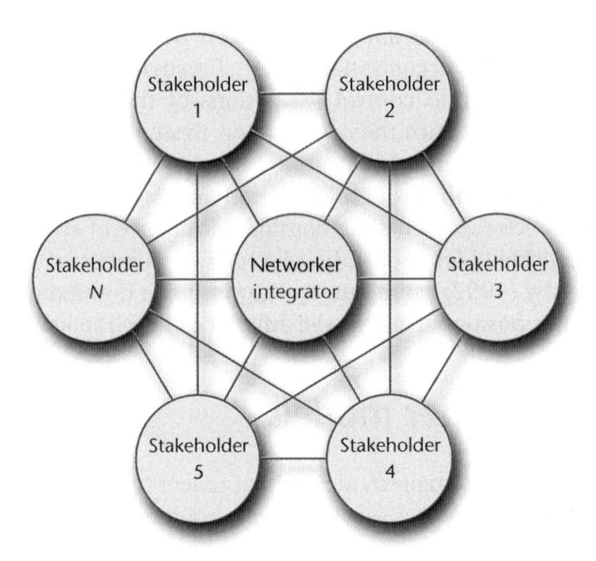

Figure 6.3 The integrator model of stakeholder management (adapted from Rowe *et al.* (1994)).

stakeholder map for WorkSpace, an office furniture manufacturer. Here it can be seen not only that WorkSpace interacts with primary and secondary stakeholders, but that there is also interaction between the different stakeholders. This application of systems theory is important, as it highlights the point that stakeholders who may be far removed or distant from an original change to the system may well be affected to a greater degree than a number of other stakeholders who are closer to the point of change. This aspect of change within a system is referred to as 'structural change' and can affect stakeholders regardless of their distance from the focus organisation or the point within the system where change was initiated.

It is also important to recognise that coalitions and individuals can belong to more than one stakeholder group. For example, Cornish fishermen and the government may be in conflict over the latter's proposal to impose tie-ups (a restriction on the number of days fishermen are allowed to operate). However, the two parties may also be locked together in fierce opposition to a European Union ruling that traditional fishing areas may only be fished with a specific licence, the numbers for which will be strictly rationed among other European fishing fleets.

Stakeholder groups can also emerge as a result of a specific event (Johnson and Scholes, 1993). This is of particular relevance to organisations planning for disaster and crisis situations. Relatives of patients who have been afflicted or harmed as a result of using particular drugs or who have been involved in an accident, such as an aircraft disaster, often form action groups when lobbying for compensation. For example, friends and relatives of the victims of the two boats, the *Marchioness* and the *Bowbelle*, which were involved in a collision on the River Thames, have acted together to have the case reopened, although the case was settled legitimately early in the 1990s.

The current position an organisation holds within the stakeholder map is partly a result of the past decisions of the organisation and its other stakeholders, and is also a

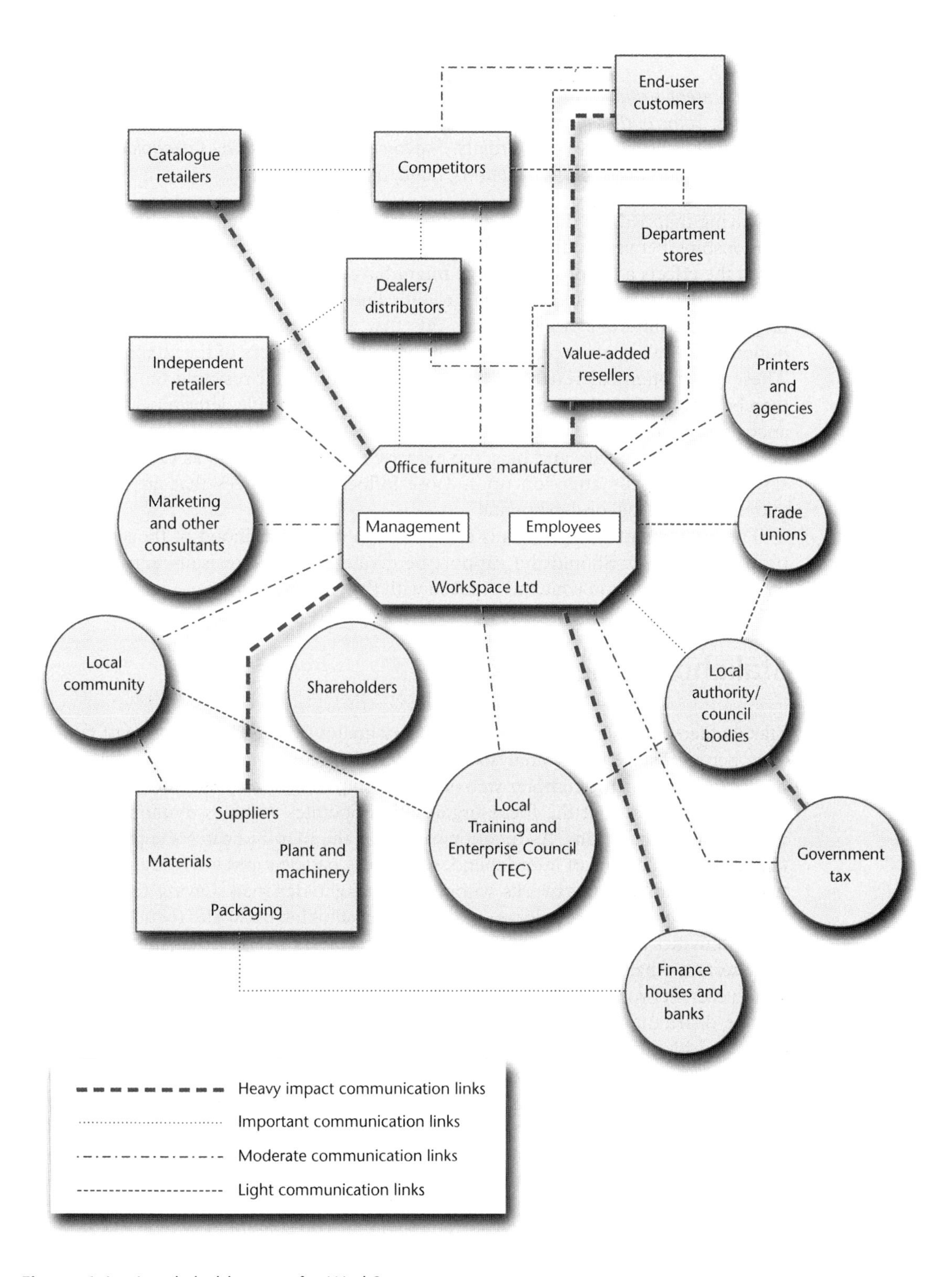

Figure 6.4 A stakeholder map for WorkSpace.

reflection of the balance of forces acting on an organisation: those that drive it forward and those that try to restrain it. As Rowe *et al.* (1994) suggest:

> *the present status of the organisation, is at best, a temporary balance of opposing forces. Some of these forces provide resources and support to the organisation, while some serve as barriers or constraints. The forces are generated by stakeholders in the course of pursuing their own interests, goals, and objectives.*

Having mapped the different stakeholders and made judgements about the interrelationships between different stakeholders, the next task is to make assumptions about the effects a proposed strategy might have on them. For example, a marketing strategy to terminate a particular product line and substitute it with one that is targeted at a different target market, one that will require different types of distribution, may well arouse opposition from particular members of the channel network. These assumptions then need to be listed as supporting or resisting the strategy and then be evaluated by the use of two simple rules. The first rule determines the importance of the assumption and the second its reliability. While the numerical analysis may be prone to subjectivity and bias, the exercise is useful because, as Greenley (1989) says, 'it helps focus attention upon those influences or forces that are likely to be extremely beneficial or detrimental'.

The outcome of this process is an evaluation of the likelihood of the success of a proposed strategy. Should the support be greater than the resistance, management has a better basis upon which to proceed with the proposed strategy.

Stakeholder networks

Stakeholders represent actors within network analysis. Indeed, the degree of congruence between stakeholder analysis and industrial network analysis is strong. Stakeholder maps reflect the complex web of relationships that all organisations weave. These maps also suggest that the focus organisation operates within a dynamic system of interacting organisations. As mentioned earlier, the map indicates the primary relationships and patterns of interdependence. These patterns and webs suggest the existence of a number of networks within each stakeholder map. Owing to the relative power positions of stakeholders, particular stakeholder networks focus upon functional activities and so have priority over others, or are perceived as more important than certain other networks. This suggests that certain organisations and individuals within each network may have a disproportionate level of power and influence.

The distribution channel is a vitally important network of organisations, and in order to distinguish between the traditional linear and vertical interpretation of distribution channels, which emphasises a bipolar and dyadic relationship (Andersson, 1992), a perspective of *a network of organisations, collaborating and working together in partnership, to provide end-user satisfaction*, is introduced as a more useful, realistic but conceptually more challenging approach. These networks not only constitute those organisations that make up the distribution channel but also seek to integrate all those other organisations that assist the distribution channel members to achieve their objectives of satisfying customer needs. Therefore a stakeholder network can be identified, which in turn can be subdivided into two major sub-networks: the performance and support networks.

The performance network consists of organisations which are directly involved with the value-adding processes in the production and distribution of the product or service. Examples would be producers, manufacturers, suppliers, distributors (such as wholesalers and retailers) and also competitors. The performance network for WorkSpace is shown in Figure 6.5.

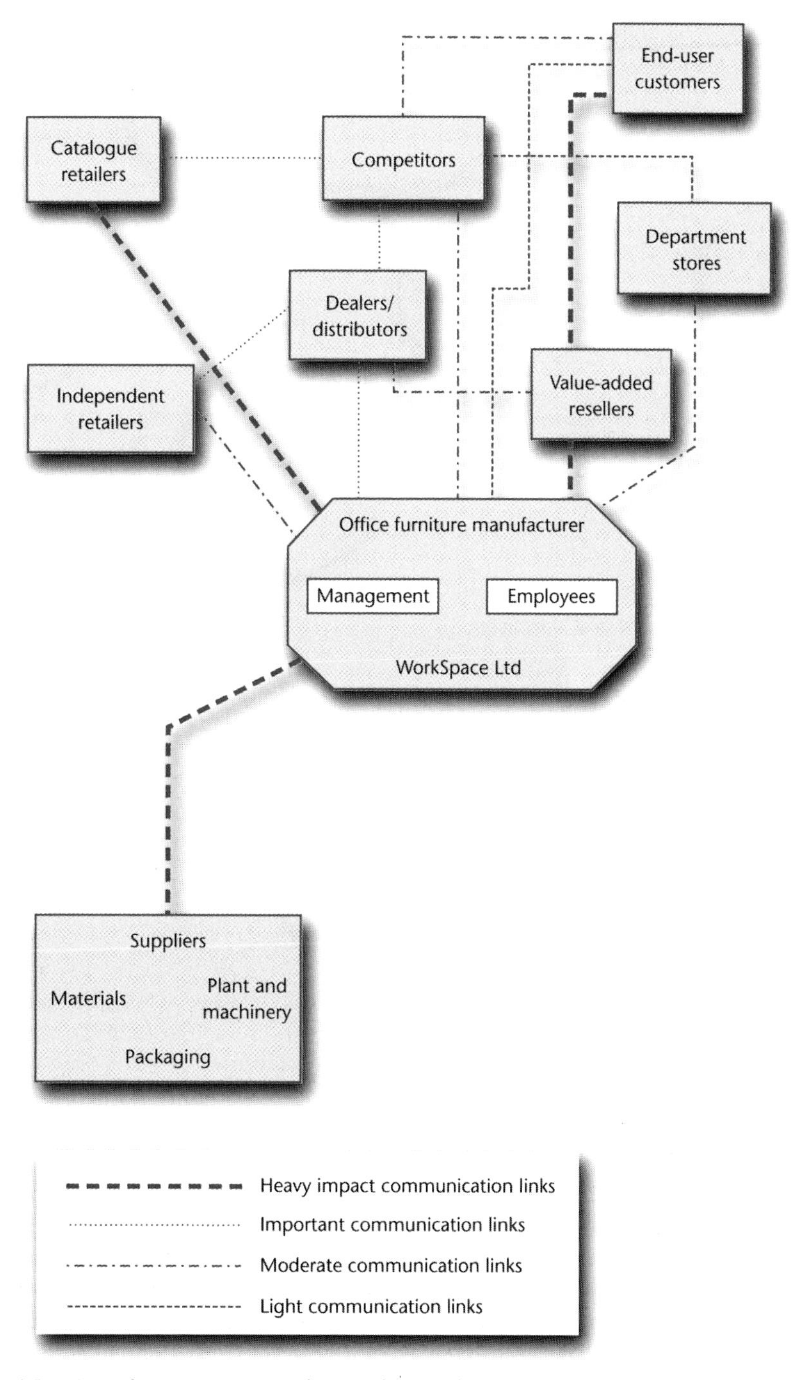

Figure 6.5 A performance network map for WorkSpace.

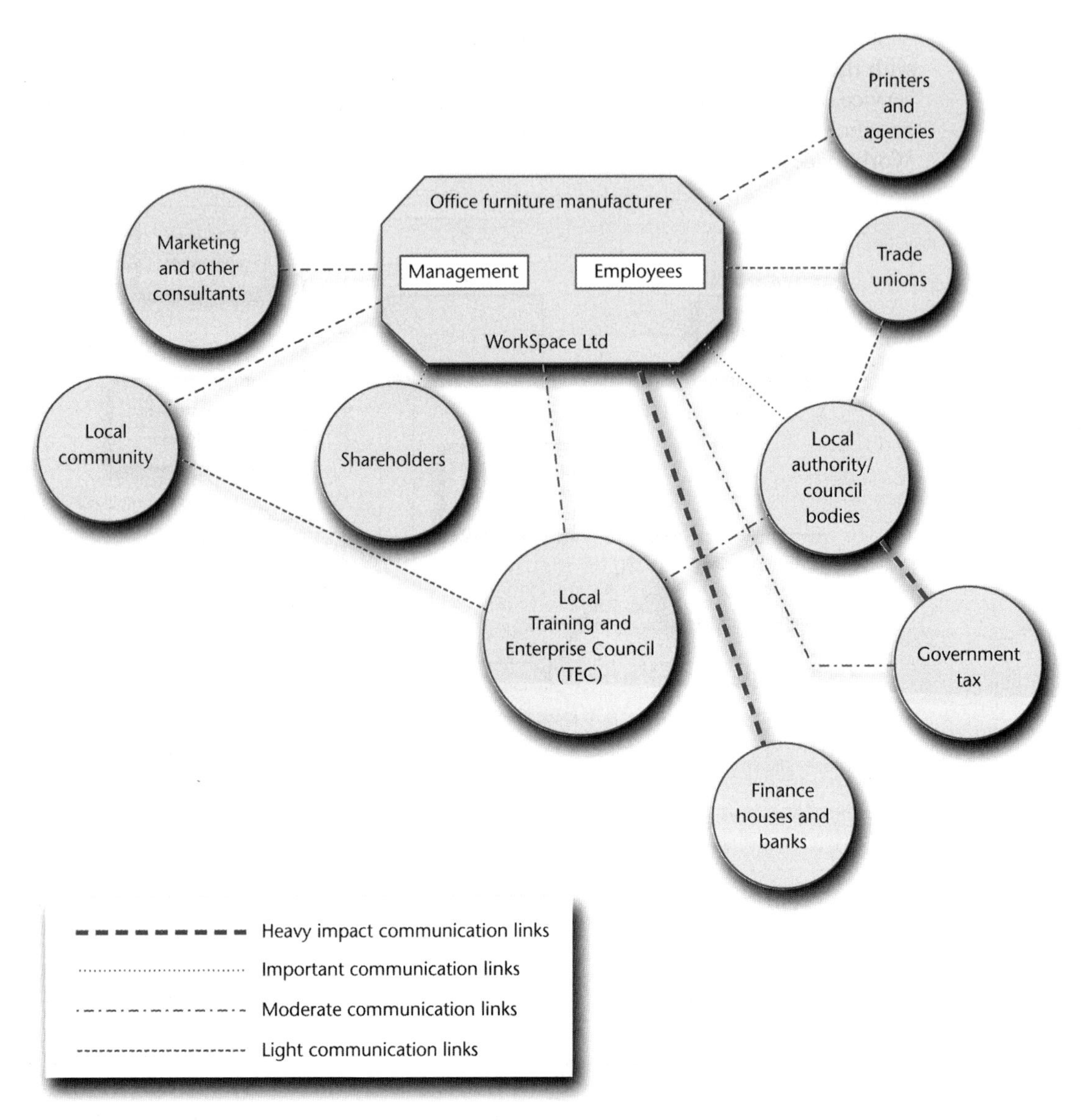

Figure 6.6 A support network map for WorkSpace.

The support network consists of those organisations or groups that influence, indirectly, the value-adding processes. For some organisations these may be financial institutions, local and national government and legislature, consultancies and support agencies, training and professional bodies, and pressure groups, such as consumer interest organisations. All of these organisations may influence the value-adding processes in an indirect way and on an irregular basis, and are characterised by their irregular, infrequent and low level of interaction in comparison with members of the performance network. Membership of the different networks will vary. For example, the government is a key stakeholder in the performance network of an NHS hospital. However, the same government is a member of the support network for a retailer or provider of wholesale services in the food or clothing markets. The support network for WorkSpace is shown in Figure 6.6.

It should be remembered that these two sub-networks are not mutually exclusive. Indeed, they are interdependent and interactive. However, for ease of analysis it is often appropriate to distinguish between the two. The identification of these networks is an important foundation for the development of marketing communications. As seen in Chapter 2, when examining communication theory, relational communication networks take into account the context in which the communication takes place, and in particular the roles participant organisations play in the network.

The context for the performance network is the interdependence between organisations in the value-adding processes, each with the common aim of satisfying buyer needs. The context for the support network is a market exchange relationship between each actor and the focus organisation, and the absence of any mutual interdependence. For example, a bank may provide loan facilities to the focus organisation, but the arrangement is relatively short term. The loan is only normally 'discussed' by both parties at the initiation and at periodic reviews and, while important, is not necessarily vital to the long-term process of adding value or to the performance of the organisation or the other organisations involved in the value chain.

Stakeholder analysis is an important concept for developing knowledge and understanding about the other organisations in the environment. From the stakeholder map it is possible to distinguish or at least derive particular networks of organisations. The performance and support networks help identify groups of organisations which have different needs and relationships, which in turn will affect the marketing communications undertaken by the focus organisation, in particular those organisations in the performance network with whom tight couplings or partnerships are formed.

Stakeholder analysis is seen, increasingly, as a significant part of corporate strategy (analysis, formulation and evaluation). However, its use as a tool within marketing communications has been overlooked, but is of importance. Of particular interest are the mapping and assumption rating exercises. Mapping is important in its own right to identify stakeholders and their interrelationships. The assumption rating exercise is important not only to evaluate the support for a particular strategy but also to evaluate the general support stakeholders have for each other and in particular for the focus organisation.

The strength of the current (or anticipated) relationships between key stakeholders and the degree of fit with corporate and competitive strategies will impact on the form, nature, strength and desired effectiveness of the marketing communications between members (Chapter 26). For example, if a pharmaceutical manufacturer experiences difficulties convincing hospital doctors that a new drug is as effective as claimed, particularly in comparison with a competitive offering, the preparation of a stakeholder map may well reveal that a number of different stakeholders interact with the hospital doctors to a greater or lesser extent. The share price may also be wavering in expectation of the success or failure of the new drug, so the financial community will be seen to have a stake and may be in need of reassurance. This information should be known prior to the launch, but what may not be known is that the strength of the relationships between certain stakeholders may have waxed or waned.

Recently, hospital pharmacists have been urged by another stakeholder, the government, to prescribe generic instead of branded drugs and, being budget-driven, have started to exert some control over the prescribing habits of hospital doctors. As a form of resistance to the management drive, the new drug is being recommended by the doctors but is being rejected by the pharmacists, who incidentally have increased powers over the hospital drugs budget. The creation of business managers, another recent development in the NHS, has established a new stakeholder, once again with budget-holding responsibilities and a vested interest in the drugs bill. Add to this the drug wholesalers, with their objectives of moving high-margin offerings such as branded drugs, and the communications tasks appear increasingly complex.

By preparing performance and support network maps, a visual interpretation of the communication tasks begins to emerge. Communications have to be targeted at the following:

1. The pharmacists, to persuade them of the efficacy and value of using the drug.
2. The doctors, to remind them that the drug represents better value effectiveness than all other offerings.
3. The financial community, to ensure continuing confidence in the manufacturer and all the manufacturer's related activities.
4. The business managers, to keep the drug at the top of their awareness, or in their evoked set.
5. The wholesalers, to keep them informed of developments, to involve them in the management of the network and to maintain their distribution facilities and stock levels.
6. The sales representatives of the manufacturer, to support and provide continuous relevant information in order that they maintain credibility with the pharmacists whom they are trying to influence.
7. The staff of the manufacturer, to maintain morale and motivation.

Channel networks

The structural pattern that any channel network assumes is a result of the relationships between the individual organisations that compose the network. The network is dynamic, so the structure should be flexible in order that it can respond to the changing environment. Two main patterns of channel networks can be identified: conventional channels and vertical marketing channels. Both are representations of the performance network described earlier.

Conventional channel networks

Traditionally, organisations group together because independently their objectives cannot be achieved. By working together each member can concentrate upon those activities that it does best. This may be retailing or manufacturing, but, whatever it is, the objectives of each organisation are best served by allowing others to perform alternative, specialist functions for them. Through this approach, organisations form temporary, often loosely aligned, partnerships with a range of organisations and retain their independence and autonomy. Bipolar relationships typify these structures, as decisions are often self-orientated and reflect the needs of just the two members of the network (Figure 6.7).

As a consequence of this self-interest, the level of control that any member has over the other members of the network is minimal, except where access to an important

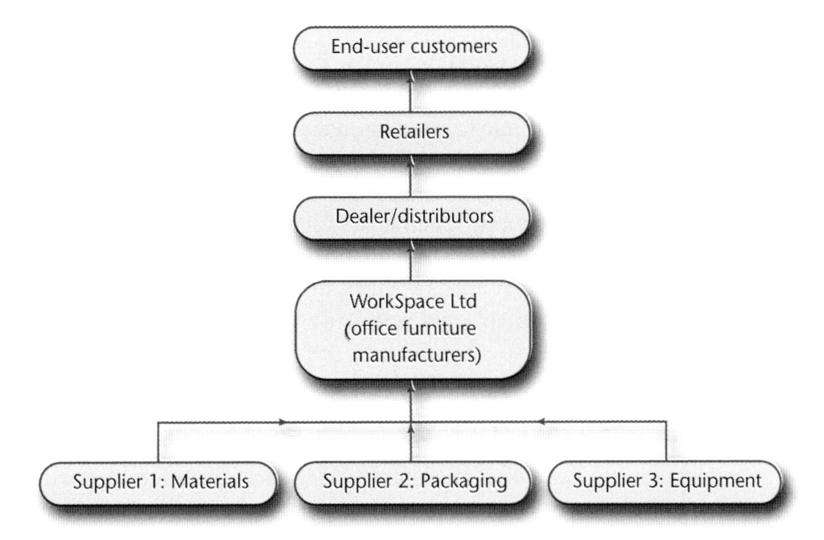

Figure 6.7 A conventional marketing channel network.

raw material or product can be affected. This framework allows offerings to move through the entire system or through parts of it. There is no single controlling organisation and the framework is viewed as a set of independent organisations working in free association with one another. The degree of connectedness is low and the coupling is loose. There is, as Oliver (1990) puts it, 'no controlled coverage of the market'. Attempts to secure coverage usually result in a loss of control in the channel network. Furthermore, the level of loyalty is low, which is indicative of the instability that exists in these types of networks (as organisations are able to enter and exit with relative freedom) and the lack of impact on the remaining actors in the overall network.

Communication within these channels is often framed within the needs of any two partners, and a wider systems perspective is absent. As a result, communications tend to be *ad hoc*, reactionary, unidirectional (in the sense that messages are not reciprocated) and do not occur on a very frequent basis.

Vertical marketing systems

Vertical marketing systems (VMSs) attempt to trade off coverage against the lack of control – more control means less coverage. They have developed since the mid-1970s and consist of vertically aligned and coordinated marketing partners. They function as a system, centrally driven by a controlling organisation, designed to achieve economies of scale and to maximise market impact in a collaborative partnership attempting to satisfy customer needs. The tighter cooperation and interdependence of member partners is formally recognised and a planned approach ensures that a greater degree of stability is achieved. The entry and exit of partners to the system is controlled to meet the needs of the channel and not any one member. The coupling between actors is tight and the level of connectedness is similarly strong.

There are three types of VMS: administered, contractual and corporate.

Administered VMS

The administered system is similar to that of the standard channel in that the participants work together, tied by the attraction of potential rewards. 'The point at which the conventional channel stops and the administered one begins must be made on the basis of judgements about the degree of effective interorganisational management taking place in the channel' (Rosenbloom, 1983).

Organisations work together to fulfil strategies developed by a limited number of network partners. These strategies are then administered through informal 'voluntary' collaborative agreements by all interested parties. It is important to recognise that members retain their own authority and that each member's commitment to the network is largely determined by self-interest, but a system-wide perspective and a view of the longer term helps bind members together.

Contractual VMS

Developing out of administered VMS are contractual partnerships which consist, essentially, of a written agreement between a dominant member and the other members of the network. These contracts set out members' rights and obligations. There are three kinds of contractual arrangement.

1. *Wholesaler-sponsored chains.* These consist of organisations which agree to work together to obtain discounts and other advantages in purchasing, distribution and promotion, e.g. Mace.
2. *Retailer-sponsored chains.* These are similar to the wholesaler chains and, for the individual organisation, represent a trade-off between independence and performance potential. The sponsored chain approach allows small and medium-sized organisations to compete against the purchasing power of many retail and wholesale multiples. Spar and VG are examples of retailer cooperatives.
3. *Franchise.* There are three forms of franchise:
   (a) Manufacturer-driven retailer systems, e.g. Ford
   (b) Manufacturer-driven wholesaler systems, e.g. Coca-Cola
   (c) Service-driven retailer systems, e.g. McDonalds.

   Franchise arrangements have grown in popularity over the last fifteen years. Under these arrangements the right to market a particular offering is agreed between two parties (a bipolar arrangement).

   There are two main approaches to franchising. The first is a *product franchise*, where the channel's dominant organisation authorises particular organisations to distribute their offering. In other words, organisations are selected into a channel and each is permitted to use the trade name and promotional materials (which are deemed to be of value to the customer) of the dominant organisation. Various German kitchen appliance and furniture manufacturers use this form of authorisation to allow particular UK retailers (independent kitchen design and fit organisations) to distribute their offerings. The second form of franchise can be referred to as a *business franchise*. Under this format not only is the product permitted to be used by the franchisee but the whole trading approach must be utilised. McDonald's restaurants are an example of the latter, with franchisees having to adopt the entire established trading style.

   What is of importance to those responsible for marketing communications is that the relationships between the franchisor and franchisee can determine the style, breadth and form of the communications between partners. For example, under the product franchise arrangement, the relationship is such that once each new franchise operation is established, contact between the two parties is limited to periodic performance review, a relationship often characterised by non-involvement and a market-structured orientation.

Under the business franchisee arrangement, a closer relationship, formed partly to protect the brand and the associated investment, means that the communications can be more relational and hence supportive, rather than market-structured. As McGrath and Hardy (1986) point out, those organisations that seek to develop understanding through substantial communications programmes will improve relationships and reduce the level of conflict in these networks. It will be shown later (Chapter 26) that the form of the relationship is an important factor in the communications strategy adopted by organisations. Whether the franchise arrangements are product or business formats is not necessarily important in itself, but the outcomes of the arrangements are important for subsequent analysis and strategy formulation.

Corporate VMS

A corporate vertical marketing system is a discrete grouping of organisations that are owned, and hence controlled, by one dominant member. This form provides for the greatest control in comparison to the other two systems. Laura Ashley not only designs and makes products but distributes them through its own retail outlets. Thomson, the tour operator, owns Lunn Poly travel agencies and Britannia Airways and in turn controls not only the distribution of its own offerings (and is not dependent upon other travel agencies) but also the carrier with whom clients travel. Another tour operator, Airtours, purchased and merged competitor travel agencies Hogg Robinson and Pickfords and relaunched them as Going Places in December 1993. Of the many benefits that this format provides, control over the information flow is an important one. Information can be dispersed to selected areas of the organisation at a time that meets management's requirements.

Corporate systems are achieved through vertical integration. Organisations can choose to integrate upstream to control their sources of supply (their inputs), or they can move downstream and seek to control the distribution of their offerings. Complete control is virtually impossible (Stern and El-Ansary, 1992) and the scale economies and cost savings that are important attractions of vertical integration can often only be achieved through large investment. Indeed some writers feel that contractual systems can provide many of the benefits that corporate systems provide and that there must be sound reasons to enter into a corporate system (Buzzell, 1983). The inherent lack of flexibility associated with corporate systems has been a prime reason for organisations to move away from such rigidity.

Channel network design

The design of a marketing channel network can only be predetermined if the focus organisation is considering the development of a VMS; otherwise, the decision is normally based upon whether to enter a particular system or how to adjust a system in which they are currently operating. These decisions need to be made on the basis of the answers to the following two questions:

1. How many sales outlets are required to provide optimal service for current and future customers?
2. How should the outlets participate in order for customer satisfaction to be achieved?

These questions are answered by the level of market coverage offered to the customer segment. There are three choices available: intensive, selective and exclusive.

1. *Intensive distribution*
   This is normally applicable to items that are low-priced and frequently purchased, where customer involvement is low and perceived risk minimal. Chewing gum, newspapers and soft drinks are good examples. By offering the product through a large number of outlets, so the wide availability promotes the opportunity for high-volume sales.
2. *Selective distribution*
   By placing the offering in a limited number of outlets a more favourable image can be generated and the producer can determine which intermediaries would be best suited to meet the needs of the channel. Customers are more involved with the purchase, and the level of perceived risk is correspondingly higher. As a result, buyers are prepared to seek out appropriate outlets, and those that best match the overall requirements of the customer will be successful. Televisions, hi-fi equipment and clothing are suitable examples of this form of distribution.

   As the costs of each channel are evaluated by a greater number of organisations, so it is likely that they will determine that the commonly accepted guide that 80% of sales are often driven by just 20% of outlets will apply. It is therefore highly probable that in the future selective distribution will be used by an increasing number of organisations.
3. *Exclusive distribution*
   Some customers may perceive a product to be of such high prestige or to be positioned so far away from the competition so that just a single outlet in a particular trading area would be sufficient to meet the needs of the channel. For example, BMW cars are normally only available from a single outlet in any one area. If the offering requires complex servicing arrangements or tight control then the exclusive form of distribution may be best, as it fosters closer relationships.

Stern and El-Ansary (1992) warn against the temptation of moving to an intensive distribution strategy in the expectation that sales volume will improve. For example, if Jaeger, manufacturers of high-quality clothing, now distributed through selective distribution outlets, decided to use multiples, discount stores and variety stores, any short-term sales improvement would rapidly fall away for the following reasons:

1. New outlets would use Jaeger products as loss leaders to attract customers. Prices generally would fall and the smaller margins might not be attractive to the original outlets.
2. Service and customer care would vary from store to store and generally deteriorate.
3. Promotion would have to be increased and more stock held by Jaeger rather than channel members. Increased costs and smaller margins would lead eventually to an unattractive business characterised by poor profitability and conditions in which no participant can win.

The selection criteria for entry to a performance network are a function of the following factors, as identified by Cravens and Woodruff (1986):

1. Anticipated revenue flows and costs.
2. Legal considerations.
3. Level of channel control required.
4. Channel availability.

To this list should be added the anticipated levels of cooperation and goodwill which will frame the relationship between members of the network. Indeed, a further question should be asked of the focus organisation itself. If accepted into an established network, will it be able to fulfil the role expected of it and what will be the form of the relationship with the other members? Will it fit in?

Channel network management

The superorganisation concept

Dibb *et al.* (1991) declare, quite rightly, that 'the marketing channel is a social system each with its own conventions and behaviour patterns'. As mentioned above, each member of the network has a role to perform, and with the role are conferred particular responsibilities, rewards and punishments. The roles of each member are understood by all partners in the channel network; therefore there are certain expectations of each organisation participating in the system. The totality of this inter-organisational behaviour is the establishment of what Stern and El-Ansary term a 'superorganisation'.

Such a label may be openly rejected by member organisations anxious to preserve their independence and autonomy, but at the end of the day they all need each other, and the more organisations require others in the channel network to perform specific functions, so the efficiency of the channel improves. Just as organisations need good management, so do superorganisations – they require direction and purpose, and they need cooperation, conflict resolution and, perhaps above all else, leadership.

Network cooperation

The term 'superorganisation' is a useful concept in that it binds constituent organisations together as a coordinated unit, and provides for a level of self-protection, purpose and direction. This in turn may foster competitive intentions, which may result in a channel network seeing itself in competition with other channel networks or superorganisations. No individual member organisation will take actions which may jeopardise the overall channel performance unless, of course, conflict has not been satisfactorily resolved. The term can also be interpreted as limiting the scope of the member organisations, one which the term 'performance network' overcomes.

As noted previously, if a network is to function effectively, cooperation between members is paramount. To work effectively and efficiently the interdependence, specialisation and expertise of individual organisations should be encouraged (Rosenbloom, 1983). However, interdependence is rarely distributed in a two-member partnership or network, in a uniform and equitable way. This inequality is a major source of power for members of the channel configuration. This disproportionate distribution means that no single organisation can have absolute power (Stern and Gorman, 1969). For example, by owning and controlling resources that are valued by another organisation, network power can be established. Relationships between members can be seen to be a reflection of the balance of power that exists between them. Emerson (1962) referred to power as a function of dependency. The more dependent X is on Y, so the greater power Y has over X. As all members of the channel network are interdependent then all members have a degree of power. It is therefore imperative that the power held by constituent members is utilised to further the development of the superorganisation and the achievement of its objectives and goals. If used otherwise, power may lead to negative consequences for the member and in turn for the channel network.

Social exchange theory is used by Stern and El-Ansary (1992) to look at the issue of dependency: 'This theory rests on two major constructs: comparison level (CL) and comparison level of alternatives (CLalt)'. The former concerns the expected performance levels of channel members based on experience. The latter is based on the expected performance of the best alternative organisation to a current channel member. As this is true for all channel members, there is a certain level of dependence upon each other. This means that each channel member can affect, by its own actions, the performance of others. It is this ability to influence the performance of others that is seen by advocates of social exchange theory as a source of power.

Sources of power

French and Raven (1959), in a classic study, determined five bases for power: rewards, coercion, expertise, legitimate and reference bases. *Rewards* are one of the more common, where, for example, a manufacturer might grant a wholesaler particular discounts dependent upon the volume of products bought during an agreed period. *Coercion* is the other side of the 'reward-based' coin, where negative measures may be brought in to sanction a channel member. If a wholesaler becomes dissatisfied with the payment cycle adopted by a retailer, deliveries may be slowed down or the discount structure revised. Power based upon *expertise*, perceived by other channel members, makes them dependent upon the flow of information from the source. Interestingly, the expert power exercised by leading pharmaceutical manufacturers is derived from the dependency of the pharmacies and general practitioners (GPs) on them and not so much on the dependency of the wholesalers. *Legitimate* power, whereby the authority to manage the channel is recognised rather like a manager recognises the authority of an executive director, is uncommon in conventional channels. Only in contractual and corporate vertical marketing systems (for example franchisors) can legitimate power be exercised. Finally, *reference* power works on the basis of association and identification – 'being in the same boat' as Rosenbloom refers to it. If members of a network are able to share and empathise with the problems of their 'network partners' then a channel-wide solution to a common problem may well result in increased understanding, collaboration and trust.

By recognising and understanding the bases of power, the levels of cooperation and the form of the relationships between members, the nature of communication, its pattern, its frequency and its style can be adjusted to complement the prevailing conditions. Furthermore, such an understanding can be useful to help shape the power relationships of the future and to enhance the corporate/marketing strategy. Once the current and anticipated power bases are determined, marketing communications can assist the shaping process. Of the power propositions provided by French and Raven, reward and coercion seem more apt for use within networks, where market exchange-based transactions predominate. Legitimate and expert power might be better applied in networks with a high level of relational exchanges.

Network conflict

Conflict within and between all channel networks is endemic. Indeed, Hunt and Nevin (1974) found conflict to be widely prevalent in channel (network) relationships. Conflict represents a breakdown or deterioration in the levels of cooperation between partners (Shipley and Egan, 1992). Cooperation is important because members of any network are, to varying degrees, interdependent; hence their membership in the first place.

The reasons for conflict need to be clearly appreciated, as identification of the appropriate cause can lead to communication strategies that remedy, or at least seek to repair, any damage. Some of the more common reasons for channel conflict, suggested by Stern and Gorman (1969), are failure to enact a given or agreed role, issues arising among the participant organisations, selective perception and inadequate communications. For example, because network members undertake particular *roles*, any failure to fulfil the expected role may be a cause of conflict. An *issue* may arise within the channel that causes conflict. For example, a wholesaler and a manufacturer may disagree about margins, training, marketing policies or, more commonly, territorial issues. McGrath and Hardy (1986) see conflict emanating from manufacturers' policies, such as sales order policies. The tighter and more constricting they are, the greater the likelihood that conflict will erupt than if the policies are flexible and can be adjusted to meet the needs of both parties.

Through the process of selective perception any number of members may react to the same stimulus in completely different and conflicting ways. The objectives of each of the network members are different, however well bonded they are to the objectives of the network. It is also likely that each member perceives different ways of achieving the overall goals, all of which are recipes for conflict. The final reason is perhaps one of the most important, and central to the issue of this particular key factor. *Communication* is a coordinating mechanism for all members of the network. Its absence or failure will inevitably lead to uncoordinated behaviour and actions that are not in the best interests of the network. The network can become destabilised through poor or inadequate communication, as the processes of selective perception can distort encoded messages and lead to conflict and disunity.

The decision by Heinz to cut out all brand television advertising and move to direct marketing seriously destabilised the partnerships between multiple grocers and manufacturers of branded products (plus the advertising agencies and television contractors). Manufacturers needed to respond to the growth of supermarket own-label lookalike products, so that they could protect their brand loyal customers. Heinz also wanted to control the discounting policy regarding its products, rather than leave it to the discretion of the supermarkets (Snoddy, 1994).

Conflict emerged in a previously stable network, as certain members saw their corporate and marketing objectives capable of being achieved through new networks which required new members and new roles. The response of the supermarkets was to threaten not to redeem any Heinz coupons that had been sent to customers via direct mail. This is against the food manufacturers' rules about misredemption, but the disequilibrium was easy to observe. The performance network broke down as a result of a shift in the perceptions of members of the best way to achieve their own objectives.

Management of channel network communications

Communications between members of marketing channels, and VMS in particular, are normally the responsibility of a particular actor in the channel network. This actor assumes this dominant role by virtue of the dependence of the other actors (members). This dependency provides for the exercise of power, as set out earlier. The organisations that are perceived to be powerful in the context of the channel network are said to be channel leaders or channel captains.

Channel leadership carries a responsibility to coordinate the activities of the other members. Therefore, all communications should be designed to assist the network as a whole and not just those of the leader. As Frazier and Sheth (1985) suggest, the objective of channel leadership is to contribute to the improved performance of the channel network. If the channel performance improves, then the channel leader is likely to benefit and its role as leader will be confirmed for a further period.

The communications that the channel leader masterminds consist of two main strands. The first is the operational data flow, enhancing the performance of the network at an operational level. The advances in information technology (IT), particularly since the early 1980s, have been crucial to the distribution of data between organisations. Indeed, IT now provides an opportunity for organisations to develop competitive advantage. For example, the installation of computerised reservation systems in travel agencies by tour operators not only helps to provide for a high level of customer satisfaction through real-time processing, but also signals the existence of a considerable mobility barrier. Those travel agents who wish to exit the network and those tour operators wishing to enter a more compelling relationship with certain travel agents must now account for all the costs of changing systems, including the hardware, software, training and support associated with information technology.

The second strand is marketing communications. This concerns the deployment of the range of tools in the promotional mix, established earlier. These flows of largely persuasive information are designed to influence organisations and individuals to take a particular course of action. Information is distributed in order to influence the decisions that members make about the marketing mix they each adopt. Particular organisations can be seen to adopt the role of channel leader and to become responsible for the discharge and regulation of the information in the network or superorganisation.

Management of organisational communications

As a broad generalisation, formal communication with all other organisations and individuals, that is all stakeholders, has been the responsibility of two individual managers, each within different departments and reporting to different senior executives.

The first of these is the brand manager, who traditionally has been responsible for the communications and, in particular, the promotion of the brand. Recently, a number of organisations have been appointing trade or channel managers, reflecting the increasing recognition of the significance and power associated with certain channel intermediaries, such as the multiple retailers. These channel managers have many responsibilities, including the establishment of suitable relationships with all organisations in the performance network.

CASE ILLUSTRATION

Royal Dutch Shell and Nigeria

This case illustration has been written by Jo Crotty, formerly a BA (Hons) Business Studies student at the University of Portsmouth and now a PhD research student at Nottingham University. Her interests are in stakeholder theory and corporate greening in Russia.

Royal Dutch Shell and Nigeria: stakeholder demands and public relations

Following the discovery of oil in the Niger Delta in 1956, Nigeria has become one of the largest oil-producing countries in the world. Today oil revenues account for over 80% of the Nigerian government's annual earnings and 90% of its foreign currency. In recent times, however, the actions of the Nigerian government towards those people living in the oil-producing regions, and the involvement and behaviour of multinational companies involved in the exploitation of Nigerian oil, have come under close international scrutiny.

The Niger Delta is populated by a plethora of minority peoples, such as the Ogoni, the Andoni and the Edo; the Ogoni number 500,000. During the 1960s, these peoples received 50% of all revenues generated from the sale of oil extracted from their lands. At this time, these revenues only accounted for approximately 10% of the government's annual income. The indigenous peoples continued to sustain themselves with traditional export industries, such as palm oil. In 1975 the proportion of oil revenues diverted to these minority peoples was reduced to 20%. Between 1970 and 1975, the Nigerian government began to rely increasingly on oil as its main source of income, increasing its dependency on these revenues from 25% of annual income in 1970 to 80% in 1975. Concurrently, the Nigerian government decided to scale down those other exporting activities that had sustained the country in the past, which many of the indigenous people of the Niger Delta had come to depend on.

In 1979, the Nigerian government entered into a joint venture agreement with Shell (30%), Elf (10%) and Agip (5%) to exploit the Nigerian oil reserves more aggressively. All land became the property of the Nigerian military governor. This agreement was followed by a further reduction in the proportion of oil revenue directed to the extraction sites, from 20% to 3%, with another 1.5% set aside for the amelioration of any ecological impact that the extraction might have on local communities. Consequently, the minority populations, such as the Ogoni, were rendered powerless. They had no control over the use of their land and little access to the funds that were accumulating as a result of the oil extraction taking place on it.

Following this joint venture, Ogoniland has borne significant environmental costs as a direct result of the oil business. Transportation pipes that would normally be placed underground in more affluent countries, have been constructed overground in a criss-cross formation making access to water problematic. There have been oil spills and gas flaring near to residential areas. The Ogoni do not have access to adequate health care or education and almost all rely completely on the land to survive.

The Ogoni writer and human rights campaigner Ken Saro-Wiwa, took up the cause of the Ogoni, forming the Movement for the Survival of Ogoni People (MOSOP). This organisation campaigned for the rights of the Ogoni people to control a fair proportion of the revenue generated from the exploitation of their land, and to protect the landscape from additional ecological destruction. As a result, Ken Saro-Wiwa and eight of his supporters were arrested and executed in November 1995.

Stakeholder response

These executions caused widespread condemnation of not only the Nigerian government, resulting in the expulsion of Nigeria from the Commonwealth, but also Shell Nigeria, who, it was claimed, could have prevented the executions by threatening to withdraw from Nigeria if the executions went ahead. Environmental non-governmental organisations, such as Greenpeace, backed by The Body Shop International, mounted a Shell consumer boycott, with the slogan 'Get The Shell Out Of Nigeria'. Greenpeace activists took to the streets and protested outside Shell petrol stations. In Germany activists went beyond the Greenpeace call for non-violent action and fire-bombed a number of Shell's petrol stations. Shell suddenly had a public relations crisis on its hands. The media, in covering what was an incident of international standing, with the additional implication that Shell could have prevented the executions, or at least could have attempted to prevent them, presented Shell in a very bad light.

At first glance it seemed that Shell faced an issue that could harm them significantly in terms of profit and credibility. When you place Shell's stakeholders on the Pearson and Mitroff (1993) 'Crisis roles for stakeholders' map (see Chapter 20), however, a different picture emerges (Figure 6.8).

Shell issued numerous press releases concerning their activity in the Niger Delta and the treatment of the Ogoni people and their land. In them they claimed to have spent over US$100 million in 1995 on environmental projects, insisting that the oil spills in the region occurred as a result of sabotage. In addition, Shell published three special booklets on the issue, entitled 'Community Development', where Shell stressed its commitment to health and education programmes in Nigeria; 'The Environment', where it stressed its commitment to environment protection, demonstrated by the replanting and regenerating of a former extraction site; and 'The Ogoni Issue', where Shell stressed that it had in fact called for clemency for Ken Saro-Wiwa, and had consulted many of its stakeholder groups in South Africa over the issue. Shell claimed that it could not have done anything more. Through these publications, Shell stressed its commitment to the community and its recognition of its environmental responsibilities.

At the same time, Greenpeace, The Body Shop International, The Rainforest Action Network, Oil Watch, Project Underground, MOSOP and the World Council of Churches produced similar booklets and pamphlets, putting the 'other side' of the story. Owens Wiwa, the brother of Ken Saro-Wiwa, began to travel the world in an attempt to muster support for a worldwide oil embargo against Nigeria, but so far he, backed by MOSOP, has been unsuccessful.

In studying the stakeholder map, one thing is immediately clear. Save for the Commonwealth, those stakeholders described as Villains and Victims are the weak players. They are charities or poor people with little or no voice. The Rescuers, the Heroes and the Protectors are, on the other hand, the groups with status and power. Shell is one on the richest companies on earth. Fortune 500 (August 1997) recently reported that Shell's profits for 1996 were in the region of US$8.9 bn, and that they have been increasing at an annual rate of 20% since 1992. Shell is also currently sitting on reserves of US$12.4 bn. Fortune 500 (August 1997) report that Shell sees the distribution of this huge reserve as the greatest strategic dilemma faced by the company at the current time. Consequently, most large pension funds hold Shell shares because they have a guaranteed return. Shell is seen as a 'safe bet' because oil is a fundamental part of our society, of the way we live. Many individual consumers may have a negative view of Shell following this incident, but how many of them actually stopped buying Shell petrol, and of the number who did not purchase it in November 1995, how many are still not purchasing it today?

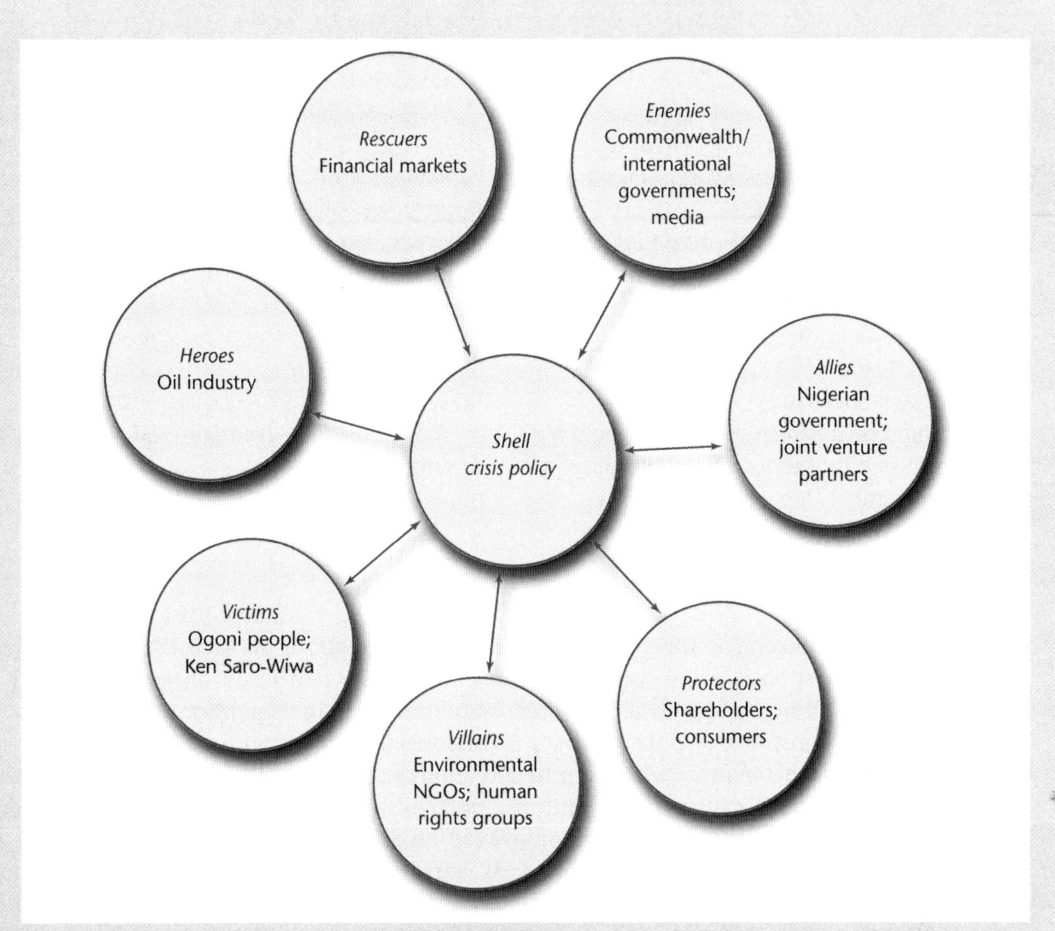

Figure 6.8 Shell's stakeholders in their crisis roles (after Pearson and Mitroff (1993)).

When considering readjustment (Pearson and Mitroff, 1993) after this crisis, Shell would have looked at the stakeholders in the crisis and would probably conclude that its *key* stakeholders, i.e. the oil industry, its shareholders and the financial community, were still with them and, what is more, had never left them. Shell may very well have concluded that it has no need to adjust its 'image' in any significant way following this event. If, however, Owens Wiwa had been successful in effecting an international oil embargo on Nigeria, then maybe things would have been very different. Only in this scenario is it realistic to assume that Shell's actions in Nigeria could have harmed it sufficiently to have forced it into adjusting its corporate policy and practice in Nigeria. Thus, it is open to question whether or not this really was a public relations crisis at all.

Bibliography:

Anon (1997) What problems face the world's most profitable company? *Fortune 500*, August, 53–7

Kretzmann, S. and Wright, S. (1997) *Human Rights and Environmental Operations Information on the Royal Dutch Shell Group Companies*. Independent Annual Report. Project Underground, Rainforest Action Network, Oil Watch.

Pearson, C.M. and Mitroff, I. (1993) From

crisis prone to crisis prepared: a framework for crisis management. *Academy of Management Executive*, **7**(1), 48–59.
Robinson, D. and Metaxa, R. (1996) *Ogoni: The Struggle Continues*. World Council of Churches, Switzerland.
Royal Dutch Shell (1997) *Health, Safety and the Environment*. The Netherlands.
Royal Dutch Shell (1995) *The Environment and the Ogoniland*. Press Release, Shell International Limited, 12 November.
Royal Dutch Shell (1995) *Response to Greenpeace Statement Regarding Execution*. Press Release, Shell International Limited, 10 November.
Royal Dutch Shell (1995) *Execution of Ken Saro Wiwa and his Co-defendants*. Press Release, Shell International Limited, 10 November.
Royal Dutch Shell (1996) *Shell Nigeria*. Annual Review.
Royal Dutch Shell (1995) *Community Development*. Nigeria Briefing.
Royal Dutch Shell (1995) *The Environment*. Nigeria Briefing.
Royal Dutch Shell (1995) *The Ogoni Issue*. Nigeria Briefing.
Rowell, A. (1996) *Green Backlash: Global Subversion of the Environmental Movement*. London: Routledge.

The second is the public relations manager, whose department has historically been responsible for communications with other non-trade organisations and the establishment of goodwill with organisations in the wider environment.

By spreading responsibility for an organisation's communications across two separate departments, each trying to accomplish different, often conflicting, objectives, organisations can only sub-optimise and fail to communicate effectively. Different and uncoordinated messages, conveyed at different times, lead to confusion and misunderstanding by stakeholders. At worst, there may be a change to a more negative perception and a fall in confidence and goodwill towards the organisation, which, unless corrected, can in the long term affect not only consumer perception and sales but also the share price and value of the organisation.

Other problems brought about by this divided approach to the management of organisational communications are changes to employees' motivation and the shared values held by the organisation. Changes in attitude and the image held of the organisation by all stakeholders, and failure to communicate corporate strategy and marketing plans to particular organisations are illustrative of further problems, as are the missed opportunities to develop strategic alliances and to satisfy changing customer needs.

Many researchers (Mallen, 1969; Rosenbloom, 1978) have concluded that channel conflict is reduced, but never eliminated, by building cooperation among members of the channel network. To help build cooperation it is essential that there is consensus about the overall objectives and sound communication. To assist the development of a cooperative network of relationships, the generation of integrated marketing communications by all members, particularly channel leaders, is fundamental. One of the first steps is to appoint a communications coordinator. This person should be responsible for the development and implementation of a communications strategy that controls all the message outputs of the organisation and assists the organisation through the complex networks to which all organisations belong.

Summary

This chapter has introduced network theory as a means of exploring some of the issues associated with an organisation's interorganisational relationships, in particular those actor organisations involved with what is traditionally viewed as the marketing channel.

Stakeholder theory provides a similar perspective to network analysis, and issues concerning the manner in which stakeholder maps can be drawn to assist marketing communications were presented. Following this, the distribution channels were presented as a network of interacting organisations, some of whom contribute directly to the value-added activities of the focus organisation (referred to as performance networks) and some of whom provide activities and services that support the focus organisation (referred to as support networks) but do not contribute directly to the channel of distribution.

Understanding who the key stakeholders are, and knowing their positions and roles in the various networks, represents an important key factor in the development of planned communications. Communications are regarded as an important element in the smooth working of, and reduction in the level of conflict in, any network. Understanding the quality and form of the current relationships helps to shape future marketing communications with members of the different networks.

Review questions

1. What are the four factors that are considered to determine the position of an organisation in a network?
2. Explain the central characteristics of industrial network analysis.
3. Determine the main stakeholders for an organisation with which you are familiar and rank them in order of importance.
4. Select those that directly influence the value-adding processes performed by the organisation.
5. Prepare a performance network map. Indicate on the map the main flows of marketing communications currently established and the promotional flows that should be in position.
6. Suggest ways in which new flows of promotional information can be established.
7. What are the differences between conventional channel networks and vertical marketing systems?
8. How might marketing communications be influenced by the type of franchise in place?
9. To what extent might the emergence of a powerful organisation reflect levels of interdependence in a network?
10. French and Raven identified several bases for power. What are they?

References

Achrol, R.S. (1997) Changes in the theory of interorganisational relations in marketing: toward a network paradigm. *Journal of the Academy of Marketing Science*, **25**(1), 56–71.

Andersson, P. (1992) Analysing distribution channel dynamics: loose and tight coupling in distribution networks. *European Journal of Marketing*, **26**(2), 47–68.

Araujo, L. and Easton, G. (1996) Networks in socioeconomic systems: a critical review, in *Networks in Marketing* (ed. D. Iacobucci). California: Sage.

Buzzell, R.D. (1983) Is vertical integration profitable? *Harvard Business Review*, **61** (January/February), 96–100.

Cravens, D.W. and Woodruff, R.B. (1986) *Marketing*. Reading MA: Addison-Wesley.

Dibb, S., Simpkin, L., Pride, W.M. and Ferrel, O.C. (1991) *Marketing*. New York: Houghton Mifflin.

Emerson, R. (1962) Power-dependence relations. *American Sociological Review*, **27** (February), 32–3.

Frazier, G.L. and Sheth, J. (1985) An attitude–behavior framework for distribution channel management. *Journal of Marketing*, **43**(3), 38–48.

Freeman, R.E. (1984) *Strategic Management*. Boston MA: Pitman.

French, J.R. and Raven, B. (1959) The bases of social power, in *Studies in Social Power* (ed. D. Cartwright). Ann Arbor: University of Michigan.

Greenley, G. (1989) *Strategic Management*. Hemel Hempstead: Prentice Hall.

Hunt, S.B. and Nevin, J.R. (1974) Power in channel of distribution: sources and consequences. *Journal of Marketing Research*, **11**, 186–93.

Johnson, G. and Scholes, K. (1993) *Exploring Corporate Strategy*, 3rd edn. Hemel Hempstead: Prentice Hall.

McGrath, A. and Hardy, K. (1986) A strategic paradigm for predicting manufacturer–reseller conflict. *European Journal of Marketing*, **23**(2).

Macneil, I.R. (1978) Contracts: adjustment of long-term economic relations under classical, neoclassical and relational contract law. *Northwestern University Law Review*, **72** (January–February), 854–905.

Mallen, B.E. (1969) A theory of retailer–supplier conflict, in *Distribution Channels: Behavioural Dimensions* (ed. L.W. Stern). New York: Houghton Mifflin.

Mattsson, L.-G. (1989) Development of firms in networks: positions and investments. *Advances in International Marketing*, **3**, 121–39.

Oliver, G. (1990) *Marketing Today*, 3rd edn. Hemel Hempstead: Prentice Hall.

Rosenbloom, B. (1978) Motivating independent distribution channel members. *Industrial Marketing Management*, **7** (November), 275–81.

Rosenbloom, B. (1983) *Marketing Channels: a Management View*. Hinsdale IL: Dryden Press.

Rowe, A.J., Mason, R.O., Dickel, K.E., Mann, R.B. and Mockler, R.J. (1994) *Strategic Management: A Methodological Approach*, 4th edn. Reading MA: Addison-Wesley.

Shipley, D. and Egan, C. (1992) Power, conflict and co-operation in brewer–tenant distribution channels. *International Journal of Service Industry Management*, **3**(4), 44–62.

Snoddy, R. (1994) Heinz drops TV adverts in move to direct marketing. *Financial Times*, 3 May, p. 1.

Stahl, M. and Grigsby, D. (1992) *Strategic Management for Decision Making*. Boston MA:P.W.S. Kent.

Stern, L. and El-Ansary, A. (1992) *Marketing Channels*, 4th edn. Englewood Cliffs NJ: Prentice Hall.

Stern, L.W. and Gorman, R.H. (1969) *Conflict in Distribution Channels: An Exploration in Distribution Channels: Behavioural Dimensions* (ed. L.E. Stern). Boston: Hougton Mifflin.

chapter 7

The communications industry

The marketing communications industry is evolving rapidly as new technology and increasing competition induces audience and media fragmentation. Clients, media and agencies continually adapt themselves to the changing environment as they attempt to understand the complexity and opportunities that are continually arising around them.

AIMS AND OBJECTIVES

The aims of this chapter are to introduce the communications industry, the various organisations involved and some of the issues affecting the operation of the industry.

The objectives of this chapter are:

1. To provide an introduction to the communications industry.
2. To consider the nature and role of the main types of organisations involved.
3. To explore relationships and methods of remuneration used within the industry.
4. To outline some of the statutory and voluntary controls used to regulate the industry.
5. To introduce some of the wider European and global issues facing the industry.
6. To anticipate some of the future trends which might affect the industry.

Introduction

The marketing communications industry consists of four principal actors. These are the media, the clients, the agencies (the most notable of which are advertising

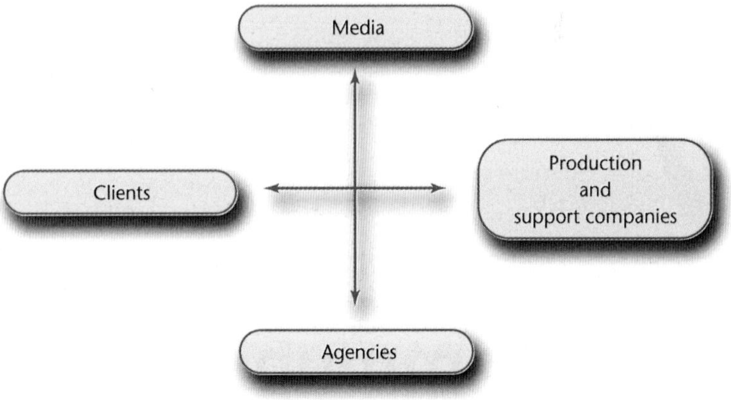

Media

Clients

Production
and
support companies

Agencies

Figure 7.1 Principal organisations in the marketing communications industry.

agencies) and finally the thousands of support organisations, such as production companies and fulfilment houses, who enable the whole process to function. It is the operations and relationships between these organisations that not only drive the industry but also form an important context within which marketing communications needs to be understood. Figure 7.1 sets out the main actor organisations in the industry.

The number of relationships that can be developed in this industry, as with others, is enormous. To further complicate matters, the slow yet enduring move towards integrated marketing communications (Chapter 29) requires participants to form new relationships and acquire new skills. The argument that marketing communications activities should be kept in-house is now weak, as manufacturing and service industry providers continue to increase their level of outsourcing activities and de-layer and hollow out their organisations even more finely. There is little or no room to maintain people with skills and expertise that are only drawn upon infrequently and where the notion of critical mass is important for media buying. Most observers would argue that it could not be done as effectively as by agencies and others who are dealing with a number of clients and are, by definition, in constant touch with developments in the industry. In the field of media buying, for example, many would argue that it is unlikely that the necessary expertise could be developed in-house. As Miles (1992) states: 'Clients... expect up-to-date information on the most cost effective media, and the muscle to buy it as cheaply as possible'. Marketing practitioners, therefore, need to use some of the organisations in the communications industry. A level of interdependence exists which requires cooperative and collaborative behaviour if the system is to function efficiently.

Growth and development of the marketing communications industry

It is useful to consider the size and value of the industry by considering the sums of money spent by clients on marketing communications. Some of these figures are acknowledged to be estimates, and there is some evidence of 'double counting' (one or more sectors claiming part of the overall spend for itself), so any figures produced

Table 7.1 Total advertising expenditure (including direct mail) £m

	1996 (£million)	1995 (£million)	1994 (£million)
Press	6,400	5,900	5,500
Television	3,300	3,100	2,900
Direct mail	1,400	1,100	1,000
Outdoor and transit	426	378	350
Radio	344	296	243
Cinema	73	69	53
Total	11,994	10,981	10,136

Source: *Advertising Statistics Yearbook*; used with kind permission.

cannot be seen as being totally accurate. That said, however, the total spend for advertising, as can be seen from Table 7.1, was nearly £12 billion in 1996.

The Institute of Sales Promotion claims that the growth of sales promotion has been 'explosive', but measuring the growth is difficult because there are no rate cards (price lists) and the breadth of activities that are attributable to sales promotion are many and varied. However, the Institute estimates that expenditure on sales promotion has grown from £5 billion in 1986 to £6.5 billion in 1992 and to £9.0 billion in 1996. Although not yet as important as advertising, this area of activity is fast catching up and, despite published figures, it is widely believed inside the industry that sales promotion has already overtaken advertising in terms of the proportion of client spend.

Estimates vary, mainly because of problems of definition, but of the other areas in the industry sponsorship has grown significantly to £500 million in 1996. Direct marketing had risen spectacularly, with direct mail alone worth £1.4 billion in 1996. Public relations has experienced steady development and was worth approximately £1.0 billion in 1996.

Other areas of the industry include direct selling (which measures its success in a growth of sales from £329m in 1985 to £796m in 1991 at a consistent growth rate); corporate entertainment, which is estimated to be worth about £500m a year (Cardwell, 1990; Thomas, 1991); and exhibitions, which were worth approximately £1,016m in 1995.

Expenditure patterns do change, albeit at different rates, and given the domination of advertising and sales promotion, the overall balance is unlikely to change dramatically in the short term. However, it is clearly important for those responsible for the future and current planning of marketing communications activities to monitor trends, particularly those in the fastest growing sectors of the industry, in order to identify and target creative opportunities.

Competitive forces

Another way of considering the industry is to apply Porter's (1980) model of competitive forces. By identifying the major industry competitive forces and assessing their impact it is possible to evaluate an organisation's present and future competitive positions. Even though competitive pressures vary from industry to industry, there are enough similarities to establish an analytical framework to gauge the nature and

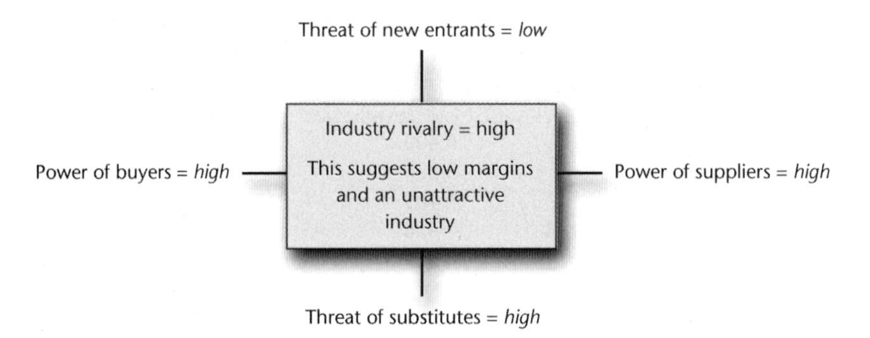

Figure 7.2 The five-forces model of competition applied to the UK Advertising Industry (Porter (1980); used with kind permission).

intensity of competition. Porter suggests that competition in an industry is a composite of the following five competitive forces, shown in Figure 7.2

Threat of new entrants

Wherever the existing barriers to entry are weak in an industry, the threat of entry by new players will be strong. So, the more difficult it is for new players to enter the industry, the stronger will be the existing organisation's competitive position. Currently entry barriers are low, so the competitive position of agencies is low.

Threat of substitute products

Very often established players fail to notice technological changes which can allow products from other industries to be substituted by their buyers for their own product (synthetic for cotton fibres in the clothing industry). In other words, the substitute has a different form, yet performs the same function. In this industry there has been a significant increase in the number and effectiveness of other products. The rise of new media options, direct marketing and sponsorship, plus much talk about integrated marketing communications and a variety of new interactive opportunities present a real threat to mass media advertising, the core product of the advertising agencies.

Power of suppliers

Suppliers in this context might be seen to be the media, as they supply the services by which agencies satisfy client needs. Suppliers tend to be powerful if there are just a few of them (as there are few alternative sources of supply) or when a particular group of suppliers constitute a major part of the total costs. The threat posed by the media owners to agencies (and clients), as expressed through media cost inflation, is large. Advertising agencies have little room to manoeuvre as long as their key product remains mass advertising.

Power of buyers

Buyers are able to exert power when there are either a few large customers or they purchase in large quantities. In addition, power can be exercised when the offering is standardised and there is little differentiation, so enabling buyers to switch supplier easily and cost effectively. This is the precise problem with advertising agencies. There is little for clients to differentiate one agency from another, other than by reputation. Consequently, a client's switching costs are low, so the power exerted by buyers can be seen to be high.

Rivalry among sellers

Despite the consolidation in the late 1980s, rivalry among advertising agencies has increased because there are a large number of agencies, many of whom are of a similar size. Margins are small, even though the billings are high, and the forces acting upon the agencies in this industry are quite strong, depressing profits and making the industry relatively unattractive to new entrants.

WPP: merging operations

In September 1997, WPP announced that it was to merge the media operations of two of its major full service agencies, J Walter Thompson and Oligvy and Mather. The new organisation, called Mindshare, offers an integrated service in addition to the media planning and buying roles. Billings for the new company will be more than $14 billion from its global activities.

The move was seen as a response to market dynamics and the need to be able to compete with other media operations. Therefore WPP can be seen to be restructuring in order to compete more effectively and manage the rivalry from competitors.

Adapted from Green and Griffiths (1997)

Porter's model allows the competitive forces to be exposed and the collective impact of the different forces determines what competition is like in the market. As a general rule, the stronger the competitive forces, the lower the profitability in the market. An organisation needs to determine a competitive approach that will allow it to influence the industry's competitive rules, protect it from competitive forces as much as possible and give it a strong position from which to compete. In this case, the power of the media suppliers, the low switching costs of buyers and the large threat of substitute products make this a relatively unattractive industry in its current form. Finer segmentation to determine markets that permit higher margins and a move to provide greater differentiation among agencies, together with a policy to reduce the threats from substitute products, perhaps through more visible alliances and partnerships, would enable the industry to recover its position and provide greater stability. It is interesting to note that many leading agencies have moved into strategic consultancy, away from the reliance on mass media, where a substantially higher margin can be generated.

Agency branding

As if to emphasise the above point about differentiation, and despite the move into strategic planning, agency marketing activity is regarded by many as inadequate.

Clients, it is reported, have difficulty in distinguishing one brand from another, with the result that agencies appear to have poor brand identities.

One of the reasons for this is poor staff training. Abrahams (1997) reports a study undertaken by Tutt's Consultancy of 40 top advertising agencies. All chairmen responded that their respective companies had a clearly defined mission and positioning and that it had been communicated clearly to all staff. However, only 20% of staff knew of the mission and positioning intentions (and fewer believed in them). Brands are developed through consistent communication, delivery and performance. Therefore, agencies need to consider internal marketing communications (Chapter 10) as a means of improving this aspect of their business and thus enhancing their opportunities to deliver a more consistent brand proposition.

Brand philosophies and values are often subsumed when working with a client's culture and values. If an agency developed a strong set of values (by which it was positioned) and took these into a client's working environment there might well be a clash or conflict, which might not be constructive or easy to resolve. So far the policy has been to smother the agency values, but this may need to change in order that agencies can provide points of differentiation for clients to identify and accept.

Selecting an agency

In the areas which have traditionally dominated marketing communications, advertising and sales promotion, there has never been a shortage of advice on how to select an agency. Articles informing readers how to select an agency (Barnett and Clarke, 1991; Young and Steilen, 1996) appear regularly, and there are a large number of publications and organisations to assist in the process.

According to Barnett and Clarke, 'while choosing an agency is rarely easy, it is often made more difficult than it need be because of the personalities of the people involved and their sometimes contradicting requirements'. The theory behind the process is relatively straightforward. A *search* is undertaken to develop a list of potential candidates. This is accomplished by referring to publications such as *Campaign Portfolio* and the *Advertising Agency Roster*, together with personal recommendations. The latter is perhaps the most potent and influential of these sources. As many as ten agencies could be included at this stage although six or seven are to be expected.

Next, the client will visit each of the short-listed candidates in what is referred to as a *credentials presentation*. This is a crucial stage in the process, as it is now that the agency is evaluated for its degree of fit with the client's expectations and requirements. The agency's track record, resources, areas of expertise and experience are reviewed, and from this a short-list of three or possibly four agencies are selected for the next stage in the process: the pitch.

To be able to make a suitable bid the agencies are given a brief and then required to make a presentation (the *pitch*) to the client. This may or may not include creative work, and the account is awarded to whichever produces the most suitable proposal. Suitability is a relative term, and a range of factors need to be considered when selecting an organisation to be responsible for a large part of a brand's visibility. A strategic alliance is being formed and therefore a strong understanding of the strategic objectives of both parties is necessary, as is an appreciation of the structure and culture of the two organisations. The selection process is a bringing together of two organisations whose expectations may be different but whose cooperative behaviour is essential for these expectations to have any chance of materialising. For example, agencies must have access to comprehensive and often commercially confidential data about products and markets if they are to operate efficiently. Otherwise, they cannot provide the service which is anticipated.

The immediate selection process is finalised when terms and conditions are agreed and the winner is announced to the contestants and made public, often through trade journals such as *Campaign*, *Marketing* and *Marketing Week*.

Agency types and structures

As with any industry, growth and development spawn new types and structures. Adaptation to the environment is important for survival. The same applies to the marketing communications industry, where, to take the advertising industry as an example, many different organisational configurations have evolved.

The first option for a client is to undertake the communications functions in-house. However, this is both costly and inefficient, and most outsource their requirements to agencies.

Full service agencies

The first and most common type of agency (advertising) is the full service agency. This type of organisation offers the full range of services that a client requires in order to advertise its products and services. Agencies such as J. Walter Thompson, Saatchi & Saatchi and Leo Burnett offer a full service consisting of strategic planning, research, creative development, production and media planning. Some of these activities may be subcontracted, but overall responsibility rests with the full service agency.

Further discussion of some of the issues concerning full service agencies follows later.

Creative shops

A derivative of this type of agency is the creative shop, which forms when creative personnel (teams) leave full service agencies to set up their own business. These 'HotShops' provide specialist services for clients who wish to use particular styles and approaches for their creative work.

Media independents

Similarly, media independents provide specialist media services for planning, buying and monitoring the purchase of a client's media schedule. There are two main forms: media independents, where the organisation is owned and run free of the direction and policy requirements of a full service agency, and media dependents, where the organisation is a subsidiary of a creative or full service organisation. The largest dependent in the UK is Zenith Media, owned originally by Saatchi & Saatchi, and the largest independent is Carat.

Norwegian media independents

In Norway, media independents have taken control of an increasingly large proportion of the media handling business. This business gain has been at the expense of advertising agencies in Europe.

Their expertise in media planning and buying has led to their growth, dominance and increased their market power. Their advantage over others is that they have refined skills in space buying and negotiation, and as media markets become more complex so the media independents' position becomes stronger.

Adapted from Helgesen (1997)

A la carte

Partly in response to the changing needs of clients and consumers, many organisations require greater flexibility in the way their advertising is managed. Consequently these clients prefer to use the services of a range of organisations. So, the planning skills of a full service agency, the creative talent of a particular HotShop and the critical mass of a media-buying independent provide an *à la carte* approach. This process needs to be managed by the client, because when the services of other marketing communications providers are included flexibility is increased while coordination and control become more complex.

The move towards integrated marketing communications (see Chapter 29) was an inevitable development to bring about greater efficiency and harmonization. Therefore, if established advertising agencies could offer all marketing communications services the client need only deliver a single brief and await results. Accordingly, WPP and Saatchi & Saatchi set about building the largest marketing communications empires in the world. According to Green (1991), Saatchi & Saatchi attempted to become the largest marketing services company in the world. The strategy adopted in the early 1980s was to acquire companies outside its current area of core competence, media advertising. Organisations in direct marketing, market research, sales promotion and public relations were brought under the Saatchi banner.

By offering a range of services under a single roof, rather like a 'supermarket', the one-stop shopping approach made intrinsic sense. Clients could put a package together, rather like eating from a buffet table, and solve a number of their marketing requirements – without the expense and effort of searching through each sector to find a company with which to work.

Green also refers to the WPP experience in the late 1980s. J. Walter Thompson and Ogilvy and Mather were grouped together under the umbrella of WPP and it was felt that synergies were to be achieved by bringing together their various services. Six areas were identified: strategic marketing services, media advertising, public relations, market research, non-media advertising and specialist communications. A one-stop shopping approach was advocated once again.

The recession of the early 1990s brought problems to both of these organisations, as well as others. The growth had been built on acquisition, which was partly funded from debt. This required considerable interest payments, but the recession brought a sharp decline in the revenues of the operating companies, and cash flow problems forced WPP and Saatchi & Saatchi to restructure their debt and their respective organisations. As Phillips (1991) points out, the financial strain and the complex task of managing operations on such a scale began to tell.

However, underpinning the strategy was the mistaken idea that clients actually wanted a one-stop shopping facility. It was unlikely that the best value for money was going to be achieved through this, so it came as no little surprise when clients began to question the quality of the services for which they were paying. There was no guarantee that they could obtain from one large organisation the best creative, production, media and marketing solutions to their problems. Many began to shop around and engage specialists in different organisations (*à la carte*) in an attempt not only to receive the best quality of service but also the best value for money. Evidence for this might be seen in the resurgence of the media specialists whose very existence depends on their success in media planning and buying. By 1990 it was estimated that in the UK 30% of market share in media buying was handled by media specialist companies.

It is no wonder then, that clients, and indeed many media people working in agencies who felt constrained to leave and set up on their own account, felt that full-service agencies were asking too much of their staff, not only in terms of providing a wide range of integrated marketing services generally, but also in giving full attention and bringing sufficient expertise to bear in each of the specific services it has to offer (account management, creative, production, media research etc.).

The debate about whether or not to use a full-service agency becomes even more crucial, perhaps, for those in specialist areas. In business-to-business marketing, for example, Yovovich and Lawler (1991) cite the experiences of a number of companies, some of which have left large agencies for smaller specialist agencies and vice versa. In many ways it comes back to the quality of relationships. They present arguments for the specialist agency based upon the point that, while there may be some convergence of approaches between consumer goods marketing and business-to-business advertising, it can be easier for a business-to-business advertising firm to do consumer advertising than it is to do the reverse.

They report that business-to-business shops survive on their ability to execute some very fundamental techniques for clients, such as direct mail or sales promotion. In contrast, the large, consumer goods-oriented shops, whose traditional skills are market research, planning and media advertising, often lack the core skills, initiative or expertise to deliver business-to-business marketing services.

The same has been said of direct marketing (Direct Marketing, 1991) where there appears to be the same sort of disenchantment with the full service agency. Criticisms include the exclusion of direct marketing experts from presentations to clients: '...a lack of education among mainstream agency types as to what direct marketing actually does, to the complaint that clients don't want to be force fed a direct marketing subsidiary that may be incompetent or inappropriate'. The experience of those involved in direct marketing is summed up thus: 'Warring account directors, poorly educated senior management and plain indifference amongst clients has meant that most of the shotgun marriages so hastily consummated between mainstream and direct marketing agencies during the 80's have failed to produce positive results'.

There is a spectrum of approaches for clients. They can find an agency which can provide all of the required marketing communication services under one roof, or find a different agency for each of the services, or mix and match. Clearly the first solution can only be used if the budget holder is convinced that the best level of service is being provided in *all* areas, and the second only if there are sufficient gains in efficiency (and savings in expenditure) to warrant the amount of additional time he or she would need to devote to the task of managing marketing communications.

Agency operations

Advertising agencies are generally organised on a functional basis. There have been moves to develop matrix structures utilising a customer orientation, but this is very inefficient and the low margins prohibit such luxuries. There are departments for planning, creative and media functions coordinated on behalf of the client by an account handler or executive.

The account handler fulfils a very important role in that these people are responsible for the flow of communications between the client and the agency. The quality of the communications between the two main parties can be critical to the success of the overall campaign and to the length of the relationship between the two organisations. Acting at the boundary of the agency's operations, the account handler needs to perform several roles, from internal coordinator and negotiator to presenter (of the agency's work), conflict manager and information gatherer. Very often account handlers will experience tension as they seek to achieve their clients' needs while trying to balance the needs of their employer and colleagues. These tensions are similar to those experienced by salespersons and need to be managed in a sensitive manner by management.

Once an account has been signed a client brief is prepared which provides information about the client organisation (Figure 7.3). It sets out the nature of the industry it operates in together with data about trends, market shares, customers, competitors and the problem that the advertising agency is required to address. This is used to inform agency personnel. In particular, the account planner will undertake research to determine market, media and audience characteristics and make proposals to the rest of the account team as to how the client problem is to be resolved.

Much of this information is translated into a creative brief for the development of copy and visuals by the appointed creative team. An example of a Creative Brief can be found in the appendices. This is a team of two, a copy writer and an art director, supported by a service team. This team is responsible for translating the proposal into an advertisement. Later, a media brief will also be generated, informing the media planning and buying department of the media required and the type of media vehicles required.

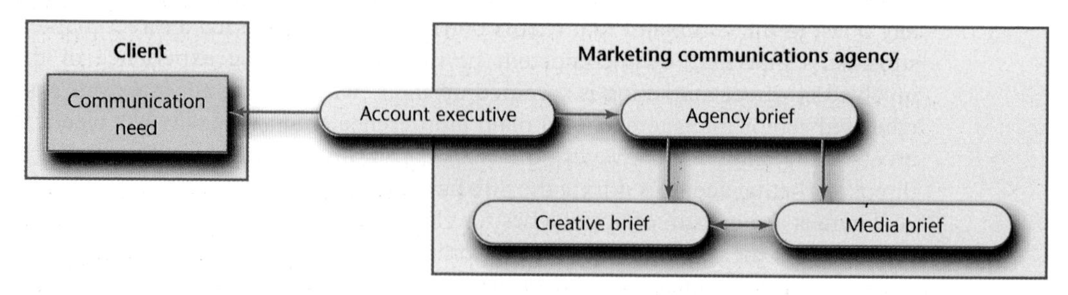

Figure 7.3 The briefing process.

Table 7.2 Some of advertising's longest held accounts

Client	Agency	Arrival
SmithKline Beecham	O & M	1896
Lever Bros	APL	1898
Brooke Bond Foods	BMP DDB	1914
Kraft	JWT	1922
Nestlé	JWT	1927
British Aerospace	BMP DDB	1938

Source: *Campaign*, 6 September 1996, p. 34.

Relationships

If the briefing process provides the mechanism for the agency operations, it is the nature of the relationships between the agency and the client that very often determines the length of the contract and the strength of the solutions advanced for the client.

There a number of agency/client relationships that have flourished over a very long period of time, and some of these are shown in Table 7.2. There are a huge number of other accounts who have excellent relationships that have lasted a long time. However, these appear to be in the minority, as many relationships appear to founder as clients abandon agencies and search for better, fresher solutions or because of takeovers and mergers between agencies, which require that they forfeit accounts that cause a conflict of interest.

From a contextual perspective these buyer/seller relationships can be seen to follow a pattern of formation, maintenance and severance, or pre-contract, contracting process and post-contract stages (Davidson and Kapelianis, 1996). Clients and agencies enter into a series of interactions (West and Paliwoda, 1996) or exchanges through which trust and commitment is developed. Hakansson (1982) identified different contexts or atmospheres within which a relationship develops. These contexts had several dimensions: closeness/distance, cooperation/conflict, power/dependence, trustworthiness and expectations. Therefore, the client/agency relationship should be seen in the context of the network of organisations and the exchanges or interactions that occur in that network. It is through these interactions that the tasks that need to be accomplished are agreed, resources made available, strategies determined and goals achieved. The quality of the agency/client relationship is a function of trust, which is developed through the exchanges and which fosters confidence. Commitment is derived from a belief that the relationship is worth continuing and that maximum effort is warranted at maintaining the relationship (Morgan and Hunt, 1994).

Poor relationships between agencies/clients are likely to result from a lack of trust and falling commitment. As it appears that communication is a primary element in the formation and substance of relational exchanges, clients might be advised to consider the agencies in their roster as an extended department of the core organisation and use internal marketing communication procedures to assist the development of identity and belonging.

Nike talks to agencies about £9m UK ad task

Nike were reported to have begun talking to UK agencies about the future of its business. This was despite the fact that the account was still placed with TBWA Simons Palmer.

Clare Dobie, the Nike UK Advertisement Manager confirmed that discussions were taking place with other agencies but stated that there were no plans to resign TBWA Simons Palmer. She said that 'it is a long time since we talked to any agencies and we want to be sure that we are working with the best people'. She went on to say that 'Park Life' (a particular football ad for Nike using football stars such as Eric Cantona, Robbie Fowler, David Seaman and Ian Wright) was, in her opinion, probably the best ever football advertisement.

This faltering commitment suggests an impending divergence of intentions, and a fall in trust between the two parties was anticipated. Indeed, in November 1997 the account was awarded to a US agency (Wieden & Kennedy) who were about to enter the UK market from its European base in Amsterdam. Nike claimed that the appointment assisted its strategy to develop a coordinated global campaign in order that it could defend its market leadership position (Barrett, 1997).

Hall (1997)

Agency remuneration

One factor that has a significant impact on the quality of the relationship between the parties is the remuneration or reward for the effort the agency makes in attempting to meet and satisfy the needs of its client. One major cause for concern and complaint among marketing managers is the uncertainty over how much their marketing communications programmes will finally cost.

According to Bennett (1993), quoting a recent report from the Incorporated Society of British Advertisers, 'One hundred and one companies, of which 63 per cent spend up to £2m on press and media buying, are greatly concerned about creative and production costs, the "confusion and complexity" of charges and a lack of business-like procedures, accountability and measurability'.

There are three main ways in which agencies are paid. These are *commission*, *fees* and *payment by results*. A fourth is a mixture or combination of these approaches.

Traditionally, advertising agencies were paid a commission by media owners for selling space in their publications. A figure of 15 per cent emerged as the norm, and seemed a fair reward for the efforts of the agency. However, as relationships between agencies and clients strengthened it seemed only reasonable that the clients should feel that agencies should act for them (and in their best interests), and not for the media owners. A number of questions were raised about whether the agency was actually being rewarded for the work it did and whether it was being objective when recommending media expenditure. As Best (1991) puts it: 'As the primary relationship and burden of paying evolved from media owner to client, the commission system survived. It still does. To a client it can seem to encourage agencies to recommend media spend regardless of his real business needs. Nor is there any logical connection between 15 per cent and the value of the agency's efforts'.

Client discontent is not the only reason why agency remuneration by commission has been called into question, and alternatives are being considered. In times of recession marketing budgets are inevitably cut, which means less revenue for agencies. Increasing competition means lower profit margins if an agency is to retain the business, and if costs are increasing at the same time the very survival of the agency is in question. As Snowden (1993) states, in an excellent review of the current debate and choices for remuneration: 'Clients are demanding more for less'. She goes on to say: 'It is clear to me that the agency business needs to address a number of issues; most important amongst them, how agencies get paid. It is the key to the industry's survival'.

During the early 1990s there was a great of discussion and energy directed towards non-commission payment systems. This was a direct result of the recession, in which clients cut budgets and there was a consequent reduction in the quantity of media purchased and hence less revenue for the agencies. Fees became more popular, and some experimented with payment by results. Interestingly, as the recession died and the economy lifted more revenue resulted in larger commission possibilities, and the death throes of the commission system were quickly replaced by its resuscitation and revival.

It is unlikely that there will be a move away completely from the payment of some commission to the agency. The system is uncomplicated and leaves the negotiations between agencies and media owners, which makes it easy for the client. Fees have been around for a long time, either in the form of retainers or on a project by project basis. Indeed, many agencies charge a fee for services over and above any commission earned from media owners. The big question is about the basis for calculation of fees (and this extends to all areas of marketing communications, not just advertising), and protracted, complicated negotiations can damage client/agency relationships.

For many, payment by results seemed a good solution. There are some problems, however, in that the agency does not have total control over its performance and the final decisions about how much is spent and which creative ideas should be used are the client's. The agency has no control over the other marketing activities of the client, which might determine the degree of success of the campaign. Indeed, this raises the very thorny question of what 'success' is and how it might be measured (Chapters 13, 17 and 24).

A different way of looking at this is to consider what the client thinks the agency does and from this evaluate the outcomes from the relationship. Jensen (1995) proposes that advertising agencies can be seen as an *ideas business* which seeks to build brands for clients. An alternative view is that agencies are *advertising factories*, where the majority of the work is associated with administration, communication, coordination and general running around to ensure that the advertisement appears on the page or screen as desired.

If the 'ideas business' view is accepted then the ideas generated add value for the client, so the use the client makes of the idea should be rewarded by way of a royalty type payment. If the 'factory concept' is adopted, then it is the resources involved in the process that need to be considered and a fee-based system is more appropriate. Both parties will actively seek to reduce costs that do not contribute to the desired outcomes. These are different approaches to remuneration and avoid the volume of media purchased as a critical and controversial area.

Controlling the marketing communications industry

There are two types of control in the marketing communications industry: statutory (the legal framework) and voluntary (or self-regulatory). This is a detailed and complex area of marketing and it is clearly beyond the scope of this chapter to give a comprehensive description of all existing controls (which are being constantly revised, updated and added to). However, what follows is intended to give the reader some idea of the nature of existing controls and reactions to them.

The self-regulatory system of advertising control in the United Kingdom has been in existence for over thirty years (Alderson, 1992a, b). The Advertising Standards Authority (ASA) oversees the non-broadcast system on which broadcast codes are based and ensures that it functions in the public interest. The Committee of Advertising Practice (CAP), the industry arm, operates in parallel to coordinate the activities of the trade and professional organisations that comprise the advertising business. Together, they ensure that the British Code of Advertising Practice functions in the interests of consumers and is observed by those who commission, prepare and publish advertisements. Finally, the Advertising Standards Board of Finance exists independently to raise a levy on advertising expenditure to fund the system.

It is to the ASA that the public and the industry complain if they suspect that a non-broadcast advertisement is less than 'Legal, Decent, Honest and Truthful'. In addition to receiving over 10,678 complaints (1997), the Authority conducts a substantial monitoring programme, scrutinising more than 15,000 advertisements. This allows the ASA to anticipate and resolve problems and to spot trends that require intervention before they are revealed by complaints. In addition it is noticeable that the copy advice service offered to advertisers is being used much more than in the past. Perhaps this is a reflection of a more sensitive and protective attitude towards customers and the public, and the need to protect brand reputation much more in harsher competitive environments. It is also interesting to note that the number of complaints received about advertisements has a distinct downward trend: see Table 7.3. Part of this fall is due to the poster industry imposing a tougher self-regulatory system, whereby any client whose advertising draws complaints will have all its subsequent advertising pre-vetted.

All advertisements investigated are adjudicated by the Council of the Authority, which consists of twelve members serving as individuals and appointed by an independent Chairman. The Council's rulings are published in a monthly report, which is widely circulated. In composition, the Council must be dominated by members who have no connection with the advertising business.

Television advertising in the UK, including satellite and cable, is governed by the Independent Television Commission (ITC), which has its own Code of Advertising Standards and Practice. In 1997, the ITC decided that 512 advertisements were adjudged to be not in good taste, were indecent or were socially irresponsible. These advertisements were withdrawn.

Advertising on radio is regulated by the Radio Authority (RA) which, likewise, has its own Code. Both bodies are statutorily regulated and both Codes therefore have

Table 7.3 Number of complaints received and advertisements withdrawn

	1995	1996	1997
Number of complaints received	12,804	12,055	10,678
Number of advertisements withdrawn	515	720	512

Source: Advertising Standards Association.

statutory force (i.e. the force of law). The ITC and the RA, as well as responding to complaints, provide advice on the interpretation of their codes.

The CAP predates the ASA and was the genesis of the self-regulatory system. In the early 1960s it was recognised by those working in the industry that effective controls were needed to set standards for those preparing and publishing advertisements. The ASA administers and the CAP formulates and updates the British Code of Advertising Practice. Any advertisement in press, posters, cinema, direct mail, viewdata, sales promotion or the management of lists and databases is governed by the rules in the Code.

In addition to the British Code of Advertising Practice, many industries have now instituted their own sectoral Codes of Practice which require observance of the CAP code but also contain more detailed rules on specialised advertisements and trading practices.

Since the Code was first published there has been a significant enlargement of the amount of legislation designed to protect the consumer. This is true not only domestically but also in relation to Directives emanating from the EU, which must be drawn into the UK's existing register of more than 80 statutes, orders and regulations affecting advertising.

The Code, and the self-regulatory framework that exists to administer it, was designed to work within and to complement those legal controls. Its scope, speed and flexibility provide an alternative, and in some instances the only, means of resolving disputes about advertisements. It also stimulates the adoption of high standards of practice in numerous areas, such as taste and decency, that are extremely difficult to judge in law but which fundamentally affect the reputation of the advertising industry.

In addition, the Office of Fair Trading, the Ministry of Agriculture, Fisheries and Food, the Department of Trade and Industry, the Home Office, the Securities and Investments Board, the Bank of England and the Department of Health (to name a diverse but not exhaustive selection) have consumer protection legislation which ranges far wider and deeper than could be executed through a judicially non-punitive Code of Practice; in some instances, companies and individuals who break the laws administered by these offices face criminal as well as civil prosecution.

The British Code of Sales Promotion Practice is published by the CAP and conforms to the principles of the International Code of Sales Promotion Practice, published by the International Chamber of Commerce. Implementation of the Code is in the hands of the CAP under the general supervision of the ASA. Day-to-day supervision of the Code, including pre-publication advice for promoters, is in the hands of the Committee's subcommittee on sales promotion, the members of which have wide experience of sales promotion matters. The Code sets out basic principles and gives general guidelines applying to all forms of sales promotion and how these apply in particular cases. The Code also lists the main legislative controls on sales promotions and associated advertising: the fifth edition (Alderson, 1990) identifies 19 acts, orders and regulations. The Institute of Sales Promotion, itself a member of the CAP, provides a recommended reading list, much of which is concerned with the regulatory framework for sales promotion and which is an invaluable guide for potential promoters. The Direct Selling Association has its own Code of Practice within which all member companies must operate. The Direct Mail Services Standards Board monitors postal advertising and unaddressed leaflet material to ensure compliance with the law and the Code. Public Relations has its own Code of Practice and there have even been suggestions (Week, 1990) that sales representatives should have their own codes of ethics.

It seems, therefore, that the consumer is well protected against any attempts to defraud, mislead or even offend. However, it does seem that these codes are constantly being challenged by clients and consumers. This may be a reflection of boundaries being tested in the name of advancement and progress, especially as offending clients are, in many cases, only lightly rebuffed and told not to do it again. But this raises the question of whether there is too much control. Some (Gray, 1992; Mills, 1990) argue that freedom of expression, freedom of speech and even freedom of choice are under threat. Others (Hill and Rawthorn, 1991) point out that even more control is on the way, talking about 'the plethora of legislation on advertising regulations now being considered by the European Commission'. The further question is, of course, does it work? The evidence, from the number of complaints and prosecutions in any one year, is that examples of malpractice are few and far between. There will always be some who are guilty (deliberately or otherwise) of 'circumventing the voluntary codes designed to regulate them' (Hoek *et al.*, 1993) and there will always be contentious issues, such as the promotion of tobacco products, especially to young people, which will, almost inevitably, lead to further controls. What is certain is that those responsible for marketing communications need to keep up to date by seeking best advice on this most important and potentially dangerous area.

Summary

This chapter has attempted to demonstrate the complex nature of the marketing communications industry by considering the size, trends, players, operations and competitive aspects. It should be noted, however, that in the space available this analysis has not attempted to be, and cannot be regarded as, a comprehensive treatment.

The structure that advertising agencies have adopted and the operational aspects may be a little outdated, and the industry might be advised to find new ways of presenting itself to its buyers. Of the many issues facing the industry one of the key ones concerns the relationships between agencies and their clients. The context that the industry presents and which influences the relationships of the main participants, the media, clients and agencies, must not be ignored.

The industry will continue to evolve and further integration between agencies and those that own and manage many of the new marketing communication tools is likely to accelerate.

Acknowledgement

The author would like to acknowledge the work of Joe Penn, whose original chapter in the first edition laid the foundation for this subsequent work.

Review questions

1. How might an organisation determine the sum to be spent on marketing communications and how might that sum be apportioned between the various activities available?
2. Which are the principal types of organisation in the marketing communication industry?
3. Write notes for a presentation explaining the different types of agency available to clients.
4. Outline the arguments for and against using an agency.
5. What factors should be taken into consideration and what procedure might be followed when selecting an agency?
6. What problems might be encountered in agency/client relationships?
7. What are the basic dimensions for the development of good agency/client relationships?
8. Write brief notes about the briefing system.
9. Explain the commission payment system, and outline alternative approaches.
10. How can an organisation best acquaint itself with the relevant controls in a chosen area of marketing communications?

References

Abrahams, B. (1997) Branding the agency. *Marketing*, 26 June, pp. 24–5.

Alderson, M. (1990) *The British Code of Sales Promotion Practice*, 5th edn. CAP.

Alderson, M. (1992a) *Advertising and Regulation*. The Advertising Standards Authority, The Advertising Association.

Alderson, M. (1992b) *ITC Annual Report and Accounts*. ITC.

Barrett, P. (1997) Nike dumps UK shop. *Marketing*, 27 November, p. 15.

Barnett, B. and Clarke, S. (1991) How to choose an agency. *Campaign*, 22 November, pp. 24–6.

Bennett, M. (1993) Called to account. *Marketing Business* (July/August), 29–32.

Best, J. (1991) Payment by results – a fad or the future? *Admap* (July), 28–35.

Cardwell, Z. (1990) How to get the client party off the ground. *Financial Director* (December), 40–3.

Davidson, S. and Kapelianis, D. (1996) Towards an organisational theory of advertising: agency–client relationships in South Africa. *International Journal of Advertising*, **15**, 48–60.

Direct Marketing (1991) The dream which never became reality. *Direct Marketing* (March), 57–9.

Gray, J. (1992) Why banning advertising is wrong. *The Campaign Report*, 25 September, pp. 41–2.

Green, A. (1991) Death of the full-service ad agency? *Admap* (January), 21–4.

Green, H. and Griffiths, A. (1997) Mindshare heralds KWT 'shake-up'. *Campaign*, 26 September, p. 1.

Hakansson, H. (1982) *International Marketing and Purchasing of Industrial Goods: an interaction approach*. Chichester: John Wiley.

Hall, E. (1997) Nike talks to agencies about £9M UK ad task. *Campaign*, 10 October, p. 2.

Helgesen, T. (1997) Advertisers and media independents—cooperation and control: a study in Norway. *International Journal of Advertising*, **16**(1), 37–47.

Hill, A. and Rawthorn, A. (1991) Persuaders gear up for challenge to EC regulations. *Financial Times*, 20 June, p. 18.

Hoek, J., Gendall, P. and Stockdale, M. (1993) Some effects of tobacco sponsorship advertisements on young males. *International Journal of Advertising*, **12**, 25–35.

Jensen, B. (1995) Using agency remuneration as a strategic tool. *Admap* (January), 20–2.

Miles, L. (1992) Going solo. *Marketing Business* (June), 41–4.

Mills, A. (1990). Advertising, a freedom under threat? *Way Ahead* (October), 8–10.

Morgan, R.M. and Hunt, S.D. (1994) The commitment–trust theory of relationship marketing. *Journal of Marketing*, **58** (July), 20–38.

Phillips, W. (1991) From bubble to rubble. *Admap* (April), 14–19.

Porter, M.E. (1980) *Competitive Strategy: Techniques for Analysing Industries and Competitors*. New York: Free Press.

Snowden, S. (1993) The remuneration squeeze. *Admap* (January), 26–8.

Thomas, H. (1991) Mixing business with pleasure. *Accountancy* (May), 104–6.

Week, W.A. (1990) Corporate codes of ethics and sales force behaviour: a case study. *Journal of Business Ethics*, **11**, 753–60.

West, D.C. and Paliwoda, S.J. (1996) Advertising client–agency relationships. *European Journal of Marketing*, **30**(8), 22–39.

Young, M. and Steilen, C. (1996) Strategy based advertising agency selection: an alternative to 'spec' presentation. *Business Horizons*, **39** (November/December), 77–80.

Yovovich, B.G. and Lawler, E.O. (1991) Big agency – small agency. *Business Marketing* (May), 13–18.

The environmental context

The environment provides a setting within which largely uncontrollable elements shape and reshape the nature and form of the marketing communications deployed by participants operating in similar markets.

AIMS AND OBJECTIVES

The aims of this chapter are to introduce some of the wider environmental factors associated with marketing communications.

The objectives of this chapter are:

1. To appreciate the complexity of the environmental context and its impact on marketing communications.
2. To understand the principal forces that operate within the context of the environment.
3. To discern the impact of societal forces on marketing communications.
4. To appreciate how technological advances have affected planned communications.
5. To provide an insight into how economic conditions affect such programmes.
6. To explore the way in which legislative changes can shape the content of promotional messages.
7. To establish the role of communications in the context of corporate responsibility.

Introduction

It has been established that organisations are open systems and that they seek to satisfy their objectives through networks of other organisations. They are, therefore, subject to the influences of these other organisations and the network as a whole. At the same time, however, the focus organisation seeks to influence different parts of the network, and much of that activity is undertaken through its promotional programme. The quality of interaction that an organisation enjoys with its environments will be a significant contribution to the success of the organisation in its attempt to meet its objectives. Planned marketing communications influence the quality of the relationships held and consequently the outcomes of the partnerships, in the form of relational exchanges.

The wider environment cannot be ignored, and is a factor in the development of planned communications. Most of the elements discussed so far are, to a large extent, capable of being controlled by the organisation. The context within which buyers and organisations function means that changes in buyer preferences and buying patterns can be determined through marketing research and programmes can be adjusted to meet changed conditions. Competitors may change the way in which they present their offerings and in doing so seek to reposition not only themselves but also some of the other players in the market.

There are opportunities to overcome these difficulties through such tools as advertising (to transmit messages to mass audiences), direct marketing (to focus messages on individual customers) and sales promotions (to stimulate purchase activity). However, there is a range of other forces which constitute a context which organisations are unable to influence to any significant degree; that is, they are largely uncontrollable, at least in the short run.

The context of these forces may be beyond the influence of an organisation and, rather than attempt to influence the source of these forces, the only feasible course of action is to adapt to the anticipated or prevailing environmental conditions. The pharmaceutical industry is now required by the European Union to list on the packaging, or on leaflets provided with drugs, many of the ingredients contained in each product. When this is considered in the light of the vast number of compounds that are used in each formulation and the requirement to provide suitable usage instructions and all necessary warnings concerning any possible side effects, it becomes apparent that the design of the label and hence promotional message associated with over-the-counter (OTC) and pharmacy only (P line) offerings becomes exceedingly complex.

The purpose of this chapter is therefore to consider the wider external environment as a context within which organisations seek to deploy planned (and unplanned) marketing communication messages. The main characteristics of this contextual element are that these forces are largely uncontrollable and that the communications activities have to be designed and implemented in a way that accommodates the key constraining and restraining forces.

The environmental context

Potentially, there are an extremely large number of elements in the environment that indirectly or directly affect the communications of an organisation. The skill of the

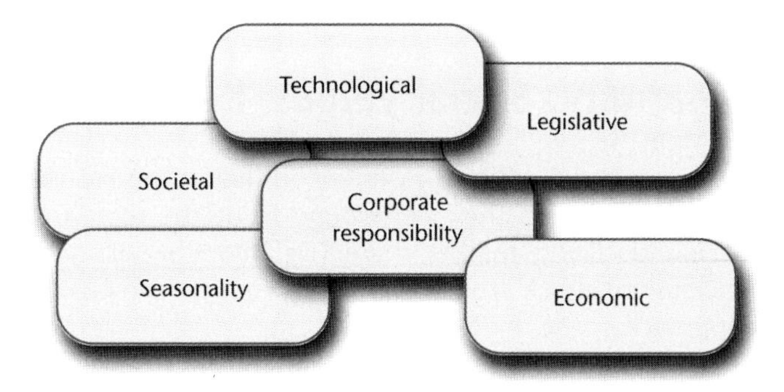

Figure 8.1 Elements of the environmental context.

communications planner is to sense those elements that may be unobtrusive now but which may gather strength and have a stronger impact on the organisation or its offerings at some point in the future. Having sensed new environmental developments and determined that their impact cannot be ignored, the next step is to adjust the way in which messages are encoded, delivered or decoded so that the impact is diffused and, where possible, used to the advantage of the organisation. The environmental context can be regarded as consisting of a number of sub-contexts within which driving and restraining forces seek to influence the established norms. The main forces are societal, technological, economic, seasonal, legislative and those of corporate responsibility (Figure 8.1).

Societal forces

One of the most significant of the environmental forces acting in the societal sub-context concerns changes in the demographic balance. The number of people in each of the age bands (e.g. 18 to 24 year olds) is changing. This demographic shift in population bands means that in the next century there will be more than three times the number of people over 60 years old than there were in the 1960s. The growth in the number of older people brings implications for the production capacity of the economy and the opening of new markets. Already the 'grey market' (over 55 year olds) is well established. In 1991 24% of the UK population was over 55 years old, and the size of this band is expected to increase into the next century (Calver *et al.*, 1993). This new segment requires different products and services from all others, as they possess different readership habits and viewing patterns. This will mean a change not only in the nature and form of products which are of value to them but also in the way products and services are presented to them.

Another force is that the number of single parent families has grown and the size and shape of the family unit are shifting as divorce rates remain high and the number of births outside the traditional family unit increases. Apart from addressing the impact that these new units have on levels of disposable income, marketing communications needs to be sensitive to the fact that the 2+2 family unit is no longer dominant. Family scenes depicted in advertisements such as those for Allied Dunbar and Oxo are not necessarily the norm, although they may of course be correct in terms of target marketing. Sales promotions that offer bonus packs or family tubs offer no value to these emerging units. Sensitivity to and awareness of these issues is more important if a message is to have credibility with the target audience.

Changing Social Values: Kellogg's

Kellogg's had traditionally positioned themselves around family values, quality and choice. In the UK they were found to be the most trusted brand, but they were facing declining market share (Datamonitor), stagnant market conditions and increasing attack from own-label products. Kellogg's needed to reconsider its approach.

In January 1998 the company announced a new positioning approach following extensive consumer research. They found from a series of focus groups that consumers believed that stress and weight control, together with family health, constituted the primary issues facing people. As a result of this they launched a radically different campaign that focused on raising awareness of the importance of diet in leading a healthy lifestyle. Their positioning is now about 'Serving the Nation's Health'.

Kellogg's claims that 'Serving the Nation's Health' is a return to the corporate philosophy established by their founder, who claimed that Kellogg's 'make quality products for a healthier world' (see Plate 8.1).

Adapted from Rogers (1998)

Further to this point and at a more subtle level, the changing nature of society brings difficulties and opportunities for advertisers. How should messages be presented to target audiences? For example, the role of women in society has changed considerably over the past decade. The traditional role of mother and housewife has changed, and there are a growing number of households where domestic chores are shared more equally (Bartos, 1983). The pattern of women's lives has changed considerably over the last twenty years. Many more are now pursuing educational qualifications before commencing careers. Increasing numbers of those who previously were unable to study are returning to education later in life. The roles women now assume at work have also changed, as a greater number now hold middle and senior management positions. Promotional messages have tried to reflect this change, and some advertisers have moved away from narrow stereotyping. Messages showing women as supercharged, multi-skilled heroines who manage homes, partners, families, business and local community activities emerged in the 1980s as a reaction to these changes in society.

When the perfume Charlie was first launched in the United Kingdom in the mid-1970s, it was the first to position itself as a fragrance for the independent woman. One of the main ways of appealing to this emerging segment was to dress the strident actress in trousers, something that had not occurred previously. This approach was soon copied by others, of course, including Chanel, who disguised their actress in a male suit and placed her unnoticed in a gentlemen's club in an attempt to position on equality and assertiveness.

The attitudes held by society have changed faster than demographics. Increasingly, towards the end of the 1980s, environmentalists became a force which businesses and consumers finally came to understand and appreciate. Organisations began to incorporate environmental issues in their communications and purchasing activities. The ecological perspective has become more important as psychographic segments become more significant, witnessed by the growth of The Body Shop, the most successful 'green retailer' (Dibb and Simpkin, 1991). The force with which ecological issues impact upon consumers and organisations can only intensify. Organisations should determine whether ecological matters present any opportunities in the form of untapped market segments, new promotional messages to reposition organisations and their brands, or new media vehicles to carry messages to this audience.

London Zoo

London Zoo experienced a marked decline in the number of visitors during the 1980s. One of the reasons for this is that the public's attitude to zoos has changed (for a variety of reasons) and they do not want animals taken out of their natural environment and caged in pens that are inappropriate. London Zoo, like many others, has tried to reposition itself as an organisation charged with the protection of endangered species, mainly through the development of breeding programmes. These actions represent a contextual adjustment. London Zoo adapted itself to the environment within which it functioned and determined a more appropriate context for its continued existence, a context that would be more acceptable to its wide array of stakeholders, most notably the paying public.

A further consideration is the way in which consumers use brands to reflect lifestyle and personality factors. In the 1980s, research indicated that brands were bought partly to reflect status and achievement, but consumers in the 1990s are more sceptical about brand claims and are considered to be more thoughtful about their purchases. This is of course a reflection of the economic conditions, but it means that the messages transmitted to target audiences need to be decoded in such a way that quality and benefits are easily understood (McMurdo, 1993). Luxury advertising is also changing as tastes change. The advertisements in glossy up-market magazines, such as *Tatler*, *Vanity Fair* and *Vogue*, can be seen to 'dwell on exclusivity and craftsmanship and the long history of their companies, rather than the materialistic imagery of the 1980s' (Rawsthorn, 1993). The context portrayed by these messages is consistent and often aspirational, motivating members of the target audience to change aspects of their lifestyle.

A further issue concerns marketing communication messages that attempt to break established conventions. In order to gain attention in cluttered markets and to be contemporary, some advertisements infringe upon societal norms and are rejected (Diesel jeans for sexual overtones, Ford Fiesta advertisements that depicted speed as the primary attribute), while others infringe yet are accepted (Tango, Wonderbra), and in so doing alter the context for future communications and expectations for advertisers, consumers and agencies either at large or within the product sector and market. The dynamism of the advertising business itself provides a mechanism by which society acts as an important context for marketing communications.

Society provides both legislative and voluntary regulatory frameworks through which marketing communications messages are designed, vetted and delivered. In a way this is a form of censorship, society's self-imposed mechanism for maintaining the contextual norms for the marketing communications we experience. Society, therefore, is a framework or context within which marketing communication messages have value, are valued and which legitimise the current culture and the marketing communications that contribute to it.

Technological forces

The pace at which technology has advanced over the past decade has had a tremendous impact upon advertisers, media owners, marketing research and advertising agencies. The principal effect has been to fragment the audience in such a way that targets can be more easily defined and reached with pinpoint accuracy. Some of the secondary effects of fragmentation are that organisations now employ different promotional mixes to reach these diverse groups. A greater emphasis has been placed on sales promotion at the expense of mass advertising. Direct marketing has attained a greater level of acceptability and more organisations are using multiple sales channels rather than only relying on the field sales force. One of the reasons for the rapid development of direct marketing has been technological advance, bringing the ability for organisations to harness computing facilities at speeds and costs that are increasing and falling respectively. For example, the surge in telemarketing activities and segmentation approaches through database management typify the advances made and society's attitudes towards to Direct Response Television (DRTV) and personalised, unsolicited mail have changed.

New technology has enabled supermarkets to scan purchases at the checkout and record the data so that in-store promotion campaigns can be run more effectively. Single-source data, that is the electronic measurement of television exposure and purchase behaviour (Assael and Poltrack, 1991), has facilitated testing the effectiveness of advertisements under semi-controlled conditions, where all the data emanate from the same household.

The explosion of video recorders and the steady growth of satellite and cable networks has reduced, and will continue to do so, the power of the central broadcast networks. This means that advertisers have more opportunities to reach particular targets and viewers are able to select a greater range of programmes. Zipping and zapping between channels enables viewers to avoid television commercials, so lowering the perceived effectiveness of the medium. Home shopping channels, while limited so far in Europe, will inevitably expand as cable and satellite penetration increases.

New on-line and interactive communications will inevitably change the way in which shopping, banking and education, for example, are undertaken and delivered to a wide variety of audiences.

Technological breakthroughs have occurred in the print industry. Colour printing for newspapers, at an economical rate, is now a commercially attractive strategy for some advertisers. Magazine publishers have developed new techniques to attract advertisers. Scent strips, for example, allow perfume houses to invite readers to try a new fragrance without them having to visit a store. Personalised magazines can now be assembled in response to reader enquiries about particular products and product categories. The advent and development of commercial radio has provided new opportunities to reach buyers, typified by the success of Classic FM and Virgin 1215.

Advertisers need to be aware of the changes that are occurring in the technological environment and be prepared to review them as they may provide better opportunities to reach their target audiences.

Economic forces

The condition of the national economy is beyond the control of any single organisation. The effects can be seen in tangible elements, such as the level of disposable income, and intangible elements, such as the confidence that organisations and consumers have to invest. The balance between an individual's propensities to save and to spend can have an immediate impact upon the way in which promotional messages are designed, delivered and received. For example, it is not uncommon for advertisers to promote economy packs and price deals during times of recession and to cut back on media expenditure. Many consumers become cautious about non-necessary expenditures and less receptive to messages inducing them to enter exchange transactions, unless there is an incentive or some form of added value associated with the purchase. When the economy is strong or gathering strength, so the desire to save gradually gives way to a greater propensity to spend. Consumers become more receptive to a variety of messages, and the content of advertising messages in particular becomes more expansive. Message appeals become more emotional and tend to replace the rational, price-orientated messages that dominate during a recession.

The 1980s was a period when the amount of credit used by consumers expanded rapidly. Shergill (1993) reports that it has been estimated by *Business Week* that citizens of the USA owed $3 trillion in 1990, compared with $1.3 trillion in 1980. This has brought about a change in buyer attitudes, where the affluence of the 1980s has given way to a value-orientated perspective in the 1990s. This change impacts upon attitudes, buying patterns and the structure of organisations as they adapt to the radically different environments and the new strategies that they seek to sustain competitiveness and viability. For example, many food manufacturers are having to adapt their products in the wake of the growing assertiveness of retailers and the success of their own brands. Marketing communications have changed, witnessed by the way in which the promotional mix is deployed and by the shift in budget away from mass advertising to sales promotions and direct marketing.

Seasonal forces

Many products have purchase cycles that are short and regular. Promotional messages can be spread across the year, according to the objectives of each campaign. Some products, however, are consumed on a seasonal basis, which impacts upon promotional strategy and media scheduling in particular. These seasonal factors may occur due to climatic and natural elements, whereas others may result from past practices or cultural norms. For example, the most important purchase period in the toy market is the period leading to Christmas; this represents a cultural determinant. However, the main sales of ice cream occur in the summer months, and gardening products sell best in the spring and early summer. These result from climatic conditions and will vary from country to country. These seasonal forces are usually uncontrollable (they cannot normally be changed), so organisations must adapt their promotional activities to meet the environmental conditions.

The market for new cars in the UK used to surge at the new registration letter date, 1 August. During this period, over 25% of each year's new car sales occurred. However, unlike the weather and climatic issues, the new car purchase and registration issue was originally induced as a societal requisite and as such was capable of change. A number of stakeholders were adversely affected by this system and a move was made to change it so that there are two points within each year when new registrations can be made. This development serves to reduce the congestion and excessive activity at car dealerships in August, but also impacts on the marketing communication schedules of car manufacturers. The nature of the competitive communication activity alters and budgets are reorganised to reflect the new market requirements. In addition to this, the activities of agencies and those involved in media planning in particular have altered, and advertising creatives need to find new ways of reminding people about their clients' products, as well as differentiating them, on perhaps a greater number of occasions each year.

Legislative forces

Some of the most important stakeholders that all organisations have are their national governments and other associated (often higher level) affiliations. In the UK the latter would be represented by the European Union, in South-East Asia by SEATO and in the USA by NAFTA. The potential force that these parties have through legislation and regulation is enormous and it is this overall context of guidelines and boundaries of behaviour that sets limits on the behaviour of organisations and the marketing communication dialogue they seek to generate and maintain.

The end of commission payments: The Prudential

Financial services company The Prudential announced in February 1998 that it was to abolish the payment of commission as a means of rewarding its sales force.

This decision can be traced back to the introduction of a legal requirement that the amount of commission earned had to be declared to consumers. Because these sums are normally taken out of the fund at the beginning of a policy term, they cut the value of the fund to be invested, and customers were unhappy at the amounts of commission declared. In addition, the drive to earn commission in the absence of adequate salaries has been regarded as a prime cause of the pension misselling that occurred in the late 1980s and early 1990s. Not only has The Prudential been admonished by the regulatory authorities and had to set aside £450 million for compensation, but it has also had its reputation severely challenged.

The changes have led to a new sales force structure with retail-style distribution based around telephone account management and a culture that encourages the development of customer relationships. As Sir Peter Davis, the Group Chief Executive, has said, 'we want to change the sales force from hunters to farmers'.

Adapted from Merrell (1998)

The processes by which new laws are developed provide opportunities for industry to put forward its views. These are normally heard formally through committee procedures and informally through lobbying practices. In this sense, legislation can be influenced and is to some extent controllable. However, the vast majority of legislation is in place and has to be complied with. The legislation regarding the promotion of products and services within a product class must always be considered

CASE ILLUSTRATION

European Union initiatives

A discussion paper issued by the European Commission debated the difficulties associated with cross-border trade and suggested that standardised EU promotional campaigns could go a long way to remedying trade restrictions.

Summers (1996) reports that pan-European TV advertising campaigns are challenged by a series of rules and regulations across a number of individual member states. For products targeted at children, advertising which is aimed at children under 10 is not allowed in Sweden. In Greece, TV toy advertising between 7:00 a.m. and 10:00 p.m. is banned; some countries require ads for sweets to carry a toothbrush symbol and others have rules intended to curb advertisers from encouraging children to exercise 'pester power'. Alcohol, tobacco, pharmaceuticals and financial services are also subject to similarly diverse regulations and rules about how much of the human body can be revealed, whether prices can be discounted for special offers, and the use of free gifts in sales promotions.

Sponsorship in the Netherlands was seen as having particularly restrictive curbs on event sponsorship, while the UK and Denmark were seen to impose strict rules on broadcasting.

> *In Germany, cash discounts to consumers are limited to 3 per cent and the advertising of special offers is also restricted. Austria, Belgium and Italy also have strict regimes. In contrast, in Scandinavia, where advertising law is more closely linked to consumer protection rather than unfair competition considerations, price advertising is encouraged – Swedish law, for example, promotes comparative price advertising between traders.*

It is suggested that savings could be made from economies of scale by standardising campaigns, as far as cultural differences allow. At the moment, under the Treaty of Rome, once a company providing services has satisfied the requirements of its own national law, no other EU state is supposed to impose further restrictions unless certain specific conditions are met.

Adapted from Summers (1996)

as a part of the planning process. Legislation changes frequently and it is important that advertisers are up-to-date and aware of current legislative requirements. These requirements not only include advertising but also packaging, sales promotions, logo and brand name issues.

The legislative framework is supplemented by the activities of the institute or trade association to which an advertiser might belong and the voluntary codes of practice that the Independent Television Commission (ITC) and the Committee of Advertising Practice (CAP) enforce as custodians of the British Code of Advertising Practice (Smith, 1993). Adherence to these guidelines is normally enforced through the threat of blacklisting and ejection from the relevant professional body. The need for members to remain within these groups can be strong. This is because membership is often regarded as a sign of credibility, which in turn is a factor that can determine whether they will continue to attract business.

Force for corporate responsibility

A fast-growing and important area of interest is the level of responsibility organisations are prepared to accept for their role in the systems in which they operate. The breadth of vision that organisations have with regard to their system responsibilities has expanded considerably over the past decade. Some would argue that there are two main driving forces behind this new vision. The first is the impact that an increased awareness and understanding of how production and consumption of resources impact upon the environment and how an organisation contributes to the cycle. The second is the recognition and acceptance that organisations need to cooperate and collaborate with other organisations, principally in their performance networks, if they are to have any strategic advantage.

One of the responses to this new vision can be seen in the proliferation of Total Quality Management programmes. These are being introduced by organisations to improve efficiency, reduce costs and increase levels of customer satisfaction. Some organisations will only collaborate with others if it can be displayed that they have an acceptable standard of quality procedures, namely a kite mark or British Standard.

Another outcome of the new vision has been the awareness and interest associated with the development of business ethics and codes of conduct. Business ethics are essentially concerned with the morality associated with the decisions that an organisation and its members make and how these decisions, both right and wrong and good and bad, affect society or particular stakeholder groups. This has been discussed at length in Chapter 3.

Issues concerning, for example, the Maxwell affair, BCCI, the Baring's Bank fraud, Matrix-Churchill, MPs' cash for questions issues and the Polly Peck financial affair all make headline news. But there are a vast number of other matters, concerning golden handshakes, insider dealing, making promises about delivery in the full knowledge that it will not be met, whistle blowing and salespersons using pressurised or misleading methods of selling, that occur frequently and which receive little public attention. One exception to this last point concerns the problems resulting from the misselling of pensions by a number of organisations in the financial services sector in the early 1990s.

Indeed, much of the work of marketing communications, and public relations in particular, is to present the organisation as a morally correct and socially responsible organisation. This is achieved by informing stakeholders of its various public good works, such as charitable donations and sponsorships, and its position on particular social issues. All of these activities or cues provide visibility so that others perceive it as an acceptable network member, one from whom they can comfortably buy goods and with whom they can sustain a viable business relationship.

Some target audiences are aware of organisations who practise good or bad business ethics, or at least, in their perception, are distinguished one way or another. Managers should not underestimate the potential for resistance or opposition by their customers, say through refusing to buy their products or use their services (Thompson, 1990). Readers are advised to refer to Chapter 3 for a deeper consideration of these and other related issues.

Summary

Organisations operate in environmental contexts that are largely controllable. Indeed, it is management's responsibility to ensure that the organisation influences its environments in order that the organisation can achieve its objectives. There are, however, areas where management has little, if any, influence. Management's task is to be aware of the nature, speed and direction of the changes that are occurring in these uncontrollable areas and to shape corporate, unit and functional strategies accordingly.

This wider environmental context is maintained by a number of forces. These forces are derived from a number of principal sources; however, many changes stem from government initiatives. Societal and cultural developments, economic conditions, technological surges and legislative frameworks continually shape the nature of the context within which organisations operate. In turn, the marketing communications undertaken by organisations need to accommodate and reflect these changes, not only in terms of the content but also the direction and speed with which they are transmitted.

Review questions

1. Identify the main forces that maintain the environmental context and which affect organisations.
2. What is the prime characteristic common to all of these forces?
3. Using an organisation with which you are familiar, identify the various forces acting upon it. How strong is each force and is the strength likely to change?
4. Suggest ways in which attitudes towards each of the following might have changed over the past thirty or forty years: cars, aftershave, margarine, package holidays, pollution and waste disposal, shopping, and criminals.
5. How have technological forces impacted upon the promotional activities of grocery retailers?
6. Write a brief report outlining some of the legislative forces that can affect particular organisations. How can marketing communications be used in this context?
7. Discuss the view that buyers are not interested in marketing communications that present an organisation and/or its products honestly and truthfully.
8. Identify three seasonal forces that are driven by natural forces and three that are driven by artificial or cultural criteria.
9. As part of the review team at an organisation of your choice, prepare a performance network map.
10. Between which of the stakeholders at IBM should marketing communications be concentrated?

References

Assael, H. and Poltrack, D.F. (1991) Using single source data to select TV programmes based on purchasing behaviour. *Journal of Advertising Research* (August/September), 9–17.

Bartos, R. (1983) Women in advertising. *International Journal of Advertising*, **2**, 33–45.

Calver, S., Vierich, W. and Phillips, J. (1993) Leisure in later life. *International Journal of Contemporary Hospitality Management*, **5**(1), 4–9.

Dibb, S. and Simpkin, L. (1991) Targeting, segments and positioning. *International Journal of Retail and Distribution Management*, **19**(3), 4–10.

McMurdo, M.W. (1993) Chasing butterflies. *Marketing Week*, 21 May, pp. 28–31.

Merrell, C. (1998) Pru has a new sales policy. *The Times*, 28 February, p. 64

Rawsthorn, A. (1993) A little luxury goes a longer way. *Financial Times*, 18 November, p. 12.

Rogers, D. (1998) Why Kellogg has crossed the thin line. *Marketing*, 5 March, pp. 12–13.

Shergill, S. (1993) The changing US media and marketing environment: implications for media advertising and expenditures in the 1990s. *International Journal of Advertising*, **12**, 95–115.

Smith, P.R. (1993) *Marketing Communications: An Integrated Approach*, London: Kogan Page.

Summers D. (1996) Management: campaigns sans frontières: Brussels would like to remove obstacles to cross-border advertising. *Financial Times*, 31 May, p. 10.

Thompson, J.L. (1990) *Strategic Management: Awareness and Change*. London: Chapman & Hall.

Marketing research

Richard Christy

In order to facilitate the development and implementation of effective marketing communications it is imperative that valid, up-to-date market and audience information is gathered and analysed. There are a huge variety of sources of secondary information and a number of methods and techniques associated with the collection of primary data. Each has advantages and disadvantages which may make them more or less suitable for particular research needs.

AIMS AND OBJECTIVES

The aim of this chapter is to consider the techniques and methods of marketing research and consider their contribution to marketing communications programmes.

The objectives of this chapter are:

1. To consider the role and contribution of marketing research.
2. To determine the types of data that can be collected and analysed.
3. To examine the principal techniques of data collection.
4. To highlight the variety of sources of information available to organisations.
5. To provide guidance concerning the relative costs associated with types of research exercises.
6. To provide an insight into the European marketing research industry.

Introduction

This chapter provides a brief review of the aims and methods of marketing research, as an important part of the marketing communications process. The role of marketing research in marketing management in general is often described as that of providing information to aid decision-making (e.g. Crimp and Wright, 1995). This chapter looks at the methods and techniques in marketing research that can support analysis and decisions to do with the creation and management of marketing communications. Later chapters in the book review the application of these techniques in planning and implementing marketing communications.

The scope of marketing research is broader than that of market research: while market research is concerned with the description and analysis of markets, marketing research may also include research into other aspects of the external environment of interest to marketing managers. The UK's Market Research Society's Code of Conduct defines research to include:

> *... the collection and analysis of data from a sample of individuals or organisations relating to their characteristics, behaviour, attitudes, opinions or possessions. It includes all forms of marketing and social research such as consumer and industrial surveys, psychological investigations, observational and panel studies"*
>
> (Market Research Society, 1997, p 50)

Baker (1991) describes the following categories of marketing research:

- Market research (market size and structure, growth trends etc.)
- Sales research (i.e. aiming to analyse and understand sales performance)
- Product research
- Advertising research
- Business economics (e.g. to do with the industry as a whole)
- Export marketing research
- Motivation research (often qualitative, rather than quantitative, data)
- Competition research

Using this broader definition, marketing research will have an important role to play at each stage of the marketing communications planning framework (MCPF) developed in this book (Chapter 30). In carrying out an initial context analysis, for example, the scope of the research is necessarily very wide, covering customers and other performance channel members, together with the rest of the external environment relevant to the organisation in question. Throughout the rest of the MCPF, information requirements are likely to cover the actual buying behaviour of customers and potential customers in the target markets, together with such aspects as:

- their present levels of awareness and understanding of the product field of interest and of the various brands within it
- the motivations that may influence their purchasing behaviour
- their awareness of and attitudes towards the organisation itself
- their attitudes towards and expectations of the organisation's brands and those of the competition

- their levels of satisfaction with the organisation's brands and/or service and with those of the competition (which may include the contribution made by individual elements of the marketing mix to the aggregate satisfaction measured)
- their present consumption of potential advertising media
- their future intentions concerning purchases in the product field in question

The organisation may also require similar information concerning members or potential members of the distribution channel. Marketing channel members often have key roles to play in the delivery of some of the added-value parts of a marketing offering (customisation, after-sales service etc.) and so may well be important targets of the communications process.

Types of marketing research

Marketing research activities can be classified in a number of ways. Kinnear and Taylor (1987), for example, identify the categories of *exploratory*, *conclusive* and *performance-monitoring* research. In the field of marketing communications research, exploratory research might include research supporting the initial context analysis, leading to the formulation and test of specific hypotheses about the market (examples of conclusive research), while performance-monitoring research would describe the range of activities designed to track and evaluate the effectiveness of the communications programme. By contrast, Crimp and Wright (1995) distinguish between:

- Descriptive research, which might provide information on, say, the target audience of a particular campaign
- Diagnostic research, which might help to analyse the effectiveness of an advertising campaign
- Predictive research, which is to do with identifying new opportunities in the market-place and forecasting the likely impact of marketing decisions

Marketing research may also be divided into *quantitative* and *qualitative* research, although any individual programme of research may integrate both (individual questionnaires often seek to collect both quantitative and qualitative information). *Quantitative* research, as its name implies, seeks to provide a quantified expression of the research findings in the area of interest and will characteristically collect and analyse data from representative surveys of the part of the market in question. Quantitative research may be used, for example, to assess the proportion of a target market that shops at a particular type of retail outlet. By contrast, *qualitative* research does not aim to provide high degrees of precision in numerical estimates. Qualitative researchers more normally work at the individual or small group level and aim to explore in greater depth the reasons *why* consumers think, feel or behave in particular ways. This type of research may be used, for example, to understand more about the meaning that a particular brand image may hold for a particular type of customer.

The various activities of marketing research can also be considered as a logical *sequence of actions* (or process) designed to identify and meet particular research objectives as cost-effectively as possible. Any such sequence must start by identifying and defining the marketing problem or decision which causes the organisation to be thinking of initiating a programme of research. Chisnall (1997), for example, describes the five sequential stages of marketing research:

- The research brief, which expresses the problem to be solved by the research
- The research proposal, which responds to the brief by defining the research objectives as clearly as possible and setting out an approach to meet those objectives
- Data collection
- Data analysis and evaluation
- Preparation and presentation of the research report

Within a simplified structure like this, there will in practice be many iterative loops: early exploratory research, for example, may well cause the research objectives to be restated in the light of the new knowledge, which may in turn modify the subsequent data collection proposals. Similarly, the piloting of the proposed data collection approach on a small number of individuals from the target market may reveal difficulties that have to be overcome before proceeding with the main survey. An important aim of this methodical and sequential approach is to ensure that all marketing research activities are matched as closely as possible to the actual marketing decisions that they are intended to support. The process also seeks to maximise value for money by defining carefully what needs to be discovered to meet the research objectives and therefore how it can best be achieved. In today's highly competitive markets, there is no merit in a commercial organisation collecting data for its own sake: like most other things in business, expenditure on marketing research has to support commercial objectives as efficiently as possible.

Primary and secondary data

In seeking maximum value for money in marketing research, an important distinction must be drawn between *primary* and *secondary* data:

- *Primary data* is collected for the first time to meet the specific needs of a particular organisation.
- *Secondary data*, by contrast, exists already, having been collected for some general purpose, and is either available to or readily obtainable by the organisation.

Primary data is relatively expensive (and sometimes time-consuming) to obtain, but can be collected to meet a specific need. Secondary data is often readily available at relatively low cost (and sometimes at no extra cost) and can provide valuable background information. Cost-effective marketing research, then, should aim to review any available secondary data early in the project, in order to:

- make maximum use of available information
- avoid expensive primary replication of that which is already known
- ensure that money spent on any primary research is directed as effectively as possible

Secondary data sources fall into two main categories: internal and external. *Internal* sources are found within the organisation itself, but are not always identified as potential sources of marketing information. Internal data sources include sales records, customer databases and past marketing research reports. Other potential sources may include operating records (e.g. transportation, installation or maintenance records) and financial data, such as sales revenue analyses and records of purchases from suppliers. In the field of corporate communications, analyses of past communication strategies adopted by the organisation may be an important resource. Internal secondary data sources may be anecdotal and oral; for example, the collective experience of the organisation's sales force. Increasingly today, organisations are making use of information technology to organise internal and external sources of data into readily accessible marketing information systems.

Internal sources of secondary data can offer valuable insights into the structure of the customer base served by the organisation, but as Crimp and Wright (1995) point out, internal sources alone may not reveal the actual size of individual customers, the extent to which customers also buy from competitors or the true nature of the potential market. Internal secondary data from different sources may also be difficult to reconcile, having been collected at different times for different purposes, with differing limitations. It is nonetheless clear that any organisation should seek to make maximum use of internal sources of potentially relevant data before spending money on new data.

External sources of secondary data are normally divided into those collected and published by government organisations and those published by other sources. Government-originated sources of secondary data cover a very wide range of topics; since April 1996, the Office for National Statistics (ONS) has been responsible for most of the government economic and social statistics in the UK. The ONS was formed from a merger of the Central Statistical Office and the Office of Population Censuses and Surveys, with a brief to 'provide Parliament, government and the wider community with the statistical information, analysis and advice needed to improve decision-making, stimulate research and inform debate' (source: ONS Web site: http://www.statsbase.gov.uk/. Information from the ONS covers such areas as population, family expenditure, social surveys and business statistics; the booklet *A Brief Guide to Sources* is available free from the ONS library. The Department of Trade and Industry also provides a list of information sources for business at its web site: http://www.dti.gov.uk/).

In addition to government-originated sources, relevant secondary data may also be obtained from a wealth of other sources, either in hard copy form or from on-line databases, which can be categorised as follows:

- Press compilation services, both general and specialist in scope
- Abstracting services covering professional and academic publications
- Market and other analyses researched and published for sale by specialist firms, such as Mintel or Euromonitor
- Research and other publications from banks, firms of accountants and other professional service providers
- Compilations of specialist data published by professional institutes or trade associations, often available at relatively low cost or free
- The various types of syndicated marketing research data (see below), collected and analysed by specialist firms and made available to subscribers to the service in question

One increasingly significant development in the availability of secondary data is the growth of information sources on the Internet. At the time of writing, the Internet appears to have achieved critical mass, with more than one million sites open, growing numbers of regular users and major investments by commercial and other organisations in the development of interesting, easy-to-use and up-to-date information sites. The search for secondary data on the Internet is aided by the availability of the various 'search engines', which can quickly provide (sometimes huge) lists of sites containing particular keywords and hot-key links, which direct the reader to other sites for further details. The more advanced sites on the Internet will include internal search engines, allowing fast location of the information needed within a large and complex structure, and sometimes also personalisation possibilities, so that frequent 'visitors' to the site can register their topics of particular interest for future reference. Clearly, a resource of this size and global scope has enormous potential for marketing research, which is evolving from one week to the next and is only really starting to be appreciated by the industry. At present, the content of the Internet strongly reflects its American (and English language) origins, but information from other regions of the world is growing fast.

The availability and suitability of secondary data may vary from one research topic to another. Information of this type is collected for general purposes and may not be available in exactly the format and with exactly the coverage required to suit the research need. In some cases, the information may not be acceptably up-to-date, especially in the case of detailed quantitative data. In many cases, the researcher will know little about the process through which data was collected, analysed and interpreted. Care should be taken in making use of such findings, especially concerning forecasts; wherever possible, a range of views from reputable and reliable sources should be reviewed.

Syndicated research services

Many of the general problems with secondary sources are much less likely to apply to the important category of syndicated marketing information sources, which are produced with the explicit aim of meeting the needs of those who subscribe to the services. Users of these services build up a valuable body of data over time, and will have plenty of experience of the value of the data in practice. Baker (1991) distinguishes several types of syndicated marketing research service, which fall into two main groups:

- The various types of *trade research*, including retail and wholesale audits, invoice analysis, distribution checks, price checks and feature checks. In developing a marketing communications programme, this type of data will help the planner to understand how the product and its competitors are moving through the various channels of distribution.
- A number of different types of consumer *panel research*, in which a sample of individuals or households from a defined market agree to record certain aspects of their behaviour over time, allowing data to be collected and analysed from the same panel at frequent intervals over time. Panel surveys of purchase behaviour ('consumer panels') include diary surveys and home audits, which help the planner to understand and analyse trends in product purchase and usage by consumers. Panel research can also be defined to include some of the *audience research* services established to measure the consumption of broadcast and other media (see below).

Table 9.1 Revenues earned by AMSO members (1996)

Audits and panels	£70m
Advertising/brand tracking	£48m
Customer satisfaction	£36m
Media (e.g. audience research)	£22m

Source: AMSO Report (1997).

Many of the larger marketing research companies run general or specialised consumer panels (see the *Market Research Society Yearbook* for a description of the services of this nature provided by MRS member organisations). Consumer panel and retail audit information is relatively expensive, but also an essential component of marketing management for major consumer goods companies. To give an impression of this, the 1997 AMSO report provides a breakdown of the revenues earned in 1996 by AMSO members – broadly, the largest UK Marketing Research companies – from the various types of continuous research, including advertising tracking studies (see Chapter 17), as shown in Table 9.1. The value, for example, of detailed information on how brands in a particular product field are moving through different types of retail outlet (retail audits) or being bought by different types of consumer (consumer panels) in planning, monitoring and evaluating marketing communications strategy is obvious, particularly since the longitudinal nature of this information allows trends to be monitored over time.

Also well-established as a source of syndicated marketing research information is the Target Group Index (TGI) produced by BMRB, one of the largest marketing research organisations in the UK. The TGI is based on a sample each year of 25,000 adults aged 15+ in Great Britain, using self-completion postal questionnaires (see below). Types of information collected include usage by respondents of over 4,000 brands in more than 500 product fields, together with readership of around 200 publications, TV viewing, attitudes and demographic characteristics of the respondents. This allows users of the service to match product usage with both media consumption and a range of respondent details, including attitudes.

As major information products of this nature continue to grow in power, coverage and specialisation, one effect is to improve the extent to which many marketing questions can be answered by marketing research information from standardised sources, rather than *ad hoc* surveys. Klaus Hehl, in his keynote speech to the 1997 ESOMAR conference, noted that the marketing research industry, like the fashion industry, should offer two types of service: off-the-peg standard solutions for standard problems, with production costs and prices as low as possible; and tailor-made solutions for the specific problems of individual clients. As marketing research becomes increasingly international in character, researchers should seek to standardise definitions and classifications in their off-the-peg products, in order to facilitate comparability and increase the value of this information (Source: ESOMAR Web site, accessed 7 January 1998).

Audience research

Audience research services are likely to be a very important source of secondary information in planning a marketing communications programme, since they provide a detailed analysis of the composition of the expected audience for the main advertising media. By using this information to select and schedule the media mix to be used in the campaign, the planner can achieve the desired coverage and weight of exposure as efficiently as possible. Each of the main media types offers some form of audience measurement, but the principal sources of information are to do with TV, press and radio advertising.

Television audience research in the UK is the responsibility of BARB: the Broadcasters' Audience Research Board. BARB is jointly owned by the ITV Association and the BBC, with additional representation from each of the main subscriber groups: the Institute of Practitioners in Advertising, Channel 4 and BSkyB (representing satellite broadcasters). Separate aspects of the research work are currently carried out by AGB and RSMB Television Research Ltd, under contract to BARB. Audience measurement is based upon a panel of UK homes; a large continuous survey is carried out nationally to determine patterns of television usage and to ensure that this panel is fully representative (BARB, undated).

The audience measurement panel comprises 4435 homes: viewing behaviour is recorded and downloaded automatically to a central computer by set-top meters, modems and telephone lines. Members of the households taking part press buttons on the meter to indicate when they enter and leave the room containing the television, allowing the system to keep a continuous record of who exactly is viewing. The system can take account of multiple TV sets in one home and is also able to record 'time-shifted' viewing from video recorders. The information from the panel is compiled and analysed to produce regular reports for users; BARB also issues a weekly press release showing viewing hours per channel and the audience figures achieved by the main programmes.

In addition to measuring viewership of TV programmes, BARB also provides reports to subscribing broadcasters on audience appreciation of these programmes. Respondents are asked to rate programmes viewed on a scale from 0 to 10, allowing an Appreciation Index to be produced from the sample. Extra *ad hoc* questions may also be asked, for example at the end of a series, or about particular presenters.

Press readership research in the UK is provided by the National Readership Survey (NRS). The NRS aims to provide high-quality readership research information for publishers and buyers of advertising space: both of these interests are represented on the Board of NRS Ltd. The NRS is currently carried out under contract by Research Services Ltd and is based upon a multi-stage probability sample (see below) of some 38,000 adults (aged 15+) carried out continuously over twelve months. The survey data are collected by Computer-Assisted Personal Interviewing: interviewers input responses directly to laptop computers and information is sent to a central computer by modem for processing, allowing results to be reported rapidly.

The NRS covers some 245 newspaper and magazine titles and aims to measure readership and to be able to match this information to a wide range of respondent details. NRS information is potentially able to be analysed in terms of the categories shown in Table 9.2. NRS subscribers receive regular standard reports and may also choose to buy further specialised reports or to commission specialised analyses of the data.

Further notable sources of information concerning the press media in the UK include British Rate and Data (BRAD), a publication listing the range of advertising media facilities, including newspapers and magazines and giving information on advertising rates and circulation figures. Circulation figures for many press publications are audited and published twice a year by the Audit Bureau of Circulations

Table 9.2 Demographic data collected by NRS (NRS Ltd Web site)

Demographics	Lifestyle data
Age; sex; social class	Business air travel
Area	Holiday-taking
Highest educational qualification obtained	Drinking
Terminal education age	Leisure (interests, activities)
Employment status	Languages spoken
Occupation and occupational status	Possession of consumer durables
Geodemographics and lifestyle groups	Motoring
Shopping activity	Financial activities
Household composition	Future expectations
Children in household	Mail order shopping
Household structure/tenure	
Income	
Marital status	
Geodemographics	

(ABC), providing potential advertisers with an objective source of information for the publications concerned.

Radio audience research in the UK has been the responsibility since 1992 of Radio Joint Audience Research (RAJAR), which measures and analyses audiences for both independent and BBC stations. RAJAR produces quarterly reports analysing radio audiences. The survey is currently carried out by Research Services Ltd and is based upon diary surveys of listening behaviour from a sample of around 47,500 adults for national radio stations in the UK and smaller samples for local radio.

Omnibus surveys

Although it is not strictly speaking a type of secondary data, it is also worth mentioning the category of *omnibus survey services*, which are often used alongside sources of secondary data in the exploratory phases of marketing research. Omnibus surveys can provide a means of obtaining answers to a series of simple initial questions from a defined audience at relatively low cost. A marketing research firm conducting an omnibus survey will construct a sample from a defined market and seek to persuade marketing companies to contribute groups of questions to a composite questionnaire. The research company will then carry out the survey and feed back the results of individual groups of questions to the client organisations.

Overall, then, the effective use of secondary data can save both time and money for the organisation. With the increasingly effective use of information technology in collecting, analysing, storing and making available a diverse range of data, secondary sources of information can be expected to become even more important in the research process as a whole.

Methods and techniques

As noted above, a key consequence of the exploratory research will be the ability to define what new information (i.e. primary data) has to be collected to meet the research objectives. This can be expressed as a subsidiary primary research objective, which will specify what information is to be discovered and from whom (the survey population or populations, who will be the source of the information). Primary data may be gathered by means of observation, experimentation or questioning. In research supporting the development of a corporate marketing communications programme, all three methods may play a part: observation techniques may be used to understand the behaviour of consumers in buying goods in a supermarket, for example, or in recording their use of TV channels, while experimentation may be used to test consumer responses to carefully controlled variations in the product's marketing mix (e.g. product formulation, pack size, advertising weight or price). This section provides a summary review of the types of technique that may be used to gather the information needed.

In designing a piece of marketing research, Crimp and Wright (1995) suggest that two key types of question have to be answered: how is the data to be collected and how is the sample to be designed? Provided that the research objectives have been correctly specified, the quality and value of the end result will depend to a large extent on the way in which these two questions are answered. In quantitative research, the aim – within the available budget for the survey – is to achieve both maximum reliability (to do with things like the precision and repeatability of the result) and validity (the extent to which the research does actually measure or illuminate the things of interest to the project). With the smaller samples normally associated with qualitative research (see below), reliability may not be attainable to the same degree, but the highest possible degree of validity is still essential.

Probability and purposive sampling

Turning firstly to the question of sampling design, this brief review does not permit a discussion in any depth of the issues to be considered in making sampling decisions: readers are referred to more specialised texts for further detail (see, for instance, Collins (1986)).

A sample aims to provide a representation in miniature of the population from which it is drawn, allowing researchers to investigate the characteristics of the whole population without the need to incur the cost and time penalty of measuring every individual in it. The information provided in the National Readership Survey (see above) about the number and types of reader of various press publications is based upon analysis of a sample of 38,000 adults, rather than a census of every adult in the UK, which would be impossibly expensive and time-consuming for these purposes. By administering a sample which is both large and well-designed, however, the NRS aims to provide its subscribers with a reliable representation of the readership of the publications surveyed over the UK population as a whole.

In the nature of sampling, it is never possible to be absolutely certain that values derived from samples are the same as the equivalent values for the population as a whole, but a well-designed and managed sample will allow the researcher to make representative estimates about the population and in some cases to make specific statements about the likely precision of the estimates.

Sampling decisions concern questions such as the size and structure of the sample to be taken and the way in which the sample is to be selected. Other things being equal, larger samples will generally provide more reliable estimates of population characteristics than smaller samples, but the way in which the sample is selected may be far more important than the number of individuals in it. A sample whose selection method involves some form of bias (systematic error) will contain a risk to validity whether the sample size is large or small. The main choice to be made in sample selection method is between an approach making use of *probability* sampling and one making use of *purposive* sampling. Probability samples are based upon random selection, in which each individual in the population has a known and non-zero chance of being selected. By contrast, the individuals in a purposive sample are selected on the basis of human judgement, often in response to pre-set criteria.

To carry out a probability sample, it is necessary to be able to identify every member of the population being sampled on a reliable and accessible list, or *sampling frame*. In some cases, useful sampling frames are readily available: at a national level in the UK, lists such as the Register of Electors or the Postcode Address File are often used in this way, for example, and more specialised frames may be available to support sampling needs at a more detailed level. Sampling frames may be critical in designing the research method: the non-availability of a suitable sampling frame may be a reason for deciding to use a purposive, rather than a probability-based, sampling design.

Probability samples are held to be theoretically preferable because they allow quantitative statements to be made about the likely closeness of the sampling estimates to the true population values. However, probability sampling procedures can be complicated, relatively time-consuming and expensive to execute in practice in marketing research, and purposive or 'quota' samples are often used in preference. As Crimp and Wright (1995) point out, the risks of bias inherent in purposive sampling can in many cases be contained to an acceptable level by careful management of the sampling design and process, despite the theoretical disadvantages.

Types of data collection method

The other main consideration in research design is the method to be used to collect data from those being surveyed. The main choice to be made is between observation, experimentation and questioning. Observational techniques include personal observation (e.g. of consumers at the point of purchase), diary methods to record the type of behaviour of interest (as used in some consumer panels, for example, although electronic methods are now widely used to streamline the process), instrumental techniques (for example the use of psychogalvanometers in laboratory research to measure emotional response to proposed marketing images) and electronic techniques, such as bar-code-based systems used in retail audits. Experimentation in marketing research might take the form of a test market, to examine the effect of introducing a particular marketing programme into a carefully selected test area and comparing it with a control area, in which no such intervention takes place. Observational and experimentation techniques generally offer relatively high objectivity, in their own terms, but will often not be capable of providing the level of understanding needed, in which case the range of questioning methodologies needs to be considered.

In planning a survey, researchers need to choose what mix of face-to-face interviews, telephone interviews and postal (or other self-completion) questionnaires will best meet the needs of the survey. As will be discussed below, each method has its own strengths and weaknesses, which will make it more or less suitable for individual situations. It is the task of the researcher to choose methods that will meet the research

Table 9.3 Data collection techniques of AMSO members

Personal interview	43.1%
Telephone interview	18.3%
Hall test	11.2%
Group discussion (e.g. focus group)	9.9%
Self-completion/postal	8.0%
Depth interviews	4.0%
Street interviews	2.6%
Mystery shopping	2.2%

objectives as cost-effectively as possible. This usually involves the consideration of three important features of the survey: the characteristics of the survey population (Are they expert in the topic to be surveyed? Are they mainly located within one area or spread across a wide area?); the demands of the material to be covered in the survey (Will there be a need to ask many open-ended questions? Are visual materials, such as showcards involved?); and the budget (in terms of both money and time-scales).

In the UK, an analysis of the data collection activities of members of the Association of Market Survey Organisations in 1996 produced the breakdown of methods by value shown in Table 9.3 (AMSO, 1997). (NB: Hall tests aim to assess customer reaction to new products or product formulations in controlled conditions, such as in a rented hall, and are not considered in this review. Depth interviews and group discussions are described below as part of the consideration of qualitative research techniques. Mystery shopping techniques involve sending a researcher anonymously to a retail outlet or other customer interface and recording the details of the interaction.)

One important aspect of the enquiry that may have a major impact on the choice of data collection method is the degree of structure that can be achieved in the questionnaire. A highly structured questionnaire will contain a series of formally worded questions to which a limited range of answers can be expected, while semi-structured or unstructured questionnaires rely far more on the skill of the interviewer to guide the progress of the conversation, probing where necessary to obtain further detail. Questionnaires may contain a mixture of 'closed' and 'open-ended' questions: closed questions specify the range of answers, allowing the interviewee to choose the most appropriate response from the selection offered. By contrast, open-ended questions allow the interviewee complete freedom of response; answers may be recorded verbatim by the interviewer or 'coded' into predetermined categories on the spot or later. The mix of closed and open questions will depend upon the nature of the subject being researched and also on the researcher's familiarity with the range of likely responses.

However the questionnaire is to be administered, care will need to be taken by the researcher in designing the questionnaire and in constructing the individual questions. Aspects of questionnaire design that must be considered include the ease with which the data collected can be tabulated and analysed to meet the research objectives, the order in which topics are dealt with in the questionnaire and the extent to which closed questions can be used in addressing each topic. Effective question wording demands a great deal of experience if the risk of unintentional bias is to be minimised. Baker (1991) summarises the ground rules for phrasing questions that are likely to be understood by respondents:

- Use everyday language.
- Use simple words rather than complex ones.
- Use simple sentences rather than complex ones.
- Keep the questions short and to the point.
- Avoid double-barrelled questions.
- Avoid double negatives.

Questions that by their wording seem to lead the respondent towards a particular answer are also to be avoided, but there are further risks of response bias to be considered that may have little to do with the way the questions are worded. Respondents may, for example, give answers that are other than 'true' because they are genuinely mistaken in their memories, or because they do not wish to give offence to the interviewer or the sponsor of the survey, or because they are embarrassed by the question, or because they wish to give an answer that they believe will reflect better on them in terms of social standing or respectability.

Piloting of draft questionnaires among a small sample of the target population helps to reveal unexpected difficulties in administering the questionnaire and may also help to ensure that any closed questions have been specified broadly enough to capture the actual range of variation in the target population.

The ability to handle relatively high proportions of open questions or unstructured enquiries is one of the important variables to be considered in choosing among the various questioning methods, as will now be discussed.

Face-to-face interviews

Face-to-face personal interviews may range from the highly structured questionnaire to the unstructured; the following paragraphs consider one-to-one interviews only, while group discussion techniques are included in the review of qualitative research techniques below. Personal interviews have always been a leading means of data collection in European marketing research: they may take place in the home, at the place of work or in public places (in the street, for example or at airports or railway stations). More recently, computer-assisted personal interviewing (CAPI) has been introduced to streamline the process of data collection, questionnaire management and information processing in personal interviews: the National Readership Survey, described under 'Audience research' above, provides one example of this. As will be seen, the personal interviewing technique is very flexible and offers many practical advantages, but the average cost per interview is relatively high, since the technique is necessarily labour-intensive and may also involve significant travelling time and expense.

In many cases, however, the strengths of the face-to-face interview technique may justify the expenditure involved (and may sometimes be the only viable approach for the data collection task in hand). With a trained and experienced interviewer, relatively good rates of agreement to participate and interview completion can be achieved. People in the UK seem to feel more comfortable with the face-to-face contact in a personal interview than with the less personal atmosphere of a telephone interview, although gradually increasing telephone usage may narrow this gap in future. For semi-structured or unstructured enquiries in both consumer and industrial marketing research, the strong interactive potential of the face-to-face interview may well be essential, as will the ability of the interviewer to probe and to guide the progress of the interview on the basis of visual as well as spoken cues.

In more structured questionnaires, open questions can be handled satisfactorily, with answers either recorded verbatim for later coding or coded on the spot. Supporting material, such as images from an advertising campaign being researched, can be used where helpful, broadening the range of questions that can be handled. The presence of an interviewer also reduces the risk that respondents will provide potentially misleading answers to questions that they do not understand or which do not apply to them. It is also possible to be sure about exactly who is answering the questions, which may not be so in other techniques. If a purposive sampling design is being used, the interviewer may also have a key role in selecting the respondents to fill the predetermined quotas.

Telephone interviews

In telephone interviews, a questionnaire is administered by an interviewer to the sample by telephone, either at home or at the place of work. Interviews conducted by telephone have become much more important in recent years with growth of CATI – computer-assisted telephone interviewing, in which interviewers at a central location can work through a screen-driven questionnaire, inputting responses directly via the keyboard. Although initial set up costs may make CATI less suitable for very small samples, the advantages of this approach are to do with speed (i.e. of covering the sample and of processing and analysing the responses), cost (although the calls cost money, no travel costs are involved and more efficient use may be made of the interviewers' time) and quality control (for suitable questionnaires, computer control helps to ensure that valid responses are entered and that correct progress is made through the questionnaire, thus minimising these potential sources of interviewer error). Even without computer assistance, telephone interviewing can also offer the advantage of convenience and relative ease of access, particularly in the context of industrial marketing research, and the ability to interview at precise times.

Telephone interviewing is, however, subject to a number of general limitations, which may restrict its value for some types of research. A key difficulty is that the technique involves higher refusal rates than for face-to-face interviewing, causing concern about the bias that will be introduced if those who refuse to take part are in some important way different from those who consent. The growth of public feeling against the dubious practice of so-called 'sugging' – selling under the guise of conducting research – in some telephone contacts has tended to worsen this problem of refusal. Similarly, the increasing use of ex-directory numbers and telephone answering equipment may also make it less easy to contact respondents in future. Although the telephone can be a useful way to contact potential business respondents, researchers may also encounter the problem of 'over-surveying' if their target decision-maker is frequently contacted with requests to take part in research questionnaires.

Bias of a different type may result from the fact that telephone penetration is very high but nonetheless incomplete in the UK; samples of telephoned households may under-represent, for example, social classes D and E in particular (although there may also be age and regional effects), unless measures are taken to allow for the uneven ownership in the survey.

The telephone interview is in some respects less flexible than its face-to-face equivalent: longer questionnaires, and those involving higher proportions of open questions are less suitable for telephone interviews and it is generally less easy to use visual support material, unless it is sent in advance by post, for example. Although a telephone contact has the feature of relative anonymity, which may help respondents to discuss some types of issue, problems may be caused for some respondents by the impersonal nature of the medium, particularly among those who do not make great use of the telephone in their normal lives.

In summary, then, the availability of CATI techniques seems likely to ensure the continued growth of telephone interviewing as a means of data collection, particularly for the more structured, simpler and shorter questionnaires that are relatively easy to conduct by telephone.

Postal questionnaires

Under this heading, the various types of self-completion questionnaires are considered: for the most part, these are mailed to respondents, but questionnaires may also be distributed by other means, such as by salespeople or from retail outlets. More recently, some marketing research firms have been gaining experience in using the Internet to distribute self-completion questionnaires (and to receive the completed responses). The creative potential of this latter innovation is clearly very high, as is the practical convenience in terms of receiving and processing the response: without doubt, the Internet will become a major data collection medium in future. However, although Internet penetration rates are growing fast (particularly among business respondents), the current low levels – and the apparent bias towards young male Internet users – mean that the general value of the technique is for the moment limited.

Postal questionnaires are mailed to those in the sample for self-completion and return. The principal advantage of this method is the low cost of achieving extensive coverage. This benefit, however, has to be set against some of the potential difficulties that have to be managed in conducting an effective postal survey.

Initial response rates may be low, although this will partly depend upon the nature of the subject and the survey population. Low response rates cause practical difficulties, but also potentially more serious concerns about non-response bias: if only, say, 5% of those in the sample respond, how sure can the researcher be that those who respond are representative of the sample as a whole (and hence of the survey population)? Much may depend upon the effectiveness of the covering letter that accompanies the questionnaire in explaining the purpose of the survey and in motivating the potential respondent to take part. Response rates may be improved by offering small gifts or other incentives to take part, and polite reminder letters may also be effective. It is obviously important in designing the survey that these activities should be allowed for in budgeting for the exercise as a whole, in order that a realistic estimate is made of the likely cost per satisfactorily completed response.

In comparing the attractions of this method of data collection with others, it should also be borne in mind that it may take significantly longer to obtain responses through postal questionnaires than through, say, telephone interviews. On the other hand, of course, the postal method does allow respondents to consider their replies or to seek information to answer the questions that may not be immediately available in a telephone or face-to-face context; this can be particularly important in some types of industrial research.

Other potential problems to be managed in postal questionnaires stem from the fact that the questionnaire itself is the main means of contact between the researcher and the sample. By and large, the researcher has to accept whatever comes back, since no probing can take place and opportunities for telephone follow-up may be limited. It is therefore of even greater-than-normal importance that the questions in the questionnaire should be clear, unambiguous and easy to understand. Since the services of a trained and experienced interviewer are by definition not available, it is also very important that the questionnaire as a whole should be easy to follow in terms of question sequence (e.g. 'if you answered "Yes", please go to question 11') and actions required (e.g. 'tick the box next to your preferred answer'; 'Please return the completed questionnaire in the enclosed stamped addressed envelope').

Further consequences of the lack of an interviewer include the inability to be sure about exactly whose views may be represented in the responses given and the inability to control the sequence in which respondents consider questions; if respondents read ahead in the questionnaire, it may bias the responses they give to earlier questions.

Overall, however, a properly designed and managed postal survey can provide a very cost-effective method of data collection, particularly in the case of longer questionnaires and provided that time is not of the essence.

Techniques in qualitative research

Much marketing research seeks to provide a numerical measure of some phenomenon of interest – how many individuals in a target market can recall a particular advertisement, for example, or how many regularly buy a particular product. Very often, however, the marketing manager needs to supplement this type of information with a deeper understanding of why, for example, customers behave in the way revealed by the survey. Qualitative techniques in marketing research have been developed to help to probe more deeply in these areas. Qualitative techniques should not be seen as a substitute for quantitative research, but rather as complementary to the research programme as a whole. The two types of technique are very often interwoven in practice: qualitative research at the exploratory stage may help to define hypotheses for investigation by quantitative methods and may also be used to aid the interpretation of quantitative findings. Indeed, it can be argued in some markets that, while detailed and high-grade quantitative information (e.g. from panels or retail audits) is essential to marketing management, it is the in-depth and non-standard information from qualitative marketing research that may give a company the insights that can form the basis of its competitive edge over its rivals.

Some aspects of consumer behaviour may be inherently difficult to research because customers, even if they are willing to cooperate with researchers, simply do not know or cannot clearly explain why they have acted in a particular way. Some qualitative techniques aim to create a context in which customers can more easily respond directly, while others use indirect techniques of investigation. Unlike some quantitative techniques, there is no possibility of calculating confidence limits around the outputs of qualitative research: the aim of this type of research effort is primarily diagnostic, and the techniques are often by design subjective, subtle and impressionistic, based upon very small samples and relying critically on the interpretive skill and experience of the researcher. For all this, however, qualitative research has established an important place in marketing research as a whole and continues to grow and develop. As competition in most product fields becomes more intense, marketing organisations need the deeper understanding of their customers that only qualitative research can bring in order to be able to target and position their offerings more effectively.

The first group of qualitative techniques can be seen as a variant of one of the main data collection techniques used in quantitative research: the face-to-face interview. So-called *depth interviews* rely upon the skill of the interviewer to prompt the respondent to talk about the subject of interest, with only a general guide as to the topics within that subject to be covered. Depth interviews may take one or two hours, depending upon the nature of the subject and the respondent. This emphasises an important characteristic of this type of research, which is its reliance on significant inputs of time by highly skilled research staff.

Focus groups or group discussions are an extension of the depth interview approach, in which a 'moderator' will lead a discussion on the theme of interest with a small group (usually between five and twelve) selected from the market in question. Focus groups may take place in homes or in conference rooms at places of work; compared with the depth interview they offer the key benefit of helping respondents to express their views or feelings as a result of the interaction between group members. Group members may be stimulated by the direction of the discussion to 'open up' and take part and may also become more willing to talk about a particular subject, once it has been raised by someone else in the group. The moderator will seek to involve all group members and can deliberately use the discussion to check or qualify points made. Focus groups are very commonly used in new product development at the concept testing stage and in marketing communications research to explore new ideas in developing a message strategy and to pre-test proposed communications. In these circumstances, the relative speed with which focus groups can be arranged and reported on is often very important.

Because some of the topics of interest in qualitative research are in their nature difficult for customers to express or embarrassing to discuss, researchers may resort to the range of *'projective' techniques*, borrowed from the world of clinical psychology, which aim to help respondents to reveal their true feelings by projecting them in the context of a hypothetical stimulus offered by the researcher. Some of these tests involve asking respondents to complete a sentence (e.g. 'Owners who give their cats dried pet food are…') or a story, or to fill in the speech balloons in a cartoon. In thematic apperception tests, respondents are asked to describe the events that might have led up to the scene in an illustration: the picture might show, for example, an angry holidaymaker at a hotel reception desk, providing a stimulus for respondents to reveal some of their real concerns about selecting and booking holidays.

Other projective techniques include word-association tests, in which respondents call out the first words that come into their heads as a result of the list of stimulus words to do with the area of interest read out by the researcher, and third person tests, in which respondents are asked to comment on some aspect of the behaviour of a third party and may indirectly provide evidence about their own feelings. Chisnall (1997) discusses the use of this type of technique – and the subsequent methodological criticisms that have been made – in seeking to surface what US consumers in the late 1940s really felt about the then new instant, as opposed to ground, coffee. The method used asked respondents to describe the type of housewife who might have prepared a sample shopping list. Respondents were given one of two lists: the lists were identical except that one included instant coffee and other ground coffee. From the differences in the descriptions provided for each type of list, researchers inferred that instant coffee buyers tended at that time to be seen as less well organised and lazier than ground coffee buyers, which provided obvious cues for marketing development.

Any classification of qualitative marketing research techniques will quickly become incomplete, since the field is highly innovative in its search for new insights from respondents. Researchers may seek to get closer to the real context in which purchase decisions are made by using techniques such as accompanying respondents on shopping trips in order to understand in more depth what happens at the vital moment of choice. Other techniques may invite respondents to draw or make models of their impressions of a particular brand, or to imagine what sort of person the brand 'personality' of a particular product might be. These approaches continue to search for insights, revelation and greater depth of understanding in areas that may be critical for marketing planning.

Clearly, there are significant risks in collecting, analysing and interpreting data in projective and other types of qualitative technique; used with care, experience and skill, however, they can greatly enhance the understanding provided by quantitative research alone and in some cases may provide the only means, however subjective and impressionistic, of researching at all.

Techniques for researching attitudes

Qualitative research and research into attitudes may tend to overlap, but an important set of methods which seek to measure attitudes can be distinguished. The importance of understanding attitudes in designing a programme of corporate marketing communications is discussed elsewhere in the book. Over the years, techniques have been developed that allow respondents to indicate their attitudes and then record the information collected on scales, allowing comparison between respondents or groups of respondents. One of the basic problems in measuring attitudes is summarised by Morton-Williams (1986):

> *...it is difficult to avoid putting words into people's mouths. It is impossible to ask someone whether he agrees or disagrees with a proposition without putting the subject of the proposition into his mind.*

Researchers must be careful to investigate the saliency of the attitudes they are measuring, often by approaching the subject of interest via general and open questions, which allow the respondent to give an indication to the interviewer of the aspects of the question that are most important.

In measuring attitudes, researchers can choose between several different scaling methods, of which the two most important in marketing research are briefly reviewed here.

Likert scales are relatively simple to apply and are regularly used in marketing research. Respondents are shown a series of attitude statements and invited to indicate on a five-point scale whether they strongly agree, agree, neither agree nor disagree, disagree or disagree strongly (three- or seven-point scales may also be used). The researcher can subsequently assign values to each response according to the positive or negative strength of the attitude expressed and sum these scores to produce an overall estimate of favourable or unfavourable disposition towards the subject in hand. Because the technique is so easy for respondents to understand, it is frequently used in questionnaires, whether or not they are administered by an interviewer. The attitude section of the Target Group Index (see above), for example, uses these scales to build up an impression of the outlook and lifestyle of survey respondents. Variants of the Likert approach may ask respondents to rate different aspects of a product or service on five-point scales from 'Very Good' to 'Very Poor' or may seek to discover how often respondents act in a certain way, using a scale from 'Always' to 'Never'. The very ease of using these scales may cause problems if care is not taken. Chisnall (1997) quotes Worcester's caveat concerning the ease of devising Likert scales:

> *All the overworked research executive has to do is to think up a few contentious statements, add a Likert agree/disagree scale and, hey presto, he has a ready-made questionnaire.*

Naturally, the reliability of the information collected will depend on how respondents understand the offered statements: researchers must ensure that the attitude statements are clear and unambiguous.

Also widely used in marketing research are *semantic differential* scales. These scales represent the range of meaning between two opposed ideas, such as 'modern and 'old-fashioned', with five- or seven-point scales separating them. Respondents are asked to indicate the point on the scale corresponding to their view of the object in question. As with Likert scales, the researcher can assign points to each response and sum them to arrive at an aggregate view of the respondent's outlook towards the issue. The technique is flexible and very easy for respondents to understand, although care should be taken to ensure as far as possible that all respondents will interpret the offered scales in the same way. In both the Likert and semantic differential approaches, researchers may use graphics imaginatively to help respondents to understand the question: a scale between 'pleasing' and 'annoying', for example, might be illustrated with a row of five cartoon faces whose expressions would communicate the intended idea.

Sometimes, researchers may wish to understand in greater depth the components of the attitudes expressed by respondents, in which case a *repertory grid* technique may be used, based upon Kelly's theory of personal constructs. The aim in this technique is to help the respondent to reveal the way in which he or she thinks about a particular object or idea, which in turn may help the researcher to understand why certain attitudes result. Indeed, the output from this technique may help to construct more appropriate semantic differential scales. If the researcher wishes to understand, for example, a respondent's way of thinking about brands in a particular product field, the repertory grid technique may be applied by showing the respondent three cards at a time, each bearing the name of one of the brands in the field. The respondent is asked to say in what way any one of the three brands differs from the other two. The answer is recorded and then a further selection of three brands is considered in the same way by the respondent. The process continues until no further reasons for difference or 'personal constructs' can be thought of by the respondent (for further details of this technique, readers should consult Sampson (1986)).

The output from this technique may be used to describe each of the brands in the product field in terms of the revealed constructs, thus allowing a comparison to be made from the point of view of the consumer. Obviously, the researcher will wish to investigate the attitudes of all of the relevant segments in the market: the personal constructs of those in one segment are very likely to differ significantly from those of other segments.

Marketing managers may use attitude data from these techniques to draw up *brand maps*, in which competing brands are located in a two-dimensional space, with the dimensions defined in terms of the attitudes expressed by consumers. In food retailing, for example, one segment of the market might have been found to

Table 9.4 Top ten MR organisations in the world (ESOMAR Web site, accessed 8 January 1998)

Organisation	Head Office	1996 turnover (US$m)
A. C. Nielsen Inc.	USA	1363
IMS International Inc.	USA/UK	907
Information Resources Inc.	USA	406
GfK	D	317
Sofrès Group	F	277
Research International	UK	248
Infratest/Burke	D	168
IPSOS Group	F	162
Millward Brown	UK	156
The Arbitron Co.	USA	154

distinguish between the various choices in terms principally of overall price level (e.g. from 'high price' to 'discount') and range of goods carried (e.g. from 'wide range' to 'narrow range'). From the information obtained, researchers could plot their own store against those of competitors and also against the 'ideal' as seen by consumers in this segment, which may help in planning a positioning campaign or in identifying gaps in the market. In other product fields, the exercise may suggest that some company brands are in fact competing with each other. In the example described here, a different segment of the market might consider the dimension of location to be more important than range carried (e.g. from 'high street' to 'out-of-town' location), leading to a different 'map' for this segment of the market.

In many cases, no two simple dimensions will adequately express the variation in attitude data collected, and researchers may resort to one of the techniques of multivariate analysis in order to reveal the patterns in the data resulting from relationships between three or more variables. A discussion of these techniques in marketing research lies beyond the scope of this book, but they can be used to reduce and simplify large amounts of data, potentially helping the marketing manager to understand the meaning of the information collected. Because of the complexity of these techniques and, above all because of the subjectivity that is often involved in interpreting the results, great care must be taken, but multivariate techniques have been widely used to segment product markets and in 'lifestyle' segmentation analyses.

Overview of the European and UK research industry

The final section of this chapter provides a brief overview of the European and UK marketing research (MR) industry. The MR industry covers a wide range of organisations, from the very large to the individual consultant. Among the larger organisations, some provide a full range of services, while others specialise in particular applications, market sectors or types of marketing research operation.

The world market for market research in 1996 was estimated by ESOMAR (source: ESOMAR Web site, accessed 7 January 1998) to have a value of more than US$11bn (about £6.5bn), representing a growth of 9% on the previous year. The European markets accounted for about 46% of the total, making Europe the largest

Table 9.5 The 1996 revenue of AMSO members analysed by source

Source of revenue	£m AMSO turnover (growth in 1996)
Food and non-alcoholic drinks	61.3 (+12%)
Media	39.6 (+9%)
Public services	35.0 (+9%)
Utilities	31.5 (+10%)
Financial services	30.3 (+9%)
Pharmaceutical companies	29.4 (+12%)
Health and beauty	27.5 (+6%)
Vehicles (business and industrial)	25.9 (+17%)
Retailers	25.9 (+40%)
Government and public bodies	20.8 (+13%)
Household products	16.4 (–2%)
Alcoholic drinks	16.2 (–2%)
Travel and tourism	14.2 (+1%)
Advertising agencies	10.1 (+4%)
Oil	5.8 (+50%)
Household durables and hardware	5.1 (–3%)
Tobacco	2.7 (–2%)
Other	48.7

Source: AMSO (1997).

MR market in the world. Within Europe, the largest national markets were those of Germany ($1171m), the UK ($1045m) and France ($883m). Annual growth rates in the European market were estimated at about 10%.

Much consolidation has taken place in an increasingly international industry; ESOMAR lists the 1996 top ten MR organisations in the world (most of which are headquartered in Europe) as given in Table 9.4.

Turning to the MR industry in the United Kingdom, the largest players have been represented by AMSO, the Association of Market Survey Organisations, which draws together some 38 companies. These organisations are also responsible for much of the syndicated marketing research and audience research information produced for subscribers in the UK market. The combined turnover of AMSO members in 1996 was £446m (AMSO, 1997), representing a growth of almost 12% over the previous year, and including strong growth in international research.

AMSO member organisations carry out more than 16 million interviews per year, together with information collected by panel and audit methods. The 1996 revenue of AMSO members can also be analysed by source, as in Table 9.5.

The industry is governed by a number of voluntary codes of practice, designed to promote high standards of professionalism and to discourage undesirable practices, such as sugging ('selling under the guise of conducting research'), which threaten the integrity and viability of 'real' information gathering and processing in marketing research. Notable among the codes of practice are those of the Market Research Society, the Association of Market Survey Associations and the ICC/ESOMAR International Code of Marketing and Survey Research Practice. These codes focus on different types of activity in the industry and are intended to be largely compatible with each other. As an example, the Market Research Society Code of Practice is designed to:

support all those engaged in marketing or social research in maintaining professional standards throughout the industry. It applies to all members of the Market research Society, whether they are engaged in consumer, business to business, social, opinion or any other type of confidential survey research. It applies to quantitative and qualitative methods as well as to mystery shopping and other techniques for data gathering. Assurance that research is conducted in an ethical manner is needed to create confidence in, and to encourage co-operation among the business community, the general public and others (MRS, 1997, p. 48)

Sections of the Code deal with responsibilities to informants, responsibilities to the general public and the business community, the mutual responsibilities of clients and agencies and the conditions of membership and professional responsibilities. Separate guidelines for handling databases containing personal details of respondents or potential respondents have also been published by the MRS.

Summary

This chapter has reviewed the marketing research methods and techniques that can help to support the decisions involved in corporate marketing communications. The scope of marketing research is very broad, covering all aspects of the external environment that may affect marketing strategy. In obtaining optimum value for money in marketing research, it is essential to manage effectively the research process as a whole. Clear research objectives are essential, as is the early process of exploratory research, which should be designed to appreciate the information that already exists and is readily obtainable (secondary data), in order to make the collection of new data for the specific research process (primary data) as effective and cost-efficient as possible.

Research design to gather primary data involves two main considerations: how the data is to be collected and what sampling approach is to be used. For reasons of convenience and cost, marketing research surveys often make use of quota sampling rather than the theoretically preferable probability sampling; careful management of quota samples can help to minimise the risk of bias in practice. Data collection methods include face-to-face personal interviewing, telephone interviewing and postal questionnaires: each method has advantages and disadvantages which may make them more or less suitable for particular research needs.

Qualitative research techniques are used to supplement quantitative research findings. Qualitative techniques are by design subjective and impressionistic, but may represent a potentially powerful way of gaining a deeper understanding of why customers think, feel and act the way they do.

A range of techniques are available to measure, analyse and compare consumer attitudes, helping researchers to understand in more depth how consumers think and feel about the organisation, its brands and those of competitors.

Review questions

1. In what ways might sources of secondary data be used in developing an advertising campaign to support the launch of a new household furniture cleaning product? What sources of information might be relevant?

2. Explain the principal characteristics of quantitative and qualitative types of information.
3. What are the advantages and disadvantages of telephone interviewing in communications research?
4. Write a short report for your manager, considering the advantages and disadvantages of using focus groups as a means of gathering information.
5. Set out the different types of syndicated sources of marketing research and evaluate their possible contribution to a corporate communications programme.
6. Describe the five main stages of marketing research.
7. A high street bank wishes to conduct a postal questionnaire survey of a sample of its personal customers, with a view to researching their attitudes towards the bank and its services. What sources of possible bias need to be borne in mind in designing the survey and what actions can the researcher take to minimise the risk of these types of bias?
8. Evaluate the role of sampling and its contribution to the marketing research
9. Prepare brief notes setting out the differences between semantic differential and Likert scales.
10. Explain briefly the main types of audience research. Why is this type of research an important aspect of marketing communications programmes?

References

Association of Market Survey Organisations (AMSO), *Annual Report* (1997).

BARB (undated) *Guide to the Broadcasters' Audience Research Board.*

Baker, M.J. (1991) *Research for Marketing.* London: Macmillan.

Chisnall, P. M. (1997) *Marketing Research*, 5th edn. London: McGraw-Hill.

Collins, M. (1986) Sampling, in *The Consumer Market Research Handbook*, 3rd edn (eds R. Worcester and J. Downham). London: McGraw-Hill, ESOMAR.

Crimp, M. and Wright, L.T. (1995) *The Marketing Research Process*, 4th edn. Hemel Hempstead: Prentice Hall.

Kinnear, T. C. and Taylor, J. R. (1987) *Marketing Research, an Applied Approach*, 3rd edn. New York: McGraw-Hill.

Market Research Society (1997) *Orgs Book 1997/8.*

Morton-Williams, J. (1986) Questionnaire design, in *The Consumer Market Research Handbook*, 3rd edn (eds R. Worcester and J. Downham). Hemel Hempstead: Prentice Hall.

Sampson, P. (1986) Qualitative and motivation research, in *The Consumer Market Research Handbook*, 3rd edn (eds R. Worcester and J. Downham). Hemel Hempstead: Prentice Hall.

Useful addresses

BARB (Broadcasters' Audience Research Board Ltd), Glenthorne House, Hammersmith Grove, London W6 0ND; Tel. 0181 741 9110; fax 0181 741 1943.

ESOMAR (European Society for Opinion and Market Research), Central Secretariat, J J Viottastraat 29, 1071 JP Amsterdam, The Netherlands; Tel. +31 20 664 21 41; fax +31 20 664 29 22; Website: http://www.esomar.nl/index.htm.

MRS (Market Research Society), 15 Northburgh Street, London EC1V 0AH; Tel. 0171 490 4911; fax 0171 490 0608; Website: http://www.marketresearch.org.uk/index.htm.

NRS (National Readership Surveys Ltd), Garden Studios, 11–15 Betterton Street, Covent Garden, London WC2H 9BP; Tel. 0171 379 0344; fax 0171 240 4399; Website: http://www.nrs.co.uk/.

RAJAR (Radio Joint Audience Research), Collier House, 163–169 Brompton Road, London SW3 1PY; Tel. 0171 584 3003; fax 0171 589 4004.

chapter 10

Intentions and targets

In order to deliver and maintain effective marketing communications it is important to communicate within the context of the organisation's corporate goals, its marketing intentions and the relevant target audience.

AIMS AND OBJECTIVES

The aim of this chapter is to examine marketing communications in the light of an organisation's corporate goals and marketing plans.

The objectives of this chapter are:

1. To appreciate the essence of corporate strategy and how the mission provides a context for the marketing (corporate) communications activities.
2. To understand the role of marketing communications in the context of corporate and business level strategies.
3. To introduce the pivotal role marketing strategy has in the development of marketing communications.
4. To appreciate how segmentation and target marketing assists the development of marketing communications.
5. To provide an example of psychographic segmentation.
6. To appraise the product life cycle and consider its contribution to marketing communications .
7. To introduce the notion of brand equity as a tool for developing marketing communications.

Introduction

The corporate and competitive strategies of organisations provide an essential backdrop for a host of other activities that organisations undertake in their attempts to satisfy their own varied objectives. These overarching goals are normally embedded within a corporate philosophy that in turn is a reflection of the dominant culture. This philosophy provides a context within which marketing (and corporate) communications are required to operate and convey the strategic intent of the organisation. In themselves the communications provide a further context for the delivery of the strategies, in particular a context whereby organisational members and non-members decode, interpret and respond to the organisation's messages.

Marketing communications is an important activity that must complement the corporate objectives and provide a context through which the philosophy and culture of the organisation are perpetuated. Therefore, marketing communications and the corporate intent are firmly intertwined. Figure 10.1 sets out the interrelationship between these two components.

The organisation's mission

The direction and strategy of the organisation are often embedded within its mission and the vision that critical members have of the organisation. The mission and philosophy form an important dimension which in itself frames the marketing (and communications) activities that follow.

According to Campbell and Yeung (1991), a mission consists of four interrelated elements: purpose, strategy, behaviour standards and values (Figure 10.2).

Purpose refers to the question about what the organisation seeks to achieve. Three types were identified. Those who are in business just to satisfy shareholders (e.g. Hanson), those who seek to satisfy a range of stakeholders (Ciba-Geigy) and those that seek to achieve or contribute toward a form of organisational self-actualisation, one where the organisation sets out to accomplish a long term aim which contributes positively to the needs of society (The Body Shop).

Strategy sets out the way in which the purpose is to be fulfilled. It determines the way the business will compete and the position and advantages it will strive to achieve.

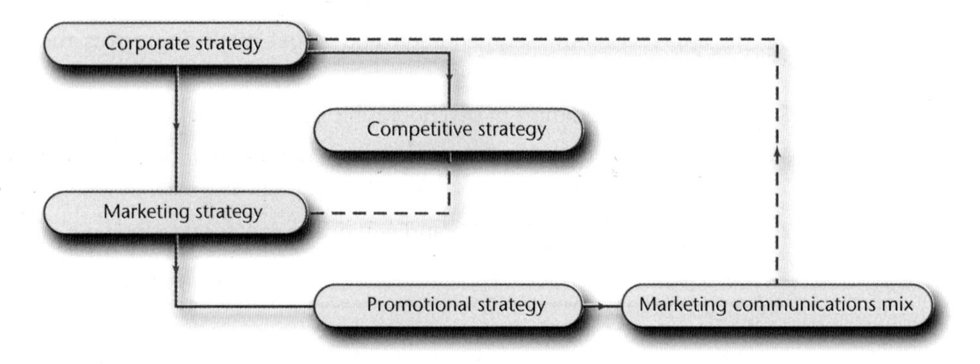

Figure 10.1 The relationship of marketing communications to corporate strategy.

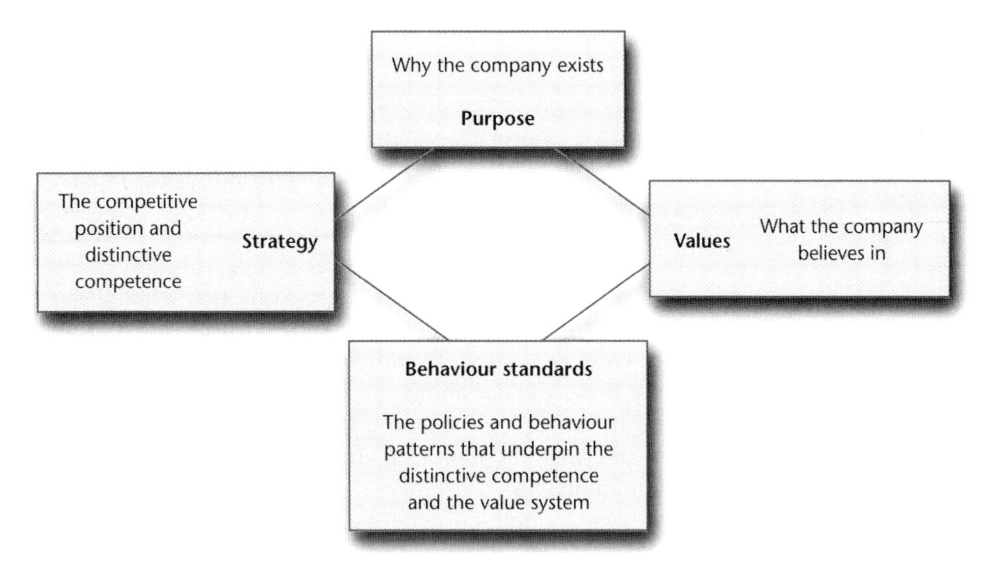

Figure 10.2 The Ashridge mission model (reprinted from Campbell and Yeung (1991), with permission from Elsevier Science).

Standards of behaviour are guidelines for the people who are required to action the strategy and to assist them to decide what to do. The authors consider the need for a 'moral rationale to run alongside the commercial rationale'. This is the way people in this organisation are expected to behave.

The final element concerns the *values* of the organisation and is an extension of the previous element. Values are the deeper-lying beliefs and moral underpinnings that are an important part of an organisation's culture. Here there is a concern for what is morally right and what is ethically the correct behaviour.

The impact and degree of emotional bond that organisational members develop with the mission and philosophy of the organisation is important because this degree of bonding is reflected in the energy and subsequent success of the organisation in achieving its aims and objectives. The communications must reflect these four elements by conveying conviction, consistency and a sense of total integration and coordination.

Marketing strategy

The marketing plan is a subset of the marketing strategy, which in turn is a part of the business plan and strategy. Marketing communications seeks to deliver the essence of the corporate goals, the direction and intention of the business plan and the conviction and detail of the marketing plan, to its target markets. In other words, marketing communications should provide a means by which the organisation communicates its offering to meet the buyer's needs. It does this in the context of the organisation's overall mission and corporate culture.

- It clarifies the role of communications in the context of particular corporate, business and marketing strategies and plans.

- It prevents duplication and confusion among those involved in the development and execution of a communication strategy.
- It anchors a communication strategy in the sense that communications are given a base, a purpose and a means of evaluating the success of the campaign.
- It provides direction to all personnel associated with the development and implementation of communication strategy.
- It focuses attention on the appropriate target audiences.

The first important point is that, by clearly segregating marketing strategy from communications strategy, the role of communications within marketing is highlighted. The role of the latter is to support and communicate the marketing strategy; that is, *not* to duplicate or formulate another approach to the market. The second point is that communications strategy should establish the most appropriate way of communicating the marketing intentions of an organisation to its various target markets and stakeholder audiences.

Marketing strategy acts as the cornerstone of the development of planned marketing communications. It sets the direction and manner in which the marketing objectives are to be achieved and guides the work of those responsible for marketing communications, those other stakeholders working inside the organisation (e.g. employees) and all stakeholders who are external to the organisation (e.g. advertising agencies).

Marketing strategy is the process whereby target markets are identified and selected. Marketing plans are developed for each selected market segment in order that the needs of buyers in each target group may be satisfied. Each marketing plan consists of the main elements of the marketing mix (see Chapter 1). Each element of this mix has the capacity to communicate in its own right (see Chapter 29 for more details). This management process is systematic and is driven by the need for an organisation to meet and exceed its corporate and marketing objectives. According to Dibb *et al.* (1991), 'A marketing strategy articulates a plan for the best use of the organisation's resources and tactics to meet its objectives'.

Many organisations are placing increasing importance on loyalty and relationship marketing as a vital part of their marketing strategies. The implementation of this strategy requires the use of marketing communications to deliver the key messages and to maintain the dialogue that is crucial to the success of the strategy.

The importance of using the marketing strategy as the base for the communications strategy and for not duplicating it must not be overlooked. This chapter will look first at the process of target market selection and review the elements of the mix in the context of communications.

Target marketing: segmentation

Segmentation is an established and acknowledged technique for dividing a mass market into identifiable sub-units, in order that the individual needs of buyers and potential buyers can be more easily satisfied.

The broad process of segmenting a market is set out in Figure 10.3. Essentially, market segmentation seeks to establish particular groups or clusters of buyers. As indicated above, target marketing is the process whereby specific segments are selected and marketing plans are then developed to satisfy the needs of the potential

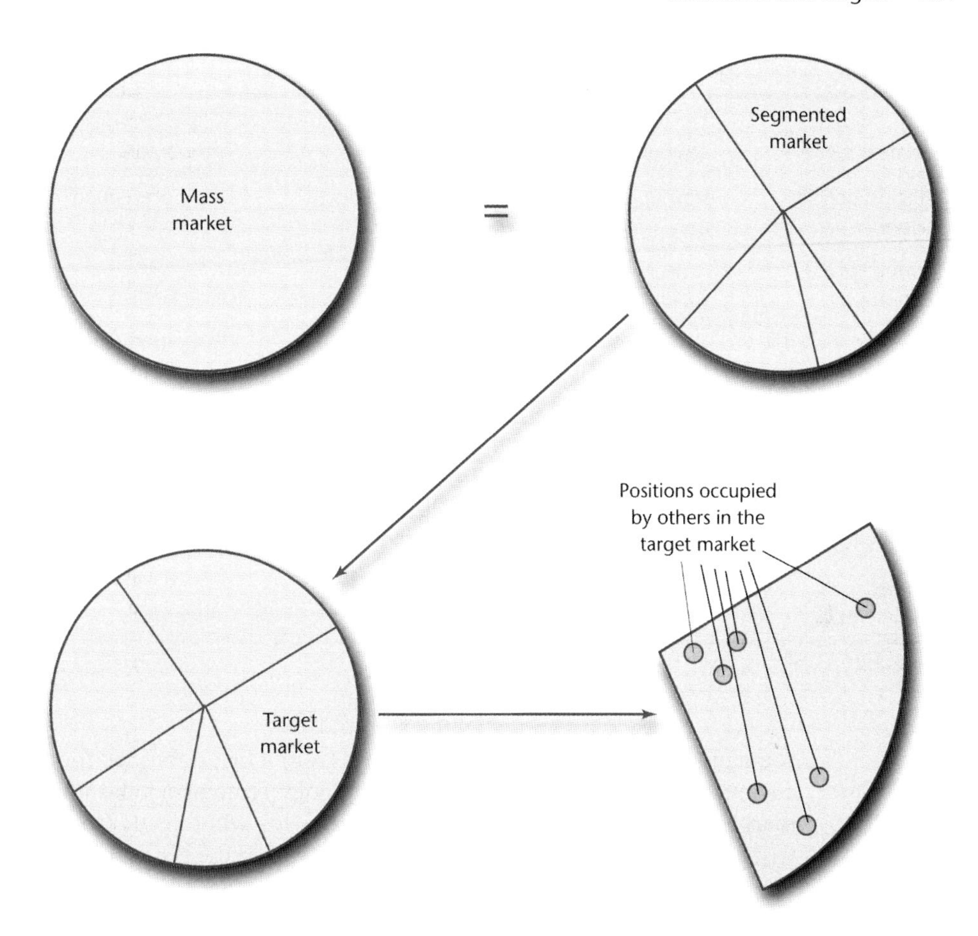

Figure 10.3 The process of target marketing.

buyers in the chosen segments. The development, or rather identification, of segments can be perceived as opportunities, and as Beane and Ennis (1987) suggest, 'A company with limited resources needs to pick only the best opportunities to pursue'.

This process of segmentation is necessary because a single product is unlikely to meet the needs of all customers in a mass market. If it were, then a single type of toothpaste, chocolate bar or car would meet all of our needs. This is not so, and there are a host of products and brands seeking to satisfy particular buyer needs. For example, ask yourself the question, 'Why do I use toothpaste?'. The answer, most probably, is one of the following:

1. You want dental hygiene.
2. You like fresh breath and you don't want to offend others.
3. You want white, shining teeth.
4. You like the fresh oral sensation.
5. Other products (e.g. water, soap) do not taste very good.

Whatever the reason, it is unlikely that given a choice we would all choose the same product. In what is now regarded as a classic study, Russell Haley (1968) undertook

Table 10.1 Benefit segments for the toothpaste market

Segment name	The senory segment	The sociables	The worriers	The independent segment
Principal benefit sought	Flavour, product appearance	Brightness of teeth	Decay prevention	Price
Demographic strengths	Children	Teens, young people	Large families	Men
Special behavioural characteristics	Users of spearmint flavoured toothpaste	Smokers	Heavy users	Heavy users
Brands disproportionately favoured	Colgate, Stripe	Macleans, Plus White, Ultra Brite	Crest	Brands on sale
Personality characteristics	High self-involvement	High sociability	High hypochondriasis	High autonomy
Lifestyle characteristics	Hedonistic	Active	Conservative	Value-oriented

Source: Haley (1968); used with kind permission.

some pioneering research in this field and from it he established four distinct types of customer. Even thirty years later this typology remains a valid interpretation of the market place. Those who bought toothpaste for white teeth (sociables), those who wished to prevent decay (worriers), those who liked the taste and refreshment properties (sensors) and finally those who bought on a price basis (independents). Each of these groups has particular demographic, behaviouristic and psychographic characteristics which can be seen in Table 10.1.

It is not surprising that a range of toothpaste products have been developed that attempt to satisfy the needs of different buyers; for example, Macleans for fresh breath, Crest for dental hygiene, Sensodyne for those sensitive to hot and cold drinks and numerous others promoted on special offers for those independent buyers looking for a low price. There are others who are not very interested in the product and have continued using a brand that others in their current or past households are comfortable with.

Buyers, therefore, can be clustered or grouped into segments. By definition, each segment has its own specific characteristics and this isolation of buyers with similar lifestyles, needs and outlook permits a greater understanding and appreciation of each cluster. Such an approach is possible with all stakeholders, although very often organisations identify buyers but fail to recognise the different needs of their other stakeholders.

The more we know and understand about all of an organisation's stakeholders and are able to develop a common realm of understanding, the more effective will be the communications with each target audience. Recognising the existence of different stakeholders, and the increasing impact some stakeholders have upon each other, means that a greater number and variety of messages have to be transmitted.

Market segmentation, therefore, is the division of a mass market into distinct groups which have common characteristics, needs and similar responses to marketing actions. How then can a market be subdivided? Some of the more common methods are as follows.

Bases for segmentation

Demographic

This is the most basic and most often used method of segmenting a market. The underlying principle is that the age, sex, occupation, level of education, religion, social class and income characteristics determine, to a large extent, a potential buyer's ability to enter into an exchange relationship or transaction. Cosmetics are largely targeted at women and toys at appropriate age groupings. Lego has developed a range of products for targeting at children at different stages in their development: Duplo for the under 4-year-olds, Lego System for the 4–8-year-olds and Lego Technic for 8–13-year-old children. All the sets are integrated with one another and continuity is maintained. Interestingly, Lego found that 5-year-old girls tended not to use the product as much as boys. The reason was found to be that girls played in a way that required their imagination to be stimulated differently from boys. Lego developed a product to meet this precise need, called Paradisa, which has been highly successful.

The advertising industry, according to Oliver (1994), was one of the first to build data on socioeconomic grade, an attempt to combine class, type of employment and income (Table 10.2). This has persisted and, despite its shortcomings, is used a great deal by a large number of marketers. The market research industry uses this approach frequently to classify markets. While this high level of credibility might promote further use, the approach can be misleading and prone to generalisations. People are, increasingly, capable of moving between groups, and the disposable income of a member of one group may well be more than that of a group above. That is, a C2 plumber may have a greater income than a C1 office administrator. The argument for their retention as valid tools of segmentation is based on the stability of the identifiable purchase patterns, the reliability of income and occupation relationships and the distinct attitude patterns that exist. For example, the ABC1 groups have a future perspective, while the C2DE groups tend to have a perspective based on present circumstances.

Geographic

This type of segmentation is based upon the premise that the needs of potential customers in one geographic area are different from those in another area. For example, it is often said that Scottish beer drinkers prefer heavy bitters, Northerners in England prefer mild, drinkers in the West prefer cider, and in the South lager is the preferred drink. This demarcation may also reflect the way in which promotional messages are received.

In Europe, perception of advertising messages is heavily influenced by the culture of particular member countries, and broad patterns of perception can be seen in Latin-based countries, as distinct from their northerly partners. In the USA it has been found that the perception of advertisements varies from the north-east to the west. The use of print advertisements is dependent very often on geographic areas rather than, say, the level of education attained by the target group. However, this method of segmentation is only useful at the broadest level. The examples given above are only broad generalisations and any marketing strategy founded on such a basis is unlikely to be very successful.

Table 10.2 Socio-economic groups in the United Kingdom (NRS)

Social grade	Social status	Occupation
A	Upper middle class	Higher managerial, administrative or professional
B	Middle class	Intermediate managerial, administrative or professional
C1	Lower middle class	Supervisory or clerical, and junior managerial, administrative or professional
C2	Skilled working class	Skilled manual workers
D	Working class	Semi- or unskilled manual workers
E	Those at the lowest levels or subsistence	State pensioners or widows (no other earner), casual or lowest grade workers

Note: The social grade of an individual is normally based on the occupation of the head of household.

Geodemographic

This type of segmentation has grown out of the need to combine the best of the two previous bases. The most well-known form of geodemographics is called Acorn (A Classification of Residential Neighbourhoods). This tool and others, such as Mosaic and Pinpoint, assume that there is a relationship between the type of housing a person lives in and their purchase behaviour. At the root of this approach is the ability to use postcodes to send similar messages to similar groups of households, on the basis that where we live determines how we live!

Geodemographics have been significant in the development of direct mail activities which allow for the accurate delivery of personal messages. Indeed, direct mail has offered advertisers and clients the opportunity to send targeted messages to the extent that it is becoming increasingly possible to achieve the ultimate form of segmentation: customization. Acorn requires the development of customer profiles, and attached to these profiles are media consumption habits, which are an important adjunct to this form of segmentation.

Psychoanalytic

Psychographics involves the subdivision of a market on the basis of personality or lifestyle (Table 10.3). This is determined by an analysis of the activities, interests and opinions (AIO) of the consumer. Lifestyles or patterns of behaviour are a synthesis of the motivations, personality and core values held by individuals. These AIO patterns are reflected in the buying behaviour and decision-making processes of individuals. By identifying and clustering common lifestyles, a correlation with a consumer's product and/or media usage patterns becomes possible. Mueller-Heumann (1992) reports that the Target Group Index (TGI) has identified six different groups of women based on the attitudes they hold. The women who constitute these groups are between 15 and 44 years of age:

1. Self-aware: concerned about fashion, appearance and exercise.
2. Fashion directed: as the self-aware, but not interested in exercise and sport.
3. Green goddess: concerned about sport and exercise but not appearance.
4. Unconcerned: neutral attitudes to all three elements.
5. Conscience-stricken: too busy with family responsibilities to be concerned with self-realization issues.

Table 10.3 Elements of lifestyle

Activities	Interests	Opinions	Demographics
Work	Family	Themselves	Age
Hobbies	Home	Social issues	Education
Social events	Job	Politics	Income
Vacation	Community	Business	Occupation
Entertainment	Recreation	Economics	Family size
Club membership	Fashion	Education	Dwelling
Community	Food	Products	Geography
Shopping	Media	Future	City size
Sports	Achievements	Culture	Stage in life cycle

Source: Plummer (1974); used with kind permission.

6. Dowdies: indifferent to fashion, cool on exercise and dress for comfort.

Bowles (1988) has shown that this segmentation base is effective in understanding shopping behaviour and media consumption.

The Values and Lifestyle programme (Vals) developed by SRI International in 1978, classified consumers according to their values and lifestyles. Both Vals 1 and the updated Vals 2 (1989) have been used successfully in the USA. Synergy Brand Values is marketing and extending a typology for use in the UK and European markets using Maslow's hierarchy of needs. Three primary motivations (sustenance, inner and outer directed) are used to cluster groups of individuals who share common characteristics. These groupings result in seven segments, each with its own distinctive attitudes, behaviours and decision-making styles. See the social value groups case illustration for more information about each of the social value groups.

Behaviouristic

In this form of segmentation the market is differentiated on the basis of the use of the offering by individuals, the benefits they derive from use, the levels of loyalty buyers display and the stage which buyers have reached in the decision-making process.

Usage

Pareto's rule states that 80% of purchases are made by just 20% of consumers. The development of customer profiles for these groups is a priority task. The main clusters should focus attention upon heavy, medium, light and non-users. In the air travel industry, business customers can be clustered according to the number of times they use particular routes or airlines. There are many outcomes to this type of segmentation, including Frequent Flier programmes and the special facilities designed for these business customers.

Usage of soft drinks can be determined in terms of purchase patterns (two bottles per week), usage situations (parties, picnics or as an alcohol substitute) or purchase location (supermarket, convenience store or wine merchant).

Benefit

Benefit segmentation refers to consumers who purchase products and services in order to satisfy specific needs and wants. The grouping of consumers on the basis of attributes sought is a widely used form of segmentation. For example, camera buyers

CASE ILLUSTRATION

Social value groups

The social value groups used by Synergy Brand Values are based on the premise that people have a set of values, beliefs and motivations that are relatively consistent through time. It has been shown that there is a strong correlation between people's values and their purchase behaviour. This is because individuals' values provide one of the primary ways of scanning their environment and of interpreting and understanding the variety of cues presented to them.

While individual experiences may shape interpretation and understanding, people who hold similar values tend to behave in a cohesive way. It is this cohesion that provides the depth and richness of this approach to segmentation. While the typologies that have emerged from various longitudinal studies in the UK (and the USA) are of direct benefit to strategic management and for identifying key changes in society and future market opportunities, the key benefits for marketing communications are for brand (re)positioning (Chapter 24), message strategy (Chapter 14), media planning (Chapter 16) and corporate identity issues (Chapter 27).

To appreciate the nature and scope of the social value groups (Figure 10.4) it is necessary to understand the broad motivational groups and sub-groups into which the population has been classified.

Inner-directed people are orientated towards personal growth and individual freedom, and are concerned about people. They tend to prefer niche, high-quality markets, and their drive for individualism may lead them to a small, round-the-corner restaurant rather than the expensive, well-known and status-orientated restaurant where 'anybody who is anybody' must be seen.

Outer-directed people have a more competitive outlook on life than the inner-directed group. They are continually seeking to improve their position and moving forward their careers and their social lives. They have a more materialistic approach and use products to signal their position.

Sustenance-driven people are concerned about the maintenance of the status quo. Consequently, safety, security and comfort are prime issues. Purchase behaviour is characterised by caution, low risk and tradition.

Readers will be able to see the similarity of these main groups with those of Maslow's hierarchy of needs (see Mullins, 1996).

The following material attempts to present a snapshot of the seven value groups into which the population has been classified. Further information can be provided by Synergy Brand Values Ltd.

Self-explorers (11% of the population)

These people cannot tolerate restriction unless it is self-imposed. They are independent and modern in outlook, economically comfortable and psychologically complex. They are driven by their needs for self-expression and personal satisfaction. They tend to be tolerant, confident, intelligent, imaginative and responsive.

Products promoted for their newness are unlikely to be received very well by this group. Promotional messages based on time saving or an environmental basis have a greater chance of success. People in this group have a low television diet but consume a lot of information in a variety of publications, which include *Marie Claire*, *Elle*, *Q* and newspapers such as the *Mail on Sunday* and *The Guardian*. 'Horizon', Classical British Costume Dramas, and 'Whose Line is it Anyway?' are the more likely television programmes watched by this group.

Core values are inner-directed.

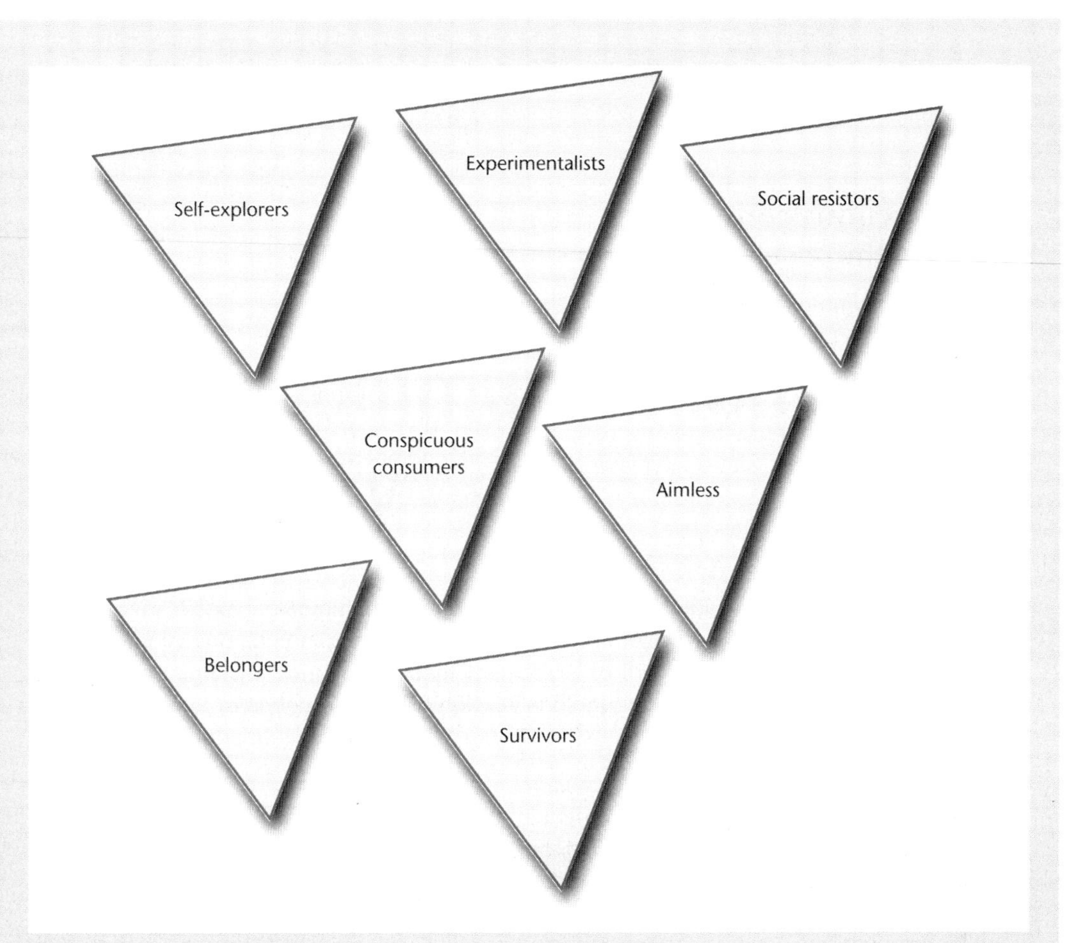

Figure 10.4 Social value groups.

Experimentalists
(10% of the population)

These people are characterised by their need for new ideas and experiences. Predominantly men in their late 20s and early 30s, experimentalists are energetic, confident, gregarious and intelligent. This group wants to find exciting approaches to life. Work is important for personal growth, but security within work is not required.

Because experimentalists enjoy an above-average level of risk-taking, new products are very attractive to them. To some extent these people are impulsive in their desire to experiment with innovations. However, they are just as likely to become bored and will drop products just as quickly. They are crucial to the development of markets, not to those that are mature or established. For example, they helped create the Häagen-Dazs market share, but cannot be relied on to be users in five years' time.

Packaging and the presentation of promotional messages are important attributes looked for by this group. Their media consumption is heavy and reveals widespread tastes. Newspapers such as the *Sun* and the *Sunday Mirror* feature a great deal. *Empire*, *Perfect Home* and various special-interest magazines are also popular. Because they are out a great deal their television consumption is light, but they prefer programmes such as 'TFI Friday', 'Big Breakfast' and 'Top of the Pops'.

Core values are combined inner- and outer-directed.

Conspicuous consumers (18% of the population)

A significant group who are marked by their strong concern for appearances, where value is expressed in the eyes of others. It is the image of themselves that is important. Energy is directed to generating a romantic notion of their own personal status through material possessions.

Conspicuous consumers use a variety of cues in order that others can develop an image of them with respect to status, personality and acceptability. Therefore, they use products that others use in order to gain respect and recognition of personal worth. Importance is attached to the opinion of others, and in advertising messages the use of the 'expert' can be useful because these people like to be able to be in the know. Work serves as an instrument in order that limited status needs are fulfilled, but is really only a means by which their standard of living can be improved.

By emphasising status, personality and lifestyle, messages aimed at this group are more likely to be received well. As decision-making is often difficult for these people, strong brand and corporate-based communications can provide reassurance and the confidence to buy. Advertisements such as those for American Express and Rolex, which feature well-known style-orientated celebrities, are powerful and effective in communicating with this group.

Living, *House Beautiful* and *Company* are popular magazines because they help to romanticise their lives. Mass soaps such as *Neighbours* and *EastEnders* are very popular, as are other mainstream programmes such as 'Men Behaving Badly' and 'The Clothes Show'.

Core values are outer-directed.

Belongers (20% of the population)

This group are strongly orientated towards the family, country and establishment, and they have a great deal of trust in large established organisations. The belonger prefers the family environment partly because of the comfort of rigid routines and the reassurance that stability brings. They are Mr and Mrs (not Ms) Average.

Work is important to members of this group, but they know their rights and place in society and do not seek to disturb the balance, as they see it. For example, it is unlikely that belongers would complain about any goods or services, and research suggests that they are more satisfied than any other group with newspapers, banks, TV and health issues.

Belongers buy large safe brands which are recommended with a parental appeal or by a figure of authority (e.g. tyres or home burglar alarms endorsed by the police force). They will also drop a brand if it lets them down or fails to get family acceptance. Belongers feel that they must do well for their children, so the parental appeal and approval is of particular significance to them. The *Mail on Sunday*, *Sun* and the *Express* are the papers most likely to be read by this group. Their television consumption is slightly above average and is geared towards the 'proper' channels, i.e. BBC and ITV, but not Channel 4 or any of the cable or satellite offerings. Nice safe programmes appear to be the most popular, e.g. *Antiques Roadshow, Dads Army* and *BBC News*. Advertisements for the Legal & General (featuring the safe protective umbrella) and Abbey National are well received by this group.

Core values are sustenance to outer driven.

Survivors (23% of the population)

These people have a strong inclination to accept the direction given by the establishment and institutions. They see the establishment as threatening and impenetrable; hence a set of values emerge that classify groups as 'Them and Us'. The establishment provides security and protection, and in return survivors offer to surrender their personal goals and ambitions (if they ever had any). The catchphrase 'the way things have always been done' serves to encapsulate their orientation towards the Them and Us position.

Survivors have a low expectation of what life will bring to them. Work, for example, is seen as necessary to make a living, but any mention of issues such as self-development and self-fulfilment can only provoke strong negative feelings. It is quite usual to find survivors remaining with organisations who are trying to become structurally flatter and slimmer. Apparently, voluntary retirement programmes tend to attract the inner- and outer-directed groups. It is unfortunate that survivors remain, because these new organisations require creativity and new approaches to work, and survivors are the least equipped to manage it.

Ownership of household items is below average and brand choices are not required as selection is invariably made on price. Therefore, survivors find little pleasure at work or through their own personal resources and turn to escapism for diversion in their lives. Papers such as the *Sun*, *Mirror* and *News of the World* are the most popular, and survivors tend to be the heaviest users of television as they search for ways to be taken out of themselves. *The Bill*, *Blind Date*, *Crimewatch UK* and *Gladiators* are preferred programmes, all of which reflect, slightly, the Them and Us disposition.

Core values are sustenance-driven.

Social resisters
(12% of the population)

This group of people believe that by maintaining the *status quo* change can be resisted for as long as possible. The need for control is vital and is achieved through stereotypical roles and acceptance of authority, so that ethical and moral codes of behaviour can be sustained.

Social resisters are driven by their sense of moral duty, which is often focused on the family. Careers or jobs are instrumental in supporting the family; there is no need for there to be any enjoyment or self-expression in work.

Reassurance and reduction of risk are achieved through the purchase of established, reliable brands. Consequently, their level of brand loyalty is high and hence difficult to change. Promotional messages should convey approval and family advantage. Social resisters approve of products that are perceived to be tried and trusted and which express values of concern and care. Television programmes such as *Songs of Praise*, *Survival* and *Family Fortunes* are preferred as are newspapers such as the *Sunday Express* and the *Sun*.

Core values are sustenance-driven.

Aimless
(6% of the population)

Without a goal or any orientation within society, the aimless resent the authorities, who are unable to provide employment for them. Unlike survivors, the aimless believe that hard work or education will not produce the rewards of work. Their world is orientated to the present, as they have no vision of the future or of the needs of others.

Work, if they have it, is perceived as a means of survival. It has no intrinsic value and they accept meaningless work much more readily than those in other groups. Their levels of self-esteem are low, they have virtually no desire for excitement and have lower levels of fear (compared with survivors) in their lives. This is because of their resigned attitude towards authority and society.

Their purchase behaviour is driven by price and their need for consumer durables is severely capped by their limited disposable income. The aimless are 70% more likely to read the *Sun* and the *News of the World* than any other group and are unlikely to read any magazines. Their average television consumption is not reflected in any dominant style, yet *Crimewatch UK*, *You've Been Framed* and the *Krypton Factor* draw a high proportion of the Aimless.

Core values are sustenance-driven.

Menumaster, a range of frozen ready-to-eat meals, used packaging with heavy red triangles and a 'bird of freedom' to symbolise the free time that these instantaneous meals provided users. Advertising messages focused upon familiarity and traditional family scenes. Sales for some of the products in the range lagged behind others. Analysis showed that the traditional recipe products, such as cottage pie and steak and kidney pie, were successful (Survivors and Belongers), but meals with slightly more esoteric recipes, such as lasagne and fish mornay, were failing to establish themselves.

A decision was made to split the brand into two brands: Menumaster and Healthy Options. The traditional recipe meals would continue to be presented to the Survivors and Belongers in the current way, under the Menumaster brand. The new recipes would be targeted at younger people and would be clearly differentiated though Healthy Options. This was accomplished by using lighter colours on the packaging and depicting couples leading a modern lifestyle, in other words appealing to the needs of different groups (Experimentalists and Self-explorers), by showing the up-to-date roles of younger, busy, often career-orientated people. The decision was successful, as these products gained market share quickly. The Menumaster brand had been re-presented to the market based upon an understanding of the values and lifestyles of the target groups. By careful coordination of the packaging and advertising images, a consistency was developed that members of the target market were able to appreciate and identify.

What is clear from the work that has been undertaken to understand psychographics is that the previous reliance on generally bland demographic data is receding. More incisive information based on the lifestyles and attitudes of people is revealing groups that are of greater potential to marketers and communications strategists.

Used with the kind permission of Synergy Brand Values Ltd

may be seeking good quality pictures, durability, ease of use, low price or a prestigious name, to name just a few benefits.

Following the Lego System example used previously, it is interesting to note that the Lego concept is built on two main benefits that children derive from using this type of product. The first main benefit is the building of the models, and the second is the play component once models are completed. Normally, the building element is of equal importance to the play component in most children's desire to use the product. However, research undertaken by Lego has discovered that certain types of children derive greater enjoyment from the play component. Consequently, a new product was launched in October 1994, called Belville. The models are relatively quick and easy to construct and the environments created (pony club, restaurants etc.) seek to maximise the play component.

Further examples of this form of segmentation can be seen in the toothpaste market, which was examined earlier, and the kitchen stove market and the different attitudes people have towards their kitchens and the impact this has on the types of cooker they might buy. See Table 10.4.

Table 10.4 Kitchen stoves – customer profiles

Group	Characteristics
Entertainers	These people like to cook at home and entertain at the same time. The kitchen will probably have a table in it.
Ostentatious non-cooks	Cooking for this group is not a pleasure, reflected in their purchase of ready-cooked prepared meals. The kitchen, however, must reflect their sense of style and design.
Traditional grandmas	This group consists of people who like to prepare family-type meals and whose cooker is changed quite infrequently. The 'eye-level' grill is a firm favourite.
Liberated home-lovers	Kitchens are an important family area to this group who believe strongly in self-sufficiency and natural products. They like lots of space in which to prepare casseroles and healthy food.
Apathetic non-cooks	Harrassed mothers preparing convenience meals for demanding children.

Source: Adapted from Lawless (1998).

Loyalty

Most markets consist of four levels of loyalty: hard core, soft core, shifting loyals and switchers. An organisation is capable of learning a great deal from analysing loyalty patterns, especially those of the hard-core loyals.

The level of loyalty shoppers have for their preferred supermarket is an important aspect of the marketing programmes developed by the major supermarkets, such as Sainsbury's, Safeway and Tesco. Increasing attention is being given to the shifting loyals in an attempt to expand the local base that each supermarket commands.

Buyer readiness stage

This refers to the stage individuals have reached as they prepare to purchase a product. It could be that they are unaware of a product's existence, that they are informed but have not formed an opinion or that they have decided they are convinced of the benefits that will come with purchase and intend buying. The numbers within each stage have an important bearing upon the communication plan.

This correlates with the process of adoption (Chapter 2) that individuals differ in the speed at which they are prepared to try new products. Marketing communications need to be targeted at those individuals who are more ready to commit themselves. Nat West Bank, working in association with Avon, an insurance company, have been offering term life assurance to clients of the bank. By gradually increasing the total value of the cover for a small percentage increment in the premiums, Avon have identified customers who are prepared to make further investments. Such an approach allows them to determine the readiness of each customer to the acceptance of each new offer.

What should be clear from this very brief overview is that no single segmentation tool will suffice. A combination of approaches is required in order that a significant and insightful consumer profile can be developed. Without this understanding, appropriate media and message development work cannot be effective, as will be seen later.

Targeting

The next task is to decide which, if any, of the segments discovered should be the focus of the marketing programme. Kotler (1997) advises that, unless the following criteria are met, it is probably unwise to continue with the segmentation plan:

- All segments should be *measurable* – is the segment easy to identify and measure?
- All segments should be *substantial* – is the segment sufficiently large to provide a stream of profits?
- All segments should be *accessible* – can the buyers be reached with promotional programmes?

To this list can be added the following:

- All segments should be *differentiable* – is each segment clearly different from other segments so that different marketing mixes are necessary?
- All segments should be *actionable* – has the organisation the capability to reach the segment?

Decisions need to be made about whether a single product is to be offered to a range of segments, whether a range of products should be offered to multiple segments or a single segment or whether one product should be offered to a single segment. Whatever the decision, always a reflection of the resources available to an organisation, a marketing mix is developed to meet the needs of the segment to be entered and be within the resource capability of the organisation.

The segmentation exercise will have been undertaken previously as part of the development of the marketing strategy. The marketing communications strategist will not necessarily need to repeat the exercise. However, work is often necessary to provide current information about such factors as perception, attitudes, volumes, intentions and usage, among others. It is the accessibility question that is paramount: how can the defined group be reached with suitable communications? What is the media consumption pattern of the target audience?

Positioning

Positioning is the natural outcome of the target marketing process and is the subject of Chapter 24. Positioning is the communications element of the segmentation process in that the marketing mix needs to be communicated to the target market buyers. This communication should be executed in such a way that the product occupies a particular position in the mind of each buyer, relative to the offerings of competitive products. As Dibb and Simkin (1991) state: 'the paying public do not always perceive a product or brand in the same way the manufacturer would like' (or believes they do). Successful positioning can only be achieved by adopting a customer perspective and by understanding how customers perceive products in the class and how they attach importance to particular attributes.

Marketing communications and segmentation

Segmentation is an important ingredient in an organisation's marketing strategy and must be fully understood by all those responsible, in whatever way, for the development of a viable promotional strategy. The process of segmentation need not be repeated by the communications team, but certain aspects of the buyer's profile need to be developed and explored in greater depth. The segmentation base must be understood if coherence, uniformity of approach and subsequent communications are to be accomplished and be successful. Rothschild's (1987) approach to the use of segmentation in the context of marketing communications is useful because he groups the various bases for segmenting markets into the following:

1. *Enduring variables*
   These variables do not change across product classes; they stay relatively constant and they live with the individual. They include demographics, geographics and psychographic variables.
2. *Dynamic variables*
   These variables, by way of contrast, change through different product classes, and therefore an individual's relationship with a product is unique. The main segmentation tools are usage, time of adoption, loyalty level and benefit sought.

It is very important, as Rothschild says, to be able to describe the consumer/stakeholder on a number of dimensions for the precise purpose of developing effective and efficient communication plans. Broadly speaking, enduring variables are used for the design of media plans (Chapter 15). These are the different media each individual prefers to read or view on a regular basis. Dynamic variables are used in message design and positioning (Chapter 14). This refers to what is said, the advertising copy and symbolism, or the sales representative's prepared introduction and product description, for example.

A further aspect of the message strategy is how it is said, the colours and fonts used, and the tone and style of the communication. The development of a positioning statement is the outcome of the review of the segmentation process and it is of vital importance if the communications strategy is to be successful.

Product life cycle

The product life cycle (PLC) is a concept that has been used exhaustively to explain and predict sales patterns of products through time. Underpinning the concept is the belief that products move through a sequential logical pattern similar to the path that life forms follow: from birth through growth to maturity, before decline and inevitable death occur. At each stage of the cycle, a set of strategies or activities can be identified that are thought to be appropriate to the development of a product. One such assembly of activities is reproduced in Figure 10.5.

Since Levitt (1965) attempted to make the PLC concept much more manageable, the popularity of the concept has been maintained. Various strategies have been devised for each stage in the PLC, very often just to legitimise the concept and continue its use as a simple, easily understood predictive tool.

However, as Lambkin and Day (1989) comment, few management concepts have been so widely accepted or thoroughly criticised as the product life cycle. Meenaghan and O'Sullivan (1986) have empirically tested the sales curve and highlighted the divergence in thinking about the PLC. The concept may have had value when market conditions were stable and relatively predictable, but the markets of the 1990s are hostile, complex and turbulent (Wood, 1990), to the extent that the PLC is rendered

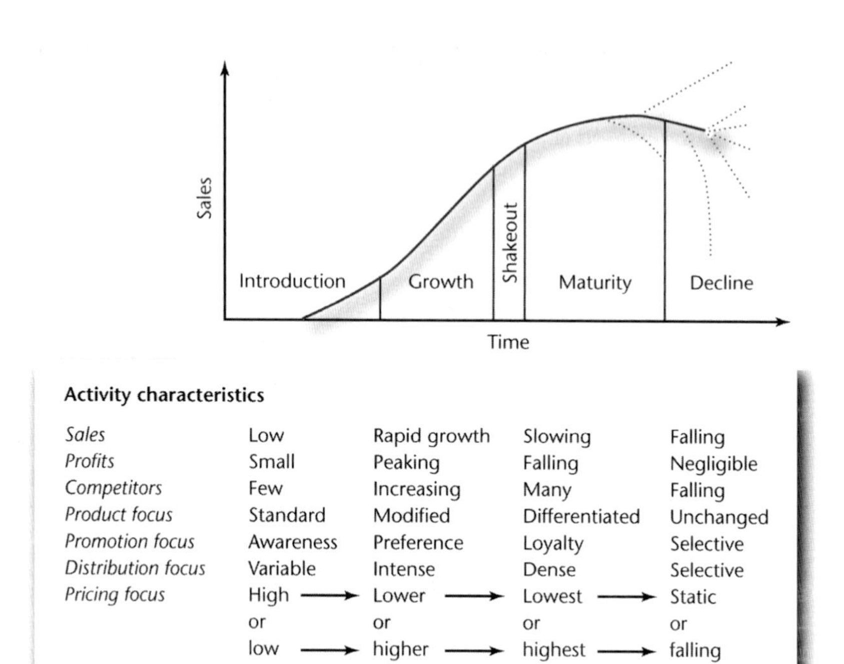

Activity characteristics

	Introduction	Growth	Maturity	Decline
Sales	Low	Rapid growth	Slowing	Falling
Profits	Small	Peaking	Falling	Negligible
Competitors	Few	Increasing	Many	Falling
Product focus	Standard	Modified	Differentiated	Unchanged
Promotion focus	Awareness	Preference	Loyalty	Selective
Distribution focus	Variable	Intense	Dense	Selective
Pricing focus	High →	Lower →	Lowest →	Static
	or	or	or	or
	low →	higher →	highest →	falling

Figure 10.5 Traditional activities associated with the PLC.

inflexible and generally irrelevant. The PLC has been exaggerated in terms of its usefulness and its use as a strategic tool. It is not an accurate reflection of the pattern of a product's life.

As a generalisation, however, it can be observed that sales increase in the initial phases of a product's life before levelling as market stagnation occurs (Tellis and Crawford, 1981). It is the mature phase that provokes most discussion, as different organisations pursue different brand strategies, there are changes in technology and buyers' preferences change. The levels of resources that have been made available to support the product vary and the marketing strategies and competitive environments in which products are expected to perform differ widely. As Lambkin and Day point out, the life-cycle frameworks fail to mention the total uncertainty about the emerging markets into which new products are launched. Furthermore, there is no account of the manner in which organisations deploy their skills and resources.

Phases of development

There is increasing acceptance that the PLC is now seen as a sterile predictive tool in marketing strategy. The concept is misleading and can lead to prescriptive approaches to strategy formulation. If it has any use, it is as an educational tool and as a means of identifying periods of past development. By conceptualising zones or phases of development, overall approaches to the development of communication strategies can be identified that aid understanding, discussion and planning (Table 10.5).

Marketing communicators need to be aware of the *phase* which the product or brand has reached within the development of the relevant product class. When sales growth

Table 10.5 Communication activities for product development phases

Introductory phase	Development phase	Established phase
Consumer		
Awareness	Differentiation	Sustain loyalty
• Advertising	• Advertising	• Sales promotion
• Public relations		• Advertising
		• Marketing public relations
		• Direct response media
Channels		
Awareness	Conviction and preference	Sustain brand exposure
• Sales promotion	• Personal selling	• Sales promotion
• Personal selling	• Direct response media	• Personal selling
• Public relations		• Merchandising
		• Joint advertising
		• Corporate public relations
		• Direct response media

slows (overall market sales slow) the effectiveness of competitive strategies becomes vitally important in shaping the sales curve in the mature phase. Strategies resulting from this knowledge should be created carefully in response to the anticipated market conditions. No set formula exists, and it is dangerous to be strategically prescriptive.

The marketing communicator needs to understand the phase in which a brand is situated. Having achieved that through the use of historical data and environmental scanning techniques, a general appreciation of the characteristics associated with marketing communications activities in the phase is of general assistance. The information may be useful to guide broad approaches to communications (awareness or persuasion), and to coordinate and focus thinking about the formulation and timing of competitive communications.

The successful development of any new offering must be accompanied by an announcement to the target market of the product's existence. Consequently, in the introductory phase, building awareness in both the consumer markets and the different channels is of paramount importance to establish the product's presence and to build distribution, respectively.

However, the nature of the brand's entering market needs to be observed perhaps with even more attention than in the past. *Brand challengers* or *entrepreneurial revolutionaries* (Cooper and Simmons, 1997) are brands that take a radical new approach to the needs of the market and break away from the frame in which brands in the sector are normally perceived. These brands have a strategy which seeks to reorientate the market to a new way of competing. Cooper and Simmons quote brands such as Virgin, Microsoft, Sony and PlayStation, to which can be added Direct Line and Toys R Us. These brands undermine those in the mature zone and jeopardise their brand values.

As development occurs and volume of sales increases, so does the number of organisations supplying the market. They have been attracted by the potential profitability, and this means that the emphasis of the communications strategy moves to the creation of differentiated awareness. In the introductory phase, demand was generated for the product concept; in the development phase, the increased number of suppliers forces demand generation to be driven by the need to create brand awareness. As this phase evolves, so the level of competitive activity intensifies, witnessed by indicators such as the level of advertising expenditure, the nature of the messages transmitted and the increasing number of players in the market.

When sales in the product class appear to level off, it could be interpreted as the onset of the established phase. The need to remain competitive remains vitally important, because sales growth in the market has possibly ceased, the market has become stagnant, and growth within individual brands will usually only be achieved by converting non-loyals and switchers into brand loyals. Where limited problem solving (Chapter 5) has created low levels of loyalty and high levels of brand switching, more funds should be moved into sales promotion at the expense of advertising. If extended problem solving has created high levels of brand loyalty, a higher level of advertising than sales promotion is required.

The termination of a product can be deliberate, the result of market forces or the development of new technology. Communication strategy will be influenced by marketing strategy. If the policy is to extinguish the product and divest of all stocks, then it is probable that there will be a dramatic withdrawal of nearly all forms of promotion. Some promotional activity will continue with the trade in an effort simply to keep open the flow and availability of products. This serves two factors: first, to reduce stocks to a minimum and so reduce the level of working capital tied up in stocks, and, secondly, it allows brand management to continue influencing the form of relationships with the members of the channel network. By seeking to support and assist channel members to attain their objectives, continuous and supportive communications will provide for future transactions.

If the policy is to allow the product to provide positive cash flows for a further period, until market forces take hold, it is probable that promotional investments will be required, albeit at lower levels than before.

Brand equity

If the PLC fails to deliver appropriate data to assist marketing management and the developmental phase approach is a little too broad, a more precise tool is required to assist the development of marketing communications.

Arising from the increasing recognition of the value that brands bring to organisations (Chapter 25) is a relatively new concept referred to as brand equity. According to Ehrenberg (1993), brand equity is just a reflection of a brand's market share. However, this is a view that excludes the composition of brands and the values that consumers place in them. There is a behavioural element and an attitudinal element (Richards, 1997). Brand equity is a measure of a number of different components, including the beliefs, images and core associations consumers have about particular brands. For example, these may be *vibrant*, *green*, *upstart*, *vigorous*, *approachable* or *caring*. These will vary between groups and represent fresh segmentation and targeting opportunities. A further component is the degree of loyalty or retention the brand is able to sustain. Measures of market penetration, involvement, attitudes and purchase intervals (frequency) are typical. In addition to these, Cooper and Simmons offer brand future as a third dimension. This is a reflection of a brand's ability to grow and remain unhindered by environmental challenges such as changing retail patterns, alterations in consumer buying methods and developments in technological and regulative fields.

Table 10.6 Five approaches to measuring brand equity

Source	Factors measured
David Aaker	Awareness, brand associations, perceived quality and market leadership, loyalty, market performance measures
Brand dynamics (Millward Brown)	Presence, relevance to consumer needs, product performance, competitive advantage, bonding
Equitrend (Total Research)	Salience, perceived quality, user satisfaction
3-D3 (TBWA Simmons Palmer)	Brand quality, quantity and future measured against a variety of stakeholders
Brand asset valuator (Young & Rubicam)	Strength (differentiation and relevance), stature (esteem and knowledge)

Source: Adapted from Cooper and Simmons (1997) and Haigh (1997).

Attempts to measure Brand Equity have to date been varied and without a high level of consensus, although the spirit and ideals behind the concept are virtually the same. Table 10.6 sets out some of the approaches adopted.

As a means of synthesing these approaches the following are considered the principal dimensions through which brand equity should be measured:

- *Brand dominance*: a measure of its market strength and performance
- *Brand associations*: measure of the beliefs held by buyers about what the brand represents and stands for
- *Brand prospects*: a measure of its capacity to grow and extend into new areas

Brand equity is considered important because of the increasing interest in trying to measure the return on promotional investments and so value brands for balance sheet purposes. A brand with a strong equity is more likely to be able to preserve its customer franchise and so fend off competitor attacks.

Summary

The corporate strategy is a foundation upon which business and functional strategies are developed. Marketing strategy is very closely allied to business strategy, and marketing communications, a sub-activity of marketing, is responsible for communicating the organisation's offering and corporate intentions to its various stakeholders, not just its customers.

To do this requires an appreciation of the needs of the buyers, non-buyers, intermediaries and other stakeholders (see Chapter 6) so that the organisation can shape its offering.

The marketing mix is an organisation's response to the identified needs of target customers. Marketing communications seek to convey the essence of the tangible and intangible elements of the offering represented in the mix. Many organisations will not have developed their marketing strategy into a form that can be formally articulated. This poses a dilemma in as much that communication planners might be drawn into developing a marketing strategy in its absence. This should be resisted, as it is not the responsibility of the marketing communications strategy to undertake this type of work.

The marketing strategy provides the communications planner with a view of the target market and a profile of the target customer, often based upon a combination of segmentation variables. Depending upon the object of the communications, whether a brand or an organisation, research can unveil the manner in which communications should be encoded and the media that need to be used to deliver the messages to the target audience. Above all else, the marketing strategy and the specification of target audiences is paramount for the development of effective marketing communications. The target audience provides a context within which marketing communications attempts to convey meaningful messages and sustain a viable dialogue with selected stakeholders.

Review questions

1. What is the difference between corporate and business level strategy?
2. Describe the elements of the Ashridge Mission Model.
3. Define marketing strategy and discuss its relevance to marketing communications.
4. Why is segmentation important?
5. How might you segment the markets for calculators, air travel, pencils, hand soaps and breakfast cereals?
6. What are enduring and dynamic segmentation variables?
7. Using the segments determined in answer to Question 5, suggest how the dynamic variables have influenced the marketing communications of organisations in these markets.
8. Comment on the utility of the product life cycle concept.
9. Identify four manufacturers' brands and suggest what types of benefits they might provide.
10. Identify three main dimensions of brand equity. What do they each measure?

References

Beane, T.P. and Ennis, D.M. (1987) Market segmentation: a review. *European Journal of Marketing*, 2, 5.

Bowles, T. (1988) Does classifying people by lifestyle really help the advertiser? *European Research* (February), 17–24.

Campbell, A. and Yeung, S. (1991) Creating a sense of mission. *Long Range Planning*, 24 August, pp. 10–20

Cooper, A. and Simmons, P. (1997) Brand equity lifestage: an entrepreneurial revolution. TBWA Simmons Palmer, Unpublished Working Paper.

Dibb, S. and Simkin, L. (1991) Targeting, segments and positioning. *International Journal of Retail and Distribution Management*, **19**(3), 4–10.

Dibb, S., Simkin, L., Pride, W.M. and Ferrel, O.C. (1991) *Marketing: Concepts and Strategies*. New York: Houghton Mifflin.

Ehrenberg, A.S.C. (1993) If you are so strong why aren't you bigger? *Admap* (October), 13–14.

Haigh, D. (1997) Brand valuation: the best thing to ever happen to market research. *Admap* (June), 32–5.

Haley, R.I. (1968) Benefit segmentation: a decision orientated research tool. *Journal of Marketing*, **32** (July), 33.

Kotler, P. (1997) *Marketing Management: Analysis, Planning Implementation and Control*, 9th edn. Englewood Cliffs NJ: Prentice Hall.

Lambkin, M. and Day, G.S. (1989) Evolutionary processes in competitive markets: beyond the product life cycle. *Journal of Marketing*, **53** (July), 4–20.

Lawless, J. (1998) Cooker buyers have wide range of tastes. *Sunday Times*, Business Section, 5 April, p. 9.

Levitt, T. (1965) Exploit the product life cycle. *Harvard Business Review* (November/December), 81–94.

Meenaghan, T. and O'Sullivan, J. (1986) The shape and length of the product lifecycle. *Irish Marketing Review*, **1**, 83–102.

Mueller-Heumann, G. (1992) Market and technology shifts in the 1990s: market fragmentation and mass customization. *Journal of Marketing Management*, **8**, 303–14.

Mullins, L.J. (1996) *Management and Organisational Behaviour*, 4th edn. London: Pitman.

Oliver, G. (1994) *Marketing Today*, 4th edn. Hemel Hempstead: Prentice Hall.

Plummer, J. (1974) The concept and application of lifestyle segmentation. *Journal of Marketing* (January), 33–7.

Richards, T. (1997) Measuring the true value of brands. *Admap* (March), 32–6.

Rothschild, M. (1987) *Marketing Communications*. Lexington MA: D.C. Heath.

Tellis, G.J. and Crawford, C.M. (1981) An evolutionary approach to product growth theory. *Journal of Marketing* (Fall), 125–32.

Wood, L. (1990) The end of the product life cycle? *Journal of Marketing Management*, **6**(2), 145–55.

chapter 11

Internal marketing communications

The concept of 'internal marketing' recognises the importance of organisational members (principally employees) as important markets in their own right. These markets can be regarded as segments (and can be segmented), each of which has particular needs and wants that require satisfaction in order that the organisation's overall goals be accomplished. Internal (marketing) communications is a contextual dialogue intended to convey managerial intentions and members' feelings and disposition towards these intentions and their own expectations.

AIMS AND OBJECTIVES

The aim of this chapter is to examine the context of internal marketing and how such issues might impact on an organisation's overall marketing communications.

The objectives of this chapter are:

1. To introduce the notion of internal marketing.
2. To understand the significance of organisational issues when developing marketing communication strategies.
3. To introduce the notion of organisational identity and the impact that employees can bring to the way that organisations are perceived by members and non-members.
4. To examine the impact of corporate culture on planned communications.
5. To provide an insight into the notion of strategic credibility and stakeholder perception of the focus organisation.
6. To appreciate the interaction and importance of corporate strategy to planned communications.

7. To examine how communication audits can assist the development of effective marketing communications.

Introduction

It was established earlier that marketing communications are concerned with the way in which various stakeholders interact with each other and with the focus organisation. Traditionally, external stakeholders (customers, intermediaries and financiers) are the prime focus of marketing communications. However, recognition of the importance of internal stakeholders as a group who should receive marketing attention has increased, and the concept of *internal marketing* emerged in the 1980s. This developed with greater impetus in the 1990s and is likely to be a major area of attention for both academics and practitioners in the first decade of the third millennium.

Berry (1980) is widely credited as the first to recognise the term 'internal marketing', in a paper that sought to delineate between product- and service-based marketing activities. The notion that the delivery of a service-based offering is bound to the quality of the personnel delivering it, has formed the foundation of a number of research activities and journal papers.

The popular view is that employees constitute an internal market in which paid labour is exchanged for designated outputs. An extension to this is that employees are a discrete group of customers with whom management interact (Piercy and Morgan, 1991), in order that relational exchanges can be maintained (developed) with external stakeholders. Therefore, as a legitimate type of customer they should be subject to similar marketing practices.

Both employees and managers impose their own constraints upon the range and nature of the activities the organisation pursues, including its promotional activities. Employees, for example, are important to external stakeholders not only because of the tangible aspects of service and production that they provide but also because of the intangible aspects, such as attitude and the way in which the service is provided: 'how much do they really care?'. Images are often based more on the intangible than the tangible aspects of employee communications.

Management, on the other hand, is responsible for the allocation of resources and the process and procedures used to create added value. Its actions effectively constrain the activities of the organisation and shape the nature and form of the communications the organisation adopts, either consciously or unconsciously. It is important, therefore, to understand how organisations can influence and impact upon the communication process.

Each organisation is a major influence upon its own marketing communications. Indeed, the perception of others is influenced by the character and personality of the organisation.

Member/non-member boundaries

The demarcation of internal and external stakeholders is not as clear as many writers suppose. The boundaries which exist between members and non-members of an organisation are becoming increasingly less clear as a new more flexible workforce emerges. For example, part-time workers, consultants and temporary workforces spread themselves across organisational borders (Hatch and Schultz, 1997) and in many instances assume multiple roles of employee, consumer (product) and financial stakeholder (e.g. Halifax or Abbey National employees, who may be borrowers or savers and now also shareholders).

According to Morgan (1997), many organisations have a problem as they do not recognise that they are themselves part of their environment. The context in which they see themselves and other organisations is too sharp. They see themselves as discrete entities faced with the problem of surviving against the vagaries of the outside world, which is often constructed as a domain of threat and opportunity. He refers to these as *egocentric* organisations. They are characterised by a fixed notion of who they are or what they can be and are determined to impose or sustain that identity at all times. This leads to an overplay of their own importance and an underplay of the significance of the wider system of relationships of which they are a part. In attempting to sustain unrealistic identities they produce identities that end up destroying important elements of the context of which they are part. The example provided by Morgan is of typewriter manufacturers who failed to see technological developments leading to electronic typewriters and then word processors.

It would appear that by redrawing or even collapsing boundaries with customers, competitors and suppliers, organisations are better able to create new identities and use internal marketing communications to better effect.

Purpose of internal marketing

What then is the purpose of internal marketing when sound HRM practices exist? Research by Foreman and Money (1995) indicates that managers see the main components of internal marketing as falling into three broad areas, namely development, reward and vision for employees. These will inevitably vary in intensity on a situational basis.

All of these three components have communication as a common linkage. Employees and management (members) need to communicate with one another and with a variety of non-members, and do so through an assortment of methods. Communication with members, wherever they are located geographically, needs to be undertaken for a number of reasons. These include the DRIP factors (Chapter 1), but these communications also serve the additional purposes of providing transaction efficiencies and affiliation needs; see Table 11.1.

Organisational identity

Organisational identity is concerned with what individual members think and feel about the organisation to which they belong. When their perception of the organisation's characteristics accords with their own self-concept then the strength of organisational identity will be strong (Dutton *et al.*, 1994). Organisational identity also refers to the degree to which feelings and thoughts about the distinctive characteristics are shared among the members (Dutton and Dukerich, 1991). There are therefore, both individual and collective aspects to organisational identity.

Table 11.1 The roles of internal marketing communications

DRIP factors	to provide information to be persuasive to reassure/remind to differentiate employees/groups
Transactional	to coordinate actions to promote the efficient use of resources to direct developments
Affiliation	to provide identification to motivate personnel to promote and coordinate activities with non-members

Table 11.2 When organisational identity is important

During the formation of the organisation
At the loss of an identity-sustaining element
On the accomplishment of an organisation's *raison d'être*
Through extremely rapid growth
If there is a change in the collective status
Retrenchment

Source: Albert and Whetten (1985).

Albert and Whetten (1985) stated that organisations must make three main decisions: who they are, what business they are in and what they want to be. In order that these decisions be made they claim that consideration must be given to what is central, what is distinctive and what is enduring about the character of the organisation.

Non-members of an organisation also develop feelings and thoughts about what the central, enduring and distinctive characteristics are. It is highly probable that there will be variances between the perceptions and beliefs of members and non-members, and this may be a cause of confusion, misunderstanding or even conflict.

This discrepancy between what Goodman and Pennings (1977) termed private and public identities can impair the 'health' of the organisation. The 'unhealthier' or greater the discrepancy, the more will be the difficulty in generating the resources required to guarantee corporate survival. In other words, the closer the member/non-member identification, the better placed the organisation will be to achieve its objectives.

Organisational identity is deemed to be important at a collective level, when an organisation is formed or when there is a major change to the continuity of the goals of the organisation or when the means of accomplishment are hindered or broken; see Table 11.2.

According to Dutton and Penner (1993), what an individual sees as important, distinctive and unique about an organisation will affect the individual's assessment of the importance of an issue facing the organisation and also the degree to which it is of personal importance.

For members, organisational identity may be conceptualised as their perception of their organisation's central and distinctive attributes, including its positional status and relevant compositional group. Consequently, external events that refute or call

CASE ILLUSTRATION

BUPA TV

The following mini-case history has been written by *Mick Hayes*, a Research Student at the University of Portsmouth, who is reading for a PhD and is researching aspects of Internal marketing.

'Amazing' internal communications

BUPA is an international health care provider employing over 25,000 people. This means that communicating a consistent message to these employees becomes a complex as well as a vital task.

BUPA utilises a number of different internal communications tools to undertake this task, including email, team briefs, a quarterly video (*BUPA TV*) and a quarterly magazine (*BUPA Life*). The issue of integration becomes important in a situation like this: if the various tools do not transmit a consistent message to the employees, confusion and dissonance may result.

One way to provide consistency is to have a single originator for all of these tools. In the case of BUPA, the PR department handles the provision of internal communications to the business.

The two quarterly issues, *BUPA Life* and *BUPA TV*, are timed so that they appear at six week intervals to increase continuity. The magazine is distributed to staff directly, while BUPA TV is distributed to managers on video to show to their staff in team briefs. The items include stories about product launches and acquisitions as well as items about individual members of staff.

A feedback form is distributed, either by email or hard copy, to the managers for their comments and suggestions, as well as feedback from the team. As a consequence of this feedback, the format has been refined: it has become more informal and now involves front-line staff as well as managers and includes contemporary music. Employees are also invited to submit items for the programme.

There is also integration with BUPA's external communications: the tag line 'You're Amazing' which has been used in the recent BUPA advertising campaign, has been adapted for use in the video. This segment informs the staff of some of their achievements. For example, the video states that 'You [the employees] are amazing, as this year you will contribute to the treatment of over 2 million people'.

The need to communicate a single ethos to a wide variety of employees complicates the role of the internal communicator. The staff of BUPA range from surgeons and nurses to sales personnel and support staff, and the communications need to encompass all of them and to show that their contributions are valued. The use of various media, coordinated through one department and integrated with both each other and the external communications is a major step towards the attainment of the goal of a staff committed to the objectives of the organisation. The collection and visible use of feedback also help towards this goal.

BUPA recognises that its staff are a major part of the organisation's success. It also recognises that the continuing commitment of its staff is essential, and effective internal communications is an important component in the process to gain this commitment.

into question these defining characteristics may threaten the perception that organisational members have of their organisational identity (Dutton and Dukerich, 1991).

Research by Elsbach and Kramer (1996) found that members of a high-ranking organisation (MBA schools) perceived a threat because the ranking devalued their central and cherished identity dimensions and so refuted their prior claims of positional status.

Members used selective categorisations to re-emphasise positive perceptions of their organisational identities for both themselves and their non-member audiences by highlighting identity dimensions or alternative groups with which they should be compared and which were not previously identified, the intention being to deflect attention.

Dutton and Dukerich state that there is a significant interdependence between individuals' social identities and their perceptions of their organisational identities. So, as they care about how their organisations are described and how they are compared with other organisations, so they experience cognitive distress (identity dissonance) when they think that their organisation's identity is being threatened by what they perceive as inaccurate descriptions or misleading (unfair) comparisons with other organisations.

In response to this distress members restore positive self-perceptions by highlighting their organisation's membership in alternative comparison groups.

It is normal to assume that identity is relatively static. However, just as organisations can experience strategic drift when the corporate strategy and performance moves further away, each period, from the intended or expected pattern, so organisations can suffer from identity drift away from the expected life cycle. Kimberley (1980) argues that this can occur for three main reasons: environmental complexity, identity divestiture and organisational success.

This indicates that care must be given to understanding and managing the organisational identity to ensure that any discrepancy between members' and non-members' perceptions of what is central, enduring and distinctive is minimised and to be aware of identity dissonance should the organisation be threatened and the values upheld by its members challenged.

Organisational culture

According to Beyer (1981), organisational identity is a subset of the collective beliefs that constitute an organisation's culture. Indeed, internal marketing is shaped by the prevailing culture, as it is the culture that provides the context within which internal marketing practices are to be accomplished.

Corporate culture, defined by Schein (1985), is 'the deeper level of basic assumptions and beliefs that are shared by members of an organisation, that operate unconsciously and define in a basic taken for granted fashion an organisation's view of its self and its environment'. A more common view of organisational culture is 'the way we do things around here'. It is the result of a number of factors, ranging through the type and form of business the organisation is in, its customers and other stakeholders, its geographical position, and its size, age and facilities. These represent the more tangible aspects of corporate culture. There are a host of intangible elements as well. These include the assumptions, values and beliefs that are held and shared by members of the organisation. These factors combine to create a unique environment, one where norms or guides to expected behaviour influence all members, whatever their role or position.

Levels of organisational culture

Corporate culture, according to Schein, consists of a number of levels. The first of these, according to Thompson (1990), is the most visible level. This includes physical

CASE ILLUSTRATION

Internal marketing – NatWest

For a long time many of the UK commercial clearing banks had failed to adopt a customer orientation. The prevailing attitude among these organisations reflected a production orientation, representative of a defensive culture. Marketing and branding for banks such as NatWest appeared not to be of central importance or of any significance. The need for brand differentiation was not recognised (Marshall, 1995), and consequently customer satisfaction levels were low and product development and innovation were also stifled, despite huge technological advances.

NatWest appointed Raoul Pinnell as its first Marketing Director in 1995. This served to elevate the role of marketing within the organisation and helped to focus staff attitudes on a new and different external approach to their business activities.

The approach to marketing in the industry had traditionally been based on above-the-line corporate image work. NatWest now demanded a new creative approach, centralised its media buying, slashed the amount spent on TV advertising from £24.5m to £7.5m and halved the number of agencies.

The bulk of the marketing budget was channelled into below-the-line work and staff training. Accompanying this programme was a huge amount of internal literature which served to inform about corporate identity cues and also reinforced the change in orientation.

The name National Westminster was replaced to support the development of the brand and its wide range of offerings. The problem according to Pinnell was that NatWest had a range of products that extended beyond those normally associated with a bank, but the organisation had failed to get the message across to their customers.

Part of the new marketing communications strategy was aimed at repositioning NatWest by dissociating itself from the banking sector with the statement 'more than just a bank'.

The emphasis on the development of customer service skills is good policy. By adjusting the product quality first (credibility factor) and then articulating the brand's credentials (raising visibility) it is more likely that long-term success can be achieved. However, the move from a defender to a prospector type organisation will not be accomplished quickly.

Adapted from Marshall (1995)

aspects of the organisation, such as the way in which the telephone is answered, the look and style of the reception area, and the general care afforded to visitors. Other manifestations of these visible aspects are the advertisements, logos, letterheads and other written communications that an organisation generates.

The second level consists of the values held by key personnel. For example, should particular sales teams who regularly better their targets have their targets increased or should certain members of the sales team be redeployed to less successful teams or new markets? If the decision is made to increase the target, and the outcome is successful, then the decision is more likely to be repeated when the same conditions arise again.

The third level in Schein's approach is achieved when the decision to increase the target becomes an automatic response to particular conditions. A belief is formed and becomes an assumption about behaviour in the organisation. This automatic approach can lead to complementary behaviour by members of the sales team. The placing of orders can become manipulated, to the extent that orders placed in month six may be 'delayed' or stuck in the top drawer of the sales representative's desk, until some point in month seven, when it is appropriate to release it.

The belief that the targets will be increased can lead to a behaviour that is referred to as 'the way we do things around here'. This behaviour leads to relative stability for all concerned and need not be disturbed unless a change is introduced, whose source is elsewhere in the system; that is, outside the team.

Culture and communication

Corporate culture is not a static phenomenon; the stronger the culture the more likely it is to be transmitted from one generation of organisational members to another, and it is also probable that the culture will be more difficult to change if it is firmly embedded in the organisation. Most writers acknowledge that effective cultural change is difficult and a long-term task. Achieving a cultural fit is necessary if an organisation wishes to embrace a strategy that is incompatible with the current mind set of the organisation. Hunger and Wheelan (1993), for example, state that to bring about cultural change, good communication, throughout the organisation, is a prerequisite for success. Mitchell (1998) considers the strong corporate culture that exists at Procter and Gamble. Depending upon one's perspective, this rigid formal hierarchical culture may be considered an advantage or a disadvantage. On the plus side it allows for strong identity, consistency and people development opportunities, as the company has a 'promote from within' policy. On the downside, the strength and penetration of the culture and need to toe the party line can restrict innovation, entrepreneurship and the use of initiative. This strength of culture and the cautious approach to risk taking may be responsible for the consistent emphasis on product performance in its advertising and communications, unlike its close rival Unilever which makes greater use of emotions in its advertising. Changing this culture will be a challenge, but to be successful senior management will, among other things, need to be 'obsessive' about communicating the following to all members of the organisation (Gordon, 1985):

1. the current performance and position of the organisation in comparison with its competition and the outlook for the future
2. the vision of what the organisation was to become and how it would achieve it
3. the progress the organisation had made in achieving those elements identified previously as important

The focus of this communication is internal, usually through training and development programmes. However, if the concept of the superorganisation is accepted (Chapter 6), then this level of communication activity should also occur in the channel networks, especially when the network is destabilised due to environmental turbulence. Certain complex offerings, such as information technology-based products, require channel members to provide high levels of training and support. It is also important to communicate the objectives of the network and to share responsibility for the performance of the channel as a whole. This is partly achieved by members fulfilling their roles as successful dealers, retailers or manufacturers, but there is still a strong requirement for the channel leader to set out what is required from each member of its different networks and to report on what has been achieved to date.

Management of the communication appropriations, through time, will show the degree to which an organisation values such investments. Brands need time, the long term, to build and develop strength. Cutting back on investment in communications, especially advertising, in times of recession and difficulty, reveals management to view such activities as an expense, a cost against short-run needs. Furthermore, the expectation of channel members may be that a certain volume of marketing communications is necessary not only to sustain particular levels of business but also because competitors are providing established levels of communication activity. What is important is that the communications planner understands the culture of the organisation and the primary networks, values, styles, motivations and norms so that the communications work with rather than against the corporate will.

Corporate strategy and communication

The relationship between corporate strategy and communications is important. Traditionally, these communications are perceived as those that make the network between an organisation's employees and its managers. This internal perspective of communications is important, particularly when organisations are in transition. This is only one part of the communication process. Employees are just one of the many stakeholders each organisation must seek to satisfy. Communications regarding strategic issues should also be targeted at members of the support and performance networks in order to gain their goodwill, involvement and understanding.

All stakeholders need to know what the objectives of the focus organisation are, particularly the mission and overriding vision the organisation has, as this will impact on the other organisations in the performance network. For example, if Heinz or Pedigree Petfoods were to announce that, in the future, all their products were to be presented in containers that are capable of being recycled, then current suppliers might need to reformulate their offerings and any future suppliers would be aware of the constraint this might place on them. The information is provided in order that others may work with them and continue supplying offerings to end users with a minimum of interruption.

Barich and Kotler (1991) suggest that the concept of positioning (the process whereby offerings are perceived by consumers relative to the competition) applies at the brand and corporate level. If an organisation is pursuing a generic strategy of differentiation, then the positioning statements of the organisation need to reflect this. The image that stakeholders have of an organisation and its offerings affects their disposition towards the organisation, their intentions to undertake market transactions and the nature of the relationships between members.

Good external communications are important because, among other benefits, they can provide a source of competitive advantage. Perrier has built its share of the mineral water market on the volume and style of its planned communications. It has dominated communications in the market and has effectively set a mobility barrier which demands that any major challenger must be prepared to replicate the size of Perrier's investment in communications. The quality of the Perrier communications has also led distributors and other network members to support and want to be involved with the organisation, as evidenced by the swift recovery in market share after all world stocks had to be withdrawn because a small number of bottles had been identified as 'contaminated'. Morden (1993) refers to these positive external perceptions as intangible benefits which help to differentiate the organisation from its competitors.

All marketing strategies, such as those to harvest, build, hold and divest, require different communication strategies and messages. Similarly, market penetration, product development, market development and product penetration strategies all require varying forms of support which must be reflected in the communications undertaken by the organisation.

Marketing research may indicate that different stakeholders do not perceive the corporate and marketing strategies of an organisation in the same way as that intended by management. Some stakeholders may perceive the performance of an organisation inaccurately. This means that the organisation is failing to communicate in an effective and consistent way, and any such mismatch will, inevitably, lead to message confusion and relative disadvantage in the markets in which the organisation operates.

The communication of strategic intent and corporate performance must be harmonised. By understating or even misleading different stakeholders, performance may be influenced, and if claims are made for an organisation which suggest a level of performance or intent beyond reality, then credibility may be severely jeopardised.

Strategic credibility

A relatively new development concerning the role of corporate strategy and corporate communications is the concept of strategic credibility. According to Higgins and Bannister (1992), strategic credibility refers to 'how favourably key stakeholders view the company's overall corporate strategy and its strategic planning processes'.

If stakeholders perceive the focus organisation as strategically capable then it is suggested that it will accrue a number of benefits. The benefits vary from industry to industry and according to each situation, but it appears from the early research that those organisations experiencing transition and who are not regulated in any way have potentially the most to gain from open corporate communication with their stakeholders. The benefits from this open attitude include improved stock market valuations and price/earnings multiples, better employee motivation and closer relationships with all members of the performance and support networks, particularly those within the financial community.

There are four main determinants of strategic credibility:

1. an organisation's strategic capability
2. past performance
3. communication of corporate strategy to key stakeholders
4. the credibility of the chief executive officer (CEO)

Strategic capability

Capability is a prerequisite for credibility. The perception that stakeholders have of the strategic processes within an organisation will influence their belief that the focus organisation can or cannot achieve its objectives. This is important in networks which are characterised by close working arrangements and high levels of interdependence.

Should one organisation indicate that it lacks the necessary capability to perform strategically, then other members of the network are likely to be affected. The sharing of a strategic vision, one that may be common to all members of the stakeholder network, is a positive indicator of the existence of the acceptance that the focus organisation is strategically capable.

Past performance

The maintenance of a sustained strategic capability profile is partly dependent upon corporate performance. Poor performance does not sustain confidence, but even the existence of a strong performance is only worthwhile if it is communicated properly. The communication should inform the target audiences that the performance was planned and that there was sound reasoning and management judgement behind the performance.

Corporate communications

Organisations should inform members of the network of their strategic intentions as well as their past performance. This requires the accurate targeting and timing of the messages at a pace suitable and appropriate to the target's requirements. Higgins and Bannister refer to financial analysts, in particular, as stakeholders in need of good information. They argue that trying to evaluate the performance of a diversified organisation operating in a number of different markets, of which many of the analysts lack knowledge and expertise, is frustrating and difficult. Good information delivered through appropriate media and at particular times can be of benefit in the development of the realm of understanding between parties.

By keeping financial analysts aware of the strategic developments and the strategic thinking of the focus organisation and the industries in which it operates, the value of the organisation is more likely to reflect corporate performance. ICI experienced a major undervaluation in the 1980s because the financial markets and other key network members were not kept informed of the new strategies and thinking behind the corporate revival in the period 1982–86.

The credibility of the CEO

The fourth element proposed by Higgins and Bannister concerns the ability of the CEO to communicate effectively with a variety of audiences. By projecting strong, balanced and positive communications, it is thought that a visible CEO can improve the overall reputation of the organisation. Coupled with the improvement will be a perception of the strategic capability of the organisation. The CEO therefore can be regarded as a major determinant of the organisation's perceived strategic credibility.

Research by Newell and Shemwell (1995) suggests that care should be taken when using CEOs as an endorser. They argue that the impact of source credibility may be reduced because of beliefs about product attributes, and this in turn may impact on behavioural intentions. Therefore, CEOs might be best used as endorsers when informationally, rather than emotionally or transformationally, based messages predominate.

For example, Richard Branson has been used as CEO endorser of the Virgin group. As Chairman he has been a focal point in the promotion of Virgin financial

CASE ILLUSTRATION

CEO endorsers – the Prudential

The Prudential, a long-established financial services organisation, had established itself through the 'the man from the Pru'. Visually this was represented by a silloutte of an archetypal sales representative who appeared friendly, approachable and caring. This approach was abandoned for being out-of-date and inappropriate for a market that embraced new players, who had developed new products and where customers had become much more financially sophisticated.

The account moved to two other agencies in relatively quick succession. However, the strategies adopted in this period either failed to reinforce the brand or were simply unliked. Faced with a changing and increasingly competitive market, where its own customers had become increasingly distant, the Prudential decided to reinstate the 'man from the Pru'. However, there was an important difference about the man. This time he was represented by the Group Chief Executive, the one person who is responsible for the range of offerings. As Andrew Williams, Advertising Manager at the Prudential, claimed: 'a personal endorsement from an executive is powerful' (see Exhibit 11.1).

The man from the Pru has always been intended to instill trust. Now, with Sir Peter Davis, the Group Chief Executive or CEO endorsing the organisation, strategic credibility as well as customer perceptions are challenged.

Adapted from Hall (1997)

Exhibit 11.1 CEO Endorser – Sir Peter Davis is now The Man from the Pru (Picture kindly supplied by the Prudential Corporation plc)

products (mainly informational messages), but has not played such a central role in the persuasive communications concerning the airline Virgin Atlantic, where emotionally based messages have been used to influence brand choice decisions. In this instance a celebrity spokesperson (actress Helen Mirren) was used to endorse the airline.

Strategic credibility is an interesting concept which can be used to develop an understanding of the perception held by key support network members of an organisation's strategic management processes.

Communication audit

Research, as we have seen, is an important element in the design of communication plans. Associated with this should be an evaluation of the most recent attempts at communicating with target audiences. The accumulation of this type of short-run information is useful because it builds into a database that can be used to identify key factors over the long run. Regression analysis can be used eventually to identify key variables in the marketing communications and marketing plans.

The communication strategies of competitors should also be measured and evaluated. Organisations and offerings do not exist in isolation from each other and competitor activities; messages, styles and levels of spend should also be taken into account. If a strategy of differentiation is being pursued it would appear pointless and wasteful to position an offering in the same way as a main competitor.

The process by which an organisation communicates with its target audiences is, as we have seen, extremely important. To assist the process of evaluating the effectiveness of past communication strategies, strategic credibility and the corporate image held by different members of all networks, a communication audit should be undertaken. Financial audits examine the processes by which organisations organise and systematically manage their financial affairs. Some of the underlying agenda items may be to prevent fraud and malpractice, but the positive aspects of the financial audit are to understand what is happening, to develop new ways of performing certain tasks and to promote efficiency and effectiveness. The same principle holds for the communication audit. How is the organisation communicating and are there better ways of achieving the communication objectives?

A communication audit is a process which can assist the communications planner in assessing whether or not an organisation is communicating with its consumers and other stakeholders in an effective and meaningful way. A further important goal of such an exercise is to determine whether the communications perceived and understood by the target audiences are the messages that were intended in the first place. Are the messages being decoded in the manner in which they were designed when they were encoded? This exercise helps organisations to develop their realm of understanding with their respective network members and includes all internal and external communications, whether overt or covert.

Procedures associated with a communication audit

All forms of printed and visual communications (brochures, leaflets, annual reports, letterheads, advertisements etc.) need to be collected and assembled in a particular location. Examples of main competitors' materials should also be brought together, as this will provide benchmarks for market evaluation. Once collated, the task is to identify consistent themes and the logic of the organisation's communications.

Plate 2.1 Dennis Fire Engines. The characteristics of the source of any marketing communication message are vitally important. The manufacturers of Dennis Fire Engines use source credibility and attractiveness as an integral part of their promotional activities. See Chapter 2 page 31. Picture reproduced with the kind permission of Dennis Fires Engines.

Plate 4.1 Beamish -Brand Personality

Plate 4.2 Beamish - Brand Personality. The development of marketing communication messages can often be directed by an association with the inner characteristics of the target market. Beamish, an Irish ale was presented reflecting two sides of the Irish character. See Chapter 4 page 75. Picture reproduced with the kind permission of Scottish Courage Ltd.

Plate 4.3 'Diet Coke'. Coca-Cola use sexual overtones to gain the attention of the target market. See Chapter 4 page 76. "Diet Coke" is a registered trade mark of The Coca-Cola Company. This image has been reproduced with kind permission from the Coca-Cola Company.

Plate 4.4 Andrex Puppy. The use of product attributes in marketing communications is long established. Here the Andrex puppy is used to symbolise (through time) the length and strength of the brand. See Chapter 4 page 85. Picture reproduced with the kind permission of Kimberley-Clark Ltd.

Plate 4.5 Skoda – Attitude Change. A major part of many marketing communication campaigns (and advertising in particular) is to either maintain or change the attitudes held by the target market towards the brand or product category. The picture shows Skoda using the VW silhouette to help change attitudes through the suggestion of reliability and trust of VW towards Skoda cars in the UK shortly after the company was bought by its German parent. See Chapter 4 page 88. Picture reproduced with the kind permission of Skoda UK Ltd.

Plate 5.1 Bose. The need to communicate rational rather than emotional based information is more important when promoting products that evoke high levels of involvement and perceived risk. See Chapter 5 page 99. Picture reproduced with the kind permission of Bose.

Plate 5.2 Virgin – Helen Mirren. The use of celebrities to help endorse and support a brand can be significant element in an individual's brand choice criteria. Helen Mirren was used by Virgin Atlantic to convey messages about product developments and advantages. See Chapter 5 page 100. Picture reproduced with the kind permission of Virgin Atlantic Ltd.

National Health Servings.

Today, nutrition, diet and the health of the nation are top of the agenda. And not a moment too soon as far as Kellogg's is concerned. Of course, there's a limit to what a Kellogg's breakfast can do. But it can make a real contribution. And we've always done everything in our power to make that contribution as big as possible.

For instance, we were the first cereal manufacturer in the UK to fortify our products with vitamins back in 1960. And we followed not long after with extra iron.

Then in 1987, before the virtues of folic acid were widely acknowledged, we started adding that as well.

What's more, at a time when half of us are officially overweight, we have now taken steps to ensure that every breakfast cereal we make will always be at least 90% fat-free. For further information and advice please phone Kellogg's 0800 626 066.

Kellogg's

Serving The Nation's Health

Plate 8.1 Kellogg's – The need to recognise and reflect social values is an important dimension when building an understanding of the target market and developing a brand's position. This picture reflects part of a campaign by Kellogg's to 'Serve the Nation's health'. The campaign was built on four pillars; weight control, disease prevention, mental and physical stimulation and winter protection. See Chapter 8 page 164. Picture reproduced with the kind permission of the Kellogg Company of Great Britain.

Plate 13.1 Orange. The latest entrant to the UK mobile phone market, was branded Orange and used a striking colour combination to help differentiate it from its competitors. See Chapter 13 page 265. Picture reproduced with the kind permission of Hutchison Telecom.

Plate 13.2 Yellow Pages – J.R. Hartley. Yellow Pages used a central character 'JR Hartley' to establish new brand values. The gentleman provoked strong levels of audience involvement and brand identification. See Chapter 13 page 269. Picture reproduced with the kind permission of Yellow Pages.

Plate 13.3 Blackcurrant Tango/Salience. Some advertising messages are designed to cut through clutter and to stand out arresting the attention of all viewers/listeners. Tango, pictured here, have used this approach to reposition the brand. See Chapter 13 page 269. Picture reproduced with the kind permission of Britvic Soft Drinks.

Plate 14.1 BMW – Shaken not Stirred. This BMW is a classic advertisement which portrays comparative product attributes, originality and message consistency. See Chapter 14 page 284. Picture reproduced with the kind permission of BMW and WCRS.

Plate 14.2 Yellow Pages – Mistletoe. The gentle use of humour is exemplified by Yellow Pages. See Chapter 14 page 292. Picture reproduced with the kind permission of Yellow Pages.

	Product A	Product B	Product C	Corporate
Literature	Assess horizontally →			
Promotions	Assess vertically ↓			
Advertising				
Direct mail				
Point-of-sale				
Stationery				
Signage				
Uniforms				
Vehicles				

Figure 11.1 A communications audit matrix (Ind (1992); used with kind permission).

Ind (1992) suggests that one way of accomplishing this is to develop a communications matrix (Figure 11.1). Information needs to be grouped by type of offering (vertically) and then by each type of medium (horizontally). The vertical grouping helps determine the variety of messages that customers receive if they are exposed to all the communications relating to a single offering. Are the messages consistent? Are the messages logically related, is the related logic one that is intended and what is the total impact of these communications? The horizontal grouping helps determine message consistency across a number of different offerings, perhaps from different divisions. If a single dealer or end user receives the communications relating to a product line or even a particular product mix, is the perception likely to be confusing?

Internal communications should be included in the audit. An analysis of official publications, such as in-house magazines, is obvious, but materials posted on noticeboards and the way in which the telephone is answered affect the perception that stakeholders have of the organisation.

The audit needs to incorporate research into the attitudes of employees to the organisation and the perceptions held by various stakeholders. This will involve both qualitative and quantitative research. The objective is to determine whether the image of the organisation reflects reality. If corporate performance exceeds the overall image, then corporate communications are not working effectively. If the image is superior to performance, then the operations of the organisation need to be improved.

In the mid-1980s, ICI's corporate performance was more advanced than its image. The organisation's communications were not working effectively. Research eventually revealed the gulf between performance and image, but had a communications audit been used on a regular basis, in conjunction with an image tracking system, then the amount of damage or loss of goodwill might have been considerably reduced.

Organisations need to understand how they are perceived by their stakeholders. A communications audit focuses attention on the totality of messages transmitted and provides a framework for corporate identity programmes.

Functional capability

The final elements to be reviewed as part of the internal marketing context are those that relate to the individual functional areas within an organisation. A firm's overall core competency may be the result of a number of competencies held at functional level. Internal marketing can be regarded as a key to providing strong external marketing performance (Greene *et al.*, 1994). This is achieved by releasing high levels of internal service provision within the functional areas. As Varey (1995) confirms: 'Internal service quality is necessary for superior external service quality'.

Financial capability

Before any communications plan can be devised in any detail, it is necessary to have a broad understanding of the financial capability of the organisation; in other words, how much money is available for communications? This is important, as it impacts upon the objectives that are to be set later and the choice of media necessary to carry the organisation's messages. For example, it is pointless asking dealers to undertake training programmes with end users if the manufacturer does not have the sales representatives and training staff to instruct the dealers in the first place. Most medium-sized tour operators do not have the capital to fund television-based campaigns, even though some of the major national tour operators regularly use television.

Manufacturing capability

One of the main aims of the communication plan is to stimulate and maintain demand. If the production resources are limited then the capacity needs to be aligned with the potential demand of a region or local area rather than nationally. Equally, the communication programme should be geared to the same area. All demand must be satisfied and likewise much of the the communication programme will be ineffective in the short term if full production capacity has been reached.

Marketing capability

Discussion so far has assumed that the available corporate and marketing expertise is of sufficient calibre not only to formulate but also to implement a marketing strategy and its associated communication requirements. This raises questions about the customer orientation of the organisation, its attitude towards marketing planning and its general disposition towards the provision of a sustained level of customer service and satisfaction. Research shows that only a minority of organisations use a formal marketing planning process (Greenley, 1985).

In a study by Doyle (1987) it was found that only 50% of UK organisations claimed to have a marketing philosophy, one where the satisfaction of customer needs predominated over either a sales-orientated or a production-orientated philosophy. There may be a variety of reasons for this, and Boydell (1977), among others, claims that the culture of the organisation may trap or constrict the organisation and reduce the effectiveness of marketing planning. This lack of belief in marketing planning is a reflection of the values and beliefs of the organisation. Leppard and McDonald (1991) conclude their study by stating that if the values of the organisation are gener-

CASE ILLUSTRATION

DERA

This mini-case history was written by *Jane Brownsord*, CIM diplomate and partner/owner of an advertising agency.

Internal communication in the Defence Evaluation and Research Agency (DERA)

Effective communication is increasingly regarded as integral to the success, even the survival, of large organisations, and yet it has only recently emerged as a management skill that can be learned and harnessed. In the past it was often unions who controlled communications, and in just about every organisation the grapevine is a force to be reckoned with. Now companies are recognising the value of managing internal communications and are using it to gain support from employees to implement new strategies, change programmes, policies and cultures.

Background to DERA

DERA is one such organisation where internal communications has proved vital in creating an environment that is responsive to change. The Defence Evaluation and Research Agency (DERA), an agency of the Ministry of Defence, has seen its fair share of change. It was formed as the Defence Research Agency (DRA) in 1991 from a merger of the four principal non-nuclear research establishments of the MOD, and later expanded to become DERA.

Its primary role was to provide scientific and technical advice to the Ministry of Defence to underpin a multi-billion pound equipment procurement programme. It also had an important objective of exploiting its wealth of knowledge for use in civil applications. With over 13,500 employees in 50 geographically spread sites, the task of transforming traditional MOD civil servants into a customer-focused income generating organisation presented a formidable communications challenge – which many years later is still ongoing.

Communications environment

The first step was to understand DERA's communications environment (or context). This had to account for the DERA staff, who were coming to terms with their newly expanded organisation and were having to adjust to commercial disciplines. The commercial environment was also new, one where DERA might be the customer, the supplier or occasionally the competitor. DERA's most important customer is the Ministry of Defence, which viewed with keen interest the changes to the organisation. Other stakeholders, such as the media, politicians and the local community, all became more significant to DERA and its activities.

Communications policy

A communication policy statement was created by the company secretary's office, in consultation with DERA senior management, to make the communications strategy visible to staff. The statement committed DERA to 'open, honest and comprehensive communication' with employees, ensuring that both local and strategic information was made available.

Implementation of the policy involved making certain organisational changes, bringing in new systems and creating communication tools to facilitate a flow of information up and down the ladder. The role of management was critical in supporting the communications programme by providing information, responding to feedback and exemplifying the culture through their behaviour. Many of the top managers attended local communication workshops to show their involvement and support.

Table 11.3 Summary of communication methods used within DERA (*Internal Communications Guide* – DERA)

The communication methods summarised below have been developed to ensure a good mix of frequent and infrequent communication and to facilitate as much two-way communication as possible.

Method	Sector	Audience	Frequency	Ownership
Talkback (*team* briefing)	All	All staff	Monthly	All managers
DERA News	All	All staff	Monthly	*DERA News* editor
Newsletters	Where published	Relevant staff	Varies	Sectors
Official notices	All	Relevant staff	As required	Issuing department
Noticeboards	All	All staff	As required	Noticeboard 'keeper'
Improvement programmes	All	All staff	As required	Originator
Focus groups	Most in some form	Teams	As required	SIMs, local managers or problem owners
Integrated Communication Environment (ICE)	All	All staff	As required	Originator
Other electronic media	All	All staff	As required	Publishing individual or sector

Early feedback

A staff attitude survey was used to understand what staff considered important in good communications. The findings of the survey and information from other sources indicated there was room for improvement in DERA's existing communications and made a number of suggestions: management needed to become more responsive to staff opinions; the amount and quality of face-to-face communication needed to increase; the language used should be free from jargon; and most importantly, staff needed to acknowledge that everyone was responsible for communicating effectively. These suggestions formed the bedrock on which DERA's communication strategy was built.

Communications strategy

An Internal Communications Working Group was formed to create and implement a communications strategy. The group were responsible for creating guidelines on the principles of good communication; implementing the effective use of team briefings, called 'Talkback'; and developing the use of electronic media (the 'DERA Intranet'). Training in communications techniques was provided for managers to give them the necessary skills, as not every manager was comfortable with speaking in public, using overhead slides and videos, and leading group discussions.

A toolkit of communication methods was formulated which managers in different parts of the organisation could choose and adapt to suit their needs (see Table 11.3). Guidelines for their effective use were provided through workshops supported by an *Internal Communications Guide* – a guidebook outlining methods of communications and how they should be used.

Where to now?

DERA has now been concentrating on improving internal communications for over six years. Most of the managers have been trained and the majority of the communication methods are in place, including focus groups, newsletters and electronic media reaching staff at all levels of the organisation. But has DERA succeeded in its communications challenge; has all its work paid off?

DERA is keen to know whether its efforts

have been effective, and Staff Attitude Surveys are frequently used. Commenting on the measurement process, Steve Parker, Sector Improvement Coordinator, says: 'Our problem is how do you *really* measure success? I think the only way you can be sure that messages are getting through is by talking to people one-to-one, because otherwise some of the messages get distorted'.

The most recent survey actually shows a decrease since 1994 from 53% to 40% in the numbers of staff with a positive attitude to communication. This is obviously disheartening after all the efforts that have been made, but it could well reflect that the context in which people are working in has changed significantly in two years. When the organisation became a trading fund in 1993, it meant that its income needed to be earned from customers, and even though 90% of those were in the MOD they still had to be persuaded that the DERA product was worth purchasing and offered value for money. That has proved a strong discipline in forcing down costs, improving efficiency and ensuring that it delivered the sort of service customers want. But out of necessity, the resulting change programme brought tremendous disruption to staff. Moving from focused scientific and technical services organisations to what is now the largest single scientific organisation in Western Europe has been a huge cultural upheaval, and staff are bound feel a loss of identity and morale.

A certain amount of disillusionment may also stem from staff frustration that thing weren't happening quickly enough – having raised their expectations through communicating openly about future plans, staff were quick to speak out when they did not immediately materialise. A further contributing factor was that in 1995, 5000 staff from the residual science and technology organisations in the MOD were taken on. This inevitably meant some dilution of the cultural improvements that DERA had already made, and in some areas DERA found itself back at square one. However, one of those organisations that joined DERA in 1995 had itself made great strides with internal communication through the formation of an internal communications team with its own newsletters, posters and guidebook. But for a time at least, the joining organisations impaired the performance of the Agency as a whole and meant that the Internal Communications Working Group had their work cut out bringing everyone to the same level and keeping momentum.

Moves are continually being made to address such issues but it's not an easy task and lessons are still being learnt in how to manage internal communications in such a vast organisation. 'The solution to an organisation's communications problems lies in the acceptance that communication is the responsibility of all managers at all levels. Formal communication structures like Talkback help, but at the end of the day, it is up to the manager to talk to his or her staff and, of equal importance, to listen to what they have to say', adds Liz Peace, Company Secretary.

Internal communications are high on the management agenda and Liz Peace has made a personal effort to accelerate improvements, including the appointment of an Internal Communications Manager and the formation of a steering group that together look at the holistic view of communications within DERA.

How can things improve?

Internal communications are not an exact science. There seems to be no right or wrong way, and no guaranteed route to success. Too little or too much information can be a dangerous thing, but how can management know in advance how to get the balance right? DERA has tried hard to follow the fundamental principles of good communications and apply them religiously, and yet staff seemed dissatisfied with DERA's internal communications.

One area where DERA may be able to improve relations and help create a feelgood factor is in its approach to communications generally. The policy of 'open, honest and comprehensive communication' seems to have really been taken literally. DERA has gone to enormous lengths to create good communications, establishing mechanisms and processes, but sometimes it can be *too* honest and open with employees. There are so many mechanisms and processes in place that staff often have too much information, sometimes too early because of management's desire to involve staff, and frequently of the wrong sort – negative.

Perhaps what DERA needs to consider is internal *marketing* communications. This would involve treating its staff in a similar way to customers in understanding that they have needs to be satisfied and expectations to be managed.

While bad news must be communicated, it should as often as possible be balanced with good news. DERA is making some great strides ahead with both technical advances and with new markets, but this doesn't always filter through. Maybe the problem is that DERA is not used to presenting and selling itself either internally or externally.

Managing the flow and type of information to keep employees informed about DERA's successes could make a very positive difference, because when employees think the organisation they work for is doing well, morale and pride are generally correspondingly high.

The new Internal Communications Manager, Steve Young, believes that DERA has turned the corner, as 'early feedback from the most recent staff survey shows a significant improvement in communications'.

'The commitment to openness and honesty plays a crucial part in building trust in DERA. Never underestimate the audience.'

He recognises the potential for information overload and the need to avoid overburdening busy people. Deciding to whom a message is vital, important or just useful is crucial for effective internal communications. In terms of measuring the effectiveness of the open communications approach the annual staff attitude survey provides the benchmark, but in addition, feedback from Talkback, correspondence to *DERA News*, and phone out and phone in polls, together with intranet newsgroups, provide important qualititative and quantitative information.

DERA realises that there is still much to do, but the challenge is to maintain the momentum.

ally consistent with the underlying values of a complete marketing planning process, then it is probable that the planning process will be adopted. The necessary values, according to Doyle, are partly driven by the CEO and his or her beliefs in marketing.

Many CEOs had a poor understanding of what marketing is: to a number of them marketing is about selling and promotion. Such a shallow perspective is unlikely to lead to an organisational culture which will support a marketing orientation. The study concluded by reference to the fact that less than half of the organisations in the study had a marketing director supporting the CEO, but 89% had a financial director.

It seems reasonable to extend these conclusions by surmising that the same values and beliefs are necessary for the successful adoption of a planned approach to marketing communications, if only because it is a subsystem of marketing planning.

Summary

Intraorganisational issues need to be appreciated when building a communications plan. One of the key factors to be considered is the corporate strategy, including the degree to which it is understood by stakeholders and the credibility that management has to manage strategic processes.

A major influence on the communication style is the prevailing culture. Culture is a reflection of the personality of the organisation, which in turn affects the corporate identity or the way in which an organisation presents itself to its stakeholders. This presentation of visual cues can be managed deliberately or left unattended. Either way, stakeholders develop a picture of the organisation which enables them to position it among others. This corporate image may well be an accurate interpretation of the real organisation. However, it may be inaccurate, in which case marketing communications need to address the problem and narrow the gap between reality and image.

Review questions

1. Write a short definition of internal marketing and explain how marketing communications needs to assume both internal and external perspectives.
2. What is the role of internal marketing communications?
3. Write short notes explaining why organisational boundaries appear to be less clear than was once thought.
4. What is organisational identity and what do Albert and Whetton (1985) consider to be the three important aspects of identity?
5. Write a brief paper explaining why an understanding of corporate culture is important for successful marketing communications.
6. Why should marketing communications accommodate corporate strategy?
7. What are the elements of strategic credibility?
8. Select different CEOs from a variety of organisations and evaluate their strategic credibility. What is the justification for selecting these individuals?
9. Prepare a communications matrix for an organisation (or brand/product) with which you are familiar.
10. Why might the functional capabilities of an organisation impact upon an organisation's marketing communications?

References

Albert, S. and Whetten, D.A. (1985) Organisational identity, in *Research in Organisational Behavior* (eds. L.L. Cummings and B.M. Staw). Greenwich CT: Jai Press.

Barich, H. and Kotler, P. (1991) A framework for marketing image management. *Sloan Management Review*, **94** (Winter), 94–104.

Berry, L.L. (1980) Services marketing is different. *Business* (May/June), 24–9.

Beyer, J.M. (1981) Ideologies, values and decision making in organisations, in *Handbook of Organisational Design* (eds. P. Nystrom and W. Swarbruck). London: Oxford University Press.

Boydell, T. (1977) BACIE Conference, London, July.

Doyle, P. (1987) Marketing and the British chief executive. *Journal of Marketing Management*, **3**(2), 121–32.

Dutton, J.E. and Dukerich, J.M. (1991) Keeping an eye on the mirror: image and identity in organisational adaptation. *Academy of Management Review*, **34**, 517–54.

Dutton, J.E., Dukerich, J.M. and Harquail, C.V. (1994) Organisational images and member identification. *Administrative Science Quarterly*, **39**, 239–63.

Dutton, J.E. and Penner, W.J. (1993) The importance of organisational identity for strategic agenda building, in *Strategic Thinking: Leadership and the Management of Change* (eds. J. Hendrey, G. Johnson and J. Newton). Chichester: Wiley.

Elsbach, K.D. and Kramer, R.M. (1996) Members' responses to organisational identity threats: encountering and countering the *Business Week* rankings. *Administrative Science Quarterly*, **41**, 442–76.

Foreman, S.K. and Money, A.H. (1995) Internal marketing: concepts, measurements and application. *Journal of Marketing Management*, **11**, 755–68.

Goodman, P.S. and Pennings, J.M. (1977) *New Perspectives on Organisational Effectiveness*. San Fransisco: Jossey-Bass.

Gordon, G. (1985) The relationship of corporate culture to industry sector and corporate performance, in *Gaining Control of the Corporate Culture* (eds. R.H. Kilman, M.J. Saxton, R. Serpa, and associates). San Francisco: Jossey-Bass.

Greene, W.E., Walls, G.D. and Schrest, L.J. (1994) Internal marketing – the key to external marketing success. *Journal of Services Marketing*, **8**(4), 5–13.

Greenley, C.E. (1985) Marketing plan utilisation. *Quarterly Review of Marketing*, **4** (Summer), 12–19.

Hall, E. (1997) Why AMV rekindled a 48-year-old ad for the Pru. *Campaign*, 21 February, p. 18.

Hatch, M.J. and Schultz, M. (1997) Relations between organisational culture, identity and image. *European Journal of Marketing*, **31**(5/6), 356–65.

Higgins, R.B. and Bannister, B.D. (1992) How corporate communication of strategy affects share price, *Long Range Planning*, **25**(3), 27–35.

Hunger, J.D. and Wheelan, T. (1993) *Strategic Management*, 4th edn. Reading, MA: Addison-Wesley.

Ind, N. (1992) *The Corporate Image: Strategies for Effective Identity Programme*, rev. edn. London: Kogan Page.

Kimberley, J. (1980) Initiation, innovation and institutionalisation in the creation process, in *The Organisational Lifecycle* (eds. J. Kimberley and R. Miles). San Francisco: Jossey-Bass.

Leppard, J.W. and McDonald, H.B. (1991) Marketing planning and corporate culture: a conceptual framework which examines management attitudes in the context of marketing planning. *Journal of Marketing Management*, **7**, 213–35.

Marshall, S. (1995) Accounting for change. *Marketing Week*, 2 June, pp. 32–5.

Mitchell, A. (1998) P&G's new horizons. *Campaign*, 20 March, pp. 34–5.

Morgan, G. (1997) *Images of Organisation*, 2nd edn. New York: Sage.

Morden, T. (1993) *Business Strategy and Planning*. London: McGraw-Hill.

Newell, S.J. and Shemwell D.J. (1995) The CEO endorser and message source credibility: an empirical investigation of antecedents and consequences. *Journal of Marketing Communications*, **1**, 13–23.

Piercy, N. and Morgan, R. (1991) Internal marketing – the missing half of the marketing programme. *Long Range Planning*, **24** (April), 82–93.

Schein, E.H. (1984) 'Coming to a new awareness of organisational culture. *Sloan Management Review*, **25** (Winter), 3–16.

Schein, E.H. (1985) *Organisational Culture and Leadership*. San Francisco: Jossey-Bass.

Thompson, J.L. (1990) *Strategic Management: Awareness and Change*. London: Chapman & Hall.

Varey, R.J. (1995) Internal marketing: a review and some interdisciplinary research challenges. *International Journal of Service Industry Management*, **6**(1), 40–63.

chapter 12

Financial resources

Organisations need to ensure that they achieve the greatest possible efficiency with each unit of resource (£s, $s, Gldrs, SKrs) they allocate to promotional activities. They cannot afford to be profligate with scarce resources and managers are accountable to the owners of the organisation for the decisions they make, including those associated with the costs of their marketing communications.

AIMS AND OBJECTIVES

The aim of this chapter is to examine the financial context within which organisations undertake promotional campaigns.

The objectives of this chapter are:

1. To determine current trends in advertising and promotional expenditure.
2. To discuss the role of the promotional budget.
3. To clarify the benefits of using promotional budgets.
4. To examine various budgeting techniques, both practical and theoretical.
5. To provide an appreciation of the advertising to sales (A/S) ratio.
6. To set out the principles where share of voice (SOV) can be used as a strategically competitive tool.
7. To consider some of the issues associated with brand valuation.

An introduction to appropriation management

The rate at which promotional expenditures, and in particular those associated with advertising, have outstripped the retail price index, has been both alarming and troublesome. This disproportionate increase in the costs of advertising has served to make it increasingly less attractive to clients and has spurred the development of other forms of promotion, most notably direct marketing.

Some advertising agencies have argued that this disproportionately high increase is necessary because of the increasing number of new products and the length of time it takes to build a brand. Large investment and commitment are required over a period of years if long-term, high-yield performance is to be achieved. Many accountants, on the other hand, view advertising from a different perspective. Their attitude has, for a long time, been to consider advertising as an expense, to be set against the profits of the organisation. Many of them see planned marketing communications as a variable, one that can be discarded in times of recession.

These two broad views of advertising and of all promotional activities, one as an investment to be shown on the balance sheet and the other as a cost to be revealed in the profit and loss account, run consistently through discussions of how much should be allocated to the promotional spend. For management, the four elements of the promotional mix are often divided into two groups. The first contains advertising, sales promotion and public relations, while the second group contains the financial aspects that relate to personal selling.

This division reflects not only a functional approach to marketing but also the way in which, historically, the selling and marketing departments have developed. This is often observed in older, more established, organisations which find innovation and change more difficult to come to terms with. Accountability and responsibility for promotional expenditure in the first group often fall to the brand or product manager. The second group is managed by a sales manager, often at national level, reporting to a sales director.

The promotional costs that need to be budgeted include the following. First, there is the air time on broadcast media or space in print media that has to be bought to carry the message to the target audience. Then there are the production costs associated with generating the message and the staff costs of all those who contribute to the design and administration of the campaign. There are agency and professional fees, marketing research, and contributions to general overheads and to expenses such as cars, entertainment costs and telephones that can be directly related to particular profit centres. In addition to all these are any direct marketing costs, for which some organisations have still to find a suitable method of cost allocation. In some cases a particular department has been created to manage all direct marketing activities, and in these cases the costs can be easily apportioned.

The budget for the sales force is not one that can be switched on and off like an electric light. Advertising budgets can be massaged and campaigns pulled at the last minute, but communication through personal selling requires the establishment of a relatively high level of fixed costs. In addition to these expenses are the opportunity costs associated with the long time taken to recruit, train and release suitably trained sales personnel into the competitive environment. For example, this process can take over 15 months in some industries, especially in the fast-changing, demanding and complex information technology markets.

Strategic investment to achieve the right sales force, in terms of its size, training and maintenance, is paramount. It should be remembered, however, that managing a sales force can be rather like turning an ocean liner: any move or change in direction has to be anticipated and actioned long before the desired outcome can be accomplished. Funds need to be allocated strategically, but for most organisations a fast return on an investment should not be anticipated.

This chapter will concentrate on the techniques associated with determining the correct allocation of funds to the first group of promotional tools and, in particular, emphasis will be placed upon the advertising appropriation. Attention will then be given to the other measures used to determine the correct level of investment in sales promotion, public relations and the field sales force. Finally, the question of brand valuation and its place on the balance sheet is considered.

Trends in advertising and promotional expenditure

It was stated earlier that advertising expenditure in the United Kingdom has risen faster than consumer expenditure. While this is true, the rapid increases in advertising spend in the 1980s came to an abrupt halt at the beginning of the 1990s.

This noticeable cutback in advertising expenditure when trading conditions tightened reflects the short-term orientation that some organisations have towards brand development. What is also of interest is the way in which the promotional mix has been changing over the past 10–15 years. For a long time the spend on media advertising dominated the promotional budget, but now over two-thirds of the promotional spend is directed towards sales promotion activities (Abraham and Lodish, 1990). The reasons for this shift in emphasis are discussed later (Chapter 18), but the change is indicative of the increasing attention and accountability that management are attaching to the promotional spend. Increasingly, marketing managers are being asked to justify the amounts they spend on their entire budgets, including advertising and sales promotion. Senior management want to know the return they are getting for their promotional investments, in order that they meet their objectives and that scarce resources can be used more effectively in the future.

The role of the promotional budget

The role of the promotional budget is the same whether the organisation is a multinational, trading from numerous international locations or a small manufacturing unit on an industrial estate outside a semi-rural community. Both organisations want to ensure that they achieve the greatest efficiency with each pound they allocate to promotional activities. Neither can afford to be profligate with scarce resources, and each is accountable to the owners of the organisation for the decisions it makes.

There are two broad decisions that need to be addressed. The first concerns how much of the organisation's available financial resources (or relevant part) should be allocated to promotion over the next period. The second concerns how much of the total amount should be allocated to each of the individual tools of the promotional mix.

Benefits of budgeting

The benefits of engaging in budgeting activities are many and varied, but in the context of marketing communication planning they can be considered as follows:

1. The process serves to focus people's attention on the costs and benefits of undertaking the planned communication activities.

2. The act of quantifying the means by which the marketing plan will be communicated to target audiences instils a management discipline necessary to ensure that the objectives of the plan are capable of being achieved. Achievement must be at a level which is acceptable and which will not overstretch or embarrass the organisation.
3. The process facilitates cross function coordination and forces managers to ensure that the planned communications are integrated and mutually supportive.
4. The process provides a means by which campaigns can be monitored and management control asserted. This is particularly important in environments that are subject to sudden change or competitive hostility.
5. At the end of the campaign, a financial review enables management to learn from the experiences of the promotional activity in order that future communications can be made more efficient and the return on the investment improved.

The process of planning the communications budget is an important one. Certain elements of the process will have been determined during the setting of the promotion objectives. Managers will check the financial feasibility of a project prior to committing larger resources. Managers will also discuss the financial implications of the communication strategy (that is, the push/pull dimension) and those managers responsible for each of the individual promotional tools will have estimated the costs that their contribution to the strategy will involve. Senior management will have some general ideas about the level of the overall appropriation, which will inevitably be based partly upon precedent, market and competitive conditions and partly as a response to the pressures of different stakeholders, among them key members of the performance network. Decisions now have to be made about the viability of the total plan, whether the appropriation is too large or too small and how the funds are to be allocated across the promotional tools.

Communication budgets are not formulated at a particular moment in a sequence of management activities. The financial resources of an organisation should be constantly referred to, if only to monitor current campaigns. Therefore, budgeting and the availability of financial resources are matters that managers should be constantly aware of and able to tap into at all stages in the development of planned communications.

Difficulties associated with budgeting for communications spend

There are a number of problems associated with the establishment of a marketing communications budget. Of them all, the following appear to be the most problematic. First, it is difficult to quantify the precise amount that is necessary to complete all the required tasks. Second, communication budgets do not fit neatly with standard accounting practices. The concept of brand value is accepted increasingly as a balance sheet item, but the concept of investment in communication to create value has only recently begun to be accepted, e.g. by Jaguar and Nestlé. Third, the diversity of the promotional tools and the means by which their success can be measured renders like-for-like comparisons null and void. Finally, the budget-setting process is not as clear-cut as it might at first appear.

As suggested earlier, there are four main stakeholder groups who contribute to the decision. These are the focus organisation, any advertising agencies, the media whose resources will be used to carry the designated messages and the target audience. It is the ability of these four main stakeholders to interact, to communicate effectively with each other and to collaborate that will impact most upon the communications budget. However, determining the 'appropriate appropriation' is a frustrating exercise for the marketing communications manager. The allocation of scarce resources across a promotional budget presents financial and political difficulties, especially where the returns are difficult to identify. Smallbone (1972) suggested that the allocation of funds for promotion is indeed one of the primary problems facing marketers, if not one of the major strategic problems.

Models of appropriation

At a broad level there are a number of models proposed by different authors concerning the appropriation of the promotional mix. Figure 12.1 shows a general model. In particular, Abratt and van der Westhuizen (1985) refer, among others, to Smallbone's (1972) and Gaedeke and Tootelian's (1983) models of promotional appropriation. Abratt and van der Westhuizen have determined, among other things, that personal selling dominated the promotion mix of all their respondents in a particular study and that the models themselves were too simplistic to be of any direct benefit.

These broad approaches to budget allocation are not therefore appropriate, and it is necessary to investigate the value of using particular techniques. It is useful to set

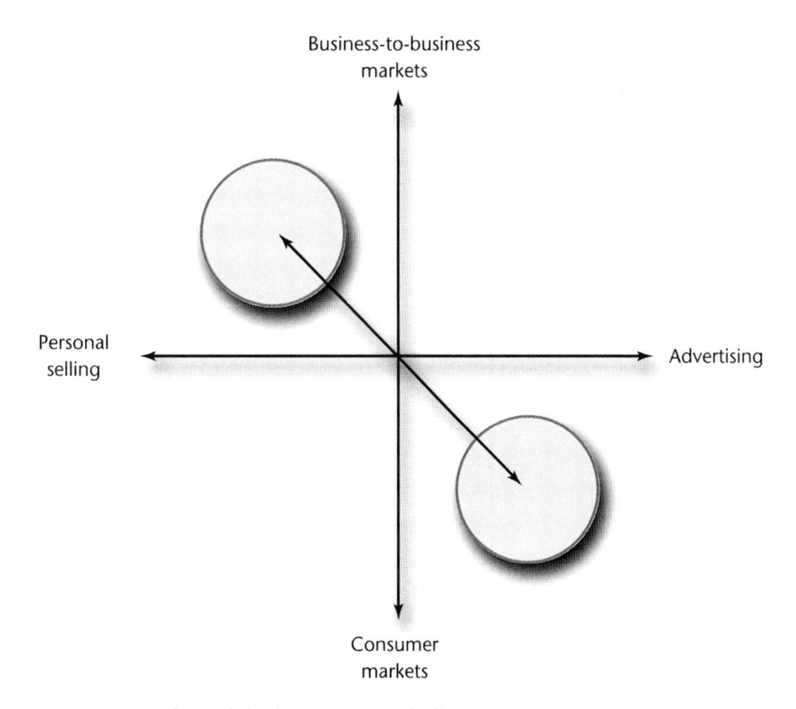

Figure 12.1 A general model of promotional allocation.

out the theoretical approach associated with the determination of communication and, in particular, advertising budgets.

Techniques and approaches

Theoretical approaches: marginal analysis and response curves

This method is normally depicted as a tool for understanding advertising expenditures, but, as Burnett (1993) points out, it has been used for all elements of the promotional mix, including personal selling, so it is included here for understanding the overall promotional allocation.

Marginal analysis enables managers to determine how many extra sales are produced from an extra unit of promotional spend. A point will be reached when an extra pound spent on promotion will generate an equal amount (a single pound worth) of revenue. At this point marginal revenue is equal to marginal costs, the point of maximum promotional expenditure has been reached and maximum profit is generated.

Another way of looking at this approach is to track the path of sales and promotional expenditure. Even with zero promotional effort some sales will still be generated. In other words, sales are not totally dependent upon formal promotional activity, a point we shall return to at a later point. When there is a small amount of promotion effort, the impact is minimal, as the majority of potential customers are either unaware of the messages or they do not think the messages are sufficiently credible for them to change their current behaviour. After a certain point, however, successive increments in promotional expenditure will produce more than proportionate increments in sales. The sales curve in Figure 12.2 can now be seen to rise steeply and the organisation moves into a position where it can begin to take advantage of the economies of scale in promotion. Eventually the sales curve starts to flatten out as diminishing returns to promotion begin to set in. This is because the majority of the potential target market have become aware of the offering and have decided whether or not to become customers.

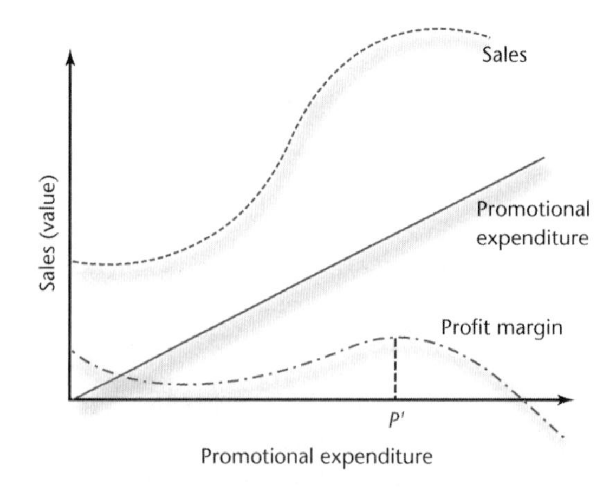

Figure 12.2 Marginal analysis for promotional expenditures. p' is the point of maximum profit, the optimum level of promotional expenditure.

Table 12.1 Difficulties with the marginal analysis as a way of setting promotional budgets

Assumes promotional activities can be varied in a smooth and uniform manner.
Requires perfect data which in reality is very difficult to obtain.
Assumes only promotional activities impact upon sales.
Does not consider all the costs associated with promotional activities.
No account is made of the actions of direct and indirect competitors.
Adstock effects are ignored.
All messages are regarded as having equal impact. No consideration is given to the quality of messages as perceived by the target audience.

This model suffers from a number of disadvantages (Table 12.1). First, it assumes that advertising can be varied smoothly and continuously. This is not the case. Second, it assumes that advertising is the only influence upon sales. As discussed previously, sales are influenced by a variety of factors, of which planned communications is but one. Controllable and uncontrollable elements in the environment influence sales. Next, no account is taken of the other costs associated indirectly with the presentation of the offering, such as those allied to distribution. Each promotional thrust will often be matched, or even bettered, by the competition. Furthermore, the actions of rivals may even affect the sales performance of all products in the same category.

It is fair to say, therefore, that the marginal approach fails to account for competitor reactions. The model assumes that sales are the result of current promotional campaigns. No attempt is made to account for the effects of previous campaigns and that adstock may well be a prime reason for a sale occurring. The time parameters used to compute the marginal analysis could be totally inaccurate.

One of the most important shortcomings of the theory is its failure to account for the qualitative effects of the messages that are transmitted. It is assumed that all messages are of a particular standard and that relative quality is unimportant. Clearly this cannot be the case.

The marginal approach is suspect in that it operates outside the real world, and it requires data and skill in its implementation that are difficult and expensive to acquire. Theoretically, this approach is sound but the practical problems of obtaining the necessary information and the absence of qualitative inputs render the technique difficult for most organisations to implement

Practical approaches

If the marginal approach is not practical then a consideration of the alternative approaches is necessary. Practitioners have developed a range of other methods which tend to reflect simplicity of deduction and operation but raise doubts over their overall contribution and effectiveness.

The following represent some of the more common approaches. It should be noted, at this point, that none of the techniques should be seen in isolation. Organisations should use a variety of approaches and so reduce any dependence, and hence risk, on any one method. The main methods are: arbitrary, inertia, media multiplier, percentage of sales, affordable, objective and task, and competitive parity.

Arbitrary

Sometimes referred to as 'chairperson's rules', this is the simplest and least appropriate of all the techniques available. Under chairperson's rules, what the boss says or guesses at is what is implemented. The fact that the boss may not have a clue what the optimal figure should be is totally irrelevant. Very often the budget is decided on the hoof, and as each demand for communication resources arrives so decisions are made in isolation from any overall strategy.

Apart from the merit of flexibility, this method has numerous deficiencies. It fails to consider customer needs, the demands of the environment or marketing strategy, and there is an absence of any critical analysis. Regretfully this approach is used often by many small organisations.

Inertia

An alternative to guesswork is the 'let's keep it the same' approach. Here all elements of the environment and the costs associated with the tasks facing the organisation are ignored.

Media multiplier

One step more advanced is the method that recognises that media rate card costs may have increased. So, in order to maintain the same impact, the media multiplier rule requires last year's spend to be increased by the rate at which media costs have increased.

Percentage of sales

One of the more common and thoughtful approaches is to set the budget at a level equal to some predetermined percentage of past or anticipated sales. Invariably, organisations select a percentage that is traditional to the organisation, such as 'we always aim to spend 5.0% of our sales on advertising'. The rationale put forward is that it is the norm for the sector to spend about 4.5–5.5% or that 5.0% is acceptable to the needs of the most powerful stakeholders or is set in recognition of overall corporate responsibilities. For example, a local authority will be mindful of the needs of its council tax payers, whose finances contribute to the funding and maintenance of local tourism activities, for example, a museum or park facilities.

There are a number of flaws with this technique. It is focused upon the sales base on which the budget rests. Planned communications, and advertising in particular, are intended to create demand, not to be the result of past sales. If the demand generators of the promotional mix are to be based on last period's performance, then it is likely that the next period's results will be similar, all things being equal. This must be the logical implication when the percentage is based on past performance.

Another way of looking at this method is to base the spend on a percentage of the next period's sales. This overcomes some of the problems, but still constrains the scope and the realistic expectations of a budget. No consideration is given to the sales potential that may exist, so this technique may actually limit performance.

Affordable

This approach is still regarded by many organisations as sophisticated and relatively free of risk. It requires each unit of output to be allocated a proportion of all the input costs and all the costs associated with the value-adding activities in production and manufacturing, together with all the other costs in distributing the output. After making an allowance for profit, what is left is to be spent on advertising and communication. In other words, what is left is what we can afford to spend.

The affordable technique is not in the least analytical, nor does it have any market or task orientation. It is a technique which is used by organisations of differing sizes (Hooley and Lynch, 1985), who are product- rather than customer-orientated. Their view of advertising is that it is a cost and that the quality of their product will ensure that it will sell itself. Organisations using this technique will be prone to missing opportunities that require advertising investment. This is because a ceiling on advertising expenditure is set and borrowings are avoided. As sales fluctuate in variable markets, the vagueness of this approach is unlikely to lead to an optimal budget.

Objective and task

The methods presented so far seek to determine an overall budget and leave the actual allocation to products and regions to some arbitrary method. This is unlikely to be a realistic, fair or optimal use of a critical resource.

The objective and task approach is different from the others in that it attempts to determine the resources required to achieve each promotion objective. It then aggregates these separate costs into an overall budget. For example, the costs associated with achieving a certain level of awareness can be determined from various media owners who are seeking to sell time and space in their media vehicles. The costs of sales promotions and sales literature can be determined and the production costs of these activities and those of direct marketing (e.g. telemarketing) and PR events and sponsorships can be brought together. The total of all these costs represents the level of investment necessary to accomplish the promotion objectives that had been established earlier in the marketing communications plan.

The attractions of this technique are that it focuses management attention upon the goals that are to be accomplished and that the monitoring and feedback systems that have to be put in place allow for the development of knowledge and expertise. On the downside, the objective and task approach does not generate realistic budgets, in the sense that the required level of resources may not be available and the opportunity costs of the resources are not usually determined. More importantly, it is difficult to determine the best way to accomplish a task and to know exactly what costs will be necessary to complete a particular activity. Very often the actual costs are not known until the task has been completed, which rather reduces the impact of the budget-setting process. What is also missing is a strategic focus. The objective and task method deals very well with individual campaigns, but is not capable of providing the overall strategic focus of the organisation's annual (period) spend. The case of Procter & Gamble illustrates this point.

The use of this approach leads to the determination of a sum of money. This sum is to be invested, in this case, in promoting the offerings of the organisation, but it could equally be a new machine or a building. To help discover whether such a sum should be invested and whether it is in the best interests of the organisation, a 'payout plan' can be undertaken.

1. *Payout plans*

   These are used to determine the investment value of the advertising plan. This process involves determining the future revenues and costs to be incurred over a two- or three-year period. The essential question answered by such an exercise is 'how long will it take to recover the expenditure'?

CASE ILLUSTRATION

Levels of marketing spend – Procter & Gamble

The strategic impact that the overall level of marketing communications spend can have is illustrated by the announcement in June 1995 that Procter & Gamble intended to reduce its long-term marketing spend from 25% to 20% of sales revenue.

Procter & Gamble released a memorandum to its regional managers in which it was stated that its marketing spend was the biggest area of cost disadvantage compared with own-label products. This was interpreted by the media as a cut in advertising and sales promotions in order to shift the focus of the overall brand strategy to a policy of everyday low prices. This policy involves money (budgets) moving from advertising and sales promotion to fund price cuts.

The company reacted by stating that the policy was to generate efficiencies in media expenditures and commercial production but also to maintain a media presence. Some value-for-money pricing was to be introduced on selected ('overpromoted') brands. However, the policy was to seek cost cuts and drive down the media and associated expenditures.

Adapted from Anon, *Marketing Week,* 23 February 1996, pp. 8 and 9

2. *Sensitivity analysis*
   Many organisations use this adjusting approach to peg back the advertising expenditure because the payout plan revealed costs as too large or sales developing too slowly. Adjustments are made to the objectives or to the strategies, with the aim of reducing the payback period.

Competitive parity

In certain markets, such as the relatively stable FMCG market, many organisations use promotional appropriation as a competitive tool. The underlying assumption is that advertising is the only direct variable that influences sales. The argument is based on the point that while there are many factors that impact on sales, these factors are all self-cancelling. Each factor impacts upon all the players in the market. The only effective factor is the amount that is spent on planned communications. As a result, some organisations deliberately spend the same amount on advertising as their competitors spend: competitive parity.

Competitive parity has a major benefit for the participants. As each organisation knows what the others are spending and while there is no attempt to destabilise the market through excessive or minimal promotional spend, the market avoids self-generated turbulence and hostile competitive activity.

There are, however, a number of disadvantages with this simple technique. The first is that, while information is available, there is a problem of comparing like with like. For example, a carpet manufacturer selling a greater proportion of output into the trade will require different levels and styles of advertising and promotion from another manufacturer selling predominantly to the retail market. Furthermore, the first organisation may be diversified, perhaps importing floor tiles. The second may be operating in a totally unrelated market. Such activities make comparisons difficult to establish, and financial decisions based on such analyses are highly dubious.

The competitive parity approach fails to consider the qualitative aspects of the advertising undertaken by the different players. Each attempts to differentiate itself, and very often the promotional messages are one of the more important means of successfully positioning an organisation. It would not be surprising, therefore, to note that there is probably a great range in the quality of the planned communications. Associated with this is the notion that when attempting to adopt different positions, the tasks and costs will be different and so seeking relative competitive parity may be an inefficient use of resources. The final point concerns the data used in such a strategy. The data are historical and based on strategies relevant at the time. Competitors may well have embarked upon a new strategy since the data were released. This means that parity would not only be inappropriate for all the reasons previously listed, but also because the strategies are incompatible.

Advertising to sales ratio

An interesting extension of the competitive parity principle is the notion of A/S ratios. Instead of simply seeking to spend a relatively similar amount on promotion as one's relative competitors, this approach attempts to account for the market shares held by the different players and to adjust promotional spend accordingly.

If it is accepted that there is a direct relationship between the volume of advertising (referred to as weight) and sales, then it is not unreasonable to conclude that if an organisation spends more on advertising then it will see a proportionate improvement in sales. The underlying principle of the A/S ratio is that in each industry it is possible to determine the average advertising spend of all the players and compare it with the value of the market. Therefore, it is possible for each organisation to determine its own A/S ratio and compare it with the industry average. Those organisations with an A/S ratio below the average may conclude that they either have advertising economies of scale working in their favour or that their advertising is working much harder, pound for pound, than some of their competitors. Organisations can also use A/S ratios as a means of controlling expenditure across multiple product areas. Budgets can be set based upon the industry benchmark, and variances quickly spotted and further information requested to determine shifts in competitor spend levels or reasons leading to any atypical performance.

Each business sector has its own characteristics, which in turn influence the size of the advertising expenditure. In 1996 the A/S ratio for female fragrances was 8.7%, coffee 3.0%, indigestion remedies 19.7%, cold treatments 14.2%, cars 2.3%, cereals 9% and jeans 0.67% (Advertising Association). It can be seen that the size of the A/S ratio can vary widely. It appears to be higher (that is, a greater proportion of revenue is used to invest in advertising) when the following are present:

1. The offering is standardised, not customised.
2. There are many end users.
3. The financial risk for the end user customer is small.
4. The marketing channels are short.

5. A premium price is charged.
6. There is a high gross margin.
7. The industry is characterised by surplus capacity.
8. Competition is characterised by a high number of new product launches.

A/S ratios provide a useful benchmark for organisations when they are trying to determine the adspend level. These ratios do not set out what the promotional budget should be, but they do provide a valuable sighter around which broad commercial decisions can be developed.

Share of voice

Brand strategy in the FMCG market has traditionally been based upon an approach which uses mass media advertising to drive brand awareness, which in turn allows premium pricing to fund the advertising investment (cost). The alternative approach has been to use price-based promotions to drive market share. This latter approach has often been regarded as a short-term approach which is incapable of sustaining a brand over the longer term.

The concept underlying the A/S ratio can be seen in the context of rival supporters chanting at a football match. If they chant at the same time, at the same decibel rating, then it is difficult to distinguish the two sets of supporters, particularly if they are chanting the same song. Should one set of supporters shout at a lower decibel rating, then the collective voice of the other supporters would be the one that the rest of the crowd, and perhaps any television audience, actually hears and distinguishes.

This principle applies to the concept of share of voice (SOV). Within any market the total of all advertising expenditure (adspend), that is all the advertising by all of the players, can be analysed in the context of the proportions each player has made to the total. Should one advertiser spend more than any other then it will be its messages that are received and stand a better chance of being heard and acted upon. In other words, its SOV is the greater. This implies, of course, that the quality of the message transmitted is not important and that it is the sheer relative weight of adspend that is the critical factor.

This concept can be taken further and combined with another, share of market (SOM). When a brand's market share is equal to its share of advertising spend, equilibrium is said to have been reached (SOV = SOM); see Figure 12.3.

Strategic implications of the SOV concept

These concepts of SOV and SOM frame an interesting perspective of competitive strategy based upon the relative weight of advertising expenditure. Schroer (1990) reports that following extensive research on the US packaged goods market (FMCG), it is noticeable that organisations can use advertising spend to maintain equilibrium and to create disequilibrium in a market. The former is established by major brand players maintaining their market shares with little annual change to their advertising budgets. Unless a competitor is prepared to inject a considerable increase in advertising spend and so create disequilibrium, the relatively stable high spend deters new entrants and preserves the *status quo*. Schroer claims that if the two market leaders maintain SOV within 10% of each other then competitive equilibrium will exist. This situation is depicted in Figure 12.3. If a market challenger launches an aggressive assault upon the leader by raising advertising spend to a point where SOV is 20–30 per cent higher than the current leader, market share will shift in favour of the challenger, as shown in Figure 12.3.

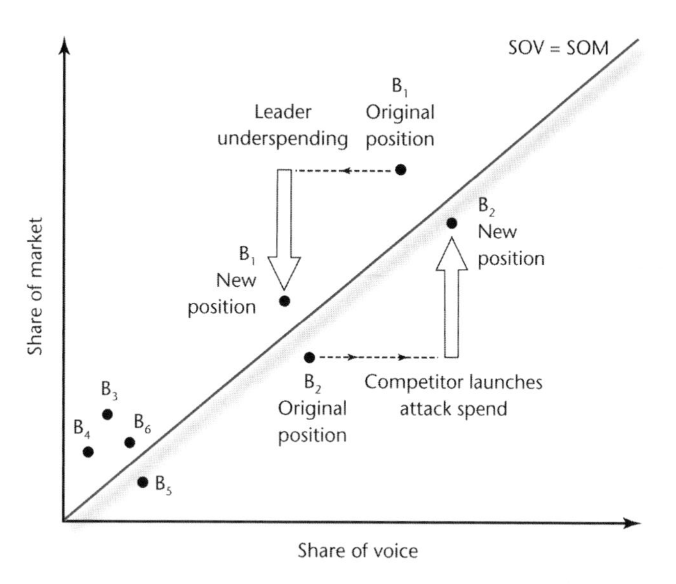

Figure 12.3 Strategy to gain market share by an increase in adspend (Schroer (1990); used with kind permission).

In Figure 12.3, Brands 1, 3, 4 and 6 have an SOM that is greater than their SOV. This suggests that their advertising is working well for them and that the larger organisations have some economies of scale in their advertising. Brands 2 and 5, however, have an SOM that is less than their SOV. This is because Brand 2 is challenging for the larger market (with Brand 1) and is likely to be less profitable than Brand 1 because of the increased costs. Brand 5 is competing in a niche market, and, as a new brand, may be spending heavily to gain acceptance in the new market environment.

This perspective brings implications for advertising spend at a strategic level. Schroer presents a matrix (Figure 12.4) which he uses to support his views that advertising spend should be varied according to the spend of the company's competitors in different markets. The implications are that advertising budget decisions should be geared to the level of adspend undertaken by competitors in particular markets at particular times. Decisions to attack or to defend are also set out. For example, promotional investments should be placed in markets where competitors are underspending. Furthermore, if information is available about competitors' costs, then decisions to launch and sustain an advertising spend attack can be made in the knowledge that a prolonged period of premium spending can be carried through with or without a counter-attack.

This traditional perspective of static markets being led by the top two actors using heavy above-the-line strategies and the rest basing their competitive thrusts on price-based promotions has been challenged by Buck (1995) by reference to a study of Superpanel data by Hamilton. In 1994, the brand leaders in many FMCG markets spent nearly 50% more than the industry average on advertising, while the number two brand spent about 8% less than the industry average. In addition, the gap with the other actors was not as significant as Schroer reported. This is of a course a comparison of European and US markets, and there is no reason why they should be identical or at least very similar. However, the data are interesting in that the challenge of Brand 2, postulated by Schroer, is virtually impossible in many of the UK, if not also in

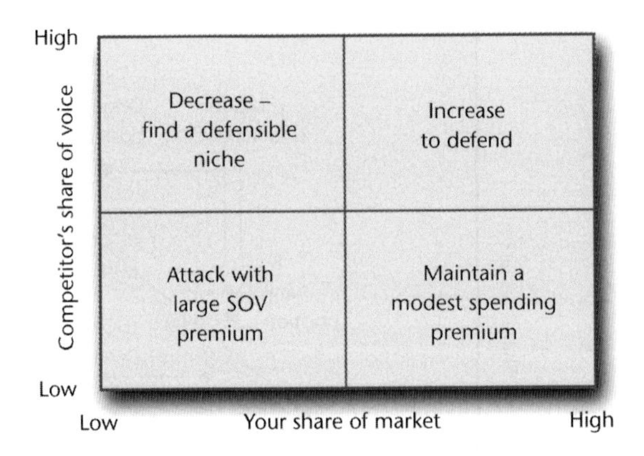

Figure 12.4 Strategies for advertising spend (Schroer (1990); used with kind permission).

European, markets. The effects of the recession in the UK may have impacted on the decision by some managers to scale down their advertising activities and as a result market leaders who continued to advertise at previously determined levels have been able to stretch their SOM advantage.

The concepts of SOV and SOM have also been used by Jones (1990) to develop a new method of budget setting. He suggests that those brands that have an SOV greater than their SOM are 'investment brands', and those that have a SOM less than or equal to their SOV are 'profit-taking brands'.

There are three points to notice. First, the high advertising spend of new brands is an established strategy and represents a trade-off between the need for profit and the need to become established through advertising spend. The result, invariably, is that smaller brands have lower profitability because they have to invest a disproportionate amount in advertising. Second, large brands are often 'milked' to produce increased earnings, especially in environments which emphasise short-termism. The third point is that advertising economies of scale allow large brands to develop with an SOV consistently below SOM.

Using data collected from an extensive survey of 1,096 brands across 23 different countries, Jones 'calculated the difference between share of voice and share of market and averaged these differences within each family of brands'. By representing the data diagrammatically (Figure 12.5), Jones shows how it becomes a relatively simple task to work out the spend required to achieve a particular share of market. The first task is to plot the expected (desired) market share from the horizontal axis; then move vertically to the intersect with the curve and read off the SOV figure from the vertical axis.

Appropriation brand types

From this approach it is possible to determine five different types of brands, based upon the amount of advertising expenditure. In each market there are brands which are promoted without the support of any advertising. These small niche players can be regarded as zero-based brands.

Where brands are supported by token advertising, which represents a small SOV, the brand is probably being milked and the resources are being channelled into other

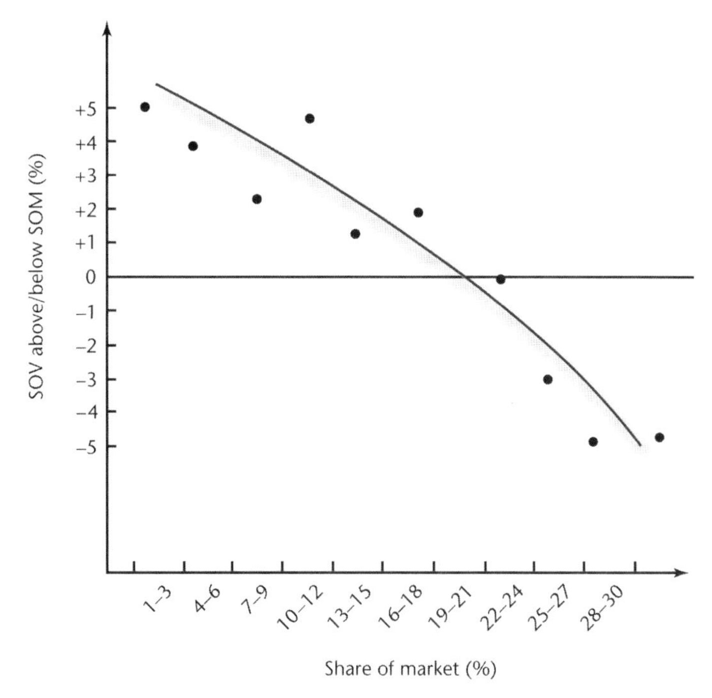

Figure 12.5 Curve comparing SOV with SOM (Schroer (1990); used with kind permission).

developing brands. New launches are typified by the heavy advertising investment necessary to get them off the ground. Here the SOV will be larger than the SOM and these can be referred to as growth brands.

In situations where the SOM is very large and the SOV much smaller, these profit-taking brands are running a risk of losing market share if a competitor spots the opportunity to invest a large sum in a prolonged attack. Finally, there is a group of brands which maintain stability by respecting each other's positions and by not initiating warfare. These brands can be referred to as equilibrium brands.

1. Zero-based brands – niche; no advertising spend.
2. Growth brands – SOV > SOM; heavy advertising.
3. Milking brands – SOV < SOM; token advertising.
4. Profit-taking brands – SOM >> SOV; relaxed advertising.
5. Equilibrium brands – SOM = SOV; maintenance advertising.

Assessing brands in the context of the advertising resources they attract is a slightly different way of reflecting their power and importance to their owners. If the SOV approach is limited by its applicability to stable, mature market conditions then at least it enables the promotional spend to be seen and used as a competitive weapon.

Which methods are most used

From this review and commentary it is necessary to draw out the degree to which these particular tools are used in practice. Mitchell's (1993) study to determine the methods and criteria used by companies to determine their advertising budgets found that 40% of respondents claimed to use the objective and task approach, 27% used percentage of future sales (8% used past sales) and 19% used a variety of company-specific methods that do not fit neatly with any one item from the list presented above.

Although the figures resulting from the study can only be used to indicate trends of overall preferences, another other set of important factors also emerged from this study. These are the range of organisational influences that impact on individual organisations. Over half the respondents reported that the method used to set these budgets actually varied, internally, across product categories. Different methods were used for new and established products

The criteria used by organisations to set their communication budgets are many and varied. Mitchell suggested that the criteria used could be grouped as *controllables* (41%), such as financial, product, production and goals; *uncontrollables* (41%), such as sales, competition, market, media and distribution; and *signals* (18%), such as national activities, experience, effectiveness of expenditures and awareness. He reported that the processes used to determine the budgets were reported as either essentially centralised or top-down (52%), decentralised or bottom-up (13.5%) or bargaining (top-down and bottom-up) (21%).

The main factors associated with the determination of marketing communications (advertising) budgets are:

1. Organisational strategy and direction, values and cultural perspective.
2. The relative amount of financial resources that are available.
3. Competitive activities and market conditions.
4. The overall level of economic confidence felt by buyers and sellers.
5. The level of product/brand development and the marketing objectives.

Over time a number of models and methods have been developed to manage these criteria in order that an appropriation be determined.

Budgeting for the other elements of the promotional mix

The methods presented so far have concentrated on the FMCG sector. The assumption has been that only one product has been considered. In reality, a range of products will need promotional finances and the allocation decision needs to reflect the needs of an organisation's portfolio of brands. Broadbent (1989) suggests that this situation and others (e.g. direct marketing, corporate advertising) require particular combinations of the approaches presented so far. The recommendation again is that no single method will help organisations to determine the optimal investment sum.

Sales promotion activities can be more easily costed in advance of a campaign than those associated with advertising. Judgements can be made about the anticipated outcomes, based upon experience, competitive conditions and the use of predictive software tools. The important variable with sales promotion concerns the redemption rate. How many of the extra pack, price deals and samples will customers demand? How much extra of a brand needs to be sold if all the costs associated with a campaign are to be covered? The production and fulfilment costs can also be determined, so in general terms a return can be calculated in advance of a sales promotion event.

However, there are a large number of sales promotion activities and these will often overlap. From a management perspective the brand management system is better, since a single person is responsible for the budget, one who is able to take a wider view of the range of activities. While the objective and task approach appears to be more easily applied to this element of the mix, other methods, such as competitive parity and fixed ratios, are often used.

The costs of *public relations* activities can also be predicted with a reasonable degree of accuracy. The staffing and/or agency costs are relatively fixed and, as there are no media costs involved, the only other major factor is the associated production costs. These are the costs of the materials used to provide third parties with the opportunity to 'speak' on the organisation's behalf. As with sales promotion, if a number of public relations events have been calculated as a necessary part of the overall promotional activities of the organisation, then the costs of the different tasks need to be anticipated and aggregated and a judgement made about the impact the events will make. The relative costs of achieving a similar level of impact through advertising or other elements of the mix can often be made, and a decision taken based upon relative values.

It has already been stated that the costs associated with the *sales force* are the highest of all the elements of the mix. This would indicate that the greatest degree of care needs to taken when formulating the size and deployment of the sales force. The different approaches to the determination of the sales force are covered in Chapter 18. The costs associated with each activity of personal selling and the support facilities (e.g. car, expenses, training) can be calculated easily, but what is more difficult to predict is the return on the investment.

These approaches to calculating the amount that should be invested in promotional activities vary in their degree of sophistication and usefulness. Of all these methods, none is the ideal answer to the question of how much should be allocated to marketing communications or, more specifically, the advertising spend. Some of the methods are too simplistic, while others are too specific to particular market conditions. For example, formulating strategy to gain market share through increasing SOV seems to ignore the dynamic nature of the markets and the fact that organisations need to satisfy a range of stakeholders and not concentrate solely on winning the greatest market share.

The reader may well have reached the conclusion that the most appropriate way forward for management is to consider several approaches in order to gather a ballpark figure. Such a composite approach negates some of the main drawbacks associated with particular methods. It also helps to build a picture of what is really necessary if the organisation is to communicate effectively and efficiently.

Of all the methods and different approaches, the one constant factor that applies to them all concerns the objectives that have been set for the campaign. Each element of the promotional mix has particular tasks to accomplish and it is these objectives that drive the costs of the promotional investment. If the ultimate estimate of the promotional spend is too high then the objectives need to be revised, not the methods used.

Brand valuation

The importance of brands cannot be understated. Indeed, many organisations have attempted (and succeeded) in valuing the worth of their brands and have had them listed as an asset on their balance sheets. While this has stimulated the accountancy profession into some debate, the concept of a brand's worth to an organisation cannot really be refuted. Among other things, companies buy the potential income streams that brands offer, not just the physical assets of plant, capital and machinery.

At the end of the promotional process, probably some period after, one of the benefits that management hope will emerge is an overall increase in the valuation of the brand. This net value arises as a result of the investment (for example, promotional expenditures) generating a return to reward those who risked the capital invested in the brand. Some believe that this value arises from these activities and that the brand itself is worth £x; this should therefore be regarded as an asset and be placed on the balance sheet.

Why then are brands valued? Birkin (1995) suggests that the reasons are quite varied, including the need to assist in merger and acquisition activities, to establish royalty rates for brand licensing, to support financing decisions (e.g. bank loans), to allocate marketing resources among brands and to formulate brand measurement systems. Perhaps the most important of these is that, through understanding the value of a brand, all those involved with the delivery of the brand are aware of the risks a brand strategy might bear and the returns most likely to be achieved on any further investment in the brand.

All this begs the questions: when does a brand add value to the organisation's overall net worth and when should it be axed? Many of the sub-brands and line extensions developed in the 1980s have become subject to investigation in the 1990s. Clarity of communication has been difficult to achieve as markets have become increasingly competitive and it is difficult to make any form of meaningful differentiation or position by which users should continue to purchase. Nestlé axed its Chambourcy yoghurt brand in 1995 and replaced it with a Nestlé-branded offering. Birds Eye phased out eight sub-brands in 1996. Part of the reasoning was to focus brand-related resources across the 'mother' brand (Birds Eye) rather than have resources spread thinly across, for example, four sub-brands in the ready meals category alone (Curtis, 1996). The equity that each of these brands held (that is, their overall value) had diminished to the point that management decided that the opportunity costs of maintaining the brand in the current context could and should not be sustained. Brand equity is discussed more fully in Chapter 10.

Summary

The task of assigning financial resources to an organisation's marketing communications is difficult and imprecise, and as yet there is no method that can be used on a prescriptive basis. Theoretically, the task can be understood and resources allocated easily. Unfortunately, the quality and availability of information required to use marginal analysis is absent and practitioners have to rely on other methods. These other methods range from the simplistic ('this is what I think we should spend') to the more complex analysis associated with the spend incurred by competitors and the relationship of share of voice with market share that some believe is operable in certain market conditions.

The decision to invest in marketing communications is a difficult one. This is because the direct outcomes are intangible and often distant, as the advertising effects are digested by potential buyers until such time as they are prepared and ready to purchase.

The methods presented in this chapter represent some of the more commonly used techniques. No one method is sufficient, and two or three approaches to the investment decision are required if management are to decide with any accuracy or confidence. Some commentators (Jones, 1990; Buzzell *et al.*, 1990) suggest that the actual amounts invested by some organisations are larger than is necessary. The consequence is that there is wastage and inefficiency, which contributes to a dilution of the profits that brands generate. Management have to make a trade-off between investing and growing the brand to secure a position compared with relaxing the promotional investment and harvesting some profit, perhaps as a reward for the previous investment activity.

Review questions

1. How might organisations benefit from adopting an appropriation-setting process?
2. What problems might be encountered when setting them?
3. Write a brief paper outlining the essence of marginal analysis. What are the main drawbacks associated with this approach?
4. Why is the objective and task method gaining popularity?
5. What is a payout plan?
6. Discuss the view that if the A/S ratio only measures average levels of spend across an industry then its relevance may be lost as individual organisations have to adjust levels of promotional spend to match particular niche market conditions.
7. How might the notion of SOV assist the appropriation-setting process?
8. What are 'profit-taking' and 'investment' brands?
9. Determining the level of spend for sales promotion is potentially difficult. Why?
10. What are the main reasons justifying the valuation of brands?

References

Abraham, M. and Lodish, L.M. (1990) Getting the most out of advertising and sales promotion. *Harvard Business Review* (May/June), 50–60.

Abratt, R. and van der Westhuizen, B. (1985) A new promotion mix appropriation model. *International Journal of Advertising*, **4**, 209–21.

Birkin, M. (1995) Why brands are valued. *Admap* (March), pp. 18–19.

Broadbent, S. (1989) *The Advertising Budget*. Henley-on-Thames: NTC Publications.

Buck, S. (1995) The decline and fall of the premium brand. *Admap* (March), 14–17.

Burnett, J. (1993) *Promotion Management*. New York: Houghton Mifflin.

Buzzell, R.D., Quelch, J.A. and Salmon, W.J. (1990) The costly bargain of sales promotion. *Harvard Business Review* (March/April), 141–9.

Curtis, J. (1996) Till death do us part. *Marketing*, 25 July, pp. 20–1

Gaedeke, R.M. and Tootelian, D.H. (1983) *Marketing: Principles and application*. St Paul MN: West.

Hooley, G.J. and Lynch, J.E. (1985) How UK advertisers set budgets. *International Journal of Advertising*, **3**, 223–31.

Jones, J.P. (1990) Ad spending: maintaining market share. *Harvard Business Review*, (January/February), 38–42.

Mitchell, L.A. (1993) An examination of methods of setting advertising budgets: practice and literature. *European Journal of Advertising*, **27**(5), 5–21.

Schroer, J. (1990) Ad spending: growing market share. *Harvard Business Review* (January/February), 44–8.

Smallbone, D.W. (1972) *The Practice of Marketing*. London: Staple Press.

part ii

Contents

chapter 13

Advertising – how it might work

Any form of ideas, goods or services paid for by an identifiable sponsor to inform, persuade, remind/reassure or influence an audience.

AIMS AND OBJECTIVES

The aims of this chapter are to explore the different views about how advertising might work and to consider the complexities associated with understanding how clients can best use advertising.

The objectives of this chapter are:

1. To consider the role advertising plays in both consumer and business-to-business markets.
2. To examine the strengths and weaknesses of the sequential models of how advertising works.
3. To introduce the principal frameworks by which advertising is thought to influence individuals.
4. To appraise the strong and weak theories of advertising.
5. To explain cognitive processing as a means of understanding how people use advertising messages.
6. To discuss the contribution that the elaboration likelihood model can make to comprehending how motivation and attitude change can be brought together.
7. To present a composite model of how advertising might work.

Introduction

The purpose of an advertising plan is to provide the means by which appropriate messages are devised and delivered to target audiences. Guidelines for the content and delivery of messages are derived from an understanding of the variety of contexts in which the messages are to be used. For example, research might reveal a poor brand image relative to the market leader, or the different or changing media habits of target consumers. The nature of the messages and the problems to be addressed will be specified in the promotional objectives and strategy.

An advertising plan is composed, essentially, of three main elements:

1. The message, or what is to be said.
2. The media, or how the message will be carried.
3. The timing, or manner in which the message will be carried.

This chapter is concerned with an exploration of how advertising might work, and introduces a number of concepts and frameworks that have contributed to our understanding. The next chapter considers the content of the advertising message, or what is to be said. Chapter 15 looks at the characteristics of the different media used to carry messages, Chapter 16 focuses upon the third issue (media planning or the timing and scheduling of the selected media) and Chapter 17 examines issues concerning the measurement and evaluation of advertising.

Role of advertising

The role of advertising in the promotional plan is an important one. Advertising, whether it be on an international, national, local or direct basis, is important, as it can inform, remind, differentiate or persuade established or potential customers of the existence of a product or organisation.

Advertising can reach huge audiences with simple messages that present opportunities to allow receivers to understand what a product is, what its primary function is and how it relates to all the other similar products. This is the main function of advertising: to communicate with specific audiences. These audiences may be consumer- or organisation-based, but wherever they are located, the prime objective is to build or maintain awareness of a product or an organisation.

Management's control over advertising messages is strong; indeed, of all the elements in the promotional mix, advertising has the greatest level of control. The message, once generated and signed off by the client, can be transmitted in an agreed manner and style and at times that match management's requirements. This means that, should the environment change unexpectedly, advertising messages can be 'pulled' immediately. For example, a campaign to build awareness of Eurostar had to be pulled for four weeks in November 1996 following the fire in the Channel Tunnel. Lying low allowed the management of Le Shuttle and Eurotunnel to concentrate on dealing with the consequences of the fire and the associated publicity the event caused, rather than the negative effects that the advertising would have caused had it been transmitted.

Advertising costs can be regarded in one of two ways. On the one hand there are the absolute costs, which are the costs of buying the space in magazines or newspapers or the time on television, cinema or radio. These costs can be enormous, and they impact directly on cash flow. For example, the rate card cost of a full page (mono) advertisement in the business section of the *Sunday Times* was £45,900 (August 1998) and a prime spot on *Yorkshire-Tyne Tees Television* for fifty seconds could cost £62,500 (rate card 1 January 1998).

On the other hand, there are the relative costs, which are those costs incurred to reach a member of the target audience with the key message. So, if an audience is measured in hundreds of thousands, or even millions on television, the cost of the advertisement spread across each member of the target audience reduces the cost per contact significantly. This aspect is developed further in Chapter 16.

The main roles of advertising are to build awareness, induce a dialogue (if only on an internal basis) and to (re)position brands, by changing either perception or attitudes. The regular use of advertising, in cooperation with the other elements of the communication mix, can be important to the creation and maintenance of a brand personality. Indeed, advertising has a significant role to play in the development of competitive advantage. In some consumer markets advertising is a dominant form of promotion. Advertising can become a mobility barrier, deterring exit and, more importantly, deterring entry to a market by organisations attracted by the profits of the industry. Many people feel that some brands sustain their large market shares by sheer weight of advertising; for example the washing powder brands of Procter & Gamble and Unilever.

Advertising can create competitive advantage by providing the communication necessary for target audiences to frame a product. By providing a frame or the perceptual space with which to pigeonhole a product, target audiences are able to position an offering relative to their other significant products much more easily. Therefore advertising can provide the means for differentiation and sustainable competitive advantage. It should also be appreciated, however, that differentiation may be determined by the quality of execution of the advertisements, rather than through the content of the messages.

Differentiation and competitive advantage

The decision by Hutchinson Telecom to enter the UK telecommunications market was seen by some at the time of entry as ambitious. The market was dominated by two main players, Cellnet and Vodafone, each with substantial market shares. The market was characterised by price competition, so margins were tight and perceptions limited.

A new brand was developed which was imbued with values that differentiated the Hutchinson offering from the price base of the others. The brand was called Orange, and the visual cue of a bright orange colour on a black background had a strong impact that was easily memorable and capable of leading to a string of triggers and brand associations.

The brand was launched with a coordinated campaign that was striking in its presentation and which has since been developed to launch new products and facilities. Market share has grown, and Orange is now a significant part of the UK market (see Plate 13.1).

Advertising in the business-to-business market is geared, primarily, to providing relevant factual information upon which 'rational' decisions can be made. Regardless of the target audience, all advertising requires a message and a carrier to deliver the message to the receiver. This text will concentrate on these two main issues, while acknowledging the wider role that advertising plays in society.

How does advertising work?

For a message to be communicated successfully, it should be targeted at the right audience, capable of gaining attention, understandable, relevant and acceptable. For effective communication to occur, messages should be designed that fit the cognitive capability of the target audience and follow 'the' model of how advertising works. Unfortunately, there is no such single model, despite years of research and speculation by a great many people. However, from all of the work undertaken in this area a number of views have been expressed, and the following sections attempt to present some of the more influential perspectives.

Sequential models

A series of models have been developed to assist our understanding of how these promotional tasks are segregated and organised effectively. Table 13.1 shows some of the better-known models.

Aida

Developed by Strong (1925), the Aida model was designed to represent the stages that a salesperson must take a prospect through in the personal selling process. This

Table 13.1 Sequential models of advertising

	Aida sequence[a]	Hierarchy of effects sequence[b]	Information processing sequence[c]
Cognitive		Awareness	Presentation
			↓
			Attention
		↓	↓
	Attention	Knowledge	Comprehension
	↓	↓	↓
Affective	Interest	Liking	Yielding
		↓	
		Preference	
	↓	↓	↓
	Desire	Conviction	Retention
Conative	↓	↓	↓
	Action	Purchase	Behaviour

[a] Strong (1925). [b] Lavidge and Steiner (1961). [c] Mcguire (1978).
Source: Adapted from Belch and Belch (1990).

model shows the prospect passing through successive stages of attention, interest, desire and action. This expression of the process was later adopted loosely as the basic framework to explain how persuasive communication, and advertising in particular, was thought to work.

Hierarchy of effects models

An extension of the progressive staged approach advocated by Strong emerged in the early 1960s. Developed most notably by Lavidge and Steiner (1961), the hierarchy of effects models represent the process by which advertising was thought to work and assume that there are a series of steps a prospect must pass through, in succession, from unawareness to actual purchase. Advertising, it is assumed, cannot induce immediate behavioural responses; rather, a series of mental effects must occur with fulfilment at each stage necessary before progress to the next stage is possible.

The information processing model

McGuire (1978) contends that the appropriate view of the receiver of persuasive advertising is as an information processor or cognitive problem solver. This cognitive perspective becomes subsumed as the stages presented reflect similarities with the other hierarchical models, except that McGuire includes a retention stage. This refers to the ability of the receiver to retain and understand information which is valid and relevant. This is important, because it recognises that marketing communication messages are designed to provide information for use by a prospective buyer when a purchase decision is to be made at some time in the future.

Difficulties with the sequential approach

For a long time the sequential approach was accepted as the model upon which advertising was to be developed. However, questions arose about what actually constitute adequate levels of awareness, comprehension and conviction and how it can be determined which stage the majority of the target audience has reached at any one point in time.

The model is based on the logical sequential movement of consumers towards a purchase via specified stages. The major criticism is that it assumes that the consumer moves through the stages in a logical, rational manner: learn, then feel and then do. This is obviously not the case, as anyone who has taken a child into a sweet shop can confirm! There has been a lot of research that attempts to give an empirical validation of some of the hierarchy propositions, the results of which are inconclusive and at times ambiguous (Barry and Howard, 1990). Among these researchers is Palda (1966), who found that the learn–feel–do sequence cannot be upheld as a reflection of general buying behaviour and provided empirical data to reject the notion of sequential models as an interpretation of the way advertising works.

The sequential approach sees attitude towards the product as a prerequisite to purchase, but as discussed earlier (Chapter 4) there is evidence that a positive attitude is not necessarily a good predictor of purchase behaviour. What is important, or more relevant, is the relationship between attitude change and an individual's intention to act in a particular way (Ajzen and Fishbein, 1980). Therefore it seems reasonable to suggest that what is of potentially greater benefit is a specific measure of attitude *towards* purchasing or *intentions* to buy a specific product. Despite measurement difficulties, attitude change is considered a valid objective, particularly in high-involvement situations.

A great deal of time and money must be spent on research, determining what needs to be measured. As a result, only large organisations can utilise the model properly: those with the resources and the expertise to generate the data necessary to exploit this approach fully.

All of these models share the similar view that the purchase decision process is one in which individuals move through a series of sequential stages. Each of the stages from the different models can be grouped in such a way that they are a representation of the three attitude components, these being cognitive (learn), affective (feel) and conative (do) orientations. This could be seen to reflect the various stages in the buying process, especially those that induce high involvement in the decision process but do not reflect the reality of low involvement decisions.

Advertising frameworks

Hall (1992) and O'Malley (1991) have suggested that there are four main advertising frameworks (Figure 13.1):

1. *The sales framework*
   This framework is based on the premise that the level of sales is the only factor that is worth considering when measuring the effectiveness of an advertising campaign. This view holds that all advertising activities are aimed ultimately at shifting product – generating sales. Advertising is considered to have a short-term direct impact on sales. This effect is measurable and, while other outcomes might also result from advertising, the only important factor is sales. On sales alone will the true effect of any advertising be felt. This view is explored further in Chapter 24.
2. *The persuasion framework*
   The second framework assumes advertising to work because it is capable of being persuasive. Persuasion is effected by gradually moving buyers through a number of sequential steps. These hierarchy of effects models assume that buyer decision-making is rational and can be accurately predicted. As discussed earlier, these models have a number of drawbacks and are no longer used as the basis for designing advertisements, despite great popularity in the 1960s and 1970s.
3. *The involvement framework*
   Involvement-based advertisements work by drawing members of the target audience into the advertisement. Involvement with the product develops as a consequence of involvement with the advertisement. Yellow Pages developed a highly successful series of television commercials that centred upon a fictional character

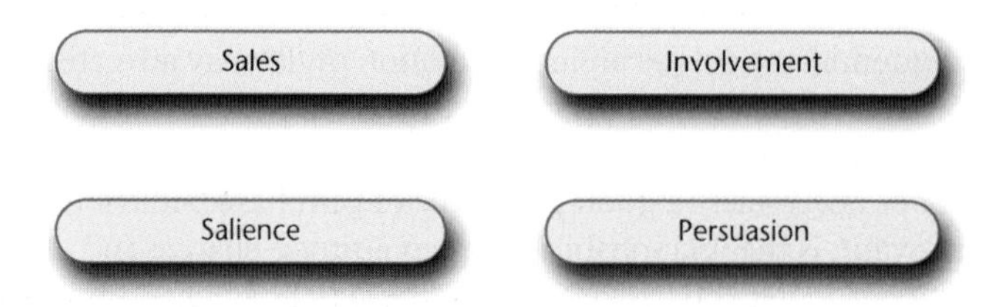

Figure 13.1 Four advertising frameworks.

called J.R. Hartley. This elderly gentleman was shown using Yellow Pages as a means of resolving a number of problems and served to provide warmth and character which involved people not only with J.R. Hartley but also helped establish brand values (see Plate 13.2).

Another example of this approach can be observed in the Nescafé Gold Blend coffee advertisements. During the late 1980s and early 1990s, UK viewers witnessed the development of a relationship between an aspirational couple with a mutual liking for the Gold Blend brand of coffee. Each advertisement, which presents particular events in the development of the couple's relationship, was eagerly anticipated by an involved and often obsessive audience. By involving the target in the drama, the brand became part of the involvement, a crucial part of each of the ritualistic playlets. Later in the decade the couple were reincarnated as a younger couple and presented in a more adventurous context. Again the theme was romance, which was allowed to unfold over a series of different advertisements.

4. *The salience framework*
Salience models are based upon the premise that advertising works by standing out, by being radically different from all other advertisements in the product class. The launch of Radion in 1990, a soap powder that used the twin propositions of cleaning and removing odours, was remarkable because of its ability to 'shout' at the audience through the use of lurid colours and striking presentations. Tango (a canned drink) was repositioned using strikingly different, zany (and interactive) messages (see Plate 13.3). Pot Noodle drew attention through presentation techniques based upon a seemingly unprofessional and off-the-wall domestic camcorder production. Alternative examples of salience advertising are the Tosh campaign by Toshiba (O'Malley) and the Benson and Hedges Silk Cut campaigns (Hall).

Acceptance of the involvement and salience frameworks is based on the assumption that the audience are active problem solvers and are perfectly capable of discrimination among brands and advertisements. Furthermore, the models bring to attention two important points about people and advertising. Advertisements are capable of generating two very clear types of response: a response to the featured product and a response to the advertisement itself. As will be seen later in this chapter, the cognitive responses that people make when exposed to advertisements and the ELM model are important means of understanding how different motivations affect decision-making.

The explanations offered to date are all based on the premise that advertising is a potent marketing force, one that is persuasive and which is done *to* people. More recent views of advertising theory question this fundamental perspective. Prominent among the theorists are Jones, McDonald and Ehrenberg, some of whose views will now be presented. Jones (1991) presented the new views as the strong theory of advertising and the weak theory of advertising.

The strong theory of advertising

All the models presented so far are assumed to work on the basis that they are capable of affecting a degree of change in the knowledge, attitudes, beliefs or behaviour of target audiences. Jones refers to this as the strong theory of advertising, and it appears to have been universally adopted as a foundation for commercial activity.

According to Jones, exponents of this theory hold that advertising can persuade someone to buy a product that they have never previously purchased. Furthermore, continual long-run purchase behaviour can also be generated. Under the strong theory, advertising is believed to be capable of increasing sales at the brand and class levels. These upward shifts are achieved through the use of manipulative and psychological techniques, which are deployed against consumers who are passive, possibly due to apathy, and are generally incapable of processing information intelligently. The most appropriate theory would appear to be the hierarchy of effects model, where sequential steps move buyers forward to a purchase, stimulated by timely and suitable promotional messages.

The weak theory of advertising

Increasing numbers of European writers argue that the strong theory does not reflect practice. Most notable of these writers is Ehrenberg (1988; 1997), who believes that a consumer's pattern of brand purchases is driven more by habit than by exposure to promotional messages.

The framework proposed by Ehrenberg is the Awareness–Trial–Reinforcement (ATR) framework. Awareness is required before any purchase can be made, although the elapsed time between awareness and action may be very short or very long. For the few people intrigued enough to want to try a product, a trial purchase constitutes the next phase. This may be stimulated by retail availability as much as by advertising, word-of-mouth or personal selling stimuli. Reinforcement follows to maintain awareness and provide reassurance to help the customer to repeat the pattern of thinking and behaviour and to cement the brand in the repertoire for occasional purchase activity. Advertising's role is to breed brand familiarity and identification (Ehrenberg, 1997).

Following on from the original ATR model (Ehrenberg, 1974), various enhancements have been suggested. However, Ehrenberg added a further stage in 1997, referred to as the nudge. He argues that some consumers can 'be nudged into buying the brand more frequently (still as part of their split-loyalty repertoires) or to favour it more than the other brands in their consideration sets'. Advertising need not be any different from before; it just provides more reinforcement that stimulates particular habitual buyers into more frequent selections of the brand from their repertoire.

According to the weak theory, advertising is capable of improving people's knowledge, and so is in agreement with the strong theory. In contrast, however, consumers are regarded as selective in determining which advertisements they observe and only perceive those which promote products that they either use or have some prior knowledge of. This means that they already have some awareness of the characteristics of the advertised product. It follows that the amount of information actually communicated is limited. Advertising, Jones continues, is not potent enough to convert people who hold reasonably strong beliefs that are counter to those portrayed in an advertisement. The time available (thirty seconds in television advertising) is not enough to bring about conversion and, when combined with people's ability to switch off their cognitive involvement, there may be no effective communication. Advertising is employed as a defence, to retain customers and to increase product or brand usage.

Advertising is used to reinforce existing attitudes not necessarily to drastically change them.

Unlike the strong theory, this perspective accepts that when people say that they are not influenced by advertising they are in the main correct. It also assumes that people are not apathetic or even stupid, but capable of high levels of cognitive processing.

In summary, the strong theory suggests that advertising can be persuasive, can generate long-run purchasing behaviour, can increase sales and regards consumers as passive. The weak theory suggests that purchase behaviour is based on habit and that advertising can improve knowledge and reinforce existing attitudes. It views consumers as active problem solvers.

These two perspectives serve to illustrate the dichotomy of views that have emerged about this subject. They are important because they are both right and they are both wrong. The answer to the question, 'How does advertising work?' lies somewhere between the two views, and is dependent upon the particular situation facing each advertiser. Where elaboration is likely to be high if advertising is to work, then it is most likely to work under the strong theory. For example, consumer durables and financial products require that advertising urges prospective customers into some form of trial behaviour. This may be a call for more information from a sales representative or perhaps a visit to a showroom. The vast majority of product purchases, however, involve low levels of elaboration, where involvement is low and where people select, often unconsciously, brands from an evoked set.

New products require people to convert or change their purchasing patterns. It is evident that the strong theory must prevail in these circumstances. Where products become established their markets generally mature, so that real growth is non-existent. Under these circumstances, advertising works by protecting the consumer franchise and by allowing users to have their product choices confirmed and re-inforced. The other objective of this form of advertising is to increase the rate at which customers reselect and consume products. If the strong theory was the only acceptable approach, then theoretically advertising would be capable of continually increasing the size of each market, until everyone had been converted. There would be no 'stationary' markets.

Considering the vast sums that are allocated to advertising budgets, not only to launch new products but also to pursue market share targets aggressively, the popularity and continued implicit acceptance of the power of advertising suggest that a large proportion of resources are wasted in the pursuit of advertising-driven brand performance. Indeed, it is noticeable that during the mid to late 1980s organisations were increasingly switching resources out of advertising into sales promotion activities. There are many reasons for this (Chapter 18), but one of them concerns the failure of advertising to produce the anticipated levels of performance: to produce market share. The strong theory fails to deliver the expected results, and the weak theory does not apply to all circumstances. Reality may be a mixture of the two.

Cognitive processing

Reference has already been made to whether buyers actively or passively process information. In an attempt to understand how information is used, cognitive processing tries to determine 'how external information is transformed into meanings or patterns of thought and how these meanings are combined to form judgements' (Olsen and Peter, 1987).

By assessing the thoughts (cognitive processes) that occur to people as they read, view or hear a message, an understanding of their interpretation of a message can be useful in campaign development and evaluation (Wright, 1973; Greenwald, 1968). These thoughts are usually measured by asking consumers to write down or verbally report the thoughts they have in response to such a message. Thoughts are believed to be a reflection of the cognitive processes or responses that receivers experience and they help shape or reject a communication.

Researchers have identified three types of cognitive response and have determined how these relate to attitudes and intentions. Figure 13.2 shows these three types of response, but readers should appreciate that these types are not discrete; they overlap each other and blend together, often invisibly.

Product/message thoughts

These are thoughts which are directed to the product or communication itself. Much attention has been focused upon the thoughts that are related to the message content.

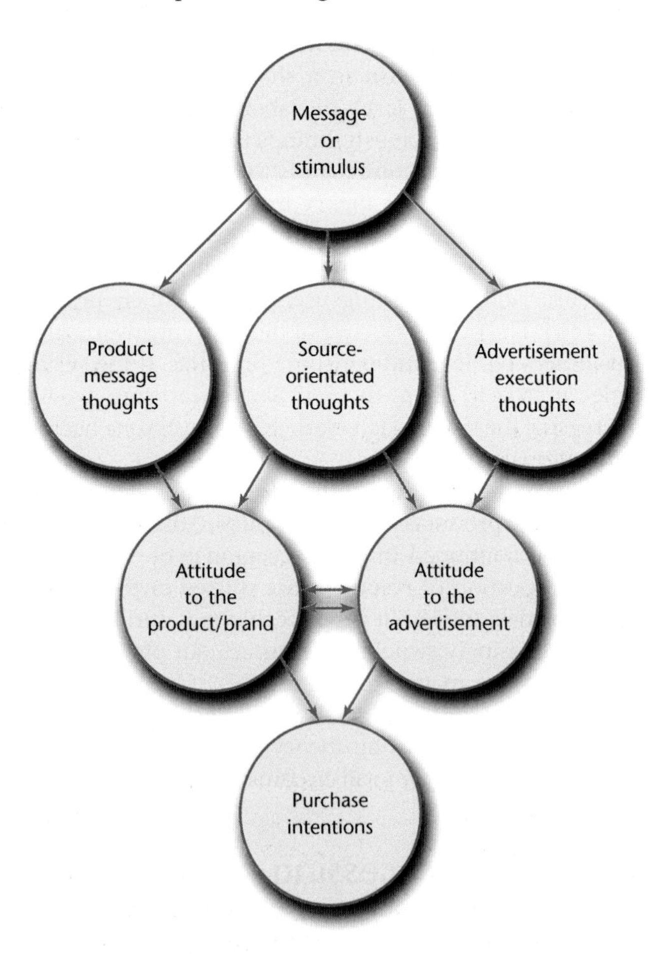

Figure 13.2 A cognitive processing model (adapted from Lutz *et al.* (1983); used with kind permission).

Two particular types of response have been considered: counter-arguments and support-arguments.

A counter-argument occurs when the receiver disagrees with the content of a message. According to Belch and Belch (1990), 'The likelihood of counter-argument is greater when the message makes claims that oppose the beliefs or perceptions held by the receiver. Not surprisingly, the greater the degree of counter-argument, the less likely the message will be accepted. Conversely, support-arguments reflect acceptance and concurrence with a message. Support-arguments, therefore, are positively related to message acceptance'. Use of the social value groups, discussed in Chapter 4, can provide important input to this aspect of message generation. Communications planners should ensure that advertisements and general communications encourage the generation of support-arguments.

Source-orientated thoughts

A further set of cognitive responses are those aimed at the source of the communication. This concept is closely allied to that of source credibility (Chapter 2), where, if the source of the message is seen as annoying or distrustful, there is a lower probability of message acceptance. Such a situation is referred to as source derogation; the converse as a source bolster.

Communication managers should ensure, during the Context Analysis, that receivers experience bolster effects to improve the likelihood of message acceptance.

Advertisement execution thoughts

This relates to the thoughts an individual may have about the advertisement or message itself. Many of the thoughts that receivers have are not product-related but are emotionally related towards the message itself. Understanding these feelings and emotions is important because of their impact upon attitudes towards the advertisement and the offering.

People make judgements about the quality of advertisements and the creativity, tone and style in which an advertisement has been executed, and, as a result of their experiences and perception, form an attitude towards the advertisement. Some suggest that attitudes towards the advertisement can be transferred to the product. An increasing proportion of advertisements appeal to feelings and emotions, as many researchers believe that attitudes towards both the advertisement and the product should be encouraged.

Elaboration likelihood model

Developed by Petty and Cacioppo (1983), the elaboration likelihood model (ELM) has helped to explain how cognitive processing, persuasion and attitude change occur when different levels of involvement are present. Elaboration refers to the extent to which an individual needs to develop and refine information necessary for decision-making to occur. If an individual has a high level of motivation or ability to process information, elaboration is said to be high. If an individual's motivation or ability to process information is poor, then his or her level of elaboration is said to be low. The ELM distinguishes two main cognitive processes, as depicted in Figure 13.3.

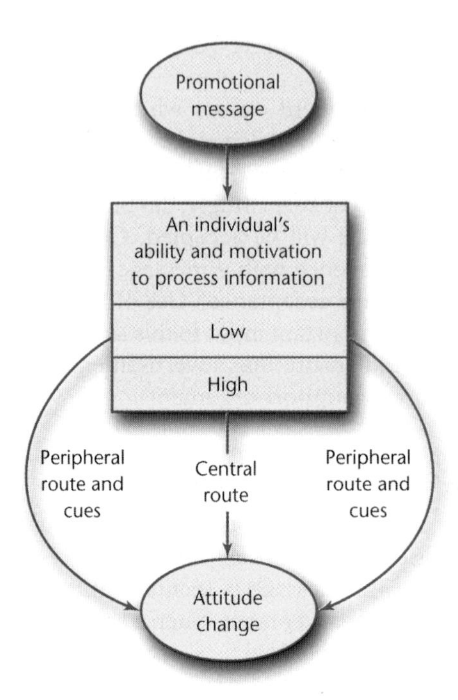

Figure 13.3 The elaboration likelihood model (based on Aaker *et al.* (1992)).

Under the central route the receiver is viewed as very active and involved. As the level of cognitive response is high, the ability of the advertisement to persuade will depend upon the quality of the argument rather than executional factors. For example, the purchase of a consumer durable such as a car or washing machine normally requires a high level of involvement. Consequently, potential customers would be expected to be highly involved and willing to read brochures and information about the proposed car or washing machine prior to demonstration or purchase. Their decision to act would depend upon the arguments used to justify the model as suitable for the individual. For the car purchase these might include the quiet engine, environmentally friendly catalytic converter, the relatively excellent consumption and other performance indicators, together with the comfort of the interior and the effortless driving experience. Whether the car is shown as part of a business executive's essential 'kit' or the commercial is flamboyant and rich will be immaterial for those in the central route.

Under the peripheral route, the receiver is seen to lack the ability to process information and is not likely to engage cognitive processing. Rather than thinking about and evaluating the message content, the receiver tends to rely upon what have been referred to as 'peripheral cues', which may be incidental to the message content.

In low-involvement situations, a celebrity may serve to influence attitudes positively. This is based upon the creation of favourable attitudes towards the source rather than engaging the viewer in the processing of the message content. For example, Gary Lineker has been used as a celebrity spokesperson to endorse Walkers crisps. The power of Gary Lineker would be more important as a major peripheral cue (more so than the nature of the product) in eventually persuading a consumer to try the brand or retaining current users. Think crisps, think Gary Lineker, think

Walkers. Where high involvement is present, any celebrity endorsement is of minor significance to the quality of the message claims.

Communication strategy should be based upon the level of cognitive processing that the target audience is expected to engage in and the route taken to affect attitudinal change. If the processing level is low (low motivation and involvement) then the peripheral route should dominate and emphasis needs to be placed on the way the messages are executed and on the emotions of the target audience. If the central route is anticipated then the content of the messages should be dominant and the executional aspects need only be adequate.

A cognitive–association model of advertising

Depending upon their level of elaboration, buyers are capable problem solvers. They can be regarded as active information processors (to varying degrees) in all product categories. Advertising is a convenient and often cost-effective way of conveying information about brands to people, who then have an opportunity to reassimilate their understanding of the brand and its related elements. This information is processed internally and is used to update their knowledge about the brand as they see it and possibly the generic category of products ('Oh, hoovers can now have a hose that coils itself automatically').

Our understanding of perception suggests that people organise filtered and selected stimuli according to the context of their current situation and their past experiences. Therefore marketing communication messages need to be consistent in order that people can organise information about a brand in the same way as they processed the information the last time they perceived the stimuli. Now, the stimuli need not be just an advertisement: it could be any element of the promotional or marketing mix, in particular the brand itself. Therefore the presence of either the product or the communication may act as a stimulus. It is not surprising that integrated marketing communications require that whatever the contact with a brand, the message should be the same and be expected in the context with which information was processed previously.

The task of marketing communications is to present key messages in such a way that the meanings that people (the target audience) ascribe to them are relevant and capable of being memorised. Advertising can be regarded as a potentially powerful means of enabling buyers to attribute meanings to messages they receive about brands. As Lannon (1992) argues, we should not be concerned with what advertising does to people (traditional view), but with what people do with advertising.

Triggers, memory and brand associations

So far in this chapter, a number of issues have been presented which, taken independently, are interesting but lack overall coherence and direction. These will now be brought together in an attempt to offer a general framework of how advertising might work.

Before proceeding any further, readers are advised that this question, 'How does advertising work?', is as complex as the question posed by Duckworth (1995): 'How does literature work?'. Think about it and describe how literature works to yourself or to a friend. Has the question any inherent validity? The same may said of advertising, and what follows is an attempt to pull together some of the strands of thought presented earlier. No formula is presented or intended, just a few ideas about the interrelationships between concepts, ideas and current research.

Advertising should be considered as a marketing (communications) tool that is used by people in one of two main ways, depending upon the context in which the message, the brand and the individual interact. Advertising messages normally pass individuals unobserved. Those that are remembered contain particular characteristics (Fletcher, 1994; Brown, 1991). These would appear to be that the product must be different or new; that the way the advertisement is executed is different or interesting; and that the message proclaims something that is personally significant to the individual in their current context. The term 'significance' means that the message is meaningful, relevant (e.g. the individual is actually looking to buy a new car or is going to buy breakfast cereals tomorrow) and is perceived to be suitably credible.

Advertising characteristics

To be successful it is necessary for advertising to :

- Present a new product or a product that is substantially different from the other products in the category.
- Be interesting and stimulating.
- Be personally significant.

The net effect of these characteristics might be that any one advertisement may be *significantly valuable* to an individual.

The strong theory of advertising may be regarded as the most applicable framework for *new brands* or those which proclaim something that is perceived to be significantly different. There is evidence that short-term sales effects can be correlated with advertising associated with these brands (Jones, 1995; McDonald, 1997). Consumers may be intrigued and interested enough to want to try the brand at the next purchase opportunity. For these people there is a high level of personal relevance derived from the message, and attitude change can be induced to convince them that it is right to make a purchase. For them the advertisement is significantly valuable and as a result may well generate a purchase decision which, from a market perspective, will drive a discernable sales increase. It may be that many of the brands that win advertising effectiveness awards fall into this category.

However, the vast majority of advertisements are about products that are not new or which are unable to proclaim or offer anything substantially different. These messages are either ignored or, if interest is aroused, certain parts of the message are filed away in memory for use at a later date. The question is, if parts are filed away, which parts are filed and why and how are they retrieved?

The weak theory suggests that advertising is really used to defend purchase behaviour. Advertising provides a rationale or explanation for why consumers (cognitive processors) have bought a brand and why they should continue buying it. Normally, advertising does not persuade – it simply reminds and reassures consumers. Or, to put it another way, consumers use advertising to remind themselves of preferred brands or to reassure themselves of their previous (and hence correct) purchase behaviour.

Consumers, particularly in FMCG markets, practise repertoire buying based on habit, security, speed of decision-making and to some extent self-expression. The brands present in any single individual repertoire normally provide interest and satisfaction. Indeed, advertising needs to ensure that the brand remains in the repertoire or is sufficiently interesting to the consumer that it is included in a future repertoire. Just consider the variety of advertising messages used by mobile phone operators, such as Cellnet, One-to-One, Vodafone and Orange. These are continually updated and refreshed using particular themes which are visually engaging.

Advertising that is interesting, immediately relevant or interpreted as possessing a deep set of personal meanings (all subsequently referred to as likeable; see Chapter 17) will be stored in long-term memory (Chapter 4). As research shows repeatably, only parts of an advertisement are ever remembered – those parts which are of intrinsic value to the recipient. The Brown (1991) example provides suitable evidence of this phenomenon.

Cadbury's Flake

This chocolate bar crumbles easily when bitten. An advertisement was devised which depicted the bar being eaten by three different people in three different contexts. The first was a secretary, who collected the crumbs in the wrapping paper. The second was a man on a train, who collected the crumbs on a plate, and the third was a small boy, who used a straw to suck up the crumbs. Each character was shown for ten seconds, but in the tracking studies that followed it was the small boy who was recalled most, in disproportion to the time of the message exposure.

Brown (1991)

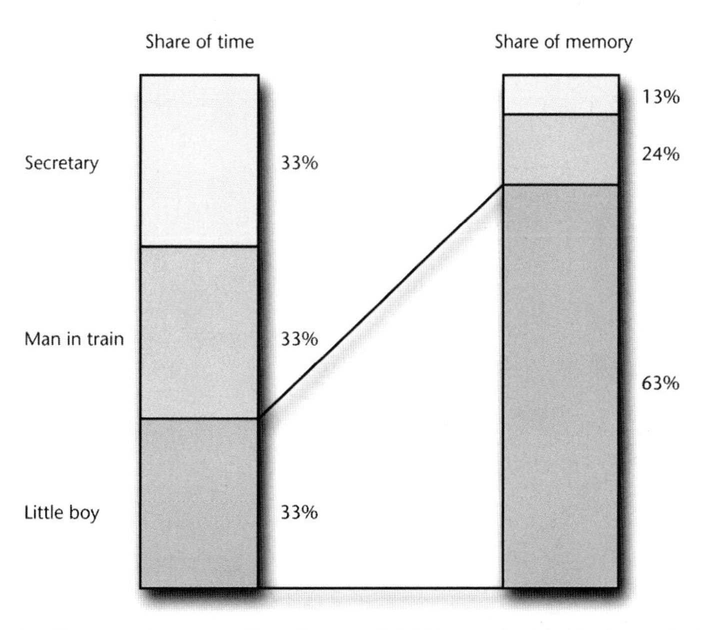

Figure 13.4 The creative magnifier (Brown (1991); used with kind permission).

This selectivity, or message take-out, is referred to as the *creative magnifier* effect. Figure 13.4 illustrates the effect that parts of a message might have on the way a message is remembered.

The implication of this is that advertising works best through the creation of interest and likeable moments, from which extracts are taken by consumers and stored away in memory. Interest is generated through fresh relevant ideas where the brand and the messages are linked together in a meaningful and relevant way. This in turn allows for future associations to be made, linking brands and advertising messages in a positive and experiential way.

Advertising is used to trigger brand associations and experiences for people, not only when seated in front of a television but also when faced with product purchase decisions. Seventy per cent of low-value FMCG purchase decisions are said to be made at the point of purchase. Advertising can be used to trigger brand associations, which in turn are used to trigger advertising messages or, rather, 'likeable' extracts.

This last point is of particular significance because advertising alone may not be sufficient to trigger complete recall of brand and advertising experiences. The brand, its packaging, sales promotion, outdoor media and POP all have an important role to play in providing consistency and interest and prompting recall and recognition. Integrated marketing communications is important, not just for message take-out or likeable extracts, but also for triggering recall and recognition and stimulating brand associations.

The model presented in Figure 13.5 attempts to bring together those elements that influence the way in which advertising might be considered to work. Stimuli act upon levels of elaboration, which in turn determine levels of cognitive processing. Likeable extracts are taken out of the messages and stored for future use. Advertising messages and/or brand experiences then allow for these extracts to be recalled. This impacts on

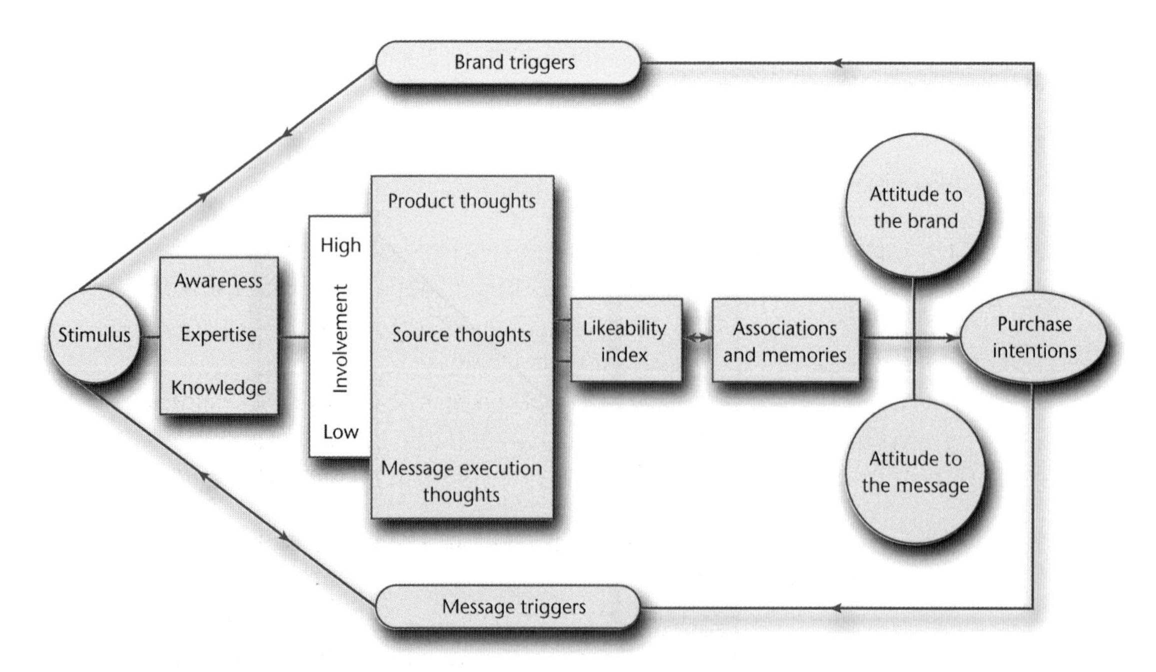

Figure 13.5 A cognitive association model of advertising/brand relationships.

the attitude to the brand and towards the advertisement, which affects purchase intentions. Therefore brands and advertising work together: one is capable of re-inforcing the other and triggers are required to action the process and to reinforce previous behaviour.

For advertisements to be effective they must be likeable (interesting, meaningful and relevant to the brand and the target audience) and therefore must be contextually compatible with the target audience and the brand.

Summary

Through time, a variety of models have been presented, each of which attempts to describe how advertising works. Aida and sequential models, such as the hierarchy of effects approach, were for a long time the received wisdom in this area. Now they are regarded as quaint but out-of-date, for a number of hard hitting reasons.

With the development of our understanding of cognitive processing and elaboration, so new views of advertising have gathered pace and increased acceptance. At the same time, many writers have become sceptical of advertising's power to persuade consumers to change their purchasing habits. When brands are perceived to have some credible value, perhaps because they are new, then advertising might be considered to work under the strong theory.

The new view is that advertising should be regarded as a means of defending customers' purchase decisions and for protecting markets, not building them. Reality suggests that the majority of advertising cannot claim to be of significant value to most people. Those messages that are of value are normally dissected so that only parts of the message are extracted and stored for future use. Messages or extracts of messages can be recalled or released from long-term memory when triggered by an association, such as new incoming advertising messages or brand experiences. Advertising and brands should be regarded as elements which need to work together if advertising is to be successful and brands are to survive.

Review questions

1. Explain the role that advertising plays within marketing communications
2. Write brief notes outlining the difference between absolute and relative costs.
3. Name three sequential models of how advertising is thought to work and evaluate the ways in which they are considered to work.
4. Which element in McGuire's model separates it from other similar models?
5. What are the essential differences between the involvement and salience frameworks of advertising? Find four advertisements (other than those described in the text) that are examples of these two approaches.
6. Write a short presentation explaining the differences between the strong and weak theories of advertising.
7. Cognitive processing is thought to be made up of three main elements. Name them.
8. Give examples of peripheral and central route cues to attitude change using the elaboration likelihood model.

9. Describe the creative magnifier effect. Why is it important?
10. What is the likely impact of triggers and brand associations in determining how advertising works?

References

Aaker, D.A., Batra, R. and Myers, J.G. (1992) *Advertising Management*, 4th edn. Englewood Cliffs NY: Prentice Hall.

Ajzen, I. and Fishbein, M. (1980) *Understanding Attitudes and Predicting Social Behaviour*. Englewood Cliffs NJ: Prentice Hall.

Barry, T. and Howard, D.J. (1990) A review and critique of the hierarchy of effects in advertising. *International Journal of Advertising*, **9**, 121–35.

Belch, G.E. and Belch, M.A. (1990) *An Introduction to Advertising and Promotion Management*. Homewood IL: Richard D. Irwin.

Brown, G. (1991) *How Advertising Affects the Sales of Packaged Goods Brands*. Millward Brown Publications.

Duckworth, G. (1995) How advertising works, the universe and everything. *Admap* (January), 41–3.

Ehrenberg, A.S.C. (1974) Repetitive advertising and the consumer. *Journal of Advertising Research*, 14 (April), 25–34.

Ehrenberg, A.S.C. (1988) *Repeat Buying*, 2nd edn. London: Charles Griffin.

Ehrenberg, A.S.C. (1997) How do consumers come to buy a new brand. *Admap* (March), 20–4

Fletcher, W. (1994) The advertising high ground, *Admap* (November), 31–4.

Greenwald, A. (1968) Cognitive learning, cognitive response to persuasion and attitude change, in *Psychological Foundations of Attitudes* (eds. A. Greenwald, T.C. Brook and T.W. Ostrom). New York: Academic Press.

Hall, M. (1992) Using advertising frameworks. *Admap* (March), 17–21.

Jones, J.P. (1991) Over promise and under-delivery. *Marketing and Research Today* (November), 195–203.

Jones, J.P. (1995) Advertising exposure effects under a microscope. *Admap* (February), 28–31.

Lannon, J. (1992) Asking the right questions – what do people do with advertising? *Admap* (March), 11–16.

Lavidge, R.J. and Steiner, G.A. (1961) A model for predictive measurements of advertising effectiveness. *Journal of Marketing* (October), 61.

Lutz, J., Mackensie, S.B. and Belch, G.E. (1983) Attitude toward the ad as a mediator of advertising effectiveness. *Advances in Consumer Research X*. Ann Arbor MI: Association for Consumer Research.

McDonald, C. (1997) Short-term advertising effects: how confident can we be? *Admap* (June), 36–9.

McGuire, W.J. (1978) An information processing model of advertising effectiveness, in *Behavioral and Management Science in Marketing* (eds. H.L. Davis and A.J. Silk). New York: Ronald/Wiley.

Olsen, J.C. and Peter, J.P. (1987) *Consumer Behaviour*. Homewood IL: Richard D. Irwin.

O'Malley, D. (1991) Sales without salience? *Admap* (September), 36–9.

Palda, K.S. (1966) The hypothesis of a hierarchy of effects: a partial evaluation. *Journal of Marketing Research*, **3**, 13–24.

Petty, R.E. and Cacioppo, J.T. (1983) Central and peripheral routes to persuasion: application to advertising, in *Advertising and Consumer Psychology* (eds. L. Percy and A. Woodside). Lexington MA: Lexington Books.

Strong, E.K. (1925) *The Psychology of Selling*. New York: McGraw-Hill.

Wright, P.L. (1973) The cognitive processes mediating the acceptance of advertising. *Journal of Marketing Research*, **10** (February), 53–62.

chapter 14

Advertising messages

The context in which people receive and interpret advertising messages must be considered thoroughly if the effectiveness of a communication is to be maximised. Ensuring that the right balance of information and emotions is achieved and that the presentation of the message is appropriate for the target audience represents a critical part of the creative process for the advertising agency and the client.

Aims and objectives

The aim of this chapter is to consider some of the ways in which advertising messages can be created by focusing on some of the principal aspects of message construction.

The objectives of this chapter are:

1. To show how messages can be constructed to account for the context in which they are to be received.
2. To examine the use of emotions and feelings in advertising messages.
3. To explore the advantages and disadvantages of using spokespersons in message presentation.
4. To consider how advertising messages might be best presented.
5. To suggest how informational and transformational motives can be used as tactical tools in an advertising plan.

Introduction

Whether advertising converts people into becoming brand-loyal customers or acts as a defensive shield to reassure current buyers, and whether central or peripheral cues

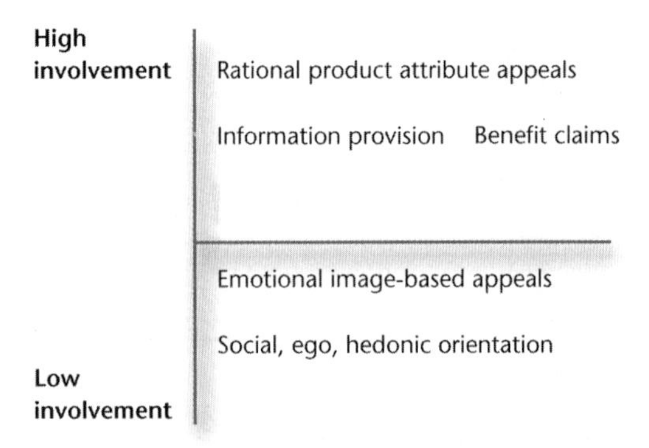

Figure 14.1 The balance of emotions and information provision.

are required, there still remains the decision about the nature and form of the message to be conveyed: the creative strategy.

In practice, the generation of suitable messages is derived from the creative brief. For the sake of discussion and analysis four elements will be considered. These concern the *balance*, the *structure*, the perceived *source* and the *presentation of the message* to the target audience.

The balance of the message

It is evident from previous discussions that the effectiveness of any single message is dependent upon a variety of issues. From a receiver's perspective, two elements appear to be significant: first, the amount and quality of the information that is communicated, and second, the overall judgement that each individual makes about the way a message is communicated.

This suggests that the style of a message should reflect a balance between the need for information and the need for pleasure or enjoyment in consuming the message. Figure 14.1 describes the two main forms of appeal. Messages can be product-orientated and rational or customer-orientated and based upon feelings and emotions.

It is clear that when dealing with high-involvement decisions, where persuasion occurs through a central processing route, the emphasis of the message should be on the information content, in particular the key attributes and the associated benefits. This style is often factual and product-orientated. If the product evokes low-involvement decision-making, then the message should concentrate upon the images that are created within the mind of the message recipient. This style seeks to illicit an emotional response from receivers.

Message style: British Airways

The new visual identity launched by BA in the summer of 1997 provides an interesting view of the balance between emotion and information inputs. The new design signals a shift away from the rational message presented by many airlines.

The traditionally factual or functionally based identities and promotional messages stress in-flight entertainment, comfort (Virgin and Helen Mirren – leg-room), size (BA – we carry more passengers etc.) and convenience. Corporate identities very often stress nationality, flags and nationhood.

BA attempted to introduce a more friendly and informal view of itself, attempting to be more approachable and probably counteract some adverse market research information. Their 'tears for joy' campaign had a global emphasis which depicted scenes of people from different parts of the world being moved to tears through happiness. Using television, press and posters the campaign used little copy, and the strikingly different tailplane designs are featured prominently.

Adapted from Trickett (1997)

Likeability

An issue that has been gaining increasing attention since the beginning of the 1990s concerns the level of likeability that an advertisement generates. Likeability is important, because learning and attitude change may be positively correlated with the degree to which consumption of the message is enjoyed. This means that the greater the enjoyment, the greater the exposure to the message and the lower the probability that the message will be perceptually zapped.

Biel (1990) found that changes in product preferences were considerably improved when receivers had 'liked the commercial a lot'. This compares with those who were less enthusiastic or neutral towards the advertisement. Haley (1990) reported that advertisements that create a belief that the product is excellent and where messages are liked are commercially more successful. In other words, a message that is well liked will sell more product than a message that fails to generate interest and liking.

This begs the question 'what makes a message liked'? Obviously, the receiver must be stimulated to become interested in the message. Having become emotionally engaged, interest can only be sustained if the credibility of the advertisement can also be maintained. The style of the message should be continued, in order that the context of the message does not require the target audience to readjust their perception. This is particularly important for low-involvement messages, where receivers have little or no interest. If the weak theory is adopted then 'liked' advertisements will tend to be those for whom the receiver has prior experience or exposure.

Otherwise, perceptual selection will ensure that messages for products of which the target has no experience, or which the target has no interest in, will be screened out regardless of the quality or the likeability of the communication.

The likeability level that an advertisement achieves is not the sole reason or measure of an advertisement's success or effectiveness (Joyce, 1991). Research from the Netherlands suggests that interest is also an important and interrelated factor. Stapel (1991) strongly suggests that advertisers should make their messages interesting, as this will probably lead to liking and overall effectiveness. However, likeability

Message consistency: BMW

When BMW (GB) was first established in 1979 it replaced a distributor who had sold a range of performance cars. The business goal was to treble sales volumes to 40,000 cars a year and maintain the high margins.

The advertising strategy was to build on the core brand values and move the perception of BMW cars from one of *performance* to one of *reward*. The line 'Ultimate Driving Machine' was first used in 1979 and has been used to underline the BMW brand since then. A consistent tone of voice was adopted whereby the advertising messages are always factually correct and removed from other types of glamour car advertising. Because of the need to focus on the technological strengths and benefits of BMW, a policy not to include any people in the advertisements was developed. The reasoning is that people are fallible, whereas BMW technology is not.

Robin Wight at WCRS, the advertising agency responsible for the continued success of BMW in the UK, leads what is referred to as a 'product interrogation' team each year. The team visits the factory and tries to uncover from the engineers new information and developments about BMW technology.

He recalls a time when he spent half a day trying to understand why six cylinder engines were smoother than those with four cylinders. The exasperated engineer was finally asked how he would convince his next-door neighbour not to buy a Mercedes (arch rival) but a BMW. He thought for a while and then said that he would place a glass of water on both engines. When revving the Mercedes the glass would not move but the imperfections in the balance of the engine would destabilise the water in the glass. No matter how much he revved the BMW the water would not move.

Wight arrived back in London, and tested the claim. It worked. Within 15 minutes the 'Shaken, not stirred' advertisement was created (see Plate 14.1).

Adapted from publicity materials kindly provided by BMW (1994) and Broadbent (1994)

and associated interest are new and interesting contributions that need to be considered when the style of an advertising message is determined.

Message structure

An important part of message strategy is the consideration of the best way of communicating the key points, or core message, to the target audience without encountering objections and opposing points of view. The following are regarded as important structural features which shape the pattern of a message.

Conclusion drawing

Should the message draw a firm conclusion for the audience or should people be allowed to draw their own conclusions from the content? Explicit conclusions are, of course, more easily understood and stand a better chance of being effective (Kardes, 1988). However, it is the nature of the issue, the particular situation and the composition of the target audience that influence the effectiveness of conclusion drawing (Hovland and Mandell, 1952). Whether or not a conclusion should be drawn for the receiver depends upon the following:

1. *The complexity of the issue*
   Healthcare products, central heating systems and personal finance services, for example, can be complex, and for some members of the target audience their cognitive ability, experience and motivation may not be sufficient for them to draw their own conclusions. The complexity of the product requires that messages must draw conclusions for them. It should also be remembered that even highly informed and motivated audiences may require assistance if the product or issue is relatively new.
2. *The level of education possessed by the receiver*
   Better-educated audiences prefer to draw their own conclusions, whereas less educated audiences may need the conclusion drawn for them because they may not be able to make the inference from the message.
3. *Whether immediate action is required*
   If urgent action is required by the receiver then a conclusion should be drawn very clearly. Political parties can be observed to use this strategy immediately before an election.
4. *The level of involvement*
   High involvement usually means that receivers prefer to make up their own minds and may reject or resent any attempt to have the conclusion drawn for them (Arora, 1985).

One and two-sided messages

This concerns whether the cases for and against an issue or just that in favour are presented to an audience. Messages that present just one argument, in favour of the product or issue, are referred to as one-sided. Research indicates that one-sided messages are more effective when receivers favour the opinion offered in the message and when the receivers are less educated.

Two-sided messages, where the good and bad points of an issue are presented, are more effective when the receiver's initial opinion is opposite to that presented in the message and when they are highly educated. Credibility is improved and two-sided messages tend to produce more positive perceptions of a source than one-sided messages (Faison, 1961).

Order of presentation

Further questions regarding the development of message strategy concern the order in which important points are presented. Messages which present the strongest points at the beginning use what is referred to as the *primacy* effect. The decision to place the main points at the beginning depends on whether the audience has a low or high level of involvement. A low level may require an attention-getting message component at the beginning. Similarly, if the target has an opinion opposite to that contained in the message, a weak point may lead to a high level of counter-argument.

A decision to place the strongest points at the end of the message assumes that the *recency* effect will bring about greater levels of persuasion. This is appropriate when the receiver agrees with the position adopted by the source or has a high positive level of involvement.

The order of argument presentation is more relevant in personal selling than in television advertisements. However, as learning through television is largely passive, because involvement is low and interest minimal, the presentation of key selling points at the beginning and at the end of the message will enhance message reception and recall.

Source of the message

The importance of source credibility was established during the discussion of communication theory in Chapter 2. The effect of source credibility on the effectiveness of the communication, and in particular the persuasiveness of a message, should not be underestimated. The key components of source credibility are, first, the level of perceived expertise (how much knowledge the source is thought to hold) and the personal motives the source is believed to possess. What degree of trust can be placed in the source concerning the motives for communicating the message in the first place? No matter what the level of expertise, if the level of trust is questionable, credibility will be adversely affected.

Establishing credibility

Credibility can be established in a number of ways. One simple approach is to list or display the key attributes of the organisation or the product and then signal trustworthiness through the use of third-party endorsements and the comments of satisfied users.

A more complex approach is to use referrals, suggestions and association. Trustworthiness and expertise, the two principal aspects of credibility, can be developed by using a spokesperson or organisation to provide testimonials on behalf of the sponsor of the advertisement. Credibility, therefore, can be established by the initiator of the advertisement or by a messenger or spokesperson used by the initiator to convey the message.

Credibility established by the initiator

The credibility of the organisation initiating the communication process is important. An organisation should seek to enhance its reputation with its various stakeholders at every opportunity. However, organisational credibility is derived from the image, which in turn is a composite of many perceptions. Past decisions, current strategy and performance indicators, level of service and the type of performance network members (e.g. high-quality retail outlets) all influence the perception of an organisation and the level of credibility that follows.

One very important factor that influences credibility is branding. Private and family brands in particular allow initiators to develop and launch new products more easily than those who do not have such brand strength. Brand extensions (such as Mars ice cream) have been launched with the credibility of the product firmly grounded in the strength of the parent brand name (Mars). Consumers recognise the name and make associations that enable them to lower the perceived risk and in doing so provide the platform to try the new product.

The need to establish high levels of credibility also allows organisations to divert advertising spend away from a focus upon brands to one that focuses upon the organisation. Corporate advertising seeks to adjust organisation image and to build reputation.

Credibility established by a spokesperson

People who deliver the message are often regarded as the source, when in reality they are only the messenger. These people carry the message and represent the true source or initiator of the message (e.g. manufacturer or retailer). Consequently, the testimonial they transmit must be credible. There are four main types of spokesperson: the expert, the celebrity, the chief executive officer and the consumer.

The expert has been used many times and was particularly popular when television advertising first established itself in the 1950s and 1960s. Experts are quickly recognisable because they either wear white coats and round glasses or dress and act like 'mad professors'. Through the use of symbolism, stereotypes and identification,

Exhibit 14.1 Richard Branson being used to endorse APA. Picture kindly supplied by APA. Photograph by Steve Pike.

these characters (and indeed others) can be established very quickly in the minds of receivers and a frame of reference generated which does not question the authenticity of the message being transmitted by such a person. Experts can also be users of products, for example, professional photographers endorsing cameras, secretaries endorsing word processors and professional golfers endorsing golf equipment (Exhibit 14.1).

Entertainment and sporting celebrities have been used increasingly in the 1990s, not only to provide credibility for a range of high-involvement (e.g. Rowan Atkinson for Barclaycard and David Ginola for Renault Laguna) and low-involvement decisions (Bob Hoskins for BT), but also to grab the attention of people in markets where motivation to decide between competitive products may be low. The celebrity enables the message to stand out among the clutter and noise that typify many markets. It is also hoped that the celebrity and or the voice-over will become a peripheral cue in the decision-making process: Bruce Forsyth for Courts, Gary Lineker for Walkers Crisps and Nannette Newman for Fairy Liquid.

Walkers Crisps

Walkers Crisps have embarked upon a series of campaigns that have incorporated a consistent communications mix. The objective was to revive and reposition the brand, and this has been achieved using television and Gary Lineker as the central spokesperson to appeal to both adults and teenagers.

Lineker has been a consistent element throughout all the campaigns and is presented and perceived as a cheeky but fun endorser for the brand. Advertisements with a number of related spokespersons, such as Paul Gascoigne and the Spice Girls, have been mixed with messages with unrelated spokespersons, such as everyday people and even a nun. These campaigns have been used to promote sales promotions such as competitions, from which a tremendous amount of PR media coverage has been generated.

The market has grown by 11%, but Walkers have achieved growth of 21%. They have revived their brand, achieved market leadership and profitability, and repositioned themselves as the number one snack food brand in the UK through the use of IMC.

There are some potential problems which advertisers need to be aware of when considering the use of celebrities. First, does the celebrity fit the image of the brand and will the celebrity be acceptable to the target audience? Consideration also needs to be given to the longer term relationship between the celebrity and the brand. Should the lifestyle of the celebrity change, what impact will the change have on the target audience and their attitude towards the brand? Witness the separation of the England football coach, Glenn Hoddle, and his wife, and the consequent termination of the Weetabix advertisement set around the family breakfast table.

This matching process can be used to change brand attitudes as well as reinforce them. BT wanted to change the attitude that men had to telephone calls. Rather than being just the bill payer and the gatekeeper of calls to other members of the family, the role Bob Hoskins had was to demonstrate male behaviour and to present a solution that was acceptable to all members of the family. Attitudes held by men towards the telephone and its use changed significantly as a result of the campaign, partly because Hoskins was perceived as a credible spokesperson, someone with whom men could identify with and feel comfortable.

The second problem concerns the impact that the celebrity makes relative to the brand. There is a danger that the receiver remembers the celebrity but not the message or the brand that is the focus of the advertising spend. The celebrity becomes the hero, rather than the product being advertised. Summers (1993) suggests that the Cinzano advertisements featuring Joan Collins and Leonard Rossiter are a classic example of the problem: 'The characters so dwarfed the product that consumers may have had trouble recalling the brand'.

Issues such as brand development can also be impeded when identification by an audience with the celebrity is strong. Sony had to fade audiences away from their association with John Cleese by using a Robot/Cleese lookalike for a period.

Richard Branson is used to promote Virgin PEP and Victor Kiam 'so liked the razor that he bought the company' (Remington). Here, the CEO openly promotes his company. This form of testimonial is popular when the image of the CEO is positive and the photogenic and on-screen characteristics provide for enhanced credibility. Bernard Mathews has established authenticity and trustworthiness with his personal promotion of Norfolk Roasts.

The final form of spokesperson is the consumer. By using consumers to endorse products the audience is being asked to identify with a 'typical consumer'. The identification of similar lifestyles, interests and opinions allows for better reception and understanding of the message. Consumers are often depicted testing similar products, such as margarine and butter. The Pepsi Challenge required consumers to select Pepsi from Coca-Cola through blind taste tests. By showing someone using the product, someone who is similar to the receiver, the source is perceived as credible and the potential for successful persuasion is considerably enhanced.

Sleeper effects

The assumption so far has been that high credibility enhances the probability of persuasion and successful communication. This is true when the receiver's initial position is opposite to that contained in the message. When the receiver's position is favourable to the message a moderate level of credibility may be more appropriate.

Whether source credibility is high, medium or low is of little consequence, according to some researchers (Hannah and Sternthal, 1984). The impact of the source is believed to dissipate after approximately six weeks and only the content of the message is thought to dominate the receiver's attention. This sleeper effect (Hovland *et al.*, 1949) has not been proved empirically, but the implication is that the persuasiveness of a message can increase through time. Furthermore, advertisers using highly credible sources need to repeat the message on a regular basis, in order that the required level of effectiveness and persuasion be maintained (Schiffman and Kanuk, 1991).

Presentation of the message

The presentation of the promotional message requires that an appeal be made to the target audience. The appeal is important, because unless the execution of the message appeal (the creative) is appropriate to the target audience's perception and expectations, the chances of successful communication are reduced.

There are two main factors associated with the presentation. Is the message to be dominated by the need to transmit product-orientated information or is there a need to transmit a message which appeals predominantly to the emotional senses of the receiver? The main choice of presentation style, therefore, concerns the degree of factual information transmitted in a message against the level of imagery thought necessary to make sufficient impact for the message to command attention and then be processed. There are numerous presentational or executional techniques, but the following are some of the more commonly used appeals.

Appeals based upon the provision of information

Factual

Sometimes referred to as the 'hard sell', the dominant objective of these appeals is to provide information. This type of appeal is commonly associated with high-involvement decisions where receivers are sufficiently motivated and able to process information. Persuasion, according to the ELM, is undertaken through the central processing route. This means that advertisements should be rational and contain logically reasoned arguments and information in order that receivers are able to complete their decision-making processes.

Slice of life

As noted earlier, the establishment of credibility is vital if any message is to be accepted. One of the ways in which this can be achieved is to present the message in such a way that the receiver can identify immediately with the scenario being presented to them. This process of creating similarity is used a great deal in advertising and is referred to as slice of life advertising. For example, many washing powder advertisers use a routine that depicts two ordinary women (assumed to be similar to the target receiver), invariably in a kitchen or garden, discussing the poor results achieved by one of their washing powders. Following the advice of one of the women, the stubborn stains are seen to be overcome by the focus brand.

The overall effect of this appeal is for the receiver to conclude the following. That person is like me; I have had the same problem as that person; he or she is satisfied using brand X; therefore, I too will use brand X. This technique is simple, well tried, well liked and successful, despite its sexist overtones. It is also interesting to note that a European-wide survey found that nearly 66% of women felt that advertisers use inappropriate stereotyping to portray females roles, these being predominantly housewife and mother roles (*Campaign*, 23 November 1993).

Demonstration

A similar technique is to present the problem to the audience as a demonstration. The focus brand is depicted as instrumental in the resolution of a problem. Headache remedies, floor cleaners and tyre commercials have traditionally demonstrated the pain, the dirt and the danger, respectively and then shown how the focus brand relieves the pain (Panadol), removes the stubborn dirt (Flash) or stops in the wet on a coin (or edge of a rooftop – Continental tyres). Whether the execution is believable is a function of the credibility and the degree of life-like dialogue or copy that is used.

Comparative advertising

Comparative advertising is a popular means of positioning brands. Messages are based upon the comparison of the focus brand with that of either a main competitor brand or all competing brands, with the aim of establishing superiority. The comparison centres upon one or two key attributes and can be a good way of entering new markets. Entrants keen to establish a presence in a market have little to lose by comparing themselves with market leaders. However, market leaders have a great deal to lose and little to gain by comparing themselves with minor competitors.

Channel crossings

When the Channel tunnel was opened it was necessary for Eurotunnel to provide a series of benefits to encourage consumers to rationalise their use of the tunnel in preference to the established ferry crossing. A series of messages were used, one of which was to suggest that the EuroStar service reduced the travel time to get to France; another was to suggest through a poster depicting a rough sea, that Eurostar was smooth and free of sea sickness discomfort. The Ferry operators responded with messages that showed the ferry crossing to be an integral part of a holiday experience and that the ferry was like a mini cruise, with all the attendant feelings associated with that type of holiday.

Appeals based upon emotions and feelings

Appeals based on logic and reason are necessary in particular situations. However, as products become similar and as consumers become more aware of the range of available products, so the need to differentiate becomes more important. Increasing numbers of advertisers are using messages which seek to appeal to the target's emotions and feelings, a 'soft sell'. Cars, toothpaste, toilet tissue and mineral water often use emotion-based messages to differentiate their products.

There are a number of appeals that can be used to solicit an emotional response from the receiver. Of the many techniques available, the main ones that can be observed to be used most are fear, humour, animation, sex, music, and fantasy and surrealism.

Fear

Fear is used in one of two ways. The first type demonstrates the negative aspects or physical dangers associated with a particular behaviour or improper product usage. Drink driving, life assurance and toothpaste advertising typify this form of appeal. The second approach is the threat of social rejection or disapproval if the focus product is not used. This type of fear is used frequently in advertisements for such products as anti-dandruff shampoos and deodorants, and is used to support consumers' needs for social acceptance and approval.

Fear appeals need to be constrained, if only to avoid being categorised as outrageous and socially unacceptable. There is a great deal of evidence that fear can facilitate attention and interest in a message and even motivate an individual to take a particular course of action: for example, to stop smoking. Fear appeals are persuasive, according to Schiffman and Kanuk (1991) when low to moderate levels of fear are induced. Ray and Wilkie (1970), however, show that should the level of fear rise too much, inhibiting effects may prevent the desired action occurring. This inhibition is caused by the individual choosing to screen out, through perceptive selection, messages that conflict with current behaviour. The outcome may be that individuals deny the existence of a problem, claim there is no proof or say that it will not happen to them.

Humour

The use of humour as an emotional appeal is attractive because it can draw attention and stimulate interest. A further reason to use humour is that it can put the receiver in a positive mood. Mood can also be important, as receivers in a positive mood are likely to process advertising messages with little cognitive elaboration (Batra and Stayman, 1990). This can occur because there is less effort involved with peripheral rather than central cognitive processing, and this helps to mood-protect. In other words, the positive mood state is more likely to be maintained if cognitive effort is avoided. Yellow Pages have used humour quietly to help convey the essence of their brand and to help differentiate it from the competition (see Plate 14.2).

It is also argued that humour is effective because argument quality is likely to be high. That is, the level of counter-argument can be substantially reduced. Arguments against the use of humour concern distraction from the focus brand, so that while attention is drawn, the message itself is lost. With the move to global branding and standardisation of advertising messages, humour does not travel well. While the level and type of humour is difficult to gauge in the context of the processing abilities of a domestic target audience, cultural differences seriously impede the transfer of jokes around the world. Visual humour (lavatorial, Benny Hill-type approaches) is more universally acceptable (Archer, 1994) than word-based humour, as the latter can get lost in translation without local references to provide clues to decipher the joke. Humour, therefore, is a potentially powerful yet dangerous form of appeal. Haas (1997) reports that UK advertising executives have significantly higher confidence in the use of humour than their US counterparts, but concludes that 'humour is a vague concept and that its perception is influenced by many factors'. These factors shape the context in which messages are perceived and the humour conveyed.

Animation

Animation techniques have advanced considerably in recent years, with children as the prime target audience. However, animation has been successfully used in many adult-targeted advertisements, such as Tetley Tea, Direct Line Insurance and electricity. The main reason for using animation is that potentially boring and low-interest/involvement products can be made visually interesting and provide a means of gaining attention. A further reason for the use of animation is that it is easier to convey complex products in a way that does not patronise the viewer.

Tax returns – self-assessment

In the two year period leading to the introduction of self-assessment, the Inland Revenue had to raise awareness of the new system and encourage the self-employed to keep tax records and meet particular deadlines for the submission of the new style accounts.

Tax matters are normally assumed to instil feelings of panic and fear and so it was decided to use an animated personality, Hector, as an approachable Tax Inspector. A campaign that used TV, Press, Direct Mail and a variety of ambient media helped drive awareness of self assessment from 26% in 1995 to 99% of the self-employed in 1997 and 96% of higher rate tax payers in November 1997. See Exhibit 14.2.

The Inland Revenue and adapted from Campbell (1997)

Sex

Sexual innuendo and the use of sex as a means of promoting products and services are both common and controversial. Using sex as an appeal in messages is excellent for gaining the attention of buyers. Research shows, however, that it often achieves little else, particularly when the product is unrelated. Therefore, sex appeals normally work well for products such as perfume, clothing and jewellery but provide for poor effectiveness when the product is unrelated, such as cars, photo-copiers and furniture. Häagan-Dazs premium ice cream entered the UK market using pleasure as central to the message appeal. This approach was novel to the product class and the direct, natural relationship between the product and the theme contributed to the campaign's success.

Exhibit 14.2 Hector the Tax Inspector – animated character used to reduce perceived risk and increase awareness of the Self-Assessment programme.

The use of sex in advertising messages is mainly restricted to getting the attention of the audience and, in some circumstances, sustaining interest. It can be used openly, as in various lingerie, fragrance and perfume advertisements, such as WonderBra and Escape; sensually, as in the Häagen-Dazs and Cointreau campaigns; and unobtrusively, as in Oxo, when Katy licks her lips as she passes a casserole to her husband and whispers 'remember Preston?' (Garrett, 1993).

Music

Music can provide continuity between a series of advertisements can and also be a good peripheral cue. A jingle, melody or tune, if repeated sufficiently, can become associated with the advertisement. Processing and attitudes towards the advertisement may be directly influenced by the music. Music has the potential to gain attention and assist product differentiation. Braithwaite and Ware (1997) found that music in advertising messages is used primarily either to create a mood or to send a branded message. In addition, music can also be used to signal a lifestyle and so communicate a brand identity through the style of music used.

Many advertisements for cars use music, partly because it is difficult to find a point of differentiation (*The Independent*, 18 October 1996), and music is able to draw attention, generate mood and express brand personality (e.g. Rover, BMW, Nissan Micra, Peugeot, Renault).

Some luxury and executive cars are advertised using commanding background music to create an aura of power, prestige and affluence, which is combined with strong visual images in order that an association be made between the car and the environment in which it is positioned. There is a contextual juxtaposition between the car and the environment presented. Readers may notice a semblance of classical conditioning, where the music acts as an unconditioned stimulus. Foxall and Goldsmith (1994) suggest that the stimulus elicits the unconditioned emotional responses that may lead to the purchase of the advertised product.

Fantasy and surrealism

The use of fantasy and surrealism in advertising has grown partly as a result of the increased clutter and legal constraints imposed on some product classes. By using fantasy appeals, associations with certain images and symbols allow the advertiser to focus attention on the product. The receiver can engage in the distraction offered and become involved with the execution of the advertisement. If this is a rewarding experience it may be possible to affect the receiver's attitudes peripherally. Readers may notice that this links to the earlier discussion on 'liking the advertisement'.

Finally, an interesting contribution to the discussion of message appeal has been made by Lannon (1992). She reports that consumers' expectations of advertisements can be interpreted on the one hand as either literal or stylish, and on the other as serious or entertaining, according to the tone of voice. This approach vindicates the view that consumers are active problem solvers and willing and able to decode increasingly complex messages. They can become involved with the execution of the advertisement and the product attributes. The degree of involvement (she argues implicitly) is a function of the motivation each individual has at any one moment when exposed to a particular message.

Advertisers can challenge individuals by presenting questions and visual stimuli that demand attention and cognitive response. Guinness challenged their consumers

Pictures reproduced with the kind permission of Gieves

Exhibit 14.3 A series of print advertisements designed to challenge readers by encouraging the question "what is going on here?"

to decode a series of advertisements which were unlike all previous Guinness advertisements and, indeed, all messages in the product class. The celebrity chosen was dressed completely in black, which contrasted with his blonde hair, and he was shown in various time periods, past and future, and environments that receivers did not anticipate. He was intended to represent the personification of the drink and symbolised the individual nature of the product. Audiences were puzzled by the presentation and many rejected the challenge of interpretation.

When individuals respond positively to a challenge, the advertiser can either provide closure (an answer) or, through surreal appeals, leave the receivers to answer the questions themselves in the context in which they perceive the message. One way of achieving this challenging position is to use an appeal that cognitively disorients the receiver (Parker and Churchill, 1986). If receivers are led to ask the question 'What is going on here'? their involvement in the message is likely to be very high. See Exhibit 14.3 for an excellent example of a print advertisement for Gieves and Hawkes that deliberately seeks to stimulate the reader to ask the questions 'What is this?'. Benetton consistently raises questions through its advertising. By presenting a series of messages that are socially disorientating, and for many disconcerting, Benetton continually presents a challenge that moves away from involving individuals into an approach where salience and 'standing out' predominates. This high-risk strategy, with a risk of rejection, has prevailed for a number of years.

The surrealist approach does not provide or allow for closure. The conformist approach, by contrast, does require closure in order to avoid any possible counter-arguing and message rejection. Parker and Churchill argue that by leaving questions unanswered, receivers can become involved in both the product and the execution of the advertisement. Indeed, most advertisements contain a measure of rational and emotional elements. A blend of the two elements is necessary and the right mixture is dependent upon the perceived risk and motivation that the target audience has at any one particular moment.

The message appeal should be a balance of the informative and emotional dimensions. Furthermore, message quality is of paramount importance. Buzzell (1964) reported that 'Advertising message quality is more important than the level of advertising expenditure'. Adams and Henderson Blair (1992) confirm that the weight of advertising is relatively unimportant, and that the quality of the appeal is the dominant factor. However, the correct blend of informative and emotional elements in any appeal is paramount for persuasive effectiveness.

Advertising tactics

The main creative elements of a message need to be brought together in order for an advertising plan to have substance. The processes used to develop message appeals need to be open but systematic.

The level of involvement and combination of the think/emotional dimensions that receivers bring to their decision-making processes are the core concepts to be considered when creating an advertising message. Rossiter and Percy (1997) have devised a deductive framework which involves the disaggregation of the emotional (feel) dimension to a greater degree than that proposed by Vaughn (1980) (see Chapter 25 for details). They claim that there are two broad types of motive that drive attitudes towards purchase behaviour. These are informational and transformational motives and these will now be considered in turn.

Informational motives

Individuals have a need for information to counter negative concerns about a purchase decision. These informational motives are said to be negatively charged feelings. They can become positively charged, or the level of concern can be reduced considerably, by the acquisition of relevant information.

Motive	Possible emotional state
Problem removal	Anger — relief
Problem avoidance	Fear — relaxation
Incomplete satisfaction	Disappointment — optimism
Mixed approach–avoidance	Guilt — peace of mind
Normal depletion	Mild annoyance — convenience

Transformational motives

Promises to enhance or to improve the user of a brand are referred to as transformational motives. These are related to the user's feelings and are capable of transforming a user's emotional state; hence they are positively charged. Three main transformational motives have been distinguished by Rossiter *et al.* (1991):

Motive	Possible emotional state
Sensory gratification	Dull — elated
Intellectual stimulation	Bored — excited
Social approval	Apprehensive — flattered

Various emotional states can be associated with each of these motives, and they should be used to portray an emotion that is appropriate to the needs of the target audience.

One of the key promotion objectives, identified earlier, is the need to create or improve levels of awareness regarding the product or organisation. This is achieved by determining whether awareness is required at the point of purchase or prior to purchase. Brand recognition (at the point of purchase) requires an emphasis upon visual stimuli, the package and the brand name, whereas brand recall (prior to purchase) requires an emphasis on a limited number of peripheral cues. These may be particular copy lines, the use of music or colours for continuity and attention-

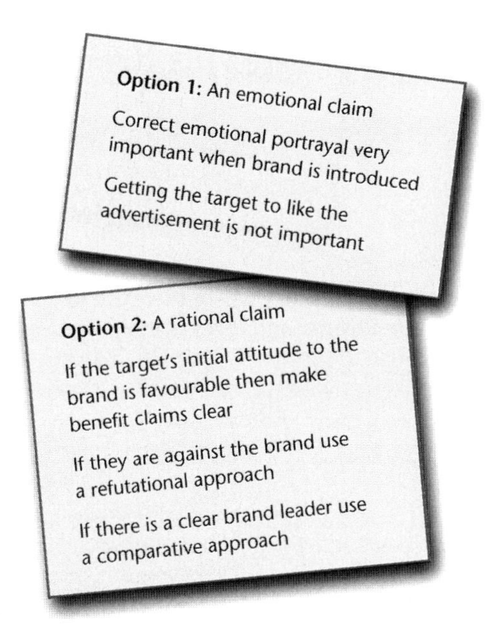

Figure 14.2 Message tactics where there are high involvement and informational motives (based on Rossiter and Percy (1997); used with kind permission).

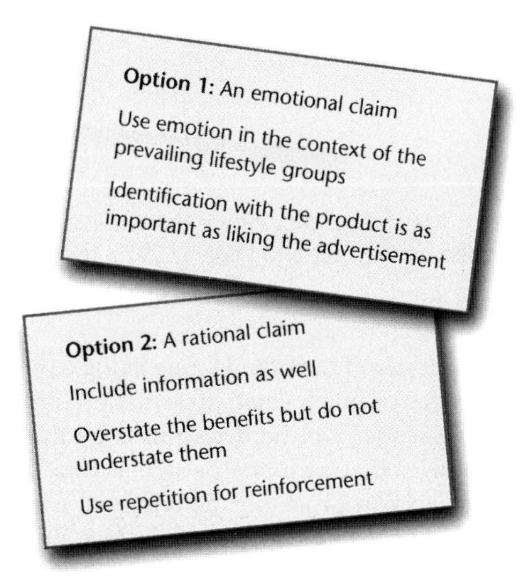

Figure 14.3 Message tactics where there are high involvement and transformational motives (based on Rossiter and Percy (1997); used with kind permission).

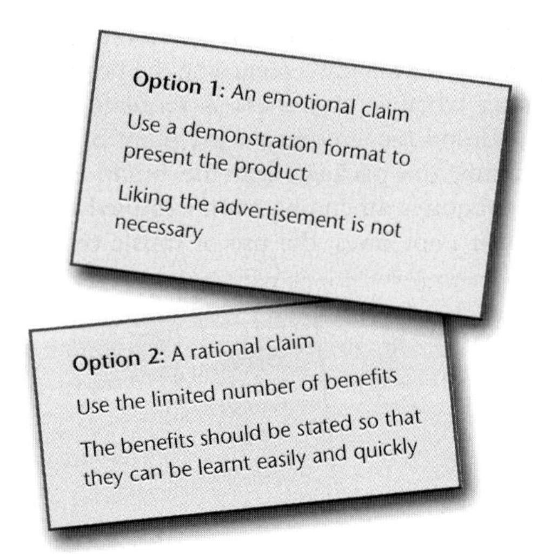

Figure 14.4 Message tactics where there are low involvement and informational motives (based on Rossiter and Percy (1997); used with kind permission).

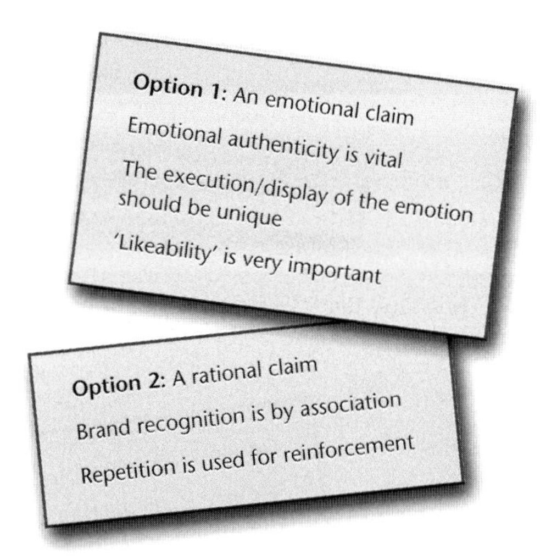

Figure 14.5 Message tactics where there are low involvement and informational motives (based on Rossiter and Percy (1997); used with kind permission).

getting frequent use of the brand name in the context of the category need, or perhaps the use of strange or unexpected presentation formats.

Advertising tactics can be determined by the particular combination of involvement and motives that exist at a particular time within the target audience. If a high-involvement decision process is determined, with people using a central processing route, then the types of tactics shown in Figures 14.2 and 14.3 are recommended by Rossiter and Percy (1997). If a low-involvement decision process is determined, with the target audience using a peripheral processing route, then the types of tactics shown in Figures 14.4 and 14.5 are recommended.

The Rossiter–Percy approach provides for a range of advertising tactics that are orientated to the conditions that are determined by the interplay of the level of involvement and the type of dominant motivation. These conditions may only exist within a member of the target audience for a certain time. Consequently, they may change and the advertising tactics may also have to change to meet the new conditions. There are two main points that emerge from the work of Rossiter and Percy. The first is that all messages should be designed to carry both rational, logical information and emotional stimuli, but in varying degrees and forms. Second, low-involvement conditions require the use of just one or two benefits in a message, whereas high-involvement conditions can sustain a number of different benefit claims. This is because persuasion through the central processing route is characterised by an evaluation of the alternatives within any one product category.

Summary

Advertising has an important role to play in most promotional plans. It is used primarily to build awareness and to usher in the other tools of the mix. The tasks that advertising is expected to achieve will have been set out in the promotional objectives and they will require communication with target consumers and organisational buyers.

Advertising is normally regarded as a tool that can persuade and change the behaviour of individuals, but there are a growing number of researchers who believe that its prime use is to defend loyal customers from the attacks of competitor products, by reinforcing attitudes.

The design and assembly of advertising messages is crucially important. Through establishment of a good realm of understanding, messages can be created in such a way that they stand a far greater opportunity of building a dialogue between members of the target audience and the brand. By appreciating the underlying emotions of the target buyer and the motivations which drive attitudes and purchase intentions, the balance and the pattern they assume can be shaped in such a way that they lead to effective advertising.

Review questions

1. Describe each of the four elements needed to create promotional messages.
2. Discuss what is meant by the term 'balance' when applied to an advertising message.
3. How might an understanding of conclusion-drawing assist the development of an advertising message?
4. What is 'likeability' when applied to advertising?
5. Select five print advertisements and comment on the nature and extent to which the order of presentation features in each of them.
6. Why do advertisers use spokespersons in their advertising?
7. Find examples of each type of spokesperson.
8. What are the main types of appeal that are used by advertisers?
9. Find examples of advertising messages for each of the main appeals identified.
10. Explain the difference between informational and transformational motivations.

References

Adams, A.J. and Henderson Blair, M. (1992) Persuasive advertising and sales accountability. *Journal of Advertising Research* (March/April), 20–5.

Archer, B. (1994) Does humour cross borders? *Campaign*, 17 June, pp. 32–3.

Arora, R. (1985) Consumer involvement: what it offers to advertising strategy. *International Journal of Advertising*, **4**, 119–30.

Batra, R. and Stayman, D.M. (1990) The role of mood in advertising effectiveness. *Journal of Consumer Research*, **17** (September), 203–14.

Biel, A. (1990) Love the ad. Buy the product? *Admap* (September), 35–40.

BMW (1994) *The BMW Break Through: 15 Years of BMW Advertising*. BMW publicity material.

Braithwaite, A. and Ware, R. (1997) The role of music in advertising. *Admap* (July/August), 44–7.

Broadbent, T. (1994) *How 15 years of consistent advertising helped BMW treble sale without losing prestige*. IPA Advertising Effectiveness Awards. London: WCRS.

Buzzel, R. (1964) Predicting short-term changes in market share as a function of advertising strategy. *Journal of Marketing Research*, **1**(3), 27–31.

Campbell, L. (1997) Is Hector's house in order? *Marketing*, 9 October, p. 20.

Faison, E.W. (1961) Effectiveness of one-sided and two-sided mass communications in advertising. *Public Opinion Quarterly*, **25** (Fall), 468–9.

Foxall, G.R. and Goldsmith, R.E. (1994) *Consumer Psychology for Marketing*. London: Routledge.

Garrett, A. (1993) The ploy of sex. *Marketing Week*, 23 April, pp. 28–31.

Haley, R.I. (1990) *Final Report of the Copy Research Validity Project*. Advertising Research Foundation Copy Research Workshop, July.

Hannah, D.B. and Sternthal, B. (1984) Detecting and explaining the sleeper effect. *Journal of Consumer Research*, 11 September, pp. 632–42.

Haas, O. (1997) Humour in advertising. *Admap* (July/August), 14–5.

Hovland, C.I. and Mandell, W. (1952) An experimental comparison of conclusion drawing by the communicator and by the audience. *Journal of Abnormal and Social Psychology*, **47** (July), 581–8.

Hovland, C.I., Lumsdaine, A. and Sheffield, F.D. (1949) *Experiments on Mass Communication*. New York: Wiley.

Joyce, T. (1991) Models of the advertising process. *Marketing and Research Today* (November), 205–12.

Kardes, F.R. (1988) Spontaneous inference processes in advertising: the effects of conclusion omission and involvement on persuasion. *Journal of Consumer Research*, **15** (September), 225–33.

Lannon, J. (1992) Asking the right questions – what do people do with advertising? *Admap* (March), 11–16.

Parker, R. and Churchill, L. (1986) Positioning by opening the consumer's mind. *International Journal of Advertising*, **5**, 1–13.

Ray, M.L. and Wilkie, W.L. (1970) Fear: The potential of an appeal neglected by marketing. *Journal of Marketing*, **34** (January), 54–62.

Rossiter, J.R. and Percy, L. (1997) *Advertising and Promotion Management*, 2nd edn. New York: McGraw-Hill.

Rossiter, J.R., Percy, L. and Donovan, R.J. (1991) A better advertising planning grid. *Journal of Advertising Research* (October/November), 11–21.

Schiffman, L.G. and Kanuk, L. (1991) *Consumer Behaviour*, 4th edn. Englewood Cliffs NJ: Prentice Hall.

Stapel, J. (1991) Like the ad.... but does it interest me? *Admap* (April), 30–1.

Summers, D. (1993) Dangerous liaisons. *Financial Times*, 18 November, p. 12.

Trickett, E. (1997) BA rethinks corporate image with M&C Saatchi campaign. *Campaign*, 13 June, p. 8.

Vaughn, R. (1980) How advertising works: a planning model. *Journal of Advertising Research*, **20**(5), 27–33.

chapter 15

The media

In order that clients can deliver their messages to specified audiences they need to utilise (and pay for) the services of particular media. There is a growing array of media to choose from, all of which have strengths and weaknesses which impact on the quality, effectiveness and meaning attributed to the message by the audience.

AIMS AND OBJECTIVES

The aim of this chapter is to establish the principal characteristics of each type of medium. This will assist understanding of the management processes by which media are selected and scheduled to deliver advertiser's messages. These planning and scheduling processes will be the subject of the next chapter.

The objectives of this chapter are:

1. To determine the variety and types of media available to advertisers.
2. To establish the primary characteristics of each type of medium.
3. To examine the strengths and weaknesses of each type of medium.
4. To provide a brief summary of the main trends in advertising expenditure on each type of medium in the United Kingdom over the 1980s and 1990s.
5. To compare the media used by direct marketeers with those of general marketeers.

Introduction

Organisations use the services of a variety of media in order that they can deliver their planned messages to target audiences. Of the many available media, six main classes can be identified. These are broadcast, print, outdoor, new, in-store and other media classes. Within each of these classes there are particular media types. For example,

Table 15.1 Summary chart of the main forms of media

Class	Type	Vehicles
Broadcast	Television	*Coronation Street, Friends*
	Radio	Virgin 1215, Classic FM
Print	Newspapers	*Sunday Times*, The *Mirror, The Daily Telegraph*
	Magazines: Consumer	*Cosmopolitan, FHM, Woman*
	Business	*The Grocer, Plumbing News*
Outdoor	Billboards	96 and 48 sheet
	Street furniture	Adshel
	Transit	London Underground, taxis, hot-air balloons
New media	Internet	Web sites, email, intranet
	Digital television	ONdigital
	Teletext	SkyText, Ceefax
	CD-ROM	Various: music, educational, entertainment
In-store	Point-of-purchase	Bins, signs and displays
	Packaging	The Coca Cola contour bottle
Other	Cinema	Pearl and Dean
	Exhibitions	Ideal Home, The Motor Show
	Product placement	Ericsson in the James Bond film *Tomorrow Never Dies*
	Ambient	Litter bins, golf tees, petrol pumps
	Guerrilla	Flyposting

within the broadcast class there are television and radio, and within the print class there are newspapers and magazines.

Within each type of medium there are a huge number of different media vehicles which can be selected to carry an advertiser's message. For example, within UK television there are the terrestrial networks (Independent Television Network, Channel 4 and Channel 5) and the satellite (BSkyB) and cable networks. In print, there are consumer and business-orientated magazines and the number of specialist magazines is expanding rapidly. These specialist magazines are targeted at particular activity and interest groups, such as *Amateur Photographer*, *Golf World* and the infamous *Sponge Divers Gazette*! This provides opportunities for advertisers to send messages to well-defined homogeneous groups which improves effectiveness and reduces wastage in communication spend. There are, therefore, three forms of media: classes, types and vehicles (Table 15.1).

One of the key tasks of the marketing communications manager is to decide which combination of vehicles should be selected to carry the message to the target audience. The means by which this decision is reached will be the subject of the following chapter. First, however, it is necessary to consider briefly the main characteristics of each media type in order that media planning decisions can be based upon some logic and rationale. The fundamental characteristics concern the costs, delivery and audience profile associated with a communication.

Costs

One of the important characteristics that need to be considered is the costs that are incurred using each type of medium. There are two types of cost: absolute and relative. Absolute costs are the costs of the time or space bought in a particular media vehicle. These costs have to be paid for and directly impact upon an organisation's cash flow. Relative costs are the costs of contacting each member of the target audience. Television, as will be seen later, has a high absolute cost, but, because messages are delivered to a mass audience, when the absolute cost is divided by the total number of people receiving the message, the relative cost is very low.

Ability to communicate a message

The way in which an advertiser's message is conveyed to the target audience varies across media types. Certain media, such as television, are able to use many communication dimensions, and through the use of sight, sound and movement can generate great impact with a message. Other types of media have only one dimension, such as the audio capacity of radio. The number of communication dimensions that a media type has will influence the choice of media mix. This is because certain products, at particular points in their development, require the use of different media in order that the right message be conveyed and understood. A new product, for example, may require demonstration in order that the audience understands the product concept. The use of television may be a good way of achieving this. Once understood, the audience does not need to be educated in this way again and future messages need to convey different types of information which may not require demonstration, so radio or magazine advertising may suffice.

Audience profile

The profile of the target audience (male, female, young or old) and the number of people within each audience that a media type can reach are also significant factors in media decisions. For example, 30% of adults in the socio-economic grade A read the *Sunday Times*. Only 4% of the C2 group also read this paper. Messages appropriate to the A group would be best placed in the *Sunday Times* and those for the C2 group transmitted through the *News of the World*, which 34% of the C2 group read. It is important that advertisers use media vehicles that convey their messages to their target markets with as little waste as possible.

The size of the industry should not be underestimated as UK advertising expenditure reached £11.99 billion in 1996. See Table 15.2 for details.

Table 15.2 UK advertising media expenditure

	1996 (£m)	1995 (£m)	1994 (£m)
Print	6,400	5,900	5,500
Television	3,300	3,100	2,900
Direct mail	1,400	1,100	1,000
Outdoor and transport	426	378	350
Radio	344	296	243
Cinema	73	69	53
Total	11,994	10,981	10,136

Source: Advertising Association (1997).

Print media

Characteristics

Of the total amount spent on advertising, across all media, most is spent on the printed word. Newspapers and magazines are the two main types of media in this class. They attract advertisers for a variety of reasons, but the most important reason is that print media are very effective at delivering a message to the target audience.

Most people have access to either a newspaper or a magazine. They read in order to keep up to date with news and events or to provide themselves with a source of entertainment. People tend to have consistent reading habits and buy or borrow the same media vehicles regularly. For example, most people read the same type of newspaper(s) each day and their regular choice of magazine reflects either their business or leisure interests, which are normally quite stable. This means that advertisers, through marketing research, are able to build a database of the main characteristics of their readers. This in turn allows advertisers to buy space in those media vehicles that will be read by the sort of people they think will benefit from their product or service.

The printed word provides advertisers with the opportunity to explain their message in a way that most other media cannot. Such explanations can be in the form of either a picture or a photograph, perhaps demonstrating how a product is to be used. Alternatively, the written word can be used to argue why a product should be used and detail the advantages and benefits that consumption will provide the user. In reality, advertisers use a combination of these two forms of communication.

The print media are most suitable for messages designed when high involvement is present in the target market. These readers not only control the pace at which they read a magazine or newspaper but also expend effort to read advertisements because they care about particular issues. Where elaboration is high and the central processing route is preferred, messages that provide a large amount of information are best presented in the printed form.

Magazines are able to reach quite specialized audiences and tend to be selective in terms of the messages they carry. In contrast, newspapers reach a high percentage of the population and can be referred to as a mass medium. The messages that newspapers carry are usually for products and services that have a general appeal.

Newspapers

Expenditure on newspaper advertising increased steadily in the 1980s, but fell back sharply with the recession in the early 1990s. Since 1986, newspaper readership has fallen, but the biggest shift has been away from the popular press with some movement towards the quality press. In 1996 expenditure on newspaper advertising reached £6.4 billion or 53.5% of the total UK advertising spend (Advertising Association, 1997).

- *Strengths*

  Newspaper advertisements are seen positively by readers because they are in control of the speed and depth of reading of the newspaper. This means that they choose which advertisements to read. This facilitates what is referred to as comparison shopping. Newspapers provide wide exposure for advertisements, and market coverage in local, regional or national papers can be extensive. These media vehicles are extremely flexible as they present opportunities for the use of colour and allow advertisements of variable sizes, insertions and coupons.

- *Weaknesses*

  The combination of a high number of advertisements and the small amount of reading time that readers give to newspapers means that most newspaper advertisements receive little exposure. Statistics show that newspaper circulation has fallen behind population growth; furthermore, teenagers and young adults generally do not read newspapers.

  Advertising costs have risen very quickly and the competition to provide news, not just from other newspapers but other sources such as cable, satellite and terrestrial television, means that newspapers are no longer one of the main providers of news. One of the consequences of this has been the development of price wars between many of the broadsheets, with *The Times* and *Sunday Times* leading the battle by discounting the Sunday and Monday papers at various times.

  Printing technologies have advanced considerably during the 1980s and 1990s, but the relatively poor quality of reproduction means that the impact of advertisements can often be lost.

Magazines

The number of consumer magazines has grown considerably in the late 1980s, and advertising revenue reached £1.6 billion (Advertising Association, 1997) in 1996, a growth of 10% on the previous year. Business magazines attract nearly twice as much advertising revenue as the consumer sector, despite being highly fragmented and complex. The fastest growing part of the consumer magazine market has been the men's lifestyle sector, where titles such as *Loaded*, *FHM* and *Men's Health* have established themselves quickly.

- *Strengths*

  The visual quality of magazines is normally very high, a result of using top-class materials and technologies. This provides advertisers with greater flexibility in the way in which the visual dimension is used to present their messages, which can be used to create impact and demand the attention of the reader.

  The large number and wide range of specialised titles means that narrow, specific target audiences can be reached much more successfully than with other media vehicles. For example, messages concerning ski equipment, clothing and resorts will be best presented in specialist ski magazines on the basis that they will be read by those who have an interest in skiing, and not knitting, snooker or fishing. Magazines can provide a prestigious and high-quality environment, with the editorial providing authority, reassurance and credibility to the advertising that they contain.

  Magazines are often passed along to others to read once the original user has finished reading it. This longevity issue highlights the difference between circulation (the number of people who buy or subscribe to a magazine) and readership (the number of people who actually read the vehicle, perhaps as a friend or partner at home, in a doctor's waiting room or at the instigation of a department head or workplace superior).

- *Weaknesses*
  Magazine audience growth rates have fallen behind the growth in advertising rates. Therefore the value of advertising in magazines has declined relative to some other types of media. The long period of time necessary to book space in advance of publication dates and to provide suitable artwork means that management has little flexibility once it has agreed to use magazines as part of the media schedule.

  Apart from specialist magazines, a single magazine rarely reaches the majority of a market segment. Several magazines must be used to reach potential users. Having reached the target, impact often builds slowly, as some readers do not read their magazine until some days after they have received it.

  The absolute and relative costs associated with magazines are fairly high, particulary costs for general interest magazines (GIMs). For special interest magazines (SIMs), however, they allow advertisers to reach their target audiences with little waste and hence high levels of efficiency.

One final form of print media yet to be discussed concerns directories. Advertising expenditure on directories has continued to increase through the 1990s. The two largest consumer directories are *Thomsons* and *Yellow Pages*.

Broadcast media

Characteristics

Broadcast media are quite young in comparison with the printed word. Fundamentally, there are two main forms of broadcast: television and radio, to which attention will be given here. Advertisers use these classes of media because they can reach mass audiences with their messages at a relatively low cost per target reached.

Approximately 98% of the population in the United Kingdom has access to a television set and a similar number have a radio. The majority of viewers use television passively, as a form of entertainment; however, new technological applications, such as digitalisation, indicate that television will be used proactively for a range of services, such as banking and shopping. Radio demands active participation, but can reach people who are out of the home environment.

Broadcast media allow advertisers to add visual and/or sound dimensions to their messages. The opportunity to demonstrate or to show the benefits or results that a particular product can bring gives life and energy to an advertiser's message. Television uses sight, sound and movement, whereas radio can only use its audio capacity to convey meaning. Both media have the potential to tell stories and to appeal to people's emotions when transmitting a message. These are dimensions that the printed media find difficulty in achieving effectively within the time allocations that advertisers can afford.

Advertising messages transmitted through the broadcast media use a small period of time, normally sixty, thirty or twenty seconds, that the owners of the media are prepared to sell. The cost of the different time slots varies throughout a single transmission day and with the popularity of individual programmes. The more listeners or viewers that a programme attracts, the greater the price charged for a slice of time to transmit an advertising message. This impacts upon the costs associated with such advertising. The time-based costs for television can be extremely large. For example, the rate card cost of a forty second spot on London Weekend Television was £66,665 (as at 1 January 1998). However, this large cost needs to be put in perspective. The actual cost of reaching individual members of the target audience is quite low, simply because all of the costs associated with the production of the message and the purchase of time to transmit the message can be spread across a mass of individuals, as discussed earlier.

The costs associated with radio transmissions are relatively low when compared with television. This reflects the lack of prestige that radio has and the pervasiveness of television.

People are normally unable, and usually unwilling, to become actively involved with broadcast advertising messages. They cannot control the pace at which they consume such advertising and as time is expensive and short, so advertisers do not have the opportunity to present detailed information. The result is that this medium is most suitable for low-involvement messages. Where the need for elaboration is low and the peripheral processing route is preferred, messages transmitted through electronic media should seek to draw attention, create awareness and improve levels of interest.

As the television and radio industries become increasingly fragmented, so the ability to reach particular market segments improves. This means that the potential effectiveness of advertising through these media increases. These media are used a great deal by consumer markets, mainly because of their ability to reach mass audiences. Messages targeted at other organisations need to be delivered by other media which are more selective and controlled more effectively.

Television

The growth in advertising expenditure on terrestrial television stopped in the early 1990s, but since 1992 it has recovered its upward trend. In 1996 television advertising was worth £3.3 billion in the UK and maintained the steady 28% of total UK advertising spend that it has attracted over the mid-1990s (Advertising Association, 1997). Food accounts for the largest single advertiser category, with nearly 20%, cosmetics and toiletries account for 7.5%, drink 8.0% and household stores 10.1% (AC Nielsen-MEAL).

The number of households connected to cable networks represented 6.5% of all homes by December 1996. More importantly, the percentage of homes connected as a percentage of the number of homes who could be connected has risen from 18.3% in 1988 to over 21% in 1996. This slow but increasing acceptance of cable television should encourage advertisers, who will be able to target their audiences much more easily and communicate with them with less wastage.

- *Strengths*

  From a creative point of view, this medium is very flexible and the impact generated by the combination of sight and sound should not be underestimated. Consumer involvement and likeability of an advertisement is dependent upon the skill of the creative team. The prestige and status associated with television advertising is higher than that of other media: in some cases, the credibility and status of a product or organisation can be enhanced significantly just by being seen to be advertising on television.

  The costs of reaching members of large target segments are relatively low, so the medium is capable of a high level of cost efficiency.

- *Weaknesses*

  Because the length of any single exposure is short, messages have to be repeated on television in order to enhance learning and memory. This increases the absolute costs of producing and transmitting television commercials, which can be large, making this medium the most expensive form of advertising.

Television audiences are increasingly fragmented as the number of entertainment and leisure opportunities expands. For example, terrestrial television networks are suffering from the competition from cable and satellite broadcasters plus video recorders and other sources of entertainment. This proliferation of suppliers has led to television clutter. In order to keep viewers, programmes are now promoted vigorously by television companies and a variety of techniques are being used to prevent viewers from channel grazing (switching).

The trend towards shorter messages has led to increased clutter. Management flexibility over the message is frustrated, as last minute changes to schedules are expensive and difficult to implement. The only choices open to decision makers are either to proceed with an advertisement or to 'pull' it, should circumstances change in such a way that it would be inappropriate to proceed.

Radio

There has been a rapid increase in the number of commercial radio services offered in the United Kingdom since 1973. Advertising expenditure on radio has recovered from a dip in the mid-1980s and in real terms levelled out in 1992. In the four years to 1996 radio advertising revenue doubled to reach £344 million, reflecting increased interest and enthusiasm for what is often regarded as an underestimeted yet versatile medium.

- *Strengths*
  Radio permits specialised programming, which in turn attracts selective audiences. Radio is a mobile medium (that is, one that can travel with audiences), so that messages can be relayed to them, for example, even when shoppers are parking their cars near to a shopping precinct. The production costs are low and radio has great flexibility, which management can use to meet changing environmental and customer needs. If it is raining in the morning, an advertiser can implement a promotional campaign for umbrellas in the afternoon.

  From a creative point of view the medium needs the active imagination of the listener. Radio has a high level of passive acceptance and the messages that are received are more likely to be retained than if they were delivered via a different medium. This combination of features makes radio an excellent support medium.
- *Weaknesses*
  Because there is an absence of visual stimuli, the medium lacks impact and the ability to hold and enthuse an audience. Levels of inattentiveness can be high, which means that a high number of messages are invariably ignored or missed. When this is combined with low average audiences, high levels of frequency are required to achieve acceptable levels of reach.

Outdoor media

Characteristics

The range of outdoor media encompasses a large number of different media, each characterised by two elements. First, they are observed by their target audiences at locations away from home. Second, they are normally used to support messages that are transmitted through the primary media: broadcast and print. Outdoor media can, therefore, be seen to be a secondary, but important support media for a complementary and effective communications mix.

Media spend on outdoor advertising declined in the earlier 1990s after steady growth in the 1980s. Growth returned to the sector as the UK economy moved out of recession and in 1996 was worth £426 million (Advertising Association, 1997).

Outdoor media consist of three main formats: street furniture, such as bus shelters; billboards, which consist primarily of 96 and 48 sheet poster sites; and Transit, which covers the Underground, buses, taxis and aerial signs (hot-air balloons).

Outdoor media accounted for approximately 3.6% of total advertising expenditure in 1996, but have been taking an increasing percentage of organisations' media spend. This is because the potential for outdoor to reinforce messages transmitted through primary media is being recognised by more and more organisations. One of the reasons for this increase is the attempt by tobacco organisations to promote their products, since they have been deprived of access to primary media. A further reason has been the technological advances which now allow electronic, inflatable and three-dimensional billboards to promote a variety of products and services. A third reason is the novelty aspect they represent and an attempt to avoid the clutter caused by the volume of advertising activity.

Billboards and street furniture

These are static displays and, as with outdoor media generally, they are unable to convey a great deal of information in the short period of time available that people can attend to the messages. However, advances in technology permit precise targeting of poster campaigns on a national, regional or individual audience basis, or by their proximity to specific outlets, such as banks, CTNs (confectioner, tobacconist and newsagent) and off-licences. Evaluation through the POSTAR system allows for measurement of not only the size and type of audience but also the traffic flows, travel patterns and even how people read posters.

- *Strengths*

  One of the main advantages of this medium springs from its ability to reach a large audience. This means that most members of a target audience are likely to have an opportunity-to-see (OTS) the message, so the cost per contact is very low. It has become recognised that outdoor media can provide tremendous support to other tools in the media mix, particularly at product launch, as backup and when attempting to build brand name recognition (see Exhibit 15.1).

  The medium is characterised by its strong placement flexibility. Messages can be placed geographically, demographically or by activity, such as on the main routes to work or shopping (see Plate 15.1). The potential impact is high, as good sites can draw the eye and make an impression. Gross rating points (GRPs; see Chapter 16) can be developed quickly by reaching a large percentage of the target audience many times in a short period.

- *Weaknesses*

  Messages transmitted by this medium do not allow for the provision of detailed information. Posters are passed very quickly and the potential attention span is therefore brief. This means that the message must be short, have a high visual impact and be capable of selling an idea or concept very quickly.

Exhibit 15.1 High impact poster campaign for Playtex – Wonderbra. (Picture kindly supplied by TBWA Simmons-Palmer.)

Printing and production lead times are long; therefore while control over message content is high, the flexibility in delivery once showings are agreed can be a limiting factor. The final disadvantage of outdoor media to be discussed is that the effectiveness of message delivery is very difficult to measure, and in an age when accountability is becoming an increasingly important factor, this drawback does not help to promote the usage of this medium.

Transit

Transit or transport advertising is best represented by the names and signs that are painted on the sides of lorries. These moving posters, which travel around the population, serve to communicate names of organisations and products to all those who are in the vicinity of the vehicle. Indeed, transport advertising includes all those vehicles that are used for commercial purposes. In addition to lorries, transport media include buses, the Underground (trains, escalators and walkways), taxis, airplanes, blimps and balloons, ferries and trains, plus the terminals and buildings associated with the means of transport, such as airports and railway stations (see Plate 15.2). The difference between outdoor and transport media is arbitrary, although the former are media static and the latter are media mobile.

Messages can be presented as inside cards, where the messages are exposed to those using the vehicle. An example of this would be the small advertising messages displayed on the curvature of the roof of London Underground trains. Outside cards are those that are displayed on the exterior of taxis, buses and other commercial vehicles (see Plate 15.3).

- *Strengths*

  The exposure time given to messages delivered via transport media can be high, but is dependent upon the journey time of the reader. The high readership scores that are recorded are due, possibly, to the boredom levels of travellers. The cost is relatively low, mainly because no extra equipment is necessary to transmit the message. Local advertisers tend to benefit most from transport advertising, as it can remind buyers of particular restaurants, theatres and shops.

- *Weaknesses*
  The medium fails to cover all market segments, as only particular groups use transportation systems. In comparison with other media it lacks status, is difficult to read (particularly in the rush hour) and suffers from the high level of clutter associated with inside cards.

New media

Recent technological advances have increased the range of new media available to advertisers to communicate with their prospects and customers. New media allow for far greater levels of interaction between the advertiser and the receiver, such that an immediate response is now possible. CD-ROM, Internet (see Chapter 23), kiosks and interactive television (below) are the leading new media opportunities. New media and interactive marketing communications (Chapter 23) complement each other.

New media are different from traditional media on a number of grounds but the most important difference is the time that elapses between message receipt and response. With new media the time is very short; response might be virtually instantaneous, and in other cases the audience may be the proactive source of the dialogue. This is unlike traditional media, where a response may be delayed for long periods: minutes, hours, days or even months.

Advertisers can target tightly clustered audiences with well-defined messages. Soon advertisers will be able to refine messages so that personal messages can be presented to individual members. This will extend any dialogue on the basis that the audience is active, interested and involved. The Goldfish Guides are one of the first examples of this new era of communication. Customers can request information about a range of products (often diverse) and within 48 hours will receive a colour brochure designed and printed to each individual's particular requirements (Dickenson, 1998). One of the major benefits of this system is that customers will receive information when they want to make purchase decisions and advertisers can now get their products in front of prospects at the right time without having to rely on distributors and dealers, whose concern is make a sale rather than push a particular manufacturer.

There are two types of new media: off-line and on-line. Off-line media are self-contained units of information (e.g. a CD-ROM) and usually have a physical presence and are hence more consumer friendly. On-line media are dynamic information communication links which are capable of providing refreshed and updated information (e.g. the Internet).

The development of credit card technology and telecommunications has enabled the development of home-based shopping via the television. Banks and financial institutions have led the way and, while there is evidence to suggest that people in the UK enjoy the traditional shopping experience and have been reluctant to adopt this approach, people in the USA actively use the medium to buy insurance, homeware and personal products. The launch of digital television in the UK in 1998 signals a change in the viewer/provider relationship. No longer will viewers have to schedule their personal timetables to coincide with the broadcast of their preferred television programmes. Digital television will allow for the personal selection of programmes at times convenient to the viewer.

Teletext facilities have expanded as the number of homes able to receive the service increases. 17 million viewers access teletext each week in the UK and over 14 million requests for information are generated through this facility each week (van Oosterom, 1996). Videotext techniques are being developed which allow users to access an electronic shopping catalogue. Viewers can leaf through pages of text via their television and telephone, select products and services and purchase them for delivery to their home.

The facsimile machine is being used increasingly in the business-to-business sector. Its ability to send personalised messages and for receivers to respond and make enquiries or raise objections has been recognised, particularly by those organisations who are adopting direct marketing approaches into their strategy. Added advantages of this new media are its speed of transmission, low absolute costs and the ability to present visual stimuli.

- *Strengths*
  The major strength of the medium rests with its ability to induce an immediate dialogue and to engage individuals with highly reduced levels of communication noise. Participants choose to use the medium, and as such are actively rather than passively involved. Interactive media allow for high levels of personalised or tailored message content.
- *Weaknesses*
  With just one in ten PCs having a modem, digital television just embarking on its commercial future and barely 40% of homes passed by cable technology, the reach of interactive media is at present limited. However, this will change quickly over the next five years as both advertisers and consumers become familiar with the benefits and costs fall further.

In-store media

Characteristics

As an increasing number of brand choice decisions are made during the shopping experience, advertisers have become aware of the need to provide suitable in-store communications. The primary objective of using in-store media is to direct the attention of shoppers and to stimulate them to make purchases. The content of messages can be easily controlled by either the retailer or the manufacturer. In addition, the timing and the exact placement of in-store messages can be equally well controlled.

As mentioned previously, both retailers and manufacturers make use of in-store media, although, of the two main forms (point-of-purchase displays and packaging), retailers control the point-of-purchase displays and manufacturers the packaging.

In-store: point-of-purchase (POP)

There are a number of POP techniques, but the most used ones are window displays, floor and wall racks to display merchandise, posters and information cards, plus counter and check-out displays. The most obvious display a manufacturer has at the point of purchase is the packaging used to wrap and protect the product until it is ready for consumption. This particular element is discussed in detail later.

Supermarket trollies with a video screen attached to them have been trialled by a number of stores. As soon as the trolley passes a particular infrared beam a short video is activated, promoting brands available in the immediate vicinity of the shopper. Other advances include electronic overhead signs, in-store videos at selected sites around the store and coupons for certain competitive products dispensed at the check-out once the purchased items have been scanned. Indirect messages can also play a role in in-store communications: for example, fresh bread smells can be circulated from the supermarket bakery at the furthest side of the store to the entrance area, enticing customers further into the supermarket. Some aroma systems allow for the smell to be restricted to just 18 inches of the display.

End-of-row bins and cards displaying special offers are POP media that aim to stimulate impulse buying. With over 75% of supermarket buying decisions made in-store, a greater percentage of communication budgets will be allocated to POP items.

- *Strengths*

  Point-of-purchase media are good at attracting attention and providing information. Their ability to persuade is potentially strong, as these displays can highlight particular product attributes at a time when shoppers have devoted their attention to the purchase decision process. Any prior awareness a shopper might have can be reinforced.

  From management's point of view the absolute and relative costs of POP advertisements are low. Furthermore, management can easily fine tune a POP advertisement to reflect changing conditions. For example, should stock levels be high and a promotion necessary to move stock out, POP displays can be introduced quickly.

- *Weaknesses*

  These messages are usually directed at customers who are already committed, at least partly, to purchasing the product or one from their evoked set. POP messages certainly fail to reach those not actively engaged in the shopping activity.

  There can be difficulties maintaining message continuity across a large number of outlets. Signs and displays can also be damaged by customers, which can impact upon the status of a product. Shoppers can therefore be negatively influenced by the temporary inconvenience of damaged and confusing displays.

  Unless rigorously controlled by store management, the large amount of POP materials can lead to clutter and a deterioration in the perception shoppers have of a retail outlet.

In-store: packaging

Characteristics

For a long time packaging has been considered a means of protecting and preserving products during transit and while they remain in store or on the shelf prior to purchase and consumption. In this sense, packaging can be regarded as an element of product strategy. To a certain extent this is still true; however, technology has progressed considerably and with consumer choice continually widening, packaging has become a means by which buyers, particularly in consumer markets, can make significant brand choice decisions. To that extent, because packaging can be used to convey persuasive information and be part of the decision-making process, yet still protect the contents, it will for the purposes of this text be considered a type of medium.

Low-involvement decision-making requires peripheral cues to stimulate buyers into action. It has already been noted that decisions made at the point of purchase,

CASE ILLUSTRATION

Unilever – Persil Power

In the mid-1990s Unilver launched a Persil brand extension called Persil Power (Omo and Skip in other European markets), which was to lead Unilever's challenge to Procter & Gamble and become market leader.

This product had an 'accelerator' which left some clothers faded and fabrics weakened under particular conditions. This defect received widespread publicity and Unilever was required to withdraw the brand.

The modern innovative design approach adopted for Persil Power was replaced by a five-year-old footballer on all Persil's detergent boxes in an attempt to replicate designs of nearly 30 years ago. Research suggested that the child is a symbol of trust and caring, an image which consumers want for reasons of familiarity and simplicity. Increasingly, consumers are ignoring new and innovative products and are reaching for boxes of the brands that are familiar – ones that they grew up with and have family-based associations.

The language used on the packaging also evolved from a 'macho language of power and acceleration' to one where 'Stain Release System', a balance of enzymes, bleaches and a polymer, was chosen to convey non-aggressive efficiency. Also introduced was a consumer advice telephone or care line. The purpose of the care line is essentially twofold: first, to provide customers with washing advice, and second to collect information and customer intelligence, such as their attitudes and in some cases comments to help rewrite instructions and evolve the new packaging.

Clothes washing habits vary widely across cultures, so Unilever was careful to allow each European market to develop its own marketing campaign. The Stain Release System is basically the same in all markets, but the timing and presentation were decided locally.

Adapted from Summers (1996)

especially those in the FMCG sector, often require buyers to build awareness through recognition. The design of packages and wrappers is important, as continuity of design in combination with the power to attract and hold the attention of prospective buyers is a vital part of point-of-purchase activity. The degree of importance that manufacturers place upon packaging and design was seen in 1994, when Sainsbury's introduced their own Cola. The reaction of the Coca-Cola company to the lookalike design of the own-label product is testimony to the value placed upon this aspect of brand personality.

There are a number of dimensions that can affect the power and utility of a package. Colour is influential, as the context of the product class can frame the purchase situation for a buyer. This means that colours should be appropriate to the product class, to the brand and to the prevailing culture if marketing overseas. For example, red is used to stimulate the appetite, white to symbolise purity and cleanliness, blue to signal freshness and green is increasingly being used to denote an environmental orientation and natural ingredients. From a cultural aspect, colours can be a problem. Buckley (1993) suggests that in Germany bright bold colours are regarded as appropriate for baby products, whereas in the United Kingdom pastel shades are more acceptable.

The shape of the package may reflect a physical attribute of the product itself. Various domestic lavatory cleaners have a twist in the neck, facilitating directable and

Exhibit 15.2 Domestos cleaning fluid – package with angled neck for easier application. Picture kindly supplied by Lever Brothers.

easier application. Research indicated that Lever Brothers should develop a product that was directable in order that it clean lavatories more effectively and economically. Domestos, a well-established brand was redesigned (Exhibit 15.2), together with the other Lever European bleach brands, in a successful attempt to harmonise packaging. The shape may also provide information about how to open and use the product, while some packages can be used after the product has been consumed for other purposes. For example, some jars can be reused as food containers, so providing a means of continual communication for the original brand in the home. Packaging can also be used as a means of brand identification, as a cue by which buyers recognise and differentiate a brand. The supreme example of this is the Coca-Cola contour bottle, with its unique shape and immediate power for brand recognition at the point of purchase (see Plate 15.4).

Package size is important, as different target markets may consume varying amounts of product. Toothpaste is available in large size family tubes and in smaller containers for those households who do not use so much.

Washing and dishwasher powder manufacturers now provide plastic refill packs which are designed to provoke brand loyalty. These packs are cheaper than the original pack, partly because some of the packaging expense has been reduced as the customer has been introduced to the product at an earlier time. Purchase of the refill pack is dependent upon product quality and customer satisfaction and, as long as the brand name is prominent for identification and reminder purposes, the decision to select the refill is quicker, as most of the risk (financial, physical and social) has been removed through previous satisfactory usage.

All packages have to carry information concerning the ingredients, nutritional values and safety requirements, including sell-by and use-by dates. Non-food packages must also attempt to be sales agents and provide all the information that a prospective buyer might need and at the same time provide conviction that this product is the correct one to purchase. Labelling of products offers opportunities to manufacturers to harmonise the in-store presentation of their products in such a way that buyers from different countries can still identify the brand and remain brand loyal. For example, Buckley suggests that Unilever decided not to change the different brands of washing powder in favour of a pan-European brand. They decided instead to retain the existing names (Omo, Skip, Via, Persil and All), and to package them in a similar way, using similar visual devices, typography and colours. This not only allows customers to remain loyal but also presents opportunities to save on advertising and design costs and gain access to satellite and other cross-border media.

Packages carry tangible and intangible messages. The psychological impact that packages can have should not be underestimated. They convey information about the product but they also say something about the quality of the product (Hall, 1991) and how it differs from competitive offerings. In some cases, where there is little to differentiate products, buyers may use the packaging on its own for decision-making purposes. Plate 15.5 indicates how packaging of the Cadbury's Milk Tray brand has evolved over the years, reflecting changing values, positioning and design preferences.

Cinema

Characteristics

There has been a revival in the level of expenditure on cinema advertising, reflecting the trends in audience sizes. In 1996 cinema advertising revenue was worth £73 million, or 0.6% of total advertising spend. With decreasing audiences until 1985, advertisers were reluctant to utilise this high-impact medium. However, since the boom years of the mid-1980s and the recessionary early 1990s, the number of people visiting cinemas in the United Kingdom has grown considerably, and attendances reached 123 million in 1996 (CAA/EDI). This growth is linked to the increase in multiplex cinemas (multiple screens at each site). With customer satisfaction levels improving, advertisers have consistently increased the adspend in this medium.

Advertising messages transmitted in a cinema have all the advantages of television-based messages. Audio and visual dimensions combine to provide high impact. However, the audience is more attentive because the main film has yet to be shown and there are fewer distractions or noise in the communication system. This means that cinema advertising has greater power than television advertisements. This power can be used to heighten levels of attention, and, as the screen images are larger than life and because they appear in a darkened room that is largely unfamiliar to the audience, the potential to communicate effectively with the target audience is strong.

- *Strengths*
  The mood of the audience is generally positive, particularly at the start of a show. This mood can be carried over into the commercials. Furthermore, the production quality of cinema messages is usually very high and transmission is often assisted by high-quality audio (digital surround sound systems) that is being installed in the new multiplex arenas.
  The production and transmission costs are quite low, which makes this an attractive media vehicle. The attention-getting ability and the power of this medium contribute to the high recall scores that this medium constantly records, often four times higher than the average recall scores for television commercials.
- *Weaknesses*
  The costs associated with reaching local audiences are low; however, if an advertiser wishes to reach a national audience, the costs can be much higher than those for television.
  The audience profile for UK cinema admissions indicates that approximately 80% of visitors are aged 15 to 34. With an increasing proportion of the population aged over 55 (the grey market), cinema advertising is limited by the audience profile and the type of products and services that can be realistically promoted.
  The third and final weakness is to some the most important. The irritation factor associated with viewing advertising messages when customers have paid to see a film has been found to be very high. Some respondents, to a number of studies, have expressed such an intensity of feelings that they actively considered boycotting the featured products. So despite the acclaim and positive reasons for using cinema advertising, advertisers are advised to be careful about the films they select to run their commercials against (audience profile will also be affected) and whether they should use this medium.

Product placement

Characteristics

One way of overcoming the irritation factor associated with advertisements screened in cinemas prior to a film showing is to incorporate the product in the film that is shown. This is referred to as product placement, which is the inclusion of products and services in films for deliberate promotional exposure, often, but not always, in return for an agreed financial sum. It is regarded by some as a form of sales promotion, but for the purposes of this text it is treated as an advertising medium because the 'advertiser' pays for the opportunity to present its product.

A wide variety of products can be placed in this way, including drinks (both soft and alcoholic), confectionery, newspapers, cars, airlines, perfume and even holiday destinations and sports equipment.

- *Strengths*
  By presenting the product as part of the film, not only is it possible to build awareness, but source credibility can be improved significantly and brand images reinforced. The audience are assisted to identify and associate themselves with the environment depicted in the film or with the celebrity who is using the product.
  Levels of impact can be very high, as cinema audiences are very attentive to large-screen presentations. Rates of exposure can be high, particularly now that cinema films are being released through video outlets and various new regional cable and satellite television organisations.
  Perhaps the major advantage is that the majority of audiences appear to approve of this form of marketing communications, if only because it is unobtrusive and integral to the film (Nebenzahl and Secunda, 1993).
- *Weaknesses*
  Having achieved a placement in a film there is still a risk that the product will run unnoticed, especially if the placements coincide with distracting or action-orientated parts of the film. Associated with this is the lack of control the advertiser has over when, where and how the product will be presented. If the product is noticed, a small minority of audiences claim that this form of communication is unethical; it is even suggested that it is subliminal advertising, which is, of course, illegal. The absolute costs of product placement in films can be extremely high, counteracting the low relative costs or cost per contact. The final major drawback concerning this form of medium concerns its inability to provide explanation, detail, or indeed any substantive information about the product. The product is seen in use and is hopefully associated with an event, person(s) or objects which provide a source of pleasure, inspiration or aspiration for the individual viewer.

Product placement is not confined to cinema films. Music videos and television films can also use this method to present advertisers' products.

Exhibitions

Characteristics

The use of exhibitions as a means of communicating with a variety of stakeholders has long been established. Organisations in both the consumer and the business-to-business markets use exhibitions as part of both pull and push strategies (Chapters 25 and 26).

There are many reasons for their use, but the primary reasons appear not to be 'to make sales' or 'because the competition is there' but because these events provide opportunities to meet potential and established customers and to create and sustain a series of relational exchanges. The main aim, therefore, is to develop long-term partnerships with customers, to build upon or develop the corporate identity and to gather up-to-date market intelligence (Shipley and Wong, 1993). This implies that exhibitions should not be used as isolated events, but that they should be integrated into a series of activities. These activities serve to develop and sustain buyer relationships.

After a tentative start to the 1990s the exhibition industry is now experiencing real growth. There were signs during and immediately after the recession that the increasing accountability of managers for their promotional budgets was being being reflected in the larger numbers of organisations who were booking late and in the reduced costs associated with stand construction and design (Wilmshurst, 1993). However, in 1996 over 10 million visitors attended 710 exhibitions (exhibition venues of over 2,000 sq ft) in the UK (Dignam, 1997).

Costs can be further reduced by using private exhibitions, where the increased flexibility allows organisations to produce mini or private exhibitions for their clients at local venues (e.g. hotels). This can mean lower costs for the exhibitor and reduced time away from their businesses for those attending. The communication 'noise' and distraction associated with the larger public events can also be avoided by these private showings.

- *Strengths*
  The costs associated with exhibitions, if controlled properly, can mean that this is an effective and efficient means of communicating with customers. The costs per enquiry need to be calculated, but care needs to be taken over who is classified as an enquirer, as the quality of the audience varies considerably. Costs per order taken are usually the prime means of evaluating the success of an exhibition. This can paint a false picture, as the true success can never really be determined in terms of orders because of the variety of other factors that impinge upon the placement and timing of orders.

  Products can be launched at exhibitions, and when integrated with a good PR campaign a powerful impact can be made. This can also be used to reinforce corporate identity.

  Exhibitions are an important means of gaining information about competitors, buyers and technical and political developments in the market, and they often serve to facilitate the recruitment process. Above all else, exhibitions provide an opportunity to meet customers on relatively neutral ground and, through personal interaction, develop relationships. Products can be demonstrated, prices agreed, technical problems discussed and trust and credibility enhanced.
- *Weaknesses*
  One of the main drawbacks associated with exhibition work is the vast and disproportionate amount of management time that can be tied up with the planning and implementation of exhibitions. However, good planning is essential if the full potential benefits of exhibition work are to be realised.

  Taking members of the sales force 'off the road' can also incur large costs. Depending upon the nature of the business these opportunity costs can soar. Some pharmaceutical organisations estimate that it can cost approximately £5,000 per person per week to divert salespeople in this way.

  The anticipated visitor profile must be analysed in order that the number of quality buyers visiting an exhibition can be determined. The variety of visitors attending an exhibition can be misleading, as the vast majority may not be serious buyers or indeed may not be directly related to the industry or the market in question.

Ambient media

Ambient media are a fairly recent innovation and represent a non-traditional alternative to outdoor media. Typical ambient media include bus tickets, golf holes, petrol pumps and litter bins. Media sites are selected on the basis of the degree of attention and surprise that messages are likely to command.

Guerrilla tactics

Guerrilla media tactics are an attempt to gain short-term visibility and impact in markets where the conventional media are cluttered and the life of the offering is very short. Traditionally, flyposting was the main method, practised most often by the music business. Now the term refers to a range of activities that derive their power and visibility from being outside the jurisdiction of the paid-for media.

Sabotage is a stronger interpretation, as the tactics require the hijacking of conventional media events. Lanigan (1996) reports on the use of spray paint to sabotage other advertisers' posters, while the launch of the *Blah Blah Blah* music magazine involved sticking speech bubbles over posters carrying messages for other advertisers.

Direct response media

Finally, this chapter on the media would not be complete without reference to direct response media. This use of the conventional media (television, print or radio) is essentially about the provision of a response mechanism or device through which consumers/buyers can follow up a message, enter into an immediate dialogue and either request further information or purchase goods. The main difference with new media is the time delay or response pause between receiving a message and acting upon it. Through direct response mechanisms the response may be delayed for as long as it takes to make a telephone call or fill out a reply coupon. However, the response pause and the use of a separate form of communication highlight the essential differences.

Estimates vary, but somewhere between 20% and 35% of all television advertisements now carry a telephone number. Direct Response Television (DRTV) is attractive to those promoting service-based offerings and increasingly FMCG brands such as Tango, Pond face creams and Pepperami are using it (Reid, 1996). Reid also reports how DRTV can be likened to a video game. Level one is viewing the commercial, while Level two requires the respondent to phone in and receive more information and derive greater entertainment value. Only at Level three will there be an attempt to sell directly to the respondent. The main purpose for all advertisers using this route is to extract personal information for the database and subsequent sales promotion and mailing purposes.

One aspect that is crucial to the success of a direct response campaign is not the number of responses but the conversion of leads into sales. This means that the infrastructure to support these promotional activities must be thought through and put in place, otherwise the work and resources put into the visible level will be wasted if customers are unable to get the information they require.

The provision of the infrastructure itself is not sufficient. The totality of the campaign should support the brand. Indeed, this is an opportunity to extend brand opportunities and provide increased brand experiences. For example, Martini used direct response to involve the consumer in the brand and to encourage greater identification with the brand and its values. By thinking through the voice and the content that respondents would hear on phoning in, it was possible to provide entertainment, add value and extend the television advertisement by providing a direct audio extension (Croft, 1996).

Summary

The importance of the media cannot be underestimated when considering planned communications. Each of the main classes and types of media that are available to advertisers has its own strengths and weaknesses. In addition, each medium type and vehicle has properties that are important to each situation faced by individual advertisers. Their selection and deployment should be based upon a contingency approach.

The general media are facing increased competition from technology-driven media, such as cable and satellite. This has resulted in fragmentation of the market and increased choice for advertisers in an attempt to customise messages for particular, precise and well-defined target audiences. Direct marketing is a relatively new approach which, through the use of direct response media and database support, permits the generation and feedback of messages for and from individual customers. The overarching objectives are to build and sustain a mutually rewarding relationship with each customer, reduce media costs and improve effectiveness and measurement.

The use of direct response media will continue to grow, while for some organisations their whole marketing approach can be built around the concept (e.g. insurance and financial services) as changes in distribution drive whole strategic shifts. Increasingly, direct response is becoming attractive to FMCG brands in an effort to provide additional brand experiences for customers.

The explosive development of interactive media means that new innovative opportunities have emerged to allow manufacturers, service providers and a whole host of organisations more personal, direct and mutually rewarding channels of communication.

Review questions

1. Explain the differences between media classes, types and vehicles. Give two examples of each to support your answer.
2. Describe the main characteristics of the print media. Find examples to illustrate your points.
3. Compare and contrast newspapers and magazines as advertising media.
4. What do you think will be the impact on broadcast television of the growth in penetration by cable television? How will this affect advertisers?
5. If radio is unobtrusive, why should advertisers use it?
6. What are the strengths and weaknesses of outdoor advertising media? Why is it sometimes referred to as the last true broadcast medium?
7. Why are the relative costs of each medium different?
8. Explain why packaging is an important advertising medium.
9. Discuss the proposition that product placement is morally unjustifiable, as it is a subliminal form of advertising.

10. New media are radically different from conventional media. What are these differences and why is this form of communication likely to become a major part of the media mix?

References

Advertising Association (1997) *Advertising Statistics Year Book.* Henley-on-Thames: NTC Publications.

Buckley, N. (1993) More than just a pretty picture. *Financial Times*, 13 October, p. 23.

Croft, M. (1996) Right to reply. *Marketing Week*, 12 April, pp. 37–42.

Dickenson, N. (1998) The brave new world of segmentation. *Campaign*, 6 February, pp. 36–7.

Dignam, C. (1997) Good show. *Marketing*, 25 September, p. 40.

Hall, J. (1991) Packaged good. *Campaign*, 18 October, pp. 21–3.

Lanigan, D. (1996) Guerrilla media. *Campaign*, 5 April, pp. 26-7.

Nebenzahl, I.D. and Secunda, E. (1993) Consumer attitudes toward product placement in movies. *International Journal of Advertising*, **12**, 1–11.

van Oosterom, J. (1996) A helicopter view of the new media. *Admap* (February), 32–35.

Reid, A. (1996) Fmcg advertisers are starting to wise up to DRTV. *Campaign*, 26 April, p. 15.

Shipley, D. and Wong, K.S. (1993) Exhibiting strategy and implementation. *International Journal of Advertising*, **12**(2), 117–30.

Summers, D. (1996) Return of the rough and tumble soap wars: familiar brands are finding favour with overloaded customers. *Financial Times*, 3 April, p. 18.

Wilmshurst J. (1993) *Below-the-line Promotion.* Oxford: Butterworth-Heinemann.

chapter 16

Media planning – delivering the message

Media planning is essentially a selection and scheduling exercise. The selection refers to the choice of media vehicles to carry the message on behalf of the advertiser. Scheduling refers to the number of occasions, timing and duration that a message is exposed, in the selected vehicles, to the target audience.

AIMS AND OBJECTIVES

The aims of this chapter are to introduce the fundamental elements of media planning and to set out some of the issues facing media planners.

The objectives of this chapter are:

1. To explain the role of the media planner and to highlight the impact of media and audience fragmentation.
2. To examine the key concepts used in media selection, reach and cover, frequency, duplication, rating points and CPM.
3. To provide an understanding of how learning and forgetting by individuals affect the selection and use of media vehicles.
4. To appreciate the concept of repetition and the debate concerning effective frequency and recency planning.
5. To understand the concepts of effectiveness and efficiency when applied to media selection decisions.
6. To introduce media source effects as an important factor in the selection and timing of advertising in magazines and television programmes.
7. To explore the different ways in which advertisements can be scheduled.

Introduction

Once a message has been created and agreed, a media plan should be determined. The aim of the media plan is to devise an optimum route for the delivery of the promotional message to the target audience. This function is normally undertaken by specialists, either as part of a full service advertising agency or as a media independent whose sole function is to buy air time or space from media owners (e.g. television contractors or magazine publishers) on behalf of their clients, the advertisers. This traditional role has changed in the early 1990s, and many media independents now provide consultancy services, particularly at the strategic level, plus planning and media research and auditing services.

Media departments are responsible for two main functions. These are to 'plan' and to 'buy' time and space in appropriate media vehicles. There is a third task – to monitor a media schedule once it has been bought – but this is essentially a sub-function of buying. The planner chooses the target audience and the type of medium, while the buyer chooses programmes, frequency, spots and distribution, and assembles a multi-channel schedule (Armstrong, 1993). In the past the media planner has been pre-eminent, but the role of the buyer is changing. Some feel the role of the buyer is in the ascendancy, but there are others who feel that the role is capable of increased automation and that many software packages now fulfil many functions of the media buyer. Such a move has implications for the type of person recruited. In the USA, for example, many housewives have been recruited on a part-time basis to do many parts of the traditional media planner's job.

Media planning is essentially a selection and scheduling exercise. The selection refers to the choice of media vehicles to carry the message on behalf of the advertiser. Scheduling refers to the number of occasions, timing and duration that a message is exposed, in the selected vehicles, to the target audience. However, there are several factors that complicate these seemingly straightforward tasks. First, the variety of available media is huge and rapidly increasing. This is referred to as media fragmentation. Second, the characteristics of the target audience are changing equally quickly. This is referred to as audience fragmentation. Both these fragmentation issues will be discussed later. The job of the media planner is complicated by one further element: money. Advertisers have restricted financial resources and require the media planner to create a plan that delivers their messages not only effectively but also efficiently.

The task of the media planner, therefore, is to deliver advertising messages through a selection of media which match the viewing and/or reading habits of the target audience at the lowest possible cost. In order for these tasks to be accomplished, three sets of decisions need to be made about the choice of media, vehicles and schedules.

Media choice

Decisions about the choice of media are complex. While choosing a single one is reasonably straightforward, choosing media in combination and attempting to generate synergistic effects is far from easy. Advances in IT have made media planning a much faster, more accurate process, one which is now more flexible and capable of adjusting to fast-changing market conditions.

The characteristics of each medium have been discussed in Chapter 15, but by way of summary they are set out in Table 16.1. It can be seen that each of the types of media has a variety of characteristics that will help or hinder the communication of an advertiser's message. In addition to this, each media vehicle will have a discrete set of characteristics that will also influence the way in which messages are transmitted and received.

McLuhan (1966) said that the medium is the message. He went on to say that the medium is the massage, as each medium massages the recipient in different ways and so contributes to learning in different ways. For example, Krugman (1965) hypothesised that television advertising washes over individuals. He said that viewers, rather than participate actively with television advertisements, allow learning to occur passively. In contrast, magazine advertising enquires active participation if learning is to occur.

Newspapers enable geographically based target audiences to be reached. The tone of their content can be controlled, but the cost per target reached is high. Each issue has a short lifespan, so for positive learning to occur in the target audience a number of insertions may be required.

A large number of magazines contain specialised material which appeals to particular target groups. These special interest magazines (SIMs) enable certain sponsors to reach interested targets with reduced wastage. General interest magazines (GIMs) appeal to a much wider cross-section of society, to larger generalised target groups. The life of these media vehicles is generally long and their 'pass along' readership high. It should not be forgotten, however, that noise levels can also be high due to the intermittent manner in which magazines are often read and the number of competing messages from rival organisations.

Television reaches the greatest number of people, but although advertisers can reach general groups, such as men aged 16 to 24 or housewives, it is not capable of reaching specific groups and incurs high levels of wastage. This blanket coverage offers opportunities for cable and satellite entrepreneurs to offer more precise targeting, but for now television is a tool for those who wish to talk to mass audiences. Television is expensive from a cash-flow perspective but not in terms of the costs per target reached.

Radio offers a more reasonable costing structure than television and can be utilised to reach particular geographic audiences. For a long time, however, this was seen as its only real strength, particularly when its poor attention span and non-visual dimensions are considered. Research in the 1990s, however, indicates that it is not destined to remain the poor relation to television, as radio has been shown to be capable of generating a much closer personal relationship with listeners, witnessed partly by the success of Classic FM and Virgin 1215, than is possible through posters, television or print.

The interesting point about outdoor and transit advertising is that exposure is only made by the interception of passing traffic. Govoni *et al.* (1986) make the point that such interception represents opportunistic coverage. Consequently the costs are low, both at investment and per contact levels.

The use of direct marketing has grown in recent years, as technology has developed and awareness has increased. The precise targeting potential of direct mail and its ability to communicate personally with target audiences is impressive. In addition, the control over the total process, including the costs, remains firmly with the sponsor.

Table 16.1 A summary of media characteristics

Type of media	Strengths	Weaknesses
Print		
Newspapers	Wide reach High coverage Low costs Very flexible Short lead times Speed of consumption controlled by reader	Short life span Advertisements get little exposure Relatively poor reproduction, gives poor impact Low attention-getting properties
Magazines	High quality reproduction which allows high impact Specific and specialised target audiences High readership levels Longevity High levels of information can be delivered	Long lead times Visual dimension only Slow build-up of impact Moderate costs
Television	Flexible format, uses sight, movement and sound High prestige High reach Mass coverage Low relative cost so very efficient (potentially)	High level of repetition necessary Short message life High absolute costs Clutter Increasing level of fragmentation
Radio	Selective audience, e.g. local Low costs (absolute, relative and production) Flexible Can involve listeners	Lacks impact Audio dimension only Difficult to get audience attention Low prestige
Outdoor	High reach High frequency Low relative costs Good coverage as a support medium Location orientated	Poor image (but improving) Long production time Difficult to measure
New media	High level of interaction Immediate response possible Tight targeting Low absolute and relative costs Flexible and easy to update Measurable	Segment specific Slow development of infrastructure High user setup costs Transaction security issues
Transport	High length of exposure Low costs Local orientation	Poor coverage Segment-specific (travellers) prestige Clutter
In-store POP	High attention-getting properties Persuasive Low costs Flexible	Segment-specific (shoppers) Prone to damage and confusion Clutter

Vehicle selection

Decisions regarding which vehicles are to carry an advertiser's message depend upon an understanding of a number of concepts, the first of which is learning.

Planning concepts

Before exploring these concepts, it is useful to appreciate the way in which people are believed to learn and forget. Following on from the discussion on learning in Chapter 4, there are several issues which are useful to media management.

Interference theory

Burke and Srull (1988) suggest that learning and brand recall can be interfered with. This may be caused either by new material affecting previously stored information or by old information being retrieved and interfered with by incoming messages. The first case, where the last message has the strongest recall, is similar to the recency effect discussed previously in the context of message design (Chapter 14).

In a competitive environment, where there are many messages being transmitted, each one negating previous messages, the most appropriate strategy for an advertiser would be to separate the advertisements from those of its competitors. This reasoning supports much of the positioning work undertaken by brand managers.

Decay

The rate at which individuals forget material assumes a pattern, as shown in Figure 16.1. Many researchers have found that information decays at a negatively decelerating rate. As much as 60% of the initial yield of information from an advertisement has normally decayed within six weeks. This decay, or wear-out, can be likened to the half-life of radioactive material. It is always working, although it cannot be seen, and the impact of the advertising reduces through time. Like McGuire's (1978) retention stage in his hierarchy of effects model, the storage of information for future use is important, but with time, how powerful will the information be and what triggers are required to promote recall?

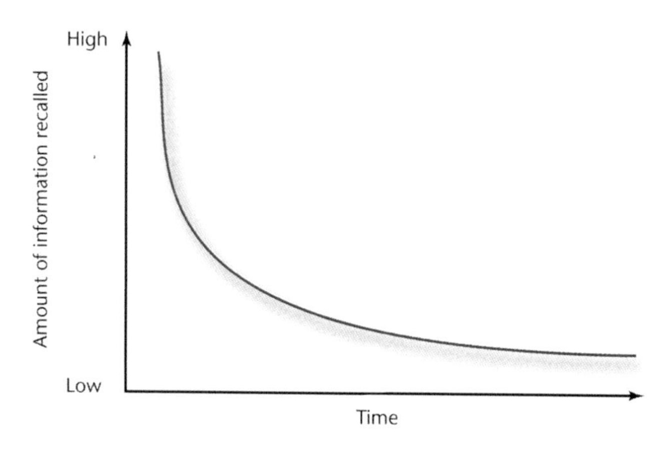

Figure 16.1 A standard decay curve.

Advertising wear-out is thought to occur because of two factors. First, individuals use selective perception and mentally switch off after a critical number of exposures. Second, the monotony and irritation caused by continued exposure leads to counter-argument to both the message and the advertisement (Petty and Cacioppo, 1979).

Advertisements for John Smith's Bitter, Gold Blend and Renault attempt to prevent wear-out by using variations on a central theme to maintain interest and yet provide consistency.

Cognitive response

Learning can be visualised as following either of the curves set out in Figure 16.2. The amount learnt 'wears out' after a certain repetition level has been reached. Grass and Wallace (1969) suggest that this process of wear-out commences once a satiation point has been reached. A number of researchers (Zielske, 1959; Strong, 1977) have found that recall is improved when messages are transmitted on a regular weekly basis, rather than daily, monthly or in a concentrated or dispersed format.

An individual's ability to develop and retain awareness or knowledge of a product will, therefore, be partly dependent not only upon the quality of the message but also on the number and quality of exposures to a planned message. To assist the media planner there are a number of concepts that need to be appreciated and used within the decisions about what, where and when a message should be transmitted. There are a number of other concepts that are of use to media planners: these are reach and coverage, frequency, gross rating points, effective frequency, efficiency and media source effects.

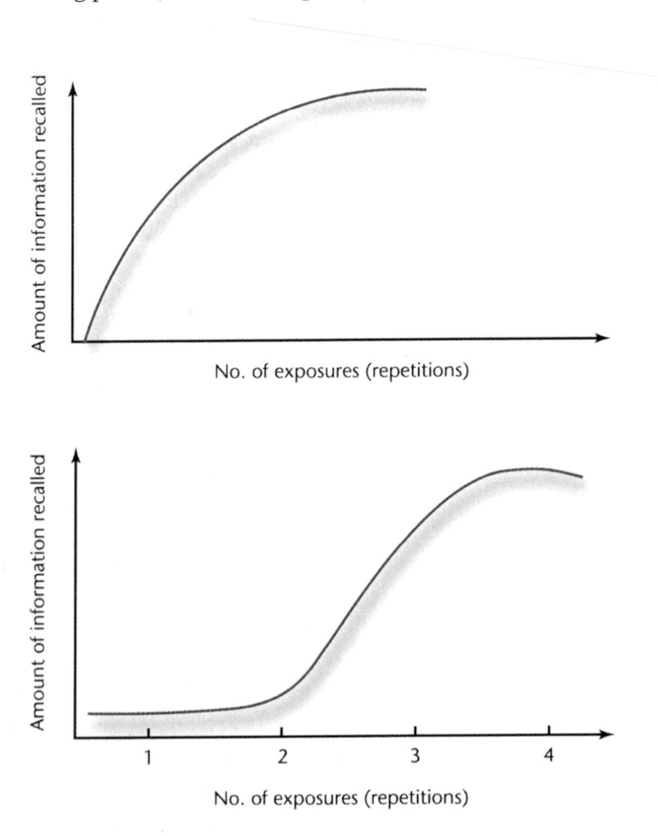

Figure 16.2 Learning curves.

Media planning concepts

Reach and coverage

Reach refers to the percentage of the target audience who are exposed to the message at least once during the relevant time period. Where 80% of the target audience has been exposed to a message, the figure is expressed as an '80 reach'.

Coverage, a term often used for reach, should not be confused or used in place of reach. Coverage refers to the size of a potential audience that might be exposed to a particular media vehicle. For media planners, therefore, coverage (the size of the target audience), is very important. Reach will always be lower than coverage, as it is impossible to reach 100% of a target population (the universe).

Building reach within a target audience is relatively easy as the planner needs to select a range of different media vehicles. This will enable different people in the target audience to have an opportunity to see the media vehicle. However, a point will be reached when it becomes more difficult to reach people who have not been exposed. As more vehicles are added, so repetition levels (the number of people who have seen the advertisement more than once) also increase.

Frequency

Frequency refers to the number of times a member of the target audience is exposed to a media vehicle (not the advertisement) during the relevant time period. It has been stated that targets must be exposed to the media vehicle, but to say that a target has seen an advertisement simply because they have been exposed to the vehicle is incorrect. For example, certain viewers hop around the channels as a commercial break starts. This has been referred to as 'channel grazing' by Lloyd and Clancy (1991). Individuals have different capacities to learn and to forget, and how much of a magazine does a reader have to consume to be counted as having read an advertisement? These questions are still largely unanswered, so media planners have adopted an easier and more consistent measure: opportunities-to-see (OTS).

This is an important point. The stated frequency level in any media plan will always be greater than the advertisement exposure rate. The term OTS is used to express the reach of a media vehicle rather than the actual exposure of an advertisement. However, a high OTS could be generated by either a large number of the target audience being exposed once (high reach) or a small number being exposed several times (high frequency).

This then raises the first major issue. As all campaigns are restricted by time and budget limitations, advertisers have to trade off reach against frequency. It is impossible to maximise both elements within a fixed budget and set period of time.

To launch a new product, it has been established that a wide number of people within the target audience need to become aware of the product's existence and its salient attributes or benefits. This means that reach is important, but as more and more people become aware, so more of them become exposed a second, third or fourth time, perhaps to different vehicles. At the outset, frequency is low and reach high, but as a campaign progresses so reach slows and frequency develops. Reach and frequency are inversely related within any period of time, and media planners must know what the objective of any campaign might be: to build reach or frequency.

Gross rating point

To decide whether reach or frequency is the focus of the campaign objective, a more precise understanding of the levels of reach and frequency is required. The term 'gross rating point' (GRP) is used to express the relationship between these two concepts. GRPs are a measure of the total number of exposures (OTS), generated within a particular period of time. The calculation itself is simply reach × frequency:

$$\text{reach} \times \text{frequency} = \text{gross rating point}$$

Media plans are often determined on the number of GRPs generated during a certain time period. For example, the objective for a media plan could be to achieve 450 GRPs in a burst (usually four or five weeks). However, as suggested earlier, caution is required when interpreting a GRP, because 450 GRPs may be the result of 18 message exposures to just 25% of the target market. It could also be an average of nine exposures to 50% of the target market!

Rating points are used by all media as a measurement tool, although they were originally devised for use with broadcast audiences. GRPs are based on the total target audience (e.g. all women aged 18 to 34, or all adults) that might be reached, but a media planner needs to know, quite rightly, how many GRPs are required to achieve a particular level of effective reach and what levels of frequency are really required to develop effective learning or awareness in the target audience. In other words, how can the effectiveness of a media plan be improved?

Effective frequency

There are a number of reasons why considering the effectiveness of a media plan has become more important. First, there is the combination of media and audience fragmentation and rising media costs. Second, there are short-termism, increased managerial accountability and intensifying competition. This latter point refers to the media planning industry itself and the restructuring and concentration of media buying around centralisation and globalisation, which have all fuelled the drive to seek more effective ways of buying media.

Frequency refers to the number of times members of the target audience have been exposed to the vehicle. It says nothing about the quality of the exposures and whether any impact was made. Effective frequency refers to the number of times an individual needs to be exposed to an advertisement before the communication is effective. Being exposed once or possibly twice is unlikely to affect the disposition of the receiver. But the big question facing media planners is how many times should a message be repeated for effective learning to occur? The level of effective frequency is generally unknown, but there has been some general agreement that, for an advertisement to be effective (to make an impact), a target should have at least three OTS. More than 10 will be ineffective and a waste of resources. The level of three is determined by messages that first provide understanding, second provide recognition and third actually stimulate action.

Determining the average frequency partially solves the problem. This is the number of times a target reached by the schedule is exposed to the vehicle over a particular period of time. For example, a schedule may generate the following:

10% of the audience is reached ten times ($10 \times 10 = 100$)
25% of the audience is reached seven times ($25 \times 7 = 175$)
65% of the audience is reached once ($65 \times 1 = 65$)
Total = 340 exposures
Average frequency = 340/100= 3.4

This figure of average frequency is misleading because different groups of people have been reached with varying levels of frequency. In the example above, an average frequency of 3.4 is achieved but 65% of the audience is reached only once. This means that the average frequency, in this example, may lead to an audience being underexposed.

Members of the target audience do not buy and read just one magazine or watch a single television programme. Consumer media habits are complex, although distinct patterns can be observed, but it is likely that a certain percentage of the target audience will be exposed to an advertisement if it is placed in two or more media vehicles. Those who are exposed once constitute unduplicated reach. Those who are exposed on two or more occasions are said to have been duplicated. Such overlapping of exposure, shown in Figure 16.3, is referred to as duplicated reach.

Duplication provides an indication of the levels of frequency likely in a particular schedule, so media plans need to specify levels of duplicated and unduplicated reach. Duplication also increases costs, so if the objective of the plan is unduplicated reach, duplication brings waste and inefficiency.

Nevertheless, it is generally agreed that a certain level of GRPs is necessary for awareness to be achieved and that increased GRPs are necessary for other communication effects to be achieved. These levels of GRPs are referred to as weights, and the weight a campaign has reflects the objectives of the campaign. For example, a burst designed to achieve 85% coverage with eight OTS would make a 680 rating, which is considered to be heavy. Such high ratings are often associated with car launches and,

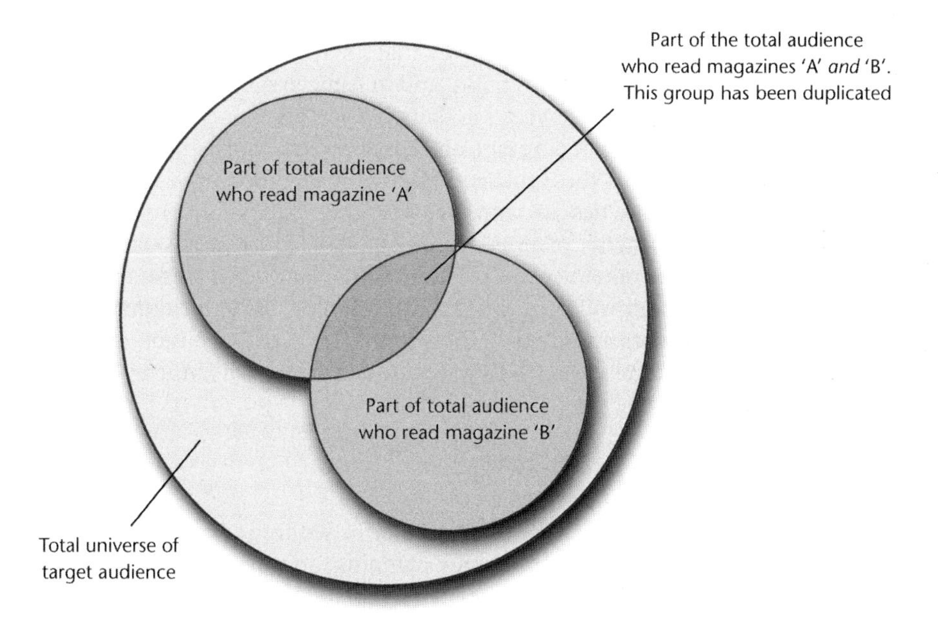

Figure 16.3 Duplication.

Table 16.2 A television laydown for a national burst

	3–9 Jan.	10–16 Jan.	17–23 Jan.	24–30 Jan.	Total (inc. satellite)
London	125	100	100	86	411
Central	125	100	100	77	402
Granada	125	112	111	111	459
North	125	100	100	68	393
STV	125	125	115	115	480
HTV	125	100	100	53	378
Meridian	125	100	100	47	372
Anglia	125	100	100	48	373
WCTV	125	100	100	41	366
Border	125	100	100	72	397
Grampian	125	118	100	100	443

for example, products that are market leaders in their class, such as Nescafé. An average rating would be one set to achieve a 400 rating, through 80% coverage and five OTS over the length of a five-week period.

Readers might be interested to know that, at deseasonalised 1997 prices, each 100 rating points cost an advertiser around £215,000 (annual spread £155,000–290,000). That means that an average five-week burst set to achieve 400 rating points will cost approximately £1 million, just for the broadcast time. Production costs and commissions need to be added to this figure.

Our understanding about how learning works can assist the quest for effective frequency levels. The amount of learning in individuals increases up to a certain point, where further exposure to material adds little to our overall level of knowledge. The same applies to the frequency level and the weightings applied to exposures. Table 16.2 shows the spread of weights for a burst bought by a major advertiser. The ratings are spread in such a way that greater weight is 'laid down' at the beginning of the campaign, to get attention, and in some areas (WCTV) the weight in week four is only 33% of the first week's activity.

The figures that coverage and reach provide only show the numbers of people who are exposed to the vehicle. Effective reach measures those that are aware of the message. This ties in with the previous discussion on effective frequency levels. Essentially, media planners recognise that effective advertising requires that, in addition to the other aspects of advertising planning, a single transmission (reach) of an advertisement will be unproductive (Naples, 1979; Krugman, 1975). A minimum of two exposures and a reach threshold of 45% of the target audience are required as a minimum level for reach to be regarded as effective (Murray and Jenkins, 1992).

Recency planning

A new perspective to counter the effective frequency model has emerged from the USA. This is known as recency planning, and has developed at a time when the weak theory of advertising has started to gain greater acceptance as the most acceptable general interpretation of how advertising works. It is also more generally accepted that advertising is not the powerful marketing tool that it was once thought to be (Jones,

Table 16.3 The differences between effective frequency and recency planning

Recency planning model	Effective frequency model
Reach goal	Frequency goal
Continuity	Burst
One week planning cycle	Four week planning cycle
Lowest cost per reach point	Lowest cost per thousand
Low ratings	High ratings

Source: Adapted from Ephron (1997).

1990) and that the timing and presentation of advertising messages need to be reconsidered in the light of the way the advertising is currently thought to work.

If it is accepted that consumer decision-making is more heavily influenced by running out of particular products (opening empty fridges and store cupboards) rather than exposure to advertising messages that are repeated remorselessly, then it follows that advertising needs to be directed at those people who are actually in the market and prepared to buy (Ephron, 1997).

As many FMCG products are purchased each week, Jones (1995) argues that a single exposure to an advertising message *in the week* before a purchase is to be made, is more important than adding further messages and so increasing frequency. Recency planning considers reach to be more important than frequency.

The goal of this new approach is to reach those few consumers who are ready to buy (in the market). To do this the strategy requires reaching as many consumers as possible in as many weeks as possible (as far as the budget will extend).

This requires a lower weekly weight and an extended number of weeks to a campaign. Advertising budgets are not cut; the fund is simply spread over a greater period of time. According to Ephron this approach is quite different from effective frequency models and quite revolutionary; see Table 16.3.

This approach has been greeted with a number of objections. It has not been accepted universally and has not been widely implemented in the UK market at the time of writing.

Gallucci (1997), among others, rejects the notion of recency planning because effectiveness will vary by brand, category and campaign. He claims that reaching 35% of a cola market (Indonesia) once a week will not bring about the same result as reaching 65% four times a week.

The debate concerning the development of recency planning and effective frequency will continue. What might be instrumental to the outcome to the debate will be a better understanding of how advertising works and the way buyers use advertising messages that are relevant to them.

Media usage and attitudes

Research by CIA MediaLab reported by Beale (1997) revealed that nearly 50% of the population have negative attitudes towards advertising. Advertising is seen by this large body of people as both intrusive and pervasive. The research led to the development of a four-part typology of personality types based upon respondents' overall attitudes towards advertising. Through an understanding of the different characteris-

Table 16.4 Advertising attitudes for media determination

Cynics (22%) This group perceives advertising as a crude sales tool. They are resentful and hostile to advertisements, although they are more likely to respond to advertisements placed in relevant media.	**Enthusiasts (35%)** Enthusiasts like to get involved with advertising and creativity is perceived as an important part of the process. Apart from newspapers, which are regarded as boring, most types of media are acceptable.
Ambivalents (22%) While creativity is seen as superfluous and irrelevant, Ambivalents are more disposed to information-based messages or those that promise cost savings. The best advertisements are those that use media that reinforce the message.	**Acquiescents (21%)** As the name suggests, this group of people have a reluctant approach to advertising. This means that they see advertising as unavoidable and an inevitable part of their world. Therefore, they are open to influence through a variety of media.

Source: Adapted from Beale (1997).

Table 16.5 Usage patterns of television consumption (Zenith Media)

	Minutes spent watching TV[a] per day
Winter	
Heavy	195–500+
Medium	106–200
Light	Less than 100
Summer	
Heavy	150–500+
Medium	60–150
Light	Less than 60

[a]ITV + CH4.

tics it is possible to make better (more informed) decisions about the most appropriate media channels to reach target audiences; see Table 16.4.

It is common for advertisers and media planners to discuss target markets in the context of heavy, medium, light and non-users of a product. It is only now that consideration is being given to the usage levels of viewers and readers. Zenith Media have determined that TV audiences can be categorised as heavy, medium and light users based upon the amount of time they spend watching television. Table 16.5 presents a breakdown of the general categories, where the amount of time spent viewing can be seen to vary considerably between the summer and winter periods.

One of the implications of this approach is that if light users consume so little television, then perhaps it is not worthwhile trying to communicate with them and resources should be directed to the medium and heavy user groups. The other side of the argument is that light users are very specific in the programmes that they watch; therefore, it should be possible to target messages at them and so use a heavy number of GRPs. Questions still remain about the number of ratings necessary for effective reach in each of these categories.

The question concerning how many rating points should be purchased was addressed by Ostrow (1981). He said that rather than use average frequency, a

Table 16.6 Issues to be considered when setting frequency levels

	Low frequency	High frequency
Marketing issues		
Newness of the brand	Established	New
Market share	High	Low
Brand loyalty	Higher	Lower
Purchase and usage cycle times	Long	Short
Message issues		
Complexity	Simple	Complex
Uniqueness	More	Less
Image versus product sell	Product sell	Image
Message variation	Single message	Multiple messages
Media plan issues		
Clutter	Less	More
Editorial atmosphere	Appropriate	Not appropriate
Attentiveness of the media in the plan	Holds	Fails to hold
Number of media in the plan	Less	More

Source: Adapted from Ostrow (1981); used with kind permission.

decision should be made about the minimum level of frequency necessary to achieve the objectives and then maximise reach at that level. Ostrow (1984) suggested that consideration of the issues set out in Table 16.6 would also assist.

The traditional approach of using television to reach target audiences to build awareness is still strong. For example, Procter & Gamble, Lever Brothers, Nestlé, Kellogg's and British Telecom all spend in excess of 75% of their budgets on television advertising. However, there are signs that some major advertisers are moving slowly from a dominant above-the-line approach to a more integrated and through-the-line approach as a more effective way of delivering messages to target audiences. Nescafé now uses 48 sheet posters and Unilever, traditionally a heavy user of television, has begun to use radio and posters as support for its television work.

Efficiency

All promotional campaigns are constrained by a budget. Therefore a trade-off is required between the need to reach as many members of the target audience as possible (create awareness) and the need to repeat the message to achieve effective learning in the target audience. The decision about whether to emphasise reach or frequency is assisted by a consideration of the costs involved in each proposed schedule or media plan.

There are two main types of cost. The first of these is the *absolute cost*. This is the cost of the space or time required for the message to be transmitted. For example, the cost of a full page single insertion colour advertisement, booked for a firm date in *The Times*, is £33,000 (March 1998). Cash flow is affected by absolute costs.

In order that an effective comparison be made between media plans the *relative costs* of the schedules need to be understood. Relative costs are the costs incurred in making contact with each member of the target audience.

Traditionally, the magazine industry has based its calculations on the cost per thousand people reached (CPT). This is often referred to as CPM, where the 'M' refers to the Roman symbol for thousand:

$$\text{CPM} = \text{space costs (absolute)} \times 1{,}000/\text{circulation}$$

The newspaper industry has used the milline rate, which is the cost per line of space per million circulation.

Broadcast audiences are measured by program ratings (USA), and television audiences in the UK are measured by television ratings or TVRs. They are essentially the same in that they represent the percentage of television households who are tuned to a specific programme. The TVR is determined as follows:

$$\text{TVR} = \text{No. of target TV households tuned into a programme} \times 100/\text{total number of target TV households}$$

A single TVR, therefore, represents 1% of all the television households in a particular area who are tuned into a specific programme.

A further approach to measuring broadcast audiences uses the share of televisions that are tuned into a specific programme. This is compared with the total number of televisions that are actually switched on at that moment. This is expressed as a percentage and should be greater than the TVR. Share, therefore, reveals how well a programme is perceived by the available audience, not the potential audience.

The question of how to measure relative costs in the broadcast industry has been answered by the use of the rating point or TVR. Cost per TVR is determined as follows:

$$\text{cost TVR} = \text{time costs (absolute costs)}/\text{TVR}$$

Intra-industry comparison of relative costs is made possible by using these formulae. Media plans which only involve broadcast or only use magazine vehicles can be evaluated to determine levels of efficiency. However, members of the target audience do not have discrete viewing habits; they have, as we saw earlier, complex media habits which involve exposure to a mix of media classes and vehicles. Advertisers respond to this mixture by placing advertisements in a variety of media, but have no way of comparing the relative costs on an inter-industry basis. In other words, the efficiency of using a *News at Ten* television slot cannot be compared with an insertion in the *Economist*. Attempts are being made to provide cross-industry media comparisons, but as yet no one formula has yet been provided that satisfies all demands. The television and newspaper industries, by using CPM in combination with costs per unit of time and space respectively, have attempted to forge a bridge which may be of use to their customers.

Finally, some comment on the concept of CPM is necessary, as there has been speculation about its validity as a comparative tool. There are a number of short comings associated with the use of CPM. For example, because each media class possesses particular characteristics, direct comparisons based on CPM alone are dangerous. The levels of wastage incurred in a plan, such as reaching people who are not targets or by measuring OTS for the vehicle and not the advertisement, may lead to an overestimate of the efficiency that a plan offers.

Similarly, the circulation of a magazine is not a true representation of the number of people who read or have an opportunity to see. Therefore, CPM may underestimate the efficiency unless the calculation can be adjusted to account for the extra or pass-along readership that occurs in reality. Having made these points, media buyers in the UK continue to use CPM/CPT and cost per rating point (CPRP) as a means of planning and buying time and space. Target audiences and television programmes are priced according to the ratings they individually generate. The ratings affect the cost of buying a spot. The higher the rating, the higher the price to place advertisements in the magazine or television programme.

Media source effects

CPM is a quantitative measure, and one of its major shortcomings is that it fails to account for the qualitative aspects associated with media vehicles. Before vehicles are selected, their qualitative aspects need to be considered on the basis that a vehicle's environment may affect the way in which a message is perceived and decoded.

An advertisement placed in one vehicle, such as *Cosmopolitan*, may have a different impact upon an identical audience from that obtained if the same advertisement is placed in *Options*. This differential level of 'power of impact', is caused by a number of source factors, of which the following are regarded as the most influential:

1. Vehicle atmosphere – editorial tone, vehicle expertise, vehicle prestige.
2. Technical and reproduction characteristics – technical factors, exposure opportunities, perception opportunities.
3. Audience and product characteristics – audience/vehicle fit, nature of the product.

Vehicle atmosphere

Editorial tone

This refers to the editorial views presented by the vehicle and the overall tone of the material contained. Govoni *et al.* (1986) describe how Procter & Gamble declared that it would not buy spots on television shows that were characterised by sex or violence. Procter & Gamble did not want any association, at either corporate or brand level, with such environments.

Vehicle expertise

Magazines and journals can reflect a level of expertise and represent source credibility. Readers who regard particular magazines, especially some of the consumer SIMs (e.g. *Golf Monthly*), business-to-business magazines (e.g. *Fire & Rescue*) and academic journals (e.g. *Harvard Business Review*), as important sources of credible information are more relaxed and open to persuasion.

Vehicle prestige

The message strategy adopted for each advertisement should be appreciated, as this can have a strong effect upon the scheduling. The prestige of a vehicle is important to some products, especially when targeted at audiences where vehicle status is important, for example, *Country Life*. Transformational advertisements have been shown to be more effective in prestige-based vehicles than in expertise-based vehicles (and vice versa for information-based advertisements).

Technical and reproduction characteristics of a vehicle

Technical factors

The technical characteristics of the vehicle, such as its visual capability, may influence the impact of the message. The use of colour, movement and sound may be necessary for the full effectiveness of a message to be realised. Other messages may need only a more limited range of characteristics, such as sound. For example, the promotion of inclusive tour holidays benefits from the communication of an impression (photograph/drawing) of the destination resort. This is important, as each destination needs to be differentiated, in the minds of the target audience, from competing destinations.

Exposure opportunities

The possibility that an advertisement will be successfully exposed to the target increases as more consideration is given to the likelihood of successful communication. Each vehicle has a number of time slots or spaces that provide opportunities for increased exposure. The back pages of magazines or facing matter often command premium advertising rates, just as prime time spots or film premieres on television always generate extra revenue for the television contractors.

Perception opportunities

Being exposed to the message does not mean that the message is perceived. A reader may not perceive an advertisement when searching for the next page of an article. Similarly, a car driver may not 'hear' a radio message because his or her attention may be on a passing car or a strange engine noise. The solution is to use strong attention-gaining materials, such as loud or distinctive music or controversial headlines. In addition, new imaginative ways of attracting attention are being developed. Car dealers have used incentives to attract audiences to test drive a car and receive vouchers for a free video film or have free subscriptions to particular magazines.

Audience/product characteristics

Audience/vehicle fit

The media plan should provide the best match between the target market and the audience reached by the vehicles in the media schedule. The more complex the target market description or consumer profile, the greater the difficulty of matching it with appropriate vehicles. Weilbacher (1984) argues that media evaluation based on product usage may be better than using demographics and psychographics. These may be inappropriate and inefficient when matching markets with audiences. As advertising is directed at influencing consumer behaviour, product usage is a more logical measure of media evaluation. This view is supported by media planners targeting heavy, medium and light users.

This perspective contrasts with the view of Rothschild (1987). He sees demographic and psychographic factors as being relatively stable and enduring factors, and thus as suitable influences upon the media selection decision. By contrast, the dynamic factors (those that vary within an individual with respect to brand choice, purchase behaviour and time of adoption between products) are seen as being more suitable for influencing media strategy.

Nature of the product

In addition to this, consideration needs to given to the nature of the product itself. Audiences have particular viewing patterns; therefore it does not make sense to advertise when it is known that the target audience is not watching (for example, promoting children's sweets late at night or photocopiers in consumer interest magazines).

Prime television spots such as *News at Ten* or major sporting occasions such as the Olympic Games will attract many major competitive brands. It may be wise to avoid competing for time and look for other suitable programmes.

Vehicle mood effects

The mood that a vehicle creates can also be an important factor. Aaker *et al.* (1992) report on the work of a number of studies in this area. These suggest that food advertisements using transformational appeals are more effective when placed in situation comedies than in thrillers and mystery programmes. Adverts for analgesics work better in both adult westerns and situation comedies (Crane, 1964).

These qualitative, vehicle-related source effects need to be considered as support for the quantitative work undertaken initially. They should not be used as the sole reason for the selection of particular media vehicles, if only because they are largely subjective.

Scheduling

This seeks to establish when the messages are transmitted in order that the media objectives be achieved at the lowest possible cost. The first considerations are the objectives themselves. If the advertising objectives are basically short-term, then the placements should be concentrated over a short period of time. Conversely, if awareness is to be built over a longer term, perhaps building a new brand, then the frequency of the placements need not be so intensive and can be spread over a period so that learning can occur incrementally.

The second consideration is the purchasing cycle. We have seen before that the optimum number of exposures is thought to be between three and ten, and this should occur within each purchasing cycle. This of course, is only really applicable to packaged goods, and is not as applicable to the business-to-business sector. However, the longer the cycle, the less frequency is required.

The third consideration is the level of involvement. If the objective of the plan is to create awareness, then when there is high involvement few repetitions will be required compared with low-involvement decisions. This is because people who are highly involved actively seek information and need little assistance to digest relevant information. Likewise, where there is low involvement, attitudes develop from use of the product, so frequency is important to maintain awareness and to prompt trial.

Finally, the placement of an advertisement is influenced by the characteristics of the target audience and their preferred programmes. By selecting compatible 'spots', message delivery is likely to improve considerably.

Timing of advertisement placements

The timing of placements is dependent upon a number of factors. One of the overriding constraints is the size of the media budget and the impact that certain placement patterns can bring to an organisation's cash flow. Putting cost to one side, many researchers have identified and labelled different scheduling patterns. Govoni *et al.* (1986), Sissors and Bumba (1989), Burnett (1993) and Kotler (1997) all suggest different approaches to scheduling. Figure 16.4 and the following are presented as a synthesis of the more common scheduling options.

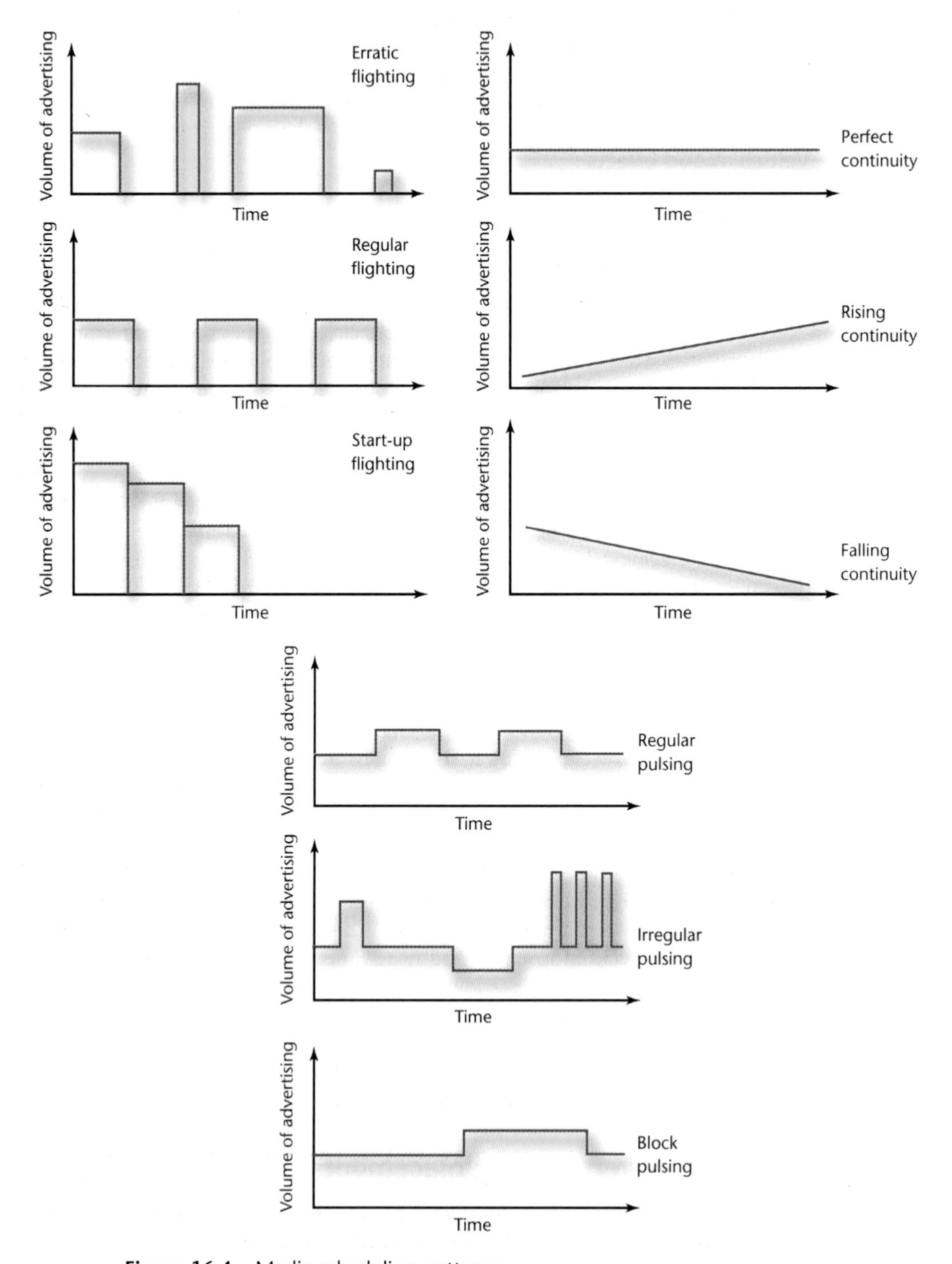

Figure 16.4 Media scheduling patterns.

Continuity patterns

Continuous patterns involve regular and uniform presentation of the message to the target audience. Over the long term, a continuous pattern is more appropriate for products and services where demand is crisis led, e.g. plumbing, or where there is a long purchase cycle. These continuous patterns are often used for mature products, where reminder advertising is appropriate. A rising pattern is used when activity centres around a particular event, such as the FA Cup Final, the Olympic Games or a general election. A fading pattern may follow an initial burst to launch a new product or to inform of a product modification.

Flighting patterns

Flighting allows advertisers the opportunity to spread their resources across a longer period of time. This may improve the effectiveness of their messages. A flighting pattern may be appropriate in situations where messages need to reflect varying demand, such as that experienced by the retail sector throughout the year. Flighting is also adopted as a competitive response to varying advertising weights applied by rivals. These schedules are used for specific events, such as support for major sales promotions and responses to adverse publicity or one-off market opportunities.

Flighting patterns can also be used in short and often heavy periods of investment activity. Because of the seasonality of the product (e.g. for inclusive tour operators), advertising at other times is inappropriate and a waste of resources. This approach can also be used to respond quickly to a competitor's potentially damaging actions, to launch new products or to provide unique information, such as the announcement of a new organisation as a result of merger activity, or to promote information about a particular event such as an impending share offer.

Pulsing patterns

Pulsing seeks to combine the advantages of both the previous patterns. As a result it is the safest of all the options, but potentially the most expensive. It allows advertisers to increase levels of message activity at certain times of the year, which is important for times when sales traditionally increase, as with car sales at the beginning of August.

Whereas flighting presents an opportunity for individuals to forget messages during periods of no advertising, pulsing helps to prevent the onset of forgetting, to build high levels of awareness and to provide a barrier that holds back competitor attack.

Summary

The task of buying the time or space in media vehicles in order that an advertising message be carried to a target audience appears seductively straightforward. It is not. It is complicated by a number of factors, ranging from the size and dispersion of the target audience to the increasing number and variety of available media. These factors are referred to as audience and media fragmentation, which bring both benefits to and difficulties for media planners and advertisers. For example, it is easier to target more specialised and compact target audiences using new and specialised media. However, audience profiles are changing rapidly and there is little control information about these audiences that allows advertising funds to be allocated 'properly' (Meuller-Heumann, 1992).

Another major difficulty, increasing in its importance, is the question of how many times a message must be repeated before an impression, awareness or learning occurs. The search for effective frequency continues, particularly by product class. However, it is generally accepted that three exposures are necessary as a minimum and ten as a maximum.

Decisions regarding the media cannot be made in isolation from the qualitative factors associated with each vehicle. Known as vehicle source effects, these are concerned with the quality of the vehicle in terms of its atmosphere, technical aspects and audience/product fit.

The final task concerns the timing or scheduling of advertisements. As with most things in life, timing is of the essence. Scheduling calls for subjectivity and, while there are numerous quantitative measures to assist decision-making, media planning is essentially about management making judgements about where best to place its client's messages to maximise their effectiveness and the efficiency of the spend.

Review questions

1. What are the main tasks facing media planners?
2. If the rate at which information decays within individuals is known, then the task of the media planner is simply to place messages at suitable intervals in the path of decay. Discuss.
3. Draw a typical learning curve and then explain interference theory.
4. Why is it important that a media planner knows whether reach or frequency is the main objective of a media plan?
5. Why are frequency levels so important? Explain the concept of effective frequency.
6. How does recency planning differ from effective frequency?
7. What is a TVR and how does it relate to GRPs?
8. How is CPM flawed as a measure of media efficiency?
9. Write a brief report outlining the principal characteristics of media source effects.
10. What are the main ways in which media plans can be scheduled?

References

Aaker, D., Batra, R. and Myers, J.G. (1992) *Advertising Management*, 4th edn. Englewood Cliffs NJ: Prentice Hall.

Armstrong, S. (1993) The business of buying: time, lads, please. *Media Week*, 3 September, pp. 26–7.

Beale, C. (1997) Study reveals negativity towards ads. *Campaign*, 28 November, p. 8.

Burke, R. and Srull, T.K. (1988) Competitive interference and consumer memory for advertising. *Journal of Consumer Research*, **15** (June), 55–68.

Burnett, J. (1993) *Promotion Management*. New York: Houghton Mifflin.

Crane, L.E. (1964) How product, appeal, and program affect attitudes towards commercials. *Journal of Advertising Research*, **4** (March), 15.

Ephron, E. (1997) Recency planning. *Admap* (February), 32–4.

Gallucci, P. (1997) There are no absolutes in media planning. *Admap* (July/August), 39–43.

Govoni, N., Eng, R. and Galper, M. (1986) *Promotional Management*. Englewood Cliffs NJ: Prentice Hall.

Grass, R.C. and Wallace, H.W. (1969) Satiation effects of TV commercials. *Journal of Advertising Research*, **9**(3), 3–9.

Jones, P. (1990) Advertising: strong or weak force? Two views an ocean apart. *International Journal of Advertising*, **9**(3), 233–46.

Jones, P. (1995) *When Ads Work: New Proof that Advertising Triggers Sales*. New York: Simon & Schuster, The Free Press/Lexington Books.

Kotler, P. (1997) *Marketing Management: Analysis, Planning, Implementation and Control*, 9th edn. Englewood Cliffs NJ: Prentice Hall.

Krugman, H.E. (1965) The impact of television advertising: learning without involvement. *Public Opinion Quarterly*, **29**(Fall), 349–56.

Krugman, H.E. (1975) What makes advertising effective? *Harvard Business Review* (March/April), 96–103.

Lloyd, D.W. and Clancy, K.J. (1991) CPMs versus CPMis: implications for media planning. *Journal of Advertising Research* (August/September), 34–44.

McGuire, W. (1978) An information processing model of advertising effectiveness, in *Behavioural and Management Science in Marketing* (eds. H.J. Davis and A.J. Silk). New York: Ronald Press.

McLuhan, M. (1966) *Understanding Media: The Extensions of Man*. New York: McGraw-Hill.

Mueller-Heumann, G. (1992) Market and technology shifts in the 1990s: market fragmentation and mass customisation. *Journal of Marketing Management*, 8, 303–14.

Murray, G.B. and Jenkins, J.R.G. (1992) The concept of effective reach in advertising. *Journal of Advertising Research* (May/June), 34–42.

Naples, M.J. (1979) *Effective Frequency: The Relationship Between Frequency and Advertising Effectiveness*. New York: Association of National Advertisers.

Ostrow, J.W. (1981) What level frequency? *Advertising Age* (November), 13–18.

Ostrow, J.W. (1984) Setting frequency levels: an art or a science? *Marketing and Media Decisions*, **24**(4), 9–11.

Petty, R.E. and Cacioppo, J.T. (1979) Effects of message repetition and position on cognitive responses, recall and persuasion. *Journal of Personality and Social Psychology*, **37** (January), 97–109.

Rothschild, M.L. (1987) *Marketing Communications*. Lexington MA: D.C. Heath.

Sissors, J.Z. and Bumba, L. (1989) *Advertising Media Planning*, 3rd edn. Lincolnwood IL: NTC Business Books.

Strong, E.C. (1977) The spacing and timing of advertising. *Journal of Advertising Research*, **17** (December), 25–31.

Weilbacher, W. (1984) *Advertising*. New York: Macmillan.

Zielske, H.A. (1959) The remembering and forgetting of advertising. *Journal of Marketing*, **23** (January), 239–43.

chapter 17

Evaluating advertising

Testing is required to ensure that an advertiser's intended messages are encoded correctly and are capable of being decoded accurately by the target audience in the context in which they are interpreted. In addition, the overall impact and effect that an advertising campaign has on a target audience needs to be reviewed in order that management can learn and better understand the impact of their advertising and their audiences.

AIMS AND OBJECTIVES

The aim of this chapter is to review the ways in which advertising can be evaluated in the context of planned marketing communications.

The objectives of this chapter are:

1. To discuss the role of evaluation as part of a marketing communications plan.
2. To explore the value of pre-testing and post-testing advertisements.
3. To provide an insight into the value of qualitative and quantitative testing techniques.
4. To determine the main methods used to evaluate advertisements at the pre-test stage.
5. To appraise the methods and tools used to evaluate advertisements at the post-test stage.
6. To appreciate the role technology plays in the assessment and evaluation of advertising.

Introduction

All organisations review and evaluate the performance of their various activities. Many undertake formal mechanisms, while others review in an informal *ad hoc* manner, but the process of evaluation or reflection is a well-established management process. The objective is to monitor the often diverse activities of the organisation so that management can exercise control. It is through the process of review and evaluation that an organisation has the opportunity to learn and develop. In turn, this enables management to refine its competitive position and to provide for higher levels of customer satisfaction.

The use of marketing communications is a management activity, one that requires the use of rigorous research and testing procedures in addition to continual evaluation. This is necessary because planned communications involve a wide variety of stakeholders and have the potential to consume a vast amount of resources.

The evaluation of planned marketing communications consists of two distinct elements. The first element is concerned with the development and testing of individual messages. For example, a particular sales promotion (such as a sample pack), has individual characteristics that may or may not meet the objectives of a sales promotion event.

An advertising message has to achieve, among other things, a balance of emotion and information in order that the communication objectives and message strategy be achieved. To accomplish this, testing is required to ensure that the intended messages are encoded correctly and are capable of being decoded accurately by the target audience. The second element concerns the overall impact and effect that a campaign has on a target audience once a communications plan has been released. This post-test factor is critical, as it will either confirm or reject management's judgement about the viability of their communications strategy. The way in which the individual components of the communications mix work together needs to be understood in order that strengths be capitalised on and developed and weaknesses negated.

This chapter examines the testing and evaluation methods that are appropriate to advertising. The testing and evaluation of advertising messages is considered from pre- and post-test perspectives. The evaluation of the other tools of the promotional mix is considered within the relevant chapters.

The role of evaluation in planned communications

The evaluation process is a key part of marketing communications. The findings and results of the evaluative process feed back into the next campaign and provide indicators and benchmarks for further management decisions. The primary role of evaluating the performance of a communications strategy is to ensure that the communications objectives have been met and that the strategy has been effective. The secondary role is to ensure that the strategy has been executed efficiently, that the full potential of the individual promotional tools has been extracted and that resources have been used economically.

Research activity is undertaken for two main reasons. The first is guidance and development and the second is prediction and evaluation (Staverley, 1993). Guidance takes the form of shaping future strategies as a result of past experiences. Development is important in the context of determining whether the communications worked as they were intended to.

Prediction and evaluation require information about options and alternatives. For example, did sales presentation approach A prove to be more effective than B, and if so, what would happen if A was used nationally? Predictably, the use of quantitative techniques is more prevalent with this latter set of reasons.

Pre-testing

Advertisements can be researched prior to their release (pre-test) or after they have been released (post-test). Pre-tests, sometimes referred to as copy tests, have traditionally attracted more attention, stimulated a greater variety of methods and generated much controversy, in comparison with post-tests.

The methods used to pre-test advertisements are based upon either qualitative or quantitative criteria. The most common methods used to pre-test advertisements are concept testing, focus groups, consumer juries, dummy vehicles, readability, theatre and physiological tests. Focus groups are the main qualitative method used and theatre or hall tests the main quantitative test. Each of these methods will be discussed later.

The primary purpose of testing advertisements during the developmental process is to ensure that the final creative will meet the advertising objectives. It is better to help shape the way an advertising message is formed, rather like potters continuously review their progress as they craft their vases, than to make a pot and then decide that it is not big enough or that the handle is the wrong shape. The practical objective of pre-testing unfinished and finished creative work is that it is more effective for an advertiser to terminate an advertisement before costs become so large and commitment too final. Changes to an advertisement that are made too late may be resisted partly because of the sunk costs and partly because of the political consequences that 'pulling' an advertisement might have.

Once a series of advertisements has been roughed or developed so that its messages can be clearly understood, advertisers seek reassurance and guidance regarding which of the alternatives should be developed further. Concept tests, in-depth interviews, focus groups and consumer juries can be used to determine which of the proposed advertisements are the better ones by using ranking and prioritisation procedures. Of those selected, further testing can be used to reveal the extent to which the intended message is accurately decoded. These comprehension and reaction tests are designed to prevent inappropriate advertisements reaching the finished stage.

Pre-testing unfinished advertisements

Concept testing

The concept test is an integral part of the developmental stage of advertising strategy. The purpose is to reduce the number of alternative advertising ideas, to identify and build upon the good ideas and to reject those that the target audience feel are not suitable.

Concept testing can occur very early on in the development process, but is usually undertaken when the target audience can be presented with a *rough* outline or *storyboard* that represents the intended artwork and the messages to be used. There are varying degrees of sophistication associated with concept testing, from the use of simple *cards* with no illustrations to *photomatics*, which is a film of individual photographs shot in sequence, and *livematics*, which is a film very close to the intended finished message. Their use will reflect the size of the advertiser's budget, the completion date of the campaign and the needs of the creative team.

Pre-testing: Kenco coffee

Kenco, who had moved into the instant coffee market, wanted to know three main things about a proposed print advertisement:

1. Its ability to generate awareness and interest.
2. The message take-out.
3. Whether the Kenco Instant brand would be perceived.

The interest factor was found to be present and the Kenco brand was also perceived. The jar of coffee, however, needed to be improved, as it did not look as if there was a jar of coffee in the cafetière or the grinder. This meant that the Instant aspect was not communicated.

Work was undertaken to highlight the jar and the tag line was reworked.

Adapted from Colinese (1997)

Concept testing, by definition, has to be undertaken in artificial surroundings, but the main way of eliciting the target's views is essentially qualitatively orientated, based upon a group discussion. This group discussion is referred to as a focus group and is a technique used by most agencies.

Focus groups

When a small number (8–10) of target consumers are brought together and invited to discuss a particular topic, a focus group is formed. By using in-depth interviewing skills, a professional moderator can probe the thoughts and feelings held by the members of the group towards a product, media vehicles or advertising messages. One-way viewing rooms allow clients to observe the interaction without the focus group's behaviour being modified by external influences.

The advantage of focus groups is that they are relatively inexpensive to set up and run and they use members of the target audience. In this sense they are representative

Exhibit 17.1 Roughs for Kraft dressings prepared by Wayne Pashley and Nigel Pollard at J. Walter Thompson. Reproduced with kind permission.

and allow true feelings and emotions to be uncovered in a way that other methods deny. They do not attempt to be quantitative and, in that sense, they lack objectivity. It is also suggested that the group dynamics may affect the responses in the 'artificial' environment. This means that there may be in-built bias to the responses and the interaction of the group members. Focus groups are very popular, but they should not be used on their own.

Consumer juries

A 'jury' of consumers, representative of the target market, is asked to judge which of a series of paste-ups and rough ideas would be their choice of a final advertisement. They are asked to rank in order of merit and provide reasons for their selections.

There are difficulties associated with ranking and prioritisation tests. First, the consumers, realising the reason for their participation, may appoint themselves as 'experts', so they lose the objectivity that this process is intended to bring. Second, the 'halo' effect can occur, whereby an advertisement is rated excellent overall simply because one or two elements are good and the respondent overlooks the weaknesses. Finally, emotional advertisements tend to receive higher scores than informational messages, even though the latter might do better in the market-place.

Pre-testing finished advertisements

When an advertisement is finished it can be subjected to a number of other tests before being released.

Dummy vehicles

Many of the pre-testing methods occur in an artificial environment such as a theatre, laboratory or meeting room. One way of testing so that the reader's natural environment is used is to produce a dummy or pretend magazine that can be consumed at home, work or wherever readers normally read magazines. Dummy magazines contain regular editorial matter with test advertisements inserted next to control advertisements. These pretend magazines are distributed to a random sample of households, who are asked to consume the magazine in their normal way. Readers are encouraged to observe the editorial and at a later date they are asked questions about both the editorial and the advertisements.

Dummy vehicle: Flora

A test Flora advertisement comprising a central figure of a gingerbread man with copy above and below was inserted in *Woman* magazine and distributed on a complimentary basis to 150 housewives. Readers were asked to read the magazine in their normal manner over the course of a week, and they were not told what the purpose of the exercise was.

Three objectives were determined for the exercise :

- The impact and branding of the advertisement.
- The level of comprehension.
- The generation of empathy toward the brand.

Results indicated that the gingerbread man provided a strong visual focus, which in turn generated empathy towards the brand. The copy line was also liked and read by an above average number of people.

However, by utilising the results the size of the visual was increased and toned while the typestyle for the copyline was softened. The amount of copy was reduced and the Flora logo was repositioned for greater exit impact.

Adapted from Colinese (1997)

The main advantage of using dummy vehicles is that the setting is natural, but, as with the focus group, the main disadvantage is that respondents are aware that they are part of a test and may respond unnaturally. Research also suggests that recall may not be the best measure for low-involvement decisions or where motivation occurs through the peripheral route of the ELM. If awareness is required at the point of sale, then recognition may be a more reliable indicator of effectiveness than recall.

Readability tests

Rudolph Flesch (1974) developed a formula to assess the ease with which print copy could be read. The test involves, among other things, determining the average number of syllables per 100 words of copy, the average length of sentence and the percentage of personal words and sentences. By accounting for the educational level of the target audience and by comparing results with established norms, the tests suggest that comprehension is best when sentences are short, words are concrete and familiar, and personal references are used frequently.

Theatre tests

As a way of testing finished broadcast advertisements, target consumers are invited to a theatre (laboratory or hall) to preview television programmes. Before the programme commences, details regarding the respondents' demographic and attitudinal details are recorded and they are asked to nominate their product preferences from a list. At the end of the viewing their evaluation of the programme is sought and they are also requested to complete their product preferences a second time.

There are a number of variations on this theme: one is to telephone the respondents a few days after the viewing to measure recall and another is to provide joysticks, push buttons and pressure pads to measure reactions throughout the viewing. The main outcome of this process is a measure of the degree to which product preferences change as a result of exposure to the controlled viewing. This change is referred to as the *persuasion shift*. This approach provides for a quantitative dimension to be added to the testing process, as the scores recorded by respondents can be used to measure the effectiveness of advertisements and provide benchmarks for future testing.

It is argued that this form of testing is too artificial and that the measure of persuasion shift is too simple and unrealistic. Furthermore, some believe that many respondents know what is happening and make changes because it is expected of them in the role of respondent. Those in favour of theatre testing state that the control is sound, that the value of established norms negates any 'role play' by respondents and that the actual sales data support the findings of the brand persuasion changes in the theatre.

A major evaluation of 400 individual advertising tests in the USA found, among many other things, that there is no clear relationship between measures of persuasion shift and eventual sales performance. This questions the use of an organisation's scarce resources and the viability of using these techniques (Lodish and Lubetkin, 1992).

This technique is used a great deal in the USA but has had limited use in the UK, until recently. However, Mazur (1993) reports that theatre testing is increasing in the UK. Agencies are concerned that the simplistic nature of recording scores as a means of testing advertisements ignores the complex imagery and emotional aspects of many messages. If likeability is an important aspect of eventual brand success, then it is unlikely that the quantitative approach to pre-testing will contribute any worthwhile information.

The increasing use of, or at least interest in, theatre tests and the movement towards greater utilisation of quantitative techniques in pre-testing procedures, runs concurrently with the increasing requirements of accountability, short-termism and periods of economic downturn. As no one method will ever be sufficient, a mix of qualitative and quantitative pre-test measures will, inevitably, always be required.

Physiological measures

A bank of physiological tests has been developed, partly as a response to advertisers' increasing interest in the emotional impact of advertising messages and partly because many other tests rely on the respondents' ability to interpret their reactions. Physiological tests have been designed to measure the involuntary responses to stimuli and so avoid the bias inherent in the other tests. There are substantial costs involved with the use of these techniques, and the validity of the results is questionable. Consequently, they are not used a great deal in practice, but, of them all, eye tracking is the most used and most reliable.

Pupil dilation

Pupil dilation tests are designed to measure the respondent's reaction to a stimulus. Pupil dilation is associated with action and interest. If the pupil is constricted then interest levels are low and energy is conserved. The level of arousal is used to determine the degree of interest and preference in a particular advertisement or package design.

On the surface, this method has a number of attractions, but it is not used very much as research has shown little evidence of success. The costs are high and the low number of respondents that can be processed limits the overall effectiveness.

Eye tracking

This technique requires the use of eye movement cameras which fire an infrared beam to track the movement of the eye as it scans an advertisement. The sequence in which the advertisement is read can be determined and particular areas which do or do not attract attention can be located; the layout of the advertisement can then be adjusted as necessary.

Galvanic skin response

This measures the resistance the skin offers to a small amount of current passed between two electrodes. Response to a stimulus will activate the sweat glands, which in turn will increase the resistance. Therefore, the greater the level of tension induced by an advertisement, the more effective it is as a form of communication.

This simple premise is, however, misguided, as the range of reactions and emotions, the degree of learning and recall, and aspects of preference and motivation are ignored. When these deficiencies are combined with the high costs and low numbers of respondents that can be processed, it is not surprising that this method of pre-testing can have little but novelty value.

Tachistoscopes

These measure the ability of an advertisement to attract attention. The speed at which an advertisement is flashed in front of a respondent is gradually slowed down until a point (about 1/100th second) is reached at which the respondent is able to identify components of the message. This can be used to identify those elements that respondents see first as a picture is exposed, and so facilitates the creation of impact-based messages.

Electroencephalographs (EEG)

This approach involves the use of a scanner which monitors the electrical frequencies of the brain. There are essentially two ways of utilising this approach (Hansen, 1988). The first, hemispheric lateralisation, concerns the ability of the left-hand side of the brain to process rational, logical information. It tends to process verbal stimuli. In contrast, the right-hand side of the brain is thought to handle visual stimuli and respond more to emotional inputs. The right is best for recognition, the left is better for recall. Advertisements should be designed to appeal to each hemisphere, but recent research now appears to reject this once-popular notion.

The second approach involves measuring levels of brain activation. It is possible to measure the level of alpha wave activity, which indicates the degree to which the respondent is aroused and interested in a stimulus. Therefore, the lower the level of alpha activity, the greater the level of attention and cognitive processing. It would follow, therefore, that by measuring the alpha waves while a respondent is exposed to different advertisements, different levels of attention can be determined.

Both these approaches have been heavily criticised; indeed, the hemispheric lateralisation theory is rejected by many researchers. Vaughn (1980) based part of his advertising planning grid (Chapter 25) on this theory, and it was regarded as an important breakthrough in our understanding of how advertising works. However, while the grid has been used extensively, there is little evidence of any commercial application.

Post-testing

Testing advertisements that have been released is generally more time-consuming and involves greater expense than pre-testing. However, the big advantage with post-testing is that advertisements are evaluated in their proper environment, or at least the environment in which they are intended to be successful.

There are a number of methods used to evaluate the effectiveness of such advertisements, and of these inquiry, recall, recognition and sales-based tests predominate.

Inquiry tests

These tests are designed to measure the number of inquiries or direct responses stimulated by advertisements. Inquiries can take the form of returned coupons and response cards, requests for further literature or actual orders. They were originally used to test print messages, but some television advertisements now carry 0800 (free) telephone numbers. An increase in the use of direct response media will lead to an increase in the sales and leads generated by inquiry-stimulating messages, so this type of testing will become more prevalent.

Inquiry tests can be used to test single advertisements or a campaign in which responses are accumulated. Using a split run, an advertiser can use two different advertisements and run them in the same print vehicle. This allows measurement of the attention-getting properties of alternative messages. If identical messages are run in different media then the effect of the media vehicles can be tested.

Care needs to be given to the interpretation of inquiry-based tests, as they may be misleading. An advertisement may not be effective simply because of the responses received. For example, people may respond because they have a strong need for the offering rather than the response being a reflection of the qualities of the advertisement. Likewise, other people may not respond despite the strong qualities of the advertisement, simply because they lack time, resources or need at that particular moment.

Recall tests

Recall tests are designed to assess the impression that particular advertisements have made on the memory of the target audience. Interviewers, therefore, do not use a copy of the advertisement as a stimulus, as the tests are intended to measure impressions and perception, not behaviour, opinions, attitudes or the advertising effect.

Normally, recall tests require the cooperation of several hundred respondents, all of whom were exposed to the advertisement. They are interviewed the day after an advertisement is screened; hence the reference to day-after-recall tests (DAR). Once qualified by the interviewer, respondents are first asked if they remember a commercial for, say, air travel. If the respondent replies 'yes, Virgin', then this is recorded as *unaided recall* and is regarded as a strong measure of memory. If the respondent says 'no', the interviewer might ask the question 'did you see an advertisement for British Airways?' A positive answer to this prompt is recorded as *aided recall*.

These answers are then followed by questions such as 'What did the advertisement say about British Airways?', 'What did the commercial look like?' and 'What did it remind you of?'. All the answers provided to this third group of questions are written down word for word and recorded as *verbatim* responses.

The reliability of recall scores is generally high. This means that each time the advertisement is tested, the same score is generated. Validity refers to the relationship or correlation between recall and the sales that ultimately result from an audience exposed to a particular advertisement. The validity of recall tests is generally regarded by researchers as low (Gordon, 1992).

Recall tests have a number of other difficulties associated with them. First, they can be expensive, as a lot of resources can be consumed by looking for and qualifying respondents. Second, not only is interviewing time expensive, but the score may be rejected if, on examination of the verbatim responses, it appears that the respondent was guessing.

It has been suggested by Zielske (1982) that thinking/rational messages appear to be easier to recall than emotional/feeling ones. Therefore, it seems reasonable to assume that recall scores for emotional/feeling advertisements may be lower. It is possible that programme content may influence the memory and lead to different recall scores for the same offering. The use of a preselected group of respondents may reduce the costs associated with finding a qualified group, but they may increase their attention towards the commercials in the knowledge that they will be tested the following day. This will inevitably lead to higher levels of recall than actually exist.

On-the-air tests are a derivative of recall and theatre tests. By using advertisements that are run live in a test area, it is possible to measure the impact of these test advertisements with DAR. As recall tests reflect the degree of attention and interest in the advertisement, this is a way of controlling and predicting the outcome of a campaign when it is rolled out nationally.

Recall tests are used a great deal, even though their validity is low and their costs are high. Wells *et al.* (1992) argue that this is because recall scores provide an acceptable means by which decisions to invest heavily in advertising programmes can be made. Agencies accumulate vast amounts of recall data which can be used as benchmarks to judge whether an advertisement generated a score that was better or less than the average for the product class or brand. Having said that, and despite their popularity, they are adjudged to be poor predictors of sales (Lodish and Lubetkin, 1992).

Recognition tests

Recall tests are based upon the memory and the ability of respondents to reprocess information about an advertisement. A different way of determining advertising effectiveness is to ask respondents if they recognise an advertisement. This is the most common of the post-testing procedures for print advertisements. Of the many services available, perhaps the Starch Readership Report is the best known.

Recognition tests are normally conducted in the homes of approximately 200 respondents. Having agreed that the respondent has previously seen a copy of the magazine, it is opened at a predetermined page and the respondent is asked, for each advertisement, 'Did you see or read any part of the advertisement?' If the answer is yes, the respondent is asked to indicate exactly which parts of the copy or layout were seen or read.

Four principal readership scores are reported. The first is *noted*, that is the percentage of readers who remember seeing the advertisement. Second is *seen-associated*, the percentage of readers who recall seeing or reading any part of the advertisement identifying the offering. Third is *read most*, the percentage of readers who report reading at least 50% of the advertisement. Finally, signature is the percentage of readers who remember seeing the brand name or logo.

The reliability of recognition tests is very high, higher than recall scores. Costs are lower, mainly because the questioning procedure is simpler and quicker. It is also possible to deconstruct an advertisement into its component parts and assess their individual effects on the reader. As with all interviewer-based research, bias is inevitable. Bias can also be introduced by the respondent or the research organisation through the instructions given or through fatigue of the interviewer.

The validity of recognition test scores is said to be high, especially after a number of insertions. However, there can be a problem of false claiming, where readers claim to have seen an advertisement but in fact have not. This, it is suggested, is because when readers confirm they have seen an advertisement, the underlying message is that they approve of and like that sort of advertisement. If they say that they have not seen an advertisement, the underlying message is that they do not usually look at that sort of advertisement. Krugman (1988), as reported by Wells *et al.* (1992) makes the important point that these readers are passing a 'consumer vote on whether the advertisement is worth more than a passing glance'. It might be that readers' memories are a reliable indicator of what the reader finds attractive in an advertisement and this could be a surrogate indicator for a level of likeability. This proposition has yet to be fully investigated, but it may be that the popularity of the recognition test is based on the validity rating and the approval that high scores give to advertisers.

Sales tests

If the effectiveness of advertisements could be measured by the level of sales that occurs during and after a campaign, then the usefulness of measuring sales as a testing procedure would not be in doubt. However, the practical difficulties associated with market tests are so large that these tests have little purpose. Only direct response counts and inquiry tests have any validity.

Practitioners have been reluctant to use market-based tests because not only are they expensive to conduct but they are also historical by definition. Sales occur partly as a consequence of past actions, including past communication strategies, and the costs (production, agency and media) have already been sunk. There may be occasions where it makes little political and career sense to investigate an event unless it has been a success, or at the very least reached minimal acceptable expectations.

For these reasons and others, advertisers have used test markets to gauge the impact their campaigns have on representative samples of the national market.

Simulated market tests

By using control groups of matched consumers in particular geographic areas, the use of simulated test markets permits the effect of advertising on sales to be observed under controlled market conditions. These conditions are more realistic than those conducted within a theatre setting and are more representative of the national market than the limited in-house tests. This market representation is thought by some to provide an adequate measure of advertising effect. Other commentators, as discussed before, believe that unless advertising is the dominant element in the marketing mix, there are usually too many other factors which can affect sales. It is therefore unfair and unrealistic to place the sole responsibility for sales with advertising.

Single-source data

With the development and advances of technology it is now possible to correlate consumer purchases with the advertisements they have been exposed to. This is known as single-source data and involves the controlled transmission of advertisements to particular households whose every purchase is monitored through a scanner at supermarket checkouts. In other words, all the research data are derived from the same households.

The advent of cable television has facilitated this process. Consumers along one side of a street receive one set of control advertisements, while the others on the other side receive test advertisements. Single-source data provide exceptionally dependable results, but the technique is expensive, is inappropriate for testing single advertisements and tends to focus on the short-term effect, failing, for example, to cope with the concept of adstock.

In the UK many independent broadcasters have set up their own research facilities. Central TV first set up Adlab in the mid-1980s. This involved a panel of 1,000 housewives, each recording their media consumption and where, when and what they purchased. HTV introduced ScatScan, which requires the use of two panels each of 1,000 housewives, either side of the Bristol Channel. It was designed to help advertisers assess their advertising effectiveness in terms of copy testing, weight testing and even the use of mixed media. The use of split regions is very important, allowing comparisons to made of different strategies.

Other tests

There is a range of other measures that have been developed in an attempt to understand the effect of advertisements. Among these are tracking studies and financial analyses.

Tracking studies

A tracking study involves interviewing a large number of people on a regular basis, weekly or monthly, with the purpose of collecting data about buyers' perceptions of the advertisements and how these advertisements might be affecting the buyers' perceptions of the brand. By measuring and evaluating the impact of an advertising campaign when it is running, adjustments can be made quickly. The most common elements that are monitored, or tracked, are the awareness levels of an advertisement and the brand; image ratings of the brand and the focus organisation; and attributes and preferences.

Tracking studies can be undertaken on a periodic or continuous basis. The latter is more expensive, but the information generated is more complete and absorbs the effect of competitor's actions, even if the effects are difficult to disaggregate. Sherwood *et al.* (1989) report that, in a general sense, continuous tracking appears more appropriate for new products and periodic tracking more appropriate for established products.

A further form of tracking study involves monitoring the stock held by retailers. Counts are usually undertaken each month, on a pre- and post-exposure basis. This method of measuring sales is used frequently. Audited sales data, market share figures and return on investment (ROI) provide other measures of advertising effectiveness.

Financial analysis

The vast amount of resources that is directed at planned communications, and in particular advertising, requires that the organisation reviews, on a periodic basis, the amount and the manner in which its financial resources have been used. For some organisations the media spend alone constitutes one of the major items of expenditure. Pedigree Petfoods, according to Hazelhurst (1988), has three main areas of expenditure, other than staffing costs. These are the cans, the raw materials that go in them and the media spend to communicate the values of the brand. He regards it as imperative that the media spend be reviewed in just the same way as any other major item is bought on a forward basis, such as the cans, capital equipment or foreign exchange.

Variance analysis enables a continuous picture of the spend to be developed and acts as an early warning system should unexpected levels of expenditure be incurred. In addition to this and other standard financial controls, the size of the discount obtained from media buying is becoming an important and vital part of the evaluation process.

Increasing levels of accountability and rapidly rising media costs have contributed to the development of centralised media buying. Under this arrangement, the promotion of an organisation's entire portfolio of brands, across all divisions, is contracted to a single media-buying organisation. Part of the reasoning is that the larger the account the greater the buying power an agency has, and this in turn should lead to greater discounts and value of advertising spend. For example, the high street retailer Boots has six major divisions, excluding Do It All, and each has traditionally been responsible for its own media spend (Izatt, 1993). In 1993 it was decided to centralise the buying under one media-buying centre. The deal, won by BMP DDB Needham, was reported to be worth £45 million a year and is intended to bring advertising economies of scale.

The point is that advertising economies of scale can be obtained by those organisations who spend a large amount of their resources on the media. To accommodate this, centralised buying has developed, which in turn creates higher entry and exit barriers, not only to and from the market but also from individual agencies.

Likeability

A major research study by the American Research Foundation (ARF) investigated a range of different pre-testing methods with the objective of determining which were best at predicting sales success. The unexpected outcome was that, of all the measures and tests, the most powerful predictor was likeability: 'how much I liked the advertisement'.

From a research perspective much work has been undertaken to clarify the term 'likeability', but it certainly cannot be measured in terms of a simple Likert scale of 'I liked the advertisement a lot', 'I liked the advertisement a little' etc. The term has a much deeper meaning and is concerned with the following issues (Gordon, 1992):

1. Personally meaningful, relevant, informative, true to life, believable, convincing.
2. Relevant, credible, clear product advantages, product usefulness, importance to 'me'.
3. Stimulates interest or curiosity about the brand; creates warm feelings through enjoyment of the advertisement.

The implication of these results is that post-testing should include a strong measure of how well an advertisement was liked at its deepest level of meaning.

Cognitive response analysis is an attempt to understand the internal dynamics of how an individual selects and processes messages, of how counter-arguing and message bolstering, for example, might be used to retain or reject an advertisement (see Chapter 14). Biel (1993) reports that there is a growing body of research evidence that links behaviour, attitude change and cognitive processing. He goes on to say that this approach, unlike many of the others, is not restricted to FMCG markets and can be deployed across service markets, durables and retailers.

One of the important points to be made from this understanding of likeability is the linkage with the concept of 'significant value' considered in Chapter 13. The degree to which advertising works is a measure of the impact a message makes with a buyer. This impact is mediated by the context in which messages are sent, received and personally managed. The main factors are that the product in question should be new or substantially different, interesting and stimulating, and personally significant. For advertising to be successful it must be effective, and to be effective it should be of personally significant value to members of the target audience (those in the market to buy a product from the category in the near future).

Summary

The evaluation of a marketing communications plan, once implemented, is an essential part of the total system. The evaluation provides a potentially rich source of material for the next campaign and the ongoing communications that all organisations operate, either intentionally or not.

The achievement of advertising objectives can only be realistically measured if the target audience is tested before and after exposure, in order that a degree of change can be determined. Such pre- and post-testing is, however, not without its problems. Is the sample random? Are the people being measured at post-test stage the same ones measured at the pre-test stage? If they are not, is the post-stage sample matched directly with the pre-test group?

There are potentially many problems with pre- and post-tests, and one way of coping with them is to control all the variables except the advertising. To achieve this, a control group and a test group are required and tests conducted so that the advertising effect can be theoretically isolated.

There are many issues involved with the assessment of advertising. There is no perfect or ideal technique, but research must be undertaken if the communication performance of an offering is to be built or maintained. An important question is why so many managers choose not to measure effectiveness. The immediate answer is that all managers do measure the effectiveness as demonstrated through their observation of the sales results at the end of each period. However, proper testing and analysis is a practice rejected for many reasons. Some of the more prevalent ones are that research uses resources which some managers would prefer to sink into the product or to building market awareness.

There can be disagreement about what is to be researched on the grounds that the many different people associated with a campaign have different needs, and as the budget is restricted the net result is that there is no research. Others argue that as it is very difficult, if not impossible, to isolate the effects of advertising, why waste resources on testing?

All these points can and should be refuted. Only by attempting to measure effectiveness will our understanding of advertising improve and lead to a more effective utilisation and more efficient use of the communication tool. Sales measurement is used most commonly because it is relatively cheap to administer and quick to implement, and to many managers sales and profits are derived from advertising, so this constitutes the only meaningful measure.

Pre- and post-testing should use a range of techniques, both qualitative and quantitative. Focus groups, concept tests, hall tests and recognition tests together with cognitive response analysis and a measure of likeability would be the ideal mixture, should time and financial resources permit.

Review questions

1. If the process is difficult and the outcomes imprecise, why should organisations evaluate and monitor their marketing communications?
2. What is pre- and post-testing?
3. What methods are used to pre-test advertisements and why are they regarded as important?
4. Explain how theatre tests work and comment on their usefulness.
5. Appraise the use of physiological tests.
6. Write a brief report comparing recall and recognition tests.
7. Suggest reasons why tracking is important. Which variables are normally monitored?
8. What are the principal dimensions of likeability as a measure of advertising effectiveness?
9. Many organisations fail to undertake suitable research to measure the success of their advertisements. Why is this and what can be done to change this situation?
10. Comment on the view that if a method of evaluation and testing lacks objectivity and testing, then the method should not be used.

References

Biel, A.L. (1993) Ad research in the US. *Admap* (May), 27–9.
Colinese, R. (1997) Pretesting in the press. *Admap* (June), 53–5.
Flesch, R. (1974) *The Art of Readable Writing*. New York: Harper & Row.
Gordon, W. (1992) Ad pre-testing's hidden maps. *Admap* (June), 23–7.
Hansen, F. (1988) Hemispheric lateralization: implications for understanding consumer behaviour. *Journal of Consumer Research*, **8**, 23–36.
Hazelhurst, L. (1988) How Pedigree Petfoods evaluate their advertising spend. *Admap* (June), 29–31.
Izatt, J. (1993) Swayed Boots. *Media Week*, 1 October, pp. 20-1.
Krugman, H.E. (1988) Point of view: limits of attention to advertising. *Journal of Advertising Research*, **38**, 47–50.
Lodish, L.M. and Lubetkin, B. (1992) General truths? *Admap* (February), 9–15.
Mazur, L. (1993) Qualified for success? *Marketing*, 23 January, pp. 20–2.
Sherwood, P.K., Stevens, R.E. and Warren, W.E. (1989) Periodic or continuous tracking studies: matching methodology with objectives. *Market Intelligence and Planning*, **7**, 11–13.
Staverley, N.T. (1993) Is it right ... will it work? *Admap* (May), 23–6.
Vaughn, R. (1980) How advertising works: a planning model. *Journal of Advertising Research* (October), 27–33.
Wells, W., Burnet, J. and Moriarty, S. (1992) *Advertising: Principles and Practice*, 2nd edn. Englewood Cliffs, NJ: Prentice Hall.
Zielske, H.A. (1982) Does day-after recall penalise 'feeling' ads? *Journal of Advertising Research*, **22**(1), 19–22.

chapter 18

Sales promotion

Sales promotion seeks to offer buyers additional value as an inducement to generate an immediate sale. These inducements can be targeted at consumers, distributors, agents and members of the sales force.

AIMS AND OBJECTIVES

The aim of this chapter is to consider the nature and role of sales promotion and to appraise its position within the marketing communications mix.

The objectives of this chapter are:

1. To explain the role of sales promotion in the promotional mix.
2. To discuss the reasons for the increased use of sales promotions.
3. To examine the way in which sales promotions are considered to work.
4. To appraise the value of this promotional tool.
5. To discuss the nature of loyalty programmes and issues associated with customer retention.
6. To appreciate how sales promotions can be used strategically.

Introduction

One of the main tasks of advertising is to develop awareness in the target audience. The main task of sales promotion is to encourage the target audience to behave in a particular way, usually to buy a product. These two tools set out to accomplish tasks at each end of the attitudinal spectrum: the cognitive and the conative elements. Just as advertising seeks to work over the long term, sales promotion can achieve short-term upward shifts in sales.

Table 18.1 Reasons for the use of sales promotions

- They are useful in securing trials for new products and in defending shelf space against anticipated and exisiting competition.
- The funds that manufacturers dedicate to them lower the distributor's risk in stocking new brands.
- They add excitement at the point-of-sale to the merchandising of mature and mundane products. They can instil a sense of urgency among consumers to buy while a deal is available.
- Since sales promotion costs are incurred on a pay-as-you-go basis, they can spell survival for smaller, regional brands that cannot afford big advertising programmes.
- Sales promotions allow manufacturers to use idle capacity and to adjust to demand and supply imbalances or softness in raw material prices and other input costs, while maintaining the same list prices.
- They allow manufacturers to price-discriminate among consumer segments that vary in price sensitivity. Most manufacturers believe that a high-list, high-deal policy is more profitable than offering a single price to all consumers. A portion of sales promotion expenditures, therefore, consists of reductions in list prices that are set for the least price-sensitive segment of the market.

Source: Buzzell *et al.* (1990).

Sales promotion seeks to offer buyers additional value, as an inducement to generate an immediate sale. These inducements can be targeted at consumers, distributors, agents and members of the sales force. A whole range of network members can benefit from the use of sales promotion.

This promotional tool is traditionally referred to as below-the-line expenditure, because, unlike advertising, there are no commission payments from media owners with this form of communication. The promotional costs are borne directly by the organisation initiating the activity, which in most cases is a manufacturer or producer. There are a number of reasons why sales promotions are used, and Buzzell *et al.* (1990) set out some of them; see Table 18.1.

There are many sales promotion techniques, but they all offer a direct inducement or an incentive to encourage receivers of the promotional messages to buy a product sooner rather than later. The inducement (for example, price-offs, coupons, premiums) is presented as an added value to the basic product and is intended to encourage buyers to act 'now' rather than later. Sales promotion is used, therefore, principally as a means to accelerate sales. The acceleration represents the shortened period of time in which the transaction is completed relative to the time that would have elapsed had there not been a promotion. This action does not mean that an extra sale has been achieved.

The role of sales promotion

Sales promotions can be targeted, with considerable precision, at particular audiences. There are three broad audiences to whom sales promotions can be targeted. These are consumers, members of the distribution or channel network, and the sales forces of both manufacturers and resellers. It should be remembered that the accuracy of these promotional tools means that many sub-groups within these broad groups can be reached quickly and accurately.

The role of sales promotion has changed significantly over recent years. At one time, the largest proportion of communications budgets was normally allocated to advertising. In many cases advertising no longer dominates the communication budget and sales promotion has assumed the focus of the communications spend, for reasons that are described below. This is particularly evident in consumer markets that are mature, reached a level of stagnation and where price and promotion work are the few ways of inducing brand switching behaviour.

Short-termism

The short-term financial focus of many industrialised economies has developed a managerial climate geared to short-term performance and evaluation, over periods as short as 12 weeks. To accomplish this, communication tools are required that work quickly and directly impact upon sales. Many see this as leading to an erosion of the brand franchise.

Managerial accountability

Following on from the previous reason is the increased pressure upon marketing managers to be accountable for their communications expenditure. The results of sales promotion activities are more easily justified and understood than those associated with advertising. The number of coupons returned for redemption and the number of bonus packs purchased can be calculated quickly and easily, with little room for error or misjudgement. Advertising, however, cannot be so easily measured either in the short or long term. The impact of this is that managers can relate the promotional expenditure to the bottom line much more comfortably with sales promotion than with advertising.

Brand performance

Technological advances have enabled retailers to track brand performance more effectively. This in turn means that manufacturers can be drawn into agreements that promulgate in-store promotional activity at the expense of other more traditional forms of mass media promotion. Barcode scanners, hand-held electronic shelf-checking equipment and computerised stock systems facilitate the tracking of merchandise. This means that brand managers can be held responsible much more quickly for below-par performance.

Brand expansion

As brand quality continues to improve and as brands proliferate on the shelves of increasingly larger supermarkets, so the number of decisions that a consumer has to make also increases. Faced with multiple-brand decisions and a reduced amount of time to complete the shopping expedition, the tension associated with the shopping experience has increased considerably over the last decade.

Promotions make decision-making easier for consumers: they simplify a potentially difficult process. So, as brand choice increases, the level of shopping convenience falls. The conflict this causes can be resolved by the astute use of sales promotions. Some feel that the cognitive shopper selects brands that offer increased value, which makes decision-making easier and improves the level of convenience associated with the shopping experience. However, should there be promotions on two offerings from an individual's repertoire then the decision-making is not necessarily made easier.

Competition for shelf space

The continuing growth in the number of brands launched in the 1980s and 1990s and the fragmentation of consumer markets mean that retailers have to be encouraged to make shelf space available. Sales promotions help manufacturers win valuable shelf space and assist retailers to attract increased levels of store traffic and higher utilisation of limited resources.

The credibility of this promotional tool is low, as it is obvious to the receiver what the intention is of using sales promotion messages. However, because of the prominent and pervasive nature of the tool, consumers and members of the trade understand and largely accept the direct sales approach. Sales promotion is not a tool that hides its intentions, nor does it attempt to be devious (which is not allowed, by regulation).

The absolute costs of sales promotion are low, but the real costs need to be evaluated once a campaign has finished and all redemptions received and satisfied. The relative costs can be high, as not only do the costs of the premium or price discount need to be determined, but also the associated costs of additional transportation, lost profit, storage and additional time spent organising and administering a sales promotion campaign need to be accounted for.

In its favour, sales promotion allows for a high degree of control. Management is able to decide just when and where a sales promotion will occur and also estimate the sales effect. Sales promotions can be turned on and off quickly and adjusted to changed market conditions. The intended message is invariably the one that is received, as there is relatively little scope for it to be corrupted or damaged in transmission.

Sales promotion plans: the objectives

The objectives of using this tool are sales-orientated and are geared to stimulating buyers either to use a product for the first time or to encourage use on a routine basis.

The main objective of sales promotion activity is to prompt buyers into action, to initiate a series of behaviours that result in long-run purchase activity. These actions can be seen to occur in the conative stage of the attitudinal set. They reflect high or low involvement, and indicate whether cognitive processing and persuasion occur via the central or peripheral routes of the ELM (Chapter 13). If the marketing objectives include the introduction of a new product or intention to enter a new market, then the key objective associated with low-involvement decisions and peripheral route processing is to stimulate trial use as soon as possible. When high-involvement decisions and central route processing are present, then sales promotions need to be withheld until a suitable level of attitudinal development has been undertaken by public relations and advertising activities.

If a product is established in a market, then a key objective should be to use sales promotions to stimulate an increase in the number of purchases made by current customers and to attract users from competing products (Figure 18.1). The objec-

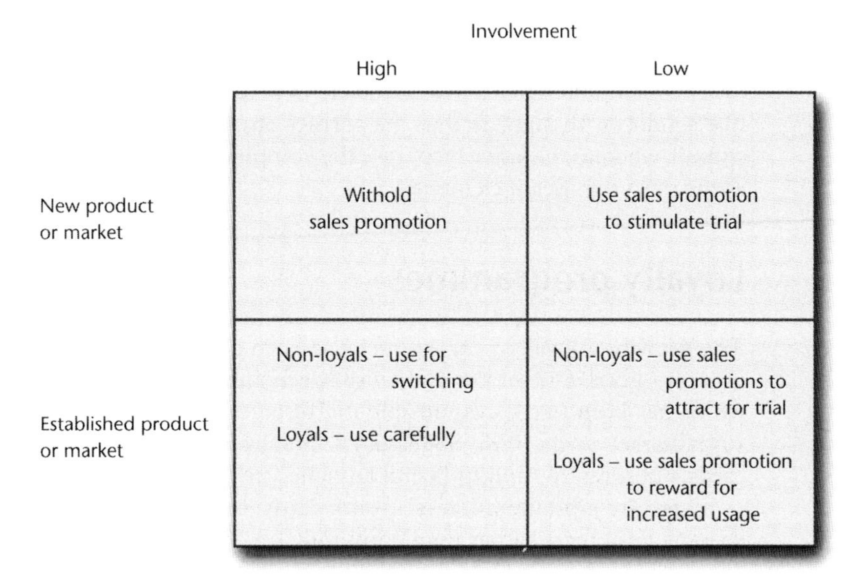

Figure 18.1 A sales promotion objectives grid.

tives, therefore, are either to increase consumption for established products or to stimulate trial by encouraging new buyers to use a product. Once this has been agreed then the desired trial and usage levels need to be determined for each of the target audiences. Before discussing these aspects, it is necessary first to review the manner in which sales promotions are thought to influence the behaviour of individuals.

An overview of how sales promotions work

If the overriding objectives of sales promotions are to accelerate or bring forward future sales, the implication is that a behavioural change is required by the receiver for the sales promotion to be effective. The establishment of new behaviour patterns is the preferred outcome. If sales promotions are to work over the longer term, that is to bring about repeat purchase behaviour, then the new behaviour patterns need to be learned and adopted on a permanent basis.

This is a complex task, and is referred to by behaviourists as shaping. The behaviourist's view is advocated, for example, by Rothschild and Gaidis (1981). They suggest that by breaking the overall task into its constituent parts, a series of smaller sequential tasks can be learned. When the successive actions are aggregated, the new desired pattern of behaviour emerges. This view emphasises the impact of external stimuli in changing the behaviour of people.

The cognitive view of the way sales promotions operate is based on the belief that consumers internally process relevant information about a sales promotion, including those of past experiences, and make a reasoned decision in the light of the goals and objectives that individuals set for themselves.

The ELM suggests that individuals using the peripheral route will only consider simplistic cues, such as display boards and price reduction signs, for example. Individuals using the central route of the ELM have a higher need for information and will develop the promotional signal to evaluate the relative price and the salient attributes of the promoted product before making a decision (Inman *et al.*, 1990).

The main difference between the views of the behaviourists and those of the cognitive school of thought is that the former stress the impact of externally generated stimuli, whereas the latter recognise the complexity of internal information processing as the most significant element.

Loyalty programmes

The growth of loyalty programmes has been a significant promotional development in recent years. One of the more visible schemes was the ClubCard offered by Tesco, which has been partly responsible for Tesco ousting Sainsbury's as the number one supermarket in the UK. Sainsbury's initial response was to publicly reject loyalty cards, but some 18 months later it launched its Reward Card.

There are a proliferation of loyalty cards, reflecting the increased emphasis upon keeping customers rather than constantly finding new ones. Whether loyalty is being developed by encouraging buyers to make repeat purchases or whether the schemes are merely sales promotion techniques that encourage extended and consistent purchasing patterns is a point that needs to be made. Customer retention is a major issue and a lot of emphasis has been given to loyalty schemes as a means of achieving retention targets.

Loyalty at one level can be seen to be about increasing sales volume; that is, fostering loyal purchase behaviour. High levels of repeat purchase, however, are not necessarily an adequate measure of loyalty, as there may be a number of situational factors determining purchase behaviour, such as brand availability (Dick and Basu, 1994).

At another level loyalty can be regarded as an attitudinal disposition. O'Malley (1998) suggests that customer satisfaction has become a surrogate measure of loyalty. However, she points out that there is plenty of evidence to show that many satisfied customers buy a variety of brands and that polygamous loyalty, as suggested by Dowling and Uncles (1997), may be a better reflection of reality.

At whichever level of loyalty, customer retention is paramount and neither behavioural nor attitudinal measures alone are adequate indicators of true loyalty. O'Malley suggests that a combination of the two is of greater use and that the twin parameters relative attitudes (to alternatives) and patronage behaviour (the recency, frequency and monetary model), as suggested by Dick and Basu, when used together offer more accurate indicators of loyalty.

The need to develop suitable attitudes and behaviours lies at the heart of loyalty programmes. It is about the provision and use of information, skilful segmentation and the development of appropriate relationships . The Cesar dog food example goes some way to illustrate this point.

Cesar dog food

Cesar dog food is a tinned food aimed at small dogs. The task facing brand management was not just to create more sales volume but to increase the purchases being made by those who were established buyers. Research revealed that pet owners regarded Cesar as a stock cupboard food to be used on those occasions that they ran out of fresh food for their pets.

In order to change this attitude it was necessary to present the product, through communications, as a mainstream brand for small dogs. To assist this, part of the communication programme included an on-pack promotion encouraging buyers to write in for a free sample, thus gaining access to their names and addresses.

Adapted from Miles (1996)

Key motivations for loyal behaviour

The concept of loyalty has attracted much research attention if only because of the recent and current popularity of this approach. Table 18.2 represents some of the more general types of loyalty that can be observed.

Loyalty schemes have been encouraged through the use of swipe cards. Users are rewarded with points each time a purchase is made. This is referred to as a 'points accrual programme', whereby loyal users are able to build up the necessary points, which are stored (often) on a card, and 'cashed in' at a later date for gifts or merchandise. The benefit for the company supporting the scheme is that the promised rewards motivate customers to accrue more points and in doing so increase their switching costs, effectively locking them into the loyalty programme and preventing them from moving to a competitor brand.

The Argos Premier Points scheme with Mobil has resulted in the issue of more than 20 million cards. Cardholders under Premier Points are not identified, as Argos claims that it is not cost-effective to track individual customers.

Recent technological developments mean that smart cards (a card that has a small microprocessor attached) can record enormous amounts of information, which is updated each time a purchase is made.

Loyalty schemes for frequent flyers (e.g. BA Executive Club and Virgin Freeway) have not only been very successful, but the cards are also used to track individual travellers. Airlines are able to offer cardholders particular services, such as special airport lounges and magazines; the card through its links to a database also enables a trav-

Table 18.2 Types of loyalty

Emotional loyalty	This is a true form of loyalty and is driven by personal identification with real or perceived values and benefits.
Price loyalty	This type of loyalty is driven by rational economic behaviour and the main motivations are cautious management of money or financial necessity.
Incentivised loyalty	This refers to promiscuous buyers: those with no one favourite brand who demonstrate through repeat experience the value of becoming loyal.
Monopoly loyalty	This class of loyalty arises where a consumer has no purchase choice due to a national monopoly. This, therefore, is not a true form of loyalty.
Inertia	This final form of loyalty arises when a buyer is disinclined to move between brands for whatever reason.

eller's favourite seat and dietary requirements to be offered. In addition, the regular accumulation of Air Miles fosters continuity and hence loyalty, through which business travellers reward themselves with leisure travel.

The potential number of applications for smart cards is tremendous. However, just like swipe cards the targeting of specific groups of buyers can be expected to become more precise and efficient and it is also easier to track and target individuals for future promotional activities.

The value of sales promotions

The increasing proportion of budgets being allocated to sales promotions has prompted concern about the costs and effects of these activities. It might be reasonable to expect that the sales curve following a sales promotion would look like that depicted in Figure 18.2. An upward shift in demand is, however, unrealistic, particularly in mature markets. Extra stock is being transferred to consumers, and therefore they have more than they require for a normal purchase cycle.

The graph shown in Figure 18.3 is more likely to occur, with sales falling in the period when consumers are loaded with stock and temporarily removed from the market. A third scenario is shown in Figure 18.4. Promotional activity does not take place in a vacuum with new products: competitors will be attracted and some customers lost to competitive offerings; in mature markets, non-loyals will take advantage of the sales promotion and then revert to competitors' sales promotions when they re-enter the market. The result is that overall demand for the product may be reduced due to the combined effects of competitive promotional activity.

Sales promotions incur a large number of hidden costs. It was stated earlier that the cost of a sales promotion is thought to be relatively low but, as Buzzell *et al.* (1990) and others have demonstrated, there are a host of other indirect costs that must be considered. Manufacturers, for example, use promotional deals to induce resellers to buy stock at a promotional price, in addition to their normal buying requirements. The additional stock is then held for resale at a later date, at regular retail prices. The

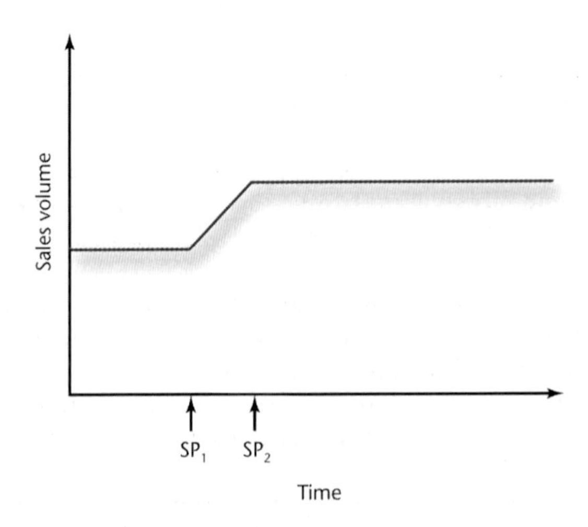

Figure 18.2 Anticipated response to a sales promotion event. SP_1 is the start of the event; SP_2 is the end.

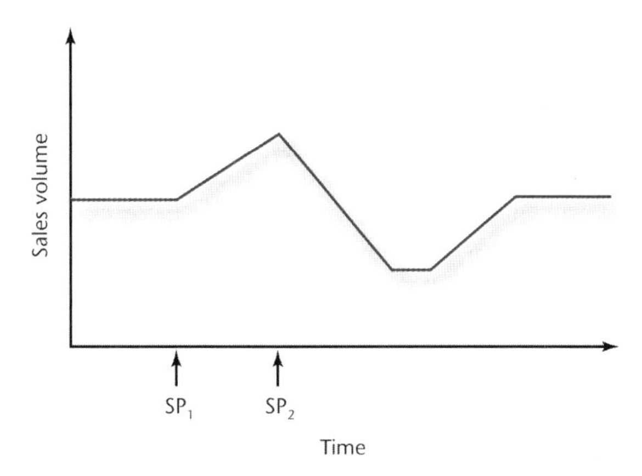

Figure 18.3 Realistic response to a sales promotion event. SP_1 is the start of the event; SP_2 is the end.

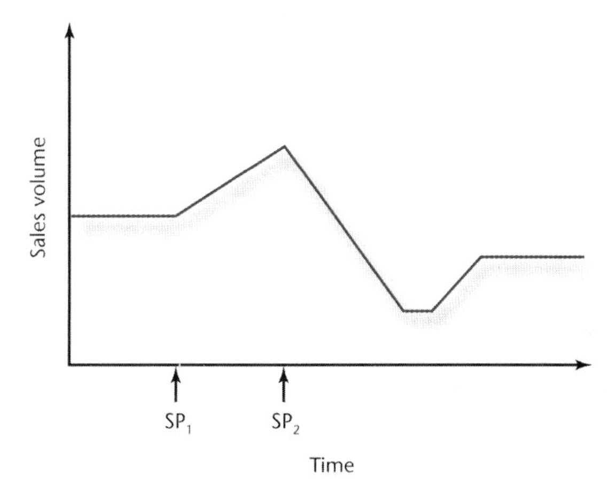

Figure 18.4 Destructive effect of competitive sales promotions.

effect of this forward buying on the costs of the reseller can be enormous. Buzzell *et al.* point out that the promotional stock attracts higher interest charges, storage costs, expenses associated with the transfer of stock to different geographical areas of the organisation and the costs associated with keeping normal and promotional stock separate. When these are added to the manufacturer's forward buying costs, it is probable, they conclude, that the costs outweigh the benefits of the sales promotion exercise.

These activities suggest that the relationship between the members of the network is market-orientated rather than relational. However, many of these extra costs are unknown, and the resellers are unaware of the costs they are absorbing as a result of the deal. In the future, resellers and manufacturers should work together on such promotions and attempt to uncover all the costs involved to ensure that the exercise is successful for both parties.

Not only the short-term costs associated with a sales promotion but also the long-term costs must be evaluated. Jones (1990) refers to this as the double jeopardy of sales promotions. He argues that manufacturers who participate extensively in short-term sales promotions, mainly for defensive reasons, do so at the expense of profit. The generation of sales volume and market share is at the expense of profit. The long-term effects are equally revealing. As the vast majority of sales promotions are temporary price reductions (TPRs), the opportunity to build a consumer franchise, where the objective is the development of brand identity and loyalty, is negated. Evidence shows that as soon as a sales promotion is switched off, so any increased sales are also terminated until the next promotion. The retaliatory effect that TPRs have on competitors does nothing to stabilise what Jones calls volatile demand, where the only outcome, for some products, is decline and obscurity.

Price war penalties

The major US producers of breakfast cereals entered a price war in April 1996. They cut prices by 20% and cut back on coupons and other sales promotions in an attempt to maintain market shares that were being eroded by own-label brands.

The price battle had little impact, as the total market for cereals fell 10% and all that the brand manufacturers achieved was a fall in profitability. When General Mills signalled the end with a price increase of 2.6% in July 1997, its share price rose significantly.

Adapted from Benezra (1997)

Sales promotions can lead consumers to depend upon the presence of a promotion before commitment to a purchase is made. If the preferred product does not carry a coupon, premium or TPR, then they may switch to a competitor's product that does offer some element of increased value. A related issue concerns the speed at which sales promotions are reduced following the introduction of a new product. If the incentives are removed too quickly, it is probable that consumers will have been unable to build a relationship with the product. If the incentives are sustained for too long, then it is possible that consumers have only identified a product by the value of the incentive, not the value of the product itself. The process by which a sales promotion is removed from a product is referred to as fading, and its rate can be crucial to the successful outcome of a product launch and a sales promotion activity.

The strategic use of sales promotions

Some writers (Davis, 1992; O'Malley, 1998) argue that sales promotions have a strategic role to play in the promotional mix. Traditionally they have been viewed as short-term tactical tools which can be used offensively to induce the trial of new products, or defensively for established products to retain shelf space and consumers. Sales promotions that do not work as intended may have been used to support inappropriate products (Rothschild, 1987) or may have been devised without adequate planning. An example of this latter issue may be the Hoover free flights misjudgement and the associated over-subscription that followed the launch of that particular sales promotion activity. There can be no doubt that sales promotions orientated to consumer deals and TPRs, in particular, do little to contribute to the overall strategy adopted for an organisation or even a product.

One of the consequences of competitive sales promotions, especially in consumer markets, is the spiral effect that retaliatory actions can have on each organisation. A sales promotion 'trap' develops when competitors start to imitate each other's activities, often based upon price reductions. This leads eventually to participants losing profitability and consumers losing value and possibly choice as some products are forced to drop out of the market.

The true strategic effect of sales promotion activities can only be achieved if they are coordinated with the other activities of the promotional mix, and this requires planning. In particular, the complementary nature of sales promotion and advertising should be exploited through the use of common themes and messages, timing, targeting and allocation of resources (in particular budgets). Sales promotions that are planned as a sequence of predetermined activities, reflecting the promotional requirements of a product over the longer term, are more likely to be successful than those sales promotions that are simply reactions to competitors' moves and market developments.

The strategic impact of sales promotions is best observed when they are designed or built into a three- to four-year plan of promotional activities, coordinated with other promotional tools and integrated with the business strategy.

Strategic promotions: Vauxhall

The advertisement reproduced in Exhibit 18.1 depicts a strategic sales promotion. The offer is a £2,000 voucher towards the purchase of another (or next) Vauxhall. With overcapacity in the car market, moving stock is important to generate cash flow and reduce working capital. By offering a large discount off the next purchase and tying the buyer into Vauxhall the strategic objective of retaining buyers and building relationships is assisted through the sales promotion device.

The manner in which many of the loyalty programmes are managed signals a move from pure sales promotion to direct marketing. The integration of these two approaches has become necessary in order that the advantages of both are realised. This does raise an interesting conflict, in that sales promotion is essentially a short-term tool, and direct marketing needs to work over the long term. The former is product-orientated (albeit giving added value to consumers) and often orientated to mass audiences, whereas the latter is based upon developing a personal dialogue (Curtis, 1996).

A further strategic issue concerns the use of joint promotions with other leading brands. Dixons, the high street electrical retailer, teamed with the cinema chain ABC. The cinema chain was being relaunched, aiming at the family market, and needed to build awareness and generate traffic. Dixons used free ABC cinema tickets to incentivise people to buy more expensive camcorders (Dwek, 1996). By twinning brand names increased promotional impact can assist both partners. However, there is a danger that such a pairing will be short-lived, and hence the strategic perspective may be limited.

IT'S ALL VERY WELL A PENSION COMPANY TELLING YOU TO PLAN FOR THE FUTURE. BUT A CAR MANUFACTURER?

£2000 off your next Vauxhall when you buy a new Vectra or Astra.

VAUXHALL'S NEW CAR 2 CAR OFFER IS PERFECT for anyone who wants a little nest egg for the future. Simply order a new Vectra or Astra between November 1 this year and February 28 1998 and we'll give you a £2000 voucher which you can use as payment towards your next new Vauxhall car.* But if you want real peace of mind, you should also take out one of the finance deals that accompany this offer. You'll get free personal accident cover; and what's more, if you then use one of our finance deals in conjunction with the voucher, we guarantee that you'll get the same interest rate as you did first time around. For further information, pester your local Vauxhall dealer for details or telephone 0345 400 800.

VAUXHALL

*PROVIDED YOU BUY YOUR NEXT CAR BETWEEN 1 AND 4 YEARS FROM THE DATE OF REGISTRATION OF YOUR FIRST CAR. CAR 2 CAR APPLIES TO PRIVATE INDIVIDUALS, NON REGISTERED BUSINESS, MOBILITY CUSTOMERS, VAUXHALL PARTNERS (EXCLUDING AUTUMN BOUNTY), FVR AND ELECT PROGRAMMES ONLY. SUBJECT TO STATUS, AVAILABILITY AND CONDITIONS. A GUARANTEE MAY BE REQUIRED.

Exhibit 18.1 Vauxhall Sales Promotion (*Source*: Daily Mail, 5 November 1997, p. 13).

together with the demographics and psychographic details compiled for panel members, enables detailed profiles to be built up about the types, timing and value of sales promotions to which different consumers respond.

Sales promotions are a competitive tool that allows for swift reaction and placement. In that sense, they are not being used as part of an overall campaign, more as an *ad hoc* sales boost. This implies that the manageability of sales promotions is very high relative to the other elements of the promotions mix and that the opportunity to pre-test might not be as large in practice as is theoretically possible (Peattie and Peattie, 1993).

The evaluation of sales promotion is potentially fast, direct, precise and easily comprehended (Doyle and Saunders, 1985). However, evaluation is not necessarily that clear-cut. The synergistic qualities of the promotion mix inevitably lead to crossover effects where the impact of other communications influences responses to particular sales promotion events. Promotions may also bring about increased awareness in addition to the trial, use and switching activities. Peattie and Peattie suggest that not only might brand and product substitution result from promotions, but store loyalty patterns might also be affected.

Of all the tools in the promotions mix, sales promotions lend themselves more easily to evaluation rather than to testing. Testing is not realistically possible in the time frames in which some organisations operate, particularly those in the FMCG sector. Activities should be planned and research built into campaigns, but it is the availability of improved IT that will continue to improve and accelerate the quality of information that management has about its sales.

Summary

Sales promotions now command the lion's share of the promotional budget. This is because it has been proved that they are very effective as a communication tool with consumers, members of the performance network and the sales force. The range of techniques and methods used to add value to offerings is enormous, but there are growing doubts about the effectiveness and profitability associated with some sales promotions.

In comparison with advertising and public relations, many of the sales promotion techniques are easier to evaluate, if only because the number of variables is smaller and they are easier to isolate. Having said this, there is a lack of effective sales promotion measurement and control. This often leads to a short-term focus. Retailers are the same, except for the evaluation on a pre- and post-test basis of their own-brand promotions. Store traffic, sales volume and consumer attitude studies prevail.

Sales promotions have a strategic role to play, particularly when they are used to complement the other activities in the promotional mix. By attempting to develop a consistent theme to a promotional plan, sales promotions can follow advertising's awareness-building activities with a series of messages that continue the theme already established. Success is much more likely when consumers are invited to take advantage of a promotion for a product that they not only are aware of but are conscious of through recent promotional messages.

Review questions

1. Why is sales promotion referred to as a below-the-line promotional tool?
2. What are the purposes of using sales promotion and why has it assumed such a large share of promotional expenditure?

3. Write a brief note explaining how shaping works.
4. Identify the major differences between the behavioural and the cognitive explanations of how sales promotions work.
5. Does sales promotion have a strategic or a tactical role to play in the promotional mix?
6. Write brief notes outlining some of the issues associated with loyalty programmes and customer retention initiatives.
7. How would you advise a newly appointed assistant brand manager on the expected outcomes of a sales promotion programme? (Choose any sector/industry of your choice.)
8. Consider four ways in which technology has contributed to the development of sales promotions. What might be the future of sales promotions as a part of the promotional mix?
9. If sales promotions dilute profitability then there seems little point in using them. Discuss.
10. Identify four ways in which sales promotions can be evaluated.

References

Benezra, K. (1997) Cereal giants call truce in price war that failed to appetise. *Campaign*, 26 September, p. 31

Buzzell, R.D., Quelch, J.A. and Salmon, W.J. (1990) The costly bargain of trade promotion. *Harvard Business Review* (March/April), 141–9.

Curtis, J. (1996) Opposites attract. *Marketing*, 25 April, pp. 28–9.

Davis, M. (1992) Sales promotions as a competitive strategy. *Management Decision*, **30**(7), 5–10.

Dick, A.S. and Basu, K. (1994) Customer loyalty: toward an integrated framework. *Journal of the Academy of Marketing Science*, **22**(2), 99–113.

Dowling, G.R. and Uncles, M. (1997) Do customer loyalty programmes really work? *Sloan Management Review* (Summer), 71–82.

Doyle, P. and Saunders, J. (1985) The lead effect of marketing decisions. *Journal of Marketing Research*, **22**(1), 54–65.

Dwek, R. (1996) Pitch for the perfect partner. *Marketing*, 17 October, pp. 35–7.

Inman, J., McAlister, L. and Hoyer, D.W. (1990) Promotion signal: proxy for a price cut? *Journal of Consumer Research*, **17** (June), 74–81.

Jones, P.J. (1990) The double jeopardy of sales promotions. *Harvard Business Review* (September/October), 145–52.

Miles, L. (1996) Why loyalty has just got personal. *Marketing – Marketing Guides*, 25 July, p. xvii.

Nielsen, A.C. (1993) Sales promotion and the information revolution. *Admap* (January), 80–5.

O'Malley, L. (1998) Can loyalty schemes really build loyalty? *Marketing Intelligence and Planning*, **16**(1), 47–55.

Peattie, K. and Peattie, S. (1993) Sales promotion – playing to win. *Journal of Marketing Management*, **9**, 255–69.

Rothschild, M.L. (1987) *Marketing Communications*. Lexington MA: D.C. Heath.

Rothschild, M.L. and Gaidis, W.C. (1981) Behavioural learning theory: its relevance to marketing and promotions. *Journal of Marketing Research*, **45**(2), 70–8.

Shultz, D.E. (1987) Above or below the line? Growth of sales promotion in the United States. *International Journal of Advertising*, **6**, 17–27.

chapter 19

Sales promotion techniques

The range and sophistication of the main sales promotion techniques reflect the variety of audiences, their needs and the tasks that need to be accomplished.

AIMS AND OBJECTIVES

The aim of this chapter is to consider the nature and characteristics of the main sales promotion tools and techniques.

The objectives of this chapter are:

1. To examine the sales promotional techniques used by manufacturers to influence resellers.
2. To examine the sales promotional techniques used by manufacturers to influence consumers.
3. To examine the sales promotional techniques used by resellers to influence consumers.
4. To examine the sales promotional techniques used by manufacturers to influence the sales force.
5. To clarify the particular objectives sales promotions seek to satisfy.

Introduction

As established in the previous chapter, sales promotions seek to offer buyers additional value, as an inducement to generate an immediate sale. These inducements can be targeted at consumers, distributors, agents and members of the sales force. A whole range of network members can benefit from the use of sales promotion.

The purpose of this chapter is to consider each of the principal sales promotion techniques.

The techniques considered in this chapter attempt to reflect the range and variety of techniques that are used to add value and induce a sale sooner rather than later. The nature and characteristics of the target audiences mean that different techniques work in different ways to achieve varying objectives. Therefore, consideration is given to the range of tasks that need to be accomplished among the following audiences: resellers, consumers and the sales force.

Sales promotions: manufacturers to resellers

Manufacturers and retailers see sales promotions as important devices to encourage trials among non-users and stimulate repeat purchase among users. Retailers prefer in-store promotions (push) instead of promotions aimed at consumers (pull) strategies. This has implications for the promotional mixes deployed by manufacturers.

Objectives for *new* products: trial

For manufacturers launching new products, the main marketing objective is to establish distribution. This is because the use of awareness advertising at the launch of a new product is pointless unless the product is available for consumers to purchase at retail outlets. Therefore, a distribution network needs to be set up in anticipation of consumer demand. The task of marketing communications is to encourage resellers to distribute a new product and to establish trial behaviour.

Objectives for *established* products: usage

Sales of established products need to be maintained and encouraged. The active support and participation of resellers is crucial. One of the main objectives of manufacturers is to develop greater exposure for their products; this means motivating distributors to allocate increased shelf space to a product thereby (possibly) reducing the amount of shelf space allocated to competitors. The task of marketing communications, therefore, is to encourage resellers to buy and display increased amounts of the manufacturer's products and establish greater usage.

It is an interesting point that the trial objective for retailers is to increase the number of new customers visiting a store. The usage objective aims to increase levels of store loyalty and the overall number of visits made by current customers. In the same way that manufacturers seek to establish brand loyalty, so retailers seek to build store loyalty.

Resellers (in particular, retailers) and manufacturers have conflicting objectives. Manufacturers want to increase the amount of shelf space and attention paid to their products, whereas resellers want to increase the numbers of people using the store; they want to develop store traffic.

Methods

The main type of sales promotion used to motivate trade customers is an *allowance*. Allowances can take many forms, some of the more common ones being buying, count and recount, buy-back allowances, merchandising and promotional allowances. Trade allowances are a means of achieving a short-term increase in sales. They can be used defensively to protect valuable shelf space from aggressive competitors. By offering to work with resellers and providing them with extra incentives, manufacturers can guard territory gained to date.

Buying allowances

The most common form of discount is the buying allowance. In return for specific orders between certain dates, a reseller will be entitled to a refund or allowance of x% off the regular case or carton price. The only factor that the reseller must consider is the timing of the order. Manufacturers often use these sales promotions so that they coincide with a main buying period, reducing risk to the distributor.

For the manufacturer, these types of allowances can lead to an increase in the average size of orders, which in turn can utilise idle capacity and also prevent competitors securing business at their expense. This technique can also be used to encourage new stores to try the manufacturer's products or to stimulate repeat usage (restocking).

Count and recount allowances

Manufacturers may require resellers to clear old stock before a new or modified product is introduced. One way this can be achieved is to encourage resellers to move stock out of storage and into the store. The count and recount method provides an allowance for each case shifted into the store during a specified period of time.

The arithmetic for this transaction is as follows:

opening stock + purchases – closing stock =
stock entitled to receive the agreed allowance

This technique can also be used to prevent a store becoming out of stock, and as such is essentially a usage-only technique. If a promotional campaign is to be launched, count and recount can prevent stock-out, loss of custom and wastage of promotional resources.

Buy-back allowances

Buy-backs can be used to follow up count and recount promotions. Under this scheme, the purchases made after the count and recount scheme (up to a maximum of the count and recount) are entitled to an allowance to encourage stores to replenish their stocks (with the manufacturer's product and not that of a competitor). By definition this is a usage-only technique.

Merchandise allowances

The previous three methods require the exchange of money, in the form of either a credit or a cash refund. Merchandising allowances benefit resellers by providing extra goods for which no payment is required. These free goods are only delivered if a reseller's order reaches a specific size. The benefit to the manufacturer is that the administrative and transportation costs for the allowance are very low and are tied to those associated with the costs of the regular order.

For resellers, the incentive is that they can earn above-average profits with the free units. Manufacturers use this type of allowance to generate trials and to open up new distributors. However, this sales promotions technique needs the support of other activities, such as advertising, to provide security and confidence before potential resellers commit themselves to a new product.

Advertising allowances

Advertising allowances can be made if resellers can show that they have undertaken a promotional campaign featuring a manufacturer's product. A percentage allowance is given against a reseller's purchases during a specified period of time. This is a useful technique in stimulating trial by new stores. By weighting the allowances, resellers can be encouraged to take stock and create shelf space for new products.

Dealer listings are advertisements and notices that identify resellers and the range of products that each carries. Issued by manufacturers to help consumers locate their nearest store, they are effective in generating store traffic and for providing source credibility.

A further refinement of the advertising allowance is a scheme which involves the collaboration of a reseller so that an advertising campaign can be jointly funded. Instead of providing an allowance against product purchases, an allowance is provided against the cost of an advertisement or campaign. Govoni *et al.* (1986) suggest that there are two forms of cooperative advertising, vertical and horizontal:

1. *Vertical advertising allowances*
   In vertical advertising, a manufacturer agrees to contribute to the reseller's campaign. A common approach is for a retailer to take out a full-page newspaper advertisement in which a number of different products are highlighted. Each manufacturer then contributes a share of the total cost, proportionate to its space/share of the advertisement. This omnibus approach is popular, as costs are shared and store traffic (usage) can be considerably improved. In addition to these benefits, manufacturers will invariably provide materials, such as artwork and schedules, to assist the promotion and coordinate the activities with their national campaigns.
   Direct mail is used increasingly, as lower unit costs and low wastage (relative to the mass appeal of advertising) encourage resellers to devote more time and resources to this form of promotion.
2. *Horizontal advertising allowances*
   In horizontal advertising, competitors join together to promote the product class and so stimulate primary demand. This form of promotion is often organised and controlled by a trade association. For example, the Milk Marketing Board's award-winning promotion of the home delivery service served to inform and remind people that the doorstep delivery service provided a range of benefits on behalf of relatively small delivery services who individually could not have undertaken the campaign and reached their target audiences so effectively.

Retailers have participated in horizontal programmes, but are normally reluctant to do so for competitive reasons. Retailers stocking products which have a territorial franchise associated with them are more willing to participate; the Southern Ford Dealers programme is a good example of retailer collaboration.

There are, of course, advantages and disadvantages with advertising allowance schemes. The manufacturer is able to buy more space, or time, for each pound spent on advertising, because the spend is often made at local, not national rates. A further factor in their favour is that the scheme encourages those who do not use advertising to participate. Finally, advertising allowances can also induce new resellers to become distributors when the objective is trial.

One of the main drawbacks concerns the cooperative aspect of the allowance arrangements. Resellers are able to assume control over the process and this can lead to circumstances where inappropriate messages and media are used. Furthermore, fraudulent claims have been submitted for advertising that either did not take place or duplicated a previous claim. This lack of control can lead to conflict, and the very scheme that was designed to foster collaborative behaviour can degenerate into a conflict of opinion and a deterioration in reseller/manufacturer relationships. It is interesting to observe that the organisations in the network that have the responsibility for distributing the manufacturer's products are the same ones which may (theoretically) be penalised by their supplier (Grey, as cited in Govoni *et al.* 1986), following abuse of sales promotions.

Hostaging

Hostaging is a process whereby a retailer/reseller is able to exert power over a manufacturer in order to pressurise or force them into providing trade promotions on a more or less continual basis. A less dependent firm may use influence strategies, such as requests and information exchange (Anderson and Narus, 1990). In contrast, the more dependent firm should seek to add value (or reduce costs) to the exchange for the partner firm, at a relatively small cost to itself.

The more dependent firm in a working relationship needs to protect its transactions-specific assets by taking various actions, such as close bonding with end-user firms. Strategies to avoid 'hostaging' would include reducing the frequency of trade deals, converting trade spending into advertising and consumer promotions, and focusing on differentiating the brand with less reliance on price (Blattberg and Neslin, 1990).

Other forms of sales promotions aimed at resellers

There are a number of other techniques that can be used to achieve sales promotion objectives. These include dealer contests, which should be geared to stimulating increased usage. By encouraging resellers to improve their performance, growth can be fostered and the reseller's attention focused on the manufacturer's products, not those of the competition. Motivation and the provision of information are necessary at the launch of new products and at the beginning of a new selling season. To assist these objectives, dealer conventions and meetings are used extensively, often in conjunction with a dealer contest. The informal interaction between the focus organisation and its resellers that these events facilitate can be an invaluable aid to the development and continuance of good relations between the two parties and, of course, at a horizontal level between resellers.

Many manufacturers provide extensive training and support for their resellers. This is an important communications function, especially when products are complex or subject to rapid change, as in the IT markets. Such coordination means that a stronger relationship can be built and manufacturers have greater control over the messages that the reseller's representatives transmit. It also means that the switching costs of the reseller are increased, since the training and support costs will be incurred again if a different supplier is adopted. Coordination through training and support can be seen as a form of marketing communications.

Dealer promotions – Reebok

In comparison with its national market share, Reebok concluded that it was under-trading in the independent sports shop sector. Research suggested that, while Reebok sales calls were not as frequent as those of Adidas and Nike, what retailers wanted was more point-of-purchase support, including materials, training on products and display and general merchandising.

Using the athlete Roger Black as an endorser, the Reebok Vector Programme sought to provide dealers with the support that was requested. Eight mailers were sent out each year to each of the 500 accredited sports retailer shops. The under-trading was corrected and market share stabilised across the independent shop sector.

Adapted from Institute of Sales Promotions (1997)

Personal selling is an important tool used to persuade buyers, the objective being to ensure that the reseller follows the guide of the manufacturer. As products become more similar and as channel power becomes concentrated in the retail sector, so resellers are able to select products from a variety of suppliers and determine the most appropriate sales promotions necessary for the markets in which they operate. This means that manufacturers can no longer assume control over members of the performance network, and they must find different ways of accessing the sales force of their distributors.

Marketing communications between manufacturers and resellers are vitally important. Sales promotions play an increasingly important role in the coordination between the two parties. Resellers look for sales promotions to support their own marketing initiatives. Supplier selection decisions depend in part upon the volume and value of the communications support. In other words, will supplier X or Y provide the necessary level of promotional support, either within the channel or direct to the consumer?

Sales promotions: resellers to consumers

Objectives

There are two overall objectives that retailers wish to achieve. The first is to promote the store as a brand. Growth at the retail level can be achieved by generating store traffic and increasing the number of people who become store (brand) loyal. This, as stated previously, is the equivalent to the *generation of trial.* To do this they need to communicate with those who are store-switchers and non-store-users. Therefore, store image advertising is undertaken by retailers and is executed away from the store. The aim is to convert switchers and non-loyals into store-loyal customers.

The second main objective, according to a study undertaken by Blattberg *et al.* (1981), is to transfer stock and its associated costs from the retailer's shelves to the cupboards and refrigerators of consumers. In an attempt to increase usage, marketing communications, and sales promotion activity in particular, are orientated to shifting particular stock at particular times. This means that turnover is increased (and targets reached) and shelves are cleared to receive new products.

Methods

Sales promotion by retailers is normally tied to the activities of manufacturers, but some price-off techniques are retailer-driven. Joint advertising and sales promotion in the local press combine to attract customers to the store. However, as discussed earlier, many of these advertising campaigns are cooperative exercises and so cannot be classed as retailer sales promotions. The attention-getting devices of in-store displays are normally regarded as merchandising, in that they are geared to gaining attention, not moving product.

Promotions that do occur in-store, regardless of origin, appear to affect non-store loyals to a greater extent than store loyals. Rossiter and Percy (1987) report the work of a Nielsen study in which sales promotions in supermarkets were tracked and sales correlated with the degree of store loyalty. The main finding was that non-store-loyals recorded a twenty-fold increase in sales following the promotion, whereas store loyals increased their sales by a factor of only ten.

Sales promotions: manufacturers to consumers

Objectives

Manufacturers use sales promotions to communicate with consumers because they can be a cost-effective means of achieving short-term increases in sales. The objectives are to stimulate trial use by new users or to increase product usage among those customers who buy the product on an occasional or regular basis.

The success of any new offering is partly dependent on the number of consumers encouraged to try the product in the first place and partly upon the number who repurchase the product at a later point in the purchase cycle. The importance of stimulating trial use cannot be underestimated. Through the use of coupons, sampling and other techniques (see below), sales promotions have become an important element in the new product launch and introduction processes.

In addition to trial, organisations need to encourage consumers to repurchase products. In markets that are mature, sales growth can only be realistically achieved by encouraging users of competitive products to switch their allegiance. This can be achieved by offering them superior benefits and added value. Attracting non-users is an alternative route, but this requires convincing them, first, that they have a need for the product class and, second, that they should try the promoted product. A more productive approach is to find new uses for the product. For example, breakfast cereals have been promoted as nourishing snacks, suitable for consumption at different times of the day. Dairies have distributed recipe books where many of the meals use milk as a prime ingredient.

Trade promotions – Mars

One of the problems faced by Mars Confectionery has been its rival's (Walls) dominance of ice cream freezer cabinets in the independent sector. Most shops have only enough space for one cabinet and that, historically, has been Walls. A promotion in 1996 was targeted at familiarising customers with the location of Mars freezers and their product range. The 'Find a Freezer' game required consumers to locate Mars freezers in 6,000 outlets. Freezers were given a name sticker and the Capital FM radio station invited listeners to find them in return for cash and Mars merchandise rewards.

Just as sales promotions are used to attract customers of competing products, so competitors use sales promotions to counter-attack and defend their markets. Sales promotions, sometimes in combination with advertising, must be used to defend a customer base from competitive attacks. By using bonus packs (extra product), price-offs, competitions and coupons to encourage increased usage, customers can be loaded with stock, effectively removing them from the market for a period longer than the normal purchase cycle.

There are two prime reasons for using sales promotions with consumers. The first is to collaborate with resellers in an attempt to defend the shelf space or franchise. This helps build a close and supportive relationship, and also creates a mobility barrier that has to be overcome by competitive organisations. The second reason is the need to transfer the cost of stock from the reseller to the consumer, boosting revenue and clearing the way for new products with better margins.

Methods for encouraging *new users* to try a product

There are three main approaches to encourage new customers to try a product for the first time: sampling, coupons and a range of consumer deals.

Sampling

When a product is introduced, whether it be a new product category or an improved or modified product, sampling is one of the most effective sales promotion techniques available. For decisions that evoke low involvement, where there is little thought or elaboration undertaken by the consumer, attitudes are confirmed as a result of product experience. It makes sense, therefore, to provide a risk-free opportunity for consumers to test a product.

Samples are very often free miniature versions of the actual product and can be used to win new customers and to protect a customer base. Samples can take the form of demonstrations, trial size packs that have to be purchased or free use for a certain period of time. The recent offers by car manufacturers to allow purchasers to return their cars after a four-week period if not satisfied provide a good example of a high-involvement decision where attitudes are formed prior to trial and are used to confirm a purchase decision. The use of scented page folds in women's magazines to demonstrate new scents and perfumes is an innovative and interesting example of making trial easier. Previously, the only method of testing perfume was through the use of samplers, available on the counters in cosmetic departments of retail outlets. Marketing communications and sales promotions in particular were aimed at enticing people to the store. Using scent folds means that it is easier for consumers to try a perfume. A far greater number of people can try a new scent, while the reader's attention can be focused on the accompanying advertisement. Readership and recall scores increase remarkably.

Sampling is expensive. Of all the available sales promotion techniques, the costs associated with sampling are the largest. To offset the high cost, the potential rewards can be equally dramatic, especially if the audience is familiar with or predisposed to the product class, and if the sample has some superior benefits. Sampling is best undertaken when the following apply:

1. Advertising alone is unable to communicate the key benefits.
2. The product has benefits that are superior to its competitors and which are clearly demonstrable.
3. Competitive attacks require loyal customers to be reminded of a product's advantages. A further use occasion of sampling is to introduce the product to customers of competitive products, in an effort to encourage them to switch.

Apart from the size, mass and degree of perishability associated with the physical characteristics, the main constraints concern the number of people who are required to receive the samples and when they are to receive them: the timing of the trial. Samples are often distributed to consumers free of charge, with the twin goals of introducing the product to new users and hopefully encouraging them to switch brands. In addition to this, sampling provides an ideal opportunity to gather valuable market research data from the field.

However, some retailers prefer miniature products which customers are expected to purchase. This approach encourages consumers to use the sample, and because they paid for it they will be likely to use it. For the retailer, this approach provides a margin in part compensation for the risk associated with any stock purchased in advance and for the floor or shelf space allocated for the trial.

Rossiter and Percy have compiled a table (Table 19.1) which sets out the main sampling media.

Coupons

Coupons are a proven method by which manufacturers can communicate with consumers and are a strong brand-switching device. They may be distributed via resellers or directly to consumers. Coupons are vouchers or certificates which entitle consumers to a price reduction on a particular product. The value of the reduction or discount is set and the coupon must be presented when purchasing the product. The objective therefore, is to offer a price deal, a discount off the full price of the product. Retailers and wholesalers act as agents for manufacturers by allowing consumers to redeem the value of coupons from them at the point of purchase. They in turn recover the cost of the deal, the value of the coupon, from the manufacturer.

Coupons provide precision targeting of price-sensitive customers, without harming those regular customers who are prepared to pay full price. In reality, however, some coupons are redeemed by regular product users, and their use reduces margins unnecessarily. The level of perceived risk experienced by new users can be reduced through the use of coupons. Users of competitive products can also be

Table 19.1 Eight methods of distributing samples

	Uses	Limitations
Door to door	■ Virtually any product can be delivered in this way	■ Most expensive means of sampling ■ Problem with leaving perishables if occupant absent ■ Illegal in some areas
Direct mail	■ Best for small, light products that are non-perishable	■ Rising postal costs
Central location	■ Best for perishables such as food, or when personal demonstration is required	■ If in-store, same offer must be made to all retailers (Robinson-Patman Act) ■ Usually involves cost of sales training ■ If in public place, may be illegal in some areas
Sample pack in stores	■ Best method for attracting retail support, because retailers sell the packs at a premium unit price	■ Requires retail acceptance like any other new product ■ May necessitate special production for trial sizes
Cross-product sampling in or on pack	■ Good for low-cost sampling of a manufacturer's other products	■ Trial limited to users of 'carrier' product ■ Restricted to large products
Co-op package distribution	■ Good for narrow audiences such as college students, military personnel, brides	■ Little appeal to trade
Newspaper or magazine distribution	■ Relatively low-cost method of sample distribution for flat or pouchable products	■ Seem to be regarded by media vehicle recipients as 'cheap' and are often disregarded, resulting in less trial than with other sampling methods ■ Obviously limited to certain product types
Any of above with coupon	■ Increases post-sample trial rate by using purchase incentive	■ Additional cost of coupon handling

Source: Rossiter and Percy (1987); used with permission.

encouraged to try the product, so coupons can be effective for product introductions and established products in stable markets.

Smart-shoppers are those consumers who feel some exclusivity and control as a result of using coupons to try new brands. They receive a psychological and economic benefit. While retailers like coupons because they merely switch the brand bought and so do not lose a sale, manufacturers are less keen, as they consider they may lose out. The evidence suggests that consumers tend to revert to their pre-coupon preferred brand after redemption of the coupon (Kahn and Louie, 1990).

This form of sales promotion allows management to set a specific period of time in which a promotion is to run. This in turn allows the other elements of the promotional mix to be integrated. For example, advertising can be used to create awareness, and print media can then be used to display a coupon for the reader to cut out for redemption at the next purchase opportunity. When attempting to generate trial, advertising must be used to create awareness, since a coupon for an unknown product will be totally ineffective and usually discarded by consumers. Personal selling can be timed to inform resellers of a forthcoming coupon offer and give time for shelves to be fully stocked when the campaign breaks. Unfortunately, it is difficult to estimate when and how many coupons will be redeemed. There are certain guides developed through experience and a redemption rate of between 3 and 5% can be considered good. The variance, however, can be marked, and the promotional cost of a stockout can be considerable.

Couponing is an expensive activity. Not only has the face value of the coupons to be considered, but the production and distribution costs must also be accounted for. General Mills, the US food group, decided to reduce the number of coupons it issues on the grounds that it sees them as a waste of money (Tomkins, 1994). At 2% redemption, the cost in terms of time, print and distribution costs plus the face value of the coupon itself means that the exercise was costing General Mills money. It has moved back to an 11% price reduction on its products instead. There are signs that the use of coupons in the USA has peaked, as there was a 12% drop in the number of coupons redeemed in 1993 and a 4% fall in the number of coupons issued. Many organisations, like General Mills, consider that a saving of 30% in the promotional budget and a cut in the price on the shelf is a better and more profitable way to do business.

There are three primary ways in which coupons can be distributed:

1. Consumer direct distribution allows management to focus the coupons upon particular target audiences. Coupons can be sent through the post or delivered on a door-to-door basis. An average redemption rate of 6% makes this one of the more effective methods of distributing coupons, although a major disadvantage is that its costs are increasing. Consequently, some manufacturers are collaborating with other manufacturers (non-competitive) to distribute coupons on a joint basis.
2. Media direct distribution allows management to gain a broad level of exposure for a product. Free-standing inserts (FSI) are a popular way of distributing coupons. These are separate sheets containing a number of different coupons. This contrasts with the normal method of printing the coupon in a newspaper or magazine. However, the redemption rates of this second approach are low because of the short life of such media vehicles, particularly newspapers, and the extra effort required by readers to cut out and store the coupon until the next purchase opportunity arises.

   Various alternative methods have been developed in response to the need to find novel ways of attracting readers' attention. On-page coupons can be found in magazines coupled with an advertisement. Pop-ups are coupons printed on card and bound into a magazine. Finally, tip-ins are coupons glued to the cover of a magazine.
3. Package direct distribution generates the highest redemption rates of all the methods available. By inserting (in) or imprinting (on) coupons on the packaging of a product (in/ons), distribution costs can be minimised. However, coupons distributed in this way only reach users; they fail, therefore, to reach non-users.

Instant coupons are an effective point-of-purchase incentive which allow purchasers literally to rip the coupon off the package for redemption at the check-out. This can generate very high levels of redemption and is administratively easier to manage than price deals, as the latter require the active participation of the reseller.

Coupons that are redeemable off the next purchase of the same item are referred to as bounce-back coupons. Coupons which are redeemable against different products are referred to as cross-ruff coupons. These are particularly effective in encouraging consumers to try other products in a manufacturer's product range. Soap, frozen foods and breakfast cereals are product ranges where this couponing approach has been successful.

A total of 213 million coupons per year at 33p each (Fields, 1997) are issued, and this represents a great deal of business activity. Fulfilment Houses undertake the work for brand managers, acting as brokers for the issuers and retailers who accept them. Manufacturers outsource coupon work, if only because it is so labour-intensive. New software systems threaten to replace some of this work, especially the tracking of vouchers, which can be undertaken in-house.

Many technological advances, and in particular the use of barcode scanners, present opportunities for manufacturers and retailers to use couponing more effectively. Fraudulent use of coupons can be cut considerably and checkout speeds increased. More importantly, however, this technology has the potential to monitor an individual customer's purchases, establish buying patterns and dispense coupons to users of competitive products at the checkout. This will lead inevitably to the identification of those customers who use coupons more frequently and the development of coupon user profiles. Manufacturers will also gain by the reduced distribution costs and the reduction in time spent handling coupons. One such system is called Catalina (see Plate 19.1).

Catalina Systems

The Catalina system, which claims a redemption rate of 6–8%, was developed in the USA and was introduced into the UK in 1993. One of the first users was Asda, who, after an initial proving period, installed the system in all 216 stores in the UK. Somerfield has 430 Catalina installations with more to follow. Catalina claims a number of advantages for both manufacturers and retailers. For manufacturers it provides for exclusivity, as only one manufacturer per product category can be installed. For retailers the overall incentive is that the system encourages return visits and increases store traffic, and volume grows.

Catalina and other similar systems provide money-off coupons plus the opportunity to deliver a variety of messages to specific shoppers. In addition, it is possible to provide incentives to the right target customers to encourage participation in research exercises. Sampling opportunities increase as well. Asda uses the system to target those customers most likely to use free telephone numbers in order to receive a free sample of a new/other product or hear a pre-recorded message. This is referred to as *confined target advertising*, or in other words a blend of sales promotion, direct marketing and advertising.

Consumer deals

These forms of sales promotion are only effective in the short term. They are not used to build consumer franchises or brand personalities. Their function is to bring about a short-term increase in sales by moving the product from the shelves of the reseller to the homes of consumers. They can encourage trial behaviour by new users and also stimulate repurchase by existing users. The techniques are as follows.

Price-offs

By far the simplest technique is to offer a direct reduction in the purchase price with the offer clearly labelled on the package or point of purchase display. These are simply referred to simply as 'price-offs'. A minimum reduction of 15% appears to be required for optimal effect (Della Bitta and Monroe, 1980). Others suggest that this figure varies according to the store and the type of brand under consideration. Research indicates that consumers are sceptical of price deals, in particular those concerning price-offs. This may result in individuals discounting the discounts (Gupta and Cooper, 1992).

The mere presence of a price-off for those with a low need for elaboration, regardless of the value of the sales promotion, appears to be sufficient to bring about a change in an individual's disposition towards the promoted product (Inman *et al.*, 1990). They suggest that it is theoretically possible to bring about an increase in sales from those with a low need for information simply by placing a promotional display without actually reducing the price!

In a study by AC Nielsen (reported by Miller, 1997) of consumer attitudes towards price-offs and sales promotions, five different types of people were identified. These are set out in Table 19.2.

Whatever the decision regarding the value of the price-off, the entire price reduction should be carried by the manufacturer, as the retailer must be continually motivated and a reduction in margin will be adversely received. Retailers see price deals as a

Table 19.2 Five types of customers and their attitude towards sales promotion

Branded EDLP[a] seekers (19%)
This group have a restricted income but are brand loyal. They therefore look around for the best deal they can get for their preferred brand. In their search for everyday low prices they ignore coupons and money-off promotions.

Low price fixture ferrets (23.3%)
Again income is restricted in this group, which is mainly populated by young families. They are very budget conscious and are store rather than product loyal. They like promotions and are quick to switch brands.

Promotion junkies (18.4%)
These people are referred to as professional shoppers because of their desire to seek out bargains. They have zero loyalty and are keen to tell their contacts of their shopping successes. They are a hazard to both manufacturers and retailers.

Stockpilers (21%)
This type of shopper is loyal to both manufacturers and retailers. They have no income difficulties and are happy to buy up large quantities of their preferred brands, regardless of the costs. Of the five types of shopper, these are the second most promotionally active, as they search for bargains but they do not switch brands for promotional reasons.

Promotionally oblivious (18.3%)
This group are totally unaware of any promotions. Described as rather old-fashioned, this group are not interested in pursuing low prices. Therefore they will buy a preferred brand regardless of the existence of a promotion and so represent a reliable group of buyers.

[a] EDLP = everyday low price.
Source: Miller (1997).

necessary activity to stimulate short-term sales. Manufacturers regard price deals as effective when tied into media advertising.

Bonus packs

Bonus packs offer more product for the regular pack price. They provide direct impact at the point of purchase, and this, combined with the lure of lower unit costs and extra value, means that this is a popular technique with consumers and manufacturers. However, resellers do not gain from bonus packs: there is no additional margin and extra shelf space is required.

Refunds and rebates

Refunds and rebates are used to invite consumers to send in a proof of purchase and in return receive a cash refund. These are very effective in encouraging the trial of new products and have proved exceptionally popular with consumer durables (rebate) as well as FMCG (refunds). The process of redeeming refunds may evoke negative feelings, as consumers do not like the trouble and inconvenience associated with claiming refunds and, when combined with the negative perception that consumers have of manufacturers who offer such rebates, the conclusion has to be that any redemption procedure should be clear, simple and easy to implement.

Methods for encouraging increased consumption – usage

There are two main ways in which sales promotions can be used to encourage increased usage: premiums (direct and self-liquidating) and contests and sweepstakes.

Premiums

Premiums are items of merchandise that are offered free or at a low cost. Premiums are used as a direct incentive to motivate people to purchase a specific product. The premium merchandise is used to add value to the product and represent an advantage over competitor products. Finding suitable low-cost premiums for the adult market, however, is difficult, as a poor premium may deter people from buying the product. Consumers are required to show proof that a purchase has been made.

Premiums are used to increase sales by attracting repeat buyers, stimulating impulse purchase and brand-switching behaviour, and to offset competitor moves. There are two main forms of premium: direct and self-liquidating.

Direct premiums are provided for the consumer at the point of purchase. They are free of charge and require the consumer to do nothing other than buy the package. The premium merchandise may be attached to the product as an on-pack premium. This can result in improving the shelf display, which is attractive to resellers as it presents an instant stimulus–response opportunity to potential buyers. Unfortunately, on-packs take up extra space, and this can mean increased labour in shelf replenishment. The extra costs involved with packaging also need to be taken into account when designing on-pack premiums.

Gillette UK attempted to switch users of competitive shaving products by offering free gel with its disposable razors. Blister packaging makes for an attractive, attention-getting display and provides an incentive for consumers to receive a free product.

Premium merchandise that is packaged inside the product is referred to as an in-pack premium. This obviously saves space and reduces costs for the manufacturer, as there is virtually no requirement to change the packaging. Breakfast cereals have traditionally used this approach.

In contrast to direct premiums, *self-liquidating* premiums require consumers to contribute to the cost of the incentive. Manufacturers seek only to cover their costs and, by buying the premium merchandise in volume, can offer the merchandise at prices considerably below the regular retail price.

The effectiveness of self-liquidating premiums is not as strong as that of direct premiums because they do not provide the same impact. There is a time delay between awareness of the offer and the reward, often a matter of weeks. Consequently, the redemption rate for these types of sales promotion is very low (0.1%). They can be used to stimulate resellers and create attention in the market, and they can deflect attention from competitor brands. Proposed new regulations from the EU threaten the abolition of self-liquidating premiums.

Manufacturers can also offer mail-in premiums to customers if they send several proofs of purchase. The premium is technically free to the customer and the multiple purchases that are stimulated generate revenue, take stock off the shelves and take customers out of the market for a period of time because they are loaded with stock.

Contests and sweepstakes

A contest is a sales promotion whereby customers compete for prizes or money on the basis of skills or ability. Entry requires a proof of purchase and winners are judged against a set of predetermined criteria. Completing the line 'I like XXX because…', writing one-line slogans, suggesting names, and drawing posters and pictures are some of the more common contests used to involve consumers with products.

A sweepstake is a sales promotion technique where the winners are determined by chance and proof of purchase is not required. There is no judging and winners are drawn at random. A variant of the sweepstake is a game which also has odds of winning associated with it. Scratchcards have become very popular games, mainly because consumers like to participate and winners can be instantly identified.

Sweepstakes are more popular than contests because they are easier to enter and, because there is no judging, administration is less arduous and less expensive. Both contests and sweepstakes bring excitement and attention to campaigns, and if the contest or sweepstake is relevant, both approaches can bring about increased consumer involvement with the product.

Great care and preparation must be put into contests and sweepstakes. Because of the legal implications and requirements of these sales promotions, many organisations contract the event to organisations that specialise in such activities.

Sales promotions: the sales force

Just as consumers and resellers benefit from the motivation provided by sales promotions, so members of the sales force can benefit too. To stimulate performance, sales promotions can be directed at the sales force of either the manufacturer or the reseller. Incentives such as contests and sales meetings are two of the most used motivators.

Contests

Contests have been used a great deal, and if organised and planned properly can be very effective in raising the performance outcomes of sales teams. By appealing to their competitive nature, contests can bring about effective new product introductions, revive falling sales, offset a rival's competitive moves and build a strong customer base. To do this, contests must be fair, so that participants have a roughly equal chance of being successful, and the winners should not be those who have high-density and high-potential territories. A further consideration is the duration of the contest: too short and the full effects may not be realised; make it too long and interest and support for the incentive may wane.

Sales meetings

Sales meetings provide an opportunity for management to provide fresh information to the sales force about performance, stock positions, competitor activities, price deals, consumer or reseller promotions, and new products. Sales training exercises can be introduced and short product training sessions can often be included. These formal agenda items are supplemented by the informal ones of peer reassurance and competitive stimulus, as well as information exchange and market analysis. Meetings can be held annually, quarterly, monthly or at local level on a weekly basis. The time that representatives are off-territory needs to be considered, but generally such meetings are of benefit to people who spend the greater part of their working week away from the office, at the boundary of the organisation.

Other sales promotion aids

Brochures are a sales promotion that can be used to assist consumers, resellers and the sales forces. Apart from the ability of the brochure to impart factual information about a product or service, brochures and sales literature stimulate purchase and serve to guide decisions. For service-based organisations, the brochure represents a temporary tangible element of the product. Inclusive tour operators, for example, might entice someone to book a holiday, but consumption may take place several months in the future. The brochure acts as a temporary product substitute and can be used to refresh expectations during the gestation period and remind significant other people of the forthcoming event (Middleton, 1989). Just as holiday photographs provide opportunities to relive and share past experiences, so holiday brochures serve to share and enjoy pre-holiday experiences and expectations. Consumption of inclusive tours, therefore, can be said to occur at the booking point, and the brochure extends or adds value to the holiday experience.

Sales literature can trigger awareness of potential needs. As well as triggering awareness, sales literature can be useful in explaining technical and complex products. For example, leaflets distributed personally at DIY stores can draw attention to a double-glazing manufacturer's products. Some prospective customers may create an initial impression about the manufacturer, based on past experiences triggered by the literature, the quality of the leaflet and the way it was presented. The leaflet acts as a cue for the receiver to review if there is a current need and, if there is, then the leaflet may be kept longer, especially where high involvement is present; value is thus added to the purchase experience.

Allied Dunbar uses sales literature at various stages in the sales process. Mailers are used to contact prospective customers, corporate brochures are used to provide source credibility, booklets about the overall market-place are left with clients after an initial discussion and product guides and brochures are given to customers after a transaction has been agreed. To help prevent the onset of cognitive dissonance, the company magazine *Outlook* is sent soon after the sale and at intermediate points throughout the year to cement the relationship between client and company.

Summary

The range of techniques and methods used to add value to offerings is enormous but there are growing doubts about the effectiveness and profitability associated with some sales promotions.

Sales promotions used by manufacturers to communicate with resellers are aimed at either encouraging resellers to try new products or purchase more of the ones they currently stock. To do this, trade allowances, in various guises, are the principal means.

Sales promotions used by resellers (largely retailers) to influence consumers are normally driven by manufacturers, although some price deals and other techniques are used to generate store traffic. The majority of sales promotions are those used by manufacturers to influence consumers. Again the main tasks are to encourage trial or increased product purchase. A range of techniques, from sampling and coupons to premiums and contests and sweepstakes, are all used with varying levels of success.

Review questions

1. Explain the objectives that manufacturers might have when encouraging resellers to take more product.
2. List the main sales promotion methods used by manufacturers and targeted at consumers.
3. Evaluate the allowance concept.
4. Consider whether hostaging is conducive to relationship marketing.
5. Collect four examples of sampling and determine whether you feel they were effective in achieving their objectives.
6. Name five different methods of distributing samples.
7. How can coupons be used to reduce levels of perceived risk?
8. Which of the two forms of premiums is generally regarded as the less successful and why do you think this is?
9. What role does the sales brochure play in marketing communications?
10. Consider the view that the sales force does not require incentivising through sales promotion as it is motivated sufficiently through other means.

References

Anderson, J.C. and Narus, J.A. (1990) A model of distributor firm and manufacturer firm working partnerships. *Journal of Marketing*, **54** (January), 42–58.

Blattberg, R.C., Eppen, G.D. and Lieberman J. (1981) A theoretical and empirical evaluation of price deals for consumer nondurables. *Journal of Marketing*, **5**(1), 116–29.

Blattberg, R.C. and Neslin, S.A. (1990) *Sales Promotion: Concepts, Methods and Strategies*. Englewood Cliffs NJ: Prentice Hall.

Della Bitta, A.J. and Monroe, K.B. (1980) A multivariate analysis of the perception of value from retail price advertisements, in *Advances in Consumer Research*, Vol. 8, (ed. K.B. Monroe). Ann Arbor MI: Association for Consumer Research.

Fields, L. (1997) Collective effort. *Marketing*, 24 July, pp. 27–8.

Govoni, N., Eng, R. and Gaper, M. (1986) *Promotional Management*. Englewood Cliffs, NJ: Prentice Hall.

Gupta, S. and Cooper, L.G. (1992) The discounting of discounts and promotion brands. *Journal of Consumer Research*, **19** (December), 401–11.

Inman, J., McAlister, L. and Hoyer, D.W. (1990) Promotion signal: proxy for a price cut? *Journal of Consumer Research*, **17** (June), 74–81.

Institute of Sales Promotions (1997) ISP Awards for 1996, *Promotions and Incentives*.

Kahn, B.E. and Louie, T.A. (1990) Effects on retraction of price on brand choice behaviour for variety seeking and last purchase-loyal-consumers. *Journal of Marketing Research*, **18** (August), 279–89.

Middleton, V.T.C. (1989) *Marketing in Travel and Tourism*. Oxford: Heinemann.

Miller, R. (1997) Does everyone have a price? *Marketing*, 24 April, pp. 30–3.

Rossiter, J.R. and Percy, L. (1987) *Advertising and Promotion Management*. New York: McGraw-Hill.

Tomkins, R. (1994) Time to cut it out. *Financial Times*, 21 April, p. 25.

Public relations

Public relations is a management activity that attempts to shape the attitudes and opinions held by an organisation's stakeholders. Through dialogue with these stakeholders the organisation may adjust its own position and/or strategy. Therefore there is an attempt to identify with, and adjust an organisation's policies to, the interests of its stakeholders. To do this it formulates and executes a programme of action to develop mutual goodwill and understanding.

AIMS AND OBJECTIVES

The aim of this chapter is to explore public relations in the context of promoting organisations and their products.

The objectives of this chapter are:

1. To discuss the role of public relations in the communications mix.
2. To clarify the differences between corporate public relations and marketing public relations.
3. To highlight the main audiences to which public relations activities are directed.
4. To provide an overview of some of the main tools used by public relations.
5. To appreciate the development and significance of corporate advertising.
6. To examine the nature and context of crisis management.
7. To determine the manner in which public relations complements the other tools of the promotional mix.

Introduction

The shift in the degree of importance given by organisations to public relations over recent years is a testimony to its power and effectiveness. An increasing number of organisations are now recognising that the role that public relations can play in the external and internal communications of organisations is a tool for use by all organisations, regardless of the sector in which they operate. Therefore, all organisations in the public, hybrid, not-for-profit and private sectors can use this tool to raise visibility, interest and goodwill.

Traditionally, public relations has been a tool which dealt with the manner and style with which an organisation interacted with its major 'publics'. It sought to influence other organisations and individuals by public relations, projecting an identity that would affect the image that different publics held of the organisation. By spreading information and improving the levels of knowledge that people held about particular issues, the organisation sought ways to advance itself in the eyes of those it saw as influential. This approach is reflected in the definition of public relations provided by the Institute of Public Relations: 'Public Relations practice is the planned and sustained effort to establish and maintain goodwill and mutual understanding between an organisation and its publics'. Another definition has been provided by delegates attending a world convention of public relations associations in 1978, entitled the Mexican Statement: 'Public Relations is the art and social science of analysing trends, predicting their consequences, counselling organisations' leadership and implementing planned programmes of action which will serve both the organisation's and the public interest' (Public Relations Educational Trust, 1991).

The main issues expressed by both these definitions are that PR is concerned with the development and communication of corporate and competitive strategies. Public relations provides visibility for an organisation, and this in turn, it is hoped, allows it to be properly identified, positioned and understood by all of its stakeholders. What these definitions do not emphasise or make apparent is that public relations should also be used by management as a means of understanding issues from a stakeholder perspective. Good relationships are developed by appreciating the views held by others and by 'putting oneself in their shoes'.

Through this sympathetic and patient approach to planned communication, a dialogue can be developed which is not frustrated by punctuated interruptions (anger, disbelief, ignorance and objections). Public relations is a management activity that attempts to shape the attitudes and opinions held by an organisation's stakeholders. It attempts to identify its policies with the interests of its stakeholders and formulates and executes a programme of action to develop mutual goodwill and understanding.

Characteristics of public relations

Public relations should, therefore, be a planned activity, one that encompasses a wide range of events. However, there are a number of characteristics that single out this particular tool from the others in the promotional mix. Public relations does not require the purchase of airtime or space in media vehicles, such as television or magazines. The decision on whether an organisation's public relations messages are transmitted or not rests with those charged with managing the media resource, not the message sponsor. Those that are selected are perceived to be endorsements or the views of parties other than management. The outcome is that these messages usually carry greater perceived credibility than those messages transmitted through paid media, such as advertising.

The degree of trust and confidence generated by public relations singles out this tool from others in the promotional mix as an important means of reducing buyers' perceived risk. However, while credibility may be high, the amount of control that management is able to bring to the transmission of the public relations message is very low. For example, a press release may have been carefully prepared in-house, but as soon as it is passed to the editor of a magazine or newspaper, a possible opinion former, all control is lost. The release may be destroyed (highly probable), printed as it stands (highly unlikely) or changed to fit the available space in the media vehicle (almost certain, if it is decided to use the material). This means that any changes will not have been agreed by management, so the context and style of the original message may be lost or corrupted.

The costs associated with public relations also make this an important tool in the promotional mix. The absolute costs are minimal, except for those organisations that retain an agency, but even then their costs are low compared with those of advertising. The relative costs (the costs associated with reaching members of the target audiences) are also very low. The main costs associated with public relations are the time and opportunity costs associated with the preparation of press releases and associated literature. If these types of activity are organised properly, many small organisations could develop and shape their visibility in a relatively inexpensive way.

A further characteristic of this tool is that it can be used to reach specific audiences, in a way that paid media cannot. With increasing media fragmentation and finer segmentation (customisation) of markets, public relations represents a cost-effective way of reaching such markets and audiences.

The main characteristics of public relations are that it represents a very cost-effective means of carrying messages with a high degree of credibility. However, the degree of control that management is able to exert over the transmission of messages can be limited.

Publics or stakeholders?

The first definition of public relations quoted earlier used, as indeed does most of the public relations industry, the word *publics*. This word is used traditionally to refer to the various organisations and groups with which a focus organisation interacts. So far, this text has referred to these types of organisation as *stakeholders*. 'Stakeholders' is a term used increasingly in the field of strategic management, and as public relations is essentially concerned with strategic issues, the word 'stakeholders' is used in this text to provide consistency and to reflect the strategic orientation and importance of this promotional tool.

The stakeholder concept has been discussed earlier, at great length, in Chapter 6. Various networks of stakeholders were identified, with each network consisting of members who are orientated towards supporting the focus organisation either in an indirect way or directly through the added-value processes.

For the purposes of this chapter it is useful to set out who the main stakeholders are likely to be. Stakeholder groups, it should be remembered, are not static and new groups can emerge in response to changes in the environment. The main core groups, however, tend to be the following.

Employees

The employees of an organisation have already been established as major stakeholders. In an internal context, employees represent a major source of word-of-mouth communications. It has long been established that employees need to be motivated, involved and stimulated to perform their tasks at a high level. Their work as external communicators is less well established, but their critical role in providing external cues as part of the corporate identity programme was discussed earlier.

Shareholders

Shareholders require regular information to maintain their continued confidence in the organisation and to prevent them changing their portfolios and reducing the value of the organisation.

Suppliers

Suppliers need to be informed of the strategies being pursued by the focus organisation, if they are to be able to provide continuity and a quality service.

Financial groups

In addition to the shareholders, there are those individuals who are either potential shareholders or those who advise shareholders and investors. These represent the wider financial community but who nevertheless have a very strong influence on the stature, strength and value that an organisation has. Financial analysts need to be supplied with information in order that they be up-to-date with the activities and performance outcomes of organisations, but also need to be advised of developments within the various markets that the organisation operates.

Organisations attempt to supply analysts with current information and materials about the organisation and the markets in which they are operating, to ensure that the potential and value of publicly quoted organisations is reflected in the share price. The success of any further attempts to increase investment and to secure any necessary capital will be determined by the confidence that the financial community has in the organisation. Public relations is an important form of communication in that it can create and shape relationships. By developing confidence in this way, the perception of risk held by investors can be lowered, funds are released and new products are developed and launched.

Media

The relationships that organisations develop with the media are extremely important. Of all the media, the press is the most crucial, as it is always interested in newsworthy items and depends to a large extent on information being fed to it by a variety of corporate press officers. Consequently, publicity can be generated for a range of organisational events, activities and developments.

Community

The local community is often the target of public relations activities because of its proximity and the influence that local citizens may have on an organisation. By attempting to keep it informed and by trying to develop a spirit of goodwill and mutual understanding, the local community can be encouraged to identify more strongly with the focus organisation. For example, it is possible to establish an environment within which an initiative to expand plant capacity will be received favourably and supported by the local community, rather than encountering public protests and hostility.

Local authorities and the government

The power and influence held by local authorities cannot be underestimated. For example, their willingness to grant planning permission for the capacity extension mentioned above will reflect the attitudes and relationships between the two parties. Organisations should seek to work with, rather than against, these stakeholder groups. As a result, public relations should be aimed at informing local authorities of their strategic intentions and seeking ways in which the objectives of both parties can be satisfied.

Where local authorities interpret legislation and frame the activities of their citizens and constituent organisations, the government determines legislation and controls the activities of people and organisations across markets. This control may be direct or indirect, but the power and influence of government is such that large organisations and trade associations seek to influence the direction and strength of legislation, because any adverse laws or regulations may affect the profitability and the value of the organisation. Recent initiatives by the UK government to reduce the length of time that new drugs are protected by patent were severely contested by representatives from drug manufacturers and their trade association, the Association of British Pharmaceutical Industries. Despite a great deal of lobbying, the action was lost, and now manufacturers have only eight years to recover their investment before other manufacturers can replicate the drug.

Customers

This stakeholder group is often the target of public relations activities, because although members of the public may not be current customers, the potential they represent is important. The attitudes and preferences towards the organisation and its products may be unfavourable, in which case it is unlikely that they will wish to purchase the product or speak positively about the organisation. By creating awareness and trust, it is possible to create goodwill and interest, which may translate into purchase activity or favourable word-of-mouth communications.

A framework of public relations

Communications with such a wide variety of stakeholders need to vary to reflect different environmental conditions, organisational objectives and form of relationship. Grunig and Hunt (1984) have attempted to capture the diversity of public relations activities through a framework. They set out four models to reflect the different ways in which public relations is, in their opinion, considered to work. These models, based on their experiences as public relations practitioners, constitute a useful approach to understanding the complexity of this form of communication. The four models are set out in Figure 20.1.

Characteristic	Model: Press agentry/publicity	Public information	Two-way asymmetric	Two-way symmetric
Purpose	Propaganda	Dissemination of information	Scientific persuasion	Mutual understanding
Nature of communication	One-way; complete truth not essential	One-way; truth important	Two-way; imbalanced effects	Two-way; balanced effects
Communication model	Source → Rec.*	Source → Rec.*	Source ⇄ Rec.* Feedback	Group ⇄ Group
Nature of research	Little; 'counting house'	Little; readability, readership	Formative; evaluative of attitudes	Formative; evaluative of understanding
Leading historical figures	P.T. Barnum	Ivy Lee	Edward L. Bernays	Bernays, educators, professional leaders
Where practised today	Sports, theatre, product promotion	Government, not-for-profit associations, business	Competitive business; agencies	Regulated business; agencies
Estimated percentage of organisations practising today	15%	50%	20%	15%

Figure 20.1 Models of public relations (Grunig and Hunt (1984); used with kind permission).
* Receiver.

The press agentry/publicity model

The essence of this approach is that communication is used as a form of propaganda. That is, the communication flow is essentially one-way, and the content is not bound to be strictly truthful as the objective is to convince the receiver of a new idea or offering. This can be observed in the growing proliferation of media events and press releases.

The public information model

Unlike the first model, this approach seeks to disseminate truthful information. While the flow is again one-way, there is little focus on persuasion, more on the provision of information. This can be best seen through public health campaigns and government advice communications in respect of crime, education and health.

The two-way asymmetric model

Two-way communication is a major element of this model. Feedback from receivers is important, but as power is not equally distributed between the various stakeholders and the organisation, the relationship has to be regarded as asymmetric. The purpose remains to influence attitude and behaviour through persuasion.

The two-way symmetric model

This represents the most acceptable and mutually rewarding form of communication. Power is seen to be dispersed equally between the organisation and its stakeholders and the intent of the communication flow is considered to be reciprocal. The organisation and its respective publics are prepared to adjust their positions (attitudes and behaviours) in the light of the information flow. A true dialogue emerges through this interpretation, unlike any of the other three models, which see an unbalanced flow of information and expectations.

The model has attracted a great deal of attention and has been reviewed and appraised by a number of commentators (Miller, 1989). As a result of this and a search for excellence in public relations, Grunig (1992) revised the model to reflect the dominance of the 'craft' and the 'professional' approaches to public relations practices. That is, those practitioners who utilise public relations merely as a tool to achieve media visibility can be regarded as 'craft'-orientated. Those organisations whose managers seek to utilise public relations as a means of mediating their relationships with their various stakeholders are seen as 'professional' practitioners. They are considered to be using public relations as a longer-term and proactive form of planned communication. The former see public relations as an instrument, the latter as a means of conducting a dialogue.

These models are not intended to suggest that communication planners should choose among them. Their use and interpretation depends upon the circumstances that prevail at any one time. Organisations use a number of these different approaches to manage the communication issues that exist between them and the variety of different stakeholder audiences with whom they interact. However, there is plenty of evidence to suggest that the press/agentry model is the one most used by practitioners and that the two-way symmetrical model is harder to observe in practice.

Structure and form of public relations

It can be seen that public relations can be involved with a range of organisational issues. This may be seen as a reflection of the potency of this form of communication. It is more than just a means of influencing other stakeholders through propaganda and/or publicity-based activities. Public relations can be used to mediate the different relationships that an organisation has with its environment and can perform a number of valuable roles, such as counsellor, diplomat and arbiter (Pieczka, 1996). For this to happen a number of environmental conditions need to exist, such as equitable information flows, a managerial predisposition to treat incoming information in an unbiased and apolitical manner, that the power bases throughout the information network are equally dispersed and that the level of connectedness is relatively stable and suitable. If these conditions prevail then public relations may be able to perform the role of a communication conduit for internal and external stakeholders more effectively than under adverse conditions.

The role that public relations should assume and its structural position within an organisation have become increasingly complex and debatable. Traditionally, public relations has been regarded as a function that reports directly to the CEO. Control over the activities of public relations is direct and the purpose is to convey appropriate

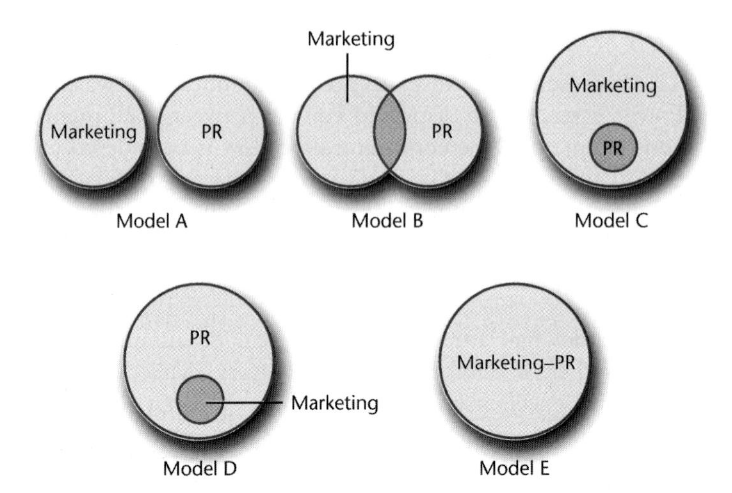

Figure 20.2 Relationships between marketing and public relations (Kotler and Mindak, (1978); used with kind permission).

information about the corporate entity and to create goodwill and understanding with other stakeholders. To that end, public relations was seen as separate to and distinct from marketing. A publication by the Public Relations Educational Trust (1991) declares that 'PR is NOT Marketing'. The substantiation for this is based on an interpretation of marketing, one that is strictly profit-orientated. This does not reflect reality, as self-help groups and organisations such as the NHS and charities would not be able to practise marketing if such a narrow perspective was supported.

Kotler and Mindak (1978) set out five ways in which organisations can manage the marketing and public relations functions. These are depicted in Figure 20.2. It can be seen that the structural relationship of marketing and public relations can range from the traditional view, where they are separate and totally unconnected, fulfilling different roles, through various other forms where one subsumes the other, to Model E. Here, both share an equal and mutually supportive relationship. In this form, both recognise the need to segment markets and to provide different satisfactions. Each function needs the support of the other and both have similar needs in terms of understanding the attitudes, perceptions and awareness held by each market or stakeholder. Internal conflict is effectively reduced, and this in turn facilitates the transmission of consistent, positive and coordinated messages to all stakeholders.

Kotler and Mindak highlight these key relationships well, but the models can also be used to depict the development of public relations and marketing in organisations. For example, local authorities have for a long time had a public relations department, but only recently have they begun to appoint marketing managers in response to their changing responsibilities, environments and new competitive orientation. Hospitals are having to focus on market needs rather than the needs of internal experts. Many are increasing the level of public relations activities and are also introducing marketing as a distinct function, partly to assist the necessary change in culture.

Many private sector organisations are making a transition from Model C to Model D or E, depending upon their experiences and organisational culture, market environments and the perspective of the CEO and senior management team towards the roles of public relations and marketing.

Corporate public relations and marketing public relations

Many writers and organisations are now challenging the traditional view of public relations. The marketing dimension of public relations has been developed considerably in recent years. This is a response to media rates increasing ahead of inflation, media and markets becoming increasingly fragmented, and marketing managers seeking more effective communication mixes. As a result, public relations is being used actively to support and reinforce other elements of the communications mix (Kitchen, 1991).

The development of integrated marketing communications has helped bring marketing and public relations closer together. The advantage of utilising a number of tools together is that through coordination message impact is improved. One of the best examples of this is the Wonderbra campaign by Playtex. It is estimated that the poster campaign was enhanced by £50 million worth of 'extra' media coverage based on the stories and publicity generated by the programme (Barrett, 1997).

It was established earlier (Chapter 6) that a performance network consists of those organisations (stakeholders) who directly influence or are influenced by the value-added processes of the focus organisation. They can engage in relational exchanges and often seek to develop long-term collaborative relationships. The support network consists of those organisations who influence and are influenced by the value-adding processes in an indirect way. They tend to engage in market exchanges which encourage a short-term perspective.

Both these networks require public relations, but in different ways. The support network needs public relations to help build and sustain goodwill between members and to create relationships which acknowledge the direction and intent of the strategy being pursued by each of them. This requires the work of a more traditional approach to public relations. The performance network needs public relations to sustain an environment where there is not only goodwill but also collaboration and trust, one where the satisfaction of particular target segments is the goal of all members. This requires a marketing orientation where there is a greater emphasis on the need to achieve certain levels of profitability as a result of meeting and satisfying customer needs.

Bearing these points in mind and recalling the professional and craft designations set out previously, it is not surprising that two types of public relations have begun to emerge: corporate public relations and marketing public relations. Corporate public relations, according to Cutlip *et al.* (1985), is 'a function of management seeking to identify, establish and maintain mutually beneficial relationships between an organisation and the various publics on whom its success and failure depend'. They define marketing public relations as 'not only concerned with organisational success and failure but also with specific publics: customers, consumers and clients with whom exchange transactions take place'.

This dichotomy is not intended to suggest that these are mutually exclusive forms of public relations, since they are not, and as Kitchen and Proctor (1991) rightly point out, they are mutually interactive. The use of corporate communications has an effect similar to that of ink being injected into a bottle of water: the diffusion produced can assist all parts of an organisation and its stakeholders, whether they be in the performance or support networks. Similarly, public relations at the product level can have an

CASE ILLUSTRATION

Marketing public relations – Raid

In 1995 Raid, a spray designed to destroy wasp nests, was introduced to the UK by Johnson Wax. Raid represented a new way to control this problem, normally handled by calling in the experts. The concept, that this problem could now be managed by the homeowner without having to call out the local council, had first to be conveyed to target audiences. In addition to this, consumers needed to be convinced that the product was easy and safe to use.

The target audiences were identified as mothers (who needed to be reassured from a hygiene standpoint), working women (who needed to know how convenient the product was to use) and men (who needed their DIY expertise and macho image protected).

These tasks were achieved using a variety of communication activities. An advertising campaign was launched through CDP, featuring comic-book bugs living in fear of the Raid shadow. The public relations company Daniel J Edelman then devised a campaign around the advertising. A Big-Bug costume was paraded around supermarkets and third-party links for credibility were made with B&Q and Marks & Spencer. Long-term weather forecasts were used to determine when to get insect experts to comment on infestations and superwasps in particular. These generated public relations stories in some of the tabloid newspapers. The public relations agency set up a national hotline and informed councils to refer consumers should they become overloaded. Over 70 referrals were achieved from a single council in less than 21 days.

One result of all this activity was that the Raid stock was sold out in all the major multiples by the end of the summer. The campaign utilised a number of promotional tools in a coordinated and integrated manner. The thrust of the campaign used marketing public relations, and by combining humour, education and endorsement achieved a remarkable launch.

Adapted from Bond (1996)

immediate effect upon the goodwill and perspective with which stakeholders perceive the whole organisation.

For example, an airline opening a new route and using marketing PR (MPR) activities focused on customers in the hinterland of each destination will impact on both the product and the airline as a whole. Further examples of MPR can be observed at Burger King, when a customer 'careline' was installed (a telephone number) that can be used by customers to contact (complain) about aspects of the company's products and services. The telephone number is printed on posters, receipts and takeaway bags, and not only serves to feed negative aspects but also, through the use of computer analysis, has enabled Burger King to develop new menu and merchandising items (Summers, 1994).

The net impact of either approach has to be reflected in the performance of the organisation, and for many that is the profitability of the unit. The identification of these two forms of public relations does not mean that this approach is a widely used practice. Indeed, at this stage only a minority of organisations recognise the benefits that this approach can bring. However, as an increasing number of organisations, in a variety of sectors, are increasing their use of PR, so more sophisticated approaches are likely to emerge, aimed at improving product, corporate and overall performance and satisfaction levels.

Objectives of a public relations plan

It can be seen that the main broad objectives of public relations activities are to provide visibility for the corporate body and support for the marketing agenda at the product level. The promotional objectives, established earlier in the plan, will have identified issues concerning the attitudes and relationships stakeholders have with an organisation and its products. Decisions will have been made to build awareness and to change perception, preferences or attitudes. The task of the public relations plan is to provide a series of programmes that develop and enhance some of the identity cues used by stakeholders to develop their image of the organisation and its products.

Public relations can be used to address issues identified within the support and performance networks. These will be concerned with communications that aim to develop positive attitudes and dispositions towards the organisation and generally concern strategic issues. Public relations can also contribute to the marketing needs of the organisation and will therefore be focused at the product level in the performance network and on consumers, seeking to change attitudes, preferences and awareness levels with respect to products and services offered. Therefore a series of programmes is necessary: one to fulfil the corporate requirements and another to support the marketing of products and services.

Whether public relations is being used in the performance, support or consumer markets, the development of levels of awareness held by particular audiences is crucial. Similarly, public relations should be used to build credibility, to motivate members of the networks and to minimise overall costs of communication.

A public relations programme consists of a number of planned events and activities that seek to satisfy communication objectives. The following represent some of the broad tools and techniques associated with public relations, but it should be noted that the list is not intended to be comprehensive.

Public relations methods and techniques

An organisation's corporate identity consists of those activities that reflect, to a large extent, the personality of an organisation (see Chapter 27). Public relations provides some of the deliberate cues which enable stakeholders to develop images and perceptions by which they understand and recognise organisations.

The range of public relations cues or methods available to organisations is immense. Different organisations use different permutations in order that they can communicate effectively with their stakeholders. For the purposes of this text a general outline is provided of the more commonly used methods.

Public relations cues are largely visual, whereas those provided by sales promotion, for example, may appeal to a broad range of senses, such as taste, touch and sight. Kitchen and Moss (1995) report how a number of FMCG companies in the UK have categorised the tools used in both these types of public relations. For these organisations, media and sports sponsorships, publicity and sales promotion tie-ups constitute the core activities of marketing public relations. Corporate public relations activities revolve around corporate publicity, issues management, public affairs, lobbying, financial/investor relations and corporate advertising. This demarcation should not be regarded as typical or indeed desirable, but it serves as a useful means

Table 20.1 Cues used by PR to project corporate identity

Cues to build credibility	Cues to signal visibility
Product quality	Sales literature and company publications
Customer relations	Publicity and media relations
Community involvement	Speeches and presentations
Strategic performance	Event management
Employee relations	Promotional messages
Crisis management skills	Media mix
Third party endorsement	Design (signage, logo, letterhead)
Perceived ethics and environmental awareness	Dress codes
Architecture and furnishing	Exhibitions/seminars
	Sponsorships

of understanding the focus of these two types of public relations. What also emerges is a profound recognition of the need to integrate the various communication activities, which itself requires objective and coordinated management attention.

No further attempt is made in this book to segregate the cues used by organisations for either marketing or corporate public relations. The main reason for this is that there is no useful benefit from such a subdivision. Cues are interchangeable and can be used to build credibility or to provide visibility for an organisation. It is the skill of the public relations practitioner that determines the right blend of techniques. The various types of cue are set out in Table 20.1.

While there is general agreement on a definition, there is a lower level of consensus over what constitutes public relations. This is partly because the range of activities is diverse and categorisation problematic. The approach adopted here is that public relations consists of a range of communication activities, of which publicity and event management appear to be the main ones used by practitioners. There are also other activities which are derived from public relations, as follows:

- lobbying (out of personal selling and publicity)
- sponsorship (out of event management and advertising)
- corporate advertising (out of corporate public relations and advertising)
- crisis management (which has developed out of issues management, a part of corporate public relations)
- investor relations (out of issues management and publicity)

Publicity

The quality of the relationship between an organisation and the media will dramatically affect the impact and dissemination of news and stories released by an organisation. The relationships referred to are those between an organisation's public relations manager and the editor and journalists associated with both the press and broadcast media.

Press releases

The press release is a common form of media relations activity. A written report concerning a change in the organisation is sent to various media houses for inclusion in the media vehicle as an item of news. The media house may cover a national area, but very often a local house will suffice. These written statements concern developments in the organisation, such as promotions, new products, awards, prizes, new contracts and customers. The statement is deliberately short and written in such a style that it attracts the attention of the editor. Further information can be obtained if it is to be included within the next publication or news broadcast.

Press conferences

Press conferences are used when a major event has occurred and where a press release cannot convey the appropriate tone or detail required by the organisation. Press conferences are mainly used by politicians, but organisations in crisis (e.g. accidents and mergers) and individuals appealing for help (e.g. police requesting assistance from the public with respect to a particular incident) can use this form of communication. Press kits containing full reproduction of any statements, photographs and relevant background information should always be available.

Interviews

Interviews with representatives of an organisation enable news and the organisation's view of an issue or event to be conveyed. Other forms of media relations concern by-lined articles (articles written by a member of an organisation about an issue related to the company and offered for publication), speeches, letters to the editor, and photographs and captions.

Media relations can be planned and controlled to the extent of what is sent to the media and when it is released. While there is no control over what is actually used, media relations allow organisations to try to convey information concerning strategic issues and to reach particular stakeholders.

Events

Control over public relations events is not as strong as that for publicity. Indeed, negative publicity can be generated by other parties, which can impact badly on an organisation by raising doubts about its financial status or perhaps the quality of its products.

Three main event activity areas can be distinguished: product, corporate and community events.

1. *Product events*
   Product-orientated events are normally focused upon increasing sales. Cookery demonstrations, celebrities autographing their books and the opening of a new store by the CEO or local MP are events aimed at generating attention, interest and sales of a particular product.
2. *Corporate events*
   Events designed to develop the corporate body are often held by an organisation with a view to providing some entertainment. These can generate a lot of local media coverage, which in turn facilitates awareness, goodwill and interest. For example, events such as open days, factory visits and donations of products to local events can be very beneficial.

3. *Community events*
   These are activities that contribute to the life of the local community. Sponsoring local fun runs and children's play areas, making contributions to local community centres and the disabled are typical activities. The organisation attempts to become more involved with the local community as a good employer and good member of the community. This helps to develop goodwill and awareness in the community.

The choice of events an organisation becomes involved with is critical. The events should have a theme and be chosen to satisfy objectives established earlier in the communications plan. See Chapter 21 for an example of sponsorship of local community events.

Lobbying

The representation of certain organisations or industries within government is an important form of public relations work. While legislation is being prepared, lobbyists provide a flow of information to their organisations to keep them informed about events (as a means of scanning the environment), but they also ensure that the views of the organisation are heard in order that legislation can be shaped appropriately, limiting any potential damage that new legislation might bring.

Moloney (1997) suggests that lobbying is inside public relations as it focuses on the members of an organisation who seek to persuade and negotiate with its stakeholders in government on matters of opportunity and or threat. He refers to in-house lobbyists (those members of the organisation that try to influence non-members) and hired lobbyists contracted to complete specific tasks.

His view of lobbying is that it is one of 'monitoring public policy-making for a group interest; building a case in favour of that interest; and putting it privately with varying degrees of pressure to public decision makers for their acceptance and support through favourable political intervention'.

The pharmaceutical industry has been actively lobbying the EU with respect to legislation on new patent regulations and to the information that must be carried in any promotional message. The tobacco industry is well known for its lobbying activities, as are ICI and many other organisations.

Corporate advertising

In an attempt to harness the advantages of both advertising and public relations, corporate advertising has been seen by some as a means of communicating more effectively with a range of stakeholders. The credibility of messages transmitted through public relations is high, but the control that management has over the message is limited. Advertising, however, allows management virtually total control over message dispersion, but the credibility of these messages is usually low. Corporate advertising is the combination of the best of advertising and the best of public relations.

Corporate advertising, that is, advertising on behalf of an organisation rather than the products or services of the organisation, has long been associated with public relations rather than the advertising department. This can be understood in terms of the

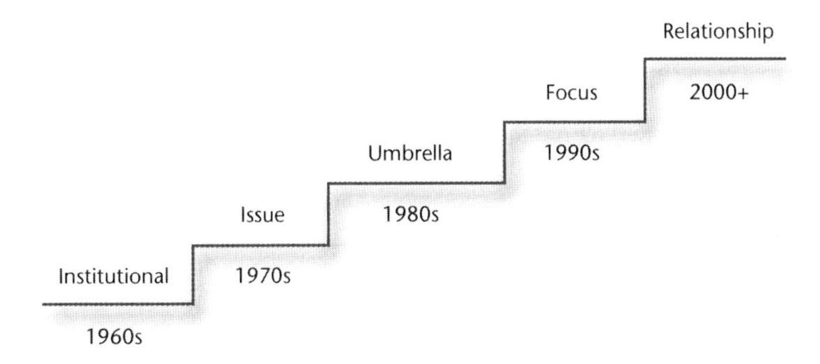

Figure 20.3 The development of corporate advertising.

origins and former use that organisations made of corporate advertising (Figure 20.3). The first major period was the 1960s, when institutional advertising became prominent. According to Stanton (1964), the primary task of institutional advertising was to create goodwill. The next period was the 1970s, when corporate image advertising became popular. During this decade, organisations used issue and advocacy advertising as a means of promoting political and social ideas in an attempt to generate public support for the position adopted by an organisation.

During the 1980s, which witnessed a large number of mergers and takeovers, there was an increase in the use of umbrella advertising. Organisations used the name of the organisation as a broad banner, under which a range of products and services were promoted. As discussed previously, there has been a movement towards the incorporation of products and services in the use of public relations. This is reflected in the use of corporate advertising in the 1990s. Although the generation of goodwill continues to be a dominant theme, there is also a need to focus upon organisations as discrete units. As many organisations de-layer and return to core business activities, so there is a need to focus communications on what they do best. Such focusing also enables them to reduce advertising expenditure on products because of increased media costs.

Corporate advertising provides some opportunity for organisations to achieve these objectives. However, the main purpose of corporate advertising appears to be the provision of cues by which stakeholders can identify and understand an organisation. This is achieved by presenting the personality of the organisation to a wide rage of stakeholders, rather than presenting particular functions or products that the organisation markets. Schumann *et al.* (1991) conclude that a number of US studies indicate that the first goal of corporate advertising is to enhance the company's reputation and the second is to provide support for the promotion of products and services. Table 20.2 sets out the six most important goals that executives see corporate advertising as responsible for satisfying.

Reasons for the use of corporate advertising

The need to improve and maintain goodwill and to establish a positive reputation among an organisation's stakeholders has already been mentioned. These are tasks that need to be undertaken consistently and continuously, with the aim of building a reputational reservoir. In addition, however, there are particular occasions when organisations need to use corporate advertising:

Table 20.2 Goals of corporate advertising

■ Enhancement of company reputation
■ Support for products and services
■ Development of business interests
■ Representation as a corporate information service
■ Advocacy of a position
■ Public communication of the company's social and environmental actions

Source: Adapted from Schumann *et al.* (1991).

- during change and transition
- when the organisation has a poor image
- for product support
- recruitment
- repositioning
- advocacy or issues

Change

When an organisation experiences a period of major change, perhaps the transition before, during and after a takeover or merger, corporate advertising can be used in a variety of ways. The first is defensively, to convince stakeholders, particularly shareholders, of the value of the organisation and of the need not to accept hostile offers; second to inform and to advise of current positions; and finally to position any 'new' organisation that may result from the merger activity. The sale of shares in the House of Fraser in the spring of 1994 was preceded by a burst of corporate advertising designed to raise awareness and to build stature and authority. This was intended to raise credibility and hence ensure a good take-up of the share offer.

Poor image

Corporate advertising can also be used to correct any misunderstanding that stakeholders might have of corporate reality (Reisman, 1989). For example, financial analysts may believe that an organisation is underperforming, but reality indicates that performance is good. As we have seen before, this can be a result of poor communication, and through corporate advertising the organisation can correct such misunderstandings and help establish strategic credibility with the financial community and other stakeholders.

Product support

Corporate advertising can also assist the launch of new products. The costs normally associated with a launch can be lowered, and it is feasible to assume, although difficult to measure, that the effectiveness of a product launch can be improved when corporate advertising has been used to establish good reputational equity.

Recruitment

Corporate advertising is used to recruit employees by creating a positive and attractive image of the organisation. The development of source credibility, in particular trust, is fundamental, and through the process of identification individuals can become attracted to the notion of working for a particular organisation and are stimulated to seek further information.

Repositioning

Organisations can be repositioned by the activities of competitor organisations. New products, new corporate messages, an improved trading performance or the arrival of a new CEO and the implementation of a new strategy can displace an organisation in the minds of its different stakeholders. This may require an adjustment by the focus organisation to re-establish itself. The Pepsi Challenge referred to earlier effectively dislodged Coca-Cola from its position as brand leader and led to a stream of product adjustments and messages from Coca-Cola aimed at repositioning itself.

Advocacy

The reasons presented so far for the use of corporate advertising are strongly related to image. A further traditional reason for the use of this tool is the opportunity for the organisation to inform its stakeholders of the position or stand that it has on a particular issue. This is referred to as advocacy advertising. Rather than promoting the organisation in a direct way, this form of corporate advertising associates an organisation with an issue of social concern, which public relations very often cannot achieve alone.

The organisation can be seen as a brand in much the same way as products and services are branded. Just as a product-based brand can be tracked, so can the corporate entity be tracked for levels of awareness, attitudes and preferences held by stakeholders.

Crisis management

A growing and important part of the work associated with public relations is crisis management. At one time, when a crisis such as a threat of takeover or workplace accident struck an organisation, the first stakeholders to be summoned by the CEOs were merchant bankers. Today the public relations consultant is first through the door. The power of corporate and marketing communications is beginning to be recognised and appreciated. Indeed, the astute CEO summons the public relations consultant in anticipation of crisis, on the basis that being prepared is a major step in diffusing the energy with which some crises can affect organisations.

Crises are emerging with greater frequency as a result of a number of factors. The first, according to Ten Berge (1991), concerns the rise of consumer groups (e.g. Greenpeace) and their ability to investigate and publicise the operations and policies of organisations. The second is that the age of instant communication, facilitated by electronic media, means that information can be disseminated throughout the world within thirty minutes of an event occurring. Third, the rate at which technology is advancing has brought about crises such as those associated with transportation systems and aircraft disasters. Human error is also a significant factor, often associated with the rate of technological change. Fourth, the climate is also changing substantially in certain parts of the world, and this can bring disaster to those who lie in the wake of natural disturbances. Finally, the economic environment is also changing as the Western world experiences stagnation and maturing markets and countries in the developing world follow a rigorous path of vitalisation and competition that has brought some organisations and industries in the West to collapse (e.g. UK shipbuilding).

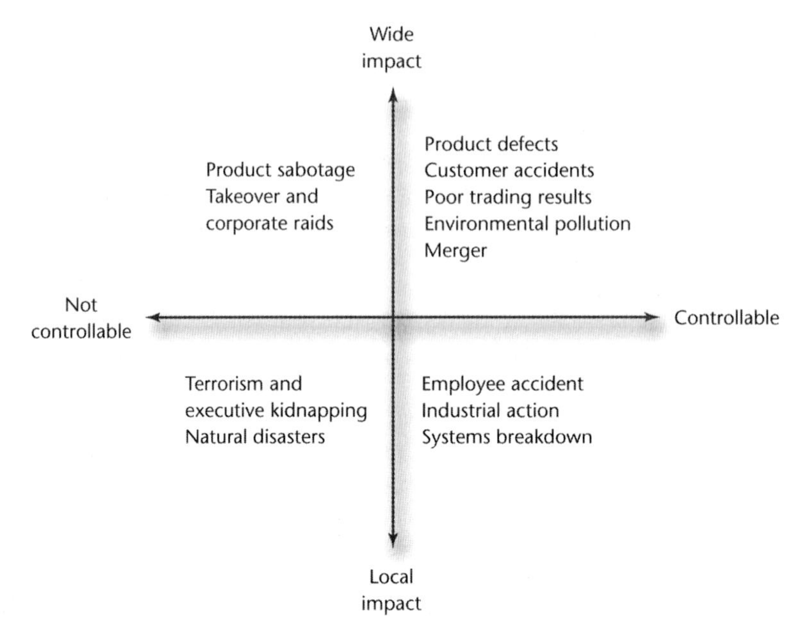

Figure 20.4 An organisational crisis matrix.

Figure 20.4 describes organisational crises in the context of two key variables. On the horizontal axis is the degree to which management has control over the origin of the crisis. Is the origin of the crisis outside management's control, such as an earthquake, or is it within its control, such as those crises associated with poor trading results? The vertical axis reflects the potential impact that a crisis might have on an organisation. All crises, by definition, have a potential to inflict damage on an organisation. However, some can be contained, perhaps on a geographic basis, whereas others have the potential to cause tremendous damage to an organisation, such as those experienced through product tampering and environmental pollution.

The increasing occurrence of crises throughout the world has prompted many organisations to review the manner in which they anticipate managing such events, should they be implicated. It is generally assumed that those organisations that take the care to plan in anticipation of disaster will experience more favourable outcomes than those that fail to plan. Quarentelli (1988) reports that there is only a partial correlation between those that plan and those that experience successful outcomes. He attributes this to the fact that only some of the organisations that take care to prepare do so in a professional way. Poor planning can only deliver poor results.

The second reason concerns the expectations of those who design and implement crisis plans. It is one thing to design a plan; it is entirely another to implement it. Crisis planning is about putting into position those elements that can effect speedy outcomes to the disaster sequence. When a crisis strikes, it is the application of contingency-based tactics by all those concerned with the event that will determine the strength of the outcome.

Crisis phases

The period over which a crisis occurs can be divided into activity phases. These are scanning, pre-impact, impact and readjustment phases. It should be remembered that the duration of each phase can vary considerably, depending upon the nature of the crisis and the manner in which management deals with the events associated with the crisis.

The first period is referred to as the scanning phase. Good strategic management demands that the environment be scanned on a regular basis to detect the first signs of significant change. Organisations that pick up signals that are repeated are in a better position to prepare for disaster than those that do not scan the environment. Those that fail to scan are often taken by surprise and have to react with less time and control to manage the events that hit them. Even if they do pick up a signal, many organisations not only ignore it, but also attempt to block it out (Pearson and Mitroff, 1993). It is as if management is attempting to deny the presence of the signals in order that any stability and certainty they may have could continue.

Many of the signals detected during the scanning phase wither and die. Some gather strength and develop with increasing force. This pre-impact phase is characterised by increasing activity and preparation in anticipation of the crisis, once its true nature and direction have been determined. Much of the activity should be geared to training and the preparation and deployment of crisis teams. The objective is not to prevent the crisis but to defuse it as much as possible, to inform significant stakeholders of its proximity and possible effects, and finally to manage the crisis process.

The impact phase is the period when the 'crisis breaks out' (Sturges *et al.*, 1991). Management is tested to the limit and if a plan has been developed it is implemented with the expectation of ameliorating the damage inflicted by the crisis. One method of reducing the impact is to contain or localise the crisis. By neutralising and constraining the event, it is prevented from contaminating other parts of the organisation or stakeholders. Pearson and Mitroff suggest that the containment of oil spills and the evacuation of buildings and aircraft are examples of containment and neutralisation. Through the necessity to talk to all stakeholders, management at this point will inevitably reveal its attitude towards the crisis event. Is its attitude one of genuine concern for the victims and stakeholders? Is the attitude consistent with the expectations that stakeholders have of the management team? Alternatively, is there a perception that management is making lame excuses and distancing itself from the event, and is this consistent with expectations?

The readjustment phase refers to the recovery and realignment of the organisation and its stakeholders to the new environment, once the deepest part of the crisis has passed. The essential tasks are to ensure that the needs of key stakeholders can still be met and, if they cannot, to determine what must be done to ensure that they can be. For example, continuity of product supply is critically important. This may be achieved by servicing customers from other locations.

Common characteristics of this phase are the investigations, police inquiries, public demonstrations, court cases and media probing that inevitably follow major crises and disasters. The manner in which an organisation handles this fall-out and tries to appear reasonable and consistent in its approach to such events can have a big impact on the perception that other stakeholders have of the organisation.

The rate at which organisations readjust is partly dependent upon the strength of the image held by stakeholders prior to the crisis occurring. If the organisation had a strong reputation then the source credibility attributed to the organisation will be high. This means that messages transmitted by the organisation would be received favourably and trusted. However, if the reputation is poor, the effectiveness of any marketing communications is also going to be low. The level of source credibility held

CASE ILLUSTRATION

Phased crises – Mercedes

In the autumn of 1997 Mercedes was in the final stages of launching a new car, the A-Class. This was no ordinary car, in that it represented a major strategic move to enter the mass car market, using the credibility and reputation of Mercedes as the main rationale for buyers. The car was revolutionary in many ways, and for some it represented the most significant development in the mass market since the Mini was launched 40 years previously.

The car was revolutionary because the engine was positioned along the bottom of the car, and although only 12 feet long the car carried four people comfortably. Initial motor journalist reaction (opinion formers) was very positive and expectations had risen as more was revealed about the A-Class. Inquiries from motorists reached 100,000 in the six months before the launch.

In Sweden a common road hazard is the elk: and 10 Swedes and over 5,500 elks were killed in 1996 from road accidents involving elks. As a result, an 'elk test' has been developed which requires a driver to swerve violently from side to side as if trying to miss one of these large animals. Most cars pass this test comfortably, but the A-Class rolled over on its roof at just 60 kph (37 mph).

Contact was made with two television stations immediately after the incident...before an ambulance was called to assist the driver. Cameras arrived within minutes to video the driver and the upturned car.

Executive reaction at Mercedes-Benz when the news broke was 'so what'? The company is reported as saying 'they did not think it necessary to issue a statement just because a car flipped over somewhere'.

Twenty-four hours later the company saw the video and began to revise its opinion of the possible consequences. How could a company those reputation was built on engineering excellence and safety have developed a car that appeared to be inherently unstable?

Mercedes blamed the tyres, a switch to the harder tyres of Michelin rather than Goodyear. But that was not enough, and within a week German magazines started to publish pictures of the car that failed the 'elk test'.

A press conference was held eight days after the incident with the company still proclaiming the car was sound. However, executives announced that an electronic stabilising system would be fitted as standard to all models. This move would cost DM 50 million alone, and so hit profits, but worse was to follow as over 3,000 orders were cancelled (although it was reported that 3,000 orders were also received, so it might be that the negative publicity also worked to the organisation's benefit).

Realising the enormity of the problem, the Board announced that all deliveries of the A-Class would be delayed until February 1998, that the chassis would be redesigned to provide greater stability and that nobody regretted the weakness more than Mercedes and that an optimal solution would be found.

Adapted from Olins and Lynn (1997)

by the organisation will influence the speed with which stakeholders allow an organisation to readjust and recover after a crisis.

The impact of the crisis at Mercedes can be seen to have progressed through a number of stages. Mercedes does not score highly when measured against the various phases of the crisis development. There was obvious poor scanning of the environment and anticipation of this basic form of car testing, and poor preparation at the pre-impact phase to diffuse the problem when or if it occurred. At the next phase, impact, can Mercedes be seen to have tried to contain the crisis and was there an atti-

CASE ILLUSTRATION

Crisis management – EuroTunnel

The fire in the Channel tunnel in November 1996 serves to illustrate a number of points about how to manage a crisis. The fire occurred on a freight-only train (Le Shuttle) at approximately 2200 hrs, a few miles into the tunnel from the French side. While there had been a full rehearsal only 10 days previously, the scale and timing (see later) of the fire caught out the crisis management team.

The first official reports from the press team were in direct conflict with the accounts of lorry drivers trapped on the train in the tunnel. The EuroTunnel chairman announced that the fire was an 'unpleasant incident', only for it to graduate to 'a serious incident' in just a few hours. The full extent of the damage, as shown to the media two days later revealed that the fire had been a major accident. At the same time announcements were being made about when the tunnel would reopen. Initially it was to be tomorrow, then Saturday, then next week, and eventually it was to be in three months. This was confusing and alarming, and could even be perceived as inept and misleading.

The EuroTunnel press team admit that the incident could have been managed more effectively. However, they suggest a number of reasons why the crisis plan that had been prepared failed to operate as planned.

1. The focus of the disaster plan had been misplaced. It was believed that the crisis would be financial, not operational.
2. The original four press offices were reduced to two, so there was little chance that the 1000+ telephone calls received in the first 24 hours could be handled effectively.
3. The public relations department was being restructured, and at the time of the accident there was no head (or front person) and only three press officers, not the normal six.
4. As the tunnel is managed by both the French and the English there had to be strict and proper coordination. This did not happen, and the media were able to bounce stories off both parties and so extend the life of the crisis.
5. The cultural differences between the French and English media also played a part. The French media saw the incident as a business story, whereas the English media took a more sensationalist position. Consequently, the French were observed to be more complacent.
6. Language difficulties resulting from mistranslation led to misinformation and an obvious feed for the media.

It is reported that with hindsight many of those involved with the disaster would have speeded up the flow of factual information and even overstated the accident when the story broke so as to earn the public's trust in the information being provided and in those providing it. EuroTunnel argues that, judging by the 90% of people either returning or intending to reuse the Shuttle and Eurostar (the passenger train) services by the following January, the crisis team were successful.

Adapted from *Marketing*, January 1997

tude of genuine concern? Yes, at later stages when the size of the crisis was fully recognised, but not at the start. The organisation's eventual recognition of the problem and decision to redesign the chassis and accept responsibility may have come too late, and the damage inflicted on the reputation of Mercedes-Benz may be a cause for much regret.

Figure 20.5 Crisis roles for stakeholders (Pearson and Mitroff (1993); used with kind permission).

Who is affected by crisis events? When a crisis hits an organisation, many different stakeholders are vulnerable to the repercussions. Pearson and Mitroff suggest that stakeholders may perceive the focus organisation adopting a particular role. This role may be as a hero, villain or even protector. Figure 20.5 depicts some of the roles that focus organisation might be cast in; in much the same way, stakeholders themselves might be cast in a role that reflects the perception of the focus organisation. It is interesting to monitor the ascribed roles and to see whether stakeholders actually fulfil their designated role or perhaps another when crisis strikes. Perhaps a move from rescuer to enemy is not uncommon!

The importance of this perspective is that attention has to be focused on the different organisations, not just the one on which the crisis has had immediate impact. The stakeholder net is wide and the sensitivity among cohesive groups in particular can be acute. The organisation that has a crisis plan of value is one that has considered the impact upon its stakeholders.

Integration of public relations in the promotional mix

Public relations has two major roles to play within the communications programme of an organisation. These are the development and maintenance of corporate goodwill and the continuity necessary for good product support.

The first is the traditional role of creating goodwill and stimulating interest between the organisation and its various key stakeholders. Its task is to provide a series of cues by which the stakeholders can recognise, understand and position the organisation in such a way that the organisation builds a strong reputation. This role is closely allied to the corporate strategy and the communication of strategic intent.

The second role of public relations is to support the marketing of the organisation's products and services, and its task is to integrate with the other elements of the promotional mix. Public relations and advertising have complementary roles. For example, the launch of a new product commences not with advertising to build awareness in target customers, but with the use of public relations to inform editors

CASE ILLUSTRATION

Marketing public relations – Ajax

During the early 1990s, the Ajax brand of domestic liquid cleaner was adjudged to be underperforming against heavy competition from Unilever and Procter & Gamble. With an initial budget of less than £100,000, Colgate-Palmolive used a marketing public relations-led approach to raise brand visibility. A public relations agency, Cohn and Wolfe, was appointed and they devised a campaign based around a change in the perceptions of cleaning. Advertising was used to convey a message that women could save time doing the cleaning by showing men doing it. This was then followed up by a number of articles in the press and broadcast media using the interest generated by the advertisements.

An advertising agency, da Costa and Co. was appointed and worked with Cohn and Wolfe to devise a series of advertisements picturing scantily dressed young men doing the cleaning. The copy ran 'How to save time doing the cleaning. Get him new Ajax Liquid'. The copy provided information about the product's ease of use and convenience, but ended with the line 'Because you don't want him to spend all his time cleaning'.

The campaign was based on half-page advertisements run in general interest magazines such as *Woman, Chat, She* and *Cosmopolitan.* The media relations activity then fed off the provocative campaign and was supplemented by primary research into domestic cleaning and later on changing social trends. Editorial coverage was achieved in a variety of broadsheet and tabloid newspapers. Broadcast coverage was achieved on Granada TV and Radio 1.

A total editorial reach of 17 million was achieved, and the comment about the campaign generated an equivalent of three times the advertising spend. As a follow-up, a sales promotion contest was added in conjunction with a Sunday paper. This integrated campaign brought marketing public relations, advertising and sales promotion together. For a total spend of less than £1 million the campaign achieved a high reach and impact and demonstrated the value of integrating the elements of the communication mix.

Adapted from a *Campaign* report, 6 May 1994

and news broadcasters that a new product is about to be launched. This news material can be used within the trade and consumer press before advertising occurs and the target buyers become aware (when the news is no longer news). To some extent this role is tactical rather than strategic, but if planned, and if events are timed and coordinated with the other elements of the promotional mix, then public relations can help build competitive advantage.

Evaluating the use of public relations

Each of the two main forms, corporate and marketing public relations, seeks to achieve different objectives and does so by employing different approaches and techniques. However, they are not mutually exclusive and the activities of one form of public relations impact upon the other; they are self-reinforcing.

Corporate public relations (CPR)

The objectives that are established at the beginning of a promotional campaign must form the basis of any evaluation and testing activity. However, much of the work of CPR is continuous, and therefore measurement should not be campaign-orientated or time-restricted but undertaken on a regular ongoing basis. CPR is mainly responsible for the identity cues that are presented to the organisation's various stakeholders as part of a planned programme of communications. These cues signal the visibility and profile of the organisation and are used by stakeholders to shape the image that each has of the focus organisation.

CPR is, therefore, focused upon communication activities, such as awareness, but there are others such as preference, interest and conviction. Evaluation should, in the first instance, measure levels of awareness of the organisation. Attention should then focus upon the levels of interest, goodwill and attitudes held towards the organisation as a result of all the planned and unplanned cues used by the organisation.

Traditionally these levels were assumed to have been generated by public relations activities. The main method of measuring their contribution to the communication programme was to collect press cuttings and to record the number of mentions the organisation received in the electronic media. These were then collated in a cuttings book which would be presented to the client. This would be similar to an explorer presenting an electric toaster to a tribe of warriors hitherto undisturbed by other civilisations! Looks nice, but what do you do with it and is it of any real use? Despite this slightly cynical interpretation, the cuttings book does provide an attempt to 'understand the level of opportunity to see' created by public relations activities (Parker, 1991).

The content of the cuttings book and the recorded media mentions can be converted into a different currency. The exchange rate used is the cost of the media that would have been incurred had this volume of communication or awareness been generated by advertising activity. For example, a 30 second news item about an organisation's contribution to a charity event may be exchanged into a 30 second advertisement at rate card cost. The temptation is clear, but the validity of the equation is not acceptable. By translating public relations into advertising currency the client is expected not only to understand but also approve of the enhanced credibility that advertising possesses. It is not surprising that the widely held notion that public relations is free advertising has grown so substantially when practitioners use this approach.

A further refinement of the cuttings book is to analyse the material covered. The coverage may be positive or negative, approving or disapproving, so the quality of the cuttings needs to be reviewed in order that the client organisation can make an informed judgement about its next set of decisions. This survey of the material in the cuttings book is referred to as a content analysis. Traditionally, content analyses have had to be undertaken qualitatively and were therefore subject to poor interpretation and reviewer bias, however well they approached their task. Today, increasingly sophisticated software is being used to produce a wealth of quantitative data reflecting the key variables that clients want evaluated.

Hauss (1993) suggests that key variables could include the type of publication, the favourability of the article, the name of the journalist, the audiences being reached and the type of coverage. All these and others can be built into programmes. The results can then be cross-tabulated so that it is possible to see in which part of the country the most favourable comments are being generated or observe which opinion formers are positively or negatively disposed.

Corporate image

The approaches discussed so far are intended to evaluate specific media activity and comment about the focus organisation. Press releases are fed into the media and there is a response which is measured in terms of positive or negative, for or against. This quality of information, while useful, does not assist the management of the corporate identity. To do this requires an evaluation of the position that an organisation has in the eyes of key members of the performance network. In addition, the information is not specific enough to influence the strategic direction that an organisation has or the speed at which the organisation is changing. Indeed, most organisations now experience perpetual change; stability and continuity are terms related to an environment that is unlikely to be repeated.

The evaluation of the corporate image should be a regular exercise, supported by management. There are three main aspects. First, key stakeholders (including employees, as they are an important source of communications for external stakeholders), together with members of the performance network and customers, should be questioned regarding their perceptions of the important attributes of the focus organisation and the business they are in (Chapter 10). Second, how does the organisation perform against each of the attributes? Third, how does the organisation perform relative to its main competitors across these attributes?

The results of these perceptions can be evaluated so that corrective action can be directed at particular parts of the organisation and adjustments made to the strategies pursued at business and functional levels. For example, in the computer retailing business, prompt home delivery is a very important attribute. If company A had a rating of 90% on this attribute, but company B was believed to be so good that it was rated at 95%, regardless of actual performance levels, then although A was doing a superb job it would have to improve its delivery service and inform its stakeholders that it was particularly good at this part of the business.

Recruitment

Recruitment for some organisations can be a problem. In some sectors, where skills are in short supply, the best staff gravitate towards those organisations that are perceived to be better employers and provide better rewards and opportunities. Part of the task of CPR is to provide the necessary communications so that a target pool of employees is aware of the benefits of working with the focus organisation and develops a desire to work there.

Measurement of this aspect of CPR can be seductive. It is tempting just to measure the attitudes of the pool of talent prior to a campaign and then to measure it again at the end. This fails to account for the uncontrollable elements in CPR, for example the actions of others in the market, but even if this approach is simplistic and slightly erroneous, it does focus attention on an issue. ICI found that it was failing to attract the necessary number of talented undergraduates in the early and mid-1980s, partly because the organisation was perceived as unexciting, bureaucratic and lacking career opportunities. A coordinated marketing communications campaign, documented elsewhere in this text, was targeted at university students, partly at repositioning the organisation in such a way that they would want to work for ICI when they finished their degrees. The results indicated that students' approval of ICI as a future employer rose substantially in the period following the campaign.

Crisis management

During periods of high environmental turbulence and instability, organisations tend to centralise their decision-making processes and their communications (Quinn and Mintzberg, 1992). When a crisis occurs, communications with stakeholders should increase to keep them informed and aware of developments. Earlier in this chapter, it was observed that crises normally follow a number of phases, during which different types of information must be communicated. When the crisis is over the organisation enters a period of feedback and development for the organisation. 'What did we do?', 'How did it happen?', 'Why did we do that?' and 'What do we need to do in the future?' are typical questions that socially aware and mature organisations, who are concerned with quality and the needs of their stakeholders, should always ask themselves.

Pearson and Mitroff (1993) report that many organisations do not expose themselves to this learning process in fear of 'opening up old wounds'. Those organisations that do take action should communicate their actions to reassure all stakeholders that the organisation has done all it can do to prevent a recurrence, or at least to minimise the impact should the origin of the crisis be outside the control of management. A further question that needs to be addressed concerns the way the organisation was perceived during the different crisis phases. Was the image consistent? Did it change, and if so why? Management may believe that it did an excellent job in crisis containment, but what really matters is what stakeholders think; it is their attitudes and opinions that matter above all else.

The objective of crisis management is to limit the effect that a crisis might have on an organisation and its stakeholders, assuming the crisis cannot be prevented. The social system in which an organisation operates means that the image held of the organisation may well change as a result of the crisis event. The image does not necessarily become negative. On the contrary, it may be that the strategic credibility of the organisation could be considerably enhanced if the crisis is managed in an open and positive way. However, it is necessary for the image that stakeholders have of an organisation to be tracked on a regular basis. This means that the image and impact of the crisis can be monitored through each of the crisis phases. Sturges *et al.* (1991) argue that the objective of crisis management is to influence public opinion to the point that 'post-crisis opinions of any stakeholder group are at least positive, or more positive, or not more negative than before the crisis event'. This ties in with the need to monitor corporate image on a regular basis. The management process of scanning the environment for signals of change and change in the attitudes and the perception held by stakeholders towards the organisation make up a joint process which public relations activities have a major role in executing.

Marketing public relations (MPR)

It was identified earlier that there is evidence of the increasing use of MPR. There are many reasons for this growth, but some of the more important ones quoted by organisations are rising media costs, audience fragmentation, changing consumer attitudes and increasing educational needs (Kitchen, 1993). By using public relations to support the marketing effort in a direct way, organisations are acknowledging that the third-party endorsement provided by MPR delivers a high level of credibility and cost-effectiveness that the other elements of the promotions mix fail to provide.

As Kitchen rightly argues, MPR cannot exist in a vacuum, it must be integrated with the other elements of the mix and provide complementarity. It is through the use of MPR as a form of product support and as part of a planned communications mix that makes this a source of high-quality leads. However, evaluating the contribution of MPR is problematic.

Some practitioners believe that this can be overcome by coding press releases as a campaign, and with the use of particular software leads can be tracked and costed. Hauss (1993) quotes Obermayer of the Inquiry Handling Service, a US-based software house. If 25 press releases were generated and the client received 4,000 inquiries the analysis ends there. With the right software, the actual cost of a press release can be input and the number of leads that come back can be measured against sales on the database.

The software can not only estimate sales but can also work out the number of leads required to make quota. The formula used is based on the rule that 45% of leads turn into sales for someone in the market within the year. The organisation's own conversion rate can be used to adjust the 45% and the quality of its lead conversion process can also be input. One of the benefits of this approach is that quantitative outcomes provide a measure of effectiveness, but not necessarily the effectiveness of the MPR campaign.

Pre- and post-test measures of awareness, preference, comprehension and intentions are a better measure of the quality and impact that an MPR campaign might have on a target audience. Measuring the conversion ratio of leads to sales is not the only measure, as it fails to isolate the other forces that impact on market performance.

MPR in business-to-business markets is directly targeted at members of the performance network. The objectives are many and include building awareness, reducing costs, satisfying educational needs and enhancing image through improving credibility. The overriding need, however, is to improve the relationship between members of the network and to provide them with a reason to continue transactions with the focus organisation. The reasons are similar to those in the personal selling buying formula (Chapter 22), namely to associate product adequacy when the appropriate problem is surfaced, and to create pleasant feelings when the name of the product or the organisation is mentioned in the same context. MPR in this situation is being used as a competitive tool to defend established positions. Measurement of the effectiveness of MPR, therefore, should be undertaken by evaluating the degree to which members support, like, endorse or prefer the focus organisation and the products it offers. This can be achieved through the use of tracking studies which plot attitudes and opinions, against which the timings of campaigns and MPR activities can be traced and evaluated.

Both CPR and MPR are difficult and elusive elements of the promotional mix to test, measure and evaluate. Practitioners use a variety of methods, but few of them provide the objectivity and validity that is necessary. As a greater number of organisations are beginning to recognise the impact that public relations can provide and establish a more credible balance to the promotional mix, so there is a greater requirement for planning and evaluation to be built into the process from the beginning (Watson, 1992).

If, at the end of the process, evaluation and testing lack objectivity, then the method should not be used.

Summary

Public relations, whether orientated primarily to product support or to the development of corporate goodwill, plays an important role within the communications mix. According to Haywood (1991), public relations can support marketing in a number of ways, from improving awareness and projecting credibility to the creation of direct sales leads and motivating the sales force and members of the performance network.

By providing all stakeholders with cues by which they can develop an image of an organisation, public relations enables organisations to position themselves and provide stakeholders with a means of identifying and understanding an organisation. This may be accomplished inadvertently through inaction or deliberately through a planned presentation of a variety of visual cues. These range from publicity through press releases to the manner in which customers are treated, products perform, events are managed and expectations are met.

Finally, the area referred to as crisis communications management has grown in significance during recent years. Public relations plays an important role in preparing for and constraining the impact of a crisis and re-establishing an organisation once a crisis has passed.

By creating campaigns targeted at individual stakeholders, or at least identifying the needs of the performance network as separate from those of the support network, the effects intended at the outset can be measured at the close of different campaigns.

Review questions

1. Define public relations and set out its principal characteristics.
2. Using an organisation of your choice, identify the main stakeholders and comment on why it is important to communicate with each of them.
3. Highlight the main objectives of using public relations.
4. What is the difference between corporate public relations and marketing public relations? Is this difference of importance?
5. Write a brief paper describing the main methods of publicity.
6. Why do you think an increasing number of organisations are using sponsorship as a part of their promotional mix?
7. Suggest occasions when corporate advertising might be best employed.
8. Identify the main phases associated with crisis management.
9. What roles might stakeholders adopt when a crisis occurs?
10. Discuss the view that public relations can only ever be a support tool in the promotional mix.

References

Barrett, P. (1997) A marriage of PR and ads. *Marketing*, 30 October, p. 15.
Bond, C. (1996) PRCA awards, in *Campaign*, 12 September, pp. 34–5.

Cutlip, S., Center, A.H. and Broom, G.J. (1985) *Effective Public Relations*. Englewood Cliffs NJ: Prentice Hall.

Haywood, R. (1991) *All About Public Relations*, 2nd edn. Maidenhead: McGraw-Hill.

Grunig, J. (ed.) (1992) *Excellence in Public Relations and Communications Management*. Hillsdale NJ: Lawrence Erlbaum.

Grunig, J. and Hunt, T. (1984) *Managing Public Relations*. New York: Holt, Rineholt & Winston.

Hauss, D. (1993) Measuring the impact of public relations. *Public Relations Journal* (February), 14–21.

Kitchen, P.J. (1991) Developing use of PR in a fragmented demassified market. *Marketing Intelligence and Planning*, **9**(2), 29–33.

Kitchen, P.J. and Procter, R.A. (1991) The increasing importance of public relations in FMCG firms. *Journal of Marketing Management*, **7**, 357–70.

Kitchen, P.J. (1993) Public relations: a rationale for its development and usage within UK fast-moving consumer goods firms. *European Journal of Marketing*, **27**(7), 53–75.

Kitchen, P.J. and Moss, D. (1995) Marketing and public relations: the relationship revisited. *Journal of Marketing Communications*, **1**, 105–19

Kotler, P. and Mindak, W. (1978) Marketing and public relations. *Journal of Marketing*, **42** (October), 13–20.

Miller, G. (1989) Persuasion and public relations: two 'Ps' in a pod, in *Public Relations Theory* (eds. C. Botan and V. Hazelton). Hilldale NJ: Lawrence Erlbaum.

Moloney, K. (1997) Government and lobbying activities, in *Public Relations: Principles and Practice* (ed. P.J. Kitchen). London: International Thomson Press.

Olins, R. and Lynn, M, (1997) A-Class disaster. *Sunday Times*, Business Focus, 16 November, p. 3.

Parker, K. (1991) Sponsorship: the research contribution. *European Journal of Marketing*, **25**(11), 22–30.

Pearson, C.M. and Mitroff, I. (1993) From crisis prone to crisis prepared: a framework for crisis management. *Academy of Management Executive*, **7**(1), 48–59.

Pieczka, M. (1996) Public opinion and public relations, in *Critical Perspectives in Public Relations* (eds. J. L'Etang and M. Pieczka). London: International Thomson Business Press.

Public Relations Educational Trust (1991) *The Place of Public Relations in Management Education*, Institute of Public Relations.

Quarantelli, E.L. (1988) Disaster crisis management: a summary of research findings. *Journal of Management Studies*, **25**(4), 373–85.

Quinn, J.B. and Mintzberg, H. (1992) *The Strategy Process*, 2nd edn. Englewood Cliffs NJ: Prentice Hall.

Reisman, J. (1989) Corporate advertising in disguise. *Public Relations Journal* (September), 21–7.

Schumann, D.W., Hathcote, J.M. and West, S. (1991) 'Corporate advertising in America: a review of published studies on use, measurement and effectiveness. *Journal of Advertising*, **20**(3), 35–56.

Stanton, W.J. (1964) *Fundamentals of Marketing*. New York: McGraw-Hill.

Sturges, D.L., Carrell, B.J., Newsom, D.A. and Barrera, M. (1991) Crisis communication management: the public opinion node and its relationship to environmental nimbus. *SAM Advanced Management Journal* (Summer), 22–7.

Summers, D. (1994) Show your customers you care. *Financial Times*, 13 January, p. 11.

Ten Berge, D. (1991) Planning for crisis: how to cope with the wolf at the door. *European Management Journal*, **9**(1), 30–5.

Watson, T. (1992) Evaluating PR effects. *Admap* (June), 28–30.

chapter 21

Sponsorship

Sponsorship is a commercial activity, whereby one party permits another an opportunity to exploit an association with a target audience in return for funds, services or resources.

AIMS AND OBJECTIVES

The aims of this chapter are to introduce and examine sponsorship as an increasingly significant form of marketing communications.

The objectives of this chapter are:

1. To appreciate the variety and different forms of sponsorship activities.
2. To understand the reasons why sponsorship has become an important part of the promotional mix.
3. To provide an insight into the main characteristics of this form of communication.
4. To consider where in the promotional mix sponsorship may be best associated.
5. To explore ways in which sponsorship can be best evaluated.

Introduction

It was mentioned earlier that community PR requires an organisation to contribute to the local community with a view to being seen as participative, caring and more involved with local affairs. The degree of control that can be levied against this type of activity is limited once a commitment has been made. By adopting a more commercial perspective, some organisations have used sponsorship, particularly of sports activities, as a means of reaching wider target audiences. Sponsorship can provide the following opportunities for the sponsoring organisation:

1. Exposure to particular audiences that each event attracts in order to convey simple awareness-based brand messages.
2. To suggest to the target audiences that there is an association between the sponsee and the sponsor and that by implication this association may be of interest and/or value.
3. To allow members of the target audiences to perceive the sponsor indirectly through a third party and so diffuse any negative effects associated with traditional mass media and direct persuasion.
4. Sponsorship provides sponsors with the opportunity to blend a variety of tools in the promotional mix and use resources more efficiently and arguably more effectively.

From this it is possible to define sponsorship as a commercial activity, whereby one party permits another an opportunity to exploit an association with a target audience in return for funds, services or resources.

It should be made clear that there is a clear distinction between sponsorship and charitable donations. The latter are intended to change attitudes and project a caring identity, with the main returns from the exercise being directed to society or the beneficiaries. The beneficiaries have almost total control over the way in which funds are used. When funds are channelled through a sponsorship the recipient has to attend to the needs of the sponsor by allowing it access to the commercial associations that are to be exploited, partly because they have a legal arrangement, but also to ensure that the exchange becomes relational and longer term; in other words, there is repeat purchase (investment) activity. The other major difference is that the benefits of the exchange are intended to accrue to the participants, not society at large.

The development of sponsorship as a communication tool has been spectacular since the early 1990s. This is because of a variety of factors, but among the most important, according to Meenaghan (1991), are the government's policies on tobacco and alcohol, the escalating costs of advertising media, the proven ability of sponsorship, new opportunities due to increased leisure activity, greater media coverage of sponsored events and the recognition of the inefficiencies associated with the traditional media.

It has been suggested that the rapid worldwide development of sponsorship is such that it is now seen as a standardised method of communicating a brand name (Witcher *et al.*, 1991). This form of communication has certainly gained popularity, but not to the extent of standardisation. Sponsorship remains a communication tool, part of the promotional mix, but as with other tools it needs to be used with a purpose and as part of an integrated communications approach. In other words, sponsorship provides a further tool which, to be used effectively, needs to be harnessed strategically. For example, many companies and brands originating in South-East Asia and Pacific regions, have used sponsorship as a means of overseas market entry in order to develop name or brand awareness (e.g. Panasonic, JVC and Daihatsu).

In addition, many sponsorships have survived recessionary periods. This may be because of the two to three year period that each sponsorship contract covers and the difficulty and costs associated with terminating such agreements. It may also be because of the impact that sponsorship might have on the core customers that continue to buy the brand during economic downturns. Easier targeting through sponsorship can also assist the reinforcement of brand messages. Readers are drawn to the weak theory of advertising (Chapter 13), and it may be that sponsorship is a means of defending a market and of providing additional triggers to stimulate brand recall/recognition.

Sponsorship objectives

There are both primary and secondary objectives associated with using sponsorship. The primary reasons are to build awareness, developing customer loyalty and improving the perception (image) held of the brand or organisation. Secondary reasons are more contentious, but generally they can be seen to be to attract new users, to support dealers and other intermediaries, and to act as a form of staff motivation and morale building (Reed, 1994).

Sponsorship is normally regarded as a communications tool used to reach external stakeholders. However, if chosen appropriately sponsorship can also be used effectively to reach internal audiences. Care is required because different audiences transfer diverse values (Grimes and Meenaghan, 1998).

A further interesting point arises from a view of a company sponsor through time. Meenaghan (1998) suggests that, at first, the sponsor acts as a donor, through the pure exchange of money in order to reach an audience. The next stage sees the sponsor acting as an investor, where, although large sums of money may well be involved, the sponsor is now actively involved and is looking for a return on the investment made. The third stage is reached when the sponsor assumes the role of an impresario. Now the sponsor is vigorously involved and seeks to control activities so that they reflect corporate/brand values and so assist the positioning process.

Following on from this is the issue about whether sponsorship is being used to support a product or the organisation. Corporate sponsorships, according to Thwaites (1994), are intended to focus upon developing community involvement, public awareness, image, goodwill and staff relations. Product- or brand-based sponsorship activity is aimed at developing media coverage, sales leads, sales/market share, target market awareness and guest hospitality. What is important is that sponsorship is not a tool that can be effective in a standalone capacity. The full potential of this tool is only realised when it is integrated with some (all) of the other tools of the promotional mix. The implementation of integrated marketing communications is further encouraged and supported when sponsorship is an integral part of the mix in order to maximise the full impact of this communication tool (see Chapter 29).

Types of sponsorship

It is possible to identify particular areas within which sponsorship has been used (Table 21.1). These areas are sports, programme/broadcast, the arts, and others which encompass activities such as wildlife/conservation and education. Out of all of these, sport has attracted most attention and sponsorship money.

Sports sponsorship

Sports activities have been very attractive to sponsors, partly because of the high media coverage they attract. Sport is the leading type of sponsorship, mainly for the following reasons:

Plate 15.1 Adshel. The use of Street Furniture such as bus shelters, as depicted here by Adshel, can be a powerful means of reaching buyers. See Chapter 15 page 309. Picture reproduced with the kind permission of Adshel.

Plate15.2 Action man – Blimp. Aerial balloons and novelty blimps can attract attention and provide visual impact. See Chapter 15 page 310. Picture reproduced with the kind permission of Virgin Airship.

Plate 15.3 London Taxis. A large number of organisations have used London Taxis to reach specific target markets. See Chapter 15 page 310. Picture reproduced with the kind permission of Taxi Media.

Plate 15.4 Coca-Cola Contour Bottle. Packaging is an important aspect of marketing communications in many sectors. Depicted here is the Coca-Cola bottle with its unique (and well protected) shape. See Chapter 15 page 315. 'Coca-Cola is a registered trade mark of the Coca-Cola Company. This image has been reproduced with the kind permission from Coca-Cola Company.

Plate 15.5 Cadbury's Milk Tray. The style and presentation of a product is most visibly seen through its packaging. Here we can see the way in which the presentation of Milk Tray has evolved. See Chapter 15 page 316. This image has been reproduced with kind permission of Cadbury's Schweppes plc.

Plate 19.1 Catalina System. The effective and efficient delivery of coupons to target consumers is significantly improved with the Catalina system. By recognising relevant products at the point of sale (through scanning) the system dispenses coupons which can be redeemed against competitive brands. See Chapter 19 page 386. Picture reproduced with the kind permission of Catalina Systems.

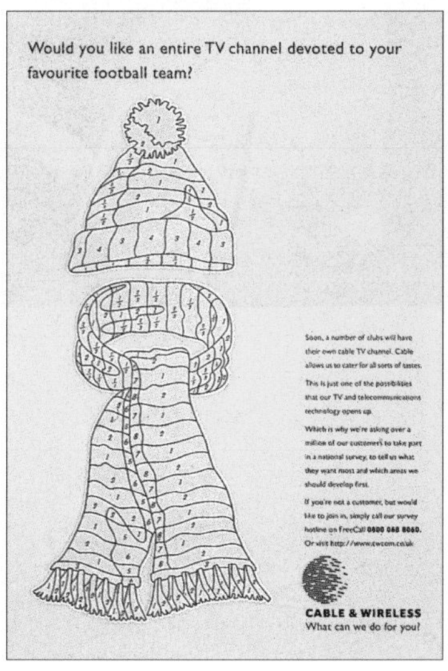

Plate 23.1 Cable & Wireless Communications. A significant part of the launch of Cable and Wireless Communications was the use of direct marketing to gather information about the market. See Chapter 23 page 472. Picture reproduced with the kind permission of C&WC.

Plate 23.2 Direct Line Telephone. The red telephone identifies Direct Line, one of the first to establish direct marketing as its principal form of marketing communications. See Chapter 23 page 481. Picture reproduced with the kind permission of Direct Line Insurance.

Plate 23.3 Apple Tango. The use of interactive communications by Apple Tango helped induce product involvement and brand identity. See Chapter 23 page 492. Picture reproduced with the kind permission of Britvic Soft Drinks.

Plate 24.1 Harveys Bristol Cream. The relaunch of Harveys Bristol Cream involved the use of blue glass, often synomous with quality glass from the area. The bottle was also reshaped to provide positive images. For a fuller account see Chapter 24 page 517. Picture reproduced with the kind permission of Harveys and Allied Domecq.

Plate 24.2 RAC. In the fiercely competitive UK vehicle breakdown and recovery market the RAC sought to reposition themselves. The campaign involved the establishment of a new visual identity. See Chapter 24 page 520. Picture reproduced with the kind permission of the RAC.

Plate 25.1 Ephrex Exhibition Stand. An exhibition stand designed to convey product attributes and the drug's main point of differentiation. See Chapter 25 page 537. Picture reproduced with the kind permission of Janssen-Cilag and Photosound Communications.

Plate 26.1 HMS *Victory*. The different organisations involved with the promotional activities of HMS *Victory* need to work together to achieve the marketing goals. See Chapter 26 page 550. Picture reproduced with the kind permission of the Royal Navy and HMS Victory.

Plate 27.1 BBC. The need for changing the BBC's corporate logo was driven by a variety of changes internal and external to the organisation. See Chapter 27 page 560. The BBC logo is a trade mark of the British Broadcasting Corporation and has been reproduced under licence.

Plate 27.2 Goldfish. The personality of an organisation is often seen in the attitude and style of its communications. The name of the credit card Goldfish partly reflects both the attitude of the organisation and the flexibility of the brand. The use of the comedian Billy Connolly to support the launch of the brand complements the preferred style of the organisation. See Chapter 27 page 566. Picture and material kindly supplied by Wolf Olins and Goldfish.

Plate 27.3 British Airways. A change of strategy needs to be communicated. British Airways changed direction and coordinated a change in corporate identity. See Chapter 27 and page 570. Picture reproduced with the kind permission of British Airways.

Plate 28.1 IBM – Solutions for a Small Planet. IBM launched a new global campaign 'solutions for a small planet' in an attempt to manage the vast network of communications once it had trimmed the number of advertising agencies working on the account from 42 to 1. See Chapter 28 page 590. Picture reproduced with the kind permission of IBM.

Table 21.1 Long-term trends in UK sponsorship market by sector, 1980–96

	Sports £m	Arts £m	Broadcast £m	Other £m	Total £m
1980	30	3	–	2	35
1985	125	22	–	20	167
1990	223	35	7	16	281
1993	250	50	60	26	386
1996	302	80	99	38	519

Source: Mintel.

1. Sport has the propensity to attract large audiences, not only at each event but more importantly through the media that attach themselves to these activities.
2. Sport provides a simplistic measure of segmentation, so that as audiences fragment generally, sport provides an opportunity to identify and reach often large numbers of people who share particular characteristics.
3. Visibility opportunities for the sponsor are high in a number of sporting events because of the duration of each event (e.g. the Olympics or the FIFA World Cup).

Carling's sponsorship of the football Premier League and the Nationwide Building Society's sponsorship of the Football League are motivated partly by the attraction of large and specific target audiences with whom a degree of fit is considered to exist. The constant media attention enables the sponsors' names to be disseminated to distant audiences, many of them on the continent.

Marshall and Cook (1992) found that event sponsorship (e.g. the Olympics or the Ideal Home Exhibition) is the most popular form of sponsorship activity undertaken by organisations. This was followed by team, league and individual support.

Sports sponsorship – Tag Heuer

Sports sponsorship is an integral and important part of the marketing communication strategies at Tag Heuer. The company manufactures precision timepieces and the policy that has been followed is that sponsorship activities must reflect the core brand values. Therefore, all sponsorship and advertising must have relevance to the product. Timed sports events, where a split second is vital to the result, are regarded as ideal. For example, Tag has been involved with Formula 1 racing, the prestigious America's Cup yachting event, and a number of other yachting and skiing events.

The marketing communications budget is split across three main areas, with approximately 60% allocated to advertising, 20% to sponsorship and 20% on various marketing and sales programmes.

Sponsorship has assisted Tag Heuer to position itself in a very competitive market, and as a result has enabled the company to become the fifth-largest Swiss watch manufacturer.

Adapted from Donkin (1995)

CASE ILLUSTRATION

Formula 1

This case illustration has been written by Paul Priddy, former BA (Hons) Business Studies student at the University of Portsmouth.

Energy drinks have profited from Formula One

In the early 1970s, Dietrich Mateschitz, today's managing partner of Red Bull GmbH, spent a lot of his time in Asia. Here he discovered that Asian managers drank a syrupy fluid before meetings in order to stay awake and concentrate through the longest of conferences. He referred to these as 'Energy Drinks'.

He developed and brought this obviously effective product to Austria, devised a marketing concept and christened the drink 'Red Bull'. In 1987, he introduced the product to the Austrian market, followed by a roll-out to a number of different Eastern European countries, the UK and the German market in 1994. Today, Red Bull is available in 20 countries – in Europe, Asia and now even in California in the USA. A total of 140 million cans were drunk throughout the world during 1996, making this the brand that opened a new drink category and enabled Red Bull to become the dominant market leader.

This unusual success can be attributable to the marketing strategy. The drink has been positioned as a drink to provide energy to those involved in sporting activities which require drive and dynamism, as exhibited in snowboarding, mountain biking, free climbing, windsurfing and motorsports, such as go-karting, Formula 3, rallying and motor-cross racing. This case illustration focuses on the relationship between two energy drinks companies and their involvement with Formula 1 motor racing teams, where this relationship is known as sponsorship.

Sport sponsorship has formed a key part of the Red Bull marketing strategy since the product's inception. Following Red Bull's involvement in other motor sporting activities (as mentioned above), the company began sponsorship in 1996 of the Sauber Formula 1 team. The deal, for an undisclosed sum, allowed Red Bull to be the racing team's title sponsor, hence the creation of the Red Bull-Sauber-Petronas team. This was seen as the logical step towards becoming an international brand. Over the 1996 and 1997 Grand Prix seasons, Red Bull has become a major brand.

The financing and promotion of motor racing in recent years has developed into a very sophisticated high-investment business, fuelled by national interests. But once businesses reach out to the Grand Prix circus, the larger the sums of sponsorship cash that are forthcoming, the greater the promise of extensive global television and media coverage.

Formula 1 is highly aspirational, and, as already mentioned, the sport attracts good media coverage. The TV audience is international and very large, demonstrated by the 350 million viewers world-wide who tuned in to watch the final Grand Prix of the 1997 season, held at Jerez, Spain. Excusing the pun, Formula 1 is a good vehicle for strong brand graphics, which offer massive opportunities for commercial exploitation.

Sponsors seek a return on their investment to exploit the opportunity fully, no matter how large the investment. It is now accepted that an association with a Formula 1 racing team can help raise a sponsor's public profile.

This interaction between sponsorship and the media has kept investment in the sport spiralling. With more and more time being given over to the sport in the form of publicity and television coverage, the more attractive it is to sponsors, at the same time generating more cash for the successful teams.

Many sponsorship deals go further than just simply selling advertising space (considered by many to be the fastest billboard on four wheels) on a racing car. 'Corporate hospitality' is another means of profiting from involvement in the sport. This form of reception is about peddling influence: by extending hospitality to customers at a Grand Prix race it assists in building confidence within the sponsor's company and helps to promote customer loyalty. With 16 or 17 events each year in as many countries, Formula 1 is an ideal vehicle to provide the backdrop for providing corporate hospitality to important or potential global customers.

Another competitor in the energy drinks market has used sponsorship in different ways to fulfil its marketing strategy by focusing its association with Formula 1. Hype (an energy drink) adorned the barge boards of the Williams FW19 (in fluorescent yellow and orange) during the first half of the 1997 Grand Prix calendar. This is a drink that is not yet available from the local supermarket, although it will be soon. Hype has been able to create global awareness of its drink products and has established itself as a brand name. This has been achieved by Hype having associated itself with Formula 1 for the past three years. Its primary objective was to raise its profile globally and so lay the foundations for a global assault on the soft/energy drinks market, which according to Managing Director David Harris has been achieved.

There is a perception by smaller companies that involvement in Formula 1 is far too expensive and a gamble. Hype, at the time, was a relatively small company, but succeeded by pretending to be big. Harris has confirmed that sponsorship within the sport has opened many doors, particularly those into the foreign markets which would otherwise have remained shut.

By being a sponsor at race meetings one can mingle with other sponsors, especially fellow sponsors of the same cars. In 1995 Benetton carried the logos of the sponsors Hype and Autogrille (an Italian roadside restaurant group). This provided an ideal outlet for Hype to gain entry to the Italian market. Similarly, Kingfisher Beer, which dominates the beer market in India, was another of Benetton's sponsors that season. It is interesting to note that Kingfisher became the distributor for Hype in that part of the world.

In little under three years, Hype has been able to establish distribution deals in 44 countries and hopes to produce 150 million cans this year. This will have been achieved without any significant sales, but would have been much harder if hype had not been involved in the sponsorship of specific Formula 1 motor racing teams.

Golf has attracted a great deal of sponsorship money, mainly because it has a global upmarket appeal and generates good television and press coverage. Golf clubs are also well-suited for corporate entertainment and offer the chance of playing as well as watching. Volvo has sponsored the European Golf Championship for the period 1996 to 2000 for £20 million. Johnny Walker has put £11 million into the game throughout the world (Wighton, 1995). Toyota supports the World Matchplay Championship at Wentworth each year because the tournament fits into a much wider promotion programme. Toyota dealers sponsor competitions at their local courses, with qualifiers going through to a final at Wentworth. The winner of that gets to play in the pro-am before the World Matchplay. Toyota incorporates the tournament into a range of incentive and promotional programmes and flies in top distributors and fleet customers from around the world. In addition the environment can be used to build customer relationships.

Programme sponsorship

While becoming established in North America in the 1980s, television programme sponsorship has only received serious attention in the UK in the 1990s. The market was worth around £95 million (estimates vary) in 1996 and is growing, partly because of a relaxation by the ITC in the regulations. However, the visibility that each sponsor is allowed is strictly controlled to certain times and before, during the break and after each programme with the credits. Masthead programming, where the publisher of a magazine such as *Amateur Photographer* sponsors a programme in a related area, such as *Photography for Beginners*, is generally not permitted, although the regulations surrounding this type of activity are being relaxed.

There are a number of reasons why programme sponsorship is appealing. First, it allows clients to avoid the clutter associated with spot advertising. In that sense it creates a space or mini-world in which the sponsor can create awareness and provide brand identity cues unhindered by other brands. Second, it represents a cost-effective medium when compared with spot advertising. It is expected that the cost of programme sponsorship will increase as the value of this type of communication is appreciated by clients (Fry, 1997). Third, the use of credits around a programme offers opportunities for the target audience to make associations between the sponsor and the programme.

Research by the Bloxam Group suggests that for a sponsorship to work there needs to be a linkage between the product and the programme. Links that are spurious, illogical or inappropriate are very often rejected by viewers. For example, Summers (1995) argues that 'Tango's sponsorship of the youth programme *The Word* was regarded as about right but the Prudential's link with *Film on Four* was not seen to link at all well'.

The same research suggests that viewers claim to own their favourite programmes. Therefore sponsors should acknowledge this relationship and act accordingly, perhaps as a respectful guest, and not intrude too heavily on the programme. They should certainly resist any active participation in the programme. 'If Pop Larkin starts asking for a cup of Tetley, then that's not right', claims Summers, and product placement issues begin to confuse matters.

Programme sponsorship is not seen as a replacement for advertising; indeed, the argument that sponsorship is not a part of advertising is demonstrated by the point that many sponsors continue with their spot advertising when running major sponsorships.

Cadbury's sponsorship of the premier UK soap opera, *Coronation Street*, in 1996 is reported to have cost £10 million each year, when all the additional promotional activities and requirements are considered. The linkage established between the two parties (Cadbury's and *Coronation Street*) exemplifies the view about the relationship and the linkages. 'The best sponsorships are those where there is an equivalence of stature between the two partners', according to Richard Frost, Cadbury's head of public relations. Research indicates that those aware of the sponsorship regarded the chocolate and the company more positively than those unaware of the linkage. Cadbury's was also awarded higher marks for being up-to-date and a supporter of the local community (Smith, 1997).

Arts sponsorship

Arts sponsorship has been very successful in the 1980s and 1990s, as responsibility for funding the arts in the UK has shifted from the government to the private sector and business in particular. Growth has slowed down, partly because of the increasing need to justify such investments, partly because of the increasing opportunities to reach target audiences and also because it is difficult to engage in these very visible activities when profits are declining and company restructuring activities are of greater concern to those being made redundant or are being displaced.

Arts sponsorship, according to Thorncroft (1996), began as a philanthropic exercise, with business giving back something to the community. It was a means of developing corporate image and was used extensively by tobacco companies as they attempted to reach their customer base. It then began to be appreciated for its corporate hospitality opportunities: a cheaper, more civilised alternative to sports sponsorship, and one that appealed more to women.

Arts sponsorship – the Cezanne exhibition

In July 1996 the Tate Gallery, with sponsorship support from Ernst & Young, an accountancy partnership, exhibited a large collection of paintings by Cezanne. The exhibition was adjudged a huge success, as revenue through admissions exceeded £2.5 million from the 450,000 visitors, and Ernst & Young made valuable contacts with a large number of current and prospective clients.

Ernst & Young had sponsored a similar exhibition of Picasso's work in 1994, and saw opportunities to build upon that success. At the Cezanne exhibition, they were able to provide a series of social events and entertained over 5,000 specific guests. The workforce requested over 10,000 complimentary tickets to support their field-based activities. In addition, the media coverage mentioning Ernst & Young far exceeded the sponsorship investment of £400,000 and the same amount spent on promotion and hospitality costs. In comparison to advertising, the sponsorship was deemed to be far more effective.

The exhibition was a good example of arts sponsorship. The sponsor took the opportunity to entertain existing and potential clients in agreeable surroundings. Employee motivation was improved considerably and the wider public also benefited.

Adapted from Thorncroft (1996)

Digital's sponsorship of the arts, and dance in particular, has been used to enhance its UK corporate status and as a means of clarifying its name as Digital, not DEC. Another important reason why Digital uses sponsorship is to establish and maintain favourable contact with key business people, mainly at board level, together with other significant public figures. Through corporate hospitality, Digital has been able to reach 75% of its targeted 8,000 key people.

Digital uses the benefits of sponsorship to enhance the corporate body, to increase awareness of the company and to change part of the corporate image. Others use sponsorship to influence image and awareness factors at the brand level, such as 7-Up, Foster's and Budweiser (Meenaghan, 1998).

Most recently, sponsorship has been used to reach specific groups of consumers. Beck's, part of Scottish & Newcastle Breweries, has used sponsorship to position the brand as an up-market beer for free-spending young professionals. To accomplish

CASE ILLUSTRATION

Community sponsorship – Royal & SunAlliance

Royal & SunAlliance has many commercial offices around the UK, but one of the more substantial is located in Horsham, West Sussex. It is by far the town's largest employer, with over 2,000 staff. For some time sections of the local community were alienated against the organisation despite the provision of considerable financial support. It transpires that one of the major reasons for the negative feelings stems from the huge building programme when the main campus building was developed in the town centre. The scale of the work was so large that the layout of the town centre was radically altered.

Royal & SunAlliance decided that it was important to generate positive, warmer feelings towards the organisation. So, in addition to the financial assistance the company now provides practical support, targeted where the community informs the company it is most needed:

- *Photocopying*: charity newsletters, church magazines event programmes, information leaflets, posters and publicity material for events.
- *Design*: production of artwork for small groups.
- *Hosting*: Provision of meeting, lecture and function rooms which are not used by the company during the weekends or evenings. Staff act as hosts and ushers as necessary.
- *Catering*: In-house facilities to support the hosting activities above.
- *Professional advice*: Business advice delivered to voluntary groups through attendance at local committees.
- *Raffle prizes*: Gifts surplus to the requirements of the direct marketing division are donated to charities for raffles to raise funds.
- *Minibuses*: Company minibuses are used regularly to support local events, such as sponsored walks, students' educational trips and taking disabled children to swimming galas.
- *Town centre events*: Major town events, such as festivals, Christmas decorations and the biennial Arts Fanfare, are rigorously supported, as are the local churches, schools, Chamber of Commerce and local health and emergency services.
- *Staff support*: The staff themselves are actively involved in voluntary activities in and around Horsham, and again the company seeks to support its employees in these pursuits.

The change from finance provider to resource facilitator appears to have had a major impact on the attitudes held by the community towards Royal & SunAlliance in Horsham. A corporate image study will be undertaken shortly to measure the degree of change. This use of sponsorship and public relations activities has been used to the benefit of all concerned and it seems that a positive dialogue has resulted in mutual understanding and goodwill.

Information kindly supplied by Ann Seabrook, Community Liaison Manager for Royal & SunAlliance in Horsham this, exhibitions by avant-garde artists such as Gilbert and George and Damien Hirst have been supported (Thorncroft, 1996).

An increasing variety of arts activities are being used as sponsorship vehicles. Barclays Bank has funded experimental drama with £100,000 for the Prudential Award for the Arts, an association with new and challenging events. Digital has given support for the populist arts (for example, it helped to bring the Cirque de Soleil to London in 1995), while gala opera performances, rock concerts and big 'events' all attract sponsorship support.

The sponsorship of the arts has moved from being a means of supporting the community to a sophisticated means of targeting and positioning brands. Sponsorship, once part of corporate public relations, has developed skills which can assist marketing public relations.

Other forms of sponsorship

It has been argued that there is little opportunity to control messages delivered through sponsorship, and far less opportunity to encourage the target audiences to enter into a dialogue with sponsors. However, the awareness and image opportunities can be used by supporting either the local community or small-scale schemes. Whitbread has been involved in supporting school programmes, environmental developments and other locally orientated activities because that is where its customers are based. Volkswagen wanted to be associated with the motoring environment rather than just the motorist. To help achieve this goal they sponsored the jackets worn by road-crossing wardens (lollipop people) so that the local authority was free to use the money once spent on uniforms on other aspects of road safety (Walker, 1995).

A fresh form of sponsorship emerged in 1997 as brands sought to leverage each other and achieve greater efficiencies and impact through association with each other. For example, Cable & Wireless (C&W) supported Barnardos in its campaign to increase awareness of current issues, generate funds and redefine the image held of the charity. C&W provided the funds for the TV campaign and in return had a credit at the end of the commercial. The integrated campaign included radio, newspapers, direct marketing and leaflets in each of the 320 Barnardos shops. C&W had previously involved Barnardos in its own launch through direct response advertisements, and also sponsored a major report published by Barnardos about child care. Its has stated its intention to become involved with local community projects (Campbell, 1997).

The majority of sponsorships, regardless of type, are not the sole promotional activity undertaken by the sponsors. They may be secondary, and used to support above-the-line work or they may be used as the primary form of communication but supported by a range of off-screen activities, such as sales promotions and (in particular) competitions. Vauxhall sponsored the Euro 96 football tournament with the deliberate objective of raising awareness. Once that had been achieved it used an advertising campaign to deliver and explain benefits (Fry, 1997).

This section would not be complete without mention of the phenomenon called 'ambush marketing'. This occurs when an organisation deliberately seeks an association with a particular event but does so without paying sponsorship fees. Such hijacking is undertaken with the purpose of influencing the audience to the extent that they believe the ambusher is legitimate. According to Meenaghan (1998) this can be achieved by overstating the organisation's involvement in the event, perhaps through major promotion activity using theme-based advertising or by sponsoring the media coverage of the event.

The position and role of sponsorship in the promotional mix

Whether sponsorship is a part of advertising, sales promotion or public relations has been a source of debate. It is perhaps more natural and comfortable to align sponsorship with advertising. Since awareness is regarded as the principal objective of using sponsorship, advertising is a more complementary and accommodating part of the mix. Sales promotion from the sponsor's position is harder to justify, although from a sponsee's perspective the value-added characteristic is interesting. The more traditional home for sponsorship is public relations (Witcher *et al.*, 1991). Sponsees, such as a football team, a racing car manufacturer or a theatre group, may be adjudged to perform the role of opinion former. Indirectly, therefore, messages are conveyed to the target audience with the support of significant participants who endorse and support the sponsor. This is akin to public relations activities.

Hastings (1984) contests that advertising messages can be manipulated and adapted to changing circumstances much more easily than those associated with sponsorship. He suggests that the audience characteristics of both advertising and sponsorship are very different. For advertising there are viewers and non-viewers. For sponsorship there are three groups of people that can be identified. First there are those who are directly involved with the sponsor or the event, the active participants. Second is a much larger group, consisting of those who attend sponsored events, and these are referred to as personal spectators. The third group is normally the largest, and comprises all those who are involved with the event through various media channels; these are regarded as media followers.

To demonstrate the potential sizes of these groups, an analysis of the sponsorship of Formula 1 racing suggests that there are approximately 3.5 million people who attended the 1995 Grand Prix championship races (active participants) and 330 million people (media followers) who saw television coverage of each race, in 160 countries (Priddy, 1997).

Exploratory research undertaken by Hoek *et al.* (1997) suggests that sponsorship is better able to generate awareness and a wider set of product-related attributes than advertising can when dealing with non-users of a product, rather than users. There appears to be no discernible difference between the impact that these two promotional tools have with users.

The authors claim that sponsorship and advertising can be considered to work in approximately the same way if the ATR model developed by Ehrenberg (1974) is adopted (Chapter 13). Through the ATR model, purchase behaviour and beliefs are considered to be reinforced by advertising rather than new behaviour patterns being established. Advertising fulfils a means by which buyers can meaningfully defend their purchase patterns. Hoek *et al.* regard this approach as reasonably analogous with sponsorship. Sponsorship can create awareness and is more likely to confirm past behaviour than prompt new purchase behaviour. The implication, they conclude, is that, while awareness levels can be improved with sponsorship, other promotional tools are required to impact upon product experimentation or purchase intentions.

It was suggested earlier that one of the opportunities that sponsorship offers is the ability to suggest that there is an association between the sponsee and sponsor which may be of value to the message recipient. This implies that there is an indirect form of influence through sponsorship. This is supported by Crimmins and Horn (1996), who argue that the persuasive impact of sponsorship is determined in terms of the strength of links that are generated between the brand and the event that is sponsored.

These authors claim that sponsorship can have a persuasive impact and that the degree of impact that a sponsorship might bring is as follows:

$$\text{persuasive impact} = \text{strength of link} \times \text{duration of the link} \times \left[\text{gratitude felt due to the link} + \text{perceptual change due to the link}\right]$$

The strength of the link between the brand and the event is an outcome of the degree to which advertising is used to communicate the sponsorship itself. Sponsors who failed to invest in advertising during the games have been shown to be far less successful in building a link with the event than those who chose to invest.

The *duration of the link* is also important. Research based on the Olympic Games shows that those sponsors who undertook integrated marketing communications long before the event itself were far more successful than those who had not. The use of mass media advertising to communicate the involvement of the sponsor, the use of event graphics and logos on packaging, and the creative use of promotional tie-ins and in-store event-related merchandising facilitated the long-term linkage with the sponsorship and added value to the campaign.

Gratitude exists if consumers realise that there is a link between a brand and an event. Sixty per cent of US adults said that they 'try to buy a company's product if they support the Olympics'. They also stated that 'I feel I am contributing to the Olympics by buying the brands of Olympic sponsors'.

Perceptual change occurs as a result of consumers being able to understand the relationship (meaning) between a brand and an event. The sponsor needs to make this clear, as passive consumers may need the links laid out before them. The link between a swimwear brand and the Olympics may be obvious, but it is not always the case. Crimmins and Horn describe how VISA's 15% perceived superiority advantage over MasterCard was stretched to 30% during the 1992 Olympics and then settled at 20% ahead one month after the games finished. The perceptual change was achieved through the messages that informed audiences that VISA was the one card that was accepted for the Olympic Games; American Express and MasterCard were not accepted.

This research, while only based upon a single event, indicates that sponsorship may bring advantages if care is taken to invest in communications long before and during the event to communicate the meaning between the brand and the event, which will leverage gratitude from a grateful audience.

Evaluating sponsorship programmes

Sponsorship has become a major part of the promotional activities of many organisations. Just as advertising and public relations campaigns are subject to rigorous evaluation, so sponsorship is also subject to close scrutiny. The problem is that the measurement of sponsorship is problematic. The ability to separate the impact of the various elements of the promotional mix can be expensive and beyond the reach of smaller brands.

Many organisations attempt to measure the size of the media audience and then treat this as an indicator of effectiveness. This is misleading, as advertising and sponsorship are considered to work in different ways and cannot be measured in a similar way. Audiences consider events (a sports match, exhibition or TV programme) as their primary focus, not which organisation is sponsoring the activity, unlike advertising, where the message either dominates the screen or a page of a magazine and viewers attend according to their perceptual filters. The focus of attention is different, and so should be the means of evaluation.

Marshall and Cook (1992) found that sports sponsors preferred to use consumer surveys to examine customer (not audience) profiles, brand-related images, attitudes and purchasing activities. This was accomplished through the use of personal interviews and telephone and postal surveys. Because the level of funding in many of the smaller sponsorships is relatively low, few if any resources are allocating to evaluative practices.

Taylor Nelson AGB provide a single-source data panel (in collaboration with TSMS media sales house and Meridian Broadcasting). The viewing habits and purchase behaviour of a representative panel of consumers are monitored through a system called TVSpan. Unlike the similar competitive offering from TGI, TVSpan uses data from the AGB SuperPanel which collects data electronically. One of its prime tasks is to enable clients to monitor purchase behaviour and test advertisements at either pre- or post-test stage. Further uses are to test new creative ideas, to test the effects of advertising with or without below-the-line support and, interestingly, to test the interaction between advertising and sponsorship (Thorncroft, 1996).

The main way in which sponsorship activities should be measured is through the objectives set at the outset. By measuring performance rigorously against clearly defined sales and communication-based measures it is more likely that a reasonable process and outcome to the sponsorship activity is likely to be established.

Summary

Sponsorship of events, activities and organisations will continue to grow in significance, if only because of its effectiveness and value as a tool of marketing communications relative to the other tools in the mix. Organisations believe that sponsorship allows them access to specific target audiences and enhances their corporate image (Marshall and Cook, 1992). Other areas will become subject to sponsorship such as the development of television programme sponsorship (for example the weather forecasts by Portman Building Society on Meridian and Tulip Computers on Sky).

There seems little doubt that the introduction of new products and brands can be assisted by the use of appropriate sponsorships. Indeed, it appears that sponsorship, in certain contexts, can be used to prepare markets for the arrival and penetration of new brands.

The evaluation of sponsorship arrangements poses a problem in that measurement is little better than that used for advertising. However, the impact and approach that sponsorship can have suggest that the two tools should be used together, coordinated, if not integrated, to develop awareness and strong brand associations and triggers. There is a warning, and that concerns the degree to which sponsorship is capable of changing purchase behaviour through persuasion. Organisations considering the use of sponsorship as a means of directly impacting upon the bottom line are likely to be disappointed. Other tools are required to stimulate behaviour; sponsorship alone is not capable of persuading target audiences to behave differently.

Review questions

1. What are the main opportunities that sponsorship opens up for organisations?
2. Why has sponsorship become such a major promotional tool in the 1990s?
3. If the objective of using sponsorship is to build awareness (among other things), then there is little point in using advertising. Discuss this view.
4. Name four types of sponsorship.
5. Why is sport more heavily sponsored than the arts or television programmes?
6. Chose eight sporting events and name the main sponsors. Why do you think they have maintained their associations with the events?
7. Consider five television programmes which are sponsored and evaluate how viewers might perceive the relationship between the programme content and the sponsor.
8. How might sponsorship have a persuasive impact on its target audiences? What is the formula used to measure this impact?
9. Explain the role of sponsorship within the promotional mix.
10. Evaluate the ways in which sponsorship can be evaluated.

References

Campbell, L. (1997) C&W underpins Barnardos ads. *Marketing*, 30 October, p. 4.

Crimmins, J. and Horn, M. (1996) Sponsorship: from management ego trip to marketing success. *Journal of Advertising Research* (July/August), 11–21.

Donkin, R. (1995) A question of good timing. *Financial Times*, 13 April, p. 23.

Ehrenberg, A.S.C. (1974) Repetitive advertising and the consumer. *Journal of Advertising Research*, **14** (April), 25–34.

Fry, A. (1997) Keeping the right company. *Marketing*, 22 May, pp. 24–5.

Grimes, E. and Meenaghan, T. (1998) Focussing commercial sponsorship on the internal corporate audience. *International Journal of Advertising*, **17**(1), 51–74.

Hastings, G. (1984) Sponsorship works differently from advertising. *International Journal of Advertising*, **3**, 171–6.

Hoek, J., Gendall, P., Jeffcoat, M. and Orsman, D. (1997) Sponsorship and advertising: a comparison of their effects. *Journal of Marketing Communications*, **3**, 21–32.

Marshall, D.W. and Cook, G. (1992) The corporate (sports) sponsor. *International Journal of Advertising*, **11**, 307–24.

Meenaghan, T. (1991) The role of sponsorship in the marketing communications mix. *International Journal of Advertising*, **10**, 35–47.

Meenaghan, T. (1998) Current developments and future directions in sponsorship. *International Journal of Advertising*, **17**(1), 3–28.

Priddy, P. (1997) An analysis and evaluation of tobacco sponsorship in motor sport, with a focus towards Formula One Grand Prix motor racing. Dissertation, BA (Hons) Business Studies, University of Portsmouth.

Reed, D. (1994) Sponsorship. *Campaign*, 20 May, pp. 37–8.

Smith, A. (1997) UK sponsors look to US. *Financial Times*, 24 March, p. 16.

Summers, D. (1995) Sponsors' careful link with TV. *Financial Times*, 2 March, p. 14.

Thorncroft, A. (1996) Business arts sponsorship: arts face a harsh set of realities. *Financial Times*, 4 July, p. 1.

Thwaites, D. (1994) Corporate sponsorship by the financial services industry. *Journal of Marketing Management*, **10**, 743–63.

Walker, J.-A. (1995) Community service. *Marketing Week*, 20 October, pp. 85–90.

Witcher, B., Craigen, G. Culligan, D. and Harvey, A. (1991) The links between objectives and functions in organisational sponsorship. *International Journal of Advertising*, **10**, 13–33.

Wighton, D. (1995). The FT Guide to Golf: the price of playing. *Financial Times*, 20 July, p. xxvii.

Personal selling

This form of marketing communication involves a face-to-face dialogue between two persons or by one person and a group. Message flexibility is an important attribute, as is the immediate feedback that often flows from use of this promotional tool.

AIMS AND OBJECTIVES

The aims of this chapter are to examine personal selling as a promotional tool and to consider management's use of the sales force.

The objectives of this chapter are:

1. To consider the different types, roles and tasks of personal selling.
2. To determine the strengths and weaknesses of personal selling as a form of communication.
3. To explore the ways in which personal selling is thought to work.
4. To establish the means by which management can organise a sales force.
5. To compare some of the principal methods by which the optimum size of a sales force can be derived.
6. To introduce the concept of multiple sales channels.
7. To discuss the future role of the sales force.

Introduction

The traditional image of personal selling is one that embraces the hard sell, with a brash and persistent salesperson delivering a volley of unrelenting persuasive messages at a confused and reluctant consumer. Fortunately, this image is receding quickly as the professionalism and breadth of personal selling become more widely recognised and as the role of personal selling becomes even more important in the communications mix.

Personal selling activities can be observed at various stages in the buying process of both the consumer and business-to-business markets. This is because the potency of personal communications is very high, and messages can be adapted on the spot to meet the requirements of both parties. This flexibility, as we shall see later, enables objections to be overcome, information to be provided in the context of the buyer's environment and the conviction and power of demonstration to be brought to the buyer when the buyer requests it.

Personal selling is different from other forms of communication in that the transmitted messages represent, mainly, dyadic communications. This means that there are two persons involved in the communication process. Feedback and evaluation of transmitted messages is possible, more or less instantaneously, so that these personal selling messages can be tailored and be made much more personal than any of the other methods of communication.

Using the spectrum of activities identified by the hierarchy of effects, we can see that personal selling is close enough to the prospective buyer to induce a change in behaviour. That is, it is close enough to overcome objections, to provide information quickly and to respond to the prospects' overall needs, all in the context of the transaction and to encourage them directly, to place orders.

Types of selling

One way of considering the types of personal selling is to examine the types of customer served through this communication process (Govoni *et al.*, 1986).

1. *Performance network*
   This involves selling offerings onward through a particular channel network to other resellers. They in turn will sell the offering to other members who are closer to the end user. For example, computer manufacturers have traditionally distributed their products through a combination of direct selling to key accounts and through a restricted number of dealers, or value-added resellers. These resellers then market the products (and bundle software) to their customers and potential customer organisations.
2. *Industrial*
   Here the main type of selling consists of business-to-business marketing and requires the selling of components and parts to others for assembly or incorporation within larger offerings. Goodman manufactures car radio systems and sells them to Ford, which then builds them into its cars as part of the final product offering.
3. *Professional*
   This type of selling process requires ideas and offerings to be advanced to specifiers and influencers. They will in turn incorporate the offering within the project(s) they are developing. For example, a salesperson could approach an architect to persuade him or her to include the alarm system made by the salesperson's organisation within the plans for a building that the architect has been commissioned to design.

4. *Consumer*
   This form of personal selling requires contact with the retail trade and/or the end user consumer.

It will be apparent that a wide range of skills and resources is required for each of these types of selling. Selling to each of these types of customer requires different skills; as a result, salespersons usually focus their activities on one of these types.

The role of personal selling

The major questions that need to be addressed when preparing a communications plan are 'What will be the specific responsibilities of personal selling?' and 'What role will it have relative to the other elements of the mix?'.

Personal selling is the most expensive element of the communications mix. The average cost per contact can easily exceed £100 when all markets and types of businesses are considered. It is generally agreed that personal selling is most effective at the later stages of the hierarchy of effects or buying process, rather than at the earlier stage of awareness building. Therefore, each organisation should determine the precise role the sales force is to play within the communication mix.

The role of personal selling is largely one of representation. In business-to-business markets sales personnel operate at the boundary of the organisation. They provide the link between the needs of their own organisation and the needs of their customers. This linkage is absolutely vital, for a number of reasons that will be discussed shortly, but without personal selling communication with other organisations would occur through electronic or print media and would foster discrete closed systems.

Many authors consider the development, organisation and completion of a sale in a market exchange-based transaction to be the key part of the role of personal selling. Sales personnel provide a source of information for buyers so that they can make the right purchase decisions. In that sense they provide a good level of credibility, but they are also perceived, understandably, as biased. The degree of expertise held by the salesperson may be high, but the degree of trustworthiness will vary, especially during the formative period of the relationship, unless other transactions with the selling organisation have been satisfactory. Once a number of transactions have been completed and product quality established, trustworthiness may improve.

As the costs associated with personal selling are high, it is vital that sales staff are used effectively. To that end, organisations are employing other methods to decrease the time that the sales force spends on administration, travel and office work and to maximise the time spent in front of customers, where they can use their specific selling skills.

The amount of control that can be exercised over the delivery of the messages through the sales force depends upon a number of factors. Essentially, the level of control must be regarded as low, because each salesperson has the freedom to adapt messages to meet changing circumstances as negotiations proceed. In practice, however, the professionalism and training that members of the sales force receive and the increasing accent on measuring levels of customer satisfaction mean that the degree of control over the message can be regarded, in most circumstances, as very good, although it can never, for example, be as high as that of advertising.

Sales force – message control

It can be argued that members of the sales team must be free to adapt messages at the point of delivery because individual clients are themselves different and have different needs and requirements. Lloyd (1997) believes that when selling to doctors, medical representatives enter into conversations that are appropriate for individual doctors.

An example concerns two products manufactured by Schering-Plough. They have two hay fever products (one nasal and the other an oral antihistamine), and sales representatives are expected to decide which to present (in detail) to doctors, based upon the representatives' knowledge and experience of each individual doctor's preferences and the needs of his or her patients.

This flexibility is framed within the context of the product strategy. Decisions that impact upon strategy are not allowed. There is freedom to adapt the manner in which products are presented, but there is no freedom for the sales representatives to decide the priority of the products to be detailed.

Adapted from Lloyd (1997)

Strengths and weaknesses of personal selling

There are a number of strengths and weaknesses associated with personal selling. It is interesting to note that some of the strengths can in turn be seen as weaknesses, particularly when management control over the communication process is not as attentive or as rigorous as it might be.

Strengths

Dyadic communications allow for two-way interaction, which, unlike the other promotional tools, provide for fast, direct feedback. In comparison with the mass media, personal selling allows for the receiver to focus attention on the salesperson, with a reduced likelihood of distraction or noise.

There is a greater level of participation in the decision process by the vendor than in the other tools. When this is combined with the power to tailor messages in response to the feedback provided by the buyer, the sales process has a huge potential to solve customer problems.

Weaknesses

One of the major disadvantages of personal selling is the cost. Costs per contact are extremely high, and this means that management must find alternative means of communicating particular messages and improve the amount of time that sales personnel spend with prospects and customers. Reach and frequency through personal selling is always going to be low, regardless of the amount of funds available.

Control over message delivery is very often low, and while the flexibility is an advantage, there is also the disadvantage of message inconsistency. This in turn can lead to confusion (a misunderstanding perhaps with regard to a product specification), the ramifications of which can be enormous in terms of cost and time spent by a variety of individuals from both parties to the contract. The quality of the relationship can, therefore, be jeopardised through poor and inconsistent communications.

When personal selling should be a major part of the promotional mix

In view of the role and the advantages and disadvantages of personal selling, when should it be a major part of the communications mix? The following is not an exhaustive list, but is presented as a means of considering some of the important issues: complexity, network factors, buyer significance and communication effectiveness.

Complexity

Personal selling is very important when there is a medium to high level of relationship complexity. Such complexity may be associated with either the physical characteristics of the product, such as computer software design, or with the environment in which the negotiations are taking place. For example, decisions related to the installation of products designed to automate an assembly line may well be a sensitive issue. This may be due to management's attitude towards the operators currently undertaking the work that the automation is expected to replace. Any complexity needs to be understood by buyer and seller in order that the right product is offered in the appropriate context for the buyer. This may mean that the buyer is required to customise the offering or provide assistance in terms of testing, installing or supporting the product.

When the complexity of the offering is high, advertising and public relations cannot always convey benefits in the same way as personal selling. Personal selling allows the product to be demonstrated so that buyers can see and, if necessary, touch and taste it for themselves. Personal selling also allows explanations to be made about particular points that are of concern to the buyer or about the environment in which the buyer wishes to use the product.

Buyer significance

The significance of the product to the buyers in the target market is a very important factor in the decision on whether to use personal selling. Significance can be measured as a form of risk, and risk is associated with benefits and costs.

The absolute cost to the buyer will vary from organisation to organisation and from consumer to consumer. The significance of the purchase of an extra photocopier for a major multinational organisation may be low, but for a new start-up organisation or for an established organisation experiencing a dramatic turnaround, an extra photocopying machine may be highly significant and subject to high levels of resistance by a number of different internal stakeholders.

The timing of a product's introduction may well be crucial to the success of a wider plan or programme of activities. Only through personal selling can delivery be dovetailed into the client's scheme of events.

Communication effectiveness

There may be a number of ways to satisfy the communication objectives other than by using personal selling. Each of the other communication tools has strengths and weaknesses; consequently differing mixes provide different benefits. Have they all been considered?

One of the main reasons for using personal selling occurs when advertising alone, or any other medium, provides insufficient communications. The main reason for this inadequacy surfaces when advertising media cannot provide buyers with the information they require to make their decision. For example, someone buying a new car may well observe and read various magazine and newspaper advertisements. The decision to buy, however, requires information and data upon which a rational decision can be made. This rationality and experience of the car, through a test drive perhaps, balances the former, more emotional, elements that contributed to the earlier decision.

The decision to buy a car normally evokes high involvement, and motivation occurs through the central route of the ELM. Therefore, car manufacturers provide a rich balance of emotional and factual information in their literature, from which the prospective buyer seeks further information, experience and reassurance from car dealers, who provide a personal point of contact. Car buyers sign orders with the presence and encouragement of sales persons. Very few cars are bought on a mail order basis!

Personal selling provides a number of characteristics that make it more effective than the other elements of the mix. As discussed, in business-to-business marketing the complexity of many products requires salespeople to be able to discuss with clients their specific needs; in other words, to be able to talk in the customer's own language, to build source credibility through expertise and hopefully trustworthiness, and build a relationship that corresponds with the psychographic profile of each member of the DMU. In this case, mass communications would be inappropriate.

There are two further factors that influence the decision to use personal selling as part of the communications mix. When the customer base is small and dispersed across a wide geographic area it makes economic sense to use salespersons, as advertising in this situation is inadequate and ineffective.

Personal selling is the most expensive element of the communication mix. It may be that other elements of the mix may provide a more cost-effective way of delivering the message.

Channel network factors

If the communication strategy combines a larger amount of push rather than pull activities then personal selling is required to provide the necessary communications for the other members of the performance network. Following on from this is the question regarding what information needs to be exchanged between members and what form and timing the information should be in. Handling objections, answering questions and overcoming misconceptions are also necessary information exchange skills.

When the number of members in a network is limited the use of a sales force is advisable, as advertising is inefficient. Furthermore, the opportunity to build a close collaborative relationship with members may enable the development of a sustainable

Table 22.1 When personal selling is a major element of the communications mix

	Advertising relatively important	Personal selling relatively important
Number of customers	Large	Small
Buyers' information needs	Low	High
Size and importance of purchase	Small	Large
Post-purchase service required	Little	A lot
Product complexity	Low	High
Distribution strategy	Pull	Push
Pricing policy	Set	Negotiate
Resources available for promotion	Many	Few

Source: Adapted from Cravens (1987).

competitive advantage. Cravens (1987) has suggested that the factors in Table 22.1 are important and determine when the sales force is an important element of the communications mix.

The roles of personal selling and the sales force are altering because the environment in which organisations operate is changing dramatically. The repercussions of these changes will become evident following the discussion of the tasks that personal selling is expected to complete.

Tasks of personal selling

The tasks of those who undertake personal selling positions vary from organisation to organisation and in accord with the type of selling activities on which they focus. It is normally assumed that they collect and bring into the organisation orders from customers wishing to purchase the offering. In this sense the order aspect of the personal selling tool can be seen as one of four order-related tasks:

1. *Order takers* are salespersons to whom customers are drawn at the place of supply. Reception clerks at hotels and ticket desk personnel at theatres and cinemas typify this role.
2. *Order getters* are sales personnel who operate away from the organisation and who attempt to gain orders largely through the use of demonstration and persuasion.
3. *Order collectors* are those who attempt to gather orders over the telephone. The growth of telesales operations is discussed later (Chapter 23), but the time saved by both the buyer and the seller using the telephone to gather repeat and low-value orders frees valuable sales personnel to seek new customers and build relationships with current customers.
4. *Order supporters* are all those people who are secondary salespersons in that they are involved with the order once it has been secured, or are involved with the act of ordering, usually by supplying information. Order processing or financial advice services typify this role.

However, this perspective of personal selling is narrow and fails to set out the broader range of activities that a sales force can be required to achieve. Salespersons do more

Table 22.2 Tasks of personal selling

Prospecting:	Finding new customers.
Communicating:	Inform various stakeholders and feed back information about the market.
Selling:	The art of leading a prospect to a successful close.
Information gathering:	Reporting information about the market and reporting on individual activities.
Servicing:	Consulting, arranging, counselling, fixing and solving a multitude of customer 'problems'.
Allocating:	Placing scarce products and resources at times of shortage.
Shaping:	Building and sustaining relationships with major customers.

than get or take orders. The organisation should decide which tasks it expects its representatives to undertake. The list in Table 22.2 is an adaptation of the work by Kotler (1988). These tasks provide direction and purpose, and also help to establish the criteria by which the performance of members of the personal selling unit can be evaluated.

Kotler (1988) quotes the sales force of IBM as responsible for 'selling, installing and upgrading customer computer equipment' and that of AT&T as responsible for 'developing, selling and protecting accounts'. The interesting point from both these examples is that responsibilities, or rather objectives, are extended either vertically upstream, into offer design, or vertically downstream, into the development and maintenance of long-term customer relationships, or both. It is the last point that is becoming increasingly important. In the business-to-business sector the sales activity mix is becoming more orientated to the need to build and sustain the relationships that organisations have with their major customers. This will be discussed later.

How personal selling works: sales processes

A number of conceptual schemes have been proposed to explain the various stages in the sale process. These can be distilled into nine main stages, set out in Figure 22.1. The alignment and rigidity of the sequence should not be overstated, as the actual activities undertaken within each of these stages will vary not only from organisation to organisation but also between salespeople.

This rather simple approach to the sales process fails to explain how a salesperson should approach a customer or why some negotiations are successful and others are not. There have been many attempts to explain how the personal selling process works. One of the first methods proposed was discussed in Chapter 13 when exploring the hierarchy of effects models. The Aida sequence put forward by Strong (1925) says that prospects must be drawn along a continuum of mental states, from attention to interest, desire and finally stimulation to act in accordance with the vendor's wishes. This approach allows for a good deal of flexibility in the salesperson's approach and permits movement around a central theme.

A further model, the stimulus–response model, suggests that if the salesperson can create the right set of circumstances then it is probable that the buyer will react in a particular way. Therefore, by controlling the circumstances of the sales process it is possible to induce the desired response. The salesperson is trained to deliver a particu-

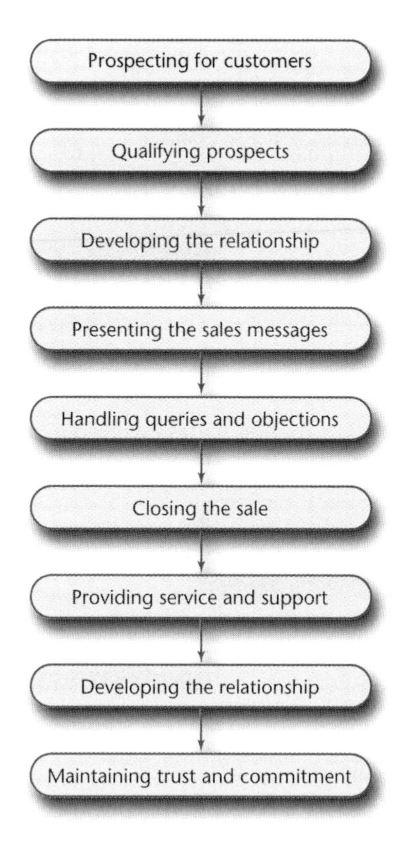

Figure 22.1 The main stages in the sales process.

lar stimulus (that is, what to say) and the buyer provides predictable responses, to which the salesperson has a number of expected responses. The sales presentation is therefore 'canned', ensuring that all aspects of the sale are covered in a logical order.

Jolson (1975) studied the results of such canned or prepared presentations with those that are personalised and determined more 'on-the-hoof'. His results indicated that buyers learned more through on-the-hoof presentations, but revealed that buyers had greater intentions to buy after the prepared presentation. This behavioural view is vendor-led and discounts the cognitive processes of the buyer in its attempt to control the process and the differing needs of different buyers.

A third model focuses upon buyers and their needs. The role of the salesperson is to assist buyers to find solutions to their problems. According to Still *et al.* (1988) the salesperson needs to understand the cognitive processes of buyers in respect of their decision to buy or not to buy. This approach has been termed the 'buying formula' and is based upon the satisfactions that a buyer experiences when placing orders as a solution to perceived problems (from work based on Strong (1938)).

The sequence of the model, therefore, is that the buyer first recognises a problem or a need. A solution is then found, which is purchased and the buyer experiences a level of satisfaction. This formula can be seen in Figure 22.2. The solution contains two components, the product or service and the name of the organisation or the salesperson who facilitated the solution. When a buying habit is formed, the formula adjusts to that in Figure 22.3. To complete the formula, buyers must regard the

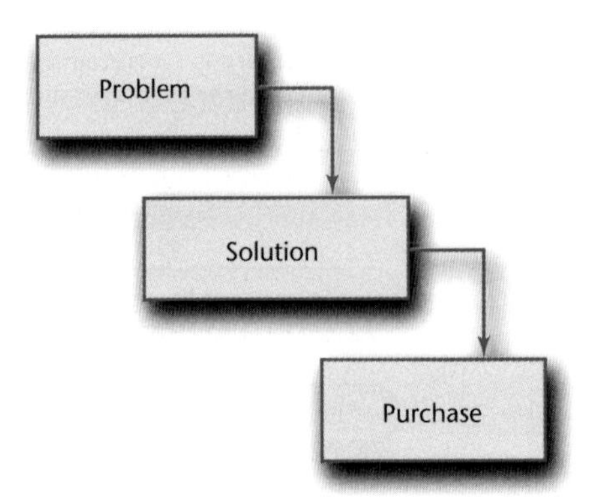

Figure 22.2 The mental stages involved in a purchase.

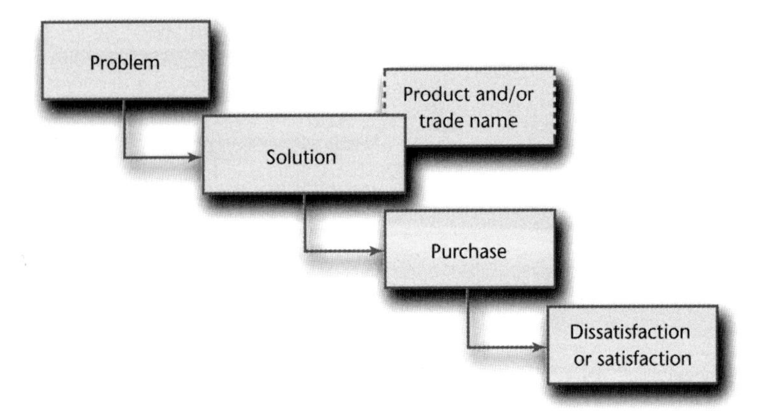

Figure 22.3 The buying formula (Still *et al.* (1988); reproduced by kind permission of Prentice Hall Inc., Englewood Cliffs NJ).

product and the source as adequate and experience pleasant feelings when thinking of the components to the solution (Figure 22.4).

Still *et al.* emphasise the need for salespersons to ensure that all the components of the buying habit are in place. For example, it is important that the buyer knows why the product is the best one for the identified problem and he or she must also have a pleasant feeling towards the source. This means that any competitor attack will be rebuffed because the current solution is deemed adequate. Reasons and pleasant feelings constitute the major elements of defence in a buying habit.

While some people might reject this approach, the essence of the buying formula approach is that a long-term relationship develops as a result of the satisfaction with the solutions offered by the salesperson. If solutions are based upon knowledge and experience that the buyer can identify and empathise with, then the strength of the relationship is likely to be reinforced. It will come as no surprise that successful salespeople appear to hold high levels of interpersonal skills, are able to relate to customer problems, have solved similar problems and are experts at solving such problems (Rothschild, 1987).

There are a host of factors that can influence the buying process, but one growing area of interest concerns the symbolic meaning of offerings and the communication

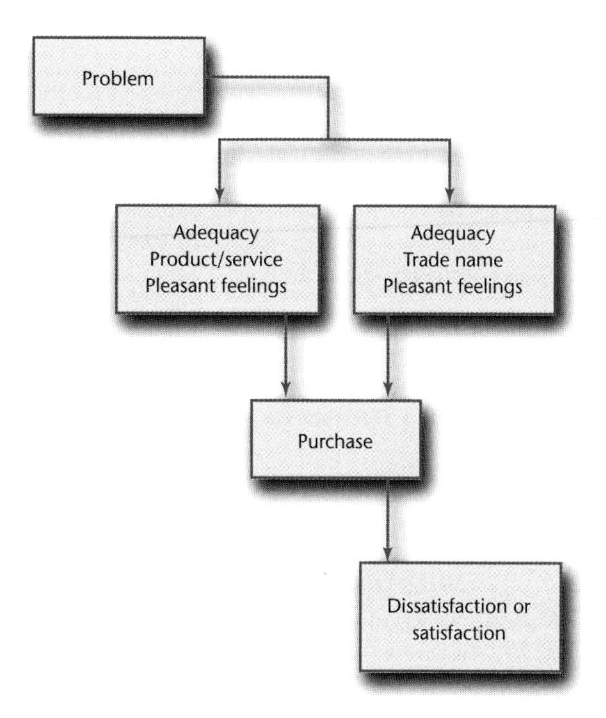

Figure 22.4 The complete buying formula (Still *et al.* (1988); reproduced by kind permission of Prentice Hall Inc., Englewood Cliffs NJ).

aspects of products and services. This is referred to as semiotics, the science of signs and meaning. Through consumption, people communicate non-verbally who they are and the roles they are playing at a particular moment. Consumption allows people self-expression. This perspective is important to the salesperson, as the perception that buyers have of them can influence the sales process. Stuart and Fuller (1991) found that a buyer's initial perception of a salesperson, the products and the organisation he or she represents is strongly influenced by the clothing worn by the representative. Dress codes and uniforms, they conclude, can be used by an organisation to shape the desired customer perceptions of an organisation's size and ethics.

The implication is that marketing communications should not ignore issues about the dress code of an organisation, just as IBM always insisted that all its representatives wore a white shirt and plain tie, dark blue suit and black shoes. The way salespeople present themselves affects the perception of others and can influence the outcome of the sales process.

Sales force management and organisation

The target market and profile of the customer will have been established previously during the development of the communication plan. In particular, the communication strategy will have indicated the degree of push and pull to be used and will have illuminated detail about the nature of the channels in which the salesperson is to operate. Such information is important, as it helps to shape the sales strategy and the messages to be transmitted. Essentially, the salesperson acts as a link between a

CASE ILLUSTRATION

De La Rue International

The following material has been written by Mark Barrett, a successful CIM student and who was Export Sales Manager for De La Rue International Ltd.

Personal selling in international business-to-business markets

In industrial markets, the marketing communications mix can vary dramatically from that in consumer and FMCG markets in particular. Often a bespoke solution is required by the customer, and even when 'off the shelf' packages are chosen, the variety of possible configurations is invariably much wider than it would be in the consumer world.

Tools that are found in consumer marketing, such as advertising, are still used, but these are frequently restricted to the trade or specialist press. High usage of brochures and exhibitions occurs, but these are really only opportunities for the organisation to raise the awareness or visibility for the customer. It would be unusual for a sale of large industrial items to be made on the strength of promotional materials alone. In these markets the promotional materials and exhibitions are the tools that are used to generate sufficient interest from the potential customer to agree to see the salesman and to allow the negotiation process to progress to the next stage.

De La Rue, the cash to cards group, is a good example of an organisation that relies considerably upon personal selling. The organisation has a near 200-year history as the world's largest printer of banknotes, traveller's cheques and other security documentation. Today, the group encompasses divisions involved with emerging technologies, such as smart cards and electronic payments, as well as the De La Rue Cash Systems division, which specialises in the manufacture and supply of banking automation equipment. De La Rue's customers include most of the world's major banks, and each solution must be exactly tailored to the bank's processes and the currency requirements of the country in question.

Having used marketing communications materials such as brochures and exhibitions to leverage De La Rue's brand and to raise the customer's awareness of specific product ranges or solutions on offer, the scene is then set for the salesperson to meet the customer and understand the customer's requirements. The ultimate challenge is to provide a solution tailored exactly to the customer's needs within all of the acceptable criteria set by the customer.

In order to do this, the Regional Sales Manager would need to spend many hours over a period of months with the customer's key decision-makers for the project in question. In different scenarios these decision-makers could hold vastly different roles within the organisation, which are primarily dictated by geographical factors as well as corporate culture. Companies involved in international business-to-business marketing such as this are making greater use of regional experts to better understand and gain benefit from the situations that are likely to be faced when meeting the customer.

No amount of sales expertise could make up for poor product quality, but it is a sign of the times that most industrial markets will be split between a handful of key players, all offering high-quality solutions. In markets such as these it can still be the relationship and understanding between the customer and the salesperson that can win the business.

Simple cultural rules are essential in building a customer relationship, but are still frequently overlooked. It is the wise and culturally aware salesperson that is often successful. Basic 'local' rules are widely documented and should always be followed. Something can always be learned from cultural awareness courses, written texts and the advice available from organisations such as the DTI in the UK. The discerning salesperson would always try to learn something new about the customer prior to a visit to demonstrate a better cultural understanding.

However, it is also true that the customer would also expect salespersons to represent something of their country and company culture. For example, De La Rue is a British PLC with a long history to be proud of. Customers often feel comfortable with this perceived 'Britishness', and displaying this discreetly will often win a customer's confidence. One way to do this can be to ensure that typical British business dress (dark suit, black shoes) is worn when first meeting a customer, regardless of the geographical location and temperature, even ignoring the customer's own culture with regard to business dress.

Decision-making units (DMUs) vary as widely as culture. For example, in Asian and African cultures it would be normal for a very senior representative of a customer's organisation to meet with the salesperson to give his or her blessing to the relationship. This person needs to receive a level of comfort with the organisation being represented, and will probably have less interest in the actual products. A presentation regarding the history of the organisation is needed, and if possible a senior member of the organisation should be introduced to the customer as a sign of the commitment being offered. Western cultures, such as that of the USA, would be much less likely to involve senior members of the organisation until a relationship has been built, with a more technical DMU being involved in initial discussions. They will be very solution focused, and a three-hour presentation on the company's history may be lost on them. Identifying the key members of the DMU is essential in preparing for the presentations and discussions required for a specific meeting. Customers will most likely be impressed by the salesperson's thoroughness in preparation if a list of attendees is provided and are unlikely to spring any nasty surprises if this courtesy has been extended. In the same way, requesting an agenda from the customer allows everyone to focus their minds on the purpose of the meeting in advance and causes less embarrassment when face to face across the table.

While a DMU always has key members, who must be identified and targeted in order to win a sale, the DMU is much larger when it comes to the fine art of losing a sale! 'Overhead on a plane/in reception/in the back of the car/at the restaurant' is an often-used phrase, but when on the customer's territory, everyone must be treated as an extension of the DMU. Misplaced comments or behaviour, however irrelevant they may seem, can ruin a deal, and the salesperson may never know why.

While corporate culture can be critical, it can also be a useful ally. International companies often have hierarchical structures stretching across territories, and the key members of a DMU may be shared between divisions. Geographical culture and therefore cultural awareness are often reduced in such an environment. Many organisations are now using Key Account Managers to understand the corporate culture of key international customers, regardless of their geographic location. Such account managers would understand the structure of the customer's organisation and also the interrelationships of the DMUs within the organisation. Relationships that have already been built in one division may help to shorten the sales cycle in other divisions. Even where this structure does not exist, the salesperson often has a 'coach' or advisor within an organisation that he or she has previously met, who may be a useful ally in identifying and introducing the key members of the DMU. These coaches should never be overlooked.

supplier and a customer, the primary role being to arrange matters so that the relationship can be continued and developed to the mutual benefit of both organisations and their participants.

In order to decide on an appropriate sales strategy, the nature of the desired communication needs to be examined. Are there to be salespersons negotiating with a single buyer or buying team? Is a sales team required in order to sell to buying teams or will conference and seminar selling achieve the desired goals? What is the degree of importance of the portfolio of accounts, and how should the organisations be contacted?

The answers to these questions and the range of issues associated with sales force management are so diverse that many of them are beyond the scope of this text. In particular, issues concerning the recruitment, selection, motivation and compensation of the sales force are not examined here. Attention is given to the way in which the sales force is organised and deployed; that is, where and in what numbers, in order that the organisation achieves its objectives. Attention is also given to the current trends in sales force management, to the new roles the sales force is expected to undertake in the 1990s and how different or multiple sales channels can improve the productivity of the sales department.

The primary and traditional sales channel is the field sales force. These are people who are recruited and trained to find prospective customers, to demonstrate or explain the organisation's products and services and to persuade prospects that they should buy the offering. Orders are then signed, and the salesperson reports the order to his or her organisation, which then fulfils the details of the customer's order, as agreed. However, while life is not this simple, this broad perspective is assumed to be the primary sales channel of many organisations, particularly those operating in the business-to-business sector.

Salespersons are like any other unit of resource in that they need to be deployed in a way that provides maximum benefit to the organisation. One of the first questions that needs to be addressed concerns the type of sales force to be used (assuming the decision has been made that some form of personal selling is required in the communications mix). Further questions are concerned with how many salespersons are required and where and how they should operate.

Decisions regarding the type, structure, size and territory of the sales force will be discussed, on the basis that this is the only sales channel used by an organisation.

Field marketing

Organisations can decide to employ a direct sales force, to use the services of a hired sales force or to use manufacturers' agents or brokers. These agents are third parties who act on behalf of a number of other organisations. Agents receive no salary, but earn commission based on their sales.

However, agents have divided loyalties and usually follow the path that will maximise their own short-term objectives rather than attempt to foster any one organisation's longer-term plans. Such potential conflict can only be realistically reduced by suitable selection and control procedures and measures designed to provide identification and loyalty towards the host organisation.

Field marketing is a relatively new sector of the industry and seeks to provide support for the sales force and merchandising personnel along with data collection and research facilities for clients. The key to field marketing is the flexibility of services provided to clients. Sales forces can be hired on short-term contracts and promotional teams can be contracted to launch new products, provide samples (both in-store and door-to-door) and undertake a range of other activities that are not part of an organisation's normal promotion endeavours.

Field marketing – Diet Pepsi

The Diet Pepsi brand was repositioned in 1997 to appeal to 18–24-year-old women. The brand was reformulated to overcome the aftertaste often associated with artificially sweetened drinks. By stressing the brand's different lifestyle positionings with 'Live life to the max' and 'Best tasting different' the campaign sought to present the brand with greater clarity and focus on the target audience.

Pepsi decided to undertake a nationwide sampling campaign entitled 'Tasting is Believing'. The goal was to reach 500,000 women in the target group, at venues such as shopping centres, parks, high streets, offices and beaches. The sampling was designed to build the brand identity and be relevant to the target audience: self-confident women. An all-girl sampling team on rollerblades, clad in combat trousers and T-shirts, was chosen ahead of an all male team, as the brand was require to talk *to* and *not at* [author's italics] women (Campbell, 1997).

In contrast to this, the relaunch of Impulse, by Elida Gibbs, used an all-male team in order that the target audience be physically attracted to and motivated to move towards the sampling team and receive a spray of the new scent (Cobb, 1997).

Adapted from Campbell (1997) and Cobb (1997)

The decision about whether to own or to hire a sales force has to be based on a variety of criteria, such as the degree of control required over not only the salesperson but also the message to be transmitted. A further criterion is flexibility. Ruckert *et al.* (1985) identified that in environments subject to rapid change, which brings uncertainty (for example because of shortening product life cycles or large technological developments), the ability to adjust quickly the number of representatives in the distribution channel can be of major strategic importance. A further criterion is cost; for some the large fixed costs associated with a sales force can be avoided by using a commission-only team of representatives.

A large number of organisations choose to have their own their sales force, but of these many use the services of a manufacturer's agents to supplement their activities. A number of pharmaceutical manufacturers use independent sales forces to supplement the activities of their own sales teams.

Sales force structure

There are a number of ways in which an organisation can structure the sales force, but there are three broad approaches (geographic, product and market/customer) which most organisations have used. The following examples are based upon Tgi PLC, which designs, manufactures and distributes loudspeaker products. These are

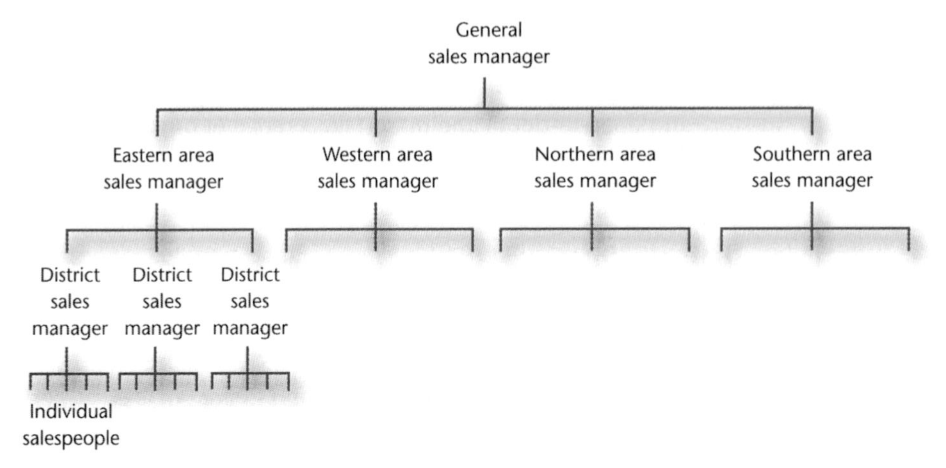

Figure 22.5 A geographic-based sales force structure.

purely examples of how they might organise their sales force, and are not intended to represent the way in which Tgi approaches its markets.

Geographic-based sales force

The most common and straightforward method of organising a sales force is to assign individuals to separate geographic territories (Figure 22.5). In this type of sales force, the salesperson is responsible for all the activities necessary to sell all products to all potential customers in the region or area in which the territory is located. This method of assignment is used by new companies; in situations where customers tend to buy a range of products; where there is little difference in the geographic spread of the products; or when resources are limited.

Strengths

This approach provides for the lowest cost, concentrates the selling effort throughout the territory and allows for a quick response to regional or local needs. This structure also ensures that customers only see one person from the selling organisation and are not at risk of becoming the recipient of multiple and conflicting messages.

Weaknesses

The level of specialised knowledge is reduced, as many products have to be promoted by each salesperson. Furthermore, salespeople under this structure tend to be allowed greater freedom in the design and execution of their working day. Consequently, the number of new customers is often low and the line of least resistance is usually pursued. This may also conflict with the objectives of the organisation, as, for example, call patterns may not be compatible with the overall goals of the sales force.

Product-based sales force

Under this type of structure, the organisation has different sales teams, each carrying a particular line of products (Figure 22.6). This is often used by organisations with large and diverse product lines. Also, organisations with highly technical and complex

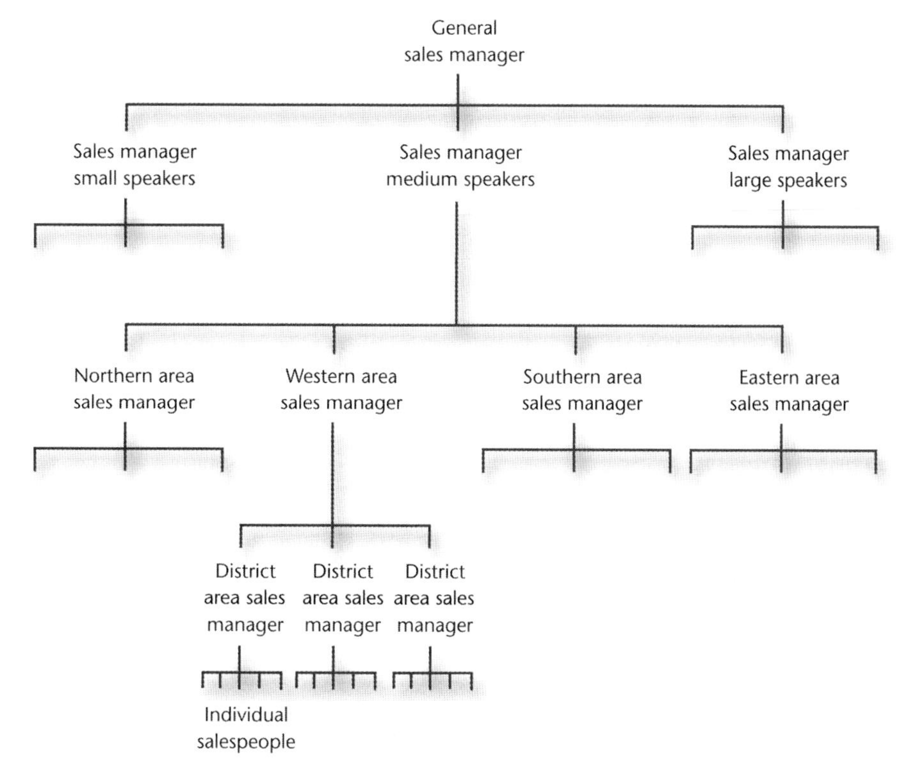

Figure 22.6 A product-based sales force structure.

products, which require specialist knowledge and particular selling techniques, prefer this form of sales force structure.

Strengths

The most important advantage of this structural approach is that it allows the development of product knowledge and technical expertise. In business-to-business markets this factor can lead to improved source credibility, since the level of expertise, and possibly trustworthiness, can be important if the messages are to be persuasive and effective. If the organisation's production facilities are organised by product (separate factories), each with a sales team operating out of the unit, then there can be increased cooperation, which in turn benefits the customer.

Sales management is better able to control the allocation of the selling effort across all products under this type of structure. If greater focus is required upon a particular product, then more salespersons can be allocated appropriately.

Weaknesses

The major disadvantage is that there is a high probability that there will be duplication of sales effort. A customer could be called on by a number of different salespeople, all from the same organisation.

Selling expenses are driven higher and management time and costs rise as the company attempts to bring coordination.

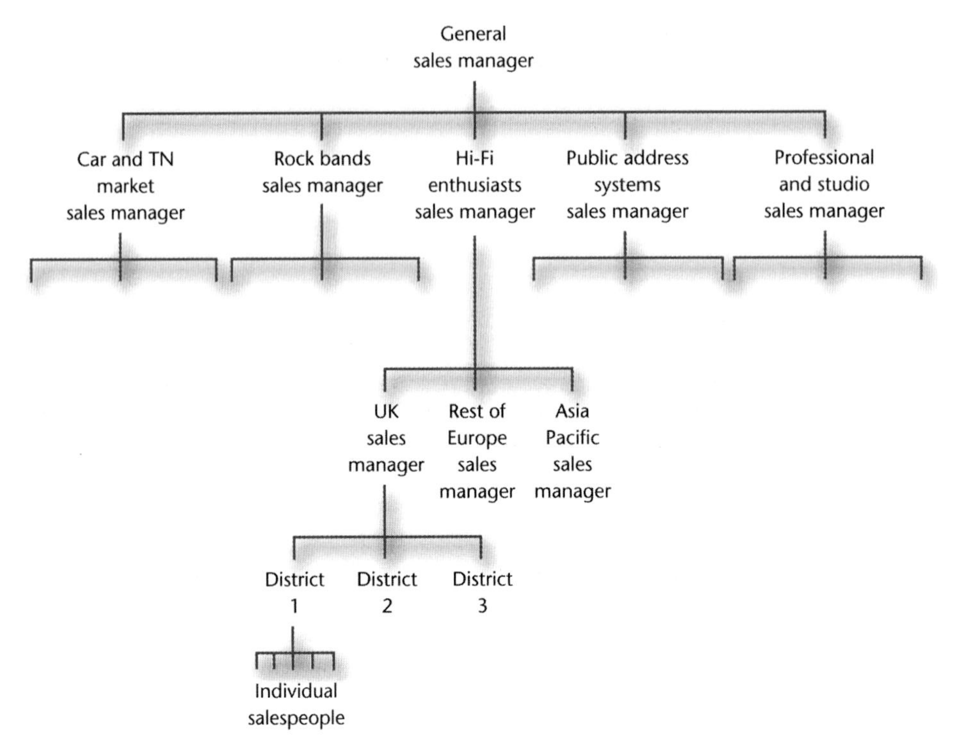

Figure 22.7 A market-based sales force structure.

Market-based sales force

Organising a sales force by market or customer type is an activity complementary to the marketing concept (Figure 22.7). This form of sales force organisation has increased in popularity, as it allows products with many applications to be sold into many different markets and hence to different customers.

Strengths

By calling on a single type of customer, a greater understanding of customer needs develops. Such customer specialisation can be used to foster specialist selling approaches for different markets. The size of the specialist sales forces can be varied by sales management in accordance with internal and external requirements. This is important for organisations operating in highly competitive and quickly changing environments.

Weaknesses

As with the product structure, duplication is a primary difficulty. The costs, however, of operating under this form of structure are higher than any of the others.

These three approaches to sales force design are not mutually exclusive, and most major organisations use a combination of them to meet the needs of their various stakeholders. As Still *et al.* (1988) state, the subdivision of the structure is usually related to primary and secondary needs for marketing success. Most organisations use geography as a subdivision, but whether this is a primary or secondary subdivision depends largely upon the importance of customer or product subdivisions for the achievement of competitive advantage. Such hybrid structures are not static and should evolve as the organisation and the environment in which it operates develop. Tgi use the customer approach not only for the sales force but at an SBU level as well.

Sales force size and shape

The size of the sales force needs to be determined on a regular basis because the environments in which sales forces are operating are changing rapidly. The decision regarding the size of the sales force presents a dilemma. Increasing the size of the sales force will increase the sales revenue, but it will also increase costs. A balance needs to be achieved, and according to Govoni *et al.* (1986) the decision is a blend of the following factors: the number of potential customers, the sales potential of each of these accounts, the geographic concentration of the customers and the availability of financial resources.

There are many different approaches to the determination of the appropriate sales force size. Many of the more recent ones are based upon sophisticated software, but these are derived essentially from three main approaches: the *breakdown*, *workload* and *sales potential* methods.

The intuitive method is a label for all of the methods not based on reason, logic, market information or, in some cases, sense. At one extreme are the hunch and the 'I have been in this business for *x* years' approach, while at the other extreme there is the 'if it is good enough for the competition, then it is good enough for us' approach. These are to be rejected.

The breakdown method

This is the simplest method. Each salesperson is viewed as possessing the same sales productivity potential per period. Therefore, divide the total anticipated sales by the sales potential and the resultant figure equates to the number of salespeople required:

$$n = \frac{sv}{sp}$$

where n is the number of salespeople required, sv is the anticipated sales volume and sp is the estimated sales productivity of each salesperson/unit.

This technique is flawed in that it treats sales force size as a consequence of sales, yet the reverse is probably true. A further difficulty concerns the estimate of productivity used. It fails to account for different potentials, abilities and levels of compensation. Furthermore there is no account of profitability as it treats sales as an end in itself.

The workload method

Underlying this method is the premise that all salespeople should bear an equal amount of the work necessary to service the entire market. The example offered is based upon work by Govoni *et al.* (1986).

The first task is to classify customers into categories based on the level of sales to each account. The ABC Rule of Account Classification holds that the first 15% of customers account for 65% of sales (A accounts), the next 20% will produce 20% of sales (B accounts) and the final 65% will yield only 15% (C accounts).

- *Task 1*: Classify customers into categories
  Class A: large/very attractive = 250
  Class B: medium/moderately attractive = 400
  Class C: small/attractive = 750
- *Task 2*: Determine the frequency and desired duration of each call for each type of account
  Class A: 15 times/pa × 95 mins/call = 23.75 hours
  Class B: 10 times/pa × 63 mins/call = 10.50 hours
  Class C: 6 times/pa × 45 mins/call = 4.50 hours
- *Task 3*: Calculate the workload in covering the market
  Class A: 250 accounts × 23.75 hours/account = 5,938 hours
  Class B: 400 accounts × 10.50 hours/account = 4,200 hours
  Class C: 750 accounts × 4.50 hours/account = 3,375 hours
  Total workload = 13,513 hours
- *Task 4*: Determine the time available per salesperson
  40 hours/week × 46 weeks/pa = 1,840 hours
- *Task 5*: Determine selling/contact time per salesperson
  Contact: 45% = 828 hours
  Travelling: 31% = 570 hours
  Non-selling: 24% = 442 hours
- *Task 6*: Calculate the number of salespersons required

$$\text{Number of salespersons} = \frac{\text{total workload}}{\text{contact hours}} \quad \frac{13{,}513}{828} = 16.32$$

A total of 16 or 17 salespeople would be required using this method. While this technique is easy to calculate, it does not allow for differences in sales response among accounts that receive the same sales effort. It fails to account for servicing and assumes that all salespersons have the same contact time. This is simply not true. One further shortcoming is that the profitability per call is neglected.

Sales potential

Semlow (1959) was one of the earliest to report the decreasing-returns principle when applied to sales force calculations. The principle recognises that there will be diminishing returns as extra salespeople are added to the sales force. For example, one extra salesperson may generate £120,000, but two more may only generate a total of £200,000 in new sales. Therefore, while the first generates £120,000, the other two only generate £100,000 each.

Semlow found, for example, that sales in territories with 1% potential generated £160,000, whereas sales in territories with 5% averaged £200,000. Therefore 1% potential in the second territory equates to £40,000 (200,000/5) and £160,000 (160,000/1) in the first.

The conclusion reached was that a higher proportion of sales per 1% of potential could be realised if the territories were made smaller by adding salespeople. As asked above, what is the optimum number of salespersons, because costs rise as more sales people are added?

Semlow's work provides the basis for some of the more sophisticated techniques and derivatives of the incremental or marginal approach. It is relatively simple in concept, but exceedingly difficult to implement. The conclusion, that a salesperson in a low-potential territory is expected to achieve a greater proportion of the potential than a colleague in a high potential territory is, as Churchill *et al.* (1990) say, 'intuitively appealing'.

Territory design

Having determined the number of salespeople that are necessary to achieve the set promotion objectives, attention must be given to the shape, potential and equality of the territories to be created. The decomposition of the total market into smaller units facilitates easier control of the sales strategy and operations. A sales territory is a grouping of customers and prospects assigned to an individual or team of salespeople. The reason for the establishment of sales territories is mainly orientated to aspects of planning and control. Sales territories enable the organisation to cover the designated market, to control costs, to assist the evaluation of salesperson performance, to contribute to sales force morale and to provide a bridge with other promotional activities, most notably advertising (Still *et al.*, 1988).

Churchill *et al.* (1990) suggest that the steps depicted in Figure 22.8 are the most appropriate. The objective is to make all territories as equal as possible with respect to, firstly, sales potential, as this facilitates performance evaluation, and, secondly, work effort, as this tends to improve morale and reduce levels of conflict.

The most basic unit is a small geographic area. Small units permit easier adjustments to be made and allow for the reassignment of accounts from one salesperson to another. Units can be based on counties, local authority areas, postcodes (important in Greater London and other metropolitan areas), cities and regions.

Once the market potential in each unit has been established, approximate territories can be set up. From this point account analysis helps to determine the call frequency and duration necessary for the larger accounts. A matrix approach, based upon the attractiveness of the account and the ability of the organisation to exploit the opportunities presented, can help this part of the management process, as in Figure 22.9. The penultimate step is to make adjustments to the boundaries of the tentative territories established earlier. These adjustments are designed to equalise potential and workload in each area.

It should be remembered that sales potential is never static, at either the market, territory or account level. In particular, potential will vary with call frequency. It will be apparent that there is a relationship between account attractiveness (AA) and account effort (AE). While AA determines how hard the account should be worked, the frequency and duration will affect the sales derived from each account. There is a need to balance potentials and workloads if computer programs, such as Callplan, are not being used.

There are several methods available. Empirically-based methods use regression analysis to represent the relationship between sales and a number of key sales variables such as the number of calls, potential or workload. Judgement-based methods require the salesperson to estimate the sales/sales call ratio so that the optimum number of calls can be made on each account. The subjective-based method involves executives making changes in call frequency to reflect changes in the market or to achieve a specific objective.

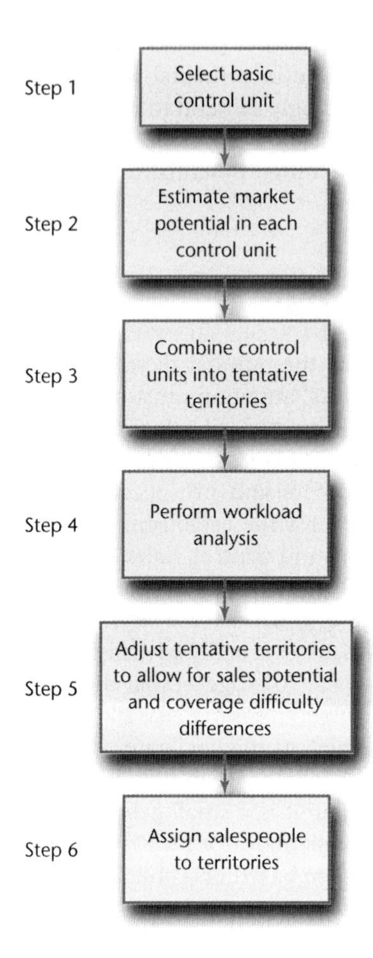

Figure 22.8 Key steps in territory design (Churchill *et al.* (1990); used with kind permission).

The final task is to assign salespeople to territories. It should be remembered that salespeople have varying levels of ability. To overcome this disparity, the most able is allocated an index of 1.00 and all others rated relative to that individual. For example, an index of 0.75 means that a salesperson could achieve 75% of the business that a salesperson with an index of 1.0 could achieve in the same territory. Salespeople can then be allocated on a basis that maximises the return to the organisation.

Other sales channels

The previous discussion of the role of the field sales force was pre-empted by the statement that this is the primary sales channel for many organisations in the business-to-business sector. There are, however, a growing number of organisations that see a different role for the sales force and that are introducing other sales channels in order to improve productivity and the bottom line. These are key accounts, team selling and direct marketing.

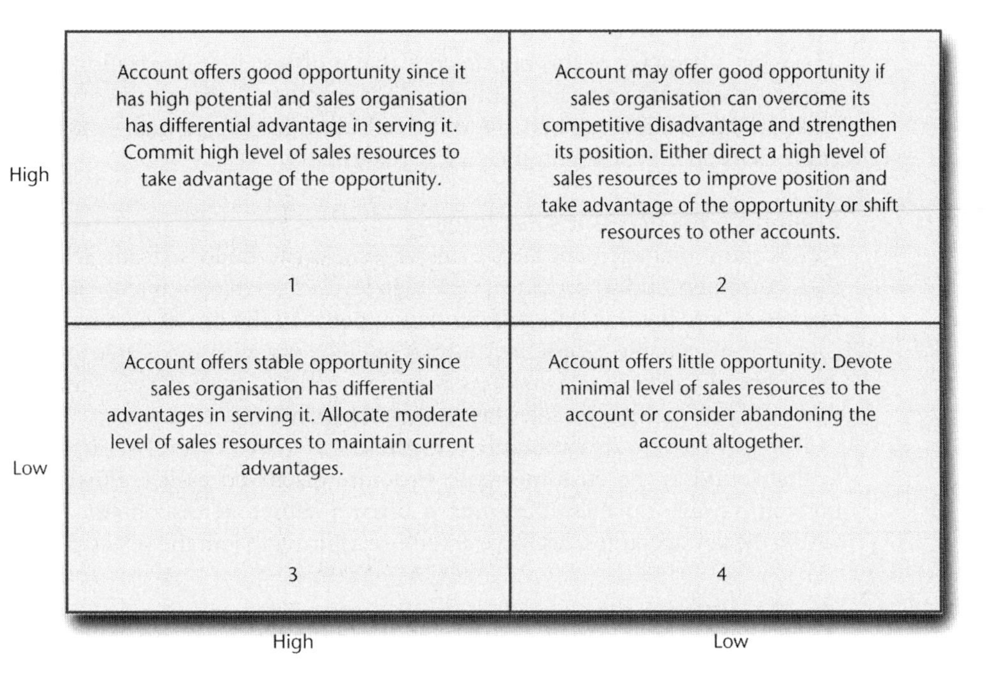

Figure 22.9 Account planning matrix (Churchill *et al.* (1990); used with kind permission).

Key accounts

The increasing complexity of both markets and products, combined with the trends towards purchasing centralisation and industrial concentration mean that a small number of major accounts have become essential for the survival of many organisations. The Pareto rule is often paramount: that 80% of sales are generated by just 20% of an organisation's customers. During the period 1985–91, Wilson (1993) reports that the number of key account managers rose by an average of 91% (Abberton Associates, 1991). This growth in the significance of key account management is expected to continue well into the 1990s. One of the results of this growth will be the change in expectations of buyers and sellers, in particular the demand for higher levels of expertise and professionalism of sales forces (Wilson, 1993).

Who in the organisation should be responsible for these key accounts? Generally there are three main responses: to assign sales executives, to create a key account division or to create a key account sales force.

Assigning sales executives

This is common in smaller organisations who do not have the resources that are available to larger organisations. Normally senior executives would assume this role, and with it they bring the flexibility and responsive service that are required. They can make decisions about stock, price, distribution and levels of customisation.

There is a tendency for key accounts to receive a disproportionate level of attention, as the executives responsible for these major customers lose sight of their own organisation's marketing strategy.

Creating a key account division

The main advantage of this approach is that it offers close integration of production, finance, marketing and sales. The main disadvantage is that resources are duplicated and the organisation can become very inefficient. It is also a high-risk strategy, as the entire division is dependent upon a few customers.

Creating a key account sales force

Key account management allows sales executives to build a strong relationship with their customers and so provide a very high level of service. In mature and competitive markets where there is little differentiation between the products, service may be the source of sustainable competitive advantage. The organisation is able to select its most experienced and able salespersons and so provide a career channel for those executives who prefer to stay in sales rather than move into management.

Administratively, this structure is inefficient as there is a level of duplication similar to that found in the customer-type structure discussed earlier. Furthermore, commission payable on these accounts is often a source of discontent, both for those within the key account sales force and those aspiring to join the select group.

Team selling

It is becoming increasingly common for organisations to assign a team of salespeople to meet the needs of key account customers. A variety of different skills are thought necessary to meet the diversity of personnel making up the DMUs of the larger organisations. Consequently, a salesperson may gain access to an organisation, after which a stream of engineers, analysts, technicians, programmers, training executives and financial experts follow.

For example, when one of Goodman's (a division of Tgi discussed earlier) car manufacturing clients plans a new model, a salesperson opens the door to provide a communication link between the two organisations. Soon, a project team evolves, consisting of engineering, manufacturing, purchasing, production and quality staff, all working to satisfy the needs of their client. Goodman even uses the same project code number as the client to provide for clarity and avoidance of confusion. It also helps to build the relationship and identification between the partners.

Most leading IT-based organisations used to sell the hardware and then leave the customer to work out how to use it. Team selling is now used by Digital, Hewlett-Packard, IBM and others to provide customised combinations of hardware, software and technical support as solutions to their customer's business problems. This requires teams of salespeople and technical experts working closely with the customer's DMU throughout the sales/purchasing cycle and beyond (Hyatt Hills, 1992).

The sales team approach requires high levels of coordination and internal communication if it is to be successful and sell across product lines from various locations (Cespedes *et al.*, 1989). The costs associated with cross-functional team selling are large, which is one of the reasons this approach is restricted to key accounts.

Evaluating personal selling performance

In contrast to the other elements of the promotional mix, personal selling requires different methods of evaluation. Pre- and post-testing the performance of each sales-

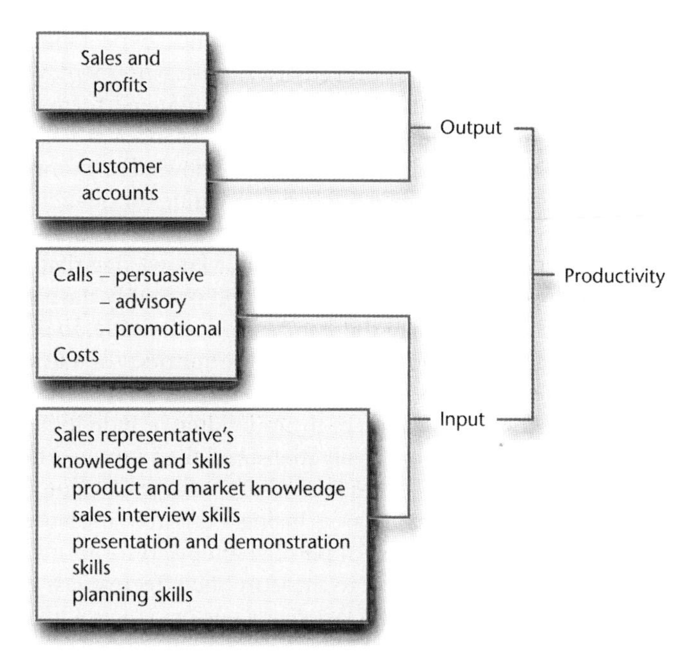

Figure 22.10 Methods for evaluating the performance of personal selling activities (Oliver, (1990); used with kind permission).

person is impractical and inappropriate. What is more pertinent for evaluation are the inputs and the effectiveness (measured as outcomes) of the personal selling process. Oliver (1990) suggests that performance can be seen as a factor of the effort and costs (inputs) that an organisation contributes. Outputs can be regarded as sales and profits resulting from exchanges with customers, while productivity can be deemed to be the ratio of inputs to outputs (see Figure 22.10).

This is a useful approach because it focuses attention on aspects of the promotional process that can be measured with the use of quantitative tools. This contrasts with the other tools, where qualitative measures generally predominate. In addition to this framework it is necessary to measure the effectiveness of the sales force as a unit and the degree to which interdepartmental cooperation is achieved in synchronising the activities of the mix.

Evaluating the performance of a salesperson

The performance of a salesperson requires the use of both qualitative and quantitative methods. There are two main types of inputs to the sales process. The first of these consists of the activities undertaken and the costs incurred as a result. The second type of input concerns the knowledge and skills necessary to achieve the required outputs. These will be examined in turn.

Measuring and then evaluating the activities of each salesperson, the inputs, is an important and frequently used measuring stick. The number of planned and unplanned sales calls, the number of presentations, the frequency with which the showroom has been used and the mix of accounts visited, plus the expenses, cost of samples used and time associated with these activities, can be measured and evaluated against organisational standards and expectations. These simple quantitative measures provide for objectivity and measurement; what they do not do is provide an insight into why the input and the ultimate performance rating did or did not achieve the required standard.

Measuring and evaluating the knowledge component of the input dimension requires greater subjectivity and reliance on qualitative measures. How well a salesperson uses his or her selling skills and presents him- or herself to customers is vitally important. In addition, the depth of knowledge that the subject has of the products, customers, territory and market will probably have a greater bearing on the performance outcome than the number of visits made. In other words, it is the quality of the sales call that is important, not the number of sales calls made. As Churchill *et al.* (1990) claim, the measurement of these qualitative aspects 'must invariably rely on the personal judgement of the individual or individuals charged with evaluation'.

Outputs are more easily measured than inputs. The most common technique used is that of the ratings attached to the volume or value of sales generated in a particular period in a designated area. Using a quota to measure achievement can be important for consistent tracking of performance and for motivational purposes. Volume analysis allows management to measure the effectiveness of the sales process, as comparisons can be drawn with last year's performance, with other sales persons (with similar territory potential) and with the potential in the territory.

Ratios provide a further insight into the overall performance and productivity of a salesperson. Expense ratios are a useful tool for understanding the way in which a salesperson is managing the territory. The cost/call ratio for example, reveals the extent to which the subject is making calls and the costs of supporting the individual in the territory. Further detailed analyses are possible, for example travel expenses/call:

$$\text{Sales expense ratio} = \frac{\text{Expenses}}{\text{Sales}}$$

$$\text{Cost per call ratio} = \frac{\text{Total costs}}{\text{Number of calls}}$$

Servicing ratios reveal the extent to which a territory's business potential has been acquired. For example, what percentage of a territory's accounts has been won, how many prospects become customers, how many customers are lost and what level of sales are achieved on average per customer or per call:

$$\text{Account penetration ratio} = \frac{\text{Accounts sold into}}{\text{Total number of available accounts}}$$

$$\text{Average order size ratio} = \frac{\text{Total sales value}}{\text{Total number of orders}}$$

$$\text{New account ratio} = \frac{\text{Number of new accounts}}{\text{Total number of accounts}}$$

The final group, activity ratios, determines the effort that is put into a territory. Calls/day, calls/account type and orders/call reveal the amount of planning and thought that is being put into an area:

$$\text{Calls/accounts ratio} = \frac{\text{Number of calls made}}{\text{Total number of accounts}}$$

$$\text{Orders/calls ratio} = \frac{\text{Number of orders}}{\text{Total number of calls}}$$

$$\text{Calls/week ratio} = \frac{\text{Number of calls}}{\text{Number of weeks worked}}$$

In isolation these ratios provide some objectivity when attempting to measure the performance of a salesperson. Used in combination they become a more powerful tool, but only to the extent that they are an aid to decision-making. One major advantage of ratio analysis is the benchmarking effect. Comparisons become possible not only across the sales force but also across the industry, as norms become established through time.

While the traditional measure has been volume, increased emphasis is being placed upon measures of profitability, an efficiency measure (Burnett, 1993). The level of gross margin achieved by each salesperson and the contribution each makes to the overall profitability of the organisation are regarded by many organisations as more important than measures of volume. The approach requires the involvement of each salesperson not only in achieving the outcomes but also in the process of setting the appropriate performance targets in the first place. This requires different types of training and skills development, which in turn will affect the expectations held by each member of the sales force.

Evaluating the performance of a sales force

The methods looked at so far have been used to evaluate the performance of individual salespersons. An overall measure of the effectiveness of the larger unit, the sales force, is also necessary. The following constitute the main areas of evaluation: the objectives set in the promotion mix, the level of interaction with the other elements of the promotion mix, activity measures and achievement against quota, the effectiveness of the sales channels used and the quality of the relationships established with customers.

The sales force, as a part of the promotion mix, has a responsibility to achieve the sales objectives set out in the promotion objectives. To do this the sales force needs the support of the other elements of the mix. Measuring this interdisciplinary factor is extremely difficult, but there is no doubt that each of the elements works more efficiently if they are coordinated with one another and the messages conveyed dovetail and reinforce each other.

Many of the measures used to evaluate the performance of individual salespersons can also be aggregated and used to evaluate the performance of the sales force as a whole. The sales force will have an overall sales budget, usually by volume and value, against which actual performance can be measured. The sales force will also be expected to open an agreed number of accounts each period and the value of business as a proportion of the potential will be watched closely.

There is no doubt that the role of the sales force is changing. If the expectations of the sales force are being adapted to new environmental conditions, it is probable that alternative measures will be required to determine the progress that a sales force is making. For example, in business-to-business markets, the traditional approach of the sales force is to manage products and their allocation to selected customers. The sales force of the future is going to be responsible, to a much greater degree, for the management of customer relationships (Wilson, 1993) and the maintenance of relational transactions that will provide organisations with strategic advantage. The use of simple quantitative techniques to measure the performance of the sales force will decline, the use of qualitative techniques will become more prevalent and the techniques themselves will become sophisticated. Measures will be required to evaluate the quality of the relationships developed by the sales force rather than the quantity of outputs achieved in a particular period. The traditional emphasis upon short-term quota achievement may well change to a focus upon long-term customer alliances and an evaluation of the strength of the relationship held between partners.

One further area of evaluation that is necessary is that of the sales channels themselves. The increased use of multiple sales channels and the contribution that direct marketing will make to the sales force cannot be ignored. Measures are required of the effectiveness of the field sales force, the key account selling team and the array of direct marketing techniques. Constant monitoring of the market is required to judge whether the classification of an account should be changed, and whether different combinations of selling approaches should be introduced.

Finally, customers need to be involved in the sales channel decision process and in the evaluation of the field sales force. If customers are happy with a sales channel then they are more likely to continue using it. It is vital that the views of customers are monitored regularly and that they contribute to the evaluation process.

The evaluation of the sales force and its individual members has for a long time been orientated to quantitative measures of input and output productivity. These are useful, as they provide for comparison within the organisation and with the industry norms. However, in future, evaluation will move from revenue to a profit perspective and a much greater emphasis will be placed upon the quality of the relationships that the sales force develops with their customers. The current imbalance between the use of quantitative and qualitative measures will shift to a position where qualitative measures become more important in evaluating the performance of the sales force.

The future role of the sales force

The performance networks of many markets are in transition; this in turn affects the structure and strategy of network members and has stimulated recognition that organisations should seek cooperative relationships (Jarillo, 1993) rather than be competitive in the manner which Porter (1985) and the Design School advocate.

Transition has also been brought about because of changing customer needs, the buoyancy of the European economy in the mid-1980s and its subsequent recession, and the shifting balance of key stakeholders. The expectations of organisational buyers and consumers have shifted so that new skills are required of a salesperson. Internally, organisations have moved their focus. For example, the manner in which performance is measured and resources are deployed has moved from a sales to a profit basis, while the sharp rise in costs of personal selling has required organisations to seek new ways of reaching and communicating with customers.

In consideration of the multiple sales channel approach and the factors that have brought significant change to the way in which field sales forces are organised, it is not surprising that the roles salespeople are expected to undertake are changing. Some of these roles are set out in Figure 22.11.

When these factors are brought together, the salesperson, who was seen earlier as working at the boundary of the organisation to generate sales, is now expected to act

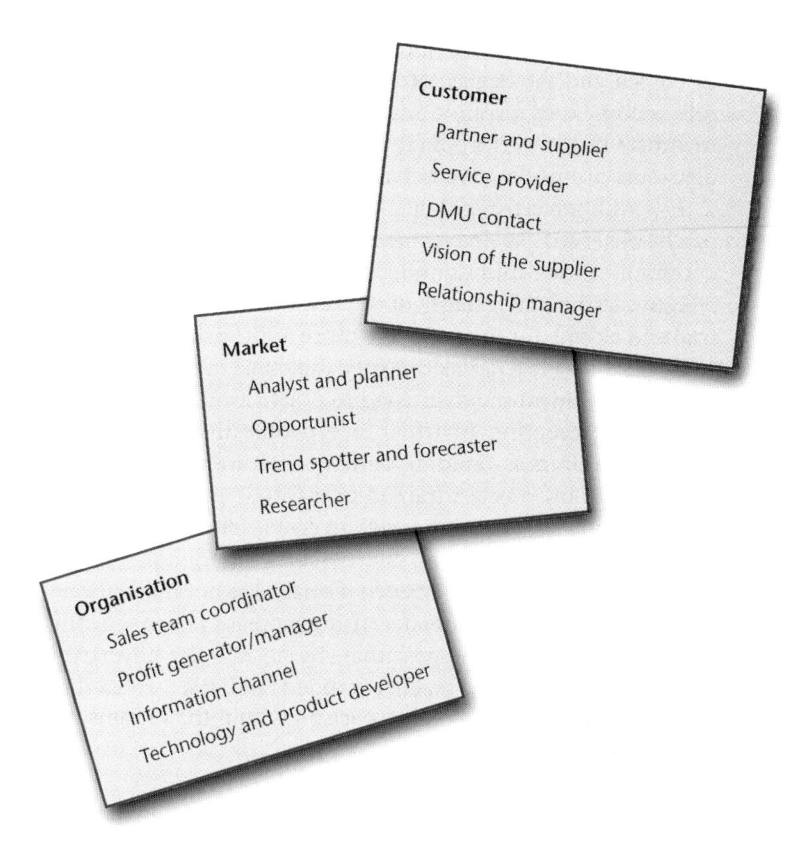

Figure 22.11 New roles for the sales force (adapted from Wilson (1993) and Anderson and Rosenbloom (1982)).

as a network coordinator and as a manager of customers (Wilson, 1993). In Chapter 26 it is identified that a collaborative communication strategy seeks to establish long-term relational transactions. The short-term market exchange perspective hinders the development of strategic advantage. Strong personal interaction with clients, based upon a problem–solution perspective to buyer needs, can provide a source of sustainable competitive advantage for organisations.

Integrating and coordinating the efforts of both the buying and the selling teams will become an important role for the salesperson, particularly as the effects of concentration lead to even greater levels of centralisation of the buying function.

The integration of personal selling with the other elements of the promotional mix

Personal selling cannot work effectively in isolation from the other elements in the promotional mix. For example, members of the sales force are literally representative of the organisation for whom they work: they are mobile PR representatives. Stakeholders perceive them and partly shape their image of the selling organisation on the way in which, for example, the salesperson dresses, speaks and handles questions, the type of car driven and the level of courtesy displayed to the support staff.

The integration and compatibility of direct marketing with the sales force has been discussed and the degree of impact should not be underestimated. The sales force's role within sales promotions can be strong, especially with activities directed at members of the performance network. Members of the sales force are often used to distribute promotional merchandise to both consumers and the trade.

It is with advertising that the strongest degree of integration with personal selling can be observed. As determined earlier, it would appear that these two elements of the communications mix complement each other in many ways. Advertising is more effective at the initial stages of the response hierarchy, but the later stages of inducing trial and closing for the order are more appropriate for personal selling.

Rothschild (1987) has reported Levitt's (1967) work which indicated that organisations that invest in advertising to create awareness are more likely to create a more favourable reception for their salespeople than those organisations which do not invest in awareness-building activities. However, those that had invested were also expected to have a better trained sales force.

Morrill (1970) found that selling costs were as much as 28% lower if the customer had been made aware of the salesperson's organisation prior to the call. Swinyard and Ray (1977) determined that even if a sale was not made for reasons other than product quality then further use of advertising increased the probability of a future sale.

All these findings suggest that, by combining advertising with personal selling, costs will be reduced, reach extended and the probability of a sale considerably improved.

Summary

The role of personal selling in the promotional mix is changing. As organisations move to more relational exchanges, so the sales force will need to play a complementary role. This role will necessitate the execution of tasks such as managing customers and integrating the activities of the performance network.

The sales force will need to be deployed in a way that optimises the resources of the organisation and realises the greatest possible percentage of the available sales and profit potential that exists in the defined area of operation. This will result in a continuance of the growth of key accounts.

The use of the field sales force as the only means of personal selling is unlikely to remain. Technological advances and the need for increasing levels of promotional effectiveness and accountability, together with tighter cost constraints, indicate that the more progressive organisations will employ multiple sales channels. This may mean the use of telemarketing and direct mail to free the sales force from non-selling activities, which will allow management to focus the time of the sales force upon getting in front of customers and prospects, with a view to using their particular selling skills.

Review questions

1. What are the different types of personal selling?
2. Describe the role of personal selling and highlight its main strengths and weaknesses.
3. Which factors need to be considered when determining the significance of personal selling in the promotional mix?

4. What are the tasks that salespersons are normally expected to accomplish?
5. Describe two ways in which the personal selling process is thought to work.
6. Write a brief report highlighting the strengths and weaknesses of each of the main ways of structuring the sales force.
7. Identify the principal differences between the workload and the sales potential methods of determining sales force size.
8. Write brief notes outlining the way in which direct marketing might be used to assist personal selling activities.
9. Suggest four new roles that salespersons might be required to adopt in the future.
10. If an organisation seeks to establish relational exchanges with its partner organisations and customers, the size of the field sales force should be increased. Discuss.

References

Abberton Associates (1991) *Balancing the Sales Force Equation: The Changing Role of the Sales Organisation in the 1990s*. CPM Field Marketing.

Anderson, R.E. and Rosenbloom, B. (1982) Eclectic sales management: strategic responses to trends in the 1980s. *Journal of Personal Selling and Sales Management* (November), 41–6.

Burnett, J. (1993) *Promotion Management*. New York: Houghton Mifflin.

Campbell, L. (1997) Sampling with added sparkle. *Marketing*, 14 August, p. 25.

Cobb, R. (1997) Sweet smell of success. *Marketing*, 9 January, pp. 22–3.

Cespedes, F.V., Doyle, S.X. and Freedman, R.J. (1989) Teamwork for today's selling. *Harvard Business Review* (March/April), 44–55.

Churchill, G.A., Ford, N.M. and Walker, C. (1990) *Sales Force Management*. Homewood IL: Richard D. Irwin.

Cravens, D.W. (1987) *Strategic Marketing*. Homewood IL: Richard D. Irwin.

Govoni, N., Eng, R. and Galper, M. (1986) *Promotional Management*. Englewood Cliffs NJ: Prentice Hall.

Hyatt Hills, C. (1992) Making the team. *Sales and Marketing Management* (February), 54–7.

Jarillo, J.C. (1993) *Strategic Networks: Creating the Borderless Organisation*. Oxford: Butterworth-Heinemann.

Jolson, M.A. (1975) The underestimated potential of the canned sales presentation. *Journal of Marketing*, **39** (January), 75.

Kotler, P. (1988) *Marketing Management: Analysis, Planning, Implementation and Control*, 6th edn. Englewood Cliffs NJ: Prentice Hall.

Levitt, T. (1967) Communications and industrial selling. *Journal of Marketing*, **31** (April), 15–21.

Lloyd, J. (1997) Cut your rep free. *Pharmaceutical Marketing* (September), 30–2.

Morrill, J.E. (1970) Industrial advertising pays off. *Harvard Business Review* (March/April), 159–69.

Oliver, G. (1990) *Marketing Today*, 3rd edn. Hemel Hempstead: Prentice Hall.

Porter, M. (1985) *Competitive Advantage*. New York: Free Press.

Rothschild, M.L. (1987) *Marketing Communications*. Lexington MA: D.C. Heath.

Ruckert, R.W., Walker, O.C. and Roering, K.J. (1985) The organisation of marketing activities: a contingency theory of structure and performance. *Journal of Marketing* (Winter), 13–25.

Semlow, W.E. (1959) How many salesmen do you need? *Harvard Business Review* (May/June), 126–32.

Still, R., Cundiff, E.W. and Govoni, N.A.P. (1988) *Sales Management*, 5th edn. Englewood Cliffs NJ: Prentice Hall.
Strong, E.K. (1925) *The Psychology of Selling*. New York: McGraw-Hill.
Strong, E.K. (1938) *Psychological Aspects of Business*. New York: McGraw-Hill.
Stuart, E.W. and Fuller, B.K. (1991) Clothing as communication in two business-to-business sales settings. *Journal of Business Research*, **23**, 269–90.
Swinyard, W.R. and Ray, M.L. (1977) Advertising–selling interactions: an attribution theory experiment. *Journal of Marketing Research*, **14** (November), 509–16.
Wilson, K. (1993) Managing the industrial sales force of the 1990s. *Journal of Marketing Management*, **9**, 123–39.

chapter 23

Direct marketing and interactive communications

Direct marketing is a strategy used to create a personal and intermediary free dialogue with customers. This should be a measurable activity and it is very often media-based, with a view to creating and sustaining a mutually rewarding relationship.

AIMS AND OBJECTIVES

The aim of this chapter is to explore the characteristics of direct marketing and develop an understanding of interactive marketing communications.

The objectives of this chapter are:

1. To introduce and define direct marketing.
2. To consider the reasons behind the growth and development of this new marketing communications tool.
3. To examine the relationship of direct brands and direct response media and their role within the marketing communications mix.
4. To appreciate the significance of the database in direct marketing.
5. To consider the value of integrating the activities of direct marketing with other elements of the mix.
6. To introduce interactive communications as a contemporary promotional tool and to consider the context in which they operate.

7. To appraise the Internet and interactive television as important new contributors to the promotional mix.

Introduction

From previous discussions about relational and marketing exchanges (Chapters 1 and 6) it should be apparent that the long-term goal of most organisations is to build a long-term relationship with each of their customers. Most of the tools of the promotional mix address mass audiences. Advertising communicates with large audiences and primarily seeks to provide certain information, affect emotions and frame intentions when the next purchase opportunity arises. Advertising is not capable of talking personally to individual customers, nor is it used to generate personal responses. Furthermore, those who choose to use advertising are constrained by the page sizes, paper types, fonts and style or the available spots, the skill of the media planner and the programmes that are available.

Sales promotions are designed to generate an immediate sale, but the information is not stored or used in such a way that a relationship is deliberately created and sustained. Public relations seeks to develop favourable interest and goodwill by piggybacking on other media. Personal selling is certainly founded upon the need to establish long-term personal relationships. However, the range of tasks that the sales force is expected to complete means that only a small percentage of its time can be focused upon generating an immediate response. Personal selling is expensive and there is variable control over the messages that are transmitted by individual members of the sales force.

In addition to these promotional tool deficiencies, the distribution element of the marketing mix was the last to receive attention. Faced with an increasing lack of product/service differentiation and margins being eroded through price competition, the marketing channel was ripe for investigation and review. It became clear that many cost advantages could be achieved through a more direct approach to the market. This meant sidelining or avoiding expensive intermediaries (channel network members) and providing opportunities to improve quality and service provision. For these main reasons, direct marketing has developed and flourished in recent years.

The role of direct marketing

In May 1994, Heinz announced that it was to cease all television advertising in the UK in support of its brands. It was its intention to use direct marketing in order to build relationships with their customers. Heinz had concluded that, in order to compete with the growth of own-label products and to communicate directly with its loyal customer base, direct mail activities in combination with sales promotions (coupons sent through the post) were going to be more effective than their £12 million annual spend on broadcast media. Television advertising would continue to be used, but as an umbrella format, stressing the overall value associated with all Heinz products (Summers, 1994).

In the beginning direct mail was the main tool, but technological advances, most notably the development of information technology and, in particular, the database, have introduced a range of other media that can be used to communicate effectively with individual customers. Indeed, all the elements of the promotional mix can be used with direct marketing to support and build meaningful relationships with consumers and members of the various stakeholder networks.

Direct marketing, therefore, is a term used to refer to all media activities that generate a series of communications and responses with an existing or potential customer. There is considerable debate about the term 'direct marketing' itself. It is often referred to as direct mail or as 'curriculum marketing, dialogue marketing, personal marketing and database marketing' (Bird, 1989). This proliferation of terms reflects the range of activities that are undertaken in an attempt to prompt a response from a customer. Terminology has begun to settle in favour of direct marketing, and this broad approach will be adopted here.

Direct marketing is a strategy used to create and sustain a personal and intermediary-free dialogue with customers. This should be a measurable activity and it is very often

Direct marketing – Cable & Wireless Communications

Cable & Wireless Communications (C&WC) was created by the merger of Mercury Communications, Bell Cablemedia, Nynex and Videotron. The company was formed with the main brief of creating a customer-orientated communications company, which was both human and credible.

The marketing communications launch had two main parts. The first was work necessary to support the stock market launch and so was targeted at the financial community.

The second phase was built around the consumer, whose indifference to cable had been part of the less than spectacular industry growth. A questionnaire was sent to customers of the founding companies asking them what they wanted. This process of asking customers what they wanted helped C&CW develop relevant products and services and also assisted the establishment of the organisation's identity and values (see Chapter 27).

On 15 September 1997, C&WC launched with the single dominating colour yellow and occupied every single colour space in the national broadsheets. Television commercials in most breaks helped position the brand, while multiple poster opportunities stressed C&WC's consultative approach and the press work developed the range of current and future services that the new organisation offered (see Plate 23.1).

Spontaneous awareness rose to 60% from nothing, and in terms of recall rates entered Millward Brown's all-time top 25. All this was achieved as a result of the direct mail questionnaire.

Adapted from Campaign Awards (1998) and information provided by Cable & Wireless Communications media-based. There are a number of important issues associated with this definition. The first is that the activity should be measurable. That is, any response(s) must be associated with a particular individual, a particular media activity and a particular outcome, such as a sale or inquiry for further information. The second issue concerns the rewards that each party perceives through participation in the relationship. The customer receives a variety of tangible and intangible satisfactions. These include shopping convenience, time utility and the satisfaction and trust that can develop between customers and a provider of quality products and services when the customers realise and appreciate the personal attention they appear to be receiving.

Underpinning the direct marketing approach are the principles of trust and commitment, just as they support the validity of the other promotional tools. If a meaningful relationship is to be developed over the long term and direct marketing is an instrumental part of the dialogue then the pledges that the parties make to develop commitment and stability are of immense importance (Ganesan, 1994).

Indeed, the concept of establishing trust is vital if relational exchanges are to be developed. Trust is a multidimensional construct (Morgan and Hunt, 1994) and the need to ensure that it is recognised and accepted by parties where direct marketing is used is highly important (Fletcher and Peters, 1997).

The direct marketer derives benefits associated with precision target marketing and minimised waste, increased profits and the opportunities to provide established customers with other related products, without the huge costs of continually having to find new customers. In addition, direct marketing represents a strategic approach to the market. It actively seeks to remove channel intermediaries, reduce costs, and improve the quality and speed of service for customers, and through this bundle of attributes presents a new offering for the market, which in itself may provide competitive advantage. First Direct, Virgin Direct and the pioneer, Direct Line, all provide these advantages, which have enabled them to secure strong positions in the market.

Types of direct brand

Direct marketing is assumed to refer to direct promotional activity, but this is only part of the marketing picture. Using direct response media in this way is an increasingly common activity used to augment the communication activities surrounding a brand and to provide a new dimension to the context in which brands are perceived.

In addition to these promotional advantages there are two main types of direct brands: *pedigree direct* brands and *hybrid direct* brands (Foster, 1996). These reflect their origins in the sense that the pedigree direct brand is developed to deliberately exploit a market-positioning opportunity. Hybrid direct brands are essentially the same except that the brand heritage is rooted in traditional distribution channels, which may well continue to be a route to market used in parallel to the direct route. Therefore, as Foster points out, the main difficulty facing the hybrid direct brand is the organisational culture: its context and heritage. With these brands there is a generally accepted approach to the market and commonality as to the way things should be done. Even the systems and processes associated with the intermediary-based approach are established and need to be altered to meet the needs of a new type of customer.

However, there is further difficulty, which lies with the image that the customer base and other stakeholders have of the hybrid direct brand. It represents a change

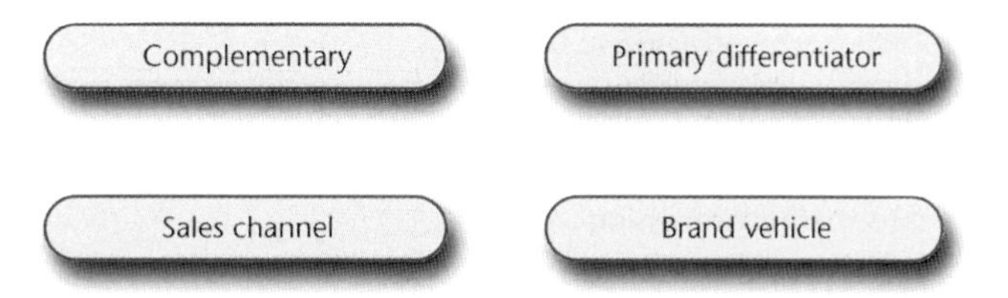

Figure 23.1 Types of direct marketing.

from the frame in which stakeholders expect to see the brand. Care therefore needs to be taken with the marketing communications to ensure that the transition is carried out in such a way that the credibility of the brand is maintained.

From this review it is possible to view direct marketing as part of one the following types (Figure 23.1). These are not hierarchical in the sense that there has to be progression from one type to another. They are reflections of the way different organisations use direct marketing and the degree to which the tool is used strategically.

Type 1: complementary tool

At this level, direct-response media are used to complement the other promotional activities used to support a brand. Their main use is to generate leads and to some extent awareness, information and reinforcement. For example, financial services companies, tour operators and travel agents use DRTV to stimulate enquiries, loans and bookings, respectively.

Type 2: primary differentiator

Rather than be one of a number of promotional tools, at this level direct response media are the primary form of communication. They are used to provide a distinct point of differentiation from competitor offerings. They are the principal form of communication. In addition to the Type 1 advantages they are used to cut costs, avoid the use of intermediaries and reach finely targeted audiences (for example, book, music and wine clubs).

Type 3: sales channel

A third use for direct marketing and telemarketing in particular concerns its use as a means of developing greater efficiency and as a means of augmenting current services. By utilising direct marketing as a sales tool, multiple sales channels can be used to meet the needs of different customer segments and so release resources to be deployed elsewhere and more effectively. This idea is developed further later in this chapter.

Type 4: brand vehicle

At this final level, brands are developed to exploit market space opportunities. These may be the pedigree or hybrid brands identified earlier (for example, Direct Line, Virgin Direct and Eagle Star Direct). The strategic element is most clearly evident at

Table 23.1 Advances in technology

Data capture and collection	
	Scanners, smart cards, loyalty schemes, marketing research
Information processing	
	Database marketing
Communication and interaction	
	Greater precision in segmentation and targeting effectiveness, direct mail, telemarketing and decline in traditional media consumption/effectiveness

this level. Indeed, the entire organisation and its culture are orientated to the development of customer relationships through direct marketing activities.

The growth of direct marketing

There can be little doubt that, of all the tools in the marketing communications mix, direct marketing has experienced the most growth in the late 1980s and 1990s. The reasons for this growth are many and varied, but two essential drivers behind the surge in direct marketing have been technological advances and changing buyer lifestyles and expectations. These two forces for change demonstrate quite dramatically how a change in the context can impact on marketing communications.

Growth driver 1: technology

Rapid advances in technology have heralded the arrival of new sources and forms of information. Technology has enabled the collection, storage and analysis of customer data to become relatively simple and straightforward. Furthermore, the management of this information is increasingly available to small businesses as well as the major blue chip organisations. Computing costs have plummeted, while there has been a correspondingly enormous increase in the power that technology can deliver.

The technological surge has in turn stimulated three major developments. The first concerns the ability to capture information, the second to process and analyse it and the third to represent part or all of the information as a form of communication to stimulate dialogue and interaction to collect further information (Table 23.1).

Organisations have been able to make increasing use of technological developments within marketing communications. Indeed, all areas of the mix have benefited as new and more effective and efficient processes and methods of communication evolve. Advances in technology are responsible for the demise of some traditional forms of communication. For example, the impact of mass communications and advertising in particular as a single device has diminished in favour of a more personalised and integrated approach to communications, enabled by technology. This gives the ability to target potential customers much more precisely at lower cost.

Growth driver 2: changing market context

The lifestyles of people in Western Europe and North American societies in particular have evolved and will continue to do so. Generally, the brash phase of *selfishness* in the

Table 23.2 Changing market context

Lifestyles and expectations
Inner directedness, pluralism, individualism
Fragmentation
Audience, media
Management requirements
Costs, accountability, competition, speed of response

1980s has given way to a more caring, society-orientated *selflessness* in the 1990s. This is reflected in brand purchase behaviour and a greater emphasis on long-term value. Continued fragmentation of the media and audiences requires finely tuned segmentation and communication devices. Direct marketing offers a solution to this splintering and micro-market scenario, and also addresses some of the changing needs of management, namely for speed of response and justification for the use and allocation of resources (Table 23.2).

The role of the database

At the hub of successful direct marketing activities is the database. A database is a collection of files held on a computer that contain data that can be related to one another and which can reproduce information in a variety of formats. Normally the data consists of information collected about prospects and customers which is used to determine appropriate segments and target markets and to record responses to communications conveyed by the organisation. It therefore plays a role as a storage, sorting and administrative device to assist direct and personalised communications: a dialogue propagator.

Increasingly, the information stored is gathered from transactions undertaken with customers, but on its own this information is not enough and further layering of data is required. The recency/frequency/monetary (RFM) model provides a base upon which lifestyle data, often bought in from a list agency, can be used to further refine the information held. Response analysis requires the identification of an organisation's best customers, and then another layer of data can be introduced which points to those that are particularly responsive to direct mail or mail order (Fletcher, 1997). It is the increasing sophistication of the information held in databases that is enabling more effective targeting and communications. The database now consists of several layers of information (Figure 23.2) whereby traditional segmentation data, which sets out customer profiles, can be fused with transactional data so that biographics (Evans, 1998) emerges as a potent new approach to developing a dialogue with individual customers.

It is through the use of the database that relationships with participants can be tracked, analysed and developed. Some tobacco companies, in anticipation of the total media ban, have invested in sales promotion activities to generate information about their heavy users, in order that they can move over to a direct marketing approach when tobacco advertising becomes illegal.

Databases provide the means by which a huge range of organisations, large and small, can monitor changes in customer lifestyles and attitudes, or, in the business-to-business

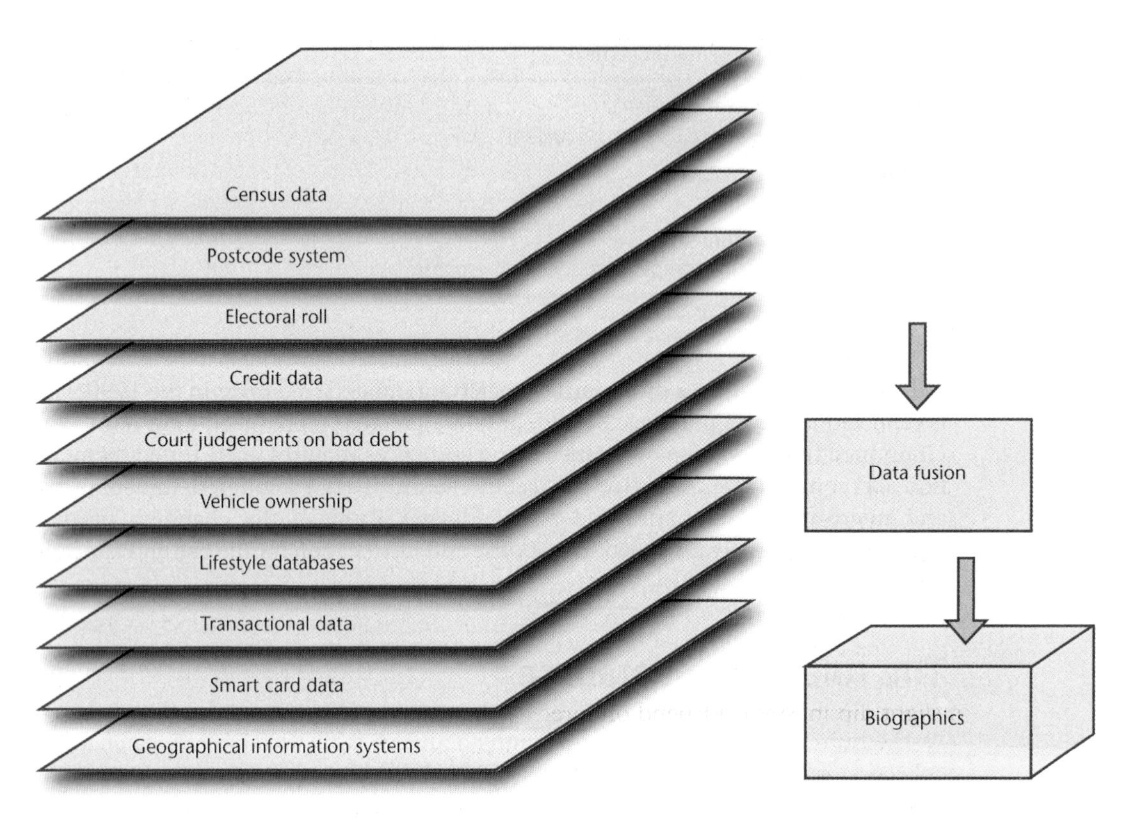

Figure 23.2 Layers of database marketing (Evans (1998); used with kind permission).

sector, the changing form of the interorganisational relationships and their impact on other members in the network as well as the market structure and level of competitive activity (Gundach and Murphy, 1993).

However, there are a number of tensions associated with the use of the database. For example, customers have varying tolerances regarding the level of privacy that a database can exploit. The tolerance or thresholds (Goodwin, 1991) vary according to the information itself, how it was collected and even who collected it. The information exists on a database very often because a customer entered into a transaction. The business entity that received the information as part of a transaction has a duty to acknowledge the confidential nature of the information and the context it was collected in before selling the details to a third party or exploiting the information to the detriment of the individual who provided it in the first place. Breaking privacy codes and making unauthorised disclosures of personal details lays open the tenuous relationship an organisation thinks it has with its 'loyal' customers.

Direct response media

The choice of media for direct marketing can be very different from those selected for general advertising purposes. The main reason for using direct response media is that direct contact is made with prospects and customers in order that a direct response is solicited and a dialogue stimulated or maintained. In reality, a wide variety of media can be used, simply by attaching a telephone number or response card. However, if broadcast media such as television and radio are the champions of the general advertiser, their adoption by direct marketers in the UK has been relatively slow. Direct mail, telemarketing and door-to-door activities are the main direct response media, as they allow more personal, direct and evaluative means of reaching precisely targeted customers.

Direct mail

The largest direct response media expenditure is direct mail, with approximately 50% of total expenditure (Rowney, 1992). Direct mail refers to personally addressed advertising that is delivered through the postal system. It can be personalised and targeted with great accuracy, and its results are capable of precise measurement.

The generation of enquiries and leads, together with the intention of building a personal relationship with customers, are the most important factors contributing to the growth of direct mail. Other factors include the increased market and media fragmentation, which have combined to reduce the overall effectiveness of general advertising. Direct mail can be expensive, at anything between £250 and £500 per 1,000 items dispatched. It should, therefore, be used selectively and for purposes other than creating awareness.

Expenditure on direct mail advertising increased rapidly in the late 1980s. Despite a slight dip in 1990, adspend on direct mail has continued to increase and demands an increasing proportion of advertisers' budgets. In 1992, £945 million was spent on direct mail, equating to 11% of total advertising expenditure (DMIS, 1993).

Organisations in the mail order catalogue and financial services sectors are the main users of this medium. However, an increasing number of other organisations are experimenting with this approach, as they try to improve the effectiveness of their promotional expenditure and reduce television advertising costs.

Direct mail: Scania

To launch its new '4-series' truck design, the Swedish truck manufacturer Scania had to communicate with dealers in over 40 different countries. As each dealer had responsibility for its own promotional activities, the problem was how to convince the dealers to use direct mail and to present Scania in a consistent and appropriate way.

The solution lay with centrally produced materials adapted for local and cultural variations.

Scania produced a complete direct mail programme with standard art design and copy translated for each country.

Adapted from Raphael (1996)

The growth in consumer-based direct mail activities has outstripped that of the business-to-business sector. The number of direct mail items sent to consumers has increased considerably (more than doubled over the ten years to 1995 alone), whereas items sent to businesses increased by less than 60%. Response rates are critical: mail order catalogues will often achieve rates of 10–15% when offering a new catalogue (Bird, 1989).

Telemarketing

An increasing number of organisations are making use of the telephone as a marketing tool. Calls can be categorised as outbound when organisations contact buyers directly, urging them to buy, asking them to provide research information or trying to interest them in the product or service so that they are prepared to buy or receive a further call or personal visit. Inbound calls are those received by organisations in response to direct response advertisements, which, for example, use 0345 or 0800 numbers.

Expenditure on telemarketing increased rapidly (40% per annum) in the late 1980s and early 1990s, but this rapid growth has not been sustained. Organisations are undertaking their outbound calls themselves rather than using tele-agencies to do the work on their behalf (Cobb, 1991).

The prime qualities of the telephone are that it provides for interaction, is flexible and permits immediate feedback and the opportunity to overcome objections, all within the same period of communication. Other dimensions of telemarketing include the development and maintenance of customer goodwill, allied to which is the increasing need to provide high levels of customer service. Telemarketing also allows organisations to undertake marketing research and is highly measurable and accountable in that the effectiveness can be verified continuously and call rates, contacts reached and the number and quality of positive and negative responses are easily recorded and monitored (Colourgraphic Group, 1992).

All of these activities can be executed by personal selling, but the speed, cost, accuracy and consistency of the information solicited through personal visits can often be improved upon by telemarketing. The complexity of the product will influence the degree to which this medium can be used successfully. However, if properly trained professional telemarketers are used, the sales results, if measured on a call basis, can outperform those produced by personal selling.

Generally there are three main ways in which telemarketing can be approached. These are canned, framed and customised. The first approach, the *canned call*, occurs when the caller follows a prepared script, often regardless of the interjections of the receiver. The same 'canned call' is presented to all in the caller's hit list, regardless of their needs and product knowledge. This rather crude approach can be quite sophisticated, as computer software prepares scripts which 'branch', as in a decision tree, to respond to a prospect's different answers (Roberts and Berger, 1989). A variation of this approach is the use of Interactive Voice Response (IVR). This enables organisations to respond quickly to incoming calls with the use of technology and remove the expense of a human operator. Data and information can be collected quickly and efficiently and calls can be routed around the organisation to the appropriate department (e.g. customer service, sales or fault reporting), so cutting queues and waiting times. However, the downside of this is that customers who are rerouted and then end up in a lengthy queue listening to background music often fail to appreciate, at that moment, the benefits of new technology.

The second approach is the *framed call*. This is similar to a semi-structured interview, where the caller has a number of topics that need to be covered but the order and the style in which the issues are dealt with are immaterial.

CASE ILLUSTRATION

Telemarketing

This mini-case history was written by Keith Gait, a CIM diploma student and who was Commercial Manager for TeleDynamics in Maidstone.

Coca-Cola

Coca-Cola requested a telemarketing campaign to support the 'Thirst for it' campaign that ran in 1997.

The 'Thirst for it' campaign was a massive on-pack promotion that ran across Coke and diet Coke. £3.5 million was spent on television, radio and the national press. Customers could win a range of instant and dream prizes when they purchased bottles, draft servings or cans of the two brands. Point of sales kits included T-shirts, posters, beer mats, scratch cards and a Coca-Cola stand.

An outbound call campaign aimed calls at the licensed trade with the goal of placing point of sale kits (and other merchandise).

The brief specified 10,000 calls to trade outlets to sell the promotional kits. A variety of tasks had to be completed:

- Order lists for the fulfilment houses had to be prepared.
- A call guide had to be produced.
- Data capture of contact name, outlet address, quantity ordered.
- Supply the data to the fulfilment house on a daily basis.
- Provide twice-weekly and end of campaign reports to cover the number of calls made, the success rate at selling the sales kits and the number of orders taken.

Teledynamics completed 8,388 calls and from this achieved 7,077 presentations. A total of 4,500 point of sale kits were ordered and 9.3 presentations/hour were made.

The campaign was a huge success and far exceeded the expectations of Coca-Cola.

The *customised call* is the telephone version of a personal sales presentation. Undertaken by professionally trained callers, the conversation is tuned to the needs of the receiver, not those of the caller. When the call is completed, regardless of whether an order has been placed, recipients replace the handset feeling satisfied that they have used their time appropriately and in full expectation that they will receive further calls.

To assist outbound callers, predictive dialling software has been shown to increase efficiency. This tool enables engaged lines, no response and answering machines to be avoided (ignored), thus allowing operators to spend an increased proportion of their time talking to potential customers rather than wasting time dialling and listening to telephones ringing. Estimates vary, but now operators can talk for 45 minutes in every hour, compared with 25 minutes before the development of predictive dialling facilities (Cook, 1997).

The costs of telemarketing are high: for example, £10 to reach a decision maker in an organisation. When this is compared with £1.50 for a piece of direct mail or £100+ for a personal sales call to the same individual, it is the effectiveness of the call and the return on the investment that determines whether the costs are really high.

Growth in telemarketing activity in the business-to-business sector has been largely at the expense of personal selling. The objectives have been to reduce costs and to utilise the expensive sales force and their skills to build on the openings and leads created by telemarketing and other lead generation activities.

Inserts

Inserts are media materials that are placed in magazines or direct mail letters. These not only provide factual information about the product or service, but also enable the recipient to respond to the request of the direct marketer. This request might be to place an order or post back a card for more information, such as a brochure.

Inserts have become more popular, but their cost is substantially higher than a four-colour advertisement in the magazine in which the insert is carried. Their popularity is based on their effectiveness as a lead generator, and new methods of delivering inserts to the home will become important to direct mailing houses in the future. Other vehicles, such as packages rather than letter mail, will be become important. For example, BT has commissioned Colleagues, a major direct mail organisation, to provide inserts to be delivered with new telephone directories.

Print

There are two main forms of direct response advertising through the printed media: first, catalogues and, second, magazines and newspapers.

Catalogues mailed direct to consumers have been an established method of selling products for a long time. Mail order organisations such as Freemans, GUS and Littlewoods have been successfully exploiting this form of direct marketing for a long time. Organisations such as Scotcade, Innovations and Kaleidoscope have successfully used mini-catalogues, but instead of providing account facilities and the appointment of specific freelance agents, their business transactions are on a cash-with-order basis.

Business-to-business marketers have now begun to exploit this medium, and organisations such as IBM now use catalogues, partly to save costs and partly to free valuable sales personnel so that they can concentrate their time selling into larger accounts.

Direct response advertising through the press is similar to general press advertising except that the advertiser provides a mechanism for the reader to take further action. The mechanism may be a telephone number (call free) or a coupon or cut-out reply slip requesting further information.

Door-to-door

This delivery method can be much cheaper than that of direct mail as there are no postage charges to be accounted for. However, if the costs are much lower, so are the response rates. Responses are lower because door-to-door drops cannot be personally addressed like direct mail, even though the content and quality can be controlled in the same way.

Avon Cosmetics is traditionally recognised as the professional practitioner of door-to-door direct marketing. Other organisations, such as Betterware, now use catalogue-based selling in combination with door-to-door delivery. The company has a sales force of 10,000 people who reach 45% of the UK population at least once every eight weeks and take orders which have an average size of approximately £8 (Milton, 1993). The growth of this company, which is now expanding into Spain and Germany, is based upon the use of a direct sales force which completes the entire cycle of catalogue delivery to the door, order-taking, product delivery and cash settlement.

Radio and television

Of the two main forms discussed earlier, radio and television, the former is used as a support medium for other advertising, often by providing enquiry numbers. Television has greater potential because it can provide the important visual dimension, but it is not used a great deal in the UK for direct marketing purposes. One of the main reasons for this has been the television contractors' attitude to pricing. However, the industry has experienced a period of great change, fuelled partly by the recessionary early 1990s. This has brought about greater pricing flexibility, and a small but increasing number of direct marketeers have used the small screen successfully, mainly by providing freephone numbers for customers.

Direct Line, originally a motor insurance organisation, has been outstanding in its use of television not only to launch but also to help propel the phenomenal growth of a range of related products (see Plate 23.2).

Integration and direct marketing

This brief review of the media used in direct marketing activities has tended to present them as separate, independent resources. Increasingly, successful direct marketing programmes are using these media in combination, as a team of complementary tools. Many organisations, regardless of whether their marketing activities are orientated solely to direct marketing or not, are using direct response media to support and supplement their other promotional activities (Emerick, 1993). For example, see the Thomas Cook illustration below.

Coordinated communications support – Thomas Cook Direct

Thomas Cook Direct was launched as a competitive alternative to the traditional process of booking vacations through travel agents and similar retailer outlets. Thomas Cook is an extremely strong brand in the travel market and has around 400 retail travel shops on high streets around the UK. However, this type of distribution was becoming more price orientated so margins had become narrow and this type of operation was increasingly unattractive in the face of competition from Going Places and Lunn Poly.

Thomas Cook Direct was a competitive strategic response, with the brand refocused around the telephone. The launch utilised several media, including press advertisements and sales brochures which communicated the availability of the service, but more importantly they allowed for the telephone number to be conveyed to the target audience. Indeed, the telephone number appeared in all advertising by Thomas Cook. Contact with their 50,000 customers (on database) is facilitated through quarterly updates and magazines. Various specialist products, such as SkiDirect, Cruise Direct and Flights Direct have evolved, partly because of the flexibility that telemarketing permits. Thus, staff allocated to the SkiDirect telephone lines, for example, are all ski enthusiasts and are able to enter into a meaningful dialogue with callers and so enhance trust and credibility. This specialist support is not feasible through mixed product high street travel agents.

Direct mail lists are used to filter potential customers, and in addition to the successful uses of Teletext, Thomas Cook Direct uses sponsorship (SkiDirect for snow forecasts) and has developed an Internet site which will provide booking facilities.

Adapted from Denny (1997)

CASE ILLUSTRATION

DRTV

This mini-case history was written by Keith Gait, a CIM diploma student and, at the time of writing, Commercial Manager for TeleDynamics in Maidstone.

National Canine Defence League (NCDL)

The NCDL launched a scheme in 1997 called 'sponsor a dog'. The idea was that members of the public could sponsor animals at their rescue centres and shelters for £1 per week. After the preliminary success of 'sponsor a dog' it was decided to roll out the project nationally, and DRTV was selcted as the most appropriate medium.

Television response handling is a complex set of activities and it was decided to outsource the work to a specialist call centre. TeleDynamics won the pitch.

The DRTV campaign was to run over four weeks in the following areas:

- Channel 4 South
- Channel 4 London
- UK Gold
- UK Living
- Granada Plus
- Discovery Home and Leisure

A single execution was generated with the the call-to-action orientated to requesting a brochure contained in a fulfilment pack. The pack consisted of a letter from the writer Jilly Cooper, a brochure, an application form and a branded freepost reply-paid envelope. The pack was fronted by a personalised letter and was despatched in a branded window envelope.

DRTV presents a number of logistical issues for a call centre, the primary one being a very large volume of calls in a very short burst (typically around 100 calls within 3 minutes of the slot).

Of course, people do not all phone straight away, choosing obscure times of the day and evening to call. Added to this is the problem that unscheduled advertisements can appear or they can go out early or late, depending upon the deal struck with the media owner by the agency. For these reasons, a specialist agency like TeleDynamics needs to be contracted, as the primary function of any DRTV campaign is to generate maximum response, and any drop-out or lost response can have serious implications. The service level agreement on the NCDL contract was to answer 85% of all calls within 12 seconds, with a call abandon rate of under 10%.

By utilising an automatic call distributor (ACD), all incomng NCDL calls were routed to the first available operator trained for NCDL calls. Call blending was used, which meant that TeleDynamics could switch operators from their outbound work one minute before the scheduled advertisement, for NCDL inbound calls, and then switch them back to outbound calls five or six minutes after the advertisement and the peak of the calls has been dealt with.

As clients are charged per second for an operator handling calls, and as call volumes vary violently, call blending is of assistance to all concerned.

It is necessary for the call centre to have the advertisement schedules not just for call blending but in order that operator breaks can be adjusted to ensure that operators are available when an advertisement goes out. To assist this a close relationship between the call centre and the media sales house ensures that an advance ad schedule is available.

For the NCDL campaign 120 operators and 15 supervisors were trained on all aspects of NCDL and the objectives of the campaign. An average call length of 90 seconds was anticipated. An automated bureau was also incorporated to take calls out of hours and cope with the peak loads, which were expected to be high in view of the emotional nature of the campaign.

Automated bureaux have a number of disadvantages, in that people are reluctant to talk to a machine and the information needs to be transcribed. This is often quite difficult, and when credit cards are involved it is very important to have accurate transcriptions. It is not surprising that abandon rates on automated bureaux are always much higher than when a live operator is taking calls and checking the data.

The NCDL campaign was completed successfully with 12,349 calls handled. The average answer time was less than 1 second and no more than 2% of calls were lost: a very successful campaign from the call-handling perspective.

Other organisations are using integrated direct marketing, which is 'the orchestration of various direct marketing vehicles so that they work together in a synergistic fashion' (Eisenhart, 1990). An example of this orchestration might be the despatch of a direct mailing using a well-qualified list followed by contacting addresses through a telemarketing programme within 24 hours of the mailer arriving. In some cases, response rates have doubled by using telemarketing in this way.

Some doubt whether organisations can justify the cost and the administrative and managerial implications of complex integrated direct campaigns. Advocates of the approach claim that each contact with a prospect helps create a wave effect, with response rates increasing at each contact.

There can be little doubt that direct response media will be used increasingly in the future as organisations realise its power and overcome built-in resistance to the direct approach. As general media rates continue to increase ahead of inflation, and as managers seek new ways of providing evidence of their astute use of marketing and, in particular, promotional resources, so direct response media will play an increasingly important role in the marketing activities of a large number of organisations. However, commitment to the direct route or to a combination of general and direct response media means that organisations must ensure that they are transmitting a consistent or complementary message through each medium used.

Supporting the sales force

In an effort to increase the productivity of the sales force and to use their expensive skills more effectively, direct marketing has provided organisations with an opportunity to improve levels of performance. In particular, the use of an inside telemarketing department is seen as a compatible sales channel to the field sales force. The telemarketing team can accomplish the following tasks: they can search for and qualify new customers, so saving the field force from cold calling; they can service existing customer accounts and prepare the field force should they be required to attend to the client personally; they can seek repeat orders from marginal or geographically remote customers, particularly if they are low-unit-value consumable items; and finally, they can provide a link between network members which serves to maintain the relationship, especially through periods of difficulty and instability. Many organisations prefer to place orders through telesales teams, as it does not involve the time costs associated with personal sales calls. The routine of such orders gives greater efficiency for all concerned with the relational exchange and reduces costs.

Direct mail activities are also becoming more important in areas where personal contact is seen as unnecessary or where limited field sales resources are deployed to key accounts. As with telesales, direct mail is often used to supplement the activities of the field force. Catalogue and electronic communications such as fax can be used for accounts which may be regarded as relatively unattractive.

All of these activities free the field sales force to increase their productivity and to spend more time with established customers or those with high profit potential.

Multiple channel selling

A number of different sales channels have been identified and many organisations, in their search to reduce costs, are trying to restructure their sales operations in an attempt to fit the anticipated needs of their stakeholders. Restructuring has often taken the form of introducing multiple sales channels with the simple objective of using less expensive channels to complete selling tasks that do not require personal, face-to-face contact, as discussed in Cravens *et al.* (1991). These authors have presented a comparison of four types of sales channel mentioned above; see Table 23.3.

Using a matrix, accounts can be categorised according to their potential attractiveness and the current strength of the relationship between two organisations (Figure 23.3). A strong relationship, for example, is indicative of two organisations engaged in mutually satisfying relational exchanges. A weak relationship suggests that the two parties have no experience of each other or, if they have, that it is not particularly satisfying. If there have been transactions it may be that these can be classified as market exchange experiences. Attractiveness refers to the opportunities a buying organisation represents to the vendor: how large or small the potential business is in an organisation.

For reasons of clarity, these scales are presented as either high or low, strong or weak. However, they should be considered as a continuum, and with the use of some relatively simple evaluative criteria accounts can be positioned on the matrix and strategies formulated to move accounts to different positions, which in turn necessitate the use of different sales channel mixes.

Table 23.3 Comparison of four types of sales channel

Sales channel	Knowledge of customer needs/ requirements	Direct access to customers	Time/customer	Cost/contact
Key account				
Coordinated sales and support activities to one or a few customers representing high-volume annual purchases	Very high level of understanding of needs/requirements	Access typically concentrated at headquarters location, and with different individuals within customer organisation	Calls are typically frequent and long	Very high because of length of contact and number of contacts within customer organisation
Field salesperson				
Field salesperson responsible for several customer/ prospects assigned on the basis of geographical area, product scope, or market scope	High to medium level of understanding (highest when needs are similar across customer base)	Face-to-face contact with assigned accounts; may include team-selling activities	Call patterns vary but are typically shorter than key account calls	High to medium depending on call duration
Telemarketing				
Assignment of large number of customers/ prospects to a salesperson who contacts accounts by phone	Medium to low level of understanding	Access by telephone and electronic support	Calls are relatively short: frequency may vary according to buying/servicing patterns	Low relative to face-to-face contact
Electronic mail contact				
Customer/ prospects contacted by computer, fax or mail	Low level of understanding unless purchasing is routine repurchase of standard items	Contacts indirect	Direct contact is not involved	Very low indirect contact costs

Source: Cravens *et al.* (1991); used with kind permission.

Using the approach of Cravens *et al.* (1991), appropriate sales channels are superimposed on the matrix in order that optimum efficiency in selling effort and costs be managed (Figure 23.4). Accounts in Section 1 vary in attractiveness, as some will be assigned key account status. The others will be very important and will require a high level of selling effort, which has to be delivered by the field sales force. Accounts in Section 2 are essentially prospects because of their weak competitive position but high attractiveness. Selling effort should be proportional to the value of the prospects: high

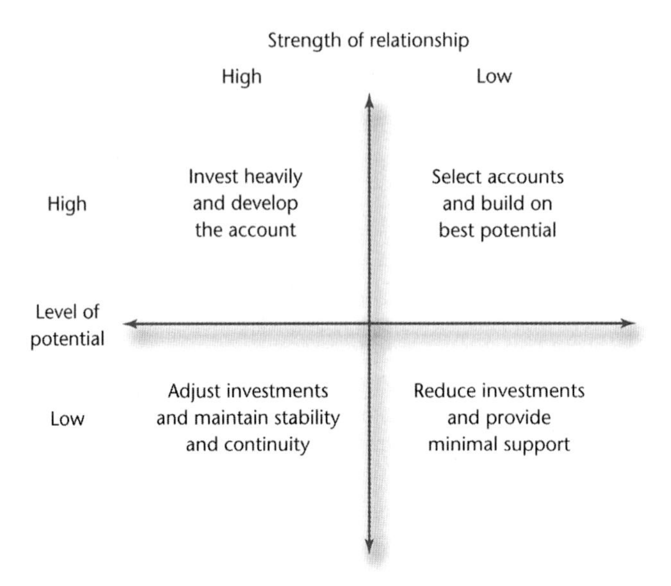

Figure 23.3 Account investment matrix.

effort for good prospects and low for the others. All the main sales channels should be used, commencing with direct mail to identify prospects, telesales for qualification purposes, field sales force selling directed at the strong prospects and telesales for the others. As the relationship becomes stronger, so field selling takes over from telesales. If the relationship weakens then the account may be discontinued and selling re-directed to other prospects.

Accounts in Section 3 are not particularly attractive and, although the relationship is strong, there are opportunities, according to Cravens *et al.*, to switch the sales channel mix by reducing, but not eliminating, the level of field force activity and to give consideration to the introduction of telesales for particular accounts. Significant cost reductions can be achieved with these types of accounts by simply reviewing the means and reasoning behind the personal selling effort. Accounts in Section 4 should receive no field force calls, the prime sales channels being telesales, direct mail and catalogue selling.

Establishing a multiple sales channel strategy based on the matrix suggested above may not be appropriate to all organisations. For example, the current level of performance may be considered as exceeding expectations, in which case there is no point in introducing change. It may be that the costs and revenues associated with redeployment are unfavourable and that the implications for the rest of the organisation of implementing the new sales channel approach are such that the transition should either be postponed or rejected. However, experience has shown, according to LaForge *et al.* (1985) that costs can be reduced through the introduction of a multiple sales channel approach and that levels of customer satisfaction and the strength of the relationship between members of the network can be improved considerably.

Interactive marketing communications

The dialogue that marketing communications seeks to generate with customers and stakeholders is partially constrained by an inherent time delay based upon the speed

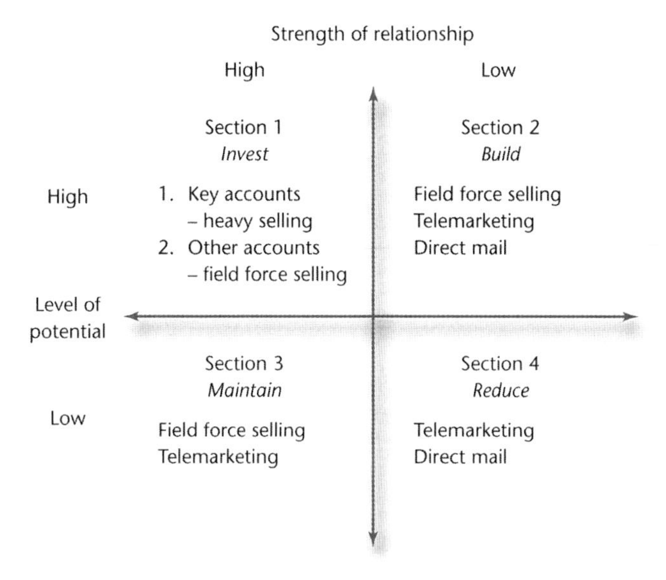

Figure 23.4 Sales channel mix allocation (adapted from Cravens *et al.* (1991)).

at which responses are generated by the participants in the communication process. Technological advances now allow participants to conduct marketing communication-based 'conversations' at electronic speeds. The essence of this speed attribute is that it allows for interactive-based communications, where enquiries are responded to more or less instantly.

One of the first and interesting points about the new communication facilities is that the context within which marketing communications occurs is redefined. Traditionally, dialogue occurs in a context which is familiar (relatively) and which is driven by providers who deliberately present their messages through a variety of communication devices into the environments that they anticipate their audiences may well pass or recognise. Providers implant their messages into the various environments of their targets. With the new computer-based communications providers become relatively passive. Their messages are presented in an environment that requires targets to use specific equipment to actively search them out. The roles are reversed, so that the drivers in the new context are active information seekers, represented by the target audience (members of the public and other information providers such as organisations), not just the information providing organisations.

A further development resulting from the use of new technology in marketing communications is the target of the communication activity. Interactivity, as stated above, has increased in speed, but interactivity can occur not only between people as a result of a message conveyed through a particular medium but can also occur with machines or cyberspace. As Hoffman and Novak (1996) state, people interactivity is now supplemented by machine interactivity. This means that the dialogue that previously occurred *through* machines now occurs *with* the equipment facilitating the communication exchanges (see Figure 23.5).

These authors refer to the work of Steuer (1992), who suggests that the principal relationship is with what is referred to as a *mediated environment* and not between sender and receiver. This is important, as it is the potential of all participants in the communication activity to mediate or influence the environment (especially the message

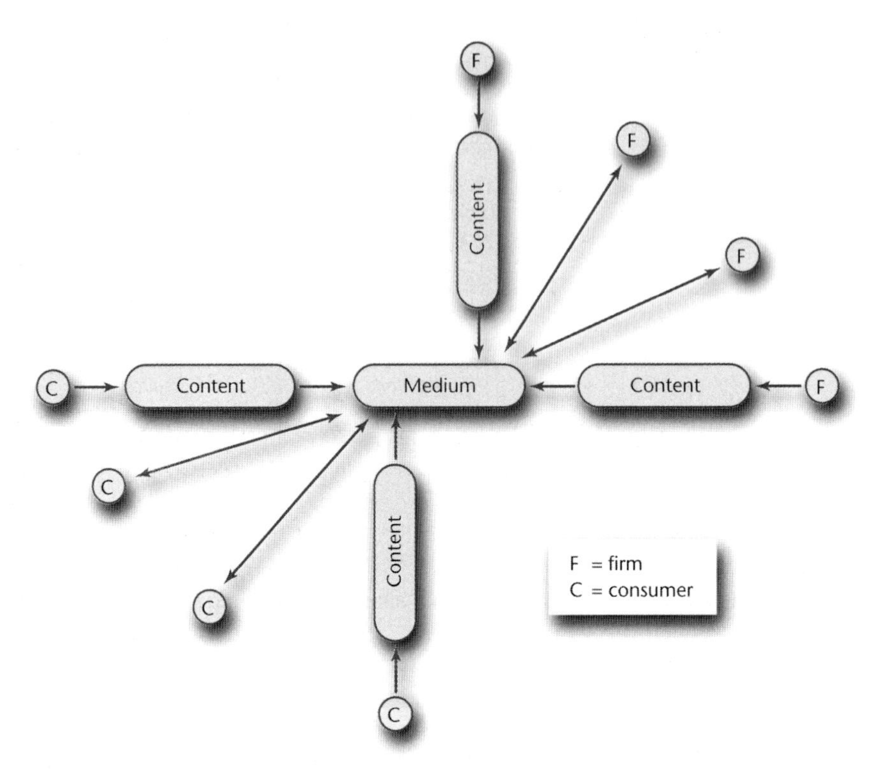

Figure 23.5 A model of marketing communications in a hypermedia computer-mediated environment (Hoffman and Novak, (1996); reprinted with permission from the *Journal of Marketing*, published by the American Marketing Association).

content) in which the dialogue occurs that makes interactive marketing communications so dynamic and such a radically revolutionary new promotional tool.

There has been considerable media attention given to the development and potential of interactive services. However, the reality is that only a very small proportion of the public have become immersed in these mediated environments, measured in terms of advertising space sold and the number of transactions undertaken interactively. As Cohen (1995) stated: 'there does remain great uncertainty as to the level of consumer demand…'.

The development of interactive services may well be best served by the identification of those most likely to adopt such services and who will encourage others in the social orbits to follow their actions. This strategy would require communication with innovators and early adopters to speed the process of adoption (Rogers, 1983). This is quite crucial, as the infrastructure and associated heavy costs require an early stream of cash flows (Kangis and Rankin, 1996).

New topologies of interactive consumers are likely to emerge, characterising their prime personality and lifestyle variables. This will in turn facilitate the provision of suitable services.

The Internet and the World-Wide Web

One of these general interactive services is the Internet. The Internet is a world-wide network of computer networks. These are linked together in such a way that users can

Table 23.4 The advantages and disadvantages of Web site ownership

Advantages
- Relatively inexpensive to create
- Equal access opportunities
- No SOV advantages
- Quick and easy to refresh and update
- Open all hours with no need for round the clock staff support
- Can provide cost efficiences (e.g. collecting information through a Web site can release staff to undertake other activities)
- Global

Disadvantages
- Varying difficulties in access
- Lack of regulation concerning the content and distribution of material made available
- Slow access and downloading time
- Possible security difficulties concerning financial transactions over the Internet
- Corporate rivalry concerning the development of technology and standards

search for, utilise and access information provided by others. The Internet provides a wide variety of activities, which include electronic mail, global information access and retrieval systems (e.g. gopher), discussion groups, multiplayer games and file transfer facilities, among others (Hoffman and Novak, 1996).

The World-Wide Web (WWW) represents the multimedia component, providing facilities such as full-colour graphics, sound and video (Berton *et al.*, 1996). The WWW can be considered as a network within which there are a number of nodes, called Web sites. These sites are created and maintained by organisations and individuals who wish to participate in Internet activities with the expectation that they can benefit (often profitably) from such participation. Web sites are intended to be visited by those browsing the Internet, and once visited the opportunity to interact and form a dialogue increases rapidly. The commercial attractiveness of a Web site is based around the opportunities to display product and company information, often in the form of catalogues, as a corporate identity cue and for internal communications; to generate leads; to provide on-screen order forms and customer support at both pre- and post-purchase points; and to collect customer and prospect information for use within a database or as a feedback link for measurement and evaluative purposes.

Barriers to entry are low for those developing Web sites. It is relatively inexpensive to create a site, and as it is the same for all participants there is an equality of entry costs. Also, because of the nature of the mediated environment no one Web site can gain a communication advantage over others as the share of voice (see Chapter 12) remains (essentially) the same.

Developing a Web site

The advantages and disadvantages of Web site ownership are set out in Table 23.4. However, many of the disadvantages are technological matters which even at the time of going to press have been or are in the process of being remedied, such is the speed at which this marketing communication tool is developing.

Many of the frameworks proposed for developing a Web site on the Internet have several deficiencies (Morgan, 1996). In an attempt to overcome these shortcomings,

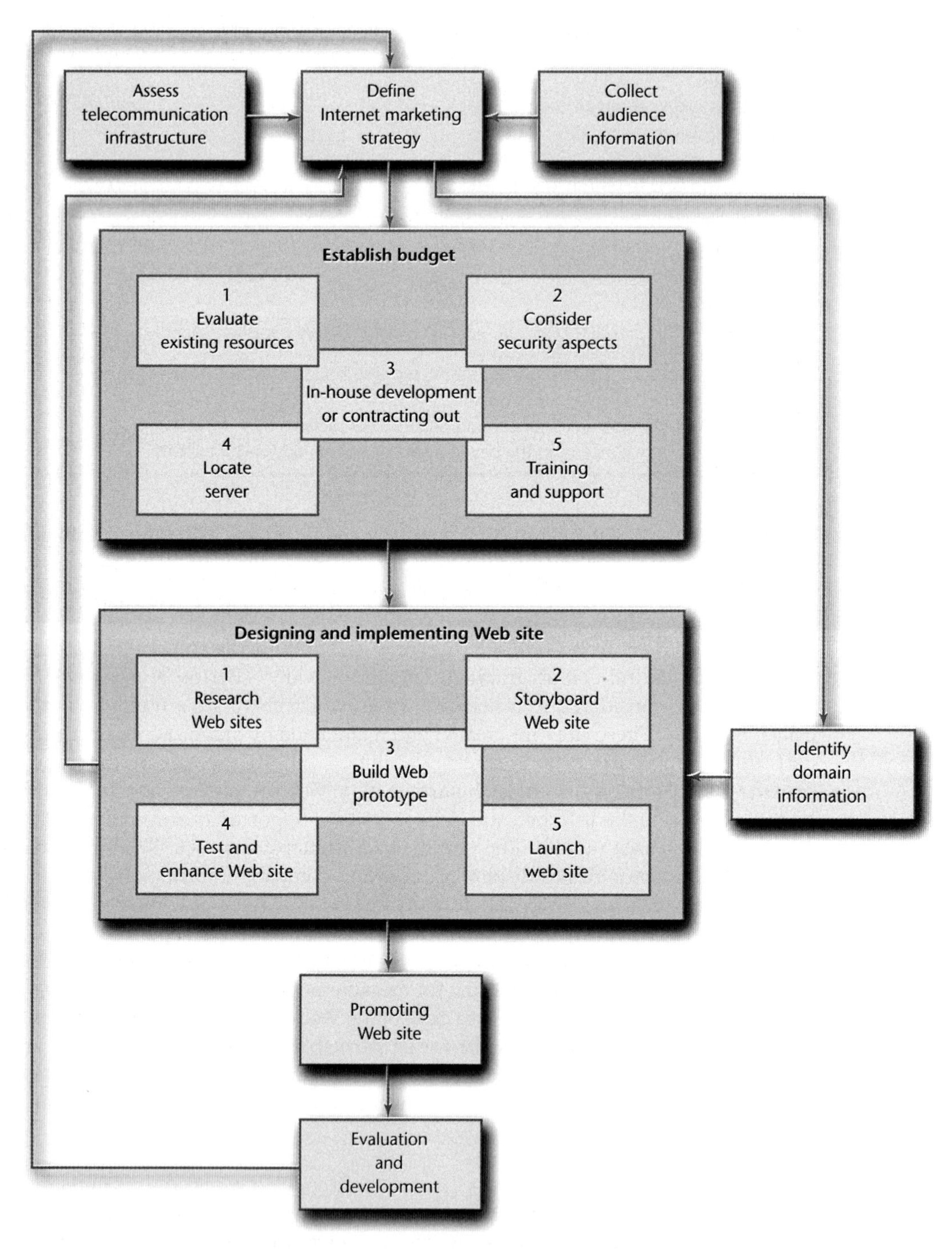

Figure 23.6 A framework for developing a site on the WWW (Ong (1995); used with kind permission).

Table 23.5 Some criteria for evaluating Web site's performance

Hits This is a request for a piece of information from the Web site server. Pages are made up of individual components, such as text, photographs and graphics. Therefore a single page request could result in several hits.
Registrations By restricting site access to those that register their details an audience profile can be developed. Care needs to be taken in using the data, as visitors may have forgotten their passwords and reregistered, and there may be many who simply visit the site once never to return.
Page requests It is easy to record the number of requests received for an individual page (or part of). This does not indicate, however, the number of people who have visited the page, although it does serve as a filter and indicate those who have more than a passing interest.
Ad specific audits Advertisers can have the number of people who have requested a page measured independently and so assist their media planning. However, this is simply an OTS measure and fails to record the number of people who actually see the advertisement.
Hot links Responses to advertisements can be measured by recording the volume of hot link activity. These are the clicks visitors can make to speed through pages and be guided through a site when searching for specific information. This facility does require the advertiser to operate a Web site, but this is not a major drawback for most advertisers.

the framework developed by Ong (1995) and presented by Morgan (Figure 23.6) is reproduced here not as a universal panacea for Web site creation but as a recognition of its attempt to overcome some of the difficulties inherent in this activity and to demonstrate the breadth of thought and vision that needs to be accommodated when developing (and reviewing) an organisation's Web presence.

Just as integrated marketing communications should have a strong link with corporate and marketing strategy, this framework requires consideration of the marketing strategy and the overall context within which the Web site is to be developed and operated. Internal resources, audience requirements, country or region telecommunications facilities have all to be evaluated prior to the design and build of the web site itself. The site's performance must also be evaluated; see Table 23.5.

Interactive television

Technological advances have made possible a range of other interactive communication opportunities. Stress so far has been placed on the Internet, but there have been many other imaginative and exciting developments and applications. One area where interactivity has been subject to experimentation is television, and some of the organisations that have experimented with interactive messages most notably are Mazda and Tango (see the case illustration below).

Among the most important is the development of digital broadcasting and the opportunities for interactive television. Digital television and interactive services are two related but different facilities. Digital services will arrive well before fully interactive services become commercially feasible.

Some believe that digital TV will overtake the Internet in terms of revenue by around 2003 or 2004 (Rosen, 1997). One of the biggest factors accelerating the consumer use of digital TV will be the entertainment possibilities that the Internet will struggle to provide. It is thought by many that digital TV will stimulate growth in home shopping. Digital television will impact on home shopping, but probably not to the extent that many popular writers assume. Research suggests that at this stage of development, rather than take an increasing proportion of total retail sales, growth in home shopping via digital television will be mainly at the expense of traditional mail order (Wade and McKechnie, 1998). There are a series of home shopping experiments being conducted by a variety of retailers. Perhaps most notably the dominant supermarkets have invested heavily in this area, and if successful the likely impact could be significant. Home shopping represents a change in buyer behaviour which may affect a range of ancillary activities. Transport and storage location facilities will need to be adjusted, and there could be alterations to employment patterns and the support and training necessary to augment new processes and procedures. It is unlikely that the retailers' high street presence will diminish significantly, as many consumers derive important entertainment and social interaction satisfaction by actively shopping.

Tango interactive

The Tango brand is often used to argue the merits of customer interaction. DRTV advertising for Tango Apple alone drew 1.3 million calls to a special Helpline in 1994. The Helpline was a fun and entertainment vehicle, but it also enabled Britvic to record and store the details of the brand's core audience.

Advertisements for the Tango Apple brand featured drinkers talking on the telephone to a Tango Apple can. The can was depicted as a seductress, tempting drinkers with her big juicy apples. The advert finished inviting viewers to call a free phone number if they felt the seduction of real Tango apples was taking over their lives. The call was answered by a 'Dr Ruth'-like character who requested them to leave details of their problem together with their names and addresses. The latter were extracted on the basis that they would be sent a money-off voucher for their next purchase of Apple Tango. With over 330,000 calls received, the strong level of interactivity between the brand and the consumer was demonstrated through this and subsequent Tango campaigns. Product involvement was increased substantially, as was top of mind awareness, important at the point of purchase (see Plate 23.3).

Anon. (1995)

The financial services sector can be expected to undergo further change as home banking in particular becomes a secure and more convenient transaction context. Entertainment possibilities will be even more attractive, as interactive games and interactive viewing through pay per view, video on demand and time shifting (which is, as Rosen points out, the option to view yesterday's programmes today) become easily accessible.

The new technology and the new communication infrastructure will enable increasing numbers of people the opportunity to experience interactive marketing communications and the new media. This may impact upon their expectations and bring changes to the way in which people lead their lives.

Summary

Direct marketing is a relatively new approach which, through the use of direct response media and database support, permits the generation and feedback of messages with individual customers. The overarching objectives are to build and sustain a mutually rewarding relationship with each customer, reduce media costs and improve effectiveness and measurement.

The use of direct marketing has grown considerably in the 1990s and will undoubtedly continue to grow during the first decade of the next century. For some organisations their whole marketing approach has been built around the direct concept (e.g. financial services) whereas for others the approach needs to be used to complement their use of the other tools in the promotional mix.

The growth of the Internet has been astonishing in recent years and represents the major form of interactive marketing communications. Interactivity *through* machines with people is now complemented with interactivity *with* machines. The development of digital television services will herald the birth of a new form of interactivity. Initially home shopping and banking facilities will be attractive to those who have access to the necessary equipment and who will benefit from the new facilities in the context of their own lifestyles. In the longer term fully interactive services will bring increased leisure and entertainment opportunities to a greater number of people.

Review questions

1. Set out a definition of direct marketing and consider the key words in the definition.
2. Explain the differences between direct response media and direct marketing.
3. Direct response media have many advantages over general mass advertising. What are they and why is this form of promotional communication increasing so quickly?
4. What are the different levels of direct marketing? What is the fundamental difference between levels?
5. Evaluate the main drivers behind the growth of direct marketing. How might these drivers change in the future?
6. Discuss the role of the database as the hub of marketing communications.
7. Telemarketing has become an integral feature of the promotional mix for reaching consumer and business-to-business markets. Why is this and what particular features of telemarketing attract clients?
8. There are many forms of interactive communication. Identify six of them.
9. How has communication theory adapted to this new form of interchange?
10. The development of Web sites has been a feature of recent organisational communications for reaching members and non-members. Prepare short notes

outlining the problems in developing such sites and argue the case for developing a Web site for a manufacturer of household electrical goods, a Premier League football club and a department store.

References

Anon. (1995) Tango case history. *Direct Response* (May), 38.

Berthon, P., Pitt, L.F. and Watson, R.T. (1996) Re-surfing W3: research perspectives on marketing communications and buyer behaviour on the Worldwide Web. *International Journal of Advertising*, **15**, 287–301.

Bird, D. (1989) *Commonsense Direct Marketing*, 2nd edn. London: Kogan Page.

Campaign Awards (1998) *Campaign Awards for 1997*, 13 February, p. 5

Cobb, R. (1991) Preparing for halcyon days. *Marketing*, 7 November, pp. 27–8.

Colourgraphic Group (1992) Telemarketing. *Marketing*, 13 February, pp. 19–22.

Cook, R. (1997) The future of telemarketing. *Campaign*, 20 June, pp. 27–8.

Cravens, D.W., Ingram, T.N. and LaForge, R.W. (1991) Evaluating multiple channel strategies. *Journal of Business and Industrial Marketing*, **6**(3/4), 37–48.

Cohen, R. (ed.) (1995) Interactive demand is not as high as believed. *Precision Marketing*, 25 September, p. 8.

Denny, N. (1997) Getting away from it all. *Marketing Direct* (June), 26–7.

DMIS (1993) *Letterbox Fact File*. Direct Mail Information Service.

Eisenhart, T. (1990) Going the integrated route. *Business Marketing* (December), 24–32.

Emerick, T. (1993) The multimedia mix. *Direct Marketing* (June), 20–2.

Evans, M. (1998) From 1086 and 1984: direct marketing into the millennium. *Marketing Intelligence and Planning*, **16**(1), 56–67.

Fletcher, K. (1997) External drive. *Marketing*, 30 October, pp. 39–42.

Fletcher, K.P. and Peters, L.D. (1997) Trust and direct marketing environments: a consumer perspective. *Journal of Marketing Management*, **13**, 523–39.

Foster, S. (1996) Defining the direct brand. *Admap* (October), 33–6.

Ganesan, S. (1994) Determinants of long-term orientation in buyer–seller relationships. *Journal of Marketing*, **58** (April), 1–19.

Goodwin, C. (1991) Privacy: recognition of a consumer right. *Journal of Public Policy & Marketing*, **10**(1), 149–66.

Gundach, G.T. and Murphy, P.E. (1993). Ethical and legal foundations of relational marketing exchanges. *Journal of Marketing*, **57** (October), 93–4.

Hoffman, D.L. and Novak, P.T. (1996) Marketing in hypermedia computer-mediated environments: conceptual foundations. *Journal of Marketing*, **60** (July), 50–68.

Kangis, P. and Rankin, K. (1996) Interactive services: how to identify and target the new markets. *Journal of Marketing Practice: Applied Marketing Science*, **2**(3), 44–67.

LaForge, R.W., Cravens, D.W. and Young, C.E. (1985) Improving sales force productivity. *Business Horizons* (September/October), 50–9.

Milton, C. (1993) Betterware's 21 per cent rise. *Financial Times*, 27 October, p. 22.

Morgan, R.F. (1996) An Internet marketing framework for the World Wide Web (WWW). *Journal of Marketing Management*, **12**, 757–75

Morgan, R.M. and Hunt, S.D. (1994) The commitment–trust theory of relationship marketing. *Journal of Marketing*, **58** (July), 20–38.

Ong, C.P. (1995) Practical aspects of marketing on the WWW. MBA Dissertation, University of Sheffield, UK.

Raphael, M. (1996) Scania chooses direct mail to keep on trucking! *Direct Marketing*, **59**(7), 30–32.

Roberts, M.L. and Berger, P.D. (1989) *Direct Marketing Management*. Englewood Cliffs NJ: Prentice Hall.

Rogers, E.M. (1983) *Diffusions of Innovations*, 3rd edn. New York: Free Press.

Rosen, N. (1997) Digital TV will soon overtake the Internet. *Revolution* (July), 6–7.

Rowney, P. (1992) Introduction to direct marketing. *Best of Direct Response Magazine*. Hertford, UK: Brainstorm Publishing.

Steuer, J. (1992) Defining virtual reality: dimensions determining telepresence. *Journal of Communication*, **42**(4), 73–93.

Summers, D. (1994) It's all in the name. *Financial Times*, 5 May, p. 20.

Wade, N. And McKechnie, S.A. (1998) The impact of digital television: will it change our shopping habits? Working paper presented at the 3rd International Conference on Marketing and Corporate Communications.

part iii

Strategies

chapter 24

Promotional objectives and positioning

The formal setting of promotional objectives is important because they provide guidance concerning what is to be achieved and when. These objectives form a pivotal role between the business/marketing plans and the marketing communications strategy.

AIMS AND OBJECTIVES

The aims of this chapter are to establish the nature and importance of the role that objectives play in the formulation of promotional strategies and to explore the concept of positioning.

The objectives of this chapter are:

1. To examine the need for organisational objectives.
2. To set out the different types of organisational goals.
3. To specify the relationship between corporate strategy and promotional objectives.
4. To determine the components of promotional objectives.
5. To examine the differences between sales- and communication-based objectives.
6. To evaluate the concept of positioning.
7. To explore the technique of perceptual mapping.
8. To understand and determine various positioning strategies.

Introduction

There are many different opinions about what it is that marketing communications seek to achieve. The conflicting views have led some practitioners and academics to polarise their thoughts about what constitutes an appropriate set of objectives. First, much effort and time has been spent trying to determine what promotion and marketing communication activities are supposed to achieve in the first place. Second, how should the success of a campaign be evaluated? Finally, how is it best to determine the degree of investment that should be made in each of the areas of the promotional mix? The process of resolving these different demands that are placed upon organisations has made the setting of promotional objectives very complex and difficult. It has been termed 'a job of creating order out of chaos' (Kriegel, 1986).

This perceived complexity has led a large number of managers to fail to set promotional objectives. Many of those that do set them do so in such a way that they are inappropriate, inadequate or merely restate the marketing objectives. The most common promotional objectives set by managers are sales-related. These include increases in market share, return on investment, sales volume increases and improvements in the value of sales made after accounting for the rate of inflation.

Such a general perspective ignores the influence of the other elements of the marketing mix and implicitly places the entire responsibility for sales performance with the promotional mix. This is not an accurate reflection of the way in which businesses and organisations work. In addition, because sales tests are too general, they would be an insufficiently rigorous test of promotional activity and there would be no real evaluation of promotional activities.

Sales volumes vary for a wide variety of reasons:

1. Competitors change their prices.
2. Buyers' needs change.
3. Changes in legislation may favour the strategies of particular organisations.
4. Favourable third-party communications become known to significant buyers.
5. General economic conditions change.
6. Technological advances facilitate improved production processes, economies of scale, experience effects and, for some organisations, the opportunity to reduce costs.
7. The entry and exit of different competitors.

These are a few of the many reasons why sales might increase, and conversely why sales might decrease. Therefore, the notion that marketing communications is entirely responsible for the sales of an offering is clearly unacceptable, unrealistic and incorrect.

The role of objectives in corporate strategy

Objectives play an important role in the activities of individuals, social groups and organisations because of the following:

1. They provide direction and an action focus for all those participating in the activity.

2. They provide a means by which the variety of decisions relating to an activity can be made in a consistent way.
3. They determine the time period in which the activity is to be completed.
4. They communicate the values and scope of the activity to all participants.
5. They provide a means by which the success of the activity can be evaluated.

It is generally accepted that the process of developing corporate strategy demands that a series of objectives be set at different levels within an organisation (Thompson, 1990; Greenley, 1989). This hierarchy or objective consists of mission, strategic business unit (SBU) or business objectives and functional objectives, such as production, finance or marketing goals.

The first level in the hierarchy (mission) requires that an overall direction be set for the organisation. If strategic decisions are made to achieve corporate objectives, both objectives and strategy are themselves constrained by an organisation's mission. Mission statements are 'management's vision of what the organisation is trying to do and to become over the long term' (Thompson and Strickland, 1990). A mission statement outlines who the organisation is, what it does and where it is headed. A clearly developed, articulated and communicated mission statement enables an organisation to define whose needs are to be satisfied, what needs require satisfying and which products and technologies will be used to provide the desired levels of satisfaction.

Conventionally, setting the mission answers the question 'What business are we in?' (Levitt, 1960). Obvious answers such as 'engineering', 'food processing', 'import and export' or 'retailing' miss the point. These are merely activities. Missions must be linked, explicitly, first and foremost to the needs met, rather than to markets or industries (Rosen, 1992). According to IBM, its original success was tied to its founder's principle of 'offering the best customer service in the world', not to technological innovation.

The mission then, should clearly identify the following:

1. The customers/buyers to be served.
2. The needs to be satisfied.
3. The products and/or technologies by which these will be achieved.

In some organisations these points are explicitly documented in a mission statement. These statements often include references to the organisation's philosophy, culture, commitment to the community and employees, growth, profitability and so on, but these should not blur or distract attention from the organisation's basic mission. The words mission and vision are often used interchangeably, but they have separate meanings. Vision refers to the expected or desired outcome of carrying out the mission over the agreed period of time.

The mission (see Chapter 10) provides a framework for the organisation's objectives, and the objectives that follow should promote and be consistent with the mission. While the word 'mission' implies a singularity of purpose, organisations have multiple objectives because of the many aspects of the organisation's performance and behaviour that contribute to the mission, and should, therefore, be explicitly identified. However, as Rosen points out, many of these objectives will conflict with each other. In retailing, for example, if an organisation chooses to open larger stores then total annual profit should rise, but average profit per square metre will probably fall.

Short-term profitability can be improved by reducing investment, but this could adversely affect long-term profitability. Organisations therefore have long-term and short-term objectives.

At the SBU level objectives represent the translation of the mission into a form that can be understood by relevant stakeholders. These objectives are the performance requirements for the organisation or unit and these in turn are broken down into objectives or targets that each functional area must achieve, as their contribution to the unit objectives. Marketing strategies are functional strategies, as are the strategies for the finance, human resource management and production departments. Combine or aggregate them and the SBU's overall target will, in reductionist theory, be achieved.

The various organisational objectives are of little use if they are not communicated to those who need to know what they are. Traditionally, such communication has focused upon employees, but there is increasing recognition that the other members of the stakeholder network need to understand an organisation's purpose and objectives. The marketing objectives developed for the marketing strategy provide important information for the communications strategy. Is the objective to increase market share or to defend or maintain the current situation? Is the product new or established? Is it being modified or slowly withdrawn? The corporate image is shaped partly by the organisation's objectives and the manner in which they are communicated. All these impact upon the objectives of the communications plan.

Promotional objectives consist of three main components. The first component concerns issues relating to the buyers of the product or service offered by the organisation. The second concerns issues relating to sales volume, market share, profitability and revenue. The third stream relates to the image, reputation and preferences that other stakeholders have towards the organisation. Each of these three streams is developed later in this chapter.

The role of promotional objectives and plans

Many organisations, including some advertising agencies, fail to set realistic (if any) promotional objectives. There are several explanations for this behaviour, but one of the common factors is that managers are unable to differentiate between the value of promotion as an expenditure and as an investment. This issue was addressed earlier (Chapter 12), but for now the value of promotional objectives can be seen in terms of the role they play in communications planning, evaluation and brand development.

The setting of promotional objectives is important for three main reasons. The first is that they provide *a means of communication and coordination* between groups (e.g. client and agency) working upon different parts of a campaign. Performance is improved if there is common understanding about the tasks the promotional tools have to accomplish. Secondly, objectives constrain the number of options available to an organisation. As Rothschild (1987) says, 'the key is to eliminate those strategies that have no chance of allowing the firm to meet its objectives'. Promotional objectives act as *a guide for decision-making* and provide a focus for decisions that follow in the process of developing promotional plans. The third reason is that objectives provide *a benchmark* so that the relative success or failure of a programme can be determined.

There is no doubt that organisations need to be flexible in order for them to anticipate and adjust to changes in their environments. This principle applies to the setting of promotional objectives. To set one all-encompassing objective and expect it to last the year (or whatever period is allocated) is both hopeful and naive; multiple objectives are necessary.

The content of promotional objectives has also been the subject of considerable debate. Two distinct schools of thought emerge: those that advocate sales-related measures as the main factors and those that advocate communication-related measures as the main orientation.

The sales school

As stated earlier, many managers see sales as the only meaningful objective for promotional plans. Their view is that the only reason an organisation spends money on promotion is to sell its product or service. Therefore, the only meaningful measure of the effectiveness of the promotional spend is in the sales results.

These results can be measured in a number of different ways. Sales turnover is the first and most obvious factor particularly in business-to-business markets. In consumer markets and the FMCG sector, market share movement is measured regularly and is used as a more sensitive barometer of performance. Over the longer term, return on investment measures are used to calculate success and failure. In some sectors the number of products sold (or cases), or volume of product shifted, relative to other periods of activity, is a common measure.

There are a number of difficulties with this view. One of these has been looked at above, that *sales result from a variety of influences*, such as the other marketing mix elements, competitor actions and wider environmental effects, such as the strength of the currency or the level of interest rates.

A second difficulty rests with the concept of *adstock or carryover*. The impact of promotional expenditure may not be immediately apparent, as the receiver may not enter the market until some later date but the effects of the promotional programme may influence the eventual purchase decision. This means that when measuring the effectiveness of a campaign, sales results will not always reflect its full impact.

Sales objectives *do little to assist the media planner, copywriters and creative team* associated with the development of the communications programme, despite their inclusion in campaign documents such as media briefs.

Sales-orientated objectives are, however, applicable in particular situations. For example, where direct action is required by the receiver in response to exposure to a message, measurement of sales is justifiable. Such an action, a behavioural response, can be solicited in direct response advertising. This occurs where the sole communication is through a particular medium, such as television or print.

The retail sector can also use sales measures, and it has been suggested that packaged goods organisations, operating in markets which are mature with established pricing and distribution structures, can build a databank from which it is possible to isolate the advertising effect through sales. For example, Sainsbury's was able to monitor the stock movements of particular ingredients used in its 'celebrity recipe' commercials. This enables it to evaluate the success of particular campaigns and particular celebrities. However, this effect is arguable on the grounds that this may ignore the impact of changes in competitor actions and changes in the overall environment. Furthermore, the effects of the organisation's own corporate advertising, adstock effects and other family brand promotions need to be accounted for if a meaningful sales effect is to be generated.

The sales school advocates the measure on the grounds of simplicity. Any manager can utilise the tool, and senior management does not wish to be concerned with information which is complex or unfamiliar, especially when working to short lead times and accounting periods. It is a self-consistent theory, but one that may mispresent consumer behaviour and the purchase process (perhaps unintentionally), and to that extent may result in less than optimal expenditure on marketing communications.

The communications school

There are many situations, however, where the aim of a communications campaign is to enhance the image or reputation of an organisation or product. Sales are not regarded as the only goal. Consequently, promotional efforts are seen as communication tasks, such as the creation of awareness or positive attitudes towards the organisation or product. To facilitate this process, receivers have to be given relevant information before the appropriate decision processes can develop and purchase activities established as a long-run behaviour.

Various models have been developed to assist our understanding about how these promotional tasks are segregated and organised effectively. These have been considered in Chapter 13 at some length and need not be repeated here. However, one particular model was developed deliberately to introduce clear objectives into the advertising development process: Dagmar.

Dagmar

Russell Colley (1961) developed a model for setting advertising objectives and measuring the results. This model was entitled 'Defining Advertising Goals for Measured Advertising Results – Dagmar'. Colley's rationale for what is effectively a means of setting communications-orientated objectives was that advertising's job, purely and simply, is to communicate to a defined audience information and a frame of mind that stimulates action. Advertising succeeds or fails depending on how well it communicates the desired information and attitudes to the right people at the right time and at the right cost.

Colley proposed that the communications task be based on a hierarchical model of the communications process:

Awareness – Comprehension – Conviction – Action

Awareness

Awareness of the existence of a product or an organisation is necessary before purchase behaviour can be expected. Once awareness has been created in the target audience it should not be neglected. If there is neglect, the audience may become distracted by competing messages and the level of awareness of the focus product or organisation may decline. Awareness, therefore, needs to be created, developed, refined or sustained, according to the characteristics of the market and the particular situation facing an organisation at any one point in time (Figure 24.1).

In situations where the buyer experiences high involvement and is fully aware of a product's existence, attention and awareness levels need only be sustained and efforts

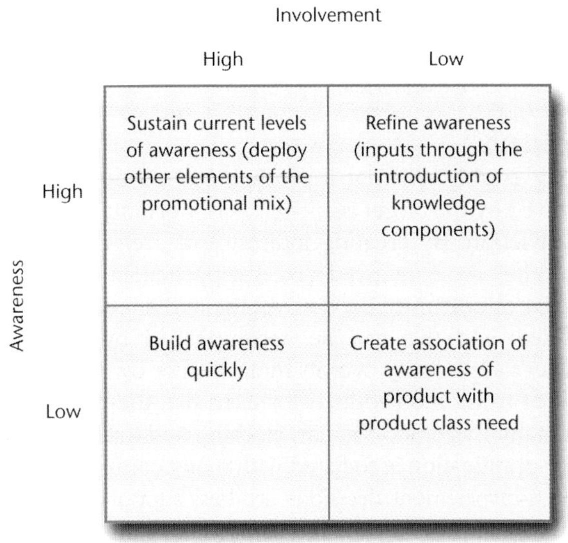

Awareness \ Involvement	High	Low
High	Sustain current levels of awareness (deploy other elements of the promotional mix)	Refine awareness (inputs through the introduction of knowledge components)
Low	Build awareness quickly	Create association of awareness of product with product class need

Figure 24.1 Awareness grid.

need to be applied to other communication tasks, which may be best left to the other elements of the communications mix. For example, sales promotion and personal selling are more effective at informing, persuading and provoking consumption of a new car once advertising has created the necessary levels of awareness.

Where low levels of awareness are found, getting attention needs to be a prime objective in order that awareness can be developed in the target audience.

Where low involvement exists the decision-making process is relatively straightforward. With levels of risk minimised, buyers with sufficient levels of awareness may be prompted into purchase with little assistance of the other elements of the mix. Recognition and recall of brand names and corporate images are felt by some (Rossiter and Percy, 1987) to be sufficient triggers to stimulate a behavioural response. The requirement in this situation would be to refine and strengthen the level of awareness in order that it provokes interest and stimulates a higher level of involvement during recall or recognition.

Where low levels of awareness are matched by low involvement the prime objective has to be to create awareness of the focus product in association with the product class.

It is not surprising that organisations use awareness campaigns and invest a large amount of their resources in establishing their brand or corporate name. For example, Pedigree Petfoods (Hazelhurst, 1988) seeks to establish 'top of mind awareness' as one of their primary objectives for their advertising spend.

Comprehension

Awareness on its own is, invariably, not enough to stimulate purchase activity. Knowledge about the product (or what the organisation does) is necessary, and this can be achieved by providing specific information about key brand attributes. These attributes and their associated benefits may be key to the buyers in the target audience or may be key because the product has been adapted or modified in some way. This means that the audience needs to be educated about the change and shown how their use of the product may be affected. For example, in attempting to persuade people to try a different brand of mineral water, it may be necessary to compare the product with other mineral water products and provide an additional usage benefit, such as environmental claims.

Conviction

Having established that a product has particular attributes which lead to benefits perceived by the target audience as important, it is then necessary to establish a sense of conviction. By creating interest and preference, buyers are moved to a position where they are convinced that one particular product in the class should be tried at the next opportunity. To do this, the audience's beliefs about the product need to be moulded, and this can be accomplished by using messages that demonstrate a product's superiority over its main rival or by emphasising the rewards conferred as a result of using the product; for example, the reward of social acceptance associated with many fragrance, fashion clothing and accessory advertisements, and the reward of self-gratification associated with many confectionery messages (Cadbury's Flake).

High-involvement decisions are best supported with personal selling and sales promotion activities, in an attempt to gain conviction. Low-involvement decisions rely on the strength of advertising messages, packaging and sales promotion to secure conviction.

Action

A communications programme is used to encourage buyers to engage in purchase activity. Advertising can be directive and guide buyers into certain behavioural outcomes; for example, to the use of toll-free numbers (0800 and 0500 in the UK), direct mail activities and reply cards and coupons. However, for high-involvement decisions the most effective tool in the communications mix at this stage in the hierarchy is personal selling. Through the use of interpersonal skills, buyers are more likely to want to buy a product than if the personal prompting is absent. The use of direct marketing activities by Avon Cosmetics, Tupperware, Betterware and suppliers of life assurance and double-glazing services has been instrumental in the sales growth experienced by organisations in these markets. Colley's dissatisfaction with the way in which advertising agencies operated led him to specify the components of a good advertising objective: 'A specific communications task to be accomplished among a defined audience to a given degree in a given period of time'. An analysis of this statement shows that it is made up of four distinct elements:

1. A need to specify the communications task.
2. A need to define the audience.
3. A need to state the required degree of change.
4. A need to establish the time period in which the activity is to occur.

Colley's statement is very clear – it is measurable and of assistance to copywriters. Indeed, Dagmar revolutionised the approach taken by advertisers to the setting of objectives. It helped to move attention from the sales effect to the communication effect school and has led to improved planning processes, due partly to a better understanding of advertising and promotional goals.

Many of the difficulties associated with sequential models (Chapter 13) are also applicable to Dagmar. In addition to problems of hierarchical progression, measurement and costs are issues concerning the sales orientation, restrictions upon creativity and short-term accountability.

Sales orientation

This criticism is levelled by those who see sales as the only valid measure of effectiveness. The sole purpose of communication activities, and advertising in particular, is to generate sales. So, as the completion of communications tasks may not result in purchases, the only measure that need be undertaken is that of sales. This point has been discussed earlier and need not be reproduced here.

Restrictions upon creativity

Dagmar is criticised on the grounds that creative flair can be lost as attention passes from looking for the big idea to concentration upon the numbers game, of focusing on measures of recall, attitude change and awareness. It is agreed that the creative personnel are held to be more accountable under Dagmar and this may well inhibit some of their work. Perhaps the benefits of providing direction and purpose offset the negative aspects of a slight loss in creativity.

Short-term accountability

To the above should be added the time period during which management and associated agencies are required to account for their performance. With accounting periods being reduced to as little as 12 weeks, the communications approach is impractical for two reasons. The first is that the period is not long enough for all of the communication tasks to be progressed or completed. Sales measures present a much more readily digestible benchmark of performance.

The second concerns the unit of performance itself. With the drive to be efficient and to be able to account for every communication pound spent, managers themselves need to use measures that they can understand and which they can interpret from published data. Sales data and communications spend data are consistent measures and make no further demands on managers. Managers do not have enough time to spend analysing levels of comprehension or preference and to convert them into formats that are going to be of direct benefit to them and their organisations. Having said that, those organisations that are prepared to invest in a more advanced management information system will enable a more sophisticated view to be taken.

The communication school approach is not accepted by some, who argue that it is too difficult and impractical to translate a sales objective into a series of specific communications objectives. Furthermore, what actually constitutes adequate levels of awareness and comprehension and how can it be determined which stage the majority of the target audience has reached at any one point in time? Details of measurement, therefore, throw a veil over the simplicity and precision of the approach taken by the communication orientation school.

From a practical perspective it should be appreciated that most successful marketing organisations do not see the sales and communications schools as mutually exclusive. They incorporate both views and weight them according to the needs of the current task, their overall experience, the culture and style of the organisation and the agencies with whom they operate.

Derivation of promotional objectives

It has been established that specific promotional objectives need to be established if a suitable foundation is to be laid for the many communication decisions that follow.

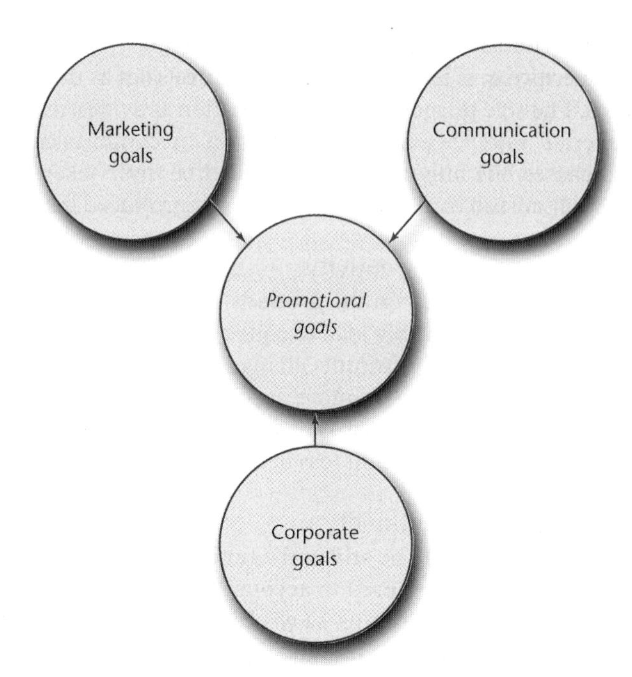

Figure 24.2 Three principal topics for promotional objective setting.

Promotional objectives are derived from understanding the overall context in which the communications will operate. Comprehending the contexts of the buyer and the organisation allows the objectives of the planned communications to be identified: the *what* that is to be achieved. For example, objectives concerning the perception that different target customers have of a brand, the perception that members of a performance network have of the organisation's offerings, the reactions of key stakeholders to previous communications and the requirements of the current marketing plan all impact upon the objectives of the communication plan. Therefore, promotional objectives evolve principally from a systematic audit and analysis of the key communication contexts, and specifically from the marketing plan and stakeholder analysis.

It was established earlier that there are three main streams of objectives. These are set out in Figure 24.2. The first concerns issues relating to the buyers of the product or service offered by the organisation. The second concerns issues relating to market share/sales volume, profitability and revenue. The third stream relates to the image, reputation and preferences that other stakeholders have towards the organisation.

All these objectives are derived from an analysis of the current situation. The marketing communication brief which flows from this analysis should specify the sales-related objectives to be achieved, as these can be determined from the marketing plan. Sales-related objectives might concern issues such as market share and sales volume.

Customer-related objectives concern issues such as awareness, perception, attitude, feelings and intentions towards a brand or product. The exact issue to be addressed in the plan is calculated by analysing the contextual information driven by the audit.

Issues related to the perception of the organisation are often left unattended or, worse, ignored. Research may indicate that the perception of particular stakeholders, in either the performance or support network, does not complement the current level of corporate performance or may be misplaced or confused. Objectives will need to be established to correct or reinforce the perception held of the organisation. The degree of urgency may be directly related to the level of confusion or misunderstanding or be related to competitive or strategic actions initiated by competitors and other members of the network. Corporate strategy may have changed and, as identified earlier, any new strategy will need to be communicated to all stakeholders.

The need for realism when setting promotional objectives

Hierarchy of effects models which specify stages of development were first proposed as far back as 1898 by E. St Elmo Lewis (Barry and Howard, 1990) and similar views were expressed by Colley (Dagmar) in 1961. Yet despite the passage of time since their publication, a large number of organisations still fail either to set any promotional objectives, or they confuse objectives with strategy. Organisations seeking to coordinate their communications need to recognise the necessity to set multiple objectives at different times in the campaign period and to be prepared to adjust them in the light of environmental changes. These changes may be due to ever-decreasing product life cycles or technological developments that may give a competitor comparative advantage, and perhaps legislative developments (or the timing of management's interpretation and implementation of certain legislation) may bring about a need to reconfigure the promotional mix.

Management's failure to set objectives is often the result of a lack of awareness of the current position, or a lack of understanding of how and why appropriate objectives need to be established. With increasingly competitive and turbulent environments, a greater number of organisations are turning their attention to ways in which they can communicate more effectively with their stakeholders. Furthermore, as more executives undertake management education programmes, so a higher level of skill is being transferred to organisations, and this in turn will bring a higher incidence of better practice.

The overall objective of any promotional programme is to increase the level of sales. While it seems unreasonable to expect the promotional mix to bear total responsibility for this, it is also unreasonable and impractical to expect the communications approach to bear total responsibility. It is imperative that organisations are willing and prepared to set promotional objectives which utilise basic communications tasks, such as awareness and intentions, and that they utilise sales benchmarks as means of determining what has been achieved and how. Promotional objectives are a derivative of both marketing and corporate strategies. Just as revenue and income targets are part of marketing strategy, so they should form part of the promotional objectives. They cannot be separated and they cannot be neglected.

Figure 24.2 shows the different types of objectives that can be set for a promotional strategy. The choice depends on the situation facing each manager and in particular whether the product or organisation is new. Establishing and maintaining levels of awareness is, however, paramount to any communications programme, and must be considered one of the primary communication objectives.

Promotional objectives need to be set which reflect the communication and sales tasks that the product or organisation needs to accomplish. It should be appreciated that promotional objectives are vitally important, as they provide the basis for a string of decisions that are to be taken at subsequent stages in the development of the communication plan.

Management's next task is to make decisions regarding which of these different promotional objectives will receive attention first. In order that decisions can be made regarding promotional strategy, the communications mix and the level of resources allocated to each promotional tool, it is necessary to rank and weight the objectives at this stage in the management process. The criteria used to weight the different objectives will inevitably be subjective. This is because they reflect each manager's perception, experience and interpretation of his or her environment. However, it is also his or her skill and judgement that are the important elements, and as long as the criteria are used and applied in a consistent manner the outcome of the communication plan is more likely to be successful.

SMART objectives

To assist management in their need to develop suitable objectives, a set of guidelines have been developed, commonly referred to as SMART objectives. This acronym stands for Specific, Measurable, Achievable, Relevant, Targeted and Timed.

The process of making objectives SMART requires management to consider exactly what is to be achieved, when, where, and with which audience. This clarifies thinking, sorts out the logic of the proposed activities and provides a clear measure for evaluation at the end of the campaign.

- *Specific*: What is the actual variable that is to be influenced in the campaign? Is it awareness, perception, attitudes or some other element that is to be influenced? Whatever the variable, it must be clearly defined and must enable precise outcomes to be determined.
- *Measureable*: Set a measure of activity against which performance can be assessed. For example, this may be a percentage level of desired prompted awareness in the target audience.
- *Achievable*: Objectives need to be attainable, otherwise those responsible for their achievement will lack motivation and a desire to succeed.
- *Realistic*: The actions must be founded in reality and be relevant to the brand and the context in which they are set.
- *Targeted and Timed*: Which target audience is the campaign targeted at, how precisely is the audience defined and over what period are the results to be generated?

For example, Toyota might have set the following marketing communication objective when launching the Avensi into the UK market in 1998. This goal is realistic, bearing in mind the marketing pedigree and resources available to Toyota.

The marketing communications objective for the period January to March 1998 (timed) is to create 65% (measurable and achievable) prompted awareness (specific) in the ABC1, male 30 to 45 year old age group and those earning £25,000 plus (targeted).

Having determined what levels of awareness, comprehension or preference are necessary or how attitudes need to be developed, the establishment or positioning of these objectives as a task for the organisation to accomplish should be seen as a primary communication objective. The attitude held or what individuals in the target market perceive, comprehend or prefer is a focus for campaign activity and subsequent evaluation.

Positioning: an introduction

Two drug manufacturers launched an identical product, Lisinopril, for the treatment of heart disease. ICI promoted its drug as Zestril and MSD promoted its as Carace. Both organisations are perceived as important and credible sources of cardiovascular expertise, their advertising or above-the-line expenditures were equal, their sales forces were of the same size and their calling rates on doctors almost identical. While their below-the-line expenditures cannot be compared directly, their activity levels appear comparable. The question raised by Cawte (1989) was, why are Zestril's sales double those of Carace's? Furthermore, why do a great many doctors prescribe Zestril when they have only seen an MSD sales representative?

This is not an isolated example, as this activity pattern has been observed elsewhere with different products from a variety of organisations and markets. There are a number of possible explanations: environmental changes, key variable adjustments such as the price/cost relationship, the level and type of training that sales representatives receive in each organisation and the form and quality of the promotional messages used to support each campaign may explain some of the differences in sales performance. However, as Cawte suggests, it appears that these are not significant and that it was the positioning of the two organisations and of their offerings that played a crucial role in the launch of these offerings.

The positioning concept

The final act in the target marketing process of segmentation and targeting is positioning. Following on from the identification of potential markets, determining the size and potential of market segments and selecting specific target markets, positioning is the process whereby information about the organisation or product is communicated in such a way that the object is perceived by the consumer/stakeholder to be differentiated from the competition, to occupy a particular space in the market. According to Kotler (1997), 'Positioning is the act of designing the company's offering and image so that they occupy a meaningful and distinct competitive position in the target customers' minds'.

This is an important aspect of the positioning concept. Positioning is not about the product but what the buyer thinks about the product or organisation. It is not the physical nature of the product that is important for positioning, but how the product is perceived that matters. This is why part of the context analysis (Chapter 30), requires a consideration of perception and the way stakeholders see brands and organisations. Of course, this may not be the same as the way brand managers intend their brands to be seen or how they believe the brand is perceived.

This perspective was originally proposed in the early 1970s by Ries and Trout (1972). They claimed that it is not what you do to a product that matters, it is what you do to the mind of the prospect that is important. They set out three stages of development: the product era, the image era and the positioning era.

The product era occurred in the late 1950s and early 1960s and existed when each product was promoted in an environment where there was little competition. Each product was accepted as an innovation and was readily accepted and adopted as a natural development. In the pharmaceutical market, drugs such as Navidex, Valium and Lasix became established partly because of the lack of competition and partly because of the ability of the product to fulfil its claims. This was a period when the features and benefits of products were used in communications; the unique selling proposition (USP) was of paramount importance.

The image era that followed was spawned by companies with established images, who introduced new me-too products against the original brands. It was the strength of the perceived company image that underpinned the communications surrounding these new brands that was so important to their success. Products such as Amoxil, Tagamet and Tenormin were launched on an image platform.

The positioning era has developed mainly because of the increasingly competitive market conditions, where there is now little compositional, material or even structural difference between products within each class. Consequently, most products are now perceived relative to each other. In most markets the level and intensity of 'noise' drives organisations to establish themselves and their offerings in particular parts of the overall market. It is now the ability of an offering to command the attention of buyers and to communicate information about how an offering is differentiated from the other competitive offerings that helps to signal the relative position the offering occupies in the market.

Drugs such as Zantac, Pepcid, Volmax and Zestril have all been launched using positioning techniques. In the consumer market, established brands from washing powders (Ariel, Daz, Persil) and hair shampoos (such as Wash & Go, Timotei), to cars (for example, Peugeot, Saab, Nissan) and grocery multiples (Sainsbury's, Tesco) each carry communications that enable receivers to position them in their respective markets.

The positioning concept is not the sole preserve of branded or consumer-orientated offerings or indeed those of the business-to-business market. Organisations are also positioned relative to one another, mainly as a consequence of their corporate identities, whether they are deliberately managed or not. The position an organisation takes in the mind of consumers may be the only means of differentiating one product from another. King (1991) argues that, given the advancement in technology and the high level of physical and functional similarity of products in the same class, so consumer's choices will be more focused on their assessment of the company they are dealing with. Therefore, it is important to position organisations as brands in the minds of actual and potential customers.

One of the crucial differences between the product and the corporate brand is that the corporate brand needs to be communicated to a large array of stakeholders, whereas the product-based brand requires a focus on a smaller range of stakeholders, in particular the consumers and buyers in the performance network.

Whatever the position chosen, either deliberately or accidentally, it is the means by which customers understand the brand's market position, and it often provides signals to determine a brand's main competitors; or (as is often the case) customers fail to understand the brand or are confused about what the brand stands for.

Developing a position

All products and all organisations have a position. The position held with each stakeholder can be managed or it can be allowed to drift. An increasing number of organisations are trying to manage the positions occupied by their brands and are using positioning strategies to move to new positions in buyers' minds and so generate an advantage over their competitors. This is particularly important in markets that are very competitive and where mobility barriers (ease of entry and exit to a market, e.g. plant and production costs) are relatively low.

Positioning is about visibility and recognition of what a product/service represents for a buyer. In markets where the intensity of rivalry and competition are increasing and buyers have greater choice, identification and understanding of a product's intrinsic values become critical. Network members have limited capacities, whether this be the level or range of stock they can carry or the amount of available shelf space that can be allocated. An offering with a clear identity and orientation to a particular target segment's needs will not only be stocked and purchased but can warrant a larger margin through increased added value.

Positioning, therefore, is the natural conclusion to the sequence of activities that constitute a core part of the marketing strategy. Market segmentation and target marketing are prerequisites to successful positioning. From the research data and the marketing strategy, it is necessary to formulate a positioning statement that is in tune with the promotional objectives.

To develop a position, managers should be guided by the following process:

1. Which positions are held by which competitors? This will almost certainly require consumer research to determine attitudes and perceptions and possibly the key attributes that consumers perceive as important.
2. From the above, will it be possible to determine which position, if any, is already held by the focus brand?
3. From the information gathered so far, will it be possible to determine a positioning strategy; that is, what is the desired position for the brand?
4. Is the strategy feasible in view of the competitors and any budgetary constraints? A long-term perspective is required, as the selected position has to be sustained.
5. Implement a programme to establish the desired position.
6. Monitor the perception held by consumers of the brand, and of their changing tastes and requirements, on a regular basis.

Perceptual mapping

In order to determine how the various offerings are perceived in a market, the key attributes that stakeholders use to perceive products in the market need to be established. A great deal of this work will have been completed as part of the research and review process prior to developing a communications plan. The next task is to determine perceptions and preferences in respect of the key attributes as perceived by buyers.

The objective of the exercise is to produce a perceptual map (brand and multi-dimensional maps) where the dimensions used on the two axes are the key attributes, as seen by buyers. This map represents a geometric comparison of how competing products are perceived (Sinclair and Stalling, 1990). Figure 24.3 shows that the key dimensions for consumers in the regional beer market could be quality and strength. Each product is positioned on the map according to the perception that buyers have of the strength of each attribute of each product. By plotting the perceived positions of each brand on the map, an overall perspective of the market can be developed.

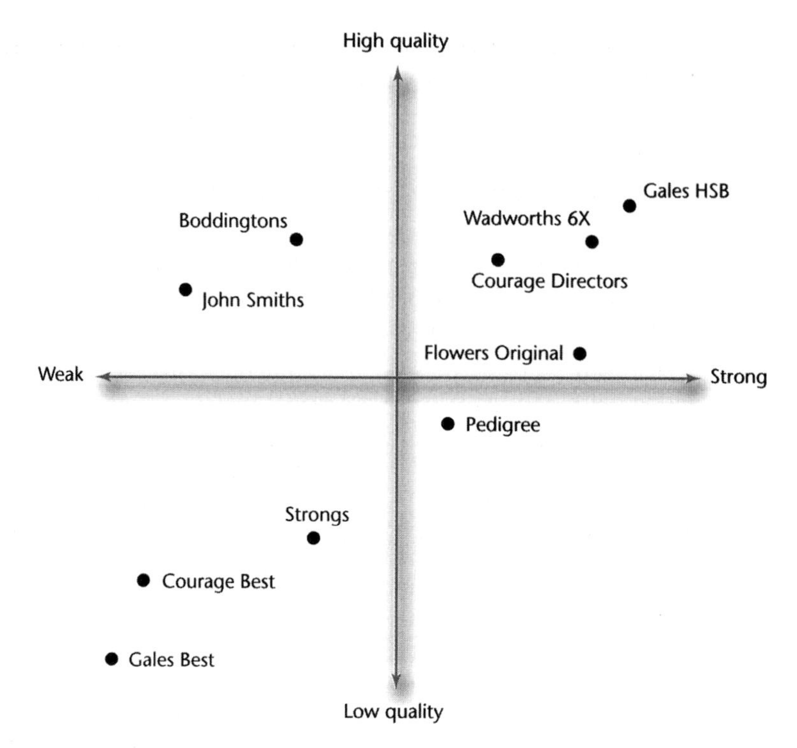

Figure 24.3 A perceptual map for regional beer market (possible positions).

The closer products are clustered together, the greater the competition. The further apart the positions, the greater the opportunity to enter the market, as competition is less intense. From the map, it can be seen that Gales HSB is perceived to be not only the strongest beer but also one which is seen to be of the highest quality. This compares with their best bitter, which is positioned as the weakest beer in the sample and one of the poorer ones in terms of quality. There is only one beer positioned in the high strength and less than average quality sector which may, subject to further research, present a market opportunity.

Substitute products are often uncovered by their closeness to each other (Day *et al.*, 1979). It is also possible to ask buyers and other stakeholders what an ideal brand would consist of. This perfect brand can then be positioned on the map, and the closer an offering is to the ideal point the greater its market share should be, as it is preferred more than its rivals. These maps are known as preference maps.

By superimposing the position of an ideal brand on the map, it is possible to extend the usefulness of the tool. Perceptions of what constitutes the right amount of each key attribute can assist management in the positioning exercise. Marketing communications can, therefore, be designed to convey the required information about each attribute and so adjust buyers' perceptions so that they are closer to the ideal position, or to the position on the map that management wants the brand to occupy. For example, Gales may wish to reposition its best bitter by changing the perception that drinkers have of the quality of the beer. Following any necessary adjustments to the product, marketing communications would emphasise the quality of the beer and hope to move it away from any association with Courage Best.

Neal (1980) offered the following reasons why perceptual mapping is such a powerful tool for examining the position of products:

1. It develops understanding of how the relative strengths and weaknesses of different products are perceived by buyers.
2. It builds knowledge about the similarities and dissimilarities between competing products.
3. It assists the process of repositioning existing products and the positioning of new products.
4. The technique helps to track the perception that buyers have of a particular product and also assists the measurement of the effectiveness of communication programmes and marketing actions, intended to change buyers' perceptions.

Perceptual mapping is an important tool in the development and tracking of promotional strategy. It enables brand managers to identify gaps and opportunities in the market and allows organisations to monitor the effects of past marketing communications. For example, in the early 1980s, none of the available brands in the newly emerging lager market was seen as refreshing. All brands were perceived as virtually the same. Heineken saw the opportunity and seized the position for refreshment, and has been able to occupy and sustain the position since then.

Positioning strategies

The development of positions which buyers can relate to and understand is an important and vital part of the marketing communications plan. In essence, the position adopted is a statement about what the brand is, what it stands for and the values and beliefs that customers (hopefully) will come to associate with the particular brand. The visual images or the position statement represented in the strap-line may be a significant trigger which buyers use to recall images and associations of the brand.

There a number of overall approaches to developing a position. These can be based on factors such as the market, the customer or redefining the appeal of the brand itself; see Table 24.1.

To implement these three broad approaches a number of strategies have been developed. The list that follows is not intended to be comprehensive or to convey the opinion that these strategies are discrete. They are presented here as means of conveying the strategic style, but in reality a number of hybrid strategies are often used.

Product features

This is one of the easier concepts and one that is more commonly adopted. The brand is set apart from the competition on the basis of the attributes, features or benefits that the brand has relative to the competition. For example, Weetabix contains all the vitamins needed each day, and the Royal Bank of Scotland promotes its credit card by extolling the benefits of its interest rate compared with those of its competitors.

Price/quality

This strategy is more effectively managed than others because price itself can be a strong communicator of quality. A high price denotes high quality, just as a low price can deceive buyers into thinking a product to be of low quality and poor value. Retail outlets such as Harrods and Aspreys use high prices to signal high quality and exclusivity. At the other end of the retail spectrum, Littlewood's, BHS and Woolworth's position themselves to attract those with less disposable income and to whom convenience is of greater importance. The price/quality appeal is best observed in

CASE ILLUSTRATION

Relaunching Harveys Bristol Cream

Harveys Bristol Cream sherry was for a long time the undisputed UK market leader, but the brand began to experience difficulties at a time when sherry consumption world-wide had fallen by 45% since the late 1970s. This was due primarily to increased competition, new lifestyles and the development of own brands. Indeed, own-label claimed 40% market share, and the emergence of a new prime competitor, Croft Original, threatened Harveys' position.

A series of research exercises were undertaken. First psychological tests indicated that the emotional sensory profile of the brand itself was inhibiting. The taste was not quite right and the packaging evoked negative imagery and product expectations. Consumers 'taste with their eyes', so what they see frames their perception and provides a context within which they experience a brand. Therefore, research suggested a change in the physical product and a change in the packaging.

The challenge was to expand the context for the brand, and this required finding a new position that provoked positive brand associations.

The next stage in the research found that people's perception of sherry as a category of drink inhibited use. What emerged were new ways of drinking sherry – with ice, long or with mixers – and this allowed new usage occasions to be identified. Sherry could now be drunk on occasions when it was socially acceptable to drink, not just at weddings and functions, but at pubs, relaxing at home and generally anywhere where drinking was expected/accepted.

From the data and information collected through focus groups and tastings, a communication hierarchy was developed (Figure 24.4). The left-hand side of the pyramid indicated the current brand image and the right-hand side suggested the new context for the brand. To utilise the brand heritage an idea emerged to use blue glass for the packaging. This type of glass originated in Bristol and was used to make high-quality products. A smaller version of the current label was transferred and after further extensive research, mainly with brand switchers and the not-so-loyals, a relaunch was confirmed. Saatchi & Saatchi were given a brief and an advertising campaign broke for

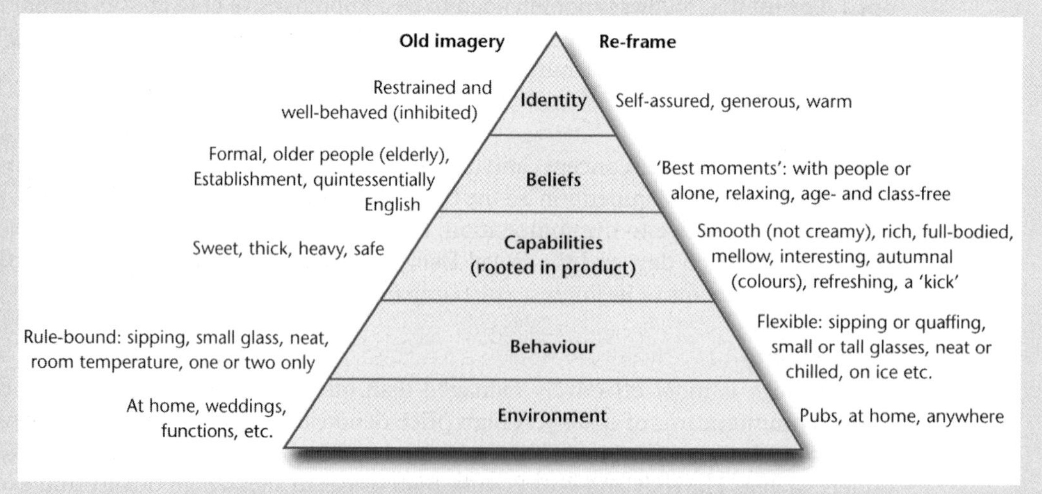

Figure 24.4 Communication hierarchy for Harveys Bristol Cream (Hodder *et al.* (1995); used with kind permission).

the Christmas market in 1994 (see Plate 24.1).

Awareness indices have all improved, the bottle is accepted in preference to the original, and sales have increased substantially, by 46% at one point. In addition, other objectives have been achieved: margins have improved against Croft and its brand leadership position has been enhanced.

Adapted from Hodder *et al.* (1995)

Sainsbury's, 'where good food costs less' and with the alcoholic lager Stella Artois, which is positioned as 'refreshingly expensive'.

Use

By informing markets when or how a product can be used, a position can be created in the minds of the buyers. For example, Kellogg's, the breakfast cereal manufacturer, has positioned itself as a snack food provider. Its marketing strategy of moving into new markets was founded on its over-dependence on breakfast consumption. By becoming associated with snacks not only is usage increased but the opportunity to develop new products becomes feasible. The launch of Pop Tarts is a testimony to this strategy. Milky Way, 'the sweet you can eat between meals', informs just when it is permissible to eat chocolate and After Eight chocolate mints clearly indicate when they should be eaten. The hair shampoo, Wash & Go, positions the brand as a quick and easy to use (convenience) product, for those whose lifestyles are full and demanding.

Product class dissociation

Some markets are essentially uninteresting, and most other positions have been adopted by competitors. A strategy used by margarine manufacturers is to dis-

Table 24.1 Positioning approaches

Approach	Type of application
Market-related	*First into a market*: Heineken was first to take the refreshment position *Redefine the market*: AA repositioned itself as the Fourth Emergency Service Miller Lite said the *lite* meant not heavy, not low alcohol
Customer-related	*A unique buying reason*: Fairy Liquid cleans 50% more dishes, so lasts longer and provides greater value *Particular type of buyer*: Tia Maria became a girl's magic password rather than just a drink to be consumed on special occasions
Appeal-related	*Distinct personality*: Pepperami became a crazy/mad 'bit of an animal' *Decision criteria*: Virgin Upper Class was presented as a sensible rational business decision, not a whim or a risk *Imaginative or interesting*: Castrol made oil into liquid engineering Lil-lets are discreet, just like the advertising

associate themselves from other margarines and associate themselves with what was commonly regarded as a superior product, butter. The Alliance and Leicester Building Society used to proclaim that 'not all building societies are the same'. The suggestion was that they were different from the rest and hence offered better services and customer care.

User

A sensible extension of the target marketing process is to position openly so that the target user can be clearly identified. Flora margarine was for men, and then it became 'for all the family'. American Express uses several leading business celebrities, including Sir Terence Conran and Anita Roddick, to suggest that users can have a lifestyle profile that complements those who use and endorse the Amex card. Some hotels position themselves as places for weekend breaks, as leisure centres or as conference centres.

Competitor

For a long time, positioning oneself against a main competitor was regarded as dangerous and was avoided. Avis, however, performed very successfully 'trying even harder' against Hertz, the industry number one. Saab contested the 'safest car' position with Volvo and Qualcast took on its new rival, the hover mower, by informing everyone that 'it is a lot less bovver than a hover', because its product collected the grass cuttings and produced the manicured lawn finish that roller-less mowers cannot reproduce.

Benefit

Positions can also be established by proclaiming the benefits that usage confers on those that consume. Sensodyne toothpaste appeals to all those who suffer from sensitive teeth, and a vast number of pain relief formulations claim to smooth away headaches or relieve aching limbs, sore throats or some offending part of the anatomy.

Cultural symbol

An appeal to cultural heritage and tradition, symbolised by age, particular heraldic devices or visual cues, has been used by many organisations to convey quality, experience and knowledge. Kronenbourg 1664, 'Established since 1803' and the use of coats of arms by many universities to represent depth of experience and a sense of permanence are just some of the historical themes used to position organisations.

Whatever the position adopted by a brand or organisation, both the marketing and promotional mixes must endorse and support the position so that there is consistency throughout all communications. For example, if a high-quality position is taken, such as that of the Ritz Carlton Hotel Group, then the product quality must be relatively high compared with competitors, the price must be correspondingly excessive and distribution synonymous with quality and exclusivity. Sales promotion activity will be minimal so as not to convey a touch of inexpensiveness, and advertising messages should be visually affluent and rich in tone and copy, with public relations and personal selling approaches transmitting high-quality, complementary cues.

The dimensions used to position brands must be relevant and important to the target audience and in the image cues used must be believable and consistently credible. Positioning strategies should be developed over the long term if they are to prove effective, although minor adaptions to the position can be carried out in order to reflect changing environmental conditions.

Repositioning

Technology is developing quickly, consumer tastes evolve and new offerings and substitute products enter the market. This dynamic perspective of markets means that the relative positions occupied by offerings in the minds of consumers will be challenged and shifted on a frequent basis. If the position adopted by an offering is strong, if it was the first to claim the position and the position is being continually reinforced with clear simple messages, then there may be little need to alter the position originally adopted.

However, there are occasions when offerings need to be repositioned in the minds of consumer/stakeholders. This may be due to market opportunities and development, mergers and acquisitions or changing buyer preferences, which may be manifested in declining sales. Research may reveal that the current position is either inappropriate or superseded by a competitor, or that attitudes have changed or preferences surpassed; whatever the reason, repositioning is required if past success is to be maintained. However, repositioning is difficult to accomplish, often because of the entrenched perceptions and attitudes held by buyers towards brands.

Repositioning: Barclaycard

In 1997 Barclaycard announced its intention to reposition itself in an attempt to defend its number one position in the UK credit card market.

Barclaycard was originally positioned on the basis of its international acceptance and related benefits, such as insurance. Rowan Atkinson had been used in various humorous campaigns to deliver these messages. However, the marketing strategy identified a need to become more synonymous with everyday purchases, as credit cards had become so much a part of society as a means of paying for goods and services.

Therefore the new communication strategy had to enable customers to perceive Barclaycard in a new way. The strap line 'Don't put it off, put it on' was designed to encourage cardholders to use their cards for small as well as large purchases. Television and posters were the media chosen to reach the target audience.

Adapted from Barrett (1997)

Perrier is positioned differently in the USA from the way it is positioned in Europe. In the USA it is presented as an expensive, stodgy and up-market mineral water, as it struggles to recover from the 1990 crisis. In Europe it is seen as a refreshing drink for young (24- to 35-year-old) adults. Perrier (US) launched a 'renaissance plan' in 1993, aimed at driving a change in the image and attracting young people with big thirsts (Browning, 1993).

Lucozade was successfully repositioned following declining sales. Originally perceived as a medicinal drink for sick children and pregnant women, the repositioning exercise, following extensive market research, led to Lucozade being offered with the promise of restoring users' energy. The target segments were changed and the messages transmitted helped to reposition Lucozade as an exciting drink for a range of different people.

CASE ILLUSTRATION

Vehicle positioning – the RAC

The United Kingdom's car recovery and driver support service market is dominated by two major players, the RAC and AA. Competition is severe, and a third competitor, Green Flag, competes with a lower cost base, as it does not support a dedicated patrol force.

The RAC is over a hundred years old and has deeply established brand values, such as trust, reliability and credibility. In the early 1990s the AA tried to reposition itself away from the RAC as the market became increasingly cluttered, more competitive and depressed as consumer spending became constricted with the recession. The RAC positioned itself as the 'knights of the road', with all the heroic rescue overtones that a knight confers, while the AA, having tried to be seen as a 'a very, very nice man', represented themselves as highly professional and demanding high standards, since a vehicle breakdown was regarded as an emergency similar in scale to that requiring the assistance of the fire, police or ambulance services. Their new position, 'to our members we are the fourth emergency service', is an attempt to be pre-eminent and gain top of mind awareness by conveying a rational benefit approach against the more emotive imagery suggested by the 'knight' (see Chapter 14).

Exhibit 24.1 The AA: the fourth emergency service. Picture and material kindly supplied by the Automobile Association.

It was against this background that the RAC sought to differentitate itself. Research indicated that while the strong brand values were still established it was necessary to modernise the organisation and avoid associations of being old-fashioned and aloof. The RAC had to become an active choice for consumers as well as providing tangible benefits to join and provide reassurance as the best breakdown assistance in the industry.

So, in April 1997 the RAC launched a new campaign that was aimed at repositioning the organisation. New values associated with being smart, modern, dynamic and customer-focused needed to be introduced but had to be sustainable and credible. Therefore, while a new colour scheme and livery was important this vsibility aspect could only be established and maintained if the operations and delivery of the service complemented this approach. It was accepted, therefore, that it was necessary to 'reposition' internally with its employees as well as with its members and non-members.

A whole raft of cultural changes have been embarked upon at the RAC to bring about a stronger customer focus and new brand values. At the same time a new corporate identity consisting of the look of the stationery, logo, vans and buildings (see Plate 24.2) has been embarked upon, together with the introduction of a premium value membership card. This card even has a contact number which can be read in any light condition. Research shows that the RAC membership card is not only highly functional but has the best 'wallet-presence' in the industry. The card also projects the new brand positioning: premium, modern and dynamic.

While the results of the post-launch research are not available at the time of going to print, this RAC case history serves to demonstrate that strong brand positions are not established through superficial images and external communications, but through a blend of internal and external communications, where the people, values and operations underpin and sustain the totality of the brand offering and in this case the corporate identity of the RAC. See Chapter 27 for further information about corporate identity.

P&O's positioning with the advent of Le Shuttle and the Channel tunnel was to 'cruise across the channel' and to present the channel crossing cleverly as an integral part of the holiday/travel experience. Another demonstration of the name change position could be observed when Marriott took over Holiday Inn in the United Kingdom. The name Marriott is perceived as a much stronger name than that of Holiday Inn. However, in order to sustain the strength of the name, yet retain the previous Holiday Inn clients who wanted a decent business class hotel but who could not afford the new rates and opulence of Marriott, a new product was created and positioned for this segment, called Courtyard by Marriott.

Summary

The use of objectives in the management process is clearly vital if the organisation's desired outcomes are to be achieved. Each of the objectives, at corporate, unit and functional levels, contributes to the formulation of the promotional objectives. They are all interlinked, interdependent, multiple and often conflicting.

The major task for the promotional objectives is twofold: first, to contribute to the overall direction of the organisation by fulfilling the communication requirements of the marketing mix; and second, to communicate the corporate thrust to various stakeholders so that they understand the focus organisation and can respond to its intentions.

Promotional objectives are derived from an initial review of the current situation and the marketing plan requirements. They are not a replication of the marketing objectives but a distillation of the research activities that have been undertaken subsequently. Such objectives consist of two main elements: sales-orientated and communication-orientated. A balance between the two will be determined by the situation facing the organisation, but may be a mixture of product and corporate tasks. These objectives, once quantified, need to be ranked and weighted in order that other components of the plan can be developed.

Part of the information generated at the research stage informs how buyers and stakeholders position the offering relative to the other players in the target market and how the product itself is perceived (see the Harveys Bristol Cream example). This aspect of the management process is very important, as the communications undertaken by the organisation help to shape the context that individuals have of the offering (or the organisation). The way in which an organisation decides to position itself and/or its offerings determines the form, intensity and nature of the messages transmitted through the promotional mix.

Review questions

1. Why do organisations use objectives as part of their planning processes?
2. What should a mission statement clearly identify?

3. Suggest three reasons why the setting of promotional objectives is important.
4. Write a brief report arguing the case both for and against the use of an increase in sales as the major objective of all promotional activities.
5. Repeat the exercise as for the previous question but this time focus upon communication-based objectives.
6. How and from where are promotional objectives derived?
7. Why is positioning an important part of marketing communications?
8. What is perceptual mapping?
9. Select four print advertisements for the same product class, and comment on the positions they have adopted.
10. What are the main positioning strategies?

References

Barrett, P. (1997) Barclaycard ad boost. *Marketing*, 20 November, p. 14.
Barry, T. and Howard, D.J. (1990) A review and critique of the hierarchy of effects in advertising. *International Journal of Advertising*, **9**, 121–35.
Browning, E.S. (1993) Perrier tries to rejuvenate stodgy image. *Wall Street Journal*, 2 September, p. 1.
Cawte, P. (1989) Positioning into the new-style market. *Pharmaceutical Marketing*, **1**(2), 13–15.
Colley, R. (1961) *Defining Advertising Goals for Measured Advertising Results*. New York: Association of National Advertisers.
Day, G., Shocker, A.D. and Srivastava, R.K. (1979) Customer orientated approaches to identifying product markets. *Journal of Marketing*, **43**(4), 8–19.
Greenley, G. (1989) *Strategic Management*. Hemel Hempstead: Prentice Hall.
Hazelhurst, L. (1988) How Pedigree Petfoods evaluate their advertising spend. *Admap* (June), 29–31.
Hodder, R., Gordon, W. and Swan, N. (1995) From four weddings and a funeral to blue velvet? *Admap* (March), 38–44.
King, S. (1991) Brand building in the 1990s. *Journal of Marketing Management*, **7**, 3–13.
Kotler, P. (1997) *Marketing Management – Analysis, Planning, Implementation and Control*. Englewood Cliffs NJ: Prentice Hall.
Kriegel, R.A. (1986) How to choose the right communications objectives. *Business Marketing* (April), 94–106.
Levitt, T. (1960) Marketing myopia. *Harvard Business Review* (July/August), 45–56.
Neal, W.D. (1980) Strategic product positioning: a step by step guide. *Business (USA)* (May/June), 34–40.
Ries, A. and Trout, J. (1972) The positioning era cometh. *Advertising Age*, 24 April, pp. 35–8.
Rosen, R. (1995) *Strategic Management: An Introduction*. London: Pitman.
Rossiter, J.R. and Percy, L. (1987) *Advertising and Promotion Management*, Lexington MA: McGraw-Hill.
Rothschild, M. (1987) *Marketing Communications*. Lexington MA: D.C. Heath.
Sinclair, S.A. and Stalling, E.C. (1990) Perceptual mapping: a tool for industrial marketing: a case study. *Journal of Business and Industrial Marketing*, **5**(1), 55–65.
Thompson, J.L. (1990) *Strategic Management: Awareness and Change*. London: Chapman & Hall.
Thompson, A. and Strickland, A.J. III (1990) *Strategic Management*. Homewood IL, Boston MA: BPI Irwin.

Communication strategies to reach consumers

A *pull* strategy is a marketing communications approach which involves the delivery of messages to members of the target audience(s). The aim is to stimulate demand by encouraging consumers to 'pull' products through the channel network. This usually means that consumers go into retail outlets (shops) to enquire about particular product(s).

AIMS AND OBJECTIVES

The aims of this chapter are to explore marketing communications strategies that enable the promotional objectives set for consumers and other end users, such as business-to-business customers, to be achieved.

The objectives of this chapter are:

1. To introduce the notion of pull-based communication strategies.
2. To examine involvement as a basis for developing promotional strategies.
3. To evaluate the FCB grid as a tool for strategy development.
4. To use the Rossiter–Percy grid as a means of creating strategic direction.
5. To explore branding as a principal strategic promotional tool for the consumer market.
6. To consider marketing communications for the business-to-business markets.

Introduction

Many writers assume marketing communication strategy to be simply the combination of activities in the communications mix. In other words, strategy is about the degree of direct marketing, personal selling, advertising, sales promotion and public relations. This is important, but it is not the essence of marketing communications strategy. From a strategic perspective, the key decisions concern the overall direction of the programme, the fit with marketing and corporate strategy and to whom primary messages should be directed.

Once promotional objectives have been established it is necessary to formulate appropriate strategies. Objectives that are focused upon consumers or end users of an offering require a different strategy from those strategies formulated to satisfy the objectives that are focused on members of the marketing channel.

If messages are to be directed at target consumers then the intention is invariably to generate increased levels of awareness, build and/or reinforce attitudes, and ultimately provoke a motivation within the target group. This motivation is to stimulate action so that the target audience expect the offering to be available to them when they decide to enquire, experiment or make a repeat purchase. This approach is known as a *pull* strategy and is aimed at encouraging consumers to 'pull' the products through the channel network. This usually means that consumers go into retail outlets (shops) to enquire about a particular product.

Communications for consumers: a pull strategy

To be effective, communication strategies for consumer markets need to be developed with an understanding of the perceptions and message response processes that target consumers' experience when moving toward a behaviour. As determined earlier (Chapter 5), involvement is a theory central to our understanding of the way in which information is processed and the way in which consumers make decisions about product purchases. It was established that there are two main types of involvement: high and low. This concept of involvement leads to two orderings of the hierarchy of effects. In decisions where there is high involvement, attitude precedes trial behaviour. In low-involvement cases this position is reversed. In the former a positive and specific position is assumed by the consumer, whereas in the latter attitudes to the product (not the product class) develop after product use.

As discussed earlier, where there is high involvement consumers seek out information because they are concerned about the decision processes and outcomes. Because they have these concerns, consumers develop an attitude prior to behaviour. Products that evoke high-involvement decision processes tend to be high cost, to be bought relatively infrequently, to be complex, to elicit feelings of risk and to be visible to others.

Where there is low involvement, consumers are content to select any one of a number of acceptable products and often rely on those that are in the individual's evoked set. Low involvement is thought to be a comfortable state, because there are too many other decisions in life to have to make decisions about each one of them, so an opportunity not to have to seek information and make other decisions is welcome.

This suggests that high and low positions are not static or permanent. Involvement is said by some (Vaughn, 1980; Ratchford, 1987), to be a continuum where con-

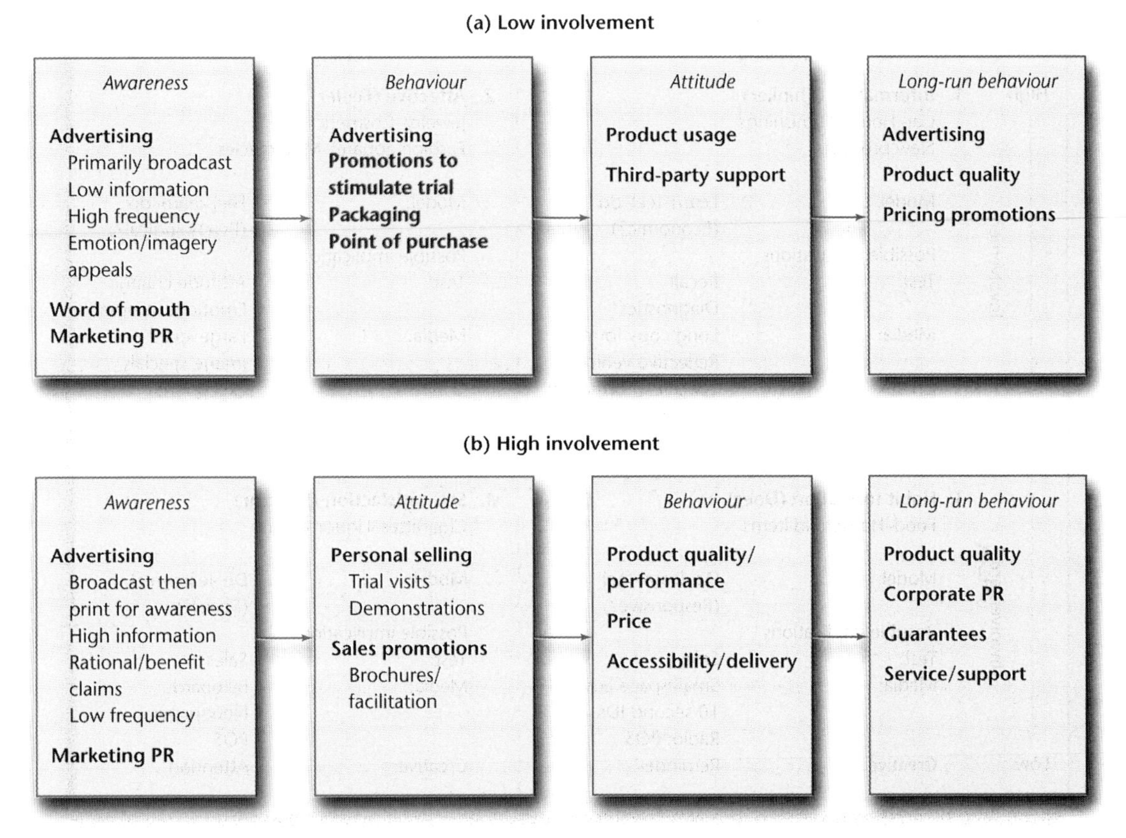

Figure 25.1 Promotional strategies for different levels of involvement.

sumers can move from a high to a low involvement position, as their experience of a product increases and their perceived risk is reduced. Figure 25.1 indicates the advertising and promotion strategies best suited for each level within both involvement spectrums.

Strategic advertising frameworks

R. Vaughn (1980) of Foote, Cone & Belding developed a matrix utilising involvement and brain specialisation theories. Brain specialisation theory suggests that the left-hand side of the brain is best handling rational, linear and cognitive thinking, whereas the right-hand side is better able to manage spatial, visual and emotional issues (the affective or feeling functions).

Vaughn proposed that by combining involvement with elements of thinking and feeling, four primary advertising planning strategies can be distinguished. These are informative, affective, habitual and self-satisfaction (see Figure 25.2). According to Vaughn, the matrix is intended to be a thought provoker rather than a formula or model from which prescriptive solutions are to be identified. The FCB matrix is a useful guide to help analyse and appreciate consumer/product relationships and to develop appropriate communication strategies. The four quadrants of the grid

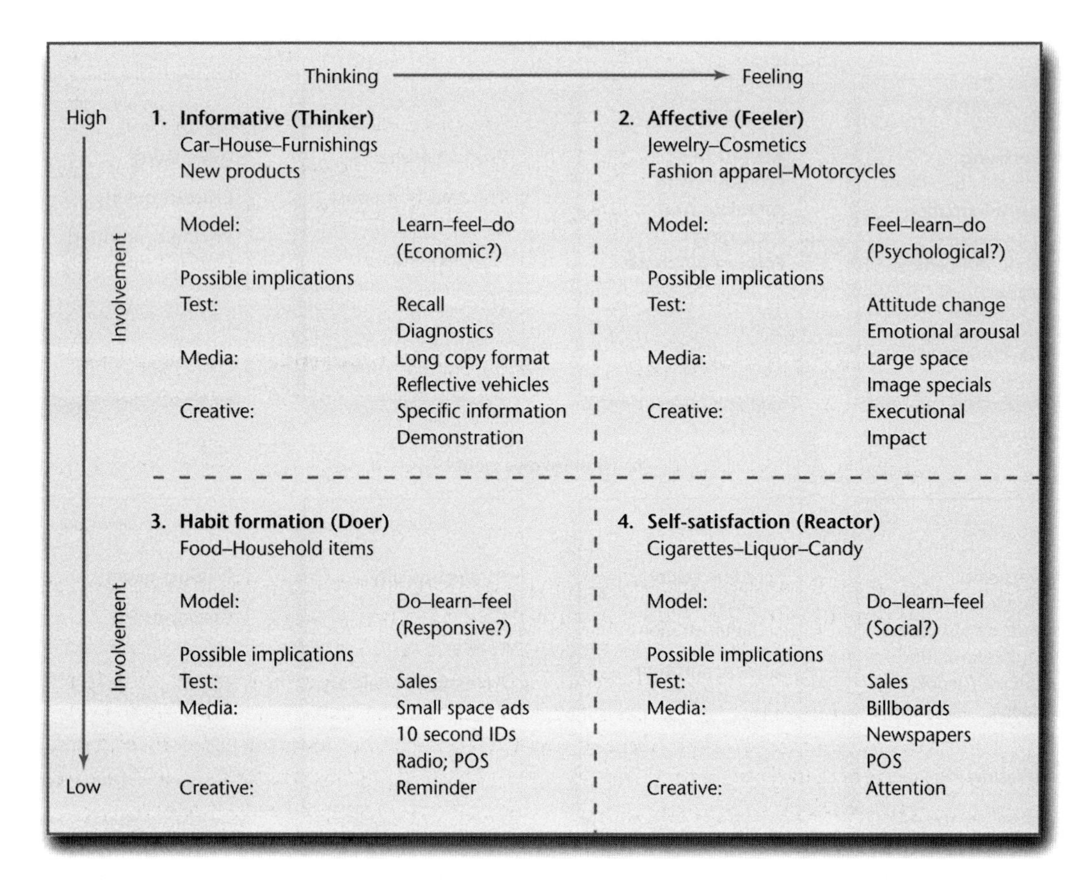

Figure 25.2 FCB grid (Vaughn (1980); used with kind permission).

identify particular types of decision-making and each requires different advertising approaches. Vaughn suggests that different orderings from the learn–feel–do sequence can be observed (see Figure 25.2). By perceiving the different ways in which the process can be ordered, he proposed that the learn–feel–do sequence should be visualised as a continuum, a circular concept. Communication strategy would, therefore, be based on the point of entry that consumers make to the cycle.

Some offerings, generally regarded as 'habitual', may be moved to another quadrant, such as 'responsive', to develop differentiation and establish a new position for the product in the minds of consumers relative to the competition. This could be achieved by the selection of suitable media vehicles and visual images in the composition of the messages associated with an advertisement. There is little doubt that this model, or interpretation of the advertising process, has made a significant contribution to our understanding of the advertising process and has been used by a large number of advertising agencies (Joyce, 1991).

Rossiter *et al.* (1991), however, disagree with some of the underpinnings of the FCB grid and offer a new one in response (revised 1997) (Figure 25.3). They suggest that involvement is not a continuum because it is virtually impossible to decide when a person graduates from high to low involvement. They claim that the FCB grid fails to account for situations where a person moves from high to low involvement and then back to high, perhaps on a temporary basis, when a new variant is introduced to

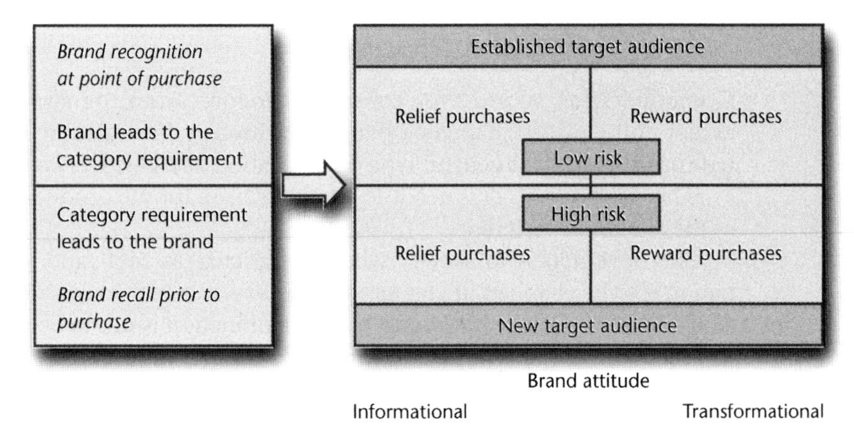

Figure 25.3 The Rossiter–Percy grid (adapted from Rossiter and Percy (1997); used with kind permission).

the market. Rossiter *et al.* regard involvement as the level of perceived risk present at the time of purchase. Consequently, it is the degree of familiarity buyers have at the time of purchase that is an important component.

A further criticism is that the FCB grid is an attitude-only model. Rossiter *et al.* quite rightly identify the need for brand awareness to be built into such grids as a prerequisite for attitude development. However, they cite the need to differentiate different purchase situations. Some brands require awareness recall because the purchase decision is made prior to the act of purchasing. Other brands require awareness recognition at the point of purchase, where the buyer needs to be prompted into brand choice decisions. Each of these situations requires different message strategies, and these are explored in Chapter 13.

The other major difference between the two grids concerns the 'think–feel' dimension. Rossiter *et al.* believe that a wider spectrum of motives must be incorporated, as the FCB 'think–feel' interpretation fails to accommodate differences between product category and brand purchase motivations. For example, the decision to use a product category may be based upon a strictly functional and utilitarian need. The need to travel to another country designates the necessity of air transport. The choice of carrier, however, particularly over the North Atlantic, is a brand choice decision, motivated by a variety of sensory and ego-related inputs and anticipated outputs. Rossiter *et al.* disaggregate motives into what they refer to as informational and transformational motives. By detailing motives into these classifications, a more precise approach to advertising tactics can be developed (Chapter 14). Furthermore, the confusion inherent in the FCB grid, between the think and involvement elements, is overcome.

It should be understood that these 'grids' are purely hypothetical, and that there is no proof or evidence to suggest that they are accurate reflections of advertising. It is true that both models have been used as the basis for advertising strategy in many agencies, but that does not mean that they are totally reliable or, more importantly, that they have been tested empirically so that they can be used in total confidence. They are interpretations of commercial and psychological activity and have been instrumental in advancing our level of knowledge. It is in this spirit of development that these models are presented in this text.

Strategic implications

Communication strategy for consumers follows from the awareness objectives set earlier in the plan (Chapters 24 and 30). Strategy formulation requires the determination of the current general type of motivation and whether involvement is regarded as either high or low. This needs to be undertaken for the product class and the brand, as they might be different.

The next step is to specify whether the current motivation/involvement combination is to be changed. If change is necessary, to which combination will the strategy lead and how will it be actioned? If the combination is not to be altered then how will the current position be maintained? In addition it is important to consider the level of elaboration (ELM, Chapter 13) present in the target audience. If the need for elaboration is high then the message strategy will be based around long copy formats and informational based messages, media vehicles that allow long exposure opportunities and low levels of repetition. If the level of elaboration is low then the peripheral route to attitudinal change is necessary. Peripheral cues will be necessary, as will short copy formats, transformational based messages and broadcast media to derive impact and high levels of repetition within the purchase cycle.

From this point the particular type of operational motive needs to be agreed. Appropriate message tactics can be developed in accordance with the motivations and perceived risk that are present during the purchase process.

There are elements in both of the frameworks reviewed earlier that have a number of strong elements of truth attached to them. However, for products that are purchased on a regular basis pull strategies should be geared to defending the rationale that current buyers use to select the brand. Heavy buyers select a particular brand more often than light users do from their repertoire. By providing a variety of consistent stimuli, and by keeping the brand alive, fresh buyers are more likely to prefer and purchase a particular brand than those that allow their brands to lose purchase currency and the triggers necessary to evoke memory impressions. For example, the long-running Renault campaign using the Nicole and Papa characters sought to use fresh ideas based on buyers' transformational motives. Normally car purchase evokes high involvement, but only at the time of purchase. In order to build reputation and positive association with the Renault brand, key messages need to be delivered in the intervening (non-purchase) period. Nicole provided a point of attention, curiosity (see Chapter 13) and consistency, while delivering messages about flair and style to be associated with Renault.

For products purchased on an irregular basis, marketing communications need only touch the target audience on a relatively low number of occasions. Strategies need to be developed that inform and contextualise the purchase rationale for consumers. This means providing lasting impressions that enable consumers to understand the circumstances in which purchase of a particular product/brand should be made once a decision has been made to purchase from the product category. Here the priorities are to communicate messages that will encourage consumers to trust and bestow expertise on the product/brand that is offered.

Branding

Branding is a particularly strong and highly successful format of the pull strategy. A successful brand is one which creates and sustains a strong positive impression in the mind of a buyer. The elements that make up this impression are numerous, but among the more important are, according to Assael (1990), the name, symbol, packaging and service reputation. Doyle (1989) claims that 'a successful brand is a name, symbol, design or some combination, which identifies the "product" of a particular organisation as having a sustainable differential advantage'.

These definitions highlight an important aspect of branding, which is that branding is a method by which buyers differentiate among similar offerings and associate certain attributes with a particular brand. Quality and satisfaction through time can lead buyers to learn to trust a brand, which leads to a priority position in the evoked set and repeat purchasing activity. The acceptance of buyers as active problem solvers means that branding can be seen as a way that buyers can reduce the amount of decision-making time and associated perceived risk. This is because brand names provide information about content, taste, durability, quality, price and performance, without requiring the buyer to undertake time-consuming comparison tests with similar offerings or other risk-reduction approaches to purchase decisions. In some categories brands can be developed through the use of messages that are entirely emotional or image-based. Many of the 'products' in FMCG sectors base their communications on imagery, assuming low involvement and the use of peripheral cues. Other sectors, such as cars or pharmaceuticals, require the image-based messages to be supported by rational information-based messages (Boehringer, 1996). In other words a blend of messages may well be required to achieve the objectives and goals of the campaign.

As a brand becomes established with a buyer, so the psychological benefits of ownership are preferred to competing offerings, and a partnership emerges. Brands are said to develop personalities and encapsulate the core values of a product. They are a strong means by which the product can be identified, understood and appreciated. Marketing communications play an important role in communicating the essence of the personality of the brand and in providing the continuity for any partnership, a necessity for a brand to be built through time.

Just as brands can provide benefits for buyers, so important direct benefits for manufacturers or resellers also exist. Brands provide a means by which a manufacturer can augment its product in such a way that buyers can differentiate the product, recognise it quickly and make purchase decisions that exclude competitive products in the consideration set. Premium pricing is permissible, as perceived risk is reduced and high quality is conveyed through trust and experience formed through an association with the brand. This in turn allows for loyalty to be developed, which in turn allows for cross-product promotions and brand extensions. Integrated marketing communications becomes more feasible as buyers perceive thematic ideas and messages, which in turn can reinforce positioning and values associated with the brand. For a summary of the benefits of branding see Table 25.1.

Biel (1997) refers to brands being composed of a number of elements. The first refers to the functional abilities a brand claims and can deliver. The particular attributes that distinguish a brand are referred to as brand skills. He quotes the cold remedy Contact, whose brand skill is to relieve cold symptoms for 12 hours.

The second element is the personality of a brand and its fundamental traits concerning lifestyle and perceived values, such as being bland, adventurous, exciting, boring or caring. The idea of brand personification is not new, but it is an important part of understanding how a brand might be imagined as a person and how the brand is different from other brands (people). Exhibit 25.1 depicts the world famous golfer

Exhibit 25.1 Hugo Boss endorsed by Sevriano Ballesteros. Picture reproduced with the kind permission of Hugo Boss Gmbh.

Sevriano Ballesteros endorsing the Hugo Boss brand. In doing so there is a measure of association between the Hugo Boss brand (and its values) and the personality of the Spanish golfing maestro.

The third branding element is about building a relationship with individual buyers. People are said to interact with brands. A two-way relationship can be realistically developed when it is recognised that the brand must interact with the consumer just as much as the consumer must interact with the brand. Blackston (1992) argues that successful branding depends on consumers' perceptions of the attitudes held by the brand towards them as individuals. He illustrates the point with research into the credit card market, where different cards share the same demographic profile of users and the same conventional brand images. Some cards provide recognition or visibility of status, which by association are bestowed upon the owner in the form of power and authority. In this sense the card enhances the user. This contrasts with other cards, where the user may feel intimidated and excluded from the card because as a person the attitudes of the card are perceived to be remote, aloof, condescending and hard to approach.

For example, respondents felt the cards were saying, 'if you don't like the conditions, go and get a different card' and 'I'm so well known and established that I can do as I want'. The implications for brand development and associated message strategies become clearer.

In line with this thinking, Biel cites Fournier (1995), who considers brand/ consumer relationships in terms of levels of intimacy, partner quality, attachment, interdependence, commitment and love.

A more recent approach to brand development work involves creating a brand experience. The Tango roadshows, which enable Tango drinkers to bungee jump, trampoline and do other out of the norm activities, are really seeking to provide extra brand-related experiences.

Retail environments based entirely around a brand have been developed, for example Levi shops. The Virgin brand can be drunk as a cola or vodka, invested as a PEP, transported by flight or rail, viewed at a cinema, listened to or simply used to get married (adapted from Croft, 1996).

Therefore, Biel sees brands as being made up of three elements: brand personality, brand skills and brand relationships. These combine to form what he regards as 'Brand Magic' and which underpins added value.

Types and forms of branding

There are many forms of branding but primarily there are manufacturer, own-label, price and generic brands.

Manufacturers' brands help identify the producer of a brand at the point of purchase. For example, Cadbury's chocolate, Ford cars and Coca-Cola are all strong manufacturers' brands. This type of brand usually requires the assistance of channel intermediaries for wide distribution, and the promotional drive stems from the manufacturer in an attempt to persuade end users to adopt the brand, which in turn stimulates channel members to stock and distribute the brand.

Own-label (or private) brands do not associate the manufacturer with the offering in any way. The own-label brand is owned by a channel member, typically a wholesaler, such as Nurdin & Peacock, or a retailer, such as Texas, Boots, Marks & Spencer, Sainsbury's and Woolworth's. This brand strategy offers many advantages to both the manufacturer, who can use excess capacity, and retailers, who can earn a higher margin than they can with manufacturers' branded goods and at the same time develop organisational (e.g. store) images. Channel members have the additional cost of promotional initiatives, necessary in the absence of a manufacturer's support. Some manufacturers refuse to make own-label products, and in the mid-1990s there was increased attention paid to this area, as some of the multiple grocers launched products that were alleged to be too similar to main manufacturer brands. Using a similar name and packaging the product in the same style has led to conflict in the channel network.

There has been considerable debate about the shift in volumes between manufacturers and own-label brands. A study by Nielsen reported by Sargent (1995) attempted to isolate the key factors that contribute to longer-term brand development. The study, which focused on 45 major UK-based FMCG markets, found a decline in the volume of manufacturer brands sales and an increase in the volume of own-label sales over the three-year period of the study. TV advertising was isolated as one of the key elements in the development of the brands that had grown (at the expense of price-based sales promotions). The study also confirmed the general view that new product development and being first into a market was of major significance when seeking brand growth over the longer term.

The growth of own-label brands at the expense of manufacturer brands need not be expected to continue unchecked. Consumers value or expect a certain level of brand choice in stores, and as some store traffic and spend per visit rates have declined, some grocery multiples have taken steps to stem the volume of their own-label brand provision and increased the volume of manufacturer brands on their shelves.

Table 25.1 Benefits of branding

Customer benefits	Supplier benefits
■ Assists the identification of preferred products	■ Permits premium pricing
■ Can reduce levels of perceived risk and so improve the quality of the shopping experience	■ Helps differentiate the product from competitors
■ Easier to gauge the level of product quality	■ Enhances cross-product promotion and brand extension opportunities
■ Can reduce the time spent making product-based decisions and in turn reduce the time spent shopping	■ Encourages customer loyalty/retention and repeat purchase buyer behaviour
■ Can provide psychological reassurance or reward	■ Assists the development and use of integrated marketing communications
■ Provides cues about the nature of the source of the product and any associated values	■ Contributes to corporate identity programmes
	■ Provides for some legal protection
	■ Provides for greater thematic consistency and uniform messages and communications

Price brands are produced by manufacturers in an attempt to compete with private brands. Tesco have used this approach to respond to the arrival of a number of low-cost retailers such as Costco and Aldi. The product is low-priced and is further characterised by an absence of any promotional support. The effect on the other brands in the manufacturer's portfolio may be to stimulate promotional support to prevent the less loyal buyers trading over to the low-priced offering.

The final type is the *generic brand*. This is sold devoid of any promotional materials and the packaging only displays information required by law. Manufacturers are even less inclined to produce these 'white carton' products than price brands. They are often sold at prices 40% below the price of normal brands. They consume very few promotional resources, for obvious reasons, but their popularity, after a burst in the 1970s, has waned considerably, particularly in the supermarket sector where they gained their greatest success. However, generics are significant in some markets. The pharmaceutical industry has experienced a growth in the use of generic products, spurred by the NHS reforms of the government (Blackett, 1992).

Branding decisions are partly a reflection of an organisation's view of the relationship of their products to each other and to the corporate body and the organisation's strategy (Gray and Smeltzer, 1985). The approach each organisation adopts shapes the marketing communications. These authors recognise five different relationships: single form, brand form, balanced form, variety form and corporate form.

Single form organisations offer a single product so that the images of the organisation and the product tend to be the same. Kwik-Fit, Pirelli, Coca-Cola and Gillette provide products and services that are keyed into a single strategic business area (SBA). Problems may be anticipated if they diversify into different areas of activity or if they deviate from their current strategies. For example, Levi failed in its attempt to move into quality men's clothing because the target market associated Levi and the Levi brand with the production of jeans. Had the brand not been so closely associated with the single product focus, there would have been a greater chance of success in its attempt to broaden the range.

The *brand form* reflects a decision not to relate the brands to the parent organisation. This *multi-brand* approach has been followed by soap manufacturers Procter & Gamble and Unilever for many years. Only recently has Unilever started to put its name on the packaging of each of its household brands. This form requires promotional expenditure to support the individual brands, but should a particular brand be damaged, the other brands in the portfolio and the corporate name are protected.

In the *balanced form*, divisions within an organisation convey individual identities, but each one is related to the corporate body. A good example of this approach is Ford UK. Each car in each of its product lines is prefixed by Ford. The Ford Fiesta 1.3L, Ford Escort 1.4GL and Ford Transit all convey the balance between the corporate name and the individual brands.

The *variety form* is identified by organisations who stress either the brand or the organisation, depending upon particular circumstances. Forte adopts this form, using Little Chef and Happy Eater brands while using the Forte umbrella to bring its hotels under one banner (e.g. Forte Crest). Gray and Smeltzer (1985) offer the example of the German organisation Bosch GmbH. This organisation identifies its spark plugs and power tools under the Bosch name, but elects to use the name Blaupunkt for its radios.

The final approach is referred to as the *corporate form*. Though the organisation may operate in a number of different SBAs, this approach requires all communications to be targeted at reinforcing the corporate image. IBM, ICI, Mars, Hewlett-Packard and Black & Decker are examples of this form.

Corporate identity, which will be looked at in detail later (Chapter 27), is also a form of branding. Woolworth's, Sainsbury's, Tesco and Marks & Spencer are examples of the growth of retail brands. All are recognised and perceived by consumers to have particular advantages and disadvantages. All have taken a long time to develop. All have invested heavily in various forms of promotion to build their brands.

There may also be a new type of brand emerging, one which seeks to provide customers with a level of trust such that the brand is strong enough to carry customers into a variety of unrelated markets. The Virgin brand has demonstrated its ability to attract customers, even though it was understood that Virgin had no prior experience of the particular market at the time it entered (for example, air travel, financial services and cosmetics). What appears to be emerging is that the Virgin brand is associated with success and is seen as one that challenges the established norms by which each market operates. By promising and delivering tangible benefits for customers, Virgin has become a people's brand that seeks out opportunities and rewrites the way markets operate.

When BMW and Daihatsu announced their separate intentions to enter the financial services sector, the corporate strategy was based upon a redefinition of their business interests and extending their brands into areas where they would be salient and strong. BMW is a trusted car brand and by moving into financial services it is in a better position to compete with (un)likely competitors such as Virgin, Marks & Spencer, Tesco and Sainsbury's. Essentially the car brand is repositioned as a service brand. With the enhanced mobility, BMW can move into new market sectors that before the redefinition would have been unavailable to them, and they might have been vulnerable to attack in their car market from new service-based brands.

Branding is a task that requires a significant contribution from marketing communications and is a long-term exercise. Organisations that cut their brand advertising

CASE ILLUSTRATION

Hula Hoops

In the mid-1990s the UK snack food segment was led by Walkers Crisps through the 'Gary Lineker – no more Mr Nice Guy' campaign. The target market was adults and children, and the humour, in the above-the-line advertising, worked in different ways for their vastly different audiences.

In an attempt to develop the Hula Hoop brand and to challenge Walkers, KP management, together with Publicis (its advertising agency) and Billington Cartmell (its Sales Promotion Agency), decided to review the marketing strategy for the brand. They decided that the brand should be specifically targeted at teenagers, a market segment in which they had dominated sales. By building on the advantage of this position, the brand was to be strengthened. To do this two main actions were undertaken.

First, the shape of the product was recognised as the central and core proposition of the Hula Hoop brand. The shape of the product was its competitive advantage, and the task of marketing communications was to communicate this strategic focus, which provided value in terms of both the crunch (taste differentiator) and the play (rings on fingers, tactile differentiator). The phrase, 'Hula Hoops are round, they're staying round, and they'll be around forever' helped to communicate the strategic importance of the shape, its position in the market relative to other snacks (by definition not round) and suggested that the brand had a heritage (25 years).

The second initiative was to position the brand in order that the target audience was able to claim ownership. This was achieved through a series of campaigns that featured the use of humour. First the hole was stolen, then square hoops emerged and certain celebrities were accused of threatening to change the shape of the Hula Hoop, before the third phase arrived, when the hoops were twisted. Unlike the universal appeal of the Walkers approach, Hula Hoops adopted the rebellious new-lad humour, and the Oi...No! campaign became part of the young teenage vocabulary. Essential to the above-the-line work was the use of the Self-Righteous Brothers (Harry Enfield and Paul Whitehouse) to support the campaigns with their 'in-yer-face' humour, which facilitated the identification of the teenage market with the values of the brand proposition.

One of the principal reasons offered to explain the campaign's success has been the integrated approach adopted by KP. Sales promotion, supported through TV work, was a significant part of the campaign. The sales promotion was strategically interwoven with the campaign, and not used merely as an add-on. Thematic advertising which supported sales promotions was perceived by the audience to have an effortless synergistic impact. Added to this was a variety of marketing public relations activities. One of these was an interview with one of the winners of the £100,000 prizes, a 15-year-old boy, on the television show *Big Breakfast*.

The 18 month campaign burst in May 1995, and sales soared by 30% through each of the three phases. A 15% market share (Nielsen Scantrack, 31 August 1996) was achieved, enabling the brand to become market leader. The campaign also achieved seven industry awards, recognition of the success and impact that the rebranding strategy achieved through tight integration.

Based on Killgren (1996)

in times of recession reduce the significance and power of their brands. The Association of Media Independents claims, not surprisingly, that the weaker brands are those that reduce or cut their advertising when trading conditions deteriorate.

Some organisations are moving the balance of their promotional mixes away from above-the-line work (advertising) towards tools below-the-line. For example, Cellnet and Orange have developed their sales promotion and direct marketing activities to provide a greater focus on loyalty and reward programmes (Campbell, 1997). These companies operate in a market where customer retention is a problem. Customer loss (or churn rate, as it is known in the telecomms business), exceeds 30%. There is, therefore, a strong need to develop marketing and communications strategies that reduce this figure.

One of the main tasks is to continually remind the market of the brand's presence, position and quality. When developing a marketing communications plan, it is vitally important to consider the information arising from a brand audit, which will include the following:

1. What the current brand image is with consumers and other significant stakeholders.
2. What brand form has been identified for the organisation.
3. How the form relates to the current and future corporate strategies.
4. How the brand is positioned in the mind of the target buyer.
5. How the brand relates to the competition in terms of market share, performance and other measures of perception and attitudes.
6. How the brand image is to be changed or reinforced.

For a brand to grow and be sustained, the functional aspects of the product must be capable of meeting the expectations of the buyer. If the quality of the product is below acceptable standards, marketing communications activities alone cannot create a brand. When Jaguar cars were first exported to the USA, the car was soon rejected by the market because the first buyers of Jaguars (innovators in the process of adoption) experienced a variety of problems. These included overheating, because thermostats failed to work, and gearboxes and clutches that needed replacing too soon. This led to a poor image of Jaguar, which meant that market penetration would be slow, at least until the product defects were corrected. A quality initiative at the production plant resulted in a car that performed at exceptionally high levels on all functions. Promotional work then built upon the new credibility, so that Jaguar became one of the most sought-after prestige cars in the USA.

Marketing communications for business-to-business markets

The business-to-business sector has traditionally been characterised by the use of a marketing communications mix whose emphasis has been placed upon personal selling, with advertising and sales promotions undertaking a relatively minor role when compared with consumer-based communication activities. The assumption is that buying centre decisions are based largely on rational decision-making, where the use of imagery and emotion in messages is either unnecessary, inappropriate or just ineffective.

CASE ILLUSTRATION

Photosound and EPREX®

This case illustration was written by Andrew Meredith, BA (Hons) Business Studies student at Portsmouth and now Projects Manager at Photosound Communications.

XIVth International Congress of Nephrology, 25–29 May 1997, Sydney

Nephrology is the branch of medicine concerned with diseases of the kidney, and ethical drug manufacturer Janssen-Cilag attended this congress with a view to reinforcing its product, EPREX®.

EPREX® is used as a treatment associated with chronic renal failure (products may not be available and/or approved in all countries. Check with your local Janssen-Cilag office for further information). In order to capitalise on the potential of the congress, Photosound Communications, a multidisciplinary communications agency, was commissioned to project manage the exhibition.

Brief

Client: Janssen-Cilag

Venue: Sydney Convention & Exhibition Centre

Attendees: 3,500

Stand space: 144 m^2 The stand space booked is unfortunately in a poor location due to the early high demand for space. Therefore it is important that the Janssen-Cilag stand is highly visible from the entrance to the exhibition hall.

Reasons for attendance: To continue positioning Janssen-Cilag as the leader in chronic renal failure applications of Epoetin-alfa. Also, in order to support new applications and dosage forms along with promoting the growing approvals and experiences with peritoneal and paediatric dialysis patients.

Overall look of stand: The exhibition stand should be welcoming and friendly, with a high impact on delegates.

Overall theme: The overriding theme for this project, which should be reflected in the graphic panels, is 'The Quality of Life'.

Graphic panels: Janssen-Cilag would like 10–12 graphic panels showing product information.

Branding: Janssen-Cilag is very keen to have a strong brand image as opposed to a corporate one. The EPREX® brand should be the most prominent, with the corporate logo in the background.

Literature/giveaways: There should be free-standing literature dispensers and they should be attached to the walls adjacent to the relevant graphic panels. Appropriate brand-associated giveaways and a stand attraction will be required.

Seating area: A general seating area was requested with tables and chairs for delegates to relax or speak to Janssen-Cilag representatives. There was no preference for a one-to-one seating area.

CD-ROM terminal: Janssen-Cilag Australia has produced a CD-ROM which will be available for delegates to view. Information on the CD includes the history of EPREX®, abstracts to read, videos of presentations etc. It is planned for a member of Janssen-Cilag Australia to be in attendance at the booth for the duration of the exhibition to deal with any delegate queries.

Planning and implementation

Once the brief had been passed on to Photosound from the client, it was allocated to a project team which consisted of an account manager, project manager, 3D designer and a graphic designer. A brainstorming session was held to source ideas for designs, themes, stand attractions and giveaways. This process enables the generation of imaginative ideas and also highlights potential problems. Once the ideas had been filtered they were then developed by the designers with the end result that a proposal was presented to the client.

Proposed design for Janssen-Cilag's EPREX® stand

From the brief and Photosound's knowledge of the client, it was clear that the design had to be very brand-oriented, clearly visible and promote the ease of administration with the auto-injector and pre-filled syringe. With this in mind the following design elements were proposed.

Design

The design of the Janssen-Cilag exhibit is dramatic and strongly reflects the EPREX® colours and logo elements. The EPREX® logo is predominantly red, white and black and consists of the product name and an arrow within two circles.

Exhibit elements

Mobile: A high-level mobile hangs over the Janssen-Cilag booth. It features a giant pre-filled syringe and auto-injector as well as product and company logos and erythrocytes. It will be visible from most parts of the exhibit hall.

Tower: A tower which carries the Janssen-Cilag logo is in the centre of the booth and a giant red arrow cuts through the centre.

Auto-injector/pre-filled syringe display: A giant auto-injector and pre-filled syringe display will attract attention and also look very dramatic.

Carpet: There are carpet cut-ins which reflect the shapes and colours in the EPREX® logo.

Ceiling: The ceiling features the red arrow of the EPREX® logo.

Detail desks: The design of the top of the detail desks is in the shape of the red arrow of the logo. The bases of the desk will carry the product and corporate logos and provide storage space for giveaways and literature.

Graphic panels: The graphic panels carry the strapline 'Embrace Energy' and 'Energy for Living'.

Technical equipment

EPREX® Climb the Mountain Challenge: An interactive game was produced which highlighted the problems which patients face when they suffer from anaemia. The game was played on one large monitor, two smaller ones set in the main wall of the booth and two free-standing play stations. All these stations were networked so the highest score overall of each session was always listed. The seats for the free-standing playstation were arrow-shaped and in the product colours. Prizes were awarded each day for the highest scoring contestants.

Entrance gift: All entrants received a gift of an EPREX® liquid mouse mat. The mouse mats were distributed from a central point and delegates were encouraged to collect theirs.

CD-ROM: As mentioned in the brief.

Giveaways: Janssen-Cilag plastic bags, pencils, branded mint rock sweets and jelly beans plus EPREX® paper clips.

Evaluation

Independent research was carried out among the congress participants, enquiring about the stands visited, the physical attractiveness of the exhibit, product interest, company image and performance. The results indicated that Janssen-Cilag's exhibit was the most aesthetically pleasing and generated above average interest and strong product recall. The product message recall scored the highest of all the exhibits at the conference. Specific points of interest were the positive feedback from physicians regarding the pre-filled syringes and the popularity of the EPREX® challenge. However, the research also showed that more clinical papers should have been available.

Janssen-Cilag and Photosound were able to evaluate this information and utilise it for future conferences and the general sales and marketing of EPREX® (see Plate 25.1).

The mix of tools used to communicate with members of buying centres has been based around personal selling, exhibitions, joint trade advertising, marketing public relations and promotions, plus advertising in specialist trade journals. The messages conveyed are informational, highlighting product features and benefits, using long copy formats and a demonstration or spokesperson appeal.

Gilliland and Johnston (1997) report that there is evidence that emotion-based copy is being used increasingly in the business-to-business service advertisements and in 30% of business-to-business product-based advertisements (Cutler and Javalgi, 1994). This should not be surprising, as use of the ELM model to predict attitude change is of equal relevance.

Buying centre involvement with particular purchase decisions (Chapter 5) varies from member to member and within an individual member, depending upon the context conditions. Gilliand and Johnston argue that when a member of the buying centre experiences high levels of goal-directed behaviour towards information processing (for whatever reason) then the central route to attitude change will be of greater relevance to those attempting to communicate with them. However, when goal-directed behaviour towards information processing is low (for whatever reason), then the peripheral route will have greater impact. Therefore the role of emotion-based copy in business-to-business marketing communications is justified and this is reflected in the changing media spend and the form of the messages used by organisations to communicate with organisational buyers.

Business to business branding

The branding concept has been used by a number of manufacturers (Intel, Teflon, Nutrasweet) to achieve two particular goals. Rich (1996) reports that the first goal is to develop an identity which final end users perceive as valuable. For example, Intel has developed their microprocessors such that PCs with the Intel brand are seen to be of high quality and credibility. This provides the PC manufacturer with an added competitive advantage.

The second goal is to establish a stronger relationship with the manufacturer. Nutrasweet works with food manufacturers advising on recipes simply because the final product is the context within which Nutrasweet will be evaluated by end users.

Business-to-business branding: ICI

ICI works with bath manufacturers and supplies them with the names and addresses of people who enquire about their Lucite material. This is simply ICI's acrylic from which 70% of European baths are made. By encouraging consumer identification with Lucite bath manufacturers, ICI has the potential to profit in the long term. ICI communicates with end users through advertisements with messages that challenge consumers to request a sample of the acrylic to see just how tough it is. It is these names and addresses that are used to support ICI customers and ultimately their customers too.

Adapted from Rich (1996)

The use of event sponsorship, whereby an organisation provides financial support for a conference or exhibition, has become increasingly popular (Miller, 1997). Mainly because of the costs involved, event organisers have sought sponsorship aid. For sponsors, events provide a means of promoting visibility within a narrowly focused target market. In addition, they provide a means of highlighting their own particular contribution within the conference or their exhibition stand.

The use of joint promotional activities between manufacturers and resellers will continue to be an important form of communication behaviour. The desire to build networks which provide cooperative strength and protection for participants will continue. Manufacturers will use joint promotional activities as a means of forging close relationships with retailers and as a means of strengthening exit barriers (routes away from relationships).

Summary

In order that the promotional objectives be accomplished, it is necessary to establish and implement a communication strategy. This aspect of planned communications has generally been neglected by researchers on the assumption that the elements of the mix constitute communication strategy. This ignores the wider dimension of promotional activities and its integration with marketing plans and corporate strategy. A more meaningful approach is to assume a stakeholder position and to develop communication strategies that enable messages to be developed and conveyed to particular groups that have meaning and purpose.

Of the main communication strategies available to organisations (push, pull and profile), the strategy used to communicate directly with consumers is a pull strategy.

Consumers need to be made aware of a product's existence, and communication strategy to this target group is very often orientated to creating or improving awareness levels. However, the communication strategy is not limited to this aspect alone. Pull strategies can also be used to help change the way in which a product/brand is perceived, to inform of new variants, to reinforce the attitudes held towards a brand (or its competitors), to reposition a brand in the minds of members of the target audience, or, as seen earlier, to reassure buyers of their purchase habits and to maintain brand purchase activity.

Understanding the level of involvement present in the target audience provides a useful base for developing promotional activities. Whether there is high or low involvement indicates when attitudes are thought to be developed. This enables a more appropriate and strategic deployment of promotional tools and messages to be achieved.

Underpinning the strategic orientation is the brand. Branding is a common pull strategy mainly because of the benefits that can accrue to both buyer and brand owner. While there are a number of brand variants and permutations, the power of the brand generally to communicate values and differentiate products and services is acknowledged and used in consumer and (increasingly) business-to-business markets.

Review questions

1. Why should separate strategies be developed for end users as opposed to intermediaries?
2. What is the difference between a promotional objective and a promotion?
3. What is a pull strategy and how does it differ from other types of strategy?

4. How might an understanding of high and low involvement assist the development of promotional strategy?
5. Select ten different products or services that you and a colleague have used recently and position them on the FCB grid using Vaughn's criteria.
6. Write brief notes outlining the differences between the Rossiter–Percy grid and the FCB grid.
7. Write brief notes explaining what branding is.
8. How do brands assist customers and suppliers?
9. Select five consumer brands and evaluate their characteristics.
10. Explain how business-to-business markets might benefit from adopting a branding approach.

References

Assael, H. (1990) *Marketing: Principles and Strategy*. Orlando FL: The Dryden Press.

Biel, A. (1997) Discovering brand magic: the hardness of the softer side of branding. *International Journal of Advertising*, **16**, 199–210.

Blackett, T. (1992) Branding and the rise of the generic drug. *Marketing Intelligence and Planning*, **10**(9), 21–4.

Blackston, M. (1993) A brand with an attitude: a suitable case for treatment. *Journal of Market Research Society*, **34**(3), 231–41.

Boehringer, C. (1996) How can you build a better brand? *Pharmaceutical Marketing* (July), 35–6.

Campbell, L. (1997) Cellnet in shift to direct work. *Marketing*, 20 November, p. 6.

Croft, M. (1996) Stretched marks. *Marketing Week*, 8 March, pp. 47–8.

Cutler, R.D. and Javalgli, R.G. (1994) Comparison of business-to-business advertising: the United States and the United Kingdom. *Industrial Marketing Management*, **23**, 117–24.

Doyle, P. (1989) Building successful brands: the strategic options. *Journal of Marketing Management*, **5**(1), 77–95.

Fournier, S. (1995) A consumer–brand relationship perspective on brand equity. Presentation to Marketing Science Conference on Brand Equity and the Marketing Mix, Tucson, Arizona, 2–3 March.

Gilliand, D.I. and Johnston, W.J. (1997) Toward a model of business-to-business marketing communications effects. *Industrial Marketing Management*, **26**, 15–29.

Gray, E.R. and Smeltzer, L.R. (1985) SMR Forum: corporate image – an integral part of strategy. *Sloan Management Review* (Summer), 73–8.

Joyce, T. (1991) Models of the advertising process. *Marketing and Research Today* (November), 205–12.

Killgren, L. (1996) The hole story. *Marketing Week*, 11 October, pp. 93–4.

Miller, R. (1997) Make an event of it. *Marketing*, 5 June, p. 28.

Ratchford, B. (1987) New insights about the FCB grid. *Journal of Advertising Research* (August/September), 24–38.

Rich, M. (1996) Stamp of approval. *Financial Times*, 29 February, p. 9.

Rossiter, J.R., Percy, L. and Donovan, R.J. (1991) A better advertising planning grid. *Journal of Advertising Research* (October/November), 11–21.

Rossiter, J.R. and Percy, L. (1997) *Advertising, Communications and Promotion Management*, 2nd edn. New York: McGraw-Hill.

Sargent, J. (1995) Building brands in the UK. *Admap* (January), 45–7.

Vaughn, R. (1980) How advertising works: a planning model. *Journal of Advertising Research* (October), 27–33.

chapter 26

Communication strategies to reach intermediaries

Communications with members of the marketing channel networks are vital if products are to be made available to end-user consumers. The purpose of these communications is encourage intermediaries to take and hold stock, to allocate scarce resources such as shelf space and to help them become advocates of the product on behalf of everyone involved in the network. In addition, good communications are regarded as important for helping to build long-term relationships with intermediaries and securing some advantage in the market system.

AIMS AND OBJECTIVES

The aims of this chapter are to introduce and explore communications that are intended to influence members of marketing channel networks.

The objectives of this chapter are:

1. To introduce the notion of *push* communication strategies.
2. To develop an understanding of push-based communications and determine how they can help communications with members of the performance network.
3. To examine trust and commitment as major components of channel-based communications.
4. To appraise the role of communication facets and channel structure as determinants of communication strategy.
5. To explore the notions of collaborative and autonomous communication strategies.

6. To consider the notion of communication quality.
7. To introduce key account management as an important strategic approach to communications with intermediaries.

Introduction

In the previous chapter the communication strategies under consideration were those where messages were targeted at end-user buyers, namely consumers and business-to-business buyers. A second group or type of target audience can be identified, called channel intermediaries (members, actors, players). Their role is to facilitate the distribution of products and services to consumers or end users. They are organisations who buy products in order to add value to them. The more common intermediaries are dealers, wholesalers, agents, value-added resellers, distributors and retailers.

The 'trade' channel has received increased attention in recent years as the strategic value of intermediaries has become more apparent. As the channel networks have developed, so has their complexity, which impacts upon the marketing communications strategies and tools used to help reach marketing goals. The expectations of buyers in these networks have risen in parallel with the significance attached to them by manufacturers. The power of multiple retailers, such as Tesco, Sainsbury's, Safeway and Asda, is such that they are able to dictate terms (including the marketing communications) to many manufacturers of branded goods. For example, many consumer-related sales promotion events are prompted by retailers in response to claims for shelf space and in-store visibility.

Effective communication is key to the satisfaction of these expectations and is the main link between an organisation and its environment. Indeed, the systems used to transfer information and meaning from people and machines, in both inter- and intra-organisational contexts, can progress or hinder the implementation of corporate and operational strategies. If the dynamics of an organisation are to be understood, for example, in order that effective and appropriate strategic change processes can be developed, then all its communication systems and networks need to be appreciated.

Once the promotional objectives and positioning statements have been determined it is necessary to establish the means by which they will be accomplished. To that end, it is necessary first to consider the communication needs from the intermediaries' perspective. What are their communication requirements in the light of the objectives that have been set, and more importantly what are their communication expectations? Once these have been considered it is possible to consider the communication strategies that may be best suited to achieving these goals and then determine the means by which strategies will be implemented.

If the promotional objectives emphasise the need to communicate with members of the 'trade' or channel network, then the strategy requires communication with members of the performance network. The purpose of these activities is to encourage intermediaries to take stock, to allocate resources (e.g. shelf space) and to help them to become fully aware of the key attributes and benefits associated with each product. This strategy is designed to facilitate resale to other members of the network and contribute to the achievement of their own objectives. This approach is known as a *push* strategy, as it is aimed at pushing the product down through the channel towards the end users. Figure 26.1 shows the targets and direction of push-based communication strategies.

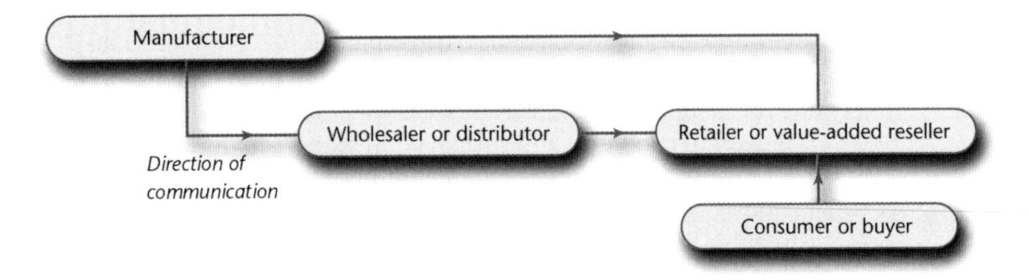

Figure 26.1 Push-based communication strategies.

The role of communication in marketing channel networks

The important role that communication plays in determining the effectiveness of any group or network of organisations is widely recognised (Grabner and Rosenberg, 1969; Stern and El-Ansary, 1992). According to Mohr and Nevin (1990), communication is 'the glue that holds together a marketing channel'. It is recognised that, from a managerial perspective, communication is important because many of the causes of tension and conflict in interorganisational relationships stem from inadequate or poor communication. Communication within networks serves not only to provide persuasive information and foster participative decision-making, but also provides for coordination, the exercise of power and the encouragement of loyalty and commitment, so as to reduce the likelihood of tension and conflict.

Jet: loyalty schemes

Jet, the petrol forecourt retailer, had been operating a customer loyalty scheme (Jetcash) for over five years. To defend its market share it planned to discontinue the scheme and use the funds saved to enter a price war.

However, the plan was met with resistance from the company's dealers, who argued that the scheme was the main reason sales volume and margin had been sustained. In view of these reaction from the dealers, their relative power and the tension likely to ensue, Jet instigated a whole review of the loyalty scheme.

Adapted from Jet loyalty plan reignited. *Marketing*, 30 October 1997, p. 12

The channel network (Chapter 6) consists of those organisations with whom others must cooperate directly to achieve their own objectives. By accepting that there is interdependence, usually dispersed unequally throughout the network, it is possible to identify organisations who have a stronger/weaker position within a network. Communication must travel not only between the different levels of dependency and role ('up and down' in a channel context) and so represent bidirectional flows, but also across similar levels of dependency and role, that is, horizontal flows. For example, these may be from retailer to retailer or wholesaler to wholesaler.

Networks and interorganisational relationships

The basic structure of any network consists of a focal organisation which is tied with a number of other functionally specialised organisations. The network uses relational exchanges to regularise and sustain cooperative activities. This is a general view and it is recognised that there are a variety of network forms, some of which were explored previously (Chapter 6). However, to repeat an important point, it is necessary to distinguish the type of networks an organisation belongs to from traditional perspectives, if only because it is now generally accepted that all organisations are networks in their own right and that there are a variety of internal and external networks to which all organisations belong.

Therefore, network organisations can be distinguished from traditional organisational forms because the exchanges are based upon membership, which encourages mutually determined relational transactions. This long-term perspective reflects the density, closeness and shared values that such networks seek to perpetuate.

Business-to-business communications: Sharwoods

Sharwood's network of independent retailers is vitally important to provide shelf space and visibility for its brand of sauces. However, it found that the sale of its Chinese sauces through the independent retailer network was low compared with those of Indian sauces. To help rectify the imbalance they used a direct marketing campaign to coincide with the Chinese New Year.

Incentivised mailpacks were sent to selected independent retail outlets, inviting them to purchase cases of Oriental products and in return receive money-off coupons. The campaign also sought to educate retailers so that they provided their customers with a breadth of suitable products. After a two-week interval, telemarketing was used to identify those retailers who had either purchased or wanted to order over the phone. A 34% take-up resulted from this approach and Sharwood's market share rose to 26% over the new year period.

Adapted from Darby (1997)

Many commentators have observed that organisations are forging relationships with other organisations that are based around a network in order to achieve new, fresh advantages. These advantages may be driven by competitive goals, but the behaviour exhibited is increasingly cooperative. These networks vary in the strength of their ties (degrees of interconnectedness), but success can be seen to be a function of the partnerships that are developed in these networks. A key question has to be what determines a successful partnership and how is success characterised and replicated?

An underlying principle of relational exchanges is the pivotal role of trust and commitment (Morgan and Hunt, 1994) (see Figure 26.2).

Commitment to a partnership, that is, the relationship with other network members, is key because of the 'enduring desire to maintain a valued relationship' (Moorman *et al.*, 1992). Of comparable importance is the degree to which partners are confident that each will act in the best interests of the relationship. *Trust*, therefore, is also regarded as a key aspect of relational exchanges and is a composite of the level of reliability and integrity that exists between partners.

Figure 26.2 The role of commitment and trust in relationship marketing (Morgan & Hunt (1994); reprinted with permission from *Journal of Marketing*, published by the American Marketing Association).

According to Mohr and Spekman (1996), partnership success is based upon three key parameters. These are the attributes the partnership exhibits, the communication behaviour and the techniques used to resolve conflict (see Figure 26.3). Their view is that partnership success is dependent upon a wider array of factors than just commitment and trust. These are recognised as important, but in addition they posit communication- and conflict-related issues. It could be argued that Mohr and Spekman define commitment and trust in a relatively narrow way, such that the other factors need to be made explicit. What is important, however, is that these authors state unequivocally that *communication problems are associated with a lack of partnership success* and that communication *might be interpreted as an overt manifestation of more subtle phenomenan such as trust and commitment.*

Elements of communications in marketing channel networks

There are some specialised messages that need to be distributed across a variety of networks, for example messages proclaiming technological advances, business

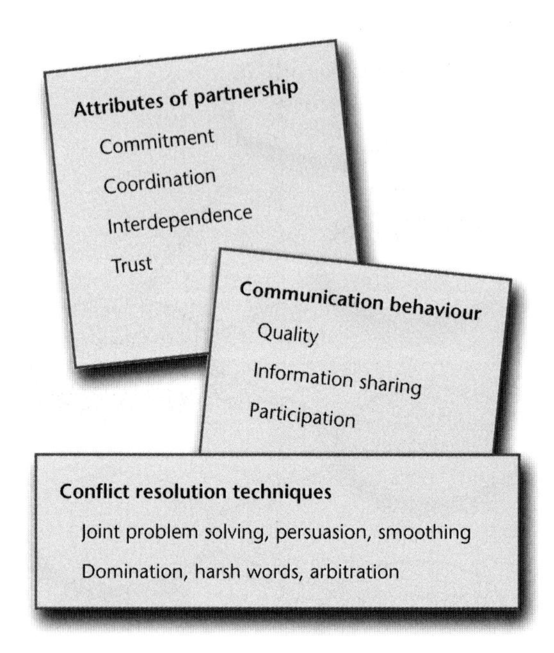

Figure 26.3 Characteristics of partnership success (Mohr and Spekman (1996); used with kind permission).

acquisitions and contracts won. It is also apparent that communication flows do not change radically over the short term. On the contrary, they become established and regularised through use. This allows for the emergence of specialised communication networks (Chapter 2). Furthermore, it is common for networks to be composed of sub-networks, overlaying each other. The complexity of an organisation's networks is such that unravelling each one would be dysfunctional.

What is necessary is the establishment of those elements that contribute to the general communications in the marketing channels. The development of a planned, channel-orientated communications strategy, a push strategy, should be based on identifiable elements that contribute to and reinforce the partnerships in the network. A number of these can be identified, namely a consideration of the movement of flows of information and in particular the timing and permanence of the flows (Stern and El-Ansary, 1992). It should also take into account the various facets of communication and the particular channel structures through which communications are intended to move (Mohr and Nevin, 1990). These will now be considered in turn.

Timing of the flows

Message flows can be either simultaneous or serial (Stern and El-Ansary). Where *simultaneous* flows occur, messages are distributed to all members so that the information is received at approximately the same time. Business seminars and dealer meetings, together with direct mail promotional activities and the use of integrated IT systems between levels (overnight ordering procedures), are examples of this type of flow. *Serial* flows involve the transmission of messages so that they are received by a preselected number of network members who then transmit the message to others at lower levels within the network. Serial flows may lead to problems concerning the management of the network, such as those concerning stock levels and production.

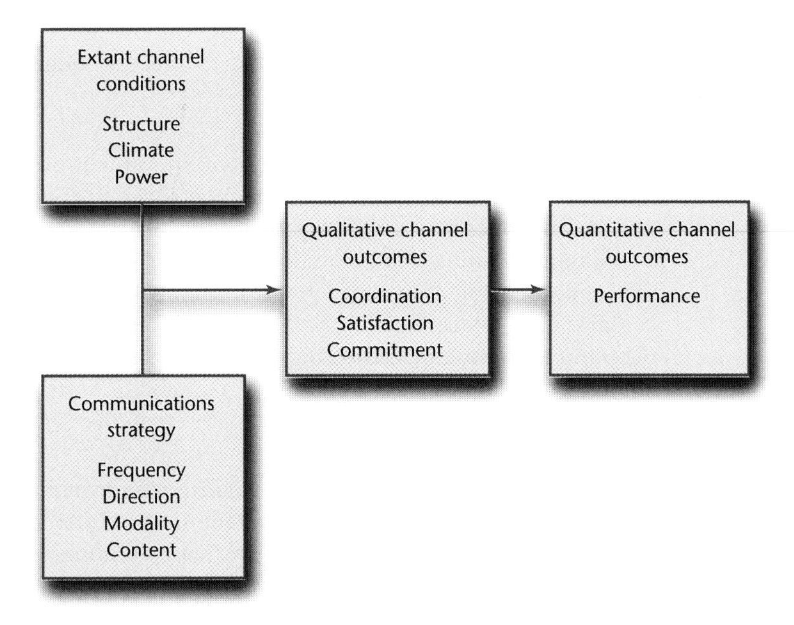

Figure 26.4 A model of communication for marketing channels (Mohr and Nevin (1990); used with kind permission).

Permanence of the flows

The degree of permanence that a message has is determined by the technology used in the communication process. Essentially, the more a message can be recalled without physical distortion of the content, the more permanent the flow. This would indicate that the use of machines to record the message content would have an advantage over person-to-person messages transmitted at a sales meeting. Permanence can be improved by recording the meeting with a tape recorder or by putting the conversation on paper and using handouts and sales literature.

Mohr and Nevin suggest that the performance outcomes of a channel network are a result of the interaction of the communication strategy used within a network and the structure of the channel within which the communications flow. Figure 26.4 depicts the relationships between strategies and structure. Therefore by examining the constituent elements and moulding the variables to meet the channel conditions, it may be possible to enhance the performance/success of the network.

Communication facets

Communication strategy results from a combination of four facets of communication. These facets are the frequency, direction, modality and content of communications.

1. *Frequency*
   The amount of contact between members of the performance network needs to be assessed. Too much information (too frequent, aggregate volume or pure repetition), can overload members and have a dysfunctional effect. Too little information can undermine the opportunities for favourable performance outcomes by failing to provide necessary operational information, motivation and support.

As a consequence, it is important to identify the current volume of information being provided and for management to make a judgement about the desired levels of communication.

2. *Direction*
This refers to the horizontal and vertical movement of communication within a network. Each network consists of members who are dependent upon others, but the level of dependency will vary: hence the dispersion of power is unequal.
Communications can be unidirectional in that they flow in one direction only. This may be from a source of power to subordinate members (for example, from a major food retailer such as Sainsbury's or Tesco to small food manufacturers). Communications can also be bidirectional, that is to and from powerful organisations. The relative power positions of manufacturer/producer and reseller need to be established and understood prior to the creation of any communication plan.

3. *Modality*
Modality refers to the method used to transmit information. Mohr and Nevin agree that there is a wide variety of interpretations of the methods used to convey information. They use modality in the sense that communications can be either formal and regulated, such as meetings and written reports, or informal and spontaneous, such as corridor conversations and word-of-mouth communications, often carried out away from an organisation's formal structures and environment.

4. *Content*
This refers to what is said. Frazier and Summers (1984) distinguish between direct and indirect influence strategies. Direct strategies are designed to change behaviour by specific request (recommendations, promises and appeals to legal obligations). Indirect strategies attempt to change a receiver's beliefs and attitudes about the desirability of the intended behaviour. This may take the form of an information exchange, where the source uses discussions about general business issues to influence the attitudes of the receiver.

Channel structures

Communication facets can be seen in the light of three particular channel conditions: structure, climate and power.

1. *Channel structure*
Channel structure, according to Stern and El-Ansary (1988), can be distinguished by the nature of the exchange relationship. These are relational and market structure relationships. Relational exchanges have a long-term perspective and high interdependence, and involve joint decision making. Market exchanges are by contrast *ad hoc* and hence have a short-term orientation where interdependence is low (Chapter 1).

2. *Channel climate*
Anderson *et al.* (1987) used measures of trust and goal compatibility in defining organisational climate. This in turn can be interpreted as the degree of mutual supportiveness that exists between channel members.

3. *Power*
Dwyer and Walker (1981) showed that power conditions within a channel can be symmetrical (with power balanced between members), or asymmetrical (with a power imbalance).

Table 26.1 The relationships between channel conditions and the facets of communication

Channel conditions	Communication facets			
	Frequency	Direction	Content	Modality
Structure				
Relational	Higher	More bidirectional	More indirect	More informal
Market	Lower	More unidirectional	More direct	More formal
Climate				
Supportive	Higher	More bidirectional	More indirect	More informal
Unsupportive	Lower	More unidirectional	More direct	More informal
Power				
Symmetrical	Higher	More bidirectional	More indirect	More informal
Asymmetrical	Lower	More unidirectional	More indirect	More informal

Source: Mohr and Nevin (1990); used with kind permission.

Table 26.1 shows the relationships between communication facets and channel conditions. This is the combination of elements identified above.

Two specific forms of communication strategy can be identified. The first is a combination referred to as a 'Collaborative communication strategy' and includes higher frequency, more bidirectional flows, informal modes and indirect content. This combination is likely to occur in channel conditions of relational structures, supportive climates or symmetrical power. The second combination is referred to as an 'Autonomous communication strategy' and includes lower frequency, more unidirectional communication, formal modes and direct content. This combination is likely to occur in channel conditions of market structures, unsupportive climates and asymmetrical power.

Communication strategy should, therefore, be built upon the characteristics of the situation facing each organisation in any particular network. Not all networks share the same conditions, nor do they all possess the same degree of closeness or relational expectations. By considering the nature of the channel conditions and then developing communication strategies that complement them, the performance of the focus organisation and other members can be considerably improved, and conflict and tension substantially reduced. Where channel conditions match communication strategy, the outcomes of the performance network are said, by Mohr and Nevin, to be enhanced. Likewise, when the communication strategy fails to match the channel conditions, the outcomes are not likely to be enhanced (Figure 26.5).

Communication quality

Recently, an interesting new perspective on marketing channel communications has emerged, namely issues concerning the quality of the communications and the success that might be attributed to the communication behaviours of the partners in any loose or tight networks.

Mohr and Sohi (1995) considered whether communication quality might be a function of the propensity to share information. The inclination among members to share information could be assumed to be positive in networks where members show high levels of trust and commitment. Frequency of communication flows, the level of

CASE ILLUSTRATION

Channel communications

This case illustration is an adapted extract from a piece of MBA coursework prepared by Janet Chard, who is Student Services Manager at the University of Portsmouth.

HMS *Victory*

Flagship Portsmouth Trust (FPT), an organisation with around 25 staff, is employed in partnership with the other heritage attractions at Portsmouth by the Royal Navy for the strategic marketing of Portsmouth's Historic Dockyard which draws over half a million people annually. The 'products' are primarily:

- HMS *Victory*: Nelson's famous flagship at the Battle of Trafalgar (recognised as the Dockyard's major attraction; owned by the MoD, which pays for restoration, upkeep and staffing).
- HMS *Warrior* (1860): Britain's first iron-hulled armoured warship (Charitable Trust).
- Henry VIII's *Mary Rose*: sunk in the Solent in 1545 and raised in 1982 (Charitable Trust).
- Royal Naval Museum: providing insight into 800 years of service to the Navy and its people. The landlord is Portsmouth Naval Base Property Trust (Charitable Trust) which receives some government funding.

The Historic Dockyard attractions are marketed as a collective package. HMS Victory draws most visitors; for example, in 1995 she generated 42.4% of total sales and is generally acknowledged as the 'primary attraction' or 'brand leader' (see Plate 26.1).

The assembly has been described as 'The finest collection of military warships in the world' which implies positioning as a key historic maritime attraction of world-wide importance, or at the very least, the 'Leading maritime attraction in the UK'. This is stressed through use of the strapline, 'The greatest historic ships in the world.' FPT's core marketing strategy is to promote the generic brand and site as a single attraction under the brand name 'Flagship Portsmouth', thereby occupying a distinctive place in consumers' minds. It is hoped that visitors are also likely to share the perception that such 'historical products' symbolise culture, age and heritage.

The Historic Dockyard is part of a mature organisation, whose protocol and culture has been established and set over hundreds of years. The configuration (Mintzberg *et al.*, 1995) seems to match that of a hierarchical, bureaucratic organisation, and the forces of efficiency synonymous with the Royal Navy draw the organisation towards the machine form, where rules and procedures dominate.

This stable, mechanistic organisation operates in the highly turbulent and competitive arena of tourism which is expanding rapidly and has many players vying for the time and money of visitors. The popular seaside resort of Southsea is no exception and, although it may be viewed as a complementary attraction, it also takes its market share, particularly in good weather. Other local competing organisations include:

- Royal Marines Museum
- The beach and pier attractions at Southsea
- Sea Life Centre
- D-Day Museum
- Marwell Zoo
- Port Solent

Recent survey data collected by FPT indicate that family groups form the largest visitor segment (52%) and, during the off-peak season, 45–54-year-olds were the biggest single group. Over 55s made up 25% during peak season and 34% off-peak.

FPT considers its main target markets to be socioeconomic groups A and B, although their

Table 26.2 Percentage of socioeconomic groups visiting the Portsmouth Historic Dockyard in 1994/1995

Grade	% of visitors 1994	% of visitors 1995
A and B	16	18
C1	26	46
C2	24	27

Visitor Survey of 1995 indicates that C1s and C2s form the majority of customers (see Table 26.2).

In order to influence members of the trade and marketing channels, FPT concentrates on regional promotion to actors such as the Southern Tourist Board and Brochure Display (a local distribution service). It also collaborates with Portsmouth City Council to target national and international markets. FPT uses a combination of push, pull and profile strategies.

The main strategy is to 'push' marketing communications literature to targeted organisations, who, in turn, promote the Historic Dockyard to potential customers. The current channel comprises the following key stakeholders:

- HMS *Victory* and the Trusts
- FPT
- Portsmouth City Council
- Southern Tourist Board
- Brochure display

The Royal Navy epitomises hundreds of years of protocol, efficiency and rules. It reflects a more formal, hierarchial organisation with which FPT would conform. Within such organisations, an endemic 'role' culture usually exists and attitudes reflect the formal structure and procedures.

The long-term partnership which exists between the Historic Dockyard and FPT encourages relational exchanges. However, market structures appear to dominate the rest of the channel. Marketing decisions are made by committee consensus and not by individual product managers, who are unable to directly influence how their products are marketed through the channel to target audiences.

The current channel functions as an administered vertical marketing system (VMS) which FPT controls, and the actors within the Dockyard have a contractual obligation. However, as key stakeholders, they are not directly dependent upon each other for business, apart from the Trusts and HMS *Victory*, who rely on one another for 'all-in' ticket sales and on FPT for their marketing communications. Communications are therefore quite formal and regulated.

The climate of decision-making and support between members of the channel is not particularly supportive. With most downstream members of the channel having a number of alternative attractions to market there is a low level of dependency on the Dockyard, despite its prominence and pulling power.

Tension may occur, as it appears that power is not evenly distributed amongst channel members. As the marketing organisation, FPT is the most powerful stakeholder, holding decision-making authority. HMS *Victory* has potential power and leverage arising from its public appeal and the highest revenue earnings on site. In this case, the channel is currently asymmetrical.

As communication strategy should be built upon the characteristics of the situation facing each organisation in any particular network, it would seem that, on this limited information, an autonomous communications strategy would appear suitable. It can be seen that FPT engages in low frequency and increased unidirectional communications. The level of formality is high, reflecting the culture of the organisations, the content is direct in nature and the style of the content is typically direct. This strategy is correct in the light of the channel conditions, which are essentially based on market structures, unsupportive climates and asymmetrical power.

Should FPT be able to develop stronger cooperation between channel members, that is, move towards closer network coupling, a more cohesive (even collaborative) marketing communications strategy might arise which would require different use of the promotional tools.

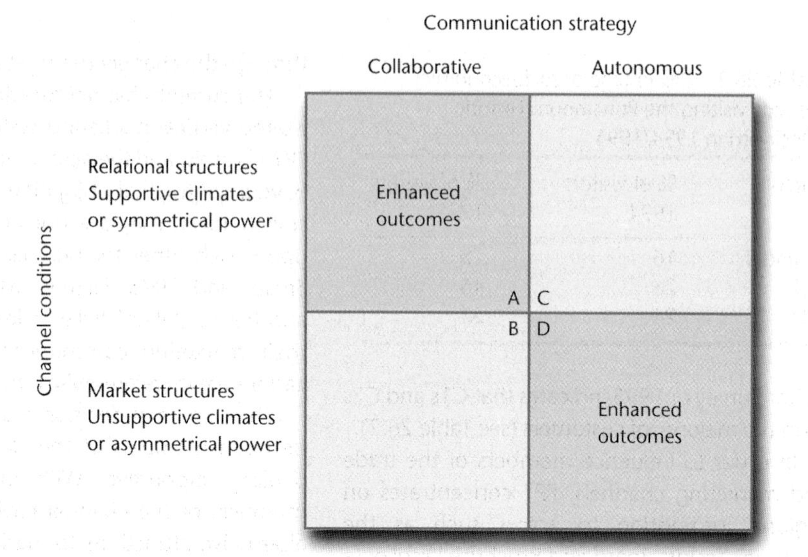

Figure 26.5 Proposed relationships between communication strategies and channel conditions. The shaded areas represent enhanced outcome levels, or where communication strategies fit channel conditions. The unshaded areas represent non-enhanced outcome levels, or where communication strategies do not fit channel conditions (Mohr and Nevin (1990); used with kind permission).

bidirectional communications in a network and the level of communication formality are assumed to be the main elements of the propensity to share information.

Another aspect considered by the researchers was the degree to which information might be withheld or distorted (deviance). Information deviance might be high when there is an absence of rules (norms) determining what information needs to communicated. Informality may lead to vagueness or inattentiveness and higher levels of deviance.

The research sought to determine whether any (or all) of the three factors indicated that there was a linkage between the variables and the quality of information perceived by channel members. The results indicated that in the sample sector (computer dealers) the only significant variable was the frequency of information. The higher the frequency of communications received by channel members, the higher the perception of the quality of the communications. Issues concerning information overload and irritance are discounted.

Satisfaction levels appear to be correlated with higher levels of bidirectional communications. So, frequency impacts on perceived quality (and hence satisfaction) and the degree of bidirectional communications is significant in determining levels of satisfaction with the communications in a channel (network) environment.

Key account management (KAM)

It has long been recognised that particular customer accounts represent an important, often large proportion of turnover. Such accounts have been referred to variously as national accounts, house accounts, major accounts and key accounts. Millman and Wilson (1995) argue that the first three are orientated towards sales, tend to the short term and are often only driven by sales management needs.

Key accounts may be of different sizes in comparison to the focus organisation, but what delineates them from other types of 'account' is that they are strategically important. Key accounts are customers who, in a business-to-business network, are willing to enter into relational exchanges and who are of strategic importance to the focus organisation.

There are two primary aspects of this definition. The first is that relational exchanges are a necessary component and the relationship is perceived by both parties as long term. The second aspect refers to the strategic issue. The key account is strategically important because the account might offer opportunities for entry to new markets, it might represent access to other key organisations or resources or it might provide symbolic value in terms of influence, power and stature.

Building inter-company relationships

Entec manufactures a range of water treatment and septic tank sytems which are sold through a range of networks. The primary intermediaries are building contractors, merchants and specifiers such as architects.

Travis Perkins is a major distributor, a building merchant through which a substantial part of Entec's sales is directed. Travis Perkins has installed an email-based order management system, and as a preferred supplier Entec has direct access. This means that leads and sales enquiries generated by Entec can be emailed to the distributor's management system, through which progress of the sales lead can be monitored through to completion.

This demonstrates the trust and commitment between the two organisations and shows how the relational transactions are reflected in the way technology has allowed them to work together to achieve their individual goals.

Points of contact

The importance of the long-term relationship as a prime part of key account identification raises questions about how these relationships are developed, what resources are required to manage and sustain them and what the long-term success and effectiveness of identifying these accounts is.

The main point of contact is through the sales force, as personal selling is the principle conduit for communication. The assignment of sales executives to these important accounts is common in smaller organisations. Those organisations that have the resources are able to incorporate the services of senior executives. They assume this role and with it they bring the flexibility and responsive service that is required as the account grows in stature. They can make decisions about stock, price, distribution and levels of customisation.

These accounts may be major or national accounts, as very often their strategic significance is not recognised. There is a tendency for these accounts to receive a disproportionate level of attention, as the executives responsible for these major customers lose sight of their own organisation's marketing strategy.

A further way of managing these accounts is to create a key account division. The main advantage of this approach is that it offers close integration of production, finance, marketing and sales. The main disadvantage is that resources are duplicated and the organisation can become very inefficient. It is also a high-risk strategy as the entire division is dependent upon a few customers.

Key account relationship cycles

A number of researchers have attempted to gain a greater understanding of KAM by considering the development cycles that relationships move through. Millman and Wilson offer the work of Ford (1980), Dwyer *et al.* (1987), Lamming (1993) and Wotruba (1991) as examples of such development cycles (Table 26.3).

Millman and Wilson have attempted to build upon the work of the others (included in Table 26.3) and have formulated a model which incorporates their own research as well as that established in the literature. This is shown in the right-hand column of the table.

The cycle develops with *Pre-KAM* where the main task is to identify those accounts that have key account potential and those that do not in order that resources can be allocated efficiently. The next stage is *Early KAM*, where the selling organisation seeks tentative agreement with prospective accounts about whether they would become 'preferred accounts'. Adaptions to the offer may need to be made.

The *Mid-KAM* stage is noted by the review process being administered by senior management, whereas the *Partnership-KAM* stage sees the establishment of joint problem solving and the sharing of sensitive information.

Synergistic-KAM is achieved when the two organisations view the relationship as consisting of one entity where they create synergistic value in the market-place. The final stage is reached when *Uncoupling-KAM* is reached and the parties decide that the relationship holds no further value. This termination can be regarded as a positive outcome, as long-term benefits may no longer be achievable if the context in which the relationship first became established has changed. For example, technological developments, change of ownership or other changes in the channel network may stimulate a reconsideration of key account status.

Table 26.3 Comparison of relational models

Ford (1980), Dwyer *et al.* (1987)	Lamming (1993)	Wotruba (1991)	Millman and Wilson (1995)
Pre-relationship awareness	Traditional	Provider	Pre-KAM
Early stage exploration	Stress	Persuader	Early-KAM
Development stage expansion	Resolved	Prospector	Mid-KAM
Long-term stage commitment	Partnership	Problem solver	Partnership KAM
Final stage institutionalisation	Beyond partnership	Procreator	Synergistic KAM
			Uncoupling KAM

Source: Millman and Wilson (1995); used with kind permission.

Summary

In order that the promotional objectives relating to members of the marketing channel network can be accomplished, it is necessary to establish and implement a communication strategy that is particular to this type of target audience.

This form of marketing communication strategy is referred to as a *push* strategy. Communication strategy in the marketing channel needs to reflect the relationships that exist between members and match prevailing conditions. Commitment and trust are important variables in determining the nature of the relational exchanges that develop in networks, but in addition communications are vitally important to help build long-term relationships.

Communication managers need to consider the specialised networks that may exist and develop those that are of potential benefit. Highly specialised networks may emerge to resolve particular issues and may keep out messages of friendship and loyalty.

There are costs associated with communication in these networks. These costs may be direct, in the form of dealer conferences and house magazines. Costs may also be indirect in nature. For example, the views of particular retailers or manufacturers' representatives may go unheard or unreported. These views might be critical to the development of particular markets and hence be of strategic importance.

An examination of the communication networks, perhaps through a channel-wide communication audit, will reveal the need to develop communication networks appropriate to the needs of each organisation and the network as a whole.

The strategic importance of key accounts has gained increased attention in recent years. One of the prime dimensions of key accounts is the long-term relationship that can develop. Millman and Wilson have developed a model which examines the various stages that key accounts move through and which recognises the strategic importance that is attached to these organisations. Marketing communications, principally through personal selling, is an important tool in fostering, nurturing and sustaining strategically important accounts.

Review questions

1. Who are the principal target audiences for push-orientated communications and how do these communications differ from pull-based communication strategies?
2. Discuss the role that trust and commitment might play in marketing communications with intermediaries.
3. What are the three parameters upon which partnership success is thought to be built?
4. Prepare notes for a short article to be included in a marketing magazine, about the importance of communications within marketing channels.
5. Describe the main elements of promotional informational flows in performance networks.
6. How can communication facets and channel structures be effectively combined?
7. What are the differences between collaborative and autonomous communication strategies?
8. Outline the concept of communication quality and identify the main dimension upon which quality is perceived to be based.

9. Identify the main difference beween house or major accounts and key accounts.
10. Explain the concept of key account relationship cycles using the Millman and Wilson model.

References

Anderson, E., Lodish, L. and Weitz, B. (1987) Resource allocation behaviour in conventional channels. *Journal of Marketing Research* (February), 85–97.

Darby, I. (1997) Korma chameleon. *Marketing Direct* (May), 29–30.

Dwyer, F.R., Shurr, P.H. and Oh, S. (1987) Developing buyer-seller relationships. *Journal of Marketing*, **51**(2), 11–28.

Dwyer, R. and Walker, O.C. (1981) Bargaining in an asymmetrical power structure. *Journal of Marketing*, **45** (Winter), 104–15.

Ford, I.D. (1980) The development of buyer–seller relationships in industrial markets. *European Journal of Marketing*, **14**(5/6), 339–53.

Frazier, G.L. and Summers, J.O. (1984) Interfirm influence strategies and their application within distribution channels. *Journal of Marketing*, **48** (Summer), 43–55.

Grabner, J.R. and Rosenberg, L.J. (1969) Communication in distribution channel systems, in *Behavioural Dimensions in Distribution Channels:A Systems Approach* (ed. L. Stern). Boston: Houghton Mifflin.

Lamming, R. (1993) *Beyond Partnership: Strategies for Innovation and Lean Supply.* Englewood Cliffs NJ: Prentice Hall.

Millman, T. and Wilson, K. (1995) From key account selling to key account management. *Journal of Marketing Practice: Applied Marketing Science*, **1**(1), 9–21.

Mintzberg, H., Quinn, J.B. and Ghoshal, S. (1995) *The Strategy Process*, revised European edition. Hemel Hempstead: Prentice Hall Europe.

Mohr, J. and Nevin, J.R. (1990) Communication strategies in marketing channels. *Journal of Marketing* (October), 36–51.

Mohr, J. and Sohi, R.S. (1995) Communication flows in distribution channels: impact on assessments of communication quality and satisfaction. *Journal of Retailing*, **71**(4), 393–416.

Mohr, J. and Spekman, R. (1994) Characteristics of partnership success: partnership attributes, communication behaviour and conflict resolution techniques. *Strategic Management Journal*, **15**, 135–52.

Morgan, R.M. and Hunt, S.D. (1994) The commitment–trust theory of relationship marketing, *Journal of Marketing*, **58** (July), 20–38.

Moorman, C., Zaltman, G. and Despande, R. (1992) Relationships between providers and users of marketing research: the dynamics of trust within and between organisations. *Journal of Marketing Research*, **29** (August), 314–29.

Stern, L. and El-Ansary, A.I. (1988) *Marketing Channels.* Englewood Cliffs NJ: Prentice Hall.

Stern, L. and El-Ansary, A.I. (1992) *Marketing Channels*, 4th edn. Englewood Cliffs NJ: Prentice Hall.

Wotruba, T.R. (1991) The evolution of personal selling. *Journal of Personal Selling and Sales Management*, **11**(3), 1–12.

chapter 27

Communication strategies to reach all stakeholders

The awareness, perception and attitudes held by stakeholders towards an organisation need to be understood, shaped and acted upon. This can be accomplished though continual dialogue, which can lead to the development of trust and commitment and enable relationships to grow. This is necessary in order that stakeholders think and act favourably towards an organisation and enable the organisation to develop strategies that are compatible with the environment and its own objectives.

AIMS AND OBJECTIVES

The aim of this chapter is to consider those communications that are designed to encourage a dialogue with stakeholders, with a view to influencing the image and reputation of the organisation.

The objectives of this chapter are:

1. To introduce the notion of corporate communications and profile strategies.
2. To appraise the term 'corporate image' and the associated concepts corporate personality, identity and reputation.
3. To explore methods of evaluating corporate image.
4. To introduce a framework incorporating corporate identity with the process of strategic management.
5. To suggest ways in which transactional analysis can assist the understanding of corporate communications.

6. To consider specialised networks as a means of communicating with members of different networks.

Introduction

As stated earlier, the promotional objectives provide a guide for many of the subsequent decisions within the development of a communications plan. So far in this text, the communications have been targeted at either end-user buyers or those within the performance network. However, the objectives may require that the organisation itself be the focus of a communications campaign where messages need to be sent to either a wide range of stakeholders or to a specific group of stakeholders, such as financial analysts, trade unions, employees or the local community.

Traditionally these activities have been referred to as corporate communications, as they deal more or less exclusively with the corporate entity or organisation. Products, services and other offerings are not normally the focus of these communications. It is the organisation and its role in the context of the particular stakeholders' activities that is important. However, it should be noted that as more corporate brands appear the distinction between corporate and marketing communications begins to become much less clear. Indeed, when considered in the light of the development and interest in internal marketing (and communications) it may be of greater advantage to consider corporate communications as part of an organisation's overall marketing communications activities. The accountability for this wider communication brief should rest with a single senior individual with dedicated responsibility.

Communications for all stakeholders: a profile strategy

The communications used to satisfy an organisation's corporate promotional goals are developed through what is referred to as a profile strategy.

This third component of communication strategy (the others being push and pull strategies) concerns the needs of all stakeholders including members of the support network. The awareness, perception and attitudes held by stakeholders towards an organisation need to be understood, shaped and acted upon. This can accomplished though continual dialogue, which will lead to the development of trust and commitment and enable relationships to grow. This is necessary in order that stakeholders act favourably towards an organisation and enable strategies to flourish and objectives be achieved.

Stakeholder analysis is used in the development of strategic plans, so if an organisation wants its communications to support the overall plan it makes sense to communicate effectively with the appropriate stakeholders. Rowe *et al.* (1994) point out that because of the mutual interdependence of stakeholders and the focus organisation, 'each stakeholder is in effect an advocate of any strategy that furthers its goals'. It follows, therefore, that it is important to provide all stakeholders with information that enables them to perceive and position the focus organisation in the desired corporate image. This requires a communication strategy that addresses these particular requirements, even though there may not be any immediately recognisable shift in performance.

However, it would be incorrect to perceive corporate communications as just a means of shaping or influencing the attitudes and behaviour of other stakeholders. Organisations exist within a variety of networks, which provide a context for the roles and actions of member organisations (Chapter 6). Bidirectional communication flows exist and organisations adapt themselves to the actions and behaviour of others in the network. Therefore, corporate communications provides a mechanism by which it can learn about the context(s) in which it exists and is itself shaped and influenced by the other stakeholders with whom it shares communications. Reference is made to the work of Grunig and Hunt (1984), considered in Chapter 20.

An organisation's corporate communications are bound by its identity. Identity is like a badge: the organisation can choose what the badge looks like, select its colours, shape and message, but once visible to the outside world the badge becomes a representation of the organisation. People form an image of the organisation based on those bits that are visible, namely the badge, regardless of whether it is still correct or distorted. In addition, it is people who wear badges, and it is the manner in which they present the badge that is important, in other words the behaviour accompanying the visible signs.

The management of the corporate identity is vital if the image held of the organisation by all stakeholders is to be consistent and accurately represent the personality of the organisation (Dowling, 1993).

The Halifax

In the summer of 1997 the Halifax converted from being the world's largest building society into a bank. The transition received a high level of media interest, mainly because of the volume and value of shares that were distributed to eligible members of the former building society.

The change in designation and status was enormous for the organisation to manage. From being a dominant player, indeed market leader, it became a smaller player in a different market, which it knew less about and in which it was far less influential.

Some months after conversion, a customer enquired whether the Halifax offered a safe deposit service, as available in the majority of other banks. The customer was informed that the Halifax did not offer such a service. 'Why not?' was the retort.

The member of staff then investigated the matter internally with the customer relations department and relayed the answer to the customer. 'Having referred your query to head office, I have been advised that Halifax plc is not a bank.'

The question therefore is, if Halifax plc is not a building society and is not a bank, what is it?

The identity crisis experienced by the few staff involved in this example may be atypical or may be replicated across the organisation. What is clear is that the personality of the organisation and the identity it wished to project are not complementary, and further self-analysis and clearer internal communication are required in order that its external communications do not lead to confusion and misunderstanding.

Adapted from Wright (1997)

Corporate communications

Corporate communications is simply a part of the process that translates corporate identity into corporate image (Ind, 1992). By attempting to control the messages that it transmits, an organisation can inform stakeholders of what it is, what it does and how it does it in a credible and consistent way. Corporate identity programmes require good management of change. Employees are probably the most important stakeholders in the sense that they are not only an audience but also an important group of communicators to external stakeholder groups. Most programmes requiring change should attempt to adapt employee perceptions first and then their attitudes and behaviour.

The gap between organisational image and identity uncovered during research determines the nature of the communications task. A communications strategy is required to address all matters of structure and internal communications and the conflicting needs of different stakeholders so as to produce a set of consistent messages, all within the context of a coherent corporate identity programme. The British Broadcasting Corporation changed its identity partly as a means of enabling it to compete more effectively in an environment that was changing quickly. With the advent of digital television, the emerging international competitive arena and the impending launch a range of new services it was important that the BBC logo became distinctive and reflected the BBC core values of quality, fairness, accuracy and artistic fairness. The previous identity was expensive (four colour), not suitable for the increasing volumes and range of applications, had become increasingly fragmented and reproduced in an inconsistent manner. In addition, it did not work on digital formats and was technically difficult to integrate with other graphics. The new identity signalled changes about the BBC and the culture, attitudes and behaviour of the people who work there (see Plate 27.1).

Analysis of the perceptions and attitudes of stakeholders towards the organisation will have revealed the size of the gap between actual and desired perception. The extent of this gap will have been determined and objectives set to close the gap. This corporate perception gap may be large or small, depending upon who the stakeholder is. Organisations have multiple images and must develop strategies that attempt to stabilise, and if possible equalize, the images held.

Using a four-cell matrix (Figure 27.1), where the vertical axis scales the size of the perceived gap and the horizontal axis the number of stakeholders who share the same perception, a series of strategies can be identified. Should a large number of stakeholders be perceived to hold an image of an organisation that is a long way from reality, then a correction strategy is required to communicate the desired position and performance of the focus organisation. Most common of these is the gap between perceived corporate performance and the real performance of the organisation when put in the context of the actual trading conditions.

If a small number of stakeholders perceive a large gap, then a targeted adjustment strategy would be required, aimed at particular stakeholder groups and taking care to protect the correct image held by the majority of stakeholders. For example, some students perceive some financial institutions (e.g. banks) as not particularly attractive for career progression or compatible with their own desired lifestyles. A targeted adjustment strategy would be necessary by the banks to alter this perception in order that they attract the necessary number of high-calibre graduates.

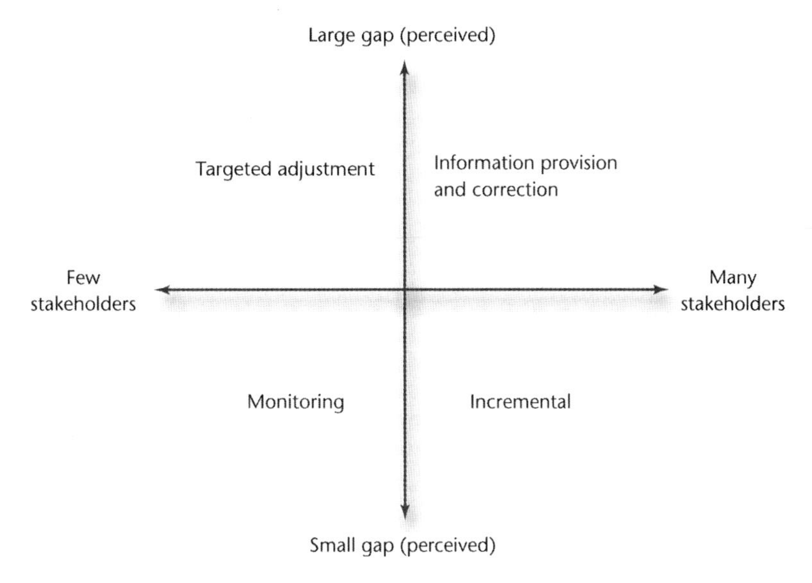

Figure 27.1 Corporate perception gap.

Should research uncover a small number of stakeholders holding a relatively small disparity between reality and image, a monitoring strategy would be appropriate and resources would be better deployed elsewhere. The best position would be if the majority of stakeholders perceived a small difference, in which case a maintenance strategy would be advisable and the good corporate communications continued. The natural extension of this approach is to use it as a base tool in the determination of the communication budget. Funds could be allocated according to the size of the perceived perception gap.

The reasons for the gap do not necessarily rest solely with stakeholders. If the image they hold is incorrect and the organisation's performance is good, then it is poor communications that are to blame, which are the fault of the organisation. If the image is correct and accurately reflects performance, then management must take the credit or the criticism for their performance as managers (Bernstein, 1984).

Management of the corporate identity

The first level denoted by Schein (1985) in his hierarchy of corporate culture concerns what are referred to as 'visible artefacts'. These are the more immediately observable aspects of the culture, such as the letterheads, logos and signage. This general view of corporate image is misplaced, and many graphic designers must accept partial responsibility for the popular misconception that the logo is the corporate image. This view is incorrect, as it fails to account for what the logo, other visible cues provided by organisations and the behaviour actually stand for, and from where they have been derived.

The image that stakeholders have of organisations is important for many reasons. They main ones are listed in Table 27.1, where it can be observed that the dimensions of corporate image are quite diverse.

Table 27.1 Dimensions of corporate identity

Dimension	
Relational dimension	Government, local community, employees, network members
Management dimension	Corporate goals, decision-making, knowledge, understanding
Product dimension	Product endorsement and support, promotional distinctiveness, competitive advantages

The relational dimension refers to the exchange of attitudes and perceptions with stakeholders of the organisation itself. As will be seen later, organisations consider who they are and what they would like to be and then project identity cues to those stakeholders who it is believed need to be informed. A more advanced understanding then allows for the adaptation of the organisation based upon the feedback or the dialogue thus created.

Management also benefit from corporate identity programmes as it encourages them to reflect upon the organisation's sense of purpose and then provides a decision framework for the decisions that they and others, perhaps functional managers, follow.

The final dimension refers to the advantages that a strong positive identity can give products and services. It is possible to develop more effective and efficient promotional programmes by focusing on the organisation's distinctiveness and then allow for the ripple to wash over the variety of offerings. Banks have traditionally used this approach, and car manufacturers have also partially attempted this strategy. Although the car marque is a very important decision determinant (e.g. Rover, Honda, BMW, VW, Nissan), it is common for particular models within the marque (brand) to be featured heavily.

The principal reason for managing the corporate identity is to make clear to all stakeholders what the values and beliefs of the organisation are and how it is striving to achieve its objectives. There are a number of secondary benefits, but these distil down to creating a supportive environment for the offerings, employees and external stakeholders associated with the focus organisation.

Abratt and Shee (1989) attempt to disentangle the confusion surrounding identity and image. They identify three main elements that are central to the development of corporate image (Figure 27.2). These are corporate personality, identity and image. Individuals and organisations project their personalities through their identity. The audience's perception of the identity is the image they have of the object, in this case, the corporate body.

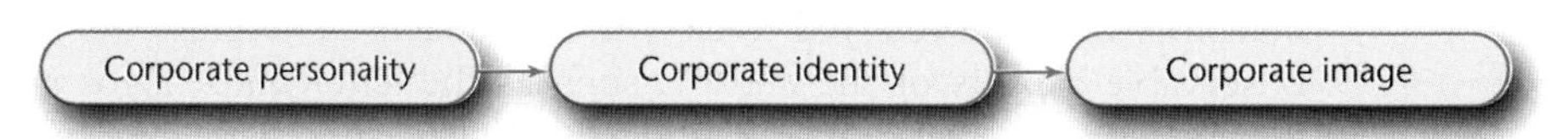

Figure 27.2 Elements of corporate identity (Abratt and Shee (1989); used with kind permission).

Corporate personality

The first of these elements requires the recognition and acceptance that organisations have personalities, or at least significant characteristics. As Bernstein (1984) states, just as individuals have personalities, so do organisations. Corporate personalities are derived partly from the cultural characteristics of the organisation: the core values and beliefs which in turn are part of a corporate philosophy. Essential to corporate personality is the strategy process adopted by the organisation. The degree to which the strategic process is either formalised and planned or informal and emergent, and whether strategy is well communicated, plays a major role in shaping the personality of the organisation.

For example, management now recognises the powerful influence that an organisation's corporate objectives have in informing and guiding the operations of each of the functional departments. The formulation of the mission statement requires management and employees to understand what the organisation seeks to achieve. To understand what the organisation wants to achieve means understanding what the organisation values and believes in, and this in turn involves and reflects the involvement of all members of the organisation, either deliberately or involuntarily.

The corporate personality can be considered to be composed of two main facets: the culture and overall strategic purpose (Markwick and Fill, 1997). Organisational culture is a composite of the various sectional interests and drives held by various key members. The blend of product offering, facilities, values and beliefs, staff, structure, skills and systems leads to the formation of particular characteristics or traits. Traits are rarely uniform in their dispersal throughout an organisation, so the way in which these interests are bound together impacts upon the form of the primary culture.

The strategic processes adopted by organisations are relatively constant because the roots of a process are embedded within the spectrum of organisational activities. Changing the strategic process is very different from changing the content of a strategy.

All members of an organisation, management and employees, are intertwined with the corporate personality; they are one and the same. The spirit and vigour with which all members of an organisation embody and articulate the mission is, according to Topalian (1984), a means by which the identity is shaped. The personality is embodied in the way the organisation carries out its business, the logic of its activities, the degree of persistence and aggression it displays in the markets in which it operates and the standards that are expected of all stakeholders.

Corporate personality is the totality of the characteristics which identify an organisation. Consider the values held by organisations such as Marks & Spencer, Hanson, Tesco, Oxfam, British Airways and Kwik-Fit. Not only are the images different but so are the values and the personalities.

IBM and Microsoft are interesting organisations to consider from a personality perspective. The turnover of IBM in 1995 was $70 billion, whereas that of Microsoft was $8.5 billion. Indeed, contrary to most people's perception, IBM, not Microsoft, is the world's largest provider of software.

IBM is a mature organisation where stability (or a return to stability) and security have long been regarded as important characteristics. Microsoft is young and vibrant, where innovation is seen as important.

Corporate personality is what an organisation actually is.

Corporate identity

The second element in the image process is corporate identity. This is the formation of the cues by which stakeholders can recognise and identify the organisation. Many

Corporate personality: British Airways

British Airways launched its new corporate identity in June 1997. It decided to inform its 58,000 staff around the world of the new identity prior to announcing it to the media and other stakeholders. At the time the organisation was seeking to cut £3 billion from its costs, so it was sensitive to the £60 million associated with the identity programme.

To cope with the change and minimise disquiet it was decided to inform staff via an internal communications programme codenamed 'The World's Biggest Secret'. The new BA wanted to be more open, interactive and less secretive. Mini-exhibitions, using video, 3D slides and virtual reality headsets were used to communicate the new identity to the entire staff in just three weeks. Each member of staff had to sign a confidentiality agreement and there were no pictures or photographs at the exhibitions which staff could take away. International staff were briefed by their managers, who flew into London and took back briefing documents.

The actual launch was held at noon GMT on 10 June 1997. It was an international affair where media representatives, travel agents, VIPs and staff watched a simultaneous global launch. Thirteen satellites were used to transmit pictures from 30 parties to 126 different audiences. As many staff as possible were included in the launch, which was hosted on the day by an ordinary member of staff to reflect the new global and caring culture that the launch was signalling. Indeed, the launch was used to signal a change in the way the organisation was to be seen by external audiences and also the way in which the organisation wanted to adapt its culture. In this way the corporate identity process can be regarded not as a reflection of the then current culture, but of what the staff (and eventually management) wanted the organisation to become. The corporate personality was in transition as management attempted to reshape the way in which the airline staff 'cared' and through them influence the way stakeholders perceived the airline.

Adapted from Curtis and Fields (1997)

organisations in recent years have chosen to pay more attention to their identity and have tried to manage these cues more deliberately.

Identity is a means by which the organisation can differentiate itself from other organisations. Bernstein (1984) makes an important point when he observes that all organisations have an identity, whether they like it or not. Some organisations choose to deliberately manage their identities, just as individuals choose not to frequent particular shops or restaurants, drive certain cars or wear specific fabrics or colours. Other organisations take less care over their identities and the way in which they transmit their identity cues, and as a result confuse and mislead members of their networks and underperform in the markets in which they operate.

According to Olins (1990a), management of the identity process can communicate three key ideas to its audiences. These are what the organisation is, what it does and how it does it. Corporate identity is manifested in four ways. These can be interpreted as the products and services that the organisation offers, where the offering is made or distributed, how the organisation communicates with stakeholders and, finally, how the organisation behaves (Olins, 1990b).

The marked development of the corporate brand has been noticeable in the 1990s. Organisations have used it as a means of differentiating their products from competitors' products, and have recognised the power of the characteristics which delineate one organisation from another. These characteristics are embodied by the organisation's personality, values and culture. The corporate brand is a means of presenting these characteristics to various audiences, such as financial markets, suppliers, employees, channel network partners, trade unions, competitors and customers.

There are three broad types of identity cues used by organisations, especially in the development of corporate brands; these are symbolism, behaviour and communication (Birkigt and Stadler, 1986).

Symbolism refers to the visual aspect and concerns the logo, letterhead and overall appearance of the design aspect associated with the company. The use of symbolism enables a level of harmonisation to be achieved by bringing together all of the identity cues.

The behavioural aspect is largely concerned with the way in which employees and managers interact with one another and, more importantly, with external members of the organisation. The tone of voice used and the actions and consideration of customer needs by employees are often represented within a customer service policy, which is as an important part of an organisation's interface with various stakeholder groups.

Communication is used to inform stakeholders quickly of episodes concerning products and the organisation. This is normally achieved through the use of visual and verbal messages. However, a broad use can be seen in communicating not only values but also the direction the organisation is heading and notable traits that the organisation wishes to inform its audiences of. For example, in the UK Volvos were seen as very safe but very dull cars driven by people who were similarly uninteresting. Communication was used to convey interest and excitement without the loss of the stable and important 'safe' attribute.

When considering the development of a corporate brand, the stewardship dimension needs also to be considered. This refers to the degree of importance that a company places on the development and maintenance of a corporate brand. The steward of the corporate brand is responsible for the consistency of the brand, in terms of the way it is presented, and for the way in which external members develop their images of the organisation. Vision and responsibility for this function often reside with 'the chairman but many companies who successfully take care of their corporate image also have one communications professional charged with the task' (Ferguson, 1996), operating at a very senior level within the organisation.

Much of this is an external perspective of identity, whereas much of the organisational behaviour literature sees identity as embedded within the organisation, with employees. Employees are members who sense identity and who are responsible for projecting their group identity to non-members, those outside the organisation. Identity develops through feelings about what is central, distinctive and enduring (Albert and Whetten, 1985) about the character of the organisation, drawn from the personality (see Chapter 11 for greater detail).

Corporate identity is the way the organisation presents itself to its stakeholders.

CASE ILLUSTRATION

Brand personality

This mini-case history has been written by Nigel Markwick, a former Portsmouth MBA student and now Project Manager at Wolf Olins.

Goldfish – the story so far

Goldfish provides an interesting case study because the brand was created so that it could be extended to cover a wide range of products and services. As such it provides some valuable insights into the creation of personality-based corporate brands. When initially launched, Goldfish offered a single product – a credit card. Since launch, the Goldfish brand has been applied to a number of other offers, all reflecting the Goldfish personality and values. This case study looks briefly at how the Goldfish brand was developed and what the personality is.

When Wolff Olins was first approached by British Gas to create a brand for a new credit card, our first reaction was 'the world isn't waiting for another credit card'. It was in this context that the Goldfish brand story starts.

The brief was to create a brand that would help launch British Gas into the world of retail financial services through a credit card, and then help it to maximise its potential in a number of new business areas where the British Gas name might not be applicable. As such, this new brand needed to have a sufficiently broad scope to allow extension into other diverse and as yet unconfirmed business opportunities.

For this reason the brand could not be simply based around a single product. Nor could it follow the pattern of other financial services if it was to be able to stand out from the crowd of hundreds of other financial service providers. The brand had to be extendible and provide a successful platform for the launch of the credit card.

Since the competitive edge could not come from the product alone, where could it come from? The answer lay in creating a brand based around personality rather than just product features. By doing this it was possible to create a distinctive brand in a very crowded 'me-too' market, evoking an emotional as well as a rational response.

An organisation's or brand's personality tells you something about 'who' you are dealing with. In the same way that the personality of an individual can be seen in how the individual behaves, the corporate or brand personality is evidenced in the behaviour of an organisation and gives an insight into its values – what it is that it stands for. The personality is also seen in the attitude and style that is adopted in communications. However, it must be more than just a glossy veneer – personality provides an insight into what the organisation is really like.

The personality for Goldfish was based around a notion of a new way of doing things, finding a clever and imaginative way of doing something that is better than that currently on offer. It is inclusive, with no boundaries – anyone should be able to associate with the Goldfish brand. It is simple and honest in the way that it talks and deals with its customers. It should have an element of surprise to it – who'd have thought of putting a fish on a credit card or calling it 'Goldfish'. (This led to the strapline 'You'll be surprised what you can do with a Goldfish'.)

The name Goldfish was chosen from a number of alternatives because it best reflected this personality. Goldfish are a familiar item in the UK – most people have had a goldfish in their homes or gardens at some stage during their lives or at least had friends who have had them. They are 'familiar' rather than 'common'. They are also beautiful, providing tremendous opportunities for distinctive creative work – important for both the design of the credit cards themselves and the associated advertising and direct mail activities (see Plate 27.2). Essentially they provide a splash of colour which was used extensively to distinguish the card from the competition.

The proposition for the credit card reflects the personality and uses the concept of 'saving as you spend' applied to home essentials, reinforcing the domestic associations of the brand. The loyalty programme for the card was based initially on money off your gas bill, but this was quickly expanded to include savings on food, DIY and even the TV licence. This emphasises the 'familiar' theme – most people have to pay a gas bill; everyone has to buy food. The loyalty programme reflects the Goldfish personality in that it is simple to understand – spend £1, gain one point, which is worth 1 penny off your gas bill.

In the case of Goldfish, the many aspects of the brand have been carefully integrated. The name, identity, credit card and communication designs and proposition have been created to align with the brand personality and values.

How successful has it been?

In its first year the Goldfish credit card attracted over half a million cardholders and achieved a brand awareness of over 70%. NOP confirmed Goldfish as the fastest growing credit card, with the highest net growth of new cardholders, exceeding that of the UK market leader, Barclaycard. Goldfish cardholders used their card more than three times the market average, indicating the strength of the product offer including the loyalty scheme.

And what of the brand personality?

Goldfish has been very successful as a single product brand. This is a result of the combination of the brand personality, design, communications and offer, including the loyalty scheme. The real test of the contribution of the brand personality to its success will be seen over the next few years as Goldfish extends to include other products and services. The link between the diverse business areas that Goldfish will operate in will be provided by how closely they align to the Goldfish personality and values. It will be interesting to follow how far the Goldfish brand will stretch over the next few years.

What is certain is that *you will be surprised what you can do with a Goldfish.*

Picture and material kindly supplied by Wolff Olins and Goldfish

Corporate image

The third and final element is corporate image. This is the perception that different audiences have of an organisation and results from the audience's interpretation of the cues presented by an organisation. As Bernstein (1984) says, 'the image does not exist in the organisation but in those that perceive the organisation'. This means that an organisation cannot change its image in a directly managed way, but it can change its identity. It is through the management of its identity that an organisation can influence the image held of it.

The image held of an organisation is the result of a particular combination of a number of different elements, but is essentially a distillation of the values, beliefs and attitudes that an individual or organisation has of the focus organisation. The images held by members of the distribution network, for example, may vary according to their individual experiences, and will almost certainly be different from those which management thinks exists. This means that an organisation does not have a single image, but may have multiple images.

For an image to be sustainable, the identity cues upon which the image is fashioned must be based on reality and reflect the values and beliefs of the organisation.

Images can be consistent, but are often based upon a limited amount of information. Images are prone to the halo effect, whereby stakeholders shape images based upon a small amount of information. The strategic credibility of Microsoft may be based largely on the image of Bill Gates rather than the current financial performance of Microsoft and the actual strategies being pursued by the organisation. Stakeholders extrapolate that Bill Gates has a high reputation for business success; therefore anything to do with Bill Gates is positive and likely to be successful.

Corporate image is what stakeholders perceive the organisation to be.

Corporate reputation

A deeper set of images comprise what is termed corporate reputation. This concept refers to an individual's reflection of the historical and accumulated impacts of previous identity cues, fashioned in some cases by near or actual transactional experiences. It is much harder and takes a lot longer to change reputation, whereas images may be influenced quite quickly. The latter is more transient and the former more embedded.

Fombrun (1996) claims that in order to build a favourable reputation four attributes need to be developed. These are credibility, trustworthiness, reliability and responsibility. Using these criteria it may be possible to speculate about the reputation developed by the food and clothing retailer, Marks & Spencer. Credibility is established through its products, which are perceived to be of high quality and have been branded. Trustworthiness has been developed through attention to customer service and workable refund policies. Reliability and consistency have been achieved by setting and adhering to particular standards of quality, and responsibility is verified through a strong ethical position and the values manifested through the company's strong customer service orientation.

Strategy and corporate identity/image

It is taken for granted that measurements of the perceptions that consumers have of brands and offerings are taken periodically. This practice varies with each organisation and industry, but the overall tendency is to take such measurements on an *ad hoc* basis. As well as measuring the strength of perception of the organisation's offerings, measurements should also be taken of the perceptions that stakeholders have of the organisation. It may be that the marketing communications have to realign perceptions of the organisation before new offerings can be launched successfully.

In Figure 27.3, the perceptions that customers have of four recruitment companies are presented. The axes used show the levels of awareness and attitude towards the service provided by each of the companies, and for the sake of discussion each company is depicted in one of the four quadrants. Recruitment company A is in the strongest position and its communications should be aimed at maintaining its current position. Recruitment company B is liked just as much as A, but only known to a limited audience. Work needs to be undertaken to improve levels of awareness by reaching a larger number of stakeholders. Recruitment company C, to those that are aware of it, is seen as a poor organisation, but fortunately only a few know about it. Management's task is to bring about improvements to their offering and delay informing stakeholders until the level of service is satisfactory. Recruitment company

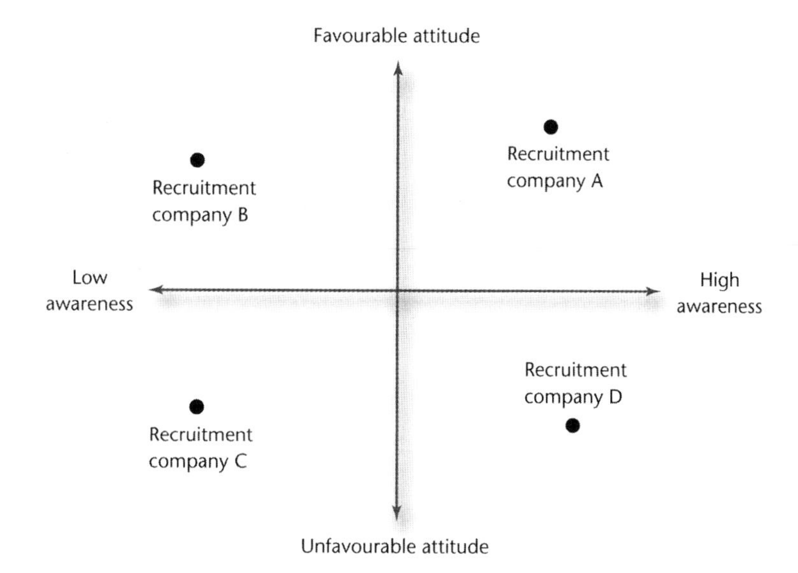

Figure 27.3 Images held by stakeholders of four recruitment companies (adapted from Barich and Kotler (1991) by permission of the publisher. Copyright 1991 by the Sloan Management Review Association. All rights reserved).

D is seen to suffer from poor service delivery and everyone knows about it. Management's task is to lower the level of awareness, or not actively increase it, and put right the service offering before seeking stakeholder attention.

This depiction is obviously a simplification, as corporate image is multidimensional (Dowling, 1986) and there is no single indicator that can adequately reflect the corporate personality. As different stakeholders will inevitably have different images, the measurement of corporate image is made difficult. Spector (1961) found that there are six main factors that account for the main dimensions that people use to articulate their image of an organisation. These are:

- Dynamic – pioneering, attention-getting, active, goal-orientated
- Cooperative – friendly, well liked, eager to please
- Business – wise, shrewd, persuasive, well organised
- Character – ethical, reputable and respectable
- Successful – financial performance, self-confidence
- Withdrawn – aloof, secretive, cautious

Spector points out that strength in one particular dimension may not be adequate, as the standard by which respondents make their judgements may be based upon an ideal or the dimension may be of little importance or significance.

In order to bring together the various aspects of corporate identity, Markwick and Fill (1997) have developed a framework entitled the corporate identity management process (CIMP) (Figure 27.4). This framework depicts the three main elements of the process: corporate personality, corporate identity and corporate image. In order for management to be able to use such a model there must be understanding of the linkages between the components. Just as the linkages in the value chain determine the extent of competitive advantage that may exist, so the linkages within the corporate

Identity and strategy: British Airways

The new corporate identity unveiled by British Airways in June 1997 was an attempt to communicate the new strategy of the airline. The variety and brightness of the new livery contrasted vividly with the royal crest, national flag and deep blue base colour which it replaced. The new design was intended to reflect the global identity that BA wanted to present, and by incorporating the colours of the Union Jack it tried to maintain a strong connection with the airline's national base. The old design reflected an affinity with royalty and nationalism that was used to herald the transition from public to private ownership. The new design reflects a multicultural nationality, more prominent and representative in the new millennium. With the airline seeking to appear more friendly and approachable, and with 50% of passengers coming from outside the UK, the 14-year-old design from Landor was no longer considered suitable, as it was too inflexible and introspective.

The mission and philosophy of BA was reviewed in the mid-1990s and was changed to 'become the undisputed leader in world travel'. With the company setting up travel products and photographic and financial services to complement the fresh goals, the new identity is a deeper and more appropriate reflection of the revised direction (and personality) of the organisation. Modern airlines are complex organisations. They are part hotelier, part travel agent, part entertainer, part ambassador, part financier, part engineer, part caterer and restauranteur, and part transporter and fulfiller of dreams. To satisfy these needs a single strong corporate brand is vitally important. British Airways had to move from being a British airline with global operations to a world airline whose headquarters happen to be in Britain (see Plate 27.3).

Adapted from BA literature and Marsh (1997)

identity process need to be understood in order to narrow the gap between reality and perception.

To assist with the linking process, van Riel's (1995) composition of corporate communication is used. These are marketing, management and organisational communication.

The first linkage is to transpose, through self-analysis, the corporate personality so that management, or those responsible for the management of the corporate identity, have a realistic perception of the corporate personality. This can be assumed to be what management thinks the personality is and the principal method is through management communication.

The second linkage is between corporate identity and the corporate image. In order that stakeholders are able to perceive and understand the organisation, the corporate identity is projected to them. The identity can be projected with orchestrated cues, planned and delivered to a timed schedule, or it can be projected as a series of random, uncoordinated events and observations. In virtually all cases, corporate identity cues are a mixture of the planned (e.g. literature, telephone style and ways of conducting business) and the unplanned (e.g. employees' comments, media views and product failures). The principal linkages are through organisation and marketing communications.

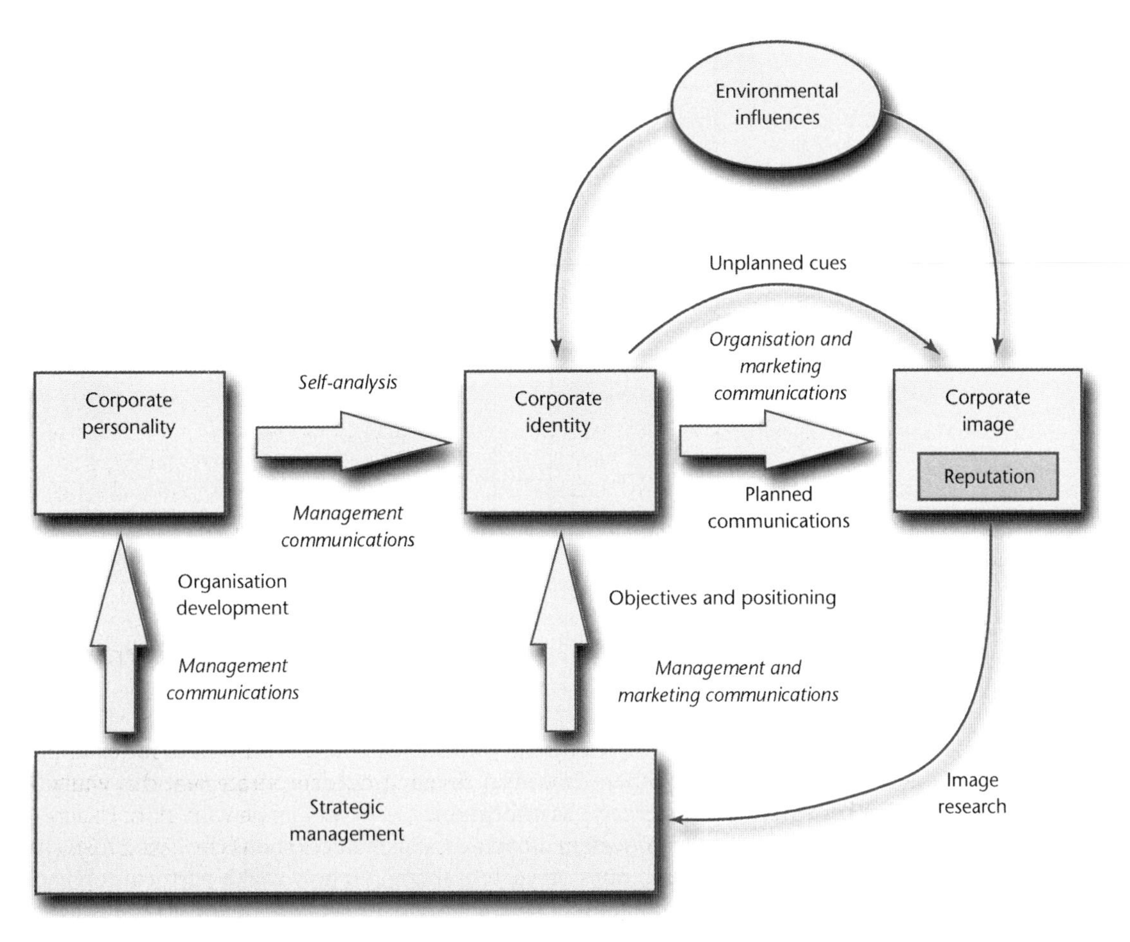

Figure 27.4 The corporate identity management process.

All organisations communicate all the time; everything they make, do, say or do not say is a form of communication. The totality of the way the organisation presents itself, and is visible, can be called its identity (Olins, 1990b). Corporate image is how stakeholders actually perceive the identity. It is, of course, unlikely that all stakeholders will hold the same image at any one point in time. Owing to the level of noise and the different experiences stakeholders have of an organisation, multiple images of an organisation are inevitable (Dowling, 1986). It is important that organisations monitor these images to ensure that the (corporate) position is maintained.

The third linkage is between the image that stakeholders have of an organisation and the corporate strategy formulation and implementation processes that an organisation adopts. This research-based linkage provides feedback and enables the organisation to adjust its personality and its identity, thus consequently affecting the cues presented to stakeholders. Image research is an important method of linking back into the strategy process.

The cues used to project the corporate identity are many and varied; some are controllable and others beyond the reach of management. These cues include the logo and letterheads, the way employees speak of the organisation, the buildings and architecture, the perception of the ability of the organisation to fulfil its obligations, its

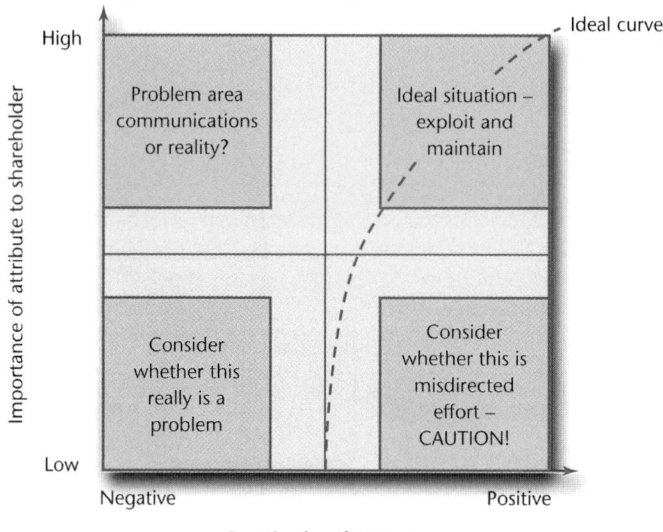

Figure 27.5 A two-dimensional attribute perception matrix (Markwick (1993); used with kind permission).

technical skills, prices, dress style and the way the telephone is answered, for example. Of all these and the many others, however, research needs to determine those attributes that key stakeholders perceive as important.

Having determined the important attributes, stakeholders should be asked to evaluate how well the organisation rates on each of them and how well it performs on each attribute in comparison with competitors. Figure 27.5 sets out the possible results of such research along two dimensions, the importance of the attribute to the stakeholder and the perceived performance of the organisation against the attribute. It can be seen that the ideal position lies to the right of the curve, and communication strategy should be aimed at achieving such a position. By introducing a third dimension, an evaluation of relative competitors against the same attributes, it is possible to determine a number of strategies that could lead to sustainable competitive advantage.

Stakeholder images can also be determined on three dimensions: the importance of attributes, organisational performance against the attributes, and performance with respect to competitors on the same attributes. A three-dimensional perception matrix (Figure 27.6) draws out the significant points. The ideal position occurs when high customer and competitor ratings are recorded for important attributes. When the attribute has a low level of importance it may be that the organisation's effort is misdirected, and management should reduce the effort spent on developing this image or seek alternative markets where this attribute has higher levels of importance. The worst position occurs when the organisation underperforms with respect to the customers' requirements and the competition on an attribute that is important. A change of strategy is required.

Effort should be concentrated on developing either corporate identity or personality in areas where the customer rating is poor and competitor rating is high on a factor that is important.

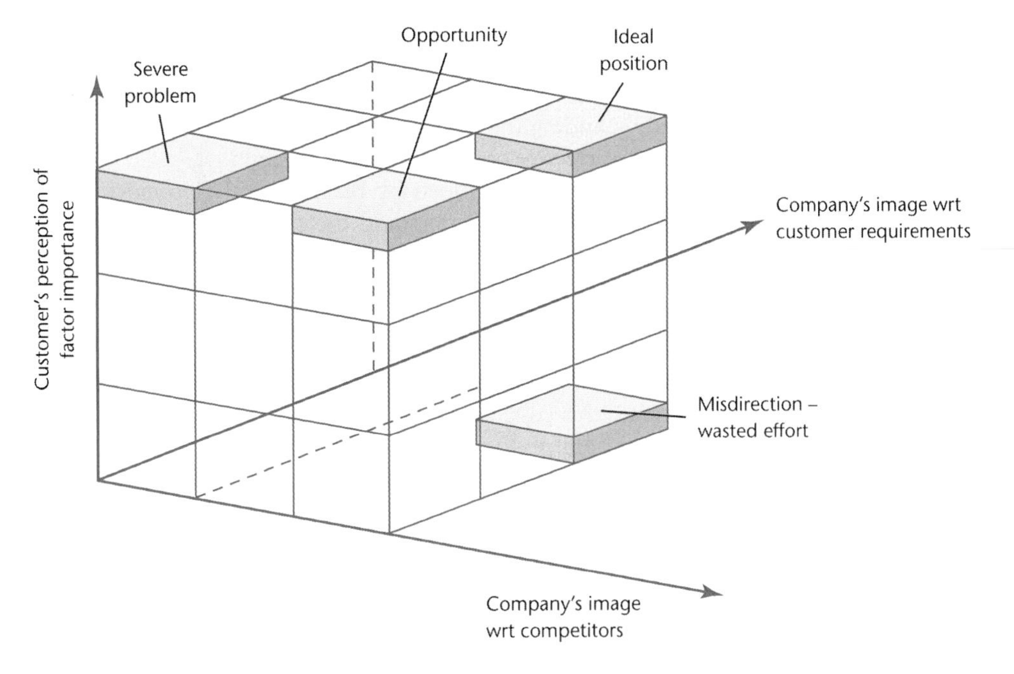

Figure 27.6 A three-dimensional attribute perception matrix (Markwick (1993); used with kind permission).

This model reveals that, by understanding the strength of images held by key stakeholders across attributes that are important to them, corrective action may be required to the personality and cues presented to stakeholders as part of the identity process. Strategic development therefore can result from an understanding of the images held about an organisation by its stakeholders.

Therefore, in order that the CIMP framework be complete, management are required to analyse and interpret the research data and then use management and marketing communications either to develop the personality or to provide adjusted corporate identity cues for positioning and goal-setting purposes.

It may be concluded that corporate identity is not a peripheral tool to be used *ad hoc*, but is a component that is central to the strategic management process. It should be used regularly by managers to understand how the organisation is being interpreted and understood by different stakeholders and to understand the essence of the organisation and whether the symbolic, behavioural and communication cues are contextually appropriate.

Network conflict

Corporate personality is a key part of the corporate image process. Just as individuals have personalities and behave in different ways, so organisations have personalities (or characteristics) and display a variety of behaviour patterns. Organisational behaviour in the collective form is partially a reflection of the events and accumulated experiences of the organisation. Part of the experience is the conflict encountered between members of the network. Successful corporate communications recognise conflict to be endemic. Conflict exists within each organisation and it also exists within the relationships that an organisation develops with its various stakeholders. While accepting that conflict need not be dysfunctional, organisations should not only seek ways of understanding the nature of any conflict but also attempt to reduce the level of any counterproductive conflict that may arise.

Transactional analysis (TA), developed by Berne (1966), provides a convenient and easy framework with which to understand the nature of conflict and indicates how conflict might be avoided or reduced in particular situations. TA also classifies behaviour into one of three groupings, each reflecting a particular state or source within the personality.

As seen in Chapter 4, Freudian theory suggests that the *ego* plays a central role in understanding personality. The ego represents reality and attempts to control the *id* and the *superego*. TA uses this psychoanalytical base to identify three ego states, each of which is roughly equivalent to the Freudian concepts. All three states are thought, by some, to exist within people, but one state may dominate. The three ego states are as follows:

1. *Child (id)* This state is characterised by very immature behaviour. The behaviour is either submissive and conforming or is insubordinate and emotional. Overall, an impulsive behaviour dominates.
2. *Adult (ego)* A rational and cool-headed approach to problems is likely to lead to logical choices being made. This behaviour is generally referred to as mature and is regarded as fair and objective.
3. *Parent (superego)* In this state behaviour is observed to be protective or critical. It is characterised by the need to establish boundaries or the parameters by which others can operate. Dominance and the setting of standards prevail.

Each ego state is composed of a series of playbacks or recordings derived from real experiences. The parent and child states are based upon experiences during the first five years of life. Everything a child's parents do and say is used by the child to develop a unique set of characteristics which will be used to form the future parent from within the child. The parent role can be 'critical' or 'nurturing'; both roles are taught (see Table 27.2). The adult role is thought to originate from the ability of the individual to discard the child and parent roles and to think in a rational and objective manner.

Here, the critical assumption is that an organisation can possess these three ego states rooted within a corporate personality. In individuals, these ego states can be observed in the gestures, tone of voice, expressions and reactions to others in our environment. Organisations can also be observed to gesticulate (Ratners, Asda), use particular styles (tones) of communication (Perrier, Peugeot, Marks & Spencer) and react in different ways to particular stimuli (Hanson, Lonrho, Glaxo). Note the way in which, for example, Tesco, Body Shop, NatWest, Virgin Atlantic and Boots express themselves and how the perceptions held of these organisations are a reflection of the reader's perception of each organisation's history and development.

Transactions

When a communication takes place a response is anticipated. The nature of these responses or *transactions* can be classified as complementary or crossed transactions.

Table 27.2 A classification of ego states

Ego state	Description	Derivation	Classification	Behaviour and verbal clues
Parent	Feeling what is proper, right and wrong. Provides discipline and protection. Dogma and control are evident.	First five years of life from external stimuli. Mainly parental stimuli. A recording of imposed unquestioned events.	*Critical parent* Critical, prejudicial, moralising or punitive *Nurturing parent* Nurturing, protective, sympathetic and comforting	Pointed finger – arms folded Head shaking – foot tapping Sighing – always, never, remember you ought to know better Pat on shoulder Consoling sound There, there, you poor thing, try again, don't worry
Adult	Gathering information. Evaluation, decision making in objective terms. Can review and monitor parent and child 'tapes'.	Begins to emerge at around 10 months old when the infant's capacity to see things in addition to the taught parent concepts and the feeling child concept.	That part of the individual that is rational and logical. This state thinks and reasons before acting.	Postures indicating interest listening and thinking. Why, what, where, when, who, how, alternatives, possible, probable, practical, feasible
Child	Part of the personality preserved from childhood. Reactions through emotions, angry, frightened, loving, carefree, adventurous, trusting and curious.	During first five years a recording of internal events take place. The feelings experienced as an infant could only be expressed as emotions.	*Natural* behaviour dictated by feelings. Impulsive, inquisitive, curious, affectionate, playful. Also fearful, self-centred and aggressive. *Adapted* toned down behaviour of natural to make it more acceptable to others.	Tears, tempers, tantrums, shoulder shrugging Look at me, nobody loves me, that's mine, can't, want, whoopee Giggling, teasing, flirting, pointing, whining Please, thank you, I wish, I'll try, I don't care, I don't know

Source: Walker and Bird (1984); used with kind permission.

Complementary transactions are achieved when a message sent from one particular ego state is reciprocated with a message from the same or expected ego state. For example, an outward adult message might be, 'the system appears to have broken down again'. An adult message in response might be 'Yes, because we have received too many orders in the last week'.

Crossed transactions are the source of a great deal of organisational conflict and occur when the message sent from a particular ego state is returned by a message from an unexpected ego state. For example, an outbound child message might be 'I wish the system wouldn't keep breaking down all the time'. A parent response could be 'Don't worry, it will be put right soon'. Crossed transactions mean that the intended communication has failed to be successfully decoded and can be regarded as ineffective.

TA can be used to understand interpersonal relationships better and its most obvious deployment is through direct selling, in terms of the promotion mix. However, there are a number of opportunities to use TA to understand the behaviour of organisations as they interact and communicate with their various stakeholders. Conflict is endemic within networks, and organisations may utilise TA as a useful means of observing and interpreting the actions of members, especially those of the channel leader.

Transactional analysis is useful as a means of understanding interpersonal relationships, as a means of developing new personal constructive behaviour patterns and as a means of understanding the way organisations communicate with their employees. An extension of this tool is to examine the manner in which organisations communicate with other organisations or stakeholders. Practical interpretations of TA are more easily observed in the specialist field of crisis management.

For example, Perrier, the mineral water brand leader, can be seen to display particularly good transactions with its UK stakeholders. It has been argued that because Perrier let each market handle the problem of contaminated water in its own way, consumers were getting different advice in different markets (Jones, 1994). However, once the contamination had been proved, there followed a slight hesitancy, presumably as it grasped the potency of the situation facing the company. It then transmitted a series of adult messages to its stakeholders, withdrawing all stocks from all world-wide locations. The response of distributors and retailers was equally adult, as they adhered to the demands of Perrier. It could also be argued that the response of their customers was equally adult, because Perrier soon recovered a large part of its European market share. Perrier was taken over by Nestlé in 1992, an indication of possible undervaluation and potential profitability within Perrier and the mineral water market.

An example of poor transactions can be observed in the EuroTunnel fire in November 1996. A fire broke out in Le Shuttle when a train was a few miles from the French end. The communications that followed from both the British and French representatives of the tunnel's managers were at times contradictory and palpably inaccurate. At one stage the public was informed that the tunnel would be closed for a few days, then weeks and then months. One statement said that it was unknown how long the tunnel would be closed or what the extent of the damage was. In contrast, the Chairman of British Midland Airways was quickly on the scene of the accident when a plane crashed on the M1 motorway in 1988, with over 40 fatalities. The Chairman's prompt appearance, acceptance of his organisation's involvement and concern for the victims and relatives can be interpreted as adult behaviour in transactional terminology. His actions were paramount in enabling the public to forgive British Midland and to ensure the continuity of the company.

Transactional analysis can be used to interpret the behaviour patterns of organisations, and if the observed behaviour is diagnosed as inappropriate a strategy can be developed to correct matters. TA provides a useful, if simple, insight into the form of the communications that exist between any two organisations or between an organisation and a range of stakeholders.

Organisations that appear to have a disproportionate number of crossed transactions will want to design a communications strategy that seeks to correct this type of imbalance. Likewise, those organisations that can be termed leaders will want to 'stroke' (a unit of recognition in TA language) certain other organisations in the network as often as possible, in order that their relationship be maintained and enhanced, which in theory, can lead to improved performance. Stroking can be seen in the form of increased discounts, seminars, joint promotional activities and various forms of corporate hospitality, aimed mainly at those individuals who work at the boundary of participant organisations.

Specialised networks embracing all key stakeholders

There are some messages that need to be distributed across all stakeholder networks, such as those proclaiming technological advances, business acquisitions and contracts won. It is also apparent that communication flows do not change radically over the short term. On the contrary, they become established and regularised through use. This allows for the emergence of specialised communication networks (Chapter 2). Furthermore, it is common for networks to be composed of sub-networks, overlaying each other. The complexity of an organisation's networks is such that unravelling each one would be dysfunctional; however, an understanding of the main forms of specialised network provides an opportunity to examine the content of the message carried.

Harold Guetzkow (1965) wrote a landmark paper on the nature of communications within organisations. Much of his work can be interpreted in the context of interorganisational and group communications. He identified five major types of network, based upon the content of the messages each network carries.

1. *Authority networks*
   These carry information in a unidirectional form, from higher to lower levels within the performance network. Authority networks are usually found within a VMS but can also be observed in non-integrated channels where the authority of the channel leader is such that procedures such as those for ordering, advertising, discounting and personal selling can be prescribed.
2. *Information exchange networks*
   In non-integrated relationships, information must flow throughout the network if coordination and the maintenance of the independent status of the members are to be maintained. This may be informal, but in most channel situations the network is formal and routinised. For example, professional and trade associations (e.g. the Association of British Pharmaceutical Industry, or the Federation of Master Builders) often provide their members with information about the 'business' or the particular environment within which they operate, often compiled from information generated by the membership!
3. *Task-expertise networks*
   These are typified by experts who cross over different hierarchical levels in the quest for a solution to a problem common to the market. The flow is bidirectional, as information has to be exchanged and disseminated at the conclusion. Examples include sales representatives selling complex offerings which require explanation and technical support on both a pre- and post-sales basis. Advertising and PR agencies and market research consultancies supply expert information and are members of the support network rather than the performance network.

4. *Friendship networks*
   Friendships may emerge as interaction through common activities develops. Those operating at the boundary of the organisation and dealing with others within the network may be able to provide information that otherwise was officially unavailable. Conferences often allow members on the same level of the channel to exchange information through a common bond of friendship.
5. *Status networks.*
   Messages may also be perceived to assign prestige to individuals and to the organisation they represent. Status may be determined by regulating who initiates and receives particular messages, and the messages themselves tend to be informal and symbolic.

Communication managers need to consider the specialised networks that may exist and develop those that are of potential benefit. Highly specialised networks may emerge to resolve particular issues and may keep out messages of friendship and loyalty.

There are costs associated with communication in these networks. These costs may be direct, in the form of dealer conferences and house magazines. Costs may also be indirect in nature. For example, the views of particular retailers or manufacturers' representatives may go unheard or unreported. These views might be critical to the development of particular markets and hence be of strategic importance.

An examination of the communication networks, perhaps through a channel-wide communication audit, will reveal the need to develop communication networks appropriate to the needs of each individual organisation and the performance network as a whole.

Summary

Communication strategies need to encompass the communication needs of all those other stakeholders, those other constituencies who might influence the organisation or be influenced by it. These approaches are referred to as Profile strategy and so completes the 3Ps for communication, Push, Pull and Profile.

Profile strategies are essentially concerned with the communication dialogue about the organisation itself rather than its products and/or services. The focus rests with the corporate body itself, who it is, what it is, what it is seeking to do and how it is important to other stakeholders.

At the root of this strategic approach is the notion of corporate identity. Organisations project themselves (as they want to be seen/understood) through a series of cues. These are then interpretated by stakeholders and used to create an image of the organisation. This corporate image may or may not be a correct interpretation of the organisation but this perception is an important one and must be treated seriously. Reputations develop from the image and can be seen to feed back to the Corporate Personality and impact upon the way members of an organisation think about themselves and determine what is central, distinctive and enduring.

Profile strategies are an important part of communication strategy and should be regarded as an integral part of any Integrated Marketing Communications approach (Chapter 29) that might be developed.

Review questions

1. Define corporate communications. What is a profile strategy?
2. Explain what a corporate brand is. How does it differ from a product brand?
3. What are the main facets of corporate personality?
4. Describe the personality or defining characteristics of five different organisations. What are their distinctive differences?
5. Prepare brief notes explaining what corporate identity is. Set out the differences between personality and identity.
6. Suggest ways in which planned and unplanned corporate identity cues are presented to stakeholders. Use an organisation with which you are familiar to illustrate your answer
7. What is corporate image and how does it differ from corporate identity?
8. Draw the CIMP model, paying particular attention to the linkages between the components.
9. Discuss the view that there is nothing intrinsically different between corporate image and reputation.
10. List the main features of transactional analysis. How might this approach assist marketing communications?

References

Abratt, R. and Shee, P.S.B. (1989) A new approach to the corporate image management process. *Journal of Marketing Management*, **5**(1), 63–76.

Albert, S. and Whetten, D.A. (1985) Organisational identity in *Research in Organisational Behaviour* (eds. L.L. Cummings and B.M. Straw). Greenwich CT: JT Press.

Barich, H. and Kotler, P. (1991) A framework for marketing image management. *Sloan Management Review*, **94** (Winter), 94–104.

Berne, E. (1966) *Games People Play: The Psychology of Human Relationships*. London: André Deutsch.

Bernstein, D. (1984) *Company Image and Reality: A Critique of Corporate Communications*. London: Holt, Rinehart & Winston.

Birkigt, K. and Stadler, M.M. (1986) Corporate identity, in van Riel, C.B.M. (1995) *Principles of Corporate Communication*. Hemel Hempstead: Prentice Hall.

Curtis, J. and Fields, L. (1997) Launched with flying colours. *Marketing*, 19 June, pp. 23–4.

Dowling, G.R. (1986) Measuring corporate images. *Industrial Marketing Management*, **15**, 109–15.

Dowling, G.R. (1993) Developing your company image into a corporate asset. *Long Range Planning*, **26**(2), 101–9.

Ferguson, J. (1996) The image. *Communicators in Business*, **9** (Summer), 11–14.

Fombrun, C. (1996) *Reputation: Realising Value from the Corporate Image*. Harvard: Harvard Business School Press.

Grunig, J. and Hunt, T. (1994) *Managing Public Relations*. New York: Holt, Rineholt & Winston.

Guetzkow, H. (1965) Communications in organisations, in *Handbook of Organisations* (ed. J.G. March). Chicago: Rand McNally & Co.

Ind, N. (1992) *The Corporate Image: Strategies for Effective Identity Programmes*. London: Kogan Page.

Jones, H. (1994) Nightmare on high street. *Marketing Week*, 16 September, pp. 28–30.

Markwick, N. (1993) Corporate image as an aid to strategic development. Unpublished MBA project, University of Portsmouth.

Markwick, N. and Fill, C. (1997) Towards a framework for managing corporate identity. *European Journal of Marketing*, **31** (5/6), 396–409.

Marsh, H. (1997) Why BA has designs on a global brand. *Marketing*, 12 June, pp. 16–17.

Olins, W. (1990a) Marketing guide: 15 corporate identity. *Marketing*, 12 April, pp. 21–4.

Olins, W. (1990b) *Corporate Identity: Making Business Strategy Visible Through Design*, London: Thames & Hudson.

van Riel, C.B.M. (1995) *Principles of Corporate Communication*. Hemel Hempstead: Prentice Hall.

Rowe, A.J., Mason, R.O., Dickel, K.E., Mann, R.B. and Mockler, R.J. (1994) *Strategic Management: A Methodological Approach*, 4th edn. Reading MA: Addision–Wesley.

Schein, E. H. (1985) *Organisational Culture and Leadership*. San Francisco: Jossey-Bass.

Spector, A.J. (1961) Basic dimensions of the corporate image. *Journal of Marketing*, 25 October, pp. 47–51.

Topalian, A. (1984) Corporate identity: beyond the visual overstatements. *International Journal of Advertising*, **3**, 55–62.

Walker, A.K. and Bird, A.M. (1984) *The First Principles of Medical Advertising*. Warner Lambert International, internal publication.

Wright, D. (1997) Comment: Halifax facts. *Sunday Times*, Money, 10 August, p. 2.

Marketing communications across borders

The management of marketing communications for audiences domiciled in two or more countries.

AIMS AND OBJECTIVES

The aim of this chapter is to examine the impact that cross-border business strategies might have on advertising agencies and marketing communications strategies.

The objectives of this chapter are:

1. To consider the development and variety of organisations operating across international borders.
2 To appraise different aspects of culture as a key variable affecting marketing communications.
3. To examine the media as a further important variable that can influence marketing communications strategy.
4. To discuss the adaptation vs. standardisation debate about advertising messages.
5. To explore the ways in which advertising agencies have developed to meet the international communication requirements of their clients.

Introduction

For organisations the differences between operating within home or domestic markets as compared with overseas or international markets are many and varied. Most of these differences can be considered within an economic, cultural, legal, technological and competitive framework. If the core characteristics of a home market (such as prices, marketing channels, finance, knowledge about customers, legislation, media and competitors) are compared with each of the same factors in the international markets which an organisation might be operating in, then the degree of complexity and uncertainty can be illuminated easily. Management might be conversant with the way of doing business at home, but as they move outside their country/regional borders areas which represent their domain of knowledge, understanding and to some extent security, so levels of control decline and risk increases.

The objective of this chapter is not to consider these particular characteristics, as time and space restrict scope. Readers interested in these issues are recommended to consult some of the many international marketing or business texts that are available. The goal of this chapter is to consider some of the issues that impact upon marketing communications when operating across international borders. To do this it is first necessary to consider the various environments and types of organisations that operate away from their home markets.

Types of cross-border organisation

Organisations can be regarded as international, multinational, global or transnational (Keegan, 1989; Bartlett and Ghoshal, 1991) and each form is a reflection of their structure and disposition towards its chosen markets (see Table 28.1).

International organisations evolve from national organisations whose origins are to serve national customers using domestic or 'home grown' resources. Some of these organisations, either by accident or design, begin to undertake a limited amount of work 'overseas'. They begin to become international, first by deploying their domestically orientated marketing mix and then later by adapting it to the needs of the new local 'overseas' market. This adaption phase signals the commencement of a *multinational strategy*. What distinguishes these organisations is that they regard the world (or their parts of it) as having discrete regions. Each country/area reports to a World Head Office, and performance is normally geared to meet financial targets.

Organisations at this stage in the evolutionary process are referred to as *global*. This is characterised by centralised decision-making, where, unlike in multinational companies, the similarities as well as the differences of each country/area are sought. Customers are seen on a global rather than a country/area basis.

Transnational organisations are an extension of global organisations. These sophisticated organisations seek to develop advantages based on efficiencies driven by serving global customers. Using technology as a key part of the infrastructure, networks allow resources to be globally derived in response to local requirements.

Organisations are far from static, and as domestic markets may stagnate and technology and communication opportunities in particular develop, so opportunities contract and expand. A further configuration reflects the need to be efficient and flexible in the organisation's use of materials and resources. The use of strategic alliances

Table 28.1 Organisational frameworks

International organisations	These organisations see their overseas operations as appendages or attachments to a central domestic organisation. The marketing policy is to serve customers domestically and then offer these same marketing mixes to other country/areas.
Multinational organisations	These organisations see their overseas activities as a portfolio of independent businesses. The policy is to serve customers with individually designed country/area marketing mixes.
Global organisations	These organisations regard their overseas activities as feeders or delivery tubes for a unified global market. The policy is to serve a global market with a single, fundamental marketing mix.
Transnational organisations	These organisations regard their overseas activities as a complex process of coordination and cooperation. The environment is regarded as one where decision-making is shared in a participatory manner. The policy is to serve global business environments using flexible global resources to formulate different global marketing mixes.

Source: Adapted from Bartlett and Ghoshal (1991) and de Mooij (1994).

and outsourcing arrangements complements this goal, and network organisations, spanning the globe, emerge.

Appreciating the different types of world-wide organisation is important, not just from a structural perspective but also for the formulation and implementation of business strategy. In addition to this, other issues concerning the products, markets and the marketing communications used by these organisations also surface.

Key variables affecting international marketing communications

There are a large number of variables that can impact upon the effectiveness of marketing communications which cross international borders. Many of these are controllable by either local or central management. However, there are a large number that are uncontrollable, and these variables need to be carefully considered before communications are attempted. The following variables (culture and media) are reviewed here because of their immediate and direct impact on organisations and their communication activities.

Culture

The values, beliefs, ideas, customs, actions and symbols that are learned by members of particular societies are referred to as culture. The importance of culture is that it provides individuals with identity and the direction of what is deemed to be acceptable behaviour. Culture is acquired through learning. If it were innate or instinctual, then everyone would behave in the same way. Human beings across the world do not behave uniformly or predictably. Therefore different cultures exist, and from this it is possible to visualise that there must be boundaries within which certain cultures, and hence behaviours and lifestyles, are permissible or even expected. These boundaries are not fixed rigidly, as this would suggest that cultures are static. They evolve and change as members of a society adjust to new technologies, government policies, changing values and demographic changes, to mention but a few dynamic variables.

Culture is passed from generation to generation. This is achieved through the family, religion, education and the media. These conduits of social behaviour and beliefs serve to provide consistency, stability and direction. The extent to which the media either move society forward or merely reflect its current values is a debate that reaches beyond the scope of the book. However, there can be no doubt as to the impact that the media have on society and the important part that religion plays in different cultures around the world.

Culture has multiple facets, and those that are of direct relevance to marketing communications are the values and beliefs associated with *symbols*, such as language and aesthetics; *institutions and groups*, such as those embracing the family, work, education, media and religion; and finally *values*, which according to Hofstede (1990) represent the core of culture. These will be looked at in turn.

Symbols

Language, through both the spoken and the non-spoken word, permits members of a society to enter into dialogue and to share meaning. Aesthetics, in the form of design and colour, forms an integral part of packaging, sales promotions and advertising. Those involved in personal selling must be aware of the symbolic impact of formal and informal dress codes and the impact that overall personal appearances and gestures, for example when greeting or leaving people, may have on people in different cultures. Advertisers need to take care that they do not infringe a culture's aesthetic codes when designing visuals or when translating copy into the local language.

Colour

Colours must be treated with care depending on the particular country where communications are being conducted. The colour of flowers can be used to illustrate this point. Purple flowers are associated with death and unhappiness in Brazil; white lilies have this association in Canada, Great Britain and Sweden; white and yellow lilies in Taiwan; and yellow lilies in Mexico. Yellow flowers stand for infidelity in France and disrespect for a woman in the (ex) Soviet Union.

Griffin (1993), p. 88

Institutions and groups

The various institutions which help form the fabric of societies and particular cultures provide a means by which culture is communicated and perpetuated through time. These groups provide the mechanisms by which the process of socialisation occurs. Of these groups, the family plays an important role. The form of the *family* is evolving in some western cultures, such that the traditional family unit is declining and the number of single-parent families is increasing. In many developing economies the extended family, with several generations living together, continues to be a central stable part of society. Marketing communication messages need to reflect these characteristics. The impact and importance of various decision-makers needs to be recognised and the central creative idea needs to be up-to-date and sensitive to the family unit.

Johnson & Johnson

Johnson & Johnson produced a global advertisement to introduce a new product. The advertisement depicted a mother with a new child which had been born in hospital. However, it was pointed out that women in Eastern Europe give birth at home and only go to hospital if there is something seriously wrong with either the mother or child. Associating a new product with serious illness was not considered a sensible strategy, and the commercial was withdrawn before release on the Polish market.

Campaign, 20 January 1995, p. 28

Work patterns vary across regions: not all cultures expect a 9 to 5 routine. This is breaking down in the UK as delayering pressurises employees to work increased hours, while in Asia-Pacific Saturday morning work is the norm.

Literacy levels can impact heavily on the ability of target audiences to understand and to ascribe meanings to marketing communication messages. The balance between visual and non-visual components in messages and the relative complexity of messages should be considered in the light of the education levels that different countries and regions have reached. In addition to these factors some target audiences in more developed economies have developed a high level of advertising sophistication. The meaning given to messages is in some part a reflection of the degree to which individuals understand commercial messages and what the source seeks to achieve. This high level of interaction with messages or advertising literacy suggests that advertisers need to create a dialogue with their audiences that recognises their cognitive processing abilities and does not seek to deceive or misinform.

Religion has always played an important part in shaping the values and attitudes of society. Links between religion and authority have been attempted based on the highly structured nature of religion and the influence that religion can play in the family, forming the gender decision-making roles and nurturing the child-rearing process. While the results of research are not conclusive there appears to be agreement that religion plays an important part in consumer buying behaviour and that marketing communications should take into account the level of religious beliefs held by the decision-maker (Delner, 1994).

Alcohol

Alcohol commercials face a variety of restrictions. In France all such advertisements are banned, while in the Czech Republic drink can be shown but it cannot be poured; nor can advertisements show people enjoying the product. In Mexico the restrictions state that food must be visible, whereas the Costa Ricans are allowed to see a glass being filled or the drink being poured ... but not both.

Similarly, mass communication technologies provide audiences with improved opportunities to understand and appreciate different religious beliefs and their associated rituals and artefacts, so care needs to be taken not to offend these groups with offensive or misinformed marketing communications.

Values

One of the most important international and culturally orientated research exercises was undertaken by Hofstede (1985, 1990). Using data gathered from IBM across 53 countries, Hofstede's research has had an important impact on our understanding of culture (Hickson and Pugh, 1995).

From this research, several dimensions of culture have been discerned. The first of these concerns the individualist/collectivist dimension. It is suggested that individualistic cultures emphasise individual goals and the need to empower, to progress and to be a good leader. Collectivist cultures emphasise good group membership and participation. Consequently, difficulties can arise when communications between these two types of culture have meanings ascribed to them that are derived from different contexts. To avoid the possible confusion and misunderstanding, an adapted communication strategy is advisable.

In addition to these challenges, comprehension (ascribed meaning) is further complicated by the language context. In high-context languages information is conveyed through who is speaking and their deportment and mannerisms. Content is inferred on the basis that it is implicit: it is known and does not need to be set out. This is unlike low-context languages, where information has to be detailed and 'spelled out' to avoid misunderstanding. Not surprisingly, therefore, when (marketing) communications occur across these contexts, inexperienced communicators may be either offended at the blunt approach of the other (of the low-context German or French for example) or intrigued by the lack of overt information being offered from the other (from the high-context Japanese or Asians for example).

A further cultural dimension concerns the role that authority plays in society. Two broad forms can be identified. In high-power-distance cultures authority figures are important and guide a high proportion of decisions that are made. In low-power-distance cultures people prefer to use cognitive processing and make reasoned decisions based on the information available. What might be deduced from this is that expert advice and clear, specific, recommendations should be offered to those in high-power-distance cultures, while information provision should be the goal of marketing communications to assist those in low-power-distance cultures (Zandpour and Harich, 1996).

People in different cultures can exhibit characteristics that suggest they feel threatened or destabilised by ambiguous situations or uncertainty. Those cultures that are more reliant on formal rules are said to have high levels of uncertainty avoidance. They need expert advice, so marketing communications that reflect these characteristics and are logical, clear and provide information in a direct and unambiguous way (in order to reduce uncertainty) are likely to be more successful.

From the adaptation/standardization perspective this information can be useful in order to determine the form of the most effective advertising messages. Zandpour and Harich used these cultural dimensions, together with an assessment of the advertising industry environment in each target country. The results of their research suggest that different countries are more receptive to messages that have high or low levels of logical, rational and information-based appeals (think). Other countries might be more receptive to psychological and dramatically based appeals (feel).

Pet food

Pet food advertisements are banned in Lithuania before 2300 hrs. The reason for this strict ruling is that food is scarce and this type of commercial could be considered offensive to humans.

Media

The rate of technological change has had a huge impact on the form and type of media that audiences can access. However, media availability is far from uniform, and the range and types of media vary considerably across countries. These media developments have been accompanied by a number of major structural changes to the industry and the way in which the industry is regulated. Many organisations (client brands, media and agencies) have attempted to grow through diversification and the development of international networks (organic growth and alliances), and there has been an increase in the level of concentration as a few organisations/individuals have begun to own and hence control larger proportions of the media industry. For example, Rupert Murdoch, Ted Turner, Time-Warner, Bertelsmann and Silvio Berlusconi now have substantial cross-ownership holdings of international media. This concentration is partly the result of the decisions of many governments to deregulate their control over the media and to create new trading relationships. As a result, this cross-ownership of the media (television, newspapers, magazines, cable, satellite, film, publishing, advertising, cinema, retailing, records) has created opportunities for client advertisers to have to go to only one media provider, who will then provide access to a raft of media across the globe. This facility, known as one-stop shopping, has been available in North America for some time, and was attempted by Saatchi & Saatchi and WPP in the 1980s from a European base, but it is only in the 1990s that this opportunity has been offered elsewhere.

Deregulation has had a profound impact on media provision in nearly all parts of the world. In Korea, for example, the number of daily newspapers has grown from 60 in 1988 to 125 in 1996, while the number of television channels has grown from 3 to 4

Table 28.2 General trends in worldwide media

- Electronic media expenditures have grown at the expense of print.
- The world-wide adspend on newspapers has fallen considerably.
- The number of general interest magazines has fallen and the number of specialist interest magazines has grown.
- The growth of satellite facilities has helped generate the development of television and cable networks.
- Television programming and distribution have become more important.
- Out-of-home media, in particular outdoor and alternative new media (e.g. ambient), have grown significantly.

Source: Based on de Mooij (1994).

terrestrial channels plus 26 cable services and one satellite broadcaster (Kilburn, 1996).

Table 28.2 sets out some of the more general world-wide trends in advertising media. The net impact of all these changes has been principally the emergence of satellite television and cable provision and the development of the international consumer press.

Cross-border communication strategy

The degree to which organisations should adapt their external messages to suit local or regional country requirements has been a source of debate since Levitt (1983) published his landmark work on global branding. The standardisation/adaptation issue is unlikely to be resolved, yet is an intuitively interesting and thought-provoking subject. The cost savings associated with standardisation policies are attractive and, when these are combined with the opportunity to improve message consistency, communication effectiveness and other internally related efficiencies such as staff morale, cohesion and organisational identity, the argument in favour of standardisation seems difficult to renounce. However, in practice there are very few brands that are truly global. Some, such as McDonald's, Coca-Cola and Levi's are able to capitalise upon the identification and inherent brand value that they have been able to establish across cultures. The majority of brands lack this depth of personality, and because individual needs vary across cultures so enterprises need to retune their messages in order that their reception is as clear and distinct as possible.

The arguments in favour of adapting messages to meet the needs of particular local and/or regional needs are as follows:

1. Consumer needs are different and vary in intensity. Assuming there are particular advertising stimuli that can be identified as having universal appeal, it is unlikely that buyers across international borders share similar experiences, abilities and potential either to process information in a standardised way or to ascribe similar sets of meanings to the stimuli they perceive. Ideas and message concepts generated centrally may be inappropriate for local markets.
2. The infrastructure necessary to support the conveyance of standardised messages varies considerably, not only across but often within broad country areas.
3. Educational levels are far from consistent. This means that buyers' ability to give meaning to messages will vary. Similarly, there will be differing capacities to

process information, so that the complexity of message content has to be kept low if universal dissemination is to be successful.

4. The means by which marketing communications are controlled in different countries is a reflection of the prevailing local economic, cultural and political conditions. The balance between voluntary controls through self-regulation and state control through legislation is partly a testimony to the degree of economic and political maturity that exists. This means that what might be regarded as acceptable marketing communication activities in one country may be unacceptable in another. For example, cold calling is not permissible in Germany and, although not popular with either sales personnel or buyers, is allowed in the Netherlands and France.
5. Local management of the implementation of standardised, centrally determined messages may be jeopardised because of a lack of ownership. Messages crafted by local 'craftsmen' to suit the needs of local markets may receive increased levels of support and motivation:

Just as the arguments for adaptation appear convincing at first glance, then so do those in favour of standardisation:

1. Despite geographical dispersion, buyers in many product categories have a number of similar characteristics. This can be supported by the various psychographic typologies that have been developed by advertising agencies for their clients. As brand images and propositions are capable of universal meaning, there is little reason to develop a myriad of brand messages.
2. Many locally driven campaigns are regarded as being of poor quality, if only because of the lack of local resources, experiences and expertise (Harris, 1996). It is better to control the total process and at the same time help exploit the opportunities for competitive advantage through shared competencies.
3. As media, technology and international travel opportunities impact upon increasing numbers of people, so a standardised message for certain offerings allows for a strong brand image to be developed.
4. Just as local management might favour local campaigns, so central management might prefer the ease with which they can implement and control a standardised campaign. This frees local managers to concentrate on managing the campaign and removes from them the responsibility of generating creative ideas and associated issues with local advertising agencies.
5. Following on from this point is one of the more enduring and managerially appealing ideas. The economies of scale that can be gained across packaging, media buying and advertising message creation and production can be enormous. In addition, the prospect of message consistency and horizontally integrated campaigns across borders is quite compelling. Buzzell (1968) argued that these economies of scale would also improve levels of profitability.

Hite and Fraser (1988) argue that the evidence indicates that, although organisations pursued standardisation strategies in the 1970s, the trend since then has been towards more local adaptation. Harris makes the point that, although the operation of a purely standardised programme is considered desirable, there is no evidence to suggest that standardisation actually works. There appears to have been little research to compare the performance of advertising that has been developed and implemented under standardisation policies with that executed under locally derived communications.

However, while a few organisations do operate at either end of the spectrum, the majority prefer a contingency approach. This means that there is a degree of standardisation, where for example creative themes, ideas and campaign planning are driven centrally and other campaign elements such as language, scenes and models are adapted to the needs of the local environment. The cosmetic manufacturer L'Oréal distributes its Studio Line of hair care products aimed at 18–35-year-olds across 50 countries. 'These are the same products with the same formulation with the same attitudinal message of personal choice' (Sennett, in Kaplan, 1994). All the advertisements have the same positioning intentions, which are developed centrally, but the executions (featuring different hairstyles) are produced locally to reflect the different needs of different markets.

IBM

In 1994 IBM sacked all of its 42 world-wide advertising agencies and gave the entire account to Ogilvy & Mather. Previously, the marketing strategy had been fragmented and there was a 'cacophony' of competing campaigns, as quoted by a senior IBM executive.

The new strategy reconfigured the marketing and sales operations into 14 teams, managed on a European and world-wide basis, targeted at vertical markets (e.g. banking, brewing, insurance industries). The new advertising campaign, 'solutions for a small planet' (Exhibit 28.1), sought to deliver a single, unified message. All the commercials, run in 40 countries over five continents, feature people speaking their native language with subtitles geared to the viewing audience (see Plate 28.1).

The creative was generated by a team based in New York, with creative input from Los Angeles and Singapore. In other words, rather than develop a campaign centrally, O&M have moved to a coordinated approach, complementing IBM's move to transnational status.

Taylor (1995)

Exhibit 28.1 IBM campaign – Solutions for a small planet (pictures reproduced with kind permission of IBM UK Ltd).

The reasons for some form of standardisation are twofold. First, there is an increasing need for improved levels of internal efficiency (and accountability) in terms of resource usage. Secondly, there is an increasing awareness of the benefits that standardised advertising may have on organisational identity, employee morale and satisfaction. The pressure to make cost savings and to develop internal efficiencies, therefore, appears to override the needs of the market.

Coca-Cola

A variation on the 'think global, act local' approach is demonstrated by Coca-Cola. The organisation develops advertisements centrally, in Atlanta, and then offers them to regional companies to use as they wish. For example, a campaign generated in April 1997 consisted of 16 different advertisements, each targeted at different audiences.

Regional companies can use them if they wish or use locally generated campaigns. Atlanta has the final say on whether they are run, and even requires these other campaigns to be developed by one of the 30 world-wide roster agencies. However, the flexibility is offered for regional companies even though brand strategy and campaign briefs are developed centrally.

Adapted from Martin (1997)

However, those who argue in favour of standardisation need to be aware that the information content will often need to be correspondingly low. Mueller (1991) observes that the greater the amount of information the greater the opportunity for buyers to discriminate among alternative purchases. Conversely, the emphasis with uninformative advertising is to use imagery and indirect (peripheral) cues. Multinational organisations prepare individual marketing mixes for individual countries/areas. Products and prices will be different, so comparisons are difficult. Likewise, key attributes will vary across countries/areas, so this means that organisations need to decide whether high levels of standardisation and low levels of information are preferred to adapted campaigns with higher levels of information content.

The criterion by which organisations should decide whether to adapt or standardise their marketing (communications) activities is normally the impact that the different strategies are likely to have on profit performance (Buzzell, 1968). The basis for these financial projections has to be a suitably sensitive segmentation analysis based on a layering of segment information. Country-only or arbitrary regional analysis is unlikely to be suitable. Cross-cultural and psychographic data need to be superimposed to provide the richness upon which to build effective communications.

Organisations rarely decide on a polarised strategy of total adaptation or complete standardisation. In practice, a policy of 'glocalisation' seems to be preferred. Under this approach, organisations develop standard messages centrally but expect the local country areas to adapt them to meet local cultural needs by adjusting for language and media components. There are, of course, variations on this theme. For example, Head Office might decide on the strategic direction and thrust of the campaign and leave the local country management to produce its own creatives.

International advertising agencies

Just as many organisations have sought to expand internationally, so many advertising agencies have attempted to grow with their clients. This process has gathered speed in the 1980s and 1990s, with varying levels of success. By trying to mirror client/brand needs and by expanding operations over increased geographic areas, organisations have experienced many financial and management challenges. These challenges have been met with varying degrees of success. The consequences of this 'natural' development are that aspects such as the structure of the industry, the configuration and work patterns of constituent agencies, the relationships between clients and advertisers and the form of advertising messages that are developed and given meaning by target audiences and agencies alike have evolved.

Agency development overseas

Operating overseas is not a recent phenomenon for advertising agencies. This strategy has been established for many decades. There are three primary routes that agencies have taken to secure international growth. These are *organic growth* through the creation of overseas subsidiaries, *acquisitive growth* through the purchase of established indigenous agencies and finally *cooperative growth*, where agencies collaborate through the formation of networks and strategic alliances.

Organic growth requires the setting up of subsidiary offices in selected regions or countries. Costs and management can be controlled, but the relatively slow speed of development has deterred many from this approach. *Acquisitive growth*, involving the merger with or purchase of advertising agencies already operating in the required market, is attractive because it is possible to use the skills and established contacts of local managers. However, these overseas operations are relatively inflexible and can incur considerable overheads as well as high initial purchase costs. *Cooperative growth* through strategic alliances and partnerships, often as part of global networks, can appear to be a more flexible and efficient approach to meeting a client's international marketing communications requirements. One of the potential problems with this approach is that the level of control over local actions can be reduced, but the reduced costs and increased speed of setup and delivery make this an attractive option.

A further variation of this method of expansion is the formation of networks of independent agencies. By contributing to a central financial fund, so giving the network a formal legal status, agencies are able to work together and provide flexibility for their clients.

International agency networks can provide clients with a number of advantages. Primarily these focus on two main areas: resource utilisation and communication effectiveness.

Resource utilisation

1. Clients and agencies help each other by avoiding costly duplication of message development work and media buying.
2. Economies of scale can reduce costs for both parties.
3. By centralising decision-making, management have increased control over the direction of campaigns and their implementation such that clients have a single main point of contact.

4. Special resources and scarce creative expertise is made available to a client globally.

Communication effectiveness

1. Creative ideas from all parts of the network can be shared and, if a largely adaptive strategy is followed, good ideas can be replicated elsewhere. Good creative ideas are rare, so by using an international agency these highly prized gems can used to the client's benefit world-wide.
2. Internal communications are improved by a common infrastructure and management information system.
3. By using a single agency operating across many markets, feedback and market analyses can be standardised (process, timing and format), thus facilitating common reporting and fast feedback of audience and competitor actions.

Freeman (1996) argues that, as manufacturers are re-evaluating the way in which they approach their customers, changes are also being brought about at business-to-business advertising agencies. Rapid technological advances in communications, global marketing of brands, shorter purchase decision-making cycles and heightened competition are forcing agencies to re-evaluate their internal organization and communications strategies. This, he suggests, has already led to a number of mergers with larger organizations and internal reorganization to better handle clients' needs.

Agency growth

The expansion of advertising agencies away from domestic markets is essentially an investment decision in which normal return on investment criteria need to be determined. Such decisions can be based upon the relative size of competitive advantage that an expanded operation might generate. Multinational agencies (MNAs) might be able to develop key advantages, such as size, access to capital, the loyalty given to them by multinational advertisers, their knowledge and skill, and their ability to use their foreign locations to service regional markets (West, 1996). Some of the growth has been motivated by the need to meet the expanding international requirements of clients. Kim (1995) cites Procter & Gamble's entry into Eastern Europe and the subsequent opening of offices in the same area by its adverting agency, Leo Burnett. Offensive and defensive business strategies, to either capitalise on or counter competitor moves, can also be regarded as prime motivating factors.

A further explanation lies with the motivations of individual managers, or agency theory. This perspective suggests that managers seek growth in order to fulfil personal needs rather than those that may be in the best interests of the organisation. These advantages nevertheless have little distinguishing power if the MNA itself is unable to coordinate its activities and lever its resources to provide client benefits of speed, creativity and media purchasing power.

Some implications of international growth

Many advertisers have been comfortable with the way in which advertising agencies have attempted to build European and international networks to complement their own global branding initiatives. There is some evidence, however, that this one-stop

CASE ILLUSTRATION

Samsung Electronics Company

Samsung Electronics is a major Korean business organisation which was founded in 1969. Because of the nature and size of the Korean market, Samsung's principal activities were export-focused from the beginning, so the time spent developing in domestic markets was not typical of many organisations in developed western economies.

International stage

OEM-branded exporting dominated Samsung's business activities, as this provided a convenient and less risky form of rapidly improving export volumes and cash flow. Until 1977 an Export Department was responsible for routine matters of shipping and courting foreign buyers. From this date an International Department was created, as a more sophisticated approach was adopted, to perform market research, some product development and overseas demand forecasting. Several foreign branches were created to encourage communication with foreign buyers, and full-scale export marketing communications, with advertising, sales promotions and exhibitions, were commenced.

Corporate messages sought to establish the size and capabilities of Samsung and were targeted at importers and OEM manufacturers. Product-based messages emphasised particular brands and were targeted at distributors and dealers in the USA, Europe, Asia, the Middle East and Central and South America.

However, the product range that Samsung offered evolved during this period so that the locus moved from televisions, radios and cassette players to microwaves and VCRs. This shift meant that Samsung had to adjust the messages it conveyed in order that the company be perceived as technologically progressive. In order to accomplish this it adopted a corporate identity programme.

Multinational stage

This signalled the commencement of the multinational stage in Samsung's development. The message was developed centrally and the same message (standardisation) was then communicated throughout all of the markets in which Samsung was active.

Trade restraints imposed by many economies led to a change in the organisation's corporate strategy. Market penetration could now only be achieved by setting up subsidiary companies in the markets in which it wished to operate. This meant that nationals with local knowledge were required to head each of these new SBUs.

The OEM emphasis gave way to own-branded exports, and, in order to support the local distribution channels and dealers, provincial marketing communications began to proliferate. Head Office developed and implemented corporate communication messages and local offices (and agencies) developed product-based communications. Problems were encountered when attempting to harmonise the company awareness campaign with the vagaries of media availability in some of the markets. The 'low-cost, high-quality' message was now targeted at consumers rather than dealers, but difficulties were encountered in getting access to appropriate media. The net result of this was that uncoordinated promotional work ensued, which was relatively ineffective in achieving its goals.

Global stage

Samsung needed to change its corporate strategy, as it was unable to continue competing on a low-cost basis, due mainly to competitors' relocation of their production facilities and the increasing labour costs in Korea. By reducing the OEM activity and promoting its own high-quality brands, Samsung was better positioned to achieve one its goals of becoming one of the world's top five electronics companies.

Corporate profitability had fallen despite increased sales revenues. The company strategy highlighted the need to coordinate its activities across the group and to reduce duplication and unnecessary investments.

The group's promotional activities were also overhauled. A coordinated global corporate and brand identity programme was established with the goal of allowing its global consumers to differentiate Samsung. Korean advertising agencies were internationalising themselves either through the establishment of overseas offices or by entering into alliances with other agencies that gave them access to global networks.

Transnational stage

It is perhaps too early to establish whether a move to transnational status has been accomplished, but it seems that Samsung might be evolving toward this form.

Adapted from Cho *et al.* (1994)

shopping approach is not entirely satisfactory (*Economist*, 1996). Some client organisations want access to a range of creative teams and also want the benefits of consolidation at the same time. The response of some MNAs has been to reorganise internally. Many of the megamergers between major agency networks have resulted in further structural changes as agencies shed accounts that cause conflicts of interest. Those clients caught up in the restructuring and consequent consolidation of the industry may well regard themselves as unwitting participants.

The relatively new position of World-wide Account Director (Farrell, 1996) is an attempt to coordinate and control the global accounts of clients such as IBM and Reebok who have centralised their international advertising activities. Another role that has emerged is that of the World-wide Creative Director (Davies, 1996). This position, it is suggested, has developed directly from clients' expectations for their agency networks to mirror their own global branding drives and management structures. But, as Martin (1996) points out, as these World-wide Creative Directors are invariably appointed with no department or resources, and are inclined to meet resistance from local management teams, the position appears to be irrelevant and impotent.

Media planning has become increasingly difficult, as not only has the provision of media services in particular regions (e.g. Asia) expanded rapidly, but at the same time there have been major social changes. Kilburn (1996) reports that in Taiwan, Ogilvy & Mather and J. Walter Thompson have formed The Media Partnership from their respective media buying operations, thus providing increased buying power for their clients in what is effectively a fragmented market.

Agency structures are evolving and adapting to the needs of their environments. The traditional perspective of control by Head Office executives over the work of local network agencies, either by a disproportionate level of standardisation policies or by rather inflexible procedures that put bureaucratic needs before market requirements, is changing. Instead of control, coordination is one of the keys to competitive advantage in MNA/agency relationships. The one factor that distinguishes transnational organisations applies equally to advertising agencies. As Banerjee (1994) suggests, agency decision-making concerning the development of major multi-

Table 28.3 Strategies associated with international advertising development

	Home	International	Multinational	Global	Transnational
Advertising stage	Domestic	Export	Multinational	Global	Transnational
Key message	Product or brand	Product and corporate	Corporate and brand	Corporate and brand	Corporate and/ or brand
Management	Standardisation	Standardisation	Standardisation and adaptation	Regional adaptation	Global adaptation
Management structure/support	Centralised	Centralised	Decentralised	Grouped centralisation	Network
Agency	Domestic	Domestic	Domestic and foreign local	Global	Transnational network

country brands will need to be collaborative in the future as 'agency power structures evolve to better reflect emerging revenue geographies'.

Stages of cross-border advertising development

Cho *et al.* (1994) propose a framework whereby the type of advertising deployed can be considered in the context of the stage of internationalisation that organisations have reached. Based upon studies of Korean firms, the authors propose that the advertising strategy is (or should be) a direct reflection of the marketing and business strategies employed. Therefore:

Domestic marketing	=	Domestic advertising
Export marketing	=	Export advertising
Multinational marketing	=	Multinational advertising
Global marketing	=	Global advertising

From this, and utilising the information about international development, it is possible to establish the key characteristics and strategies associated with each stage of international growth (Table 28.3).

Summary

As organisations saturate domestic markets and seek growth opportunities overseas, so they meet new challenges and embark upon fresh strategies. Organisations operating across a number of international and/or regional borders evolve through international, multinational, global and transnational phases and forms. The differentiating characteristics appear pronounced and convincing as growth drivers impel development.

Two of the main variables that impact upon the marketing communications deployed by organisations across these different forms are culture and the media. Culture is a composite of a number of elements, ranging from symbols such as language, groups and education, through values represented in language context and power distance.

The media are also significant drivers which have been influenced by both technological drivers and political initiatives to deregulate and open up accessibility.

The strategies used to communicate with cross-border audiences focus upon either standardisation or total adaptation to the needs of the local audience. While the debate is interesting and practice varied, the evidence suggests that a mixture of the two approaches, glocalisation, is the preferred practice of many global and transnational organisations.

Advertising agencies have had to respond to the initiatives driven by their clients. Global advertising agency development has taken a variety of forms; however, there appears to be a match between the marketing strategies pursed by client organisations and the consequent advertising strategies to support them.

Review questions

1. There are four types of organisation reflecting their structure and disposition to their markets. Name them and their key characteristics.
2. Prepare some brief notes explaining how culture impacts upon an organisation's marketing communications.
3. Select two countries of your choice. Compare the significance of cultural symbols and provide examples of how these are used.
4. Explain high- and low-context languages.
5. Discuss how deregulation of media ownership has affected marketing communications.
6. You have been asked to make a presentation to senior managers on the advantages and disadvantages of standardising the marketing messages delivered for your brand throughout the world. Prepare notes for each of the slides you will use.
7. Evaluate the different ways in which advertising agencies can grow.
8. International advertising agencies provide resource utilisation and communication effectiveness as their main advantages. Explain the detail associated with these two characteristics.
9. Determine the four stages of cross-border advertising development.
10. What are the key differences between each of the these four stages?

References

Banerjee, A. (1994) Transnational advertising development and management: an account planning approach and a process framework. *International Journal of Advertising*, **13**, 95–124.

Bartlett, C. and Ghoshal, S. (1991) *Managing Across Borders: The Transnational Solution.* Cambridge MA: Harvard Business School Press.

Buzzell, R. (1968) Can You Standardise Multinational Marketing? *Harvard Business Review*, **46** (November/December), 102–13.

Cho, D-S., Choi, J. and Yi, Y. (1994) International advertising strategies by NIC multinationals: the case of a Korean firm. *International Journal of Advertising*, **13**, 77–92.

Davies, J. (1996) The rise of the super-creative. *Campaign*, 1 November, p. 18.

Delner, N. (1994) Religious contrast in consumer decision behaviour patterns: their dimensions and marketing implications. *European Journal of Marketing*, **28**(5), 36–53.

Economist (1996) A passion for variety. *Economist*, 30 November, pp. 68–71; UK, pp. 104–7.

Farrell, G. (1996) Suits: the world is their ad oyster. *Adweek*, **37**(8), 29–33.

Freeman, L. (1996) Client-driven change alters agency strategies. *Advertising Age – Business Marketing*, **81**(2), 1–20.

Griffen, T. (1993) *International Marketing Communications*. Butterworth Heinemann.

Harris, G. (1996) International advertising: developmental and implementational issues. *Journal of Marketing Management*, **12**, 551–60.

Hickson D.J. and Pugh, D.S. (1995) *Management Worldwide*. London: Penguin.

Hite, R.E. and Fraser, C. (1988) International advertising strategies of multinational corporations. *Journal of Advertising Research*, **28** (August/September), 9–17.

Hofstede, G. (1980) *Culture's Consequences: International Differences in Work Related Values*. Sage.

Hofstede, G. (1991) *Cultures and Organisations*. London: McGraw-Hill.

Hofstede, G., Neuijen, B., Ohayv, D.D. and Sanders, G. (1990) Measuring organisational cultures: a qualitative and quantitative study across twenty cases. *Administrative Science Quarterly*, **35**(2), 286–316.

Kaplan, R. (1994) Ad agencies take on the world. *International Management* (April), 50–2.

Keegan, W.J. (1989) *Global Marketing Management*. Englewood Cliffs NJ: Prentice Hall.

Kilburn, D. (1996) Asia rising. *Adweek*, **37**(34), 22–6.

Kim, K.K. (1995) Spreading the net: the consolidation process of large transnational advertising agencies in the 1980s and early 1990s. *International Journal of Advertising*, **14**, 195–217.

Levitt, T. (1983) The globalization of markets. *Harvard Business Review* (May/June), 92–102.

Martin, M. (1996) How essential is the role of a worldwide creative director? *Campaign*, 9 February, p. 45.

Martin, M. (1997) How Coca-Cola's 'think global, act local' approach pays off'. *Campaign*, 6 June, p. 27.

Mooij de, M. (1994) *Advertising Worldwide*. Hemel Hempstead: Prentice Hall.

Mueller, B. (1991) An analysis of information content in standardised vs. specialised multinational advertisements. *Journal of International Business Studies* (First Quarter), 23–39.

Taylor, P. (1995) What's the big idea? *Financial Times*, 2 March, p. 14.

West, D.C. (1996) The determinants and consequences of multinational advertising agencies. *International Journal of Advertising*, **15**(2), 128–39.

Zandpour, F. and Harich, K. (1996) Think and feel country clusters: a new approach to international advertising standardization. *International Journal of Advertising*, **15**, 325–44.

Integrated marketing communications

Integrated marketing communications are more likely to occur when organisations attempt to enter into a coordinated dialogue with their various internal and external audiences. The communication tools used in this dialogue and the messages conveyed should be internally consistent with the organisation's objectives and strategies. The target audiences should perceive the communications and associated cues as coordinated, likeable and timely.

AIMS AND OBJECTIVES

The aims of this chapter are to explore the concept of integrated marketing communications with a view to appreciating the complexities associated with this relatively new stategic approach.

The objectives of this chapter are:

1. To introduce integrated marketing communications (IMC) and establish a need for this new concept.
2. To understand the possible meanings that lie behind IMC.
3. To illustrate the breadth and depth of IMC as applied to organisations.
4. To explain the manner in which the marketing mix communicates.
5. To consider how the structures and frameworks of advertising agencies might need to change in order that they are better able to work with IMC.
6. To appraise the reasons for the development of IMC and the main drivers propelling its growth.
7. To set out some of the main reasons why IMC is resisted and how such resistance might be best overcome.

Introduction

Promotional tools have often been regarded by practitioners and academics as separate, individualistic techniques, that offer particular benefits for buyers. Through the use of each promotional tool, clients were able to achieve impacts or effects *on* buyers and only each particular tool was able to achieve these impacts. Consequently, clients were required to deal with a variety of functionally different and independent organisations in order to communicate with their various audiences.

As a result, clients and suppliers of the promotional tools saw specialisation as the principal means to achieve communication effectiveness. This resulted in a proliferation of advertising agencies and the development of sales promotion houses. Public relations specialists stood off from any direct association with marketing. Personal selling evolved as a discrete function within organisations. This specialist approach was further emphasised by the development of trade associations and professional management groups (for example the Institute of Practitioners in Advertising (UK) and the Institute of Sales Promotion (UK)) which seek to endorse, advance, protect and legitimise the actions of their respective professions and members. One of the results of this constrained perspective and functional development of the marketing communications industry has been the inevitable opposition to the desire for change driven by clients. Improvements and new approaches to create and sustain a dialogue with buyers are now central requirements. The structural inadequacies of the marketing communication industry have restrained the means by which client organisations can achieve their marketing and marketing communication objectives.

It is interesting that the rapid development of direct marketing initiatives since the latter half of the 1980s has coincided with a move towards what has become regarded as integrated marketing communications (IMC). A further significant development has been the shift in marketing philosophies, from transaction to relationship marketing. These will be considered later.

IMC has emerged partially as a reaction to the structural inadequacies of the industry and the realisation by clients that their communication needs can (and should) be achieved more efficiently and effectively than previously. In other words, just as power has moved from brand manufacturers to multiple retailers, so some power is shifting from agencies to clients.

While the origins of IMC might be found in the prevailing structural conditions and the needs of particular industry participants, an understanding of what IMC is or should be is far from being resolved and is evolving as the industry matures.

What does integration mean?

The trend away from traditional communication strategies, based largely on mass communication delivering generalised messages, has started to give way to more personalised, customer-orientated and technology-driven approaches, referred to as integrated marketing communications. Duncan and Everett (1993) recall that this new (media) approach has been referred to variously as *orchestration*, *whole egg* and *seamless communication*.

However defined, the development is marked by an increased realisation that multidisciplinary approaches are required to achieve marketing and business objectives. To that end the synergistic benefits are perceived as not only achievable but also desirable.

One of the more popular and intrinsically satisfying views of IMC is that the messages conveyed by each of the promotional tools should be harmonised in order that audiences perceive a consistent set of messages. An interpretation of this perspective, at one level, is that the key visual triggers (design, colours, form and tag line) used in advertising should be replicated across the range of promotional tools used, including POP and the sales force. A further interpretation, at a deeper level, is that the theme and set of core messages used in any campaign should be determined initially and then deployed across the promotional mix (sometimes referred to as synergy). One of the differences is the recognition that mass media advertising is not always the only way to launch consumer or business-to-business promotional activities, and that a consideration of the most appropriate mix of communication forms might be a better starting point when formulating campaigns.

What runs through both these approaches is the belief that above-the-line and below-the-line communications need to be moulded into one cohesive bundle, from which tools can be selected and deployed as conditions require.

It was determined earlier that marketing communications success is not determined solely by the activities or use of the promotional tools. The elements of the marketing mix, however configured, also communicate (Smith, 1996). The price and associated values; the product, in terms of the quality, design and tangible attributes; the manner and efficiency of the service delivery people; and where and how it is made available, for example the location, retailer/dealer reputation and overall service quality (Bucklin, 1966) are brand identity cues with which recipients develop images and through time may shape brand reputations.

Communication through the marketing mix

The target marketing process requires the development and implementation of a distinct marketing mix to meet the requirements of the selected target markets. The elements are mixed together in such a way that they should meet the needs of the target segment. Each element of the marketing mix has a variable capacity to communicate (Figure 29.1).

Product

A product is more than its physical components. It represents the potential to satisfy a range of conscious and unconscious customer needs. Products consist of a combination of physical and service elements, and the balance between the two will vary. At one extreme, for example, a Waterman pen provides tangible attributes of grip and writing facilities. However, it also possess a further dimension which is the prestige and status that such a pen bestows (or is thought to bestow) upon the owner. In contrast, the owner of a common disposable pen would normally only perceive the tangible aspects of the pen's writing facilities.

Offerings therefore consist of tangible and intangible attributes. The marketing communication task is to ensure that the perception of the offering and/or the organisation is the desired one. One of the most important aspects of perception, in this context, is that of perceptual cues. These are the means by which individual judgements are made about products and organisations.

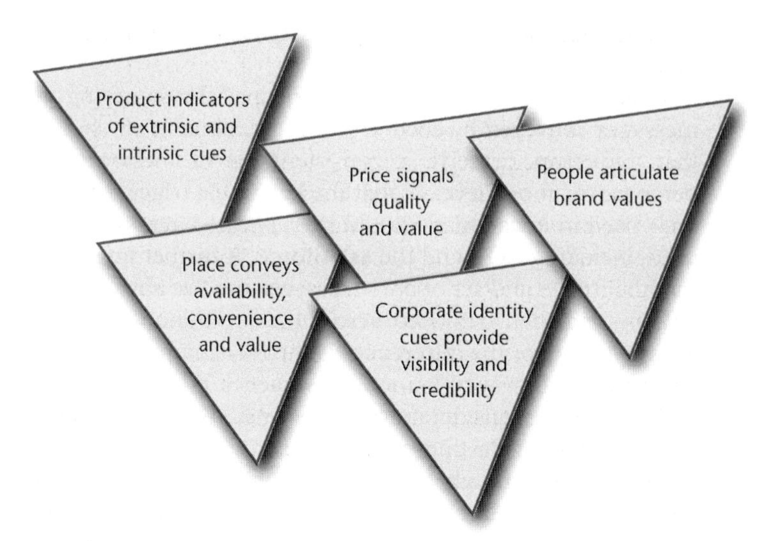

Figure 29.1 The marketing mix communicates.

Intrinsic cues are related to the physical characteristics of the offering. These may be size, colour, flavour or shape. Very often these cues are used to make judgements about quality. When Guinness attempted to redesign its label, tests revealed that Guinness drinkers were unable to distinguish the bottles with the new round label from all the other bottles on the shelves. The cue for ordering a Guinness had been removed, and so was the new design.

Extrinsic cues have normally been concerned with price, store image and the manufacturer. Retail outlets have their own images, and these influence the perception of the offerings they carry. One way of providing consistency is the use of own-label products.

In a similar way, consumers make judgements about offerings based on the perception of the retail outlets where it is available. Organisations (including manufacturers) who are perceived positively will generate higher levels of stakeholder confidence (especially consumer confidence). This can lead to an earlier acceptance of new products in comparison with those organisations whose image is neutral or worse. Marketing communications need to establish favourable images to build confidence and to facilitate the spread of positive word-of-mouth communications from opinion formers and leaders. Furthermore, research shows that offerings that are heavily promoted are perceived as higher in quality than those that are not advertised or promoted and consumers prefer to buy advertised brands, particularly if they have been recommended through personal communications as well.

Price

Marketing communications have the responsibility of informing the target audience about the price of an offering. This can be undertaken via advertising, personal selling and sales promotion activity, or through in-store merchandising and packaging-based communications. Buyers may concern themselves with price, but this is used in combination with other cues, such as the shape, size, smell and colour, to determine a perception of the value that the offering represents. Price is an important contributor to perceived value. Is an expensive offering overpriced, or does it represent exceptional value and bestow high status upon those who are seen to have purchased the product? The answer to this type of question depends upon a number of factors, including the level of disposable income available to the buyer, the perception by the buyer of competitive offerings and the changing expectations of buyers.

Price can prevent purchase because the potential buyer may be unable or unwilling to enter into the exchange process. The stated price may also be seen as too low, and so represent low value and hence low quality. Decision-making by buyers in unfamiliar markets is often based upon price. For example, the first purchase of a camera or a power tool can be anchored on the relative prices of each of the offerings being considered. Price can, therefore, be a major cue in the purchase decision process.

The pricing strategy needs to be reflected in the communications undertaken by the organisation. The prominence that price receives depends on a large number of factors (target audience, level of involvement and attitude to risk, complexity and technicality of the offering and the importance of price in the decision-making process), but it should be sensitive to the expectations of the target audience and the positioning strategy.

People

As the service element becomes increasingly important as a means of differentiating organisations and their product offerings, so the value employees bring to the customer/company interface becomes a vital aspect of the marketing mix.

The significance of internal marketing communications has been explored earlier in Chapter 11 and so will not be repeated here. However, the impact that people make or bring to the marketing communication process is substantial in terms of organisational identity issues and the projection of corporate identity cues.

Place

The use of intermediaries to make available products and services to members of the target market has been discussed earlier (Chapters 6 and 26). These organisations, who cooperate in order that they achieve their business goals, represent a significant target audience for all involved in the marketing channel system.

Communication activities need to be coordinated and synchronised in such a way that the best possible impact is derived from an organisation's attempt to communicate effectively. When Cadbury's launched the Wispa bar on a test market in the North of England, demand outstripped supply. The new bar had to be withdrawn and all promotion ceased. The result of this mismatch within the marketing strategy was a six-month delay in resuming supplies and an opportunity for competitors to take the initiative in the newly identified and exposed market. For marketing communications it is very important to have adequate levels of stock in the distribution system at the launch of a new offering, and to achieve that requires a coherent set of formal and informal internal and external communication networks.

As discussed earlier, the customer's perception of the store, point-of-purchase or the other organisations in the performance channel will affect the attitudes and purchase behaviour of customers. It is important at this point to appreciate what the marketing communications planner needs to do:

Table 29.1 Elements involved in integrating marketing communications

Promotional mix	Above-the-line and below-the-line
Marketing mix	Price, product, people, place and promotion
Business strategy	Philosophy, objectives and mission, content
Outsourced providers	Agencies, production and material suppliers, fulfilment houses
The organisation	Employees and management, whether located at HO, SBUs, departments or overseas divisions

1. Liaise with channel members to ensure that stock is available.
2. Be aware of the needs of channel members who may require the support of your organisation's marketing communications. This will be stated in the marketing plan.
3. Provide consistency for all communications used in the channel.
4. Understand and act in accordance with the communications strategy.
5. Ensure that all members of the organisation understand, support and are empowered to implement the concept. The use of internal marketing communications is important to ensure that the blend of internal and external communications is appropriate.
6. Coordinate actions with any main agencies involved with the communications programme.

This brief look at the marketing strategy serves to remind us that the communications plan can only be successfully developed if the key factors within the marketing plan are clearly identified and developed. It can therefore be established that IMC cannot be achieved just by saying the same message through a variety of promotional tools; the marketing mix is also a strong communicator.

If marketing communications is to be used effectively then there is a need to communicate aspects of the direction in which the organisation intends moving and how it intends to achieve this. In other words, the business philosophy and its aims and objectives, often expressed formally through mission and vision statements (Chapter 10), need to be communicated to particular audiences in a way that is synchronised and coordinated with the organisation's other communication endeavours.

Table 29.1 sets out the main elements that need to be considered and managed when developing IMC. The breadth and depth of these elements suggests that the organisation as a whole needs to accommodate many changes and that IMC is not just a matter of transmitting uniform marketing communications messages.

Reasons for the development of IMC

The explosion of interest in IMC has resulted from a variety of drivers. Generally they can be grouped into three main categories: those drivers (or opportunities) that are market based, those that arise from changing communications, and those that are driven from opportunities arising from within the organisation itself. These are set out in Table 29.2.

Table 29.2 Drivers for IMC

Organisational drivers for IMC
- Increasing profits through improved efficiency
- Increasing need for greater levels of accountability
- Rapid move towards cross-border marketing and the need for changing structures and communications
- Coordinated brand development and competitive advantage
- Opportunities to utilise management time used more productively
- Provide direction and purpose

Market-based drivers for IMC
- Greater levels of audience communications literacy
- Media cost inflation
- Media and audience fragmentation
- Stakeholders' need for increasing amounts and diversity of information
- Greater amounts of message clutter
- Competitor activity and low levels of brand differentiation
- Move towards relationship marketing from transaction-based marketing
- Development of networks, collaboration and alliances

Communication-based drivers for IMC
- Technological advances (Internet, databases, segmentation techniques)
- Increased message effectiveness through consistency and reinforcement of core messages
- More effective triggers for brand and message recall
- More consistent and less confusing brand images
- Need to build brand reputations and to provide clear identity cues

The opportunities offered to organisations that contemplate moving to IMC are considerable and it is somewhat surprising that so few organisations have been either willing or able to embrace the approach. One of the main organisational drivers for IMC is the need to become increasingly efficient. Driving down the cost base enables managers to improve profits and levels of productivity. By seeking synergistic advantages through its communications and associated activities and by expecting managers to be able to account for the way in which they consume marketing communication resources, so integrated marketing communications becomes increasingly attractive. At the same time, organisation structures are changing more frequently and the need to integrate across functional areas reflects the efficiency drive.

From a market perspective the predominant driver is the reorientation from transaction-based marketing to relationship marketing. The extension of the brand personality concept into brand relationships (Hutton, 1996) requires a customer consideration in terms of asking not only 'What do our customers want?', but also 'What are their values, do they trust us and are we loyal to them?' By adopting a position designed to enhance trust and commitment (Morgan and Hunt, 1994) an organisation's external communications need to be consistent and coordinated, if only to avoid information overload and misunderstanding.

From a communication perspective the key driver is to provide a series of triggers by which buyers can understand the values a brand stands for and a means by which they can use certain messages to influence their activities. By differentiating the marketing communications, often by providing clarity and simplicity, advantages can be attained. The adage 'What does advertising do to people?' is no longer viable (Lannon, 1996). The question to be asked, she says, is 'What do people do *with* advertising?' (marketing communications).

Integrated marketing strategy and communications – Häagen-Dazs

Häagen-Dazs demonstrated the effective use of IMC when it entered the UK market. Ice cream was traditionally a seasonal children's food, and the market had experienced little growth or innovation. The business strategy adopted was to create a new market segment, one that has become referred to as the super-premium segment.

The positioning intention was to present Häagen-Dazs as a luxury, fashion-orientated food for adults. To achieve the business goals, the entire marketing mix was coordinated: the product reflected high quality, the high price induced perceived quality, and the distribution in the launch was through up-market restaurants in prestige locations and five-star hotels where Häagen-Dazs was the only branded ice cream on the menu.

The promotional campaign used celebrities from many walks of life as opinion leaders to create a word-of-mouth ripple effect. The quality of the media used and messages themselves reflected the same quality theme. The brand has since become firmly established and, although the arrival of Ben & Jerry's and other up-market brands has increased competition and rivalry, the brand remains distinctive and continues to use an integrated approach to its communications.

An integrated approach should attempt to provide a uniform or consistent set of messages. These should be relatively easy to interpret and to assign meanings to. This enables target audiences to think about and perceive brands within a consistent context and so encourage behaviour as anticipated by the source. Those organisations that try to practise IMC understand that buyers refer to and receive messages about brands and companies from a wide range of information sources. Harnessing this knowledge is a fundamental step towards enhancing marketing communications.

Resistance to integration

The adoption of IMC by organisations has not been as widespread as the amount of discussion around the subject has been. As with many aspects of change, there has been substantial resistance to its incorporation, and, if sanctioned, only partial integration has been achieved. This is not to say that integration is not possible or has not been achieved, but the path to IMC is far from easy.

One of the key issues encouraging the establishment of IMC has been the willingness of some public relations practitioners to move closer to the marketing department. As Miller and Rose (1994) comment, the previously held opposition to integration by public relations practitioners has begun to dissolve as the more enlightened agencies see it as 'a reality and a necessity'.

Resistance to change is partly a reflection of the experiences and needs of individuals for stability and the understanding of their environments. However, it is also a reflection, again, of the structural conditions in organisations and industry, which have help determine the expectations of managers and employees. The following represent some of the more common reasons for the resistance to the incorporation of IMC.

Financial structures and frameworks

Resistance through finance-led corporate goals, which have dominated industry performance and expectations, has been particularly significant. The parameters set around it and the extent to which marketing communications are often perceived as a cost rather than an investment have provided a corporate environment where the act of preparing for and establishing integrative activities is disapproved of at worst, or room for manoeuvre restricted at best. Furthermore, the period in which promotion activities are expected to generate returns works against the principles of IMC and the time needed for the effects to take place.

Opposition/reluctance to change

The attitudes and opinions of staff are often predictable in the sense that any move away from tried and proven methods to areas which are unknown and potentially threatening is usually rejected. Change has for a long time been regarded with hostility and fear, and as such is normally resisted. Our apparent need for stability and general security has been a potent form of resistance to the introduction of IMC. This is changing as change itself becomes a familiar aspect of working life. Any move towards IMC therefore represents a significantly different approach to work, as not only are the expectations of employees changed but so also are the working practices and the associated roles with internal customers and, more importantly, those providing outsourcing facilities.

Traditional hierarchical and brand management structures

Part of the reluctance to change is linked with the structure and systems inherent in many organisations. Traditional hierarchical structures and systems are inflexible and slow to cope with developments in their fast-adapting environments. These structures stifle the use of individual initiative, slow the decision-making process and encourage inertia. The brand management system, so popular and appropriate in the 1970s and early 1980s, focuses upon functional specialism, which is reflected in the horizontally and vertically specialised areas of responsibility. Brands now need to be managed by flexible teams of specialists, who are charged with responsibilities and the resources necessary to coordinate activities across organisations in the name of integration.

Attitudes and structure of suppliers and agencies

One of the principal reasons often cited as a barrier to integration is the relationship that clients have with their agencies, and in particular their advertising agencies. Generally, advertising agencies have maintained their traditional structures and methods of operating, while their clients have begun to adapt and reform themselves. The thinking behind this is that advertising agencies have tried to maintain their dominance of mass advertising as the principal means of brand development. In doing so they seek to retain the largest proportion of agency fee income, rather than having these fees diluted as work is allocated below the line (to other organisations). The establishment of IMC threatens the current role of the main advertising agencies. This is not to say that all agencies think and act in this way. They do not, as witnessed by the innovative approaches to restructuring and the provision of integrated resources for their clients by agencies such as St Lukes. So, while clients have seen the benefits of integrated marketing communications, their attempts to achieve them have often been thwarted by the structures of the agencies they need to work with and by the attitudes of their main agencies.

Perceived complexity of planning and coordination

The complexity associated with integrating any combination of activities is often cited as a means for delaying or postponing action. Of greater significance are the difficulties associated with coordinating actions across departments and geographic boundaries. IMC requires the cooperation and coordination of internal and external stakeholder groups. Each group has an agenda which contains goals that may well differ from or conflict with those of other participants.

For example, an advertising agency might propose the use of mass media to address a client's needs, if only because that is where its specialist skills lie. However, direct marketing might be a more appropriate approach to solving the client's problem, but because there is no established mechanism to coordinate and discuss openly the problem/solution, the lead agency is likely to have its approach adopted in preference to others.

How to overcome the restraints

The restraints that prevent the development of IMC need to be overcome. Indeed, many organisations that have made significant progress in developing IMC have done so by instigating approaches and measures that aim to reduce or negate the impact of the barriers that people put up to prevent change. The main approaches to overcoming the barriers are as follows.

Adopting a customer-focused philosophy

The adoption of a customer-focused approach is quite well established within marketing departments. However, this approach needs to be adopted as an organisation-wide approach, a philosophy that spans all departments and which results in unified cues to all stakeholders. In many cases, agencies need to adopt a more customer-orientated approach and be able and willing to work with other agencies, including those below the line.

Harnessing the benefits of training and staff development programmes

A move towards IMC cannot be made without changes in the expectations held by employees within the client and agency sectors. Some of the key processes that have been identified as important to successful change management need to be used. For example, the involvement and participation of all staff in the process is in itself a step to providing motivation and acceptance of change when it is agreed and delivered.

Appointment of change agents

The use of change agents, people who can positively affect the reception and implementation of change programmes, is important. As IMC should span an entire organisation, the change agent should be a senior manager in order to signal the importance and speed at which the new perspective is to be adopted.

Planning to achieve SCA (Sustainable Competitive Advantage)

In order to develop competitive advantages some organisations have restructured by removing levels of management, introduced business reprocessing procedures, and even set up outsourcing in order that they achieve cost efficiencies and effectiveness targets. Prior to the implementation of these delayering processes, many organisations were (and many still are) organised hierarchically.

As Brown (1997) rightly states, the emergence and establishment of IMC will only have a real chance of success once the industry matures, becomes market orientated and leaves behind issues concerning client–agency complications.

Incremental approaches

In view of the evidence that IMC has not been totally established in any single organisation, it suggests that the changes required to achieve IMC are large and that the barriers are strong. What can be observed are formative approaches to IMC and that organisations have experimented and tried out various ideas within their resource and cultural contexts.

It seems logical that moves towards the establishment of IMC must be undertaken in steps: an incremental approach (Figure 29.2). What has been achieved so far can

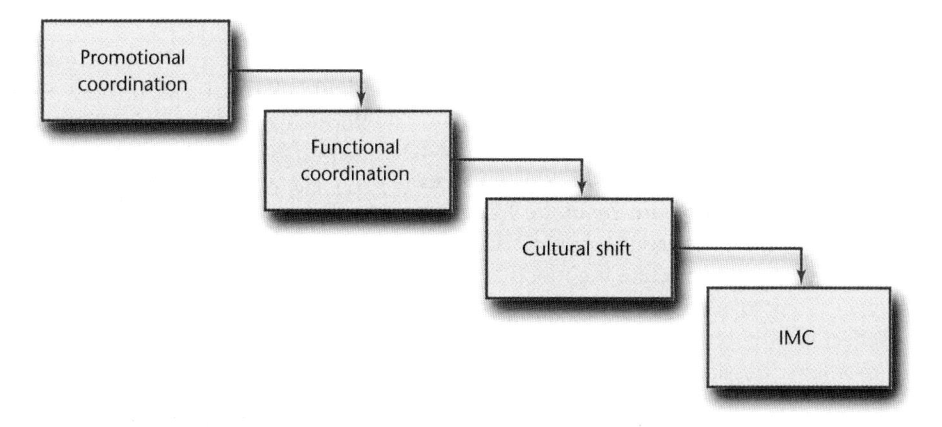

Figure 29.2 An incremental approach to the establishment of IMC.

be recognised as forms of coordination. Different organisations have coordinated various aspects of their communications activities. The majority have focused upon their promotional activities and have tried to bring together their communications to provide consistency and thematic harmonisation.

Therefore, it seems that the starting point in the move towards IMC is at the level of the promotional mix. From *promotional coordination*, progress through to *functional coordination* seems likely, where different parts of the organisation are introduced to the notion of internal marketing relationships and where internal marketing communications plays an important part of the process.

The next stage is characterised by the organisation moving towards a strong(er) customer orientation. This requires a *cultural shift* of values and beliefs, whereby organisational and brand identity issues become paramount. This can only be implemented at this stage, as the internal systems, procedures and employee mind set need to be in place if the strategy is to be credible to customers and other stakeholders.

CASE ILLUSTRATION

National brewery chain

This case illustration was written by Pat Dade who is a director of Synergy Consulting, a division of Synergy Brand Values Ltd.

The purchase, refurbishment, stocking and running of a public house is an expensive experience. Many pubs nowadays can easily cost £500,000 just to set up. It is therefore vital that the brewery industry gain accurate and useful information from the field. However, this information is rarely quantified and many decisions are based on random visits, past experience and gut reaction. With the development of theme pubs and their unique differentiated positions, this is less acceptable because of the high costs of entry and the necessary high turnover.

Synergy began working with a national brewery chain (name disguised) to develop ways of classifying pubs by usage and understanding the motivations behind the visits. These motivations dictate the mood and ambience required inside the pub and will have a big effect on the type of alcohol that is sold. For example, busy pubs tend to sell packaged drinks because apart from their trendy – therefore desirable – appearance, they are quick and easy to order and difficult to spill.

A survey of 100 pubs was undertaken in which interviews with customers and publicans were supplemented with catchment area analyses, ambience evaluation, brand usage studies, behaviour monitoring and till surveys.

From this Synergy were able to develop a framework derived from the Social Value Group system (see Chapter 10), from which it was possible to determine the best pub concept in any given catchment area or location.

Inner directed

These people prefer to use a range of pubs rather than just a local. They will actively search for new experiences and are quite comfortable with the unknown and untested. To this group people create the ambience they prefer. The same pub/club can be different each night for them and so be acceptable, if not desirable.

Outer directed

These people prefer to go to the right place, the 'in place', the place to be seen. If the pub/club matches this profile they will go; if not they tend to avoid being seen there. They are traditionally aspirational and are only truly comfortable with a branded proposition. An Australian pub isn't interesting to them until it is part of a chain.

Sustenance driven

These people don't want international themed pubs of any description (Australian, German, French, etc.). They want a traditional British pub, with traditional beer (ales, stouts and lagers) on tap and with no jukebox if you please. Brewers have alienated many of these drinkers over the recent years in the drive for modernization. The newer purchasers of pub chains such as J.D. Wetherspoon, J.J. Moon and the Firkin Chain, have all seen this alienation and drawn a new generation of these loyal people back into the 'new local'.

The framework was used to drive a range of marketing initiatives that served to provide a foundation for integrated marketing communications. For example, decisions regarding new site purchases, the development of new concepts, the drinks mix (the ratio of premium to standard), promotional messages and media selection, pricing and the overall ambience and theme of the pubs are all derived from the initial motivational studies. Such a common base of information provides for the development of integrated marketing communications. Indeed, this work was instrumental in devising the Australian theme pubs that have been so successful.

The gut instinct of the field operator can obviously never be replaced, but this model provided back up and a framework for building new propositions, making new acquisitions and for providing for the development of integrated marketing communications.

Finally, total *IMC* (integration of all marketing and corporate communications) is achieved when all external agencies, outsourcing providers and partners work with the organisation in such a way that customers perceive consistency in the promises and actions the organisation makes and are satisfied with the organisation's attempts to anticipate and satisfy customer needs and the results that they seek from their relationships with the brand or organisation.

Agency structures and IMC

In order for messages to be developed and conveyed through an integrated approach, the underlying structure supporting this strategy needs to be reconsidered. Just as the structure of the industry had a major impact on the way in which messages were developed and communicated as the industry developed, so the structural underpinning needs to adapt to the new and preferred approaches of clients in the 1990s and the new millennium.

The use of outside agencies who possess skills, expertise and purchasing advantages which are valued by clients is not new and is unlikely to change. However, the way in which these outsourced skills are used and how they are structured has been changing. Aspects of client–agency relationships are important, and are considered in Chapter 7. What is important for this part of the text is a consideration of the way in which those organisations who provide outsourcing facilities and contribute to a client's IMC can be configured to provide optimal servicing and support. Gronstedt and Thorsen (1996) suggest five ways in which agencies could be configured to

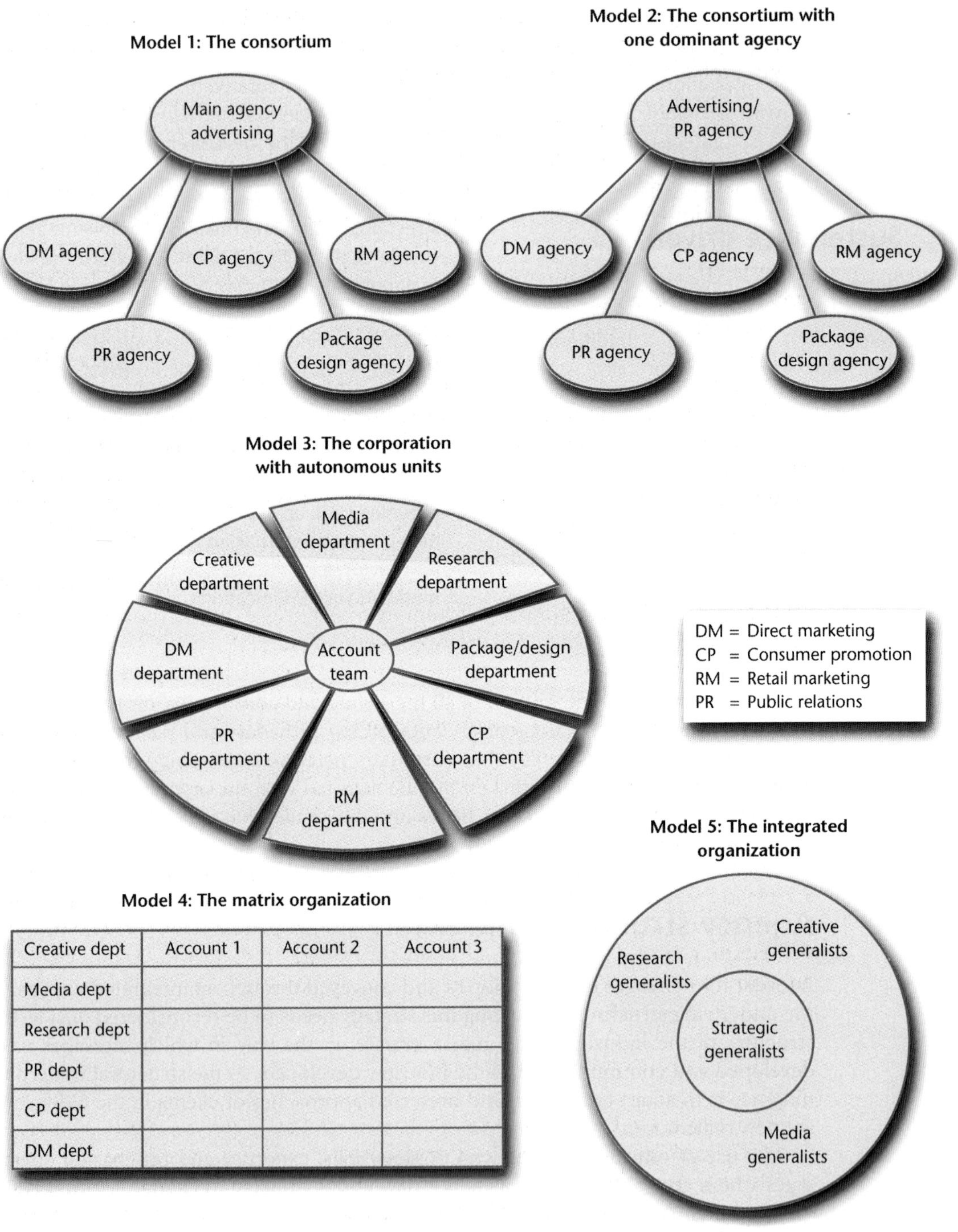

Model 1: The consortium

Main agency advertising

DM agency

CP agency

RM agency

PR agency

Package design agency

Model 2: The consortium with one dominant agency

Advertising/ PR agency

DM agency

CP agency

RM agency

PR agency

Package design agency

Model 3: The corporation with autonomous units

Account team

Media department

Research department

Package/design department

CP department

RM department

PR department

DM department

Creative department

DM = Direct marketing
CP = Consumer promotion
RM = Retail marketing
PR = Public relations

Model 4: The matrix organization

Creative dept	Account 1	Account 2	Account 3
Media dept			
Research dept			
PR dept			
CP dept			
DM dept			

Model 5: The integrated organization

Creative generalists

Research generalists

Strategic generalists

Media generalists

Figure 29.3 An overview of the five agency structures (Gronstedt and Thorson (1996); used with kind permission).

provide integrated marketing communications. The research is based upon US-based advertising agencies, so while not immediately transferable to the European, Asian or other regional markets, their proposals provide a base from which other agencies might evolve in other geographic markets.

The models are presented in Figure 29.3, and although the authors acknowledge that a mix of forms could be identified, one particular form tended to dominate each agency. The forms denote a continuum, at one end of which is a highly centralised organisation that can provide a high level of integration for a variety of communication disciplines. Staffed by generalists with no particular media bias, these organisations are structured according to client needs, not functional specialisms. Total integration is offered at the expense of in-depth and leading-edge knowledge in new and developing areas.

At the other end of the continuum are those providers who group themselves in the form of a network. Often led by a main advertising agency which has divested itself of expensive overheads, the independent yet interdependent network players each provide specialist skills under the leadership of the main contractor agency. One of the two main weaknesses associated with this model concerns the deficiency associated with communications across the players in the network. This horizontal aspect means that individual members of the network tend to identify with their own area of expertise and advance their specialism, possibly at the expense of the client's overriding requirements. The other main weakness concerns the transitory or temporary nature of a member organisation's involvement within such networks. Therefore, the level of potential integration is possibly weakest in this model, although the level of expertise available to clients is highest at this end of the continuum.

One of the essential points emerging from this research is that there seems to be a trade-off between levels of integration and the expertise provided by different agencies. Clients who want to retain control over their brands and to find an integrated agency where all the required services are of the exact level and quality demanded may be expecting too much. The inevitability of this position is that clients may choose to select marketing communication expertise from a variety of sources, and the integrated agency may well lose out.

Furthermore, environmental factors should not be ignored, and it may be that clients in the future will state their preferred structural requirements at the pitching or client briefing stage of the agency–client relationship. Increasingly, agencies may well be required to mix and match their structures and provide structural flexibility to meet the varying needs of their clients.

Client structures and IMC

The final aspect to be considered in IMC concerns the structure of the client organisation. The hierarchical structures common in many organisations in the period up to 1970s have been subject to attack. In search of survival in recession and increasing profits and dividends in times of plenty, organisations have sought to restructure and realign themselves with their environment. Hierarchies delivered a management structure that delegated authority in compartmentalised units. The brand management system that accompanied this structural approach provided a straitjacket and gave only partial authority to incumbents. At the same time, responsibility for pricing, channel management, personal selling and public relations activities was split off and allocated to a number of others. It follows from this that the likelihood of internal integration has been hampered by the structure of the organisation and the way in which structural units were assembled.

The restructuring process has resulted in organisations that are delayered and leaner. This means that the gap between senior management and those within the operating core (Mintzberg, 1996) is both smaller and now capable of sustaining viable internal communications that are truly two-way and supportive.

Increasingly organisations are operating in overseas or cross-border markets. For a deeper account of the issues concerning international marketing communications, readers are referred to Chapter 28. However, as organisations develop structurally, from international to multinational to global and transnational status, so the need to coordinate internally and to integrate internal communications becomes ever more vital to sustain integrated marketing communications (Grein and Gould, 1996). Internal marketing (Chapter 11) is becoming more popular with clients (and agencies) as it is realised that employees are important contributors to corporate identity programmes and invaluable spokespersons for the products they market. Internal communications can help not only to inform and remind/reassure but also to differentiate employees in the sense that they understand the organisation's direction and purpose, appreciate what the brand values are and so identify closely with the organisation as a whole. This is a form of integration from which marketing communications can benefit.

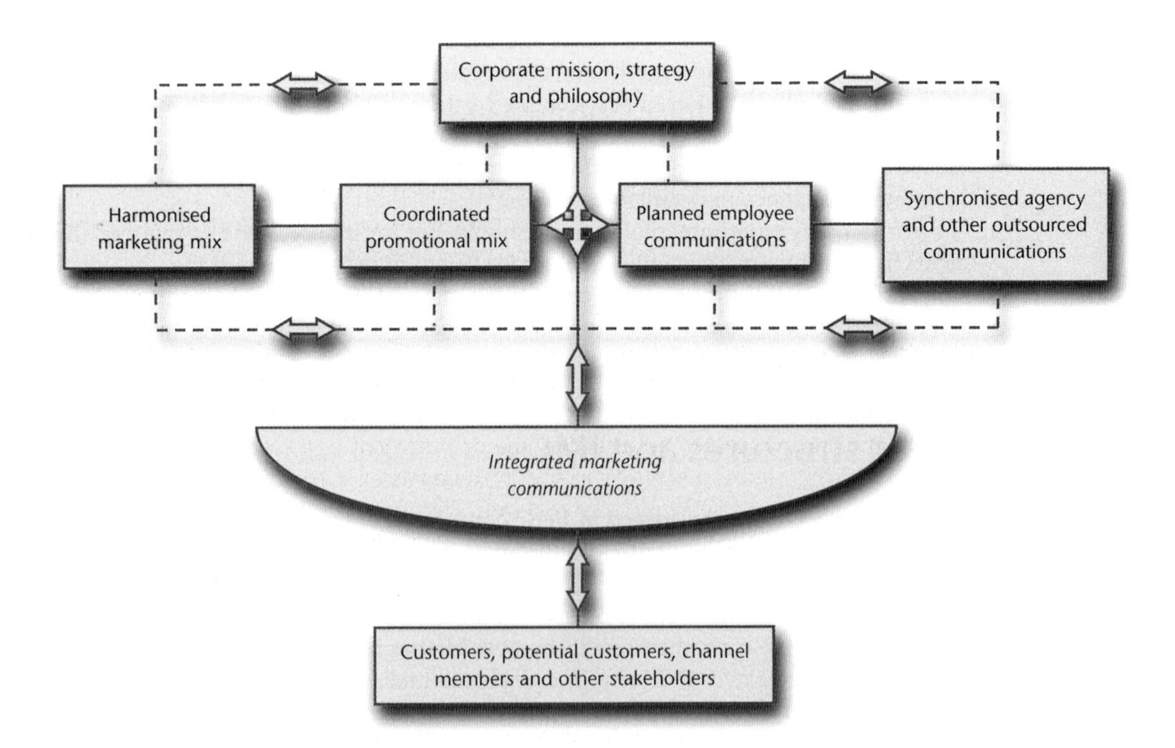

Figure 29.4 A model of integrated marketing communications.

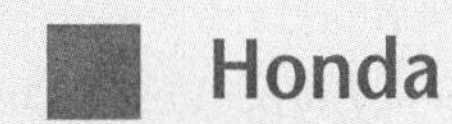

Honda

When Honda launched its five-door Civic in 1995 it used TV advertisements, direct marketing and sales promotion activities. All the tools used the same branding and visuals and the agencies used were required to work together.

O'Sullivan (1996)

Integrated marketing communications are more likely to occur when organisations attempt to enter into a coordinated dialogue with their various internal and external audiences. The communication tools used in this dialogue and the messages conveyed should be internally consistent with the organisation's objectives and strategies. The target audiences should perceive the communications and associated cues as coordinated, likeable and timely.

Integrated Marketing Communications means different things to different people. However, if it is to be a significant development for organisations then the term should embrace the marketing mix, the promotional mix, internal communications and all those outsourced providers who contribute to the overall marketing communication process. As Figure 29.4 demonstrates, all of these elements should be linked to the overall purpose of the organisation, normally encapsulated and framed in the strategy, philosophy and mission of the organisation.

Summary

The development of IMC can be seen as resulting naturally from two main factors. The first concerns the way in which the tools of the promotional mix have been deployed. Their use, in the past, has been largely singular in that they have been departmentalised and managed, internally and externally, as separate and independent items. By combining tools and enabling the communication strengths of one tool to reinforce those of another, target audiences are more likely to benefit, along with the organisation.

Secondly, and following on from this first point, has been the drive for business efficiency and increased effectiveness. IMC offers opportunities to improve effectiveness and deliver messages in a more productive manner. Now that a genuine mixture of tools can be assembled, many managers can see IMC as a way of putting right a number of problems across the organisation, many of them structural or communication-orientated.

While the concept of IMC is attractive, the development of the approach in practical terms has to date not been very encouraging. There has been a great deal of debate and some attempt to coordinate the content and delivery of marketing communication messages. Most organisations have yet to achieve totally integrated marketing communications; only partial or coordinated levels of activity have so far been achieved.

Review questions

1. Discuss the main reasons for the development of IMC.
2. Prepare brief notes setting out what IMC means.

3. Write a definition of IMC and prepare notes for a colleague explaining how the elements of the McCarthy marketing mix communicate.
4. Explain with the aid of a rough diagram how different agency structures can be developed to accommodate IMC.
5. What are the principal reasons for the development of IMC?
6. List the main drivers for the growth of IMC.
7. Appraise the main reasons offered for the failure of organisations to develop IMC.
8. What is the incremental approach to establishing IMC?
9. Evaluate the view that IMC is principally an internal marketing tool.
10. Prepare the outline for an essay arguing whether IMC is a strategic approach or just a means to correct internal operational difficulties and to reduce media costs.

References

Brown, J. (1997) Impossible dream or inevitable revolution: an exploration of integrated marketing communications. *Journal of Communication Management*, **12**(1), 70–81

Bucklin, (1966) *A Theory of Distribution Channel Structure*. Berkeley CA: IBER Publications.

Duncan, T. and Everett, S. (1993) Client perceptions of integrated marketing communications. *Journal of Advertising Research*, **3**(3), 30–9.

Grein, A.F. and Gould, S.J. (1996) Globally integrated communications. *Journal of Marketing Communications*, **2**, 141–58.

Gronstedt, A. and Thorsen, E. (1996) Five approaches to organise an integrated marketing communications agency. *Journal of Advertising Research* (March/April), 48–58.

Hutton, J.G. (1996) Integrated relationship-marketing communications: a key opportunity for IMC. *Journal of Marketing Communications*, **2**, 191–9.

Lannon, J. (1996) Integrated communications from the consumer end. *Admap* (February), 23–6.

Miller, D.A. and Rose, P.B. (1994) Integrated communications: a look at reality instead of theory. *Public Relations Quarterly* (Spring), 13–16.

Mintzberg, H. (1996) *The Strategy Process*, European edition. Englewood Cliffs NJ: Prentice Hall.

Morgan, R.M. and Hunt, S.D. (1994) The commitment–trust theory of relationship marketing. *Journal of Marketing*, **58** (July), 20–38.

O'Sullivan, T. (1996) Positive linking. *Marketing Week*, 15 March.

Smith, P. (1996) Benefits and barriers to integrated communications. *Admap* (February), 19–22.

Developing marketing communication plans

The Marketing Communications Planning Framework (MCPF) aims to enable managers and students to bring together the various elements of marketing communications into a logical sequence of activities where the rationale for promotional decisions is built upon information generated at previous levels in the framework. It also provides a checklist of activities that need to be considered.

The MCPF represents a way of understanding the different promotional components, of appreciating the way in which they relate to one another and a means of writing coherent marketing communications plans for work or for examinations, such as those offered by the Chartered Institute of Marketing in the Marketing Communications Strategy paper.

AIMS AND OBJECTIVES

The aim of this final chapter is to bring together the different elements of marketing communications and to suggest an approach to writing and developing a promotional plan.

The objectives of this chapter are:

1. To consider the different elements of marketing communications and identify linkages between the elements.
2. To present a framework for the development of marketing communication plans.
3. To highlight key areas of such plans.
4. To present an example of a promotional plan based upon a case study.
5. To evaluate some of the problems associated with this type of exercise.

Introduction

This text has considered a wide range of elements that contribute to our understanding of marketing communications. All marketing managers (and others) need to understand these elements and appreciate how they contribute to the satisfaction of business, marketing and promotional objectives.

To help students and managers comprehend the linkages between the elements and to understand how these different components complement each other, this chapter deals exclusively with the development of marketing communication plans. To that extent it will be of direct benefit to managers seeking to build plans for the first time or for those familiar with the activity to reconsider current practices. Secondly, the chapter should also be of direct benefit to Chartered Institute of Marketing students who are currently required to design such a plan as part fulfilment of the examination in Marketing Communications Strategy at the Diploma level.

The Marketing Communications Planning Framework

It has been established (Chapter 1) that the principal tasks facing marketing communications managers are to decide:

1. Who should receive the messages.
2. What the messages should say.
3. What image of the organisation/brand receivers are expected to retain.
4. How much is to be spent establishing this new established image.
5. How the messages are to be delivered.
6. What actions the receivers should take.
7. How to control the whole process once implemented.
8. What was achieved.

Note that more than one message is transmitted and that there is more than one target audience. This is important, as recognition of the need to communicate with multiple audiences and their different information requirements, often simultaneously, lies at the heart of marketing communications. The aim is to generate and transmit messages which present the organisation and their offerings to their various target audiences, encouraging them to enter into a dialogue. These messages must be presented consistently and they must address the points stated above. It is the skill and responsibility of the marketing communications planner to blend the communication tools and to create a mix that satisfies these elements.

A framework for integrated marketing communications plans

To enable managers and students to bring together the various promotional elements into a cohesive plan, which can be communicated to others, an overall framework is required.

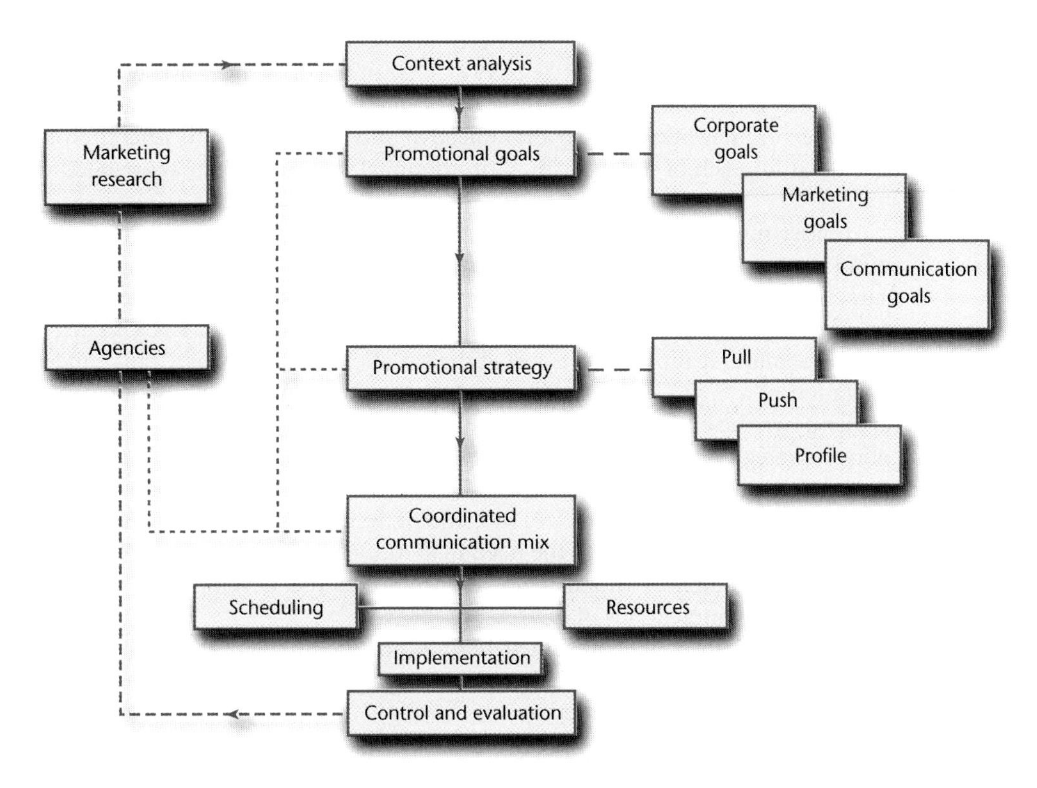

Figure 30.1 The Marketing Communications Planning Framework.

The Marketing Communications Planning Framework (MCPF) (Figure 30.1), seeks to achieve this by bringing together the various elements into a logical sequence of activities where the rationale for promotional decisions is built upon information generated at a previous level in the framework. Another advantage of using the MCPF is that it provides a suitable checklist of activities that need to be considered.

The MCPF represents a sequence of decisions that marketing managers undertake when preparing, implementing and evaluating communication strategies and plans. It does not mean that this sequence reflects reality; indeed many marketing decisions are made outside any recognisable framework. However, as a means of understanding the different components, appreciating the way in which they relate to one another and bringing together various aspects for work or for answering examination questions such as those offered by the Chartered Institute of Marketing in the Marketing Communications Strategy paper, this approach has many advantages and has been used by a number of local, national and international organisations.

Marketing communications requires the satisfaction of promotional objectives through the explicit and deliberate development of communication strategy. The MCPF will be used to show first the key elements, second some of the linkages and third the integrated approach that is required.

The process of marketing communications, however, is not linear, as depicted in this framework, but integrative and interdependent. To that extent, this approach is a recognition of the value of stakeholder theory and of the requirement to build partnerships with buyers and other organisations networked with the organisation.

Other 'decision sequences' have been advanced, in particular one by Rothschild (1987) and another by Engel *et al.* (1994). One of the difficulties associated with their frameworks is that they fail to bring strategy into the development of the promotional mix. Their frameworks rely on the objective and task approach, whereby plans are developed for each of the individual promotional tools, and then aggregated to form strategy.

Another more recent framework is the SOSTAC approach. This is essentially a sound system and moves closer than most of the others to achieving suitable marketing communication plans. However, as the framework is multipurpose and is intended for application to a variety of planning situations, there is a strong danger that the communication focus is lost at the situation analysis phase. This can lead to a reiteration of a SWOT and/or a general marketing plan, with subsequent problems further down the line in terms of the justification and understanding of the communications strategy and promotional mixes that need to be deployed. As CIM Senior Examiner in this subject I have read a great number of examination scripts where students have made these errors of judgement. In addition, the SOSTAC model does not give sufficient emphasis to the need to identify and understand the characteristics of the target audience, which is so important for the development of a coherent marketing communications plan.

The MCPF approach presented here is not intended to solve all the problems associated with such plans, but is robust enough to meet the needs of employers and examiners, and is recommended.

Elements of the plan

Marketing communications plans consist of the elements in the MCPF, as set out in Table 30.1.

Context analysis

The MCPF consists of a number of elements, the first of which is the context analysis (CA). The purpose of compiling a CA is to determine and understand the key market and communication drivers which are likely to influence (or already are influencing) a brand (or organisation) and either help or hinder its progress towards meeting its long-term objectives. This is different from a situation analysis, because the situation analysis considers a range of wider organisational factors, most of which are normally considered in the development of marketing plans (while the communication focus is lost). Duplication is to be avoided, as it is both inefficient and confusing.

Table 30.1 Elements of a marketing communications plan

Context analysis
Promotional objectives
Marketing communications strategy
Promotional mix (methods and tools)
Budget
Schedule
Evaluation and control

The compilation of a CA is very important, as it presents information and clues about what the promotional plan needs to achieve. Information and market research data about target audiences (their needs, perception, motivation, attitudes and decision-making characteristics), the media and the people they use for information about offerings, the marketing objectives and time-scales, the overall level of financial and other resources that are available, the quality and suitability of agency and other outsourced activities, and the environment in terms of societal, technological, political and economic conditions, both now and at some point in the future, all need to be considered.

At the root of the CA is the marketing plan. This will already have been prepared and contains important information about the target segment, the business and marketing goals, competitors and the time-scales on which the goals are to be achieved.

The rest of the CA seeks to elaborate and build upon this information so as to provide the detail in order that the plan can be developed and justified.

The CA provides the rationale for the plan. It is from the CA that the marketing objectives (from the marketing plan) and the marketing communications objectives are derived. The type, form and style of the message are rooted in the characteristics of the target audience, and the media selected to convey the messages will be based upon the nature of the tasks, the media habits of the audience and the resources available.

The main components of the context analysis are:

1. **The business context**
   Corporate and marketing strategy and plans
   Brand/organisation analysis
   Competitor analysis
2. **The customer context**
   Segment characteristics
   Levels of awareness, perception and attitudes towards the brand/organisation
   Level of involvement
   Types of perceived risk
   DMU characteristics and issues
3. **The stakeholder context**
   Who are the key stakeholders and why are they important?
   What are their communication needs?
4. **The organisational context**
   Financial constraints
   Organisation identity
   Culture, values and beliefs
   Marketing expertise
   Agency suitability
5. **The environmental context**
   Social, political, economic and technological restraints and opportunities

Promotional objectives

Promotional objectives consist of three main elements:

- **Corporate objectives**: these are derived from the business or marketing plan. They refer to the mission and the business area that the organisation believes it should be in.

- **Marketing objectives**: these are derived from the marketing plan and are output-orientated. Normally these can be considered as sales-related objectives, such as market share, sales revenues, volumes, ROI and profitability indicators.
- **Marketing communication objectives**: these are derived from an understanding of the current context in which a brand exists and the future context in the form of where the brand is expected to be at some point in the future. These will be presented as awareness levels, perception, comprehension/knowledge, attitudes towards and overall degree of preference for the brand. The choice of communication goal depends upon the tasks that need to be accomplished. In addition, most brands need either to maintain their current brand position or reposition themselves in the light of changing contextual conditions. A comment on positioning intentions should be made at this point.

Both the marketing and marketing communication goals need to be set out in SMART terminology.

Communication strategy

The communication strategy should be customer orientated not method orientated. Therefore, the strategy depends upon whether the target is the trade, the end user or all stakeholders. Figure 30.2 depicts promotional strategy as a triangulation of strategic forces and that any one particular strategy represents a combination of forces. A single point can be (conceptually) identified within the triangle which represents the particular strategic combination of forces necessary to complete the prevailing promotional objectives. In most cases there is an element of all three forces, but the emphasis will usually be upon the trade or the consumer/buyer, in which case the strategic approach will be a combination of the push and pull strategies, as denoted by the point A. Point B represents a strategy which features a heavy profile strategy, used perhaps at the introduction of a new company (perhaps Cable and Wireless Communications) which might then be followed by a strategy which is focused more on point A. This sets the overall thrust and direction of the marketing communication activities and provides a means by which the budget can be allocated.

At this point the positioning intentions are to be developed. These will be related to the market, the customers or some other dimension. The justification for this will arise from the CA.

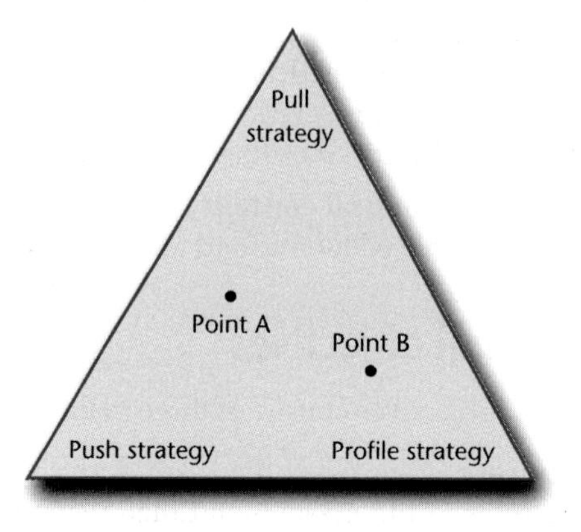

Figure 30.2 Triangle of strategic options.

Having formulated, stated and justified the required position, the next step is to present the basic form and style of the key message that is to be conveyed. Is there to be a lot of copy or just a little? Is there to be a rational or emotional approach or some weighting between the two? What should be the tone of the visual messages? Is there to be a media blitz (e.g. a Microsoft-type day, as used for the launch of Windows 95, or Cable & Wireless yellow saturation)? It is at this point that those responsible for the development of these plans can be imaginative and try some new ideas. Trying to tie in the message to the strategic orientation is the important part, as the advertising agency will refine and redefine the message and the positioning.

Promotional methods

At this point, the promotional mixes need to be considered *for each* of the strategies proposed; that is, a mix for the consumer strategy, a mix for the trade strategy and a distinct mix for the communications to reach the wider array of stakeholders.

The choice of promotional methods should clearly state the methods and the media to be used. A short paragraph justifying the selection is very important, as the use of media in particular is to a large extent dependent upon the nature of the goals, the target audience and the resources.

The schedule

The next step is to schedule the use of the methods and the media. This is best achieved by the production of a Gantt chart (see the suggested answer later in the chapter).

Events should be scheduled according to the goals and the strategic thrust. So, if it necessary to communicate with the trade prior to a public launch, those activities tied into the push strategy should be scheduled prior to those calculated to support the pull strategy.

Similarly, if awareness is a goal then, if funds permit, it may be best to use television and posters first before sales promotions (unless sampling is used), direct marketing, point of purchase, and personal selling.

Budget

This is a vitally important part of the plan, one that is often avoided or forgotten about. The cost of the media and methods can either be allocated in a right-hand column of the Gantt chart, or a new chart can be prepared. Preferably, actual costs should be assigned, although percentages can be allocated if examination time is at a premium. What is of importance is the relative weighting of the costs and that there is a recognition and understanding of the general costs associated with the proposed individual activities.

It must be understood that a television campaign cannot be run for less than £1.5 million and that the overall cost of the strategy should be in proportion to the size of the client organisation, its (probable) level of profitability and the size and dynamics of the market in which it operates.

Control and evaluation

Unless there is some form of evaluation there will be no dialogue and no true marketing communications. There are numerous methods to evaluate the individual

Table 30.2 Linkages within the MCPF

Objectives	From the marketing plan, from the customer, stakeholder network and competitor analysis and from an internal marketing review
Stategic balance between push, pull and profile	From an understanding of the brand, the needs of the target audiences including employees and all other stakeholders and the marketing goals
Brand positioning	From users' and non-users' perceptions, motivations, attitudes and understanding about the brand and its direct and indirect competitors
Message content and style	From an understanding about the level of involvement, perceived risk, DMU analysis, information processing styles and the positioning intentions
Promotional tools and media	From the target audience analysis of media habits, involvement and preferences, from knowledge about product suitability and media compatibility, from a competitor analysis and from the resource analysis

Table 30.3 The role of promotional objectives

Balance of the promotional strategy
Positioning requirements
Promotional methods in terms of the most appropriate tools and media
Schedule (that is, when particular activities need to be completed)
Evaluation of what was achieved

performance of the tools and the media used, and for examination purposes these should be stated. In addition, and perhaps more meaningfully, the most important measures are the promotional objectives set in the first place. The success of a promotional strategy and the associated plan is the degree to which the objectives set are achieved.

Links and essential points

It was mentioned earlier that there are a number of linkages associated with different parts of the promotional plan. These are some of the more prominent ones.

The Contextual Analysis feeds the items shown in Table 30.2.

The promotional objectives derived from the CA feed the items shown in Table 30.3.

The promotional strategy is derived from an overall appreciation of the needs of the target audience (and stakeholders) regarding the brand and its competitive position in the market.

To help explain the MCPF and the linkages there follows a mini-case study for which a marketing communications plan is required. It is suggested that you prepare one using the material in this chapter as a guide. Further on, there is a suggested answer which you can use to compare with your own response. The answer I have prepared is not the only possible answer: there are other plans which could be of equal significance and use.

MINI CASE

Porridge matters

Alternative Health Foods Ltd (AHF) was formed in the early 1980s when the F-Plan diet was first spawned on a wave of publicity. The high level of interest shown by the public in fibre, oat and natural products (such as All-Bran) spurred Roger Tomkinson to develop his own cereal mixes for his family and then local consumption. Using a high proportion of various natural ingredients, many locally sourced, he developed a small range of cereal mixes.

He was soon encouraged to supply local health food shops with small quantities of three of his cereal mixes. From this point AHF has grown substantially and is now a major supplier of cereals to health food shops, chemists and a number of hotels.

The cereal products are sold under the Rainbow Foods brand and all are made from natural ingredients, with no additives or preservatives. Many of the ingredients are sourced in the UK. The breakfast cereal range consists of four main products: three muesli and one porridge mix. The three muesli are Natural (sweet), Organic (low salt and sugar) and Coated (honey clusters). A range of cereal bars has also been developed successfully under the Snappy brand. All products command a premium price, which is consistent with their position in the health foods sector.

The cereals are packaged in recycled cardboard containers with simple and straightforward labels in toning green, beige and other natural colours.

AHF also supplies a range of own-label products for many of the main supermarket multiples. The ingredients for the own-label products are significantly different from those for the branded market. The own-label muesli mixes need fewer ingredients but have to be either richer or stronger in taste. Prices are much lower on the own-label range, reflected in a 30% margin compared with 65% earned on the branded 'Rainbow Foods' range sold into the chemists and health food shops.

Turnover reached £22 million last year and profitability was a respectable 12%. Market share in the breakfast cereal market had reached 8% and it had been clearly articulated by the directors that this was expected to rise over the next three years (to 12%) as the company prepared to grow organically and through acquisition. Promotional expenditure was approximately 7% of turnover.

Currently the branded products are supplied to approximately 2,300 independent retail outlets throughout the UK. These are a mix of health food shops, independent chemists and hotels. Many of the hotels supplied are located in metropolitan areas, in contrast to the chemists and health food shops, which are often located close together in the same street in suburban areas.

Own-label products are distributed to 18 accounts in the UK. There are some export sales to Europe, looked after by a Swiss agent who has substantial contacts in the French, Swiss and German supermarket businesses.

Consumer research indicated that Rainbow muesli was perceived as a high-quality brand by muesli users. Fifty-two per cent of all muesli users are aware of the Rainbow brand; however, levels of awareness in non-user segments was low. Current consumers are mainly women, in the 40–60 age band, well educated, ABC1, with an active interest in healthy foods. Their slightly conservative approach to life was reflected in their comfortable lifestyle and their dietary need to eat muesli and similar nutritious foods.

The market was changing however, as an increase in consumption of muesli by younger people, mainly in the 18–35 band had been detected. Some were interested in the health aspect but others in this emerging segment saw the value for money associated with muesli products. As a number commented at a series of focus groups 'not only was it good for you, but it is quick to prepare, fills you up and can be eaten at any time'. A report in a Sunday paper commented that a number of television advertisements for different snack foods were stressing speed and satisfaction and were obviously targeted at young and busy executives.

Recently, a government report found that the food content in most packaged breakfast cereals was so low as to be of little or no value. Some commentators revived the old joke that the cardboard container was more nutritious than the contents. At around the same time, however, reports from the USA were suggesting that a high intake of oats was an important factor in preventing certain diseases and had been shown to speed recovery from illness and major operations.

After much discussion and consultation, AHF decided that the Rainbow brand should be repositioned to appeal to the emerging younger market. In the short term, however, the brand should not be positioned so as to alienate current customers.

Suggested marketing communications plan for 'Porridge matters'

Contents

Marketing communications plan for AHF

- Executive summary
- Contextual analysis
- Promotional objectives
- Strategy
- Promotional methods
- Scheduling
- Budgets
- Control and evaluation
- Prepared by:
- Date:

Executive summary

The ambitious plan to increase market share by 50% over the next three years requires a communication strategy that repositions the Rainbow brand as a nutritious yet quick to prepare snack food. Using a push, pull and profile strategy, the Rainbow brand should have increased penetration through the independent sector and establish stronger brand values with a new market segment.

Context analysis

Business context

The organisation produces cereals under the Rainbow Foods brand (four products, of which three are muesli) and also produces many own-label products for the leading supermarket chains.

Established in the 1980s, AHF is relatively young in life-cycle terms and might be most comfortably placed in the growth stage.

A growing turnover of £22 million, net profits of about 12% and market share at 8% rising to 12% over the next three years are indicative of an ambitious and well-managed organisation.

Distribution to over 2,300 independent retail outlets suggests wide geographic coverage and nationwide demand.

The marketing strategy requires that Rainbow be repositioned to meet the needs of the growing nutrious snack food market.

Customer context

The current target market is ABC1 women, aged 40–60, who have an active interest in healthy foods.

The emerging market, however, is characterised by people aged 18–35 who lead busy active lives and who perceive muesli products as a fast yet nutritious food which complements their lifestyle.

Positioned as a high-quality brand, premium pricing is sustained and the healthy food perception is a key factor in the brand's success to date.

Involvement in the purchase decision is relatively low, but the quality of the product and the health-based messages that have accompanied the brand to date have enabled buyers to reduce their functional risk and have used Rainbow to discriminate against competitor products. This has been a source of competitive advantage.

Stakeholder context

Little is revealed about the stakeholders, but it is said that it is intended to grow the organisation and a combination of debt and equity will be sought from external financial sources to fund the policy. This means that it is necessary to develop suitable relationships with the financial markets and to communicate mission, strategies and performance results with these stakeholders.

It is necessary to communicate with the intermediaries on a regular basis to gain their cooperation and goodwill. In addition it is important to communicate with the other organisations in the network and in the communities in which AHF operates, or is likely to operate, with a view to building the reputation of the organisation.

Organisational context

Financially AHF seems well placed, but the promotional appropriation will be limited to approximately £1.7 million next year and £1.8 million the year after, assuming revenue growth of 10%.

Little is said about the internal marketing communication needs, but as a strong reputation is required it will be necessary to develop good employee morale and identification with the aims and needs of the organisation. This means that resources must be diverted into good training programmes and good formal and informal communication systems.

Research activity appears limited, but the Government report about nutrition presents an opportunity for the Rainbow brand to disassociate itself from the breakfast cereal market. This will allow for repositioning.

Awareness of the brand is 52% (current muesli users), but awareness among regular cereal buyers is much lower. Attitudes and perceptions are unknown and research in these areas is required.

Environment context

There appear to be trends towards healthier eating habits, but paradoxically working lives are becoming more demanding. A tension between the need to work and the need to live (eat) sensibly suggests opportunities for products that relieve the guilt associated with hard work and neglecting proper food intake.

Promotional objectives

The promotional objectives are derived from the preceding analysis of the key communication factors facing AHF at the moment. In addition to the corporate objectives, two other sets of promotional objectives can be determined.

Corporate objectives

Over the next three years the corporate objectives are:

1. To increase turnover by 10% per annum. This level of performance for revenue and profits is justified on the basis of the increasing demand for health foods in many Western economies. This interest has recently received increased impetus from the media reports following the publication of the US report into health and cereal products.
2. To move into related markets with new products.

Marketing objectives

These are:

1. To double the Rainbow market share in the branded muesli market. This is justified by Rainbow's strong market position, positive perceptions held by independent grocery buyers towards AHF and the good levels of current buyer satisfaction.
2. To increase the purchase frequency of Rainbow muesli by current users from 5 to 7 packets per year.
3. To increase the penetration level of independent stockists who sell Rainbow muesli from 2,300 to 3,000 over the next three years.
4. To improve ROI by 15% per annum.

This can be achieved by utilising a more efficient promotional mix and by driving other internal efficiency measures.

Marketing communication objectives

These are:

1. To raise levels of prompted awareness among current muesli consumers from 52% to 65% over the next 12 months.
2. To raise prompted and spontaneous awareness of Rainbow muesli among the emerging market of 18–35-year-old ABC1 males and females over the six months finishing 31 March next year.
3. To reposition Rainbow muesli among the current and emerging markets as a healthy, invigorating and life-enhancing all-purpose snack/food.
4. To achieve 60% of independent stockists preferring Rainbow as their first choice muesli product.

Positioning

The market size for muesli and health foods is very likely to increase by anything from 12 to 16% per annum over each of the next five years, according to latest independent reports.

In order to compete and achieve the stated objectives it will be necessary to reposition the brand and provide a stronger point of differentiation for consumers. This will be achieved by identifying the brand as a product that not only satisfies the health expectations of buyers but is also perceived as a snack food for anytime consumption. Key messages will require minimal copy, due to the low level of involvement, but strong visual messages associating work and healthy food will be crucial.

The use of a strong spokesperson will be important for both internal and external audiences.

Promotional strategies

All three promotional strategies are required.

Pull strategy

A pull strategy will be required to achieve the awareness levels stated above and to reposition the brand as specified.

Such credibility can be enhanced with the use of suitable endorsers to assist cognitive processing, which is most likely to be via the peripheral route. A strategy to utilise significant opinion leaders will be necessary.

Table 30.4 The promotional mix to support the pull strategy

Advertising	Advertising is required to meet the awareness and repositioning goals. This is best achieved through an integrated approach. Television advertising is not possible because of the relatively small financial resources available. Radio, however, may provide suitable opportunities. Posters are to be used to build awareness (48 sheet and Adshel). To raise awareness in the emerging market of 18–35-year-olds, advertisements need to be placed in suitable general interest magazines, such as *Cosmopolitan, Marie Claire, Loaded* and *FHM*. Celebrity opinion leaders need to be seen to use and endorse the brand. In order to reach current buyers, specialist consumer interest magazines should be used to convey the health and vitality message.
Sales promotion	Promotional leaflets available through health food and other independent high street outlets, providing not only health information but also advice about diet and recipes using Rainbow oats. Sampling will be a major part of the repositioning exercise from which public relations opportunities will arise.
Sponsorship	Sponsorship opportunities to reinforce the positioning intentions need to be located.
Direct marketing	A database needs to be set up. Using a sales promotion (competition) to engage the new market will provide names and addresses for future mailings.
Public relations	Marketing public relations activities need to focus on the sponsorship opportunities and the celebrity opinion leaders.

Table 30.5 The promotional mix to support the push strategy

Personal selling	Personal selling will be important not only to achieve the sales output targets but also to reinforce the revised brand position. This will require training and a review of the skill requirements necessary to penetrate the sector and develop new relationships with significant accounts.
Sales promotion	High-quality sales literature will be used to reinforce the brand attributes and the positioning intentions. In an attempt to get strong self-presence, case discounts and advertising allowances should be offered to larger retailers and groups. Incentive schemes, such as competitions, are to be developed to encourage retailer involvement.
Advertising	Restricted use with most effort placed in leading trade journals (e.g. *The Grocer*). Promotional materials specific to the European markets will need to be prepared in order to support the Swiss agent. Independent retailers need to be supported with promotional materials including point-of-purchase materials.
Direct marketing	Direct mail facilities to be used to reach independent retailers and telemarketing to be used to service low-potential accounts.
Public relations	Marketing public relations are to be used to communicate the values and benefits of the Rainbow brand.

Messages should strengthen the position that Rainbow muesli is a healthy snack food that fits in with busy lifestyles. To assist educating audiences, the use of recipes and innovative meals might be of assistance, together with sponsorship of appropriate events to which the 18–35-year-old market can relate.

The US report and other data will be used to substantiate benefit claims.

Fifty per cent of available resources are notionally allocated to pull.

Push strategy

A push strategy is necessary in order that the marketing objectives of an increased number of outlets can be achieved. Also, the communications objectives to achieve the required 60% preference rate among independent outlets need to be supported through consistent and high-quality communications.

Profitability targets are more likely to be achieved if margin does not have to be given away in the form of discounts to get shelf presence.

Thirty-five per cent of available resources are notionally allocated to a push strategy.

Profile

A profile strategy is necessary in order to build interest and understanding of AHF by various significant stakeholders, such as the financial sector, employees and the local community.

The key messages are that AHF is an environmentally aware, strategically credible and financially sound organisation which represents a good investment opportunity. In addition, the accent is to communicate high levels of service and deliver through positive employee identification.

While only 15% of available resources are to be allocated over the next 12 months, this figure will rise over the following two years.

The promotional mix

In the light of the desired strategies it is necessary to formulate three promotional mixes and allocate funds accordingly (Tables 30.4–30.8). These costs are approximate and the objective and task approach method will be required to determine actuals before implementation.

Table 30.6 The promotional mix to support the profile strategy

Public relations	The regular use of Corporate Public Relations to reach all stakeholders is important. AHF should endeavour to understand the attitudes and disposition of significant stakeholders and should consider adjusting its stance as necessary. The use of press releases and events will be important.
Sponsorship	AHF should use sponsorship to develop awareness with potential investors and key stakeholders.
Newsletters	These are to be used to reach employees, intermediaries and others associated with the organisation.
Employee conferences	Employee conferences, as a reward, as a motivational factor and as a means of disseminating information, need to be held on a regular basis.
Training	Training for all employees in terms of providing high levels of customer service.

Table 30.7 The schedule

	Year 1				Year 2			
	Q1	Q2	Q3	Q4	Q1	Q2	Q3	Q4
Pull strategy								
Advertising	√	√	√	√	√	√	√	√
Sales promotion		√		√		√		√
Sponsorship			√	√	√	√	√	√
Database	√	√	√	√	√	√	√	√
Public relations		√			√	√	√	
Push strategy								
Personal selling	√	√	√	√	√	√	√	√
Trade (sales) promotions	√	√		√	√		√	√
Advertising	√		√			√	√	
Direct marketing		√	√	√		√	√	√
Public relations	√	√	√	√	√	√	√	√
Profile strategy								
Public relations	√	√	√	√	√	√	√	√
Sponsorship			√	√	√	√	√	√
Newsletters		√		√		√		√
Employee conferences		√		√		√		√
Training	√		√		√		√	

Table 30.8 The promotional budget (amounts in £000)

	Year 1	Year 2	Total
Pull strategy			
Advertising	480	330	810
Sales promotion	170	180	350
Sponsorship	nil	100	100
Direct marketing	75	150	225
Public relations	45	50	95
Research	80	90	170
Total pull cost	*850*	*900*	*1,750*
Push strategy			
Personal selling	(separate budget)		
Trale (sales) promotions	310	320	630
Advertising	110	90	200
Direct marketing	95	125	220
Public relations	35	40	75
Research	50	55	105
Total push cost	*600*	*630*	*1,230*
Profile strategy			
Public relations	40	45	85
Sponsorship	50	60	110
Newsletters	10	15	25
Employee conferences	50	55	105
Training	70	70	140
Research	30	25	55
Total profile cost	*250*	*270*	*520*
Total cost of promotional plan	*£1.7 million*	*£1.8 million*	*£3.5 million*

Control and evaluation

In order that the plan remain on target, control procedures are required. These will be implemented partly by external agencies responsible for their respective parts of the plan, but we will be responsible for the overall delivery and control.

Variance analysis will be used on a quarterly basis to monitor budgetary spend levels and a series of quantitative and qualititive measure will be used evaluate the effectiveness of the individual elements as well as the overall impact of the promotional activities.

Focus groups, tracking studies (awareness and perception) and recall tests will be used to monitor the development of the Rainbow brand and the reputation of AHF.

In particular, the objectives set for both the marketing and marketing communications components will be assessed regularly and will be the main form of evaluation of the campaign as an integrated marketing communications plan.

References

Engel, J.F., Warshaw, M.R. and Kinnear, T.C. (1994) *Promotional Strategy*, 8th edn. Homewood IL: Richard D. Irwin.

Rothschild, M. (1987) *Marketing Communications*, Lexington MA: DC Heath.

Mini-cases

The mini-cases that follow are intended to allow readers the opportunity to apply some of the techniques and approaches used in this text. At the end of each case there are some questions which should be attempted in order to assist understanding, help develop levels of knowledge and foster skills in the practical identification and implementation of marketing communications.

All the cases are based either on real organisations or situations that have occurred in different markets. In some of the cases individuals, organisations and brands have been renamed or disguised. Some of the material has been adapted from different sources, and where brand names have been used, whether real or fictitious, all figures are imaginary and are not intended to represent actual positions.

CASE

Sharpe views ahead

Panorama airways is an airline with a mission – to fly!

Located at Gatwick Airport, London Panorama's fleet of Boeing 747s, 737s and Lockheed Tristars are meticulously maintained to provide their 1.75 million passengers (last year's figures) with smooth, safe and trouble-free journeys.

The staff at Panorama, some 2,300 people, identify closely with the business and over 45% have been with Panorama for over five years.

As a subsidiary of a major British Airline, Panorama has access to a wealth of expertise in engineering, operations and safety. Panorama moves business and holiday passengers through scheduled services to 21 European destinations and its international charter flights. It is the fifth largest airline in the UK holiday market.

Much of its work involves engineering and servicing for other airlines at Gatwick and Chicago, its only foreign location. This work contributes to its financial strength and, in part, to the quality image it has developed.

Panorama is, however, best known among travel agents and operators as a holiday airline, one associated with sun, sea and sand.

At a recent press conference, Mike Sharpe, the Managing Director of Panorama, outlined that one of Panorama's goals was the development of the long-haul market, which increased by 23% in the last 12 months. In addition to the established transatlantic routes, the Far East and Australasia were key targets.

The public image of Panorama is recognised as having an effect upon the business, and as Mike Sharpe said, Panorama's livery is of 'paramount importance'. Staff are encouraged, indeed trained, to respect the needs of individual customers, whether they be trade or end user. Many UK travel operators use Panorama because of its attention to detail at all stages of its operations and its ability to handle large numbers of passengers easily.

Sharpe is aware of the increasingly competitive market and the pressure being applied to Panorama's margins. He has set marketing objectives of building market share by 1.25% over the next year without diluting profitability. One of his marketing communications objectives is to build levels of awareness in the trade and to business and leisure travellers. (Based on an idea by G. Lancaster)

Task

Develop an outline marketing communications plan to enable Panorama achieve its stated objectives.

CASE

Nurella – soft soap isn't all flannel

Introduction

Brian Cranshaw was delighted when he was invited to join Fulcross Ltd, a soap manufacturer, as Marketing and Sales Director. He was already one of three national line sales managers for a leading FMCG food organisation, and he was ambitious to take full responsibility for the sales and marketing of a single company.

The soap market

For a standard toilet bar, prices range from 20p for a very inexpensive retailer brand soap, through 44p for a typical leading national brand, to 95p for a high-quality name brand. Some specialist soaps retail at over £2.00. Several brands dominate the market, with Lux, Palmolive and Imperial Leather enjoying shares of around 9% and Camay, Zest, Fairy and Lifebuoy shares of about 6%. Fresh and Knight's Castile follow with 3–5% each and the remainder of the market is divided equally between 'own brands' and 'others'.

Two-thirds of all soap sales pass through the supermarket segment when Boots, with 14% of the market, is included with supermarkets and self-service groceries. This leaves only small shares of 14% from the remaining grocery outlets, 8% from other chemists and 12% from departmental and variety stores.

Fulcross Ltd

Fulcross offers two main brands: Caress, a soap in toilet and bath size packages, and Splash, a shower gel. Both brands are distributed throughout the UK. The recommended retail price for a Caress toilet bar is 68p. This places the brand in the upper third by price among the quality brands, although some soaps are considerably more expensive. The Splash brand has been positioned in a similar way in the top third.

Group net turnover was about £9.2 million last year, giving Fulcross less than 2% of the national market. By using the retail price index as a deflator, Cranshaw calculated that in real terms Fulcross's sales appear to have been decreasing by around 5% per annum over the past four years. Nevertheless, the Caress brand is widely recognised and the firm made a profit before tax of 4% on sales last year. The Caress brand has been sold for over 50 years and has a good sound quality image, appealing to AB women in the grey market (50+ year olds) with above average disposable incomes. Distribution is through the independent sector, not supermarkets. The Splash shower gel was launched in 1988, but has failed to establish a strong position in the market. It is seen by supermarket buyers as a third-rate product, and so far they have failed to list it, let alone devote shelf space to it.

Both the Caress and Splash brands are targeted at the independent sector (high street chemists, retail chains) and most are serviced through wholesalers who are invoiced at list prices less 20%, then less 10%. It is expected that the 20% margin is passed on to the retailer. Very large chains are able to buy direct from Fulcross and they normally receive both discounts. Warehousing and distribution represent a large overhead, averaging 11% of sales.

During the Second World War, Fulcross had been forced to use general manufacturers' representatives working on commission to cover its accounts. Thereafter, Fulcross never fully returned to an employee sales force. The firm now operates through a field marketing organisation in six regions, although its own Sales Director covers a seventh – London Western – operating from the head office at Ealing. Representatives work on 2% commission for all orders from their regions, including national, wholesale and retail chains who purchase for delivery to other regions. Fulcross then supplies the orders from bulk warehouse stocks, which are maintained at four sites and are replenished from Ealing. The six regions covered by the representatives are London Eastern, South-Western, Midlands, Scotland and Northern Ireland.

Research

When he arrived at Fulcross, Cranshaw was confident he could change the situation by repositioning both brands. He is on first-name terms with many of the buyers for national supermarket and retail chains, comes into frequent contact with them to arrange special deals and promotions, and has entertained and been 'out on the town' with a number of them.

One of Cranshaw's first actions on joining his new company was to appoint a new advertising agency, Parsons, Smith and Brown (PSB). They commissioned a series of research activities including a special Nielsen-type study of the representation of the Fulcross brands in different outlets and their share of the market through those outlets. The results confirmed that Caress (and to a lesser extent Splash) has a strong presence in the independent chemist sector, a very poor share of the grocery outlets, and little representation through the major multiples.

Even more revealing were PSB's findings about people's attitudes towards the Caress and Splash brands. Research indicated that while a substantial market existed for the Caress brand (for those who wished to reward themselves with a luxury soap), a new segment was emerging for technology-based products. The target market appears to be characterised by ABC1 women, aged 18–35, who have busy careers and who pursue modern lifestyles. This group want a soap product that has a highly technical formulation, provides reassurance and protection for sensitive skin, and hints at some expression of the user's awareness of environmental issues.

Several competitors spent double the Caress percentage on advertising, but Cranshaw has said that he is not impressed with the advertising strategies being used to try to increase market share.

He referred to the heavy advertisers as 'men of the eighties'. These strategies were based on highly emotional messages where differentiation was based upon self-indulgence and reward.

Virtually all housewives buy toilet soap and some 9% – disproportionately grouped in the 35–44 age bracket – were classified as heavy users. To get at these heavy users, PSB argued that there was no substitute for brand advertising. Cranshaw recognised the argument, but favoured a heavy emphasis on supermarket display and point of purchase activities.

The Nurella brand

In the light of PSB's report Cranshaw planned to introduce a new brand to enter the supermarket sector. He wanted to introduce both a soap and a shower gel under the Nurella brand.

Cranshaw's idea is to withdraw Splash from the market, continue with Caress and launch a soap brand as Nurella. A new shower gel should then follow, to be called 'Nurella Protein Plus', thus extending the Nurella brand. Cranshaw saw the Nurella brand positioned as a scientific, hi-tech, modern and credible product. The new gel would be a green liquid in a grey/red container. Cranshaw believes that he can reposition Fulcross in the toiletries sector and establish Nurella as a technologically based brand. Access to supermarket shelves should be possible with Nurella, as long as Fulcross is prepared to invest in a promotional campaign to support the multiple grocers. Meanwhile, the Caress brand would be unaffected, so the risk to Fulcross, he reasons, is limited to the possible loss of the current volume of Splash sales through the independent sector.

The rebranding decision has been agreed in principle by the board, and most production difficulties associated with the new brand overcome. PSB and Cranshaw agree that a promotional campaign is a priority next step for the launch. To take the campaign forward Cranshaw is preparing a marketing communication plan.

(*Note* : Fulcross Ltd is a fictitious company and all figures are intended to give an impression of the size and shape of the market. They are included as a means of illustrating particular points and stimulating thought and discussion. They are not intended to represent the actual market shares of the real brands mentioned in the case.)

Review questions

1. What are the possible positioning opportunities for the Nurella brand? Which of these strategies (Chapter 24) are the more plausible in the light of the information available?
2. Write a brief paper outlining the branding issues concerning the Caress, Splash and Nurella brands.
3. Prepare a marketing communications plan for the Nurella brand.

CASE

A case of the grass is always greener

Bricut, a long established medium-sized engineering company, had important decisions to make about the promotion of its range of lawnmowers.

Distribution was originally directed through ironmongers and garden centres and by 1980 over a thousand accounts were being serviced and 11 salespersons were employed. Its distribution was particularly successful and at the time was regarded as a major competitive strength. This success was attributed to the high reputation which had been established within the trade; the product, service, delivery and above all the company were all perceived to be trustworthy and very reliable.

Growth of sales volume was aided by the introduction of two new models: the Super County, a much bigger machine, and the County Junior, a small version of the original product (the County). These additions were prompted by sales force suggestions as a result of growing competition.

By the mid-1980s, Bricut believed it had good products, an established sales force and a wide distribution network. A marketing department had been established which was geared to servicing the garden centres and ironmongers with sales literature, leads and joint promotions with key accounts. The operation was very successful, profitable and the envy of many of its traditional competitors. But the industry, the market and the trade entered a period of turmoil. Indeed technological advances in the early 1980s had created opportunities for manufacturers to produce a cost-effective hover mower that could be within the financial reach of most consumers. Initially, Bricut had thought it could maintain a niche strategy with its petrol mowers, and so did not attempt to follow the large-volume firms who were introducing new electric hover models. However, there were changes in the marketing channels, as Bricut found increasingly that its traditional outlets were being reduced in number as industry-wide distribution moved more to discount stores, hypermarkets and DIY superstores.

There were two significant events which had helped to destabilise Bricut. First, a leading chain of ironmongers was upgrading all its outlets, closing many of them and opening much larger stores. In its rationalisation it decided not to stock Bricut.

Secondly, research had shown that a new generation of convenience gardeners had emerged. This group wanted a lawnmower that would be simple to use, lightweight, produce rolled out 'stripes' across a cut lawn and be easy to store. Electric mowers with grass collection facilities appeared to satisfy the needs of the convenience gardener.

Bricut had been aware of the growth of the convenience gardener, but had deliberately not attempted to develop the technology and enter this market segment. However, by the end of the 1980s management believed that they could no longer ignore this market segment and, as a response to these now established market requirements, had entered into an alliance with a leading department store group to develop and launch a new range of electric rotary mowers, to be sold under the store label. These were called the Riviera range. Bricut believed that it should develop the technology and that this would enable it to meet the needs of the new generation of gardeners. The design of the Riviera was jointly agreed and Bricut proceeded to develop a small range of electric mowers that it sold in a similar way in cooperation with other specialist retail outlets. Sales growth and profitability continued to be very encouraging. The electric mower market in the UK was dominated by Qualcast and Flymo, with machines made in Italy, France and the Far East, but Bricut had established a reasonable 5% share of the electric mower market by 1996. So, by the end of 1996 Bricut was targeting its County range of petrol mowers at the traditional gardener and its range of electric rotary mowers to the convenience gardener through retail outlets as own-label products.

Information compiled from guarantee registration cards indicated that customers of the County range had much larger gardens than average and that two-thirds were in the south and west of England. Wanting to learn more about its users, Bricut included several questions in a national omnibus survey. From this and other secondary sources, market shares were estimated (see table).

Bricut also gleaned from this research that owners of Super County and County machines tended to be over 45 years old and agreed that 'they took gardening seriously' and 'gardening is my main hobby'. They also found that Bricut users valued its solid design and reliability and they agreed that they intended to buy a County if they had to purchase another machine. They thought electric machines, particulary hover mowers, were flimsy and inappropriate for serious gardeners. In the same segment, only 32% of non-users of Bricut machines were aware of Bricut and the County range.

Performance Data for the County Range 1996

1996	County Junior	County	Super County
Price range	under £200	£200 to £450	over £450
Sales volume	12,000	7,800	5,200
Market share	3%	8%	22%
Contribution	(6%)	17%	43%

The product line was also being evaluated after it was concluded that the Super County was making a significant profit, the original County was making a small contribution and the County Junior was making a loss (see table).

The electric rotary mower range, including the Riviera, was also profitable. A recent complication was that a Japanese manufacturer was known to be looking for a British distributor for its revolutionary new robotic machines. Bricut thought this might allow it to develop a stronger competitive advantage and be first into the new technology.

The marketing plan for 1998 requires the simultaneous development of both the petrol-based County brand range and the rotary electric brands. Market share for the Super County and the County is set to increase, but serious consideration is being given to the phasing out of the County Junior, which will be replaced by either the robotic or rotary mowers alternatives. In the light of these developments Bricut is reviewing its marketing communications.

Based on an idea by Gordon Oliver.

Review questions

1. Consider the communication issues that might arise within the marketing channels currently employed by Bricut.
2. Develop a promotional mix for Bricut that would enable it to communicate with its traditional customers and the newly emerging segment of convenience gardeners.
3. Prepare a paper that sets out the key issues that marketing communications will need to address.

The following document is the Creative brief used by USP Advertising in Bournemouth (used with kind permission).

Creative brief

Client:
Project:
Review date:
Presentation date:
Release date:

Version no:
Date USP briefed:
USP brief issued:
Job no:
Author/Owner:

[ad, brochure, leaflet, mailer, etc]

The background

Briefly, what is the background for this proposed activity? Where does it fit within the overall marketing and communications mix? Provide relevant samples of advertising and promotional activity (both client's and competitors') to enable us to view this activity in context, and to consider opportunities for integration of messages, look-and-feel, etc.

The product

Provide information on the specific product/brand to be advertised, features and benefits, pricing, distribution/sales channels, packaging, seasonality, etc.

The objectives

Why are we advertising? To gain a specific response? To increase enquiries/sales/awareness? To present news about the product? To create/change/reinforce attitudes about the product? What targets are to be set for response rates, conversion rates, etc?

The target audience

Identity: Traditionally, consumer audiences have been defined in socio-economic terms, e.g. ABC1 males aged 30–45. More revealing is a definition of the typical customer in terms of age, sex, outlook, job, interests, education, income, personal or work needs in relationship to our product offering, status and role in the decision-making/influencing process.

Perceptions: What are their current perceptions of our product, levels of understanding, etc. Does research exist: within USP, with the client, or via other means?

The proposition

In no more than 25 words, state the single-minded proposition that sums up what we are saying. This should be the single main 'buying reason' that is likely to persuade our audience to buy/switch to our product, compared with the competition – phrased in plain English as if you were talking directly to a member of the target audience. Remember, it is the one reason we wish to highlight. There will be others, but they will be subsidiary to this.

The support

What supporting information or arguments do we need to include to convince the audience of the above proposition; to further develop our sales message; to overcome any threat from a competitive product; and to get our audience to respond positively to our communication?

The competition

What competition exists? Does our client's product offer benefits or attributes that are not present in competitors' products? Do competitors' products offer benefits or attributes not found in our client's product?

The tone of voice

Is there any particular way we should talk to our audience that would aid communication of our proposition? Authoritative? Urgent? Friendly? Cheeky? Irreverent? etc.

The desired response

What *exactly* do we want our audience to do as a result of seeing our communication? Include details of specific calls to action and response mechanisms such as coupons, FreeCall numbers, fax-backs, Freepost/Business Reply Service cards etc.

The measurement of the work

How will the success of this piece be measured? What needs to be included to cater for this?

The media and creative requirements

Is this a press ad? A brochure? A direct mail piece? A one-off? Part of a campaign? What is needed? Concepts? Scamps? Rough Visuals? Finished Marker/Mac Visuals? Copy outline or platform? Full copy? Be specific.

The production requirements

Such as type and size of media, no. of pages, black and white, no. of colours, 5-colour Language Black artwork or other special print requirements, tear-off cards, tip-ons etc. Mechanicals: page size, bleed etc., film/electronic file requirements. Approx. print/mailing quantities, if appropriate.

The mandatories

Corporate ID/look-and-feel issues, typefaces, logos, sign-offs, codes, publication numbers etc.

The budget

What is the budget in both financial and time terms? Are there budget factors which govern our approach to this creative work, or which preclude original photography or illustration, use of library transparencies, etc? What hours have been estimated for each stage of the job?

Project schedule

What are the key timings for this project (you may wish to expand on the basic timings in the header section).

Author index

Subject index

Note: Page references in *italics* refer to Figures; those in **bold** refer to Tables

MANAGEMENT

CONCEPTS & PRACTICES